THE
PELOPONNESIAN
WAR

THUCYDIDES

THE PELOPONNESIAN WAR

Translated, with introduction, notes, and glossary by
STEVEN LATTIMORE

Hackett Publishing Company, Inc.
Indianapolis/Cambridge

Printed in the United States of America

09 08 07   3 4 5 6 7

Corrections were introduced in the second printing.

For further information, please address

Hackett Publishing Company, Inc.
P.O. Box 44937
Indianapolis, Indiana 46244–0937

www.hackettpublishing.com

Text design by Dan Kirklin

Cover art: Vasari, *The Opposing Fleets of the Turks and the Holy League at Lepanto*. Photo: Vatican Museums.

Library of Congress Cataloging-in-Publication Data

Thucydides.
    [History of the Peloponnesian War. English]
    The Peloponnesian War/Thucydides; translated, with introduction, notes, and glossary by Steven Lattimore.
        p.   cm.
    Includes bibliographical references and index.
    ISBN 0–87220–394–8 (pbk.)   ISBN 0–87220–395–6 (cloth)
    1. Greece—History—Peloponnesian War, 431–404 B.C.
I. Lattimore, Steven. II. Title.
DF229.T5L38 1998
938'.05—dc21   97-46084
                                                  CIP

ISBN-13: 978-0-87220-395-2 (cloth)
ISBN-13: 978-0-87220-394-5 (pbk.)

For Judith, Nicholas, and Isabel

CONTENTS

Book 8

INTRODUCTION

Interest in the fifth-century Athenian writer Thucydides has probably never been higher than in the last third of the twentieth century, to judge from the amount of scholarly publications devoted to him during that period. His topic is one of enduring importance; in 431 B.C.E. the Greek world, at the peak of its intellectual and cultural development, was engulfed in the Peloponnesian War, which ended twenty-seven years later with the defeat and overthrow of the Athenian empire by a Spartan-led coalition. Thucydides wrote as a contemporary of these events.

He starts by identifying himself as an Athenian who began writing a record of the war when it broke out because he realized at once that it would be the most momentous known to history; he claims to have done considerable research on early Greek history to reinforce this judgment. He later states that he lived to see the end of the war, and several passages verify this. He did not complete his book; our text ends abruptly while recording events of the late summer of 411, and since three fourth-century historians began their histories at exactly this stopping place, it is very unlikely that a Thucydidean account of the years 410–404 ever existed. His presentation of the first twenty years, however, divided since the Hellenistic period into eight books, is impressively detailed and is certainly our most authoritative source on this period of the war. Thucydides' *Peloponnesian War* has long been valued for setting unprecedented standards of objectivity and consequent accuracy.

What has characterized recent Thucydidean scholarship, however, is an emphasis on Thucydides the man. A "postmodernist" Thucydides has emerged, an author whose unquestionable power is derived from his artistic ambition and genius and from intense personal emotions that sometimes led him far away from the objectivity he professed.[1] It follows

1. For the term "postmodernist" and an insightful essay on the changed approach to Thucydides, see Connor 1977 (I would call Connor 1984 an example of the new scholarship at its finest and the most valuable single volume on Thucydides); cf. Grant 1974 and Rawlings 1981, pp. 263–72.

that Thucydides' historical accuracy is now being more consistently and acutely challenged than ever before, in part by scholars who believe that artistic intentions dominated Thucydides' version of events,[2] also leading him to magnify the importance of his topic unduly,[3] in part by those who find him deeply biased, notably in favor of Athens and against Sparta.[4] Thucydides' readers, then, should include (as they always have) those with no particular interest in the Peloponnesian War; and those who read him primarily to learn about the war should question everything they read. Still, it should be stressed that scholars who attempt to correct Thucydides usually—and avowedly—rely on evidence supplied elsewhere in Thucydides' text.[5] As for bias, it is true that Thucydides' depiction of the Spartans is critical, perhaps overwhelmingly negative (although an occasional scholar has found Thucydides to be an admirer of Sparta); yet the devious and callous Spartans of *The Peloponnesian War* are not wholly incompatible with the Spartans of the years 410–362 in the *Hellenika* of the ardently pro-Spartan Xenophon.[6] As for the Athenians, they are at the center of the book, and Thucydides' attitude toward them takes on much of the complexity of his attitude toward war and empire; his partiality has not precluded reporting instances of Athenian misconduct as well as folly.

Certainly, all would acknowledge that our most credible information about Thucydides himself comes from his own book. He was an adult when the war started. In book 2, describing the horrible plague that struck Athens in 430, he states that, in addition to observing the symptoms in others, he had the plague himself. Toward the end of book 4, referring to himself as the son of Oloros, he tells us that he was a general in 424, stationed at Thasos, off the coast of Thrace (where he had rights to working gold mines there and, consequently, great influence with the locals), when he received orders to relieve the Athenians defending Amphipolis; he was

2. E.g., Hunter 1973.

3. See 1.1n.

4. E.g., Badian 1993; like many sceptics of Thucydides' veracity, Badian is a professed admirer of his artistry.

5. See 1.96n. Disconcertingly, Dover (1973, p. 4) points out that when independent evidence is discovered, it tends to contradict rather than confirm Thucydides; such evidence, however, is in such short supply as to suggest chance as a major factor in this.

6. See, however, Bradford 1994, pp. 76–78.

unable to save the town,[7] and in book 5 he informs us that he was exiled for twenty years "after" his command, soberly commenting that he could thus associate with persons on both sides, especially Peloponnesians; the end of his exile would then have coincided with the end of the war.[8] Several sources from the Roman period say that Thucydides was murdered before he could finish the book, but their stories differ from one another and probably represent nothing more than hypotheses based on the book's unfinished state;[9] the tendency in antiquity to construct spurious biographies of literary figures by such inferences must serve as a warning to modern scholars. There is, however, somewhat more valid evidence suggesting that Thucydides lived into the 390s.[10] But even if he barely outlived the war, it is clear that he eventually gave priority to revising what he had previously written rather than recording the final six years of the war.

In the book as it stands, the most notable event is the Sicilian expedition, to which books 6 and 7 are almost completely devoted; it has been very plausibly argued that books 1 through (especially) 4 were revised to their extant form to foreshadow the Athenian disaster of 413.[11] Conversely, as far as can be judged from an account that does not go beyond 411 (but, as noted previously, it is suggestive that it does not), the defeat of 405–404 had a lesser impact on Thucydides, who tends to write about the Spartans contemptuously rather than resentfully. If he lived as late as 393 (which does not seem at all impossible), he could have witnessed the death in battle of Lysander, the victorious Spartan admiral; the disintegration of the Spartan alliance; the incipient revival of Athenian sea power and empire; and the rebuilding of the famous "long walls" joyously pulled down by the victors in 404.

7. It has been argued with some plausibility that his account is designed to deny his culpability; see 4.103–7n.

8. For controversies about his exile, see 5.26n. and 8.68n. He is likely to have spent much of his time in Corinth; see Stroud 1994.

9. According to the late antique biographical information that has come down under the name of Marcellinus, a tomb in Athens, possibly a cenotaph, was inscribed with the names of Thucydides son of Oloros from the deme of Halimos, and of his son Timotheos; the same source records the suggestion that an unnamed daughter of Thucydides composed book 8.

10. See 2.100n, 6.3n, and 8.84n.

11. See especially Hunter 1977, pp. 282–91; this article also presents a useful review of the composition problem or "Thucydidean question." At least portions of even the "Sicilian" books 6 and 7 may have been written late; see 6.3n.

This is admittedly very speculative. There is general agreement among scholars, however, that Thucydides must have been born around 460 or slightly later. Another consensus, that he was born into the aristocratic and wealthy clan of the Philaidai, is based on the name of his father, which is also that of a Thracian king whose daughter married into this family in the late sixth century.[12] The Philaidai's long-term interests in Thrace would account for Thucydides' gold-mining rights there. The Philaidai were politically conservative as well as wealthy, and it has been maintained that Thucydides "ended his life as he had begun it, a confirmed oligarch who never renounced the creed of his fathers."[13] Even if Athens' early war leader Perikles is defined as a conservative, and a conservative in Thucydides' eyes (which is the view of the author of the statement just quoted), however, the admiration expressed for him by Thucydides in book 2 is enough to show a sharp break with his family background; the totality of his more overtly political views reflects a complex man formed by a complex age and society. Briefly, Thucydides seems to have regarded democracy as, in Churchill's phrase, "the worst form of government except for all the others." He often remained aristocrat enough to express admiration for oligarchic leaders (even when condemning their cause) and criticize the people and, especially, popular leaders (even when approving of their cause). At times he commended the more conservative governments for a stability generally lacking in democracies, but he stresses the vigor and achievements that were possible when a larger sector of the population was actively engaged; *sophrosyne* (prudence, moderation: a conservative watchword) was not enough.[14] Among oligarchic politicians and thinkers, Thucydides gives Antiphon the most striking praise, and although the suggestion made in antiquity and sometimes renewed by modern scholars that Antiphon was his teacher may well have originated as another biographical inference drawn from his writing, there is some credibility in it, especially if this Antiphon was the same man as the "sophist."[15]

But at various points Thucydides appears to reflect not only the sophists but also all the other elements of the extraordinary intellectual atmosphere

12. Herodotos, *Histories* 6.39; see Rusten 1989, pp. 2–3.

13. This is the concluding sentence of McGregor 1956.

14. On Thucydides' political views, see notes on 2.65, 4.21, 6.54–59, 7.55, 8.1–2, 68, 95–96, 97; cf. also Connor 1984, pp. 221–29; Farrar 1988, pp. 126–91; and Pope 1988.

15. See 8.68n.

that characterized Athens during the later fifth century; the problem is one of determining which influences were direct and which were decisive.[16] At the risk of some oversimplification, I would suggest that his assessment of overall situations owes a debt to the Hippocratic school of medical writing,[17] but that his presentation and analysis of events, through pervasive irony and emphasis on reversals,[18] are more akin to tragedy.[19] The author to whom he ultimately has the closest affinity, however, and whose text he appears to have taken with him in his travels, is Homer.[20] I would restrict this name to the poet of the *Iliad*; while to Thucydides, as to his contemporaries, "Homer" denoted considerably more than the two "Homeric" epics, the *Iliad* was at once his most formidable rival and his most inspiring model. Although the choice of a war as subject was perhaps inevitable for an ancient Greek writer of an ambitious and emulous nature, his opening paragraph, in its dual emphasis on death and suffering and on causality, can be compared with the proem of the *Iliad* (and contrasted with the Odyssean opening of Herodotos' *Histories*). Separately, Thucydides' skillful variation of conventional phrases and sentiments, his use of cross-referencing[21] and foreshadowing, his apparent "digressions" that build suspense and add resonance,[22] his balancing of the specific and the generic, his austere emphasis on his subject, relieved by vignettes from more normal life (reminiscent of many Homeric similes), might be incidental points in common with Homer; taken together, they appear more than coincidental.

His writing style, however, is unique.[23] Working at least some of the time in isolation, whatever his educational and literary background, he car-

---

16. Cf. Dover 1973, pp. 9–13, Finley 1967, pp. 55–117, Jung 1991.

17. See now Reichenauer 1991, but cf. also the cautionary remarks of Parry 1969. See 6.14n and 6.18n.

18. On Thucydides' use of irony, see Tompkins 1983 and Connor 1984, p. 36 (cf. Stahl 1966, p. 93); for reversals, see especially book 4.

19. Cf. Stahl 1966, especially pp. 125–26, 137, Finley 1967, pp. 1–54, Rawlings 1981, pp. 264–65, Macleod 1983, pp. 140–58, and Lapini 1991, especially pp. 128–30; Macleod believes that the influence of Herodotos, "another tragic historian," was more direct, see also Hunter 1973, e.g., p. 164.

20. See Macleod 1983, pp. 157–58 and, for a discussion of a number of probable direct allusions, Mackie 1996.

21. See Rengakos 1996.

22. E.g., 4.32; for Homeric digressions, see Austin 1966.

23. See especially Rusten 1989, pp. 21–28, also Dover 1973, pp. 9–13.

ried to extremes such contemporary practices as interlaced word order, variation of balanced words and clauses, and use of abstract verbal and substantive nouns and of rare, often poetic words; he strained and sometimes broke the rules of Greek grammar; and he added his specialty: sentences of inordinate length, which are anything but artless, sometimes piling up subordinate clauses of various functions that convey the overall situation in which the action—itself usually described with sudden directness—occurs; others begin with the action, reversing the formal, and hence the psychological, pattern. Another writer might have used a page to indicate a similar complexity of interrelated events; Thucydides' method is incomparably more intense when it succeeds, but he occasionally passes beyond concentration into congestion. It might be noted that these complicated sentences may occur in the narrative as well as in the speeches (which represent more than a quarter of the book and are celebrated for their difficulty) and in the analytical passages. Above and beyond his perception that events were seldom simple, he shows a restless wish to avoid the obvious, a reluctance to state anything too conventionally or predictably. "Thucydides was an intensely self-conscious artist, eclectic and experimental, ambitious to impress, but not always sufficiently critical to read what he had written with the eyes of someone who could not know what train of thought had run through the writer's mind."[24]

It has also been well said that "No author who writes like Thucydides is trying to scare away readers,"[25] and I would place great emphasis on the word "readers." Not only difficulty, remarked in antiquity, but difficulty often created by unpredictability and by variation for its own sake would have worked strongly against successful oral presentation, at least in public (Thucydides appears to acknowledge this),[26] and in such presentation at least some of his foreshadowing and elaborate cross-referencing would have gone unappreciated. The practical problems, in ancient Greece, of writing for a readership (as well as revising, which evidently took up much of Thucydides' time) would have been considerable,[27] but during his exile

24. Dover 1973, p. 13. I know of no better demonstration of the deep purpose usually underlying Thucydides' apparently capricious use of Greek than Macleod 1979, pp. 60–64 (= 1983, pp. 131–35).

25. Grant 1974, p. 82; he believes that Thucydides "wanted his work to be a popular success," see *infra*.

26. See 1.22; on Thucydides as an author who wrote for readers, see Edmunds 1993 and Crane 1996.

27. See Flory 1995 and Small 1995.

he apparently had both leisure and financial assets, and he was unquestionably dedicated to his work. By any account of literacy in Classical Greece, the readership of a book as demanding as Thucydides' would have been small and well-educated, heavily upper-class, perhaps predominantly Athenian. Thucydides may well have hoped for occasional wider exposure; some extended passages, especially those describing battles and other vigorous action, are packed with picturesque storyteller's detail and could have been recited very effectively. Even these, however, gain much of their meaning from the intricate context to which they belong.

Thucydides took an extreme chance with his unprecedented book. He was driven by his obvious, very Greek, and especially very Athenian competitiveness and, even more, by his dismay that current events received less thoughtful attention than those continuously retold from the legendary past. It is not necessary, and probably wrong, to believe that he was as indifferent to Greek literary and artistic accomplishments as his silence (even in Perikles' hymn of praise to contemporary Athens) would suggest. He saw that the tragedians and above all Homer had achieved their lasting impact by stark concentration on human motivation and experience, and on these terms he attempted to make the Peloponnesian War as unforgettable as the Trojan War. Over the years, the readers he sought will maintain that he succeeded. For them, somehow, Brasidas will always be approaching the bridge at Amphipolis as the snow falls and shortly before Thucydides.

TRANSLATOR'S NOTE

The translator's fundamental responsibility, at least in dealing with a prose work of nonfiction, is to give the reader the most accurate information possible about what is in the text. I have at all times attempted to fulfill this responsibility, benefitting in the process from the enormous amount of important, variegated, and stimulating research on Thucydides that has been published during the past few decades. My principal motivation for translating Thucydides, however, was to convey to the reader with little or no knowledge of Greek a comparably accurate impression of Thucydides as an artist, in all his demanding originality. Both translators and readers will differ over the proper methodology for reproducing the spirit of an author, and there are situations in which the aims of fidelity, clarity, and readability come into conflict with one another. My priority has been fidelity, and although I have not always been entirely literal in reproducing Greek syntax or idiom, I have tended to be most literal where I feel that

Thucydides is at his most distinctive and idiosyncratic; in particular, I have resisted subdividing his unusually—and intentionally—long sentences. When I am not sure that the results are clear, I have had recourse to the footnotes. I felt that some Greek terms were better left untranslated and have listed these in a glossary (sometimes with a reference to a note giving additional information). As for readability, I can only hope that my approach has not been counterproductive, that I have not at times made Thucydides appear less readable than he actually is; my plea is that, while no translation other than the freest paraphrase could ever turn *The Peloponnesian War* into easy reading, Thucydides is at almost all times an exciting writer, not least when he is struggling to express novel or complicated ideas. I in turn have often struggled in the attempt to capture this excitement. In spelling I have preferred Greek, but not when a more latinized or anglicized version reflects the pronunciation or the near-universal usage of English-speaking classicists (Alcibiades, Syracuse). In the translation I refer to Hellas, Hellenes, and Lacedaemonians; in the introductions and the footnotes, to Greece, Greeks, and Spartans.

The footnotes have several functions and as a consequence are not uniform in tone or scale. Some serve to furnish the reader with additional information required for a full understanding of a passage; some are intended to explore the implications of a passage, including the problems it may pose, and in these notes I have given priority to the most recent Thucydidean scholarship, sometimes adding my own suggestions; my emphasis has been on elucidating Thucydides as a literary artist rather than as a historian.

For the Greek text, my starting point has always been the edition of J. Classen as revised by J. Steup; the footnotes indicate most of the various other editions I consulted. Like all of these, I observe the canonical (and on the whole sensible and convenient) division of *The Peloponnesian War* into eight books; I have supplied a short introduction for each of them (a single one for books 6 and 7) summarizing its contents and chief characteristics. I have also followed the standard subdivision of the books into chapters, with which the endnotes are correlated, but I have not used the further subdivisions of chapters into sections or lines (the former, however, are regularly used in the secondary literature I cite).

I am deeply grateful to Hackett Publishing Company for honoring me with the opportunity to translate Thucydides and for giving helpful advice and friendly encouragement at every stage along the way. The anonymous readers for Hackett were invaluable, sympathetic towards my intentions and rigorous and constructive in showing me where I was subverting these; I shudder to think what my work would have been like without their critiques. Over the years, I have gained considerably from conversations and correspondence about Thucydides with Stanley Burstein, Mortimer Chambers, Paula Arnold Debnar, Carolyn Dewald, Andrew Dyck, Michael Haslam, Mabel Lang, Donald Lateiner, Richmond Lattimore, Stephen Rhodes, Frank Russell, Thomas Scanlon, Michael Seaman, Daniel Tompkins, and many of my students at UCLA; during my own student days, the stimulating teaching of Norman Doenges and the late William Wallace precluded any possibility that I would fail to develop a special interest in Thucydides. Some other instances of indebtedness are mentioned in my footnotes. Elian Chuaqui and Mary Eike gave generous and efficient help with proofreading.

In preparing corrections to the first printing, I benefited from suggestions by several alert and sympathetic readers, particularly Chuck Bennett and Professor Simon Hornblower.

BOOK ONE

INTRODUCTION

In a long and characteristically intricate sentence, Thucydides begins by intro-ducing himself and his subject. For the latter, he claims a unique magnitude, jus-tifying this in part by putting forward what he regards as the first reasonably accurate survey of early Greek history, the "Archaeology"; sea power, a great leitmotif in book 1, is given special prominence. The methods he uses here illus-trate the ones he intends to follow throughout his work: objectivity, careful ex-amination of all evidence, avoidance of mythology and story-telling; the speeches, however, must not be taken as transcripts of all that was said. The first two of these (Thucydidean speeches are frequently paired) are in the context of the events leading to the outbreak of war. Thucydides expresses his hope to have made clear for all time the causes, both immediate and long-term, of the Peloponnesian War. The most important of these, the growth of Athenian power and Spartan fear of it, lead him to survey the period of ca. 479–433 B.C.E., the "Pentakontaetia." Returning to the immediately prewar period, he describes the assembly at Sparta in which the Peloponnesian alliance reached the decision to declare war. Final negotiations with Athens are the occasion for the prewar sto-ries of Kylon, Pausanias, and Themistokles, told in an uncharacteristically straightforward and entertaining style (this does not necessarily reflect Hero-dotean influence and would not necessarily be early writing on that account). At the conclusion of the book is the first of three speeches Thucydides gives Perikles, notable for its optimistic assessment of Athenian strength and concom-itant intransigence.

Book 1 is the most ambitious and original portion of Thucydides' work; it is also the most controversial of the eight books. Book 1 confronts the reader squarely with the so-called Thucydidean question: Which passages were com-posed at which date? Equally central is the newer, "post modernist" question: What sort of historian was Thucydides, and how accurate? Every major feature of book 1 has been called seriously flawed. The justification of his subject has been seen as rhetorical exaggeration; the "Archaeology," as full of naive anach-ronisms and overcredulous (despite Thucydides' several disclaimers) in its use of

1

Homer. Thucydides policy on recording speeches has been found confused, even contradictory; his practice, deficient in whatever accuracy he meant to claim. Rather than proving definitive, his analysis of the causes of the war has been controversial enough to generate exhaustive modern debate, and some have seen here something less pardonable in a historian than confusion or obscurity: an attempt, after the event, at an apologia for Periklean Athens, even a programmatic falsification of genuine Spartan attempts to avoid the conflict. The stories about Kylon, Pausanias, and Themistokles are conceded more charm than authenticity.

For all its problems and controversies, the survival of book 1 alone would have assured us that Thucydides was a writer of exceptional intellectual and artistic power.

BOOK ONE

[1] Thucydides, an Athenian, recorded the war between the Peloponnesians and the Athenians, writing how they waged it against each other and beginning his work as soon as the war broke out in expectation that it would be a major one and notable beyond all previous wars, basing this assumption on the fact that both sides came into it flourishing in overall preparedness and on seeing that the rest of the Hellenes were aligning themselves with one or the other, some immediately and others at least intending to. This was certainly the greatest disturbance to affect the Hellenes and a considerable number of barbarians—one might say the majority of mankind.

While it was impossible, because of the amount of time elapsed, to discover clearly what happened in the previous era or the still more remote past, I believe—using the evidence I have come to trust by investigating as far back as possible—that these events were not on a large scale either regarding warfare or in other respects. [2] For it is clear that what is now called Hellas was not a land securely settled long ago, but that there were

1.1. Whatever Thucydides called his untitled work, it would not have been "History," a word he carefully avoided (see especially Loraux 1986a). His first sentence suggests a title, too long to be convenient; "Peloponnesian War" has become a conventional abbreviation, and if it is Athenocentric, that is not fundamentally misleading. His subsequent practice is to refer simply to "this war." Woodman 1988, pp. 1–69, while I think exaggerating rhetoric as a component in Thucydides' writing and thought, convincingly shows how his preface has many verbal echoes of Herodotos and how, more generally, he vies with Homer as well as the older historian in magnifying his theme (see also 1.23). See also Moles 1993.

1.2–19. These chapters are commonly called the "Archaeology": not in the modern sense (despite 1.10) but as generally used in antiquity to refer (often as a title) to accounts of very ancient history or lore. The term here (first attested in a scholion on 1.12) does Thucydides some disservice in misrepresenting his specific purpose (despite a few digressions) of justifying his initial statement about the war's importance and of demonstrating his methodology in the process. As an introduction, 1.2–19 are severe to the point of forbidding, as was complained in antiquity; modern scholars have more often been inclined to criticize substantive shortcomings such as credulous use of poets as evidence or anachronisms resulting from

migrations in former times and each group readily abandoned its territory
under pressure from anyone more numerous at the time. In the absence of
commerce (they didn't associate with one another on either land or sea
with any confidence), utilizing their native resources to the level of a bare
living without possessing surplus goods and without planting crops (since
it was uncertain when someone else would come and take these from people who also had no fortifications) and supposing that they could obtain
the minimal daily subsistence anywhere, they each emigrated without hesitation and accordingly were strong neither in the size of their cities nor in
the rest of their preparation. It was especially the finest land that constantly changed population: what is now called Thessaly, Boiotia, most of
the Peloponnesos except Arkadia, and the best parts elsewhere in Hellas.
For on account of the fertility of the land, there were individual gains
bringing about factional strife that ruined the people living there, and it
also made them all the more the object of plots from outside. Attica, in any
case, was without faction from remotest times because of its poor soil, and
the same people always occupied it. And here is not the worst evidence for
arguing that the failure of other parts of Hellas to grow in the same way as
Attica was due to migrations. For of the people driven from the rest of
Hellas by war or faction, the most capable took refuge among the Athenians, considering it secure, and because from the start they immediately
became citizens, they made the city's population even larger, so that later,
with Attica insufficient, the Athenians also sent out colonies to Ionia.

[3] And the following also shows me clearly the weakness of early soci-
eties: before the Trojan War, the Hellenes are not known to have accomplished anything in common. Nor, it seems to me, did they share the name
Hellas yet; rather, in the days before Hellen, the son of Deukalion, this
title in fact did not even exist, and the various tribes, most extensively the

---

arguments by analogy. Hornblower 1991, pp. 7–56, however, makes many effective points in defense of this account of Greek prehistory and early history, rightly
stressing (pp. 7–8) how little Thucydides had to work with. Some other recent discussions of the Archaeology are Connor 1984, pp. 20–32, Allison 1989, pp. 11–27,
and Ellis 1991

1.2. "Without planting crops": Thucydides must be referring to planting trees
such as olive, which took time to produce; cf. *HCT* I and Hornblower 1991 *ad*
1.2.2. "And here is . . . due to migrations:" this important sentence is unfortunately
one of the most obscure in Thucydides, and other interpretations are possible (see
Hornblower *ad* 1.2.6); characteristically, Thucydides has accompanied compressed expression of several thoughts with extremely abstract language.

Pelasgian, gave their names to the areas, but when Hellen and his sons became powerful in Phthiotis and were called in to help other cities, each tended now to be called Hellenes through the association, although it was a long process for this to prevail for all. And Homer is the best evidence; born long after even the Trojan War, he never uses this term collectively nor for any except Achilles' followers from Phthiotis (precisely the first Hellenes) but refers in his poems to Danaans, Argives, and Achaians. He does not even speak of barbarians, in my opinion because the Hellenes had not yet been comparably distinguished by a single name. The Hellenes, then, as they increasingly came to be called, both city by city (all speaking the same language) and later as a whole, accomplished nothing together before the Trojan War on account of weakness and lack of contact with one another. But it was only when they were becoming more experienced in seafaring that they united even for this expedition.

[4] Minos was the earliest known in our tradition to acquire a navy, and he controlled most of the sea now called Hellenic, ruled the Cyclades, and in most cases was also their first colonizer, driving out the Karians and installing his sons as governors. He also naturally cleared the seas of piracy as far as possible to direct revenues toward himself instead. [5] For the Hellenes in early times, as well as the barbarians along the coast and all who were islanders, turned to piracy as soon as they increased their contacts by sea, some of the most powerful men leading the way for their own profit and to support the needy. Falling on unwalled cities consisting of villages, they plundered them and made their main living from this, the practice not yet bringing disgrace but even conferring a certain prestige; witness those mainlanders even of the present who glory in successful raiding, also the request everywhere in early poetry that men arriving by sea say whether they were pirates, as though those questioned would not deny the practice nor would those who wanted to know blame them. They also raided each other on land. Much of Hellas still lives in the old way up to the present, Ozolian Lokris, Aitolia, Akarnania, that part of the mainland generally, and for these mainlanders the habit of carrying weapons has survived as a result of the old-style plundering. [6] For all Hellas used to carry weapons because their settlements were unprotected and their routes unsafe, and they spent their ordinary daily life under arms, like barbarians.

1.3. The most authoritative antique date for the fall of Troy, 1184, has considerable support from archaeological evidence. "All speaking the same language" might, as a new element, fit in more naturally after "as a whole": for possible dislocation in the text, cf. Classen/Steup I and *HCT* I *ad* 1.3.4.

Those parts of Hellas that still live in this way are an indication of what was also the former way of life for all alike. The Athenians were the first to put weapons aside and make their lives more sumptuous as well as more relaxed, and the elder of their rich men only recently gave up the indulgence of wearing linen tunics and tying up their hair in a knot fastened with gold grasshoppers; from the influence of kinship, the same fashion lasted for a long time among Ionian elders. By contrast, it was the Lacedaemonians who first dressed simply in the present style, and in general their wealthy men began to live most like common people. They were also the first to strip publicly for athletics and anoint themselves with oil afterward; the old way was for athletes to compete with their genitals covered, even in the Olympic games, and this ended quite recently. Even now, there are some barbarians, especially Asians, who hold boxing and wrestling contests and do it wearing loincloths. And one might point to many other ways in which early Hellenic life resembled that of barbarians today.

[7] As for cities, those built later in a time of increased seafaring and with more abundant wealth were fortified establishments right on the coast and occupied the isthmuses for trade as well as defense against their neighbors. The old cities, however, on account of the long survival of piracy, were usually built away from the sea, whether on the islands or the mainland (for the pirates raided both one another and the nonseafaring populations of the coast), and are inland settlements to this day. [8] Islanders were the most active pirates, both Karians and Phoenicians. These settled most of the islands, and here is proof: when Delos was purified by the Athenians in this war and all the burials on the island removed, more than half proved to be Karian, recognizable by the weaponry used as grave furnishings and by the method of burial which is still in use. When the navy of Minos was established, communication by sea improved, since his colonization of most of the islands involved expelling the lawless elements, and coastal populations now increasingly proceeded to acquire wealth and live more securely, some even building city walls as a reflection of their new prosperity. Love of profit caused the

1.6. "More sumptuous": for this passage (and the Archaeology in general) as a challenge to Herodotos, see Georges 1994, pp. 136–137. There is some evidence, by no means conclusive, from both testimonia and art that "athletic nudity" (whose origins are still much debated) was a much earlier institution than Thucydides believed; cf. Bonfante 1989, McDonnell 1991, and Percy 1996, p. 73.

1.8. For the possibility that Thucydides along with others misidentified Greek Geometric pottery (ca. 900–700 B.C.E.) as Karian, see Snodgrass 1980, p. 66.

weaker to submit to the domination of the strong and the more powerful, with their abundant wealth, to make the smaller cities subject to them. It was after they had already entered this stage that they later campaigned against Troy.

[9] And Agamemnon, as I see it, assembled his force more by surpassing his contemporaries in power than by leading suitors bound by the oaths to Tyndareus. Those Peloponnesians who have received the clearest account through ancestral tradition say that first Pelops acquired power through the enormous wealth he brought with him among a poor population when he came from Asia and gave his name to the land, even though he was an immigrant, and that later the position of his descendants was even greater when Eurystheus was killed in Attica by the Herakleidai after entrusting his kingdom to his maternal uncle Atreus (banished by his father, as it happened, because of the death of Chrysippos) at the start of his campaign on account of their kinship, and when Eurystheus never came back, Atreus with the consent of the Mycenaeans, since they feared the Heraklidai, and he was considered powerful and had also cultivated the common people, succeeded as king of Mycenae and all Eurystheus' other holdings, and the descendants of Pelops became greater than the descendants of Perseus. I think that Agamemnon, combining this inheritance with greater naval strength than anyone else, assembled and launched the expedition less because of good will than because he was feared. For he obviously brought with him the greatest number of ships and in addition supplied the Arkadians, as Homer, if he is good enough evidence, has stated clearly. And he says further, in the "Transmission of the Scepter," that "he was lord over many islands and all Argos"; now as a mainlander he wouldn't have ruled any but offshore islands (and these wouldn't be "many") unless he had possessed a navy. It is this campaign that must be used to gauge what earlier ones were like.

[10] And the fact that Mycenae was a small place or that some other town of that period does not seem impressive now is not a reliable basis for anyone to doubt that the expedition was fully as large as the poets have said and tradition maintains. For if the city of the Lacedaemonians were

1.9. Several ancient sources state, as Thucydides implies in a single "long but not shapely sentence" (*HCT* I *ad* 1.9.2), that Atreus (with his brother Thyestes) murdered his illegitimate half-brother Chrysippos; for this and other traditions about his death, see Gantz 1993, pp. 488–90; the parenthetical mention of Atreus' exile adds irony to Thucydides' emphasis on wealth, since Pelops could not have anticipated how profitable exile would prove for Atreus.

deserted and the shrines and foundations of buildings preserved, I think that after the passage of considerable time there would eventually be widespread doubt that their power measured up to their reputation (and yet they occupy two-fifths of the Peloponnesos and preside over the whole of it as well as numerous allies beyond; nevertheless, since the city is not unified nor furnished with elaborate shrines or public buildings but settled in villages in the old Hellenic way, it would look inferior), but that if the Athenians were to suffer the same fate their power would be estimated, from the city's pure appearance, as twice what it is.

It is therefore reasonable to avoid the skepticism that comes from looking at the appearance of cities rather than their military resources and to believe that the Trojan expedition was greater than previous ones—yet fell short of those of the present, again if it is right to trust Homer's poetry here as well, where he probably embellished with exaggerations, being a poet; even if we do trust him, it is still obvious that the expedition was not very strong. For out of twelve hundred ships he puts those of the Boiotians at a hundred and twenty men and those of Philoktetes at fifty, in my opinion indicating the largest and the smallest crews; at any rate, he does not mention other sizes in the "Catalogue of Ships." That the rowers were also fighters he has made clear regarding Philoktetes' ships, since he says all the oarsmen were archers. It is not probable that many except kings and those of the highest rank sailed as passengers, especially since they had to cross the sea with military equipment, moreover using boats that had no decks but were built in the old piratical style. Now if one takes an average from the largest and the smallest ships, those who sailed do not seem numerous considering that they were sent out by Hellas as a whole.

[11] The reason was not so much shortage of men as shortage of money. On account of low supplies, they led an army limited to the size they considered capable of living off the land while campaigning, and even after winning a battle when they arrived (as they clearly did, or they could not have built a wall for their camp), they apparently did not use their whole force but turned to cultivating the Chersonesos and to plundering—

1.10. "Rather than their military resources" confuses the argument, which should be: "I am demonstrating the right and wrong ways to estimate military resources"; the phrase may have been added as a gloss, so Classen/Steup *ad* 1.10.3. In this chapter we have "perhaps the first ever expression of the idea of 'poetic license'" (Hornblower 1991 *ad* 1.10.3); Thucydides himself bears watching, since the "twelve hundred" ships were actually 1186). For a total of 102,000 men and sensible discussion of Thucydides' arguments, see *HCT* I *ad* 1.10.5.

because of low supplies. And with their army divided in this way, the Trojans were the more able to hold out for ten years of active warfare, since they were a match for whatever forces were left to face them. If they had come with abundant supplies and carried on the war in unison and continuously without plundering or cultivating land, they would easily have conquered in battle and captured the city, since they actually held their own without using all their forces but only the detachment on hand at any time; if they had settled down and pressed the siege, they would have taken Troy with less time and effort. Instead, because of lack of funds, not only were previous efforts feeble, but even this very one which became so renowned in comparison is actually revealed by the facts as less significant than its reputation and the idea about it, which now prevails on account of the poets.

[12] Even after the Trojan War, of course, Hellas was still going through migrations and incursions that prevented its untroubled development. The delayed return of the Hellenes from Troy caused much turmoil, and there was widespread faction in the cities, creating refugees who established new ones. The present-day Boiotians, sixty years after the capture of Troy, were driven from Arne by the Thessalians and settled the land now called Boiotia, formerly Kadmeis (there was also a contingent in this land earlier, including some who campaigned against Ilion). And in the eightieth year after the fall of Troy, the Dorians and the Herakleidai took over the Peloponnesos. After a long period of difficulty, Hellas was securely pacified, without further population changes, and sent out colonies; the Athenians colonized most of Ionia and the islands, whereas the Peloponnesians sent out most of the colonies in Italy and Sicily as well as some elsewhere in Hellas.

All these settlements were after the Trojan War. [13] When Hellas became stronger and placed even more emphasis on acquiring wealth, tyrannies were set up in most of the cities as a result of increased revenues (previously, there were hereditary monarchies with formally restricted powers), and the Hellenes equipped navies and were more active at sea. The Corinthians are said to have been the first to develop ships almost like today's, and Corinth was the first place in Hellas where triremes were built. And Ameinokles, a Corinthian shipwright, evidently built four ships for the Samians; it is about three hundred years from the end of this war since he went to Samos. The earliest sea battle we know of involved Corinthians against Corcyreans; this was about two hundred and sixty years before the same date. For the Corinthians, with their city situated on the isthmus, were always engaged in commerce from the earliest times, since the Hellenes within the Peloponnesos and beyond gained access to one another through their territory, at first on land rather than by sea, and Corinth was powerful through affluence, as the ancient poets confirm by calling the place "wealthy." And as Hellenic seafaring increased, they provided themselves with ships and put down piracy, and with involvement in both kinds of commerce they kept their city strong by revenues. Later, the Ionians also acquired great naval strength in the time of Cyrus, the first Persian king, and his son Kambyses and for some time controlled the sea in their area when they were fighting against Cyrus. Polykrates the tyrant of Samos, whose navy flourished in the time of Kambyses, subjected many of the islands and on seizing Rheneia dedicated it to the Delian Apollo. And the Phokaians, when they colonized Massilia, defeated the Carthaginians at sea.

[14] This accounts for the strongest navies, and it seems that even these, many generations after the Trojan War, used few triremes but were still equipped with pentekonters and long boats, just like the earlier fleets. It was shortly before the Persian Wars and the death of Dareios, king of Persia after Kambyses, that the tyrants in Sicily and the Corcyreans had large numbers of triremes, and these were the last important navies established in Hellas before Xerxes' campaign. As for the Aiginetans and the Athenians, they and a few others had acquired modest fleets consisting mostly of pentekonters. It was at the last minute that Themistokles persuaded the Athenians, not only at war with the Aiginetans but in expectation of the barbarian as well, to build those same ships they used to fight in the Persian War; even these were still without full decks.

[15] Such were Hellenic navies in the earliest times and later on. Nevertheless, it was those who developed them who consolidated the greatest gains in both revenues and rule over others; especially if their land was insufficient, they sailed to the islands and subjugated them. On land, no war that resulted in any concentration of military forces took place. All wars that did occur were individual affairs over boundaries; the Hellenes did not leave their own territories for expeditions abroad aiming at conquest, since they did not unite as subjects of the most important cities, any more than they joined in expeditions as equal partners, but rather made war individually against neighbors. The war fought at some early date between the Chalkidians and the Eretrians did the most to divide the rest of Hellas into alliances with one side or the other.

[16] The various states also encountered various obstacles to their growth, and in the case of the Ionians, whose power was making great

1.13. Cyrus ruled from 559 to 530; Kambyses, from 530 to 522.

strides, Cyrus and the Persian kingdom, after conquering Croesus and all that lay between the Halys river and the sea, campaigned against them and made the mainland cities his subjects, and Dareios later added the islands by overpowering them with the Phoenician navy. [17] And wherever there were tyrannies in the Hellenic cities, they looked no farther than the personal interests of individual well-being and the enrichment of their households, ran their cities with the maximum security, and only against neighboring peoples did they accomplish anything at all significant; the ones in Sicily made the greatest advances in power. And so in every way Hellas was long held down so that nothing notable was achieved in common, and cities had little enterprise.

[18] After the last tyrants almost everywhere except in Sicily, both those in Athens and those in the rest of Hellas (which was mostly under tyrants long before Athens), were expelled by the Lacedaemonians (for even though their land went through the longest known period of faction after its conquest by the Dorians who now occupy it, they have still been well ordered by laws longer than anyone else and never under tyranny, in fact using the same form of government for over four hundred years since this war ended, and consequently powerful enough to settle the affairs of other cities as well), it was only a few years until the battle of Marathon between the Persians and the Athenians.

Ten years later, the barbarian came back with the great armada intended to enslave Hellas. When this great danger was impending, the Lacedaemonians as the preeminent power became the leaders of the Hellenes who joined in the fight, while the Athenians, resolving as the Persians advanced to abandon their city and embarking on their ships after they had cleaned it out, became a seaborne people. Although the Hellenes in common drove out the barbarian, it was not much later that both the allies and those who had revolted from the king separated into two groups under the Athenians and the Lacedaemonians, since these stood out as the greatest powers: one strong on land, the other through ships. For a short time, the league held together, and then the Lacedaemonians and the Athenians quarreled and made war on each other, joined by their allies; wherever the other Hellenic states were at odds, they now moved into these two alliances. And so over the whole time from the Persian wars to this war, sometimes making truces, otherwise fighting either each other or any allies that revolted, they became well prepared militarily and grew more experienced by getting their training in combat. [19] The Lacedaemonians did not dominate their allies by making them pay tribute but by taking great pains to have them governed through oligarchies, the Athenians by taking over the fleets of the allied cities, Chios and Lesbos excepted, in the course of time and assigning amounts of money for each to pay. So both as a result had greater preparedness for this war individually than the strongest power they ever enjoyed with their alliance intact.

[20] Such, then, I found to be the nature of early events, although with difficulty in trusting every piece of evidence. For men accept one another's accounts of the past, even about their native countries, with a uniform lack of examination. For example, the Athenians commonly believe that Hipparchos was tyrant when he was killed by Harmodios and Aristogeiton and do not know that Hippias as the eldest son of Peisistratos was the ruler, Hipparchos and Thessalos being his brothers, but Harmodios and Aristogeiton, suspecting at the last minute on that very day that Hippias had received some information from their fellow conspirators, kept away from him as forewarned, but since they could accept their danger only if they actually accomplished something before being arrested, when they found Hipparchos by the sanctuary called the Leokoreion organizing the Panathenaic procession they killed him. And there is a great deal more, from the present as well as the dimly remembered past, that the other Hellenes too are wrong about, such as that each king of the Lacedaemonians casts two votes instead of one, or that they have a Pitanate army division, which never existed. So devoid of effort is most people's search for the truth, and they would rather turn toward what is readily available. [21] In light of the evidence I have cited, however, no one would go wrong in supposing that the early events I have related happened much in that way: not believing that the past was more like what the poets have sung, embellishing with their exaggerations, or the prose chroniclers have composed more for attractive listening than for truthfulness, in versions that cannot be checked and for the most part have forfeited credibility over time by winning victories as patriotic fiction, but regarding my discoveries from the clearest possible evidence as adequate for what concerns antiquity. And this war—even though men always consider the war on hand the most important while

1.20. Hipparchos was assassinated in 514. Regarding "a great deal more . . . wrong," it is not clear whether Thucydides is primarily criticizing authors or their public. Among the former, he seems to have Herodotos very much in mind, so Hornblower 1991 *ad* 1.20.3, *pace HCT* I *ad* 1.20.3; both scholars review the possibility that Herodotos (6.57.5 and 9.53.2) was not actually in error.

1.21. Flory 1990 has argued persuasively that by "the mythical element" Thucydides means more specifically "patriotic fiction" of the sort that won many "victories" among audiences; cf. Hornblower 1991 *ad* 1.3.2 and 1.21.1.

they are fighting but once they have ended it are more impressed by ancient ones—will nevertheless stand out clearly as greater than the others for anyone who examines it from the facts themselves.

[22] Insofar as these facts involve what the various participants said both before and during the actual conflict, recalling the exact words was difficult for me regarding speeches I heard myself and for my informants about speeches made elsewhere; in the way I thought each would have said what was especially required in the given situation, I have stated accordingly, with the closest possible fidelity on my part to the overall sense of what was actually said. About the actions of the war, however, I considered it my responsibility to write neither as I learned from the chance informant nor according to my own opinion, but after examining what I witnessed myself and what I learned from others, with the utmost possible accuracy in each case. Finding out the facts involved great effort, because

1.22. Speech is too important a part of the evidence to be left out, yet this is a special case, which presents obstacles even to the most conscientious, and Thucydides has just been defining and stressing responsibility on the part of both writer and reader; even though his approach to the speeches must be a compromise, he claims overall accuracy for his combination of summarizing and inventing. The institutionalization of contemporary rhetoric might reduce the subjectivity of the latter component, see Hornblower 1987, p. 46, and cf. Cole 1991, pp. 104–12. The degree of self-contradiction possibly involved in Thucydides' policy for the speeches continues to be exhaustively discussed; Wilson 1982b is a useful summary, pointing out that whether Thucydides actually carried out his policy is quite another question (a number of speeches have been called implausible both as summaries of what was said and as conjectures as to what would predictably have been said). Cf. also Cogan 1981, Hornblower 1987, pp. 45–72, Rusten 1989, pp. 7–17, Heath 1990, Badian 1992, Swain 1993, and Rengakos 1996. Reporting events called for a different policy, and a contrast is drawn but should not be overestimated (on this point and more generally, Gomme's long note in *HCT* I, pp. 140–48 is still invaluable); even though Thucydides was careful to mention his own presence at some events, it is not likely that he was implying that these required less scrutiny (any more than he considered a speech safely recorded if he had heard it himself). Hanson 1993 argues that the speeches attributed to commanders before battle are a literary convention that Thucydides himself invented; it should be noted that as a group these are the speeches most expressly integrated with actions, sometimes in considerable detail. In the last three sentences ("Yet if they are judged useful . . ."), the abstract impersonality is remarkable; there is no first-person vocabulary nor term translatable as "my work." His "single, Olympian boast" (Finley 1942, p. 110) exalts not his individual powers but his principles; others ("who wish") can use these, and the reader can share the ability, which Thucydides claims with careful qualification, to understand what is likely to happen in the future (see especially Ste. Croix 1972, pp. 30–33).

eye-witnesses did not report the same specific events in the same way, but according to individual partisanship or ability to remember. And the results, by avoiding patriotic storytelling, will perhaps seem the less enjoyable for listening. Yet if they are judged useful by any who wish to look at the plain truth about both past events and those that at some future time, in accordance with human nature, will recur in similar or comparable ways, that will suffice. It is a possession for all time, not a competition piece to be heard for the moment, that has been composed.

[23] The Persian War was the greatest action of the past, yet it had a quick resolution in two battles on sea and two on land. But this war not only was great by its extended length but also was accompanied by such sufferings as never afflicted Hellas in any comparable period of time. For never had there been so many cities captured or left desolate, some by barbarians and others by the Hellenes as they fought each other (and some cities even changed population after they were taken), nor were there so many men exiled or slaughtered, both in the war itself and because of faction. And things formerly known from hearsay accounts, less often from factual confirmation, could now be believed, such as earthquakes, since these came without parallel in their wide distribution as well as severity, along with eclipses of the sun, which occurred more frequently than in any memories of the past, also droughts in some parts and the famines caused by them, and the disease that did the most damage and destroyed a large number: the plague. All these descended in conjunction with this war.

The Athenians and the Peloponnesians began it by breaking the Thirty-Year Peace that they made after the capture of Euboia. As to why

1.23. The Thirty-Year Peace was concluded in 446/5. "That no one may ever search . . . begin the war": the literature on this obviously crucial passage is immense; useful recent discussions are Rhodes 1987, Ostwald 1988, pp. 1–5, and Hornblower 1991 *ad* 1.23.6. It is not simply that the precise reasons for the war, especially the question of Athenian vs. Spartan responsibility, are still debated after all, but that (typically) Thucydides' thought and language have become a controversial topic in their own right. I am inclined to agree that "the explicit formulation of a distinction between profound and superficial causes is arguably Th.'s greatest single contribution to later history-writing" (Hornblower, p. 65), yet also to doubt that he distinguished between "cause" and "charges" either absolutely or semantically; cf. 1.118 and 1.145–46. It has often been objected that the "truest cause" was, on Thucydides' own showing, hardly neglected in speech; but what Thucydides apparently means (also in 1.88 and 1.118) is that Spartan *fear* (i.e., of a threat to Sparta's own security) was decisive (Sparta was not dragged into war by its allies) but downplayed among Spartans and Spartan allies (not necessarily by others, cf. 1.33). That Thucydides was referring to retrospective discussion (Richardson 1990, p. 158) seems very unlikely.

they broke the peace, I have first written an account of the complaints and disputes so that no one may ever search for the reasons that so great a war broke out among the Hellenes. For I consider the truest cause the one least openly expressed, that increasing Athenian greatness and the resulting fear among the Lacedaemonians made going to war inevitable. The following are the openly stated charges made by each side that caused them to break the peace and begin the war.

[24] Epidamnos is a city on the right for a voyager into the Ionian gulf; the Taulantians, barbarians of the Illyrian race, are the neighboring population. While the Corcyreans colonized it, the founder was Phalios son of Eratokleides, a Corinthian belonging to the descendants of Herakles, who was called in from the mother city in full accordance with ancient custom; and there were some Corinthians as well as other Dorians among the colonists. As time passed, the power of the Epidamnians became great, strengthened by a large population, but after many years of internal conflict, according to reports, they were exhausted by war with the neighboring barbarians and lost much of their power. In the final years before this war, the common people expelled the members of the upper class, who combined with the barbarians in attacking the occupants of the city, plundering them on both land and sea. Since the Epidamnians in the city were getting the worst of it, they sent an embassy to Corcyra as the mother city urging the Corcyreans not to look on while they were destroyed but reconcile them with the exiles as well as bringing the barbarian war to an end; this they begged as suppliants seated in the sanctuary of Hera. Instead of accepting their supplication, the Corcyreans sent them away without results.

[25] When the Epidamnians realized that they would get no help from Corcyra, they were at a loss to deal with the situation and sent to Delphi to ask the gods whether they should give the city over to the Corinthians as its founders and try to find some sort of aid from them. The god's response to them was that they should hand over the city and make the Corinthians their leaders. The Epidamnians went to Corinth and handed over the city as the oracle directed, pointing out that their founder was from Corinth as well as disclosing the oracle, and begged them not to look on while they were being destroyed but to come to their rescue. And the Corinthians promised the requested help, partly as a duty, since they thought the colony was as much theirs as the Corcyreans', but partly also out of hatred for the Corcyreans because they were colonists of theirs who slighted them, neither giving them the customary honors at the festivals they shared nor

---

1.24–55. The Epidamnians sent their embassy to Corcyra in 435. On the war brought on by their plight, see Kagan 1969, pp. 205–50 and Wilson 1987.

offering the first portion of sacrifices to a Corinthian as their other colonies did but looking down on them from a position combining financial power comparable to that of the richest states of the time with stronger military preparedness, also boasting of their marked superiority at sea, sometimes even through Corcyra's early occupation by the Phaeacians of naval fame (and accordingly they built up their fleet all the more and were anything but weak; they had one hundred and twenty triremes when they went into the war). [26] With all these grievances, then, the Corinthians gladly sent help to Epidamnos, inviting anyone who wanted to go as a settler in addition to a detachment of Ambracians, Leukadians, and their own troops. They made their way on land to Apollonia, a Corinthian colony, fearing obstruction by the Corcyreans if they crossed by sea.

When the Corcyreans learned that the settlers and troops had reached Epidamnos and the colony had been made over to the Corinthians, they reacted violently. Sailing immediately with twenty-five ships, later joined by a second force, they abusively ordered them to take back the exiles (who had come to Corcyra, pointed to their ancestral tombs, and appealed to these and their ties of friendship as they begged the Corcyreans to restore them) and send away the troops and the settlers the Corinthians had sent in. With none of their demands met, the Corcyreans opened hostilities against the Epidamnians with forty ships, joined by the exiles they intended to restore and by additional forces from Illyria. Occupying a position in front of the city, they made a proclamation that any Epidamnian who wanted to leave and the foreigners as well could go away unharmed; otherwise, they would treat them as enemies. Since there was no compliance, the Corcyreans laid siege to the city (which is on an isthmus), [27] and the Corinthians, when messengers from Epidamnos reported the siege, prepared an expedition and at the same time formally announced the colonization of Epidamnos on a fair and equal basis for anyone who wanted to go; anyone unwilling to sail with them right away but wishing to take part in the colony could make a deposit of fifty Corinthian drachmas and stay behind. A large number sailed and a large number put down the money. They also asked the Megarians to join them in a naval escort in case their voyage was obstructed by the Corcyreans; Megara furnished them with eight ships for the escort, and likewise Pale in Kephallenia four. They asked the Epidaurians, who supplied five, likewise Hermione one, Troizen two, Leukas ten, and Ambracia eight. They requested money from the Thebans and Phleiasians, both money and ships without crews from the Eleans. Thirty ships and three thousand hoplites were supplied by the Corinthians themselves.

[28] When the Corcyreans learned about these preparations, they went to Corinth with Lacedaemonian and Sikyonian representatives they had called in as supporters and ordered the Corinthians to withdraw both their troops and the settlers, since they had no claim to Epidamnos. If the Corinthians wanted to contest this, they were willing to accept arbitration in the Peloponnesos by any cities both parties agreed on; these were to go unchallenged, whichever party was awarded the colony. They were also willing to submit the case to the oracle at Delphi. They advised the Corinthians not to begin a war; otherwise, if the Corinthians chose force, for their own part they would be compelled to find friends not of their preference, different from those they had now but necessary for self-defense. The Corinthians answered that if they removed their ships and the barbarian forces from Epidamnos there could be deliberations; meanwhile, it was unthinkable that they would be negotiating while the Epidamnians were under siege. The Corcyreans countered that they would comply if the Corinthians also withdrew their men in Epidamnos; they were also ready to let both sides stay in place and to make a truce until a settlement was reached.

[29] The Corinthians accepted neither proposal. Instead, when their ships were manned and their allies on hand, first sending ahead a herald to declare war on the Corcyreans and then setting out with seventy-five ships and two thousand hoplites, they sailed for Epidamnos to confront the Corcyreans in battle. The commanders of the ships were Aristeus son of Pellichos, Kallikrates son of Kallias, and Timanor son of Timanthes, and of the infantry Archetimos son of Eurytimos, and Ischaridas son of Ischaros. When they reached Aktion in the territory of Anaktorion at the mouth of the Ambracian gulf, where the sanctuary of Apollo is, the Corcyreans sent a herald in a small boat ordering the Corinthians not to sail against them and at the same time manned their ships, reinforcing the old ones to make them seaworthy and getting the others in full readiness. When the herald reported no sign of peace from the Corinthian side, and their ships were fully manned, numbering eighty (since forty were besieging Epidamnos), they put out to sea against the Corinthians and fought a battle; the Corcyreans won decisively and destroyed fifteen Corinthian ships. On the same day, their men besieging Epidamnos also succeeded in forcing it to surrender on terms allowing them to sell the foreign elements into slavery while holding the Corinthians prisoner until there was a further decision. [30] After the sea battle, the Corcyreans set up a trophy at Leukimme, a promontory in their territory, and killed their other prisoners of war but held the Corinthians in captivity.

Afterward, when the Corinthians and their allies had taken their ships home in defeat, the Corcyreans were in control of the entire sea in that area; sailing to the Corinthian colony on Leukas, they ravaged the land, and they burned Kyllene, the shipyard of the Eleans, because they had furnished ships and money to the Corinthians. And for most of the period after the sea battle, they maintained control of the sea and plundered the Corinthian allies by sea attacks, until the Corinthians at the beginning of summer sent out ships and an army because their allies were suffering, and they set up camp at Aktion and around Cheimerion in Thesprotia for the protection of both Leukas and all other friendly cities. The Corcyreans set up an opposing camp at Leukimme with both ships and infantry. Neither sailed against the other, but throughout that summer they remained in their opposing positions, and with the approach of winter each went home.

[31] During the year after the sea battle and the following year the Corinthians, furious over the war with the Corcyreans, built ships and prepared the strongest naval force they could, collecting crews not only from the Peloponnesos but also from the rest of Hellas by the attraction of pay. When the Corcyreans learned about their preparations, they were alarmed and decided (since they were not allied with any of the Hellenes, having enrolled in neither the Athenian nor the Lacedaemonian alliance) to go to the Athenians and try to become their allies and find help there. When the Corinthians learned about this, they also came to Athens to present their case, lest the addition of the Athenian to the Corcyrean navy prevent them from settling the war as they chose. After an assembly was called, the two sides gave opposing speeches, and the Corcyreans spoke as follows:

[32] "Athenians, there are reasonable obligations for people who, like ourselves at present, come before neighbors to ask for help when there is no prior claim based on great service or an alliance: they should demonstrate first, as well as possible, that their request will actually offer advantages, otherwise that at least it will not bring harm; next, that their gratitude can be relied on; and if they do not prove any of these points clearly, they should not be outraged at not getting what they requested. The Corcyreans have sent us because they were confident that in requesting an alliance they could also make these arguments convincingly. But it has come about that the same policy is both inconsistent, from your standpoint, regarding our request and disadvantageous regarding our own situation at present. For we who by our own choice never entered into an alliance with anyone in the past are here to ask this of others and at the same time, as a consequence, have come to be isolated in our present war with the Corinthians.

"And what formerly seemed prudence on our part, that we did not share, through foreign alliance, the risks brought on by the other party's judgment, now stands revealed as folly and weakness. It is true that in the sea battle we threw back the Corinthians by ourselves, unaided. But since they are moving against us with a large force from the Peloponnesos and the rest of Hellas and we see that we cannot survive through our own strength alone and, moreover, the danger is a terrible one should we fall into their power, we are forced to ask for help from you and every other source and should be pardoned if we take initiatives that break with our former heedlessness, not with criminal intentions but rather because we were mistaken in our judgment.

[33] "The circumstances of our request, if you grant it, will be advantageous for you in many respects: first because you will be helping those who are being treated unjustly, and next because by receiving those in the greatest danger you will earn in the securest possible way their gratitude in undying memory; and we have built up the largest navy except for yours. Consider this: what success could be more exceptional, or more painful to your enemies, if that very force which you would have wanted on your side at a high cost in both money and gratitude comes over to you of its own accord, offering itself without risks or expense and even beyond that bringing you a widespread reputation for generosity, the gratitude of those you will be defending, and a direct benefit in strength? In all of time, all these things in combination have befallen few men, and few have come seeking an alliance who can offer their benefactors no less security and honor than they will receive.

"As to the actual war in which we would be invaluable, if there is anyone among you who does not believe it is coming, his judgment is at fault, and he is not aware that in their fear of you the Lacedaemonians are ready for war, that the Corinthians have strong influence there and are your enemies, and that they are making our subjection the preliminary to an attack on you, lest we stand together in common enmity against them and they fail to gain either of two initial advantages, damaging us or making their own position secure. Conversely, the right course for us is to take the initiative by our offer of alliance and your acceptance of it and to anticipate rather than to react to them in planning.

[34] "And if they say it is not right for you to receive their colonies as allies, they ought to know that every colony honors the mother city when it is treated properly but is alienated when treated unjustly; colonists are not sent out to be the slaves of those who stay behind but their equals. The unjust behavior of the Corinthians is obvious, since they preferred to settle

their grievances by war rather than by fair standards. And let their actions against us, their kinsmen, be a warning to you, so that you are neither misled by their deceit nor won over by their requests made openly. It is the one with the least regrets over concessions to the enemy who will continue in the greatest security. [35] You will not break the treaty with the Lacedaemonians by receiving us, the allies of neither side. It is specified in the treaty that any Hellenic state allied with neither side is allowed to come over to whichever it pleases. And it is intolerable if they have the opportunity to recruit crews from your allies and the rest of Hellas in addition, and last but not least from your own subjects, yet they can cut us off from the alliance which is open to all, and from any other source of help, and then call it illegal if you grant our request.

"But we will have a much deeper complaint if we fail to persuade you. For you will be rejecting us even though we are in danger and not your enemies, while providing no opposition to the other side, enemies of yours and aggressors, but actually allowing them to build up strength from your empire. There is no justice in this, but in either denying them hired combatants from your empire or sending us as well whatever aid you think fit, but particularly in helping us by openly accepting us as allies. We have shown, as we suggested at the start, that the advantages would be numerous, the most important being that we have the same enemies (the strongest basis for trust), and these are not weak but more than able to punish defectors. And to spurn a naval alliance is not like rejecting an alliance on land; by all means, keep anyone else from having a fleet if possible, otherwise pick the strongest as your friend.

[36] "And if anyone is thinking that there are advantages in what we have said but fears to break the treaty by acting on this conviction, let him understand that while his fear combined with strength will contribute to the enemy's fear, confidence in a position of weakness after rejecting us will appear less threatening to strong enemies, and understand further that he is not planning now any more about Corcyra than about Athens and not showing effective foresight on her behalf, when in confronting the war which is imminent and all but here, he looks only at the immediate situation and hesitates over acquiring a site of critical importance whether in friendly or hostile hands. For its placement on the route to Italy and Sicily is ideal for keeping a fleet from there from reinforcing the Peloponnesians or being sent there from here, and in general highly advantageous.

"By this briefest of summaries of both the overall situation and the details, you will realize that we must not be abandoned. There are three Hellenic navies of real importance: yours, ours, and the Corinthians'. If you do nothing to prevent two of these from being formed into a single one, then you will fight at sea against the Corcyreans and the Corinthians combined; by accepting our alliance, you will be able to oppose them with our ships added to your own."

Such was the Corcyrean speech, and the Corinthians then spoke as follows. [37] "Since these Corcyreans have not only spoken about acceptance of their alliance but stated that we are aggressors and they are unfairly involved in war, it is necessary for us to refer to these points as well before going on to the rest of our argument, so that you may comprehend the claims on our side more completely and then refuse their request with sound reasons. They say that it was out of prudence that they never entered into an alliance, but they have followed this policy with evil intentions, not out of virtue, and did not want to have an ally as witness to their crimes nor to face disgrace by calling one in. And in this connection there is also their state's autonomy through its location, which empowers them to be the sole judges of injuries they inflict rather than being controlled by agreements, since they make very few voyages to their neighbors while very frequently encountering others obliged to put into their ports. It is in this context that they speciously justify a nonalignment that serves their purpose, not to avoid involvement in the wrongdoing of others but to commit wrongs unaided, and to use force where they have control, take advantage where they can escape detection, and feel no shame over whatever gains they make. Yet if they were really the honorable men they claim to be, the more unaccountable they are to others, the more opportunity they would then have to give their high character the greatest visibility by offering and accepting just settlements.

[38] "But they are not that sort in their relations either with others or with us, and although they are our colonists, they have been rebellious all along and are now at war with us, saying that they were not sent out to be mistreated. For our part, we maintain that we did not found colonies to be insulted by them but to be recognized as leaders and receive the proper signs of respect. Our other colonies certainly honor us, and we are greatly beloved by our colonists; it is obvious that if we are acceptable to the majority, there is no good reason for us to be unacceptable to them alone, and that we would not be taking the abnormal step of going to war with them if we had not also suffered extraordinary wrongs.

"Even if we had actually been in error, it would have been noble on their part to yield to our wrath, and disgraceful on ours to abuse their moderation; but in the insolence of wealth they have wronged us in many ways, and in particular, even though they did not lay claim to Epidamnos, which

is ours, when it was being injured, they seized it when we came to the rescue and now hold it by force. [39] And of course they say that they were
willing to submit to arbitration first, but this can certainly not be regarded
as a meaningful claim when invoked from a secure position by someone
who has seized an advantage rather than by one who puts himself on an
equal basis, in deeds as well as words, before contesting the issue. These
people, with their attractive proposal of arbitration, did not bring it forward before they besieged the place but only after they realized that we
would not stand aside.

"They have now come here, not only in the wrong themselves over Epidamnos but expecting you to be not their allies but their accomplices in
crime, and to receive them when they are at war with us. When they
should have approached you was at the time of their greatest security, not
in a situation in which we have been wronged and they are in danger, and
in which you who had no share of their power then will now be sharing
your aid and without being involved in their crimes will be equally responsible to us, even though they should long since have included you in their
power as well as its consequences.

[40] "That we have come with valid complaints, then, and that the Corcyreans are violent and grasping has been made clear; it is now essential
that you know that you cannot justly receive them. For if it is stated in the
treaty that any city not already included may join whichever side it wishes,
this is not a provision for those who take this action in order to harm others
but for anyone whose request for protection does not involve deserting
someone else and does not bring those who accept the alliance, if they
reflect on it, war instead of peace.

"This would be in store for you in the present situation unless you follow our advice. You would not simply become their auxiliaries but our
enemies instead of our partners in a treaty. For if you join their cause, our
defensive operations will necessarily involve you. And yet the right course
for you is certainly to remain uninvolved with either side, unless you
choose the alternative of joining us against them (since you are actually a
party to a treaty with the Corinthians but have never had so much as a
truce with the Corcyreans), and avoid establishing a principle that allows
alliances with defectors. We can argue that at the time of the Samian
revolt, when the vote of the Peloponnesians was divided over whether to
come to the defense of the Samians, we did not cast our vote against you
but told them plainly that in disciplining allies everyone is on his own.
Now if you are going to start harboring and abetting the wrongdoers, it is
obvious that there are just as many on your side who will come over to us,

and you will be establishing the principle more against yourselves than against us.

[41] "Accordingly, we have these rightful expectations from you, more than sufficient by Hellenic standards, and also advice concerning the following claim to gratitude which we, not being enemies to the point of injuring you nor again friends to the point of your taking liberties, maintain you should satisfy in the present situation. At one time, when you were short of warships in your war with Aigina, before the Persian invasion, you received twenty ships from Corinth. This favor, and the one that kept the Peloponnesians from helping the Samians, made the conquest of the Aiginetans and the punishment of the Samians possible for you, and our actions also came at those crucial times when men engaged against their enemies are indifferent to everything except winning; they regard anyone who is of service as a friend, even if previously hostile, and anyone opposing them as an enemy even if he happens to be a friend, since they neglect even considerations of kinship in their obsession with immediate victory.

[42] "Reflecting on this, which is something the younger can learn from the older, acknowledge that you should requite us with comparable behavior, and do not suppose that there is justice in what we say, but expediency, if it comes to war, is another matter. Expediency is the consequence of making the fewest mistakes, and the imminence of war, which the Corcyreans use to frighten you when they urge you toward injustice, is still veiled in uncertainty and not a valid reason for an emotional decision that would bring upon you the hatred of the Corinthians, not imminent but with immediate certainty, when the prudent course is to mitigate the suspicion already existing over Megara. For the most recent favor, however slight, can cancel a more substantial grievance when it comes at the right moment. And do not be swayed by the argument that they are offering a mighty naval alliance; to avoid wronging one's equals is a more secure basis of strength than can be found by grasping a dangerous advantage when incited by the immediate prospects.

[43] "Since we find ourselves in the same situation as the one at Lacedaemon, when we declared that each should punish his own allies, we now expect to get as much from you in return, and that you not injure us by your vote when you were helped by ours. Give us the same consideration you receive, with the understanding that the crisis on hand is one that decisively identifies the benefactor as a friend and the opponent as an

1.41. "Considerations of kinship": usually translated "their own interests"; I have followed *HCT* I *ad* 1.43.1.

enemy. Do not go against us by receiving the Corcyreans and do not defend them in their course of injustice. By refusing them, you will be acting correctly and also making the best plans on your own behalf."

[44] This is what the Corinthians said, and the Athenians, after hearing both speeches and meeting in assembly, even for a second time, inclined in the first assembly toward accepting the arguments of the Corinthians but in the later one reconsidered and made an alliance with the Corcyreans, not going so far as to have the same enemies and friends (since if the Corcyreans requested them to sail with them against the Corinthians they would be breaking the treaty with the Peloponnesians) but forming a defensive pact for mutual assistance if anyone attacked Corcyra, Athens, or an ally of either. For they considered war with the Peloponnesians a certainty in any case and did not want Corcyra to reinforce Corinth with a fleet of such size but rather for them to wear each other down as much as possible, so that if it came to war, they would meet weakened opposition from Corinth and other naval powers. At the same time, the island's favorable location on the coastal route to Italy and Sicily was clear to them.

[45] It was for these reasons that the Athenians accepted the alliance with the Corcyreans, and soon after the departure of the Corinthians they sent ten ships to help them. Commanding these were Lakedaimonios son of Kimon, Diotimos son of Strombichos, and Proteas son of Epikles. They were instructed not to fight against the Corinthians unless they sailed against Corcyra and were about to land there or on some other part of their territory, and in that case to prevent them by every means; these instructions were intended to avoid breaking the treaty. [46] The ships arrived at Corcyra, and the Corinthians, after their preparations were complete, set sail for Corcyra with one hundred fifty ships. There were ten from Elis, twelve from Megara, ten from Leukas, twenty-seven from Ambracia, one from Anaktorion, and ninety from the Corinthians themselves; each city had its own commanders, and the Corinthians had five, with Xenokleides son of Euthykles in charge.

When they had reached the mainland across from Corcyra in their voyage from Leukas, they anchored at Cheimerion in Thesprotian territory.

1.44. "The Athenians . . . reconsidered": Plutarch's statement (*Perikles* 29.1) that Perikles (see 1.139–45) persuaded them is probably correct. That Thucydides omitted this detail to mitigate Perikles' responsibility for the Peloponnesian War (see Kagan 1969, pp. 237–39 and especially Badian 1993, pp. 160–61) seems to me unlikely. He may, however, have wanted to protect Perikles' reputation for far-sightedness (a quality Thucydides particularly admired; see 2.65), since the Corcyreans did not prove valuable allies later on.

There is a harbor there, and above it some distance inland is the city of Ephyre in the Elaian district of Thesprotis. Nearby, the Acherousian lake empties into the sea; the Acheron river from which it is named flows through Thesprotis and into the lake. The course of the Thyamis river is also here, forming the boundary between Thesprotis and Kestrine, and the promontory of Cheimerion rises between these rivers. It was at this point on the mainland that the Corinthians anchored and made camp. [47] Meanwhile, when the Corcyreans heard they were approaching, they manned one hundred ten ships commanded by Mikiades, Aisimides, and Eurybatos and made their camp on one of the islands that are called Sybota, and the Athenian ships were with them. Their land forces were at the promontory of Leukimme, also a thousand hoplites from Zakynthos who had come as reinforcements. On the mainland, the Corinthians also had many auxiliaries from the barbarians, since the mainlanders in that area had always been friendly to them.

[48] When the Corinthians had finished their preparations, they set out from Cheimerion at night with three days' provisions planning on a sea battle, and at dawn, in the course of their voyage, they sighted the Corcyrean fleet at sea and coming toward them. After they saw each other, they formed their battle lines, the Attic ships on the right wing of the Corcyreans, who occupied the rest of the line in three divisions, each under one of the commanders. This was the Corcyrean formation, and on the Corinthian side the Megarian and Ambracian ships held the right wing, the rest of the allies were grouped in the middle, and the Corinthians, with the ships that were the best sailers, held the left wing opposite the Athenians and the Corcyrean right.

[49] After the lines met, with signals raised on both sides, they began a sea battle, and both fleets had great numbers of hoplites as well as archers and javelin-throwers on deck, still prepared in their inexperience for old-fashioned tactics. And the battle was a fierce one, not because of skill but more in the manner of a battle on land. When their ships came into contact, they did not readily separate because of the number and crowding of the ships and since they placed most of their hopes for victory on the hoplites on the decks, who took up fighting positions as the ships stood still;

1.49–50. Even though Thucydides is perhaps the captious Athenian in describing the efforts of the second-greatest and third-greatest Greek navies, he is credible on the formidable effects of Athenian naval reputation (made all the more impressive to readers by Athenian prescience about the battle's outcome); the Spartans exercised a comparable spell over opponents on land, see 4.34. On Sybota the harbor (not the islands), see Hornblower 1991 *ad* 1.50.3.

there were no maneuvers through the lines, but they fought instead with more courage and vigor than technique. This resulted in plenty of shouting on all sides and a disordered sea battle, during which the Athenian ships would frighten their opponents by coming up to the Corcyreans wherever they were in trouble but did not take the offensive, since the commanders were concerned about their orders from Athens. The right wing of the Corinthians was in particular distress, since the Corcyreans with twenty ships, after routing their opponents and pursuing them to land in disarray, burned the empty tents and plundered their supplies. So here the Corinthians and their allies were defeated and the Corcyreans victorious. But where the Corinthians themselves were, on the left wing, they had a decisive success, since the Corcyreans, out of a smaller number of ships overall, were without the twenty involved in the pursuit.

When the Athenians saw the Corcyreans hard pressed, they began to help with less hesitation, although at first they avoided any ramming. When the rout became pronounced, however, and the Corinthians were pushing ahead, everyone finally took a full part in direct action, and the distinction was no longer maintained in the face of a situation so extreme that Corinthians and Athenians were compelled to fight against each other.

[50] After the rout was complete, the Corinthians, instead of tying up and towing the hulls of whatever ships they had disabled, turned toward slaughtering the men rather than taking captives, sailing in and out and killing their own friends in ignorance, since they did not realize that those on the right wing had been defeated. Because there had been a large number of ships on both sides covering a considerable expanse of water, the combatants, once they had met, did not easily recognize which were winning and which were losing. For in number of ships the sea battle was larger than any previously fought between Hellenes.

After the Corinthians had pursued the Corcyreans to shore, they turned to the wrecks and their own dead, recovering most of these and bringing them to Sybota, a deserted harbor in Thesprotis, where the land army of barbarians had been waiting in their support. When they had finished with this, they formed their line again and sailed at the Corcyreans. The Corcyreans responded by sailing out to oppose them with every ship still seaworthy and their reserves, accompanied by the Athenians, since they feared an attempt to land on their territory.

By this time it was late, and the paian had been sung for action, and suddenly the Corinthians backed water, since they had caught sight of twenty Athenian ships approaching, ones the Athenians had sent out later to reinforce the ten, afraid of exactly what happened, that the Corcyreans would be defeated and their ten too few to help. [51] So the Corinthians, seeing them in the distance and suspecting that they were from Athens, and not only the ones they could see but more, withdrew. The ships were not apparent to the Corcyreans, since their approach came from a less visible angle, and they were amazed that the Corinthians were backing water, until some of them could see and called, "ships approaching over there!" Then they also withdrew, since it was already growing dark and the Corinthians had turned away and ceased hostilities. In this way the enemies separated, and the battle ended with nightfall. While the Corinthians were encamped at Leukimme, the twenty ships from Athens led by Glaukon son of Leagros and Andokides son of Leogoras, approaching through the corpses and wrecks, sailed into the camp soon after they were sighted. Since it was dark, the Corcyreans were afraid that they were enemies but then recognized them, and the ships came to anchor.

[52] On the following day, the thirty Athenian ships as well as all Corcyrean ships still seaworthy set sail for the harbor at Sybota where the Corinthians were anchored to see whether they were going to fight. The Corinthians cleared the shore and formed a line in the open sea but took no action, unwilling to begin a battle if they could avoid one, since they saw that fresh ships had come from Athens as reinforcements and that they faced many problems in having prisoners to guard on board and no way to repair ships in a deserted location; how to make their voyage home was an even greater consideration, since they feared that the Athenians, on the assumption that the treaty had been broken because they had come into conflict, would not let them leave.

[53] They decided to put some men in a small boat and send them to the Athenians without a herald's staff to test their intentions. They sent them with this declaration: "You are in the wrong, Athenians, starting a war and breaking the treaty; when we are taking vengeance on our enemies, you are standing in our way under arms. If it is your intention to prevent our sailing to Corcyra or wherever else we please, if you are breaking the treaty, start here by taking us prisoner and treating us as enemies." This was their statement; while there was an outcry from all the Corcyrean forces within hearing that they should immediately be seized and put to death, the Athenians gave the following answer: "Peloponnesians, we are not starting a war, and we are not breaking the treaty. We have come to

1.51. On the names of the Athenian commanders, see Hornblower 1991 *ad* 1.51.4: "This is an exceedingly rare instance of a factual statement in Thucydides which can be shown from an inscription to be wrong."

help these Corcyreans as our allies. If you wish to sail elsewhere, we are not preventing you; if you are going to sail against Corcyra or any of its territory, we will not hesitate to stop you by force."

[54] After this reply from the Athenians, the Corinthians made preparations to sail home and also set up a trophy at Sybota on the mainland. As for the Corcyreans, they gathered their wrecked ships and their dead, which had been carried in their direction by the current and a wind which came up during the night and scattered them everywhere, and they set up their own trophy at Sybota of the islands, as though they had won. Each side had the following reasons for claiming victory: the Corinthians set up their trophy because they had had the upper hand in the battle until night, which had enabled them to bring in most of their wrecked ships and dead, and they had taken at least a thousand prisoners and sunk about seventy ships; the Corcyreans, since they had destroyed about thirty ships, and after the arrival of the Athenians, gathered the wrecks and dead of their own coast, and because the Corinthians had backed water after they saw the Athenian ships and had not sailed out from Sybota to meet them after the arrival of the Athenians, used all these reasons for setting up a trophy.

[55] So both sides claimed to be victorious; on their way home, the Corinthians employed treachery to take Anaktorion, a place on the mouth of the Ambracian gulf where they and the Corcyreans had common rights, and after establishing a Corinthian settlement there, they departed for home. Of their Corcyrean prisoners, they sold eight hundred who were slaves but kept two hundred and fifty in captivity and treated them with consideration, intending that they should return and bring Corcyra over to Corinth; most of them happened to be among the leading men of the city. So in this way the Corcyreans survived in the war against Corinth, and the Athenian ships left their territory. But for the Corinthans this became the first reason for war with the Athenians, that while they were under treaty obligations they fought with the Corcyreans against them.

[56] Immediately after this, the following also turned into a dispute between the Athenians and the Peloponnesians leading them into war. While the Corinthians were thinking of ways to get revenge, the Athenians, since they suspected Corinthian hostility, ordered the Potidaians, who inhabit the isthmus of Pallene and were Corinthian colonists but tributary Athenian allies, to pull down their fortifications toward Pallene and send hostages to Athens, also to expel their Corinthian magistrates and in the future not to accept those sent out annually, acting out of fear that the Potidaians might revolt under the influence of Perdikkas and the Corinthians and draw the other allies in the Thracian area into their revolt.

[57] The Athenians took these measures immediately after the sea battle at Corcyra; for the Corinthians were now openly at odds with them, and Perdikkas son of Alexandros, king of Macedon, formerly an ally and friend, had been turned into an enemy. He became an enemy because the Athenians had made an alliance with his brother Philippos and with Derdas, who had united against him. Perdikkas in alarm was both communicating with the Lacedaemonians in order to bring Athens into a war with the Peloponnesians and approaching the Corinthians about a Potidaian revolt. He was also proposing to the Chalkidians in Thrace and the Bottiaians that they join in the revolt, thinking that if he had the alliance of these places that were adjacent to him, he could conduct the war more easily with their cooperation. Alert to all this and wanting to head off the revolt of the cities, the Athenians, who were at just this time dispatching thirty ships and a thousand hoplites toward his territory under the command of Archestratos son of Lykomedes and two others, instructed the ship commanders to take hostages from the Potidaians and tear down their fortifications, also to keep a close watch on the cities to prevent their revolt.

[58] The Potidaians had not only sent representatives to Athens, in case there was any chance of persuading them to make no major changes in policy towards them, but had also gone to Lacedaemon with the Corinthians to have help available if they needed it, and when after long negotiations the Athenians made no concessions and their ships sailed against Macedon and the Potidaians alike, while the Lacedaemonian authorities promised that if the Athenians attacked Potidaia they would invade Attica, it was then that the Potidaians saw the right time to revolt, forming a confederacy with the Chalkidians and the Bottiaians. And Perdikkas persuaded the Chalkidians along the coast to abandon and level their cities and move inland to Olynthos, making this a single stronghold; to those who left he gave land of his own in Mygdonia around Lake Bolbe to cultivate as long as war against the Athenians lasted. So they moved inland, destroying their cities, and prepared for war.

[59] The thirty Athenian ships arrived in the Thracian area and found Potidaia and the other places in a state of revolt. Considering it impossible to fight against both Perdikkas and the combined cities in revolt, the generals turned toward Macedon, their original destination, established their base, and carried on the war along with Philippos and Derdas' brothers, whose forces had invaded from the interior. [60] At this point, with

1.57. "Archestratos son of Lykomedes and two others": the text is corrupt and the actual number uncertain; I have followed *HCT* I and Hornblower 1991 *ad* 1.57.6.

Potidaia in revolt and the Athenian ships off Macedon, the Corinthians feared for the place and felt its danger as their own, and they sent Corinthian volunteers and other Peloponnesians induced by pay, totalling sixteen hundred hoplites and four hundred light-armed. Their leader was Aristeus son of Adeimantos, whose popularity because of his long-standing service to the Potidaians was the main reason most of the volunteers joined the expedition. They reached Thrace forty days after Potidaia revolted.

[61] The Athenians also received the news immediately that the cities had revolted, and when they learned as well that Aristeus' men were advancing they sent two thousand of their own hoplites and forty ships to the places in revolt, with Kallias son of Kalliades and four others in command. They first reached Macedon and found that the thousand troops sent earlier had just taken Therme and were besieging Pydna. At first they themselves joined the siege of Pydna, but then, making an agreement and alliance with Perdikkas because Potidaia was a pressing concern and Aristeus had arrived, they withdrew from Macedon, proceeding to Beroia and from there to Strepsa, which they initially tried to take without success, and marched overland to Potidaia with their three thousand citizen hoplites besides many from their allies, and with six hundred cavalry who had accompanied Philippos and Pausanias; seventy ships were with them, sailing along the coast. Advancing in short stages, they reached Gigonos on the third day and set up camp.

[62] Expecting the Athenians, the Potidaians and the Peloponnesians with Aristeus made their camp on the isthmus near Olynthos and established their commissary outside the city. The allies chose Aristeus as commander of all the infantry and Perdikkas (who had immediately withdrawn from his alliance with the Athenians and was fighting alongside the Potidaians, appointing Iolaos as ruler in his absence) of the cavalry. It was Aristeus' plan to keep his army on the isthmus to guard against an Athenian attack while the Chalkidians, the other allies from beyond the isthmus, and the two hundred cavalry from Perdikkas waited in Olynthos and, whenever the Athenians moved against his forces, reinforced him from the rear and placed the enemy between their armies. The Athenian commander Kallias and his colleagues, however, sent off the Macedonian cavalry and

1.61. "They . . . set up camp": Badian 1993, p. 177, in rejecting theories that involve making ships the subject, argues that "only men could do that"; but in 4.26, "ships" eat meals.

a few allies to Olynthos to hold off any reinforcements coming from that area, and they themselves broke camp and moved on Potidaia.

When they reached the isthmus and saw their opponents preparing for battle, they formed their own ranks, and almost immediately the two armies engaged. Aristeus' wing and all the Corinthian and other picked troops next to him routed the opposing wing and went after it a long way in pursuit, but the rest of the army of Potidaians and Peloponnesians was defeated by the Athenians and fled to the city. [63] And when Aristeus returned from pursuit and saw that the rest of the army had been defeated, he was at a loss as to his chances of proceeding in either way, toward Olynthos or toward Potidaia. He decided to make his formation as compact as possible and force his way through to Potidaia at a run. He passed along the sea by the breakwater under missile fire and was roughly handled, losing a number of his men but saving most. And when the battle was beginning and signals were raised, the forces for supporting the Potidaians from Olynthos (about sixty stades away and in clear sight) advanced a short distance to reinforce them, and the Macedonian cavalry took up their position opposite them to prevent this; but when the Athenian victory was quickly accomplished and the signals were lowered, the reinforcements withdrew to their fortifications and the Macedonians to the Athenians; cavalry were not engaged on either side. After the battle, the Athenians set up a trophy and gave the Potidaians back their dead under truce. Of the Potidaians and their allies, just under three hundred were killed; of the Athenians, one hundred fifty citizens and their general Kallias were killed.

[64] The Athenians immediately built and manned a counterwall to the northern wall on the isthmus. They built no counterwall toward Pallene; they did not feel strong enough to cross over to Pallene and build a wall in addition to manning the one on the isthmus, fearing that the Potidaians and their allies would fall on them while their forces were divided. The Athenians at home learned that Pallene was not walled off and eventually sent sixteen hundred citizen hoplites and Phormio son of Asopios as general. Arriving at Pallene and using Aphytios as a base, he led his army to Potidaia, advancing gradually and ravaging the country. When no one came out to meet him in battle, he walled off the fortifications on the Pallene side. Consequently, Potidaia was now under heavy siege on both sides and from the sea by blockading ships. [65] Aristeus, now that the city was walled off and he had no hope for its salvation except possibly from the Peloponnesians or from some other unexpected development, recommended that all except five hundred wait for a wind and sail out, so that food might last longer, and he was willing to be one of those who stayed.

Unable to convince them and wanting to arrange whatever suited the circumstances and would result in the best possible situation on the outside,
he eluded the Athenian guard and sailed out. Remaining among the
Chalkidians, he helped them fight in many ways, such as killing a number
of the Sermylians by setting an ambush near their city, and also negotiated
with the Peloponnesians for a way some help might arrive. After Potidaia
was walled off, Phormio and his sixteen hundred hoplites laid waste the
territory of the Chalkidians and captured some of their towns.

[66] For the Athenians and the Peloponnesians, these charges were
added against one another: for the Corinthians, that the Athenians were
besieging Potidaia, which was their colony and had Corinthians and other
Peloponnesians inside; for the Athenians against the Peloponnesians, that
they had caused the revolt of a city of theirs, allied and tributary, and had
come to fight them openly with the Potidaians. Even so, the war had not
yet broken out, but there was still a truce; for the Corinthians had taken
these actions independently. [67] But with Potidaia besieged, they did not
let matters stand, since their own men were inside and besides they feared
for the place. Immediately calling the allies to Lacedaemon, they came and
denounced the Athenians on the grounds that they had broken the truce
and were committing aggression against the Peloponnesos. The Aiginetans, represented not publicly but secretly, out of fear of the Athenians,
particularly joined the Corinthians in promoting war, saying that they did
not have the autonomy guaranteed by the treaty. The Lacedaemonians,
issuing an additional invitation to anyone, ally or not, who claimed to have
suffered from Athenian aggression, called their regular assembly and told
them to speak. Among those who came forward and one by one made their
accusations were the Megarians, who pointed to a number of grievances
but especially their exclusion from both the ports of the Athenian empire
and the market of Attica in violation of the treaty. The Corinthians came
forward last, after letting the others inflame the Lacedaemonians, and
spoke as follows:

[68] "Lacedaemonians, your trust in your own constitution and society
renders you less trusting toward others if they have something to tell you,

---

1.68–86. For the debate at Sparta in 432, Thucydides uniquely records four
speeches. It has long been noted that the third speech is framed as an answer to the
first, the fourth as an answer to the second, and consequently it is sometimes suggested that the second and fourth are later additions, but see 1.84n. and 1.86n.;
Hornblower 1987, p. 60, and 1991 *ad* 1.78.1, 1.86.1–3 makes an effective case for
the unity of the four speeches (all four may well have been written relatively late).
Cf. *HCT* I, pp. 252–55.

and you derive your prudence from it but also behave with the greater ignorance regarding things outside your state. We say this who many times announced to you in advance the injuries we were to suffer at the hands of the Athenians, and each time, instead of taking the lesson from our instruction, you suspected the speakers of being motivated by their own private quarrels. And this explains why it is not before we suffered but while we are in the midst of suffering that you have convened these allies, among whom we have a right to speak corresponding to the magnitude of our grievances, since we have been outraged by the Athenians and disregarded by you. Now if at any point they had been secretive about their aggression against Hellas, there would still be need for the instruction one gives the uninformed. But as it is, why are lengthy speeches necessary from men you can see are either enslaved or, even among your allies, the objects of plots by those who have long since prepared themselves to face war at any time? Otherwise, they would not have defied us by appropriating and holding Corcyra, nor would they be laying siege to Potidaia, the most useful base in connection with Thracian affairs—and Corcyra would have furnished the largest navy to the Peloponnesians.

[69] "And you are to blame for this situation, first by allowing the Athenians to fortify their city after the Persian War and set up the long walls subsequently, and by constantly, up to the present, withholding freedom not only from those enslaved by the Athenians but now even from your own allies. For it is not the enslaver but the one who has the power to stop him but looks on who more truly does the deed, even if he bears a reputation for virtue as the liberator of Hellas. Only now have we managed to meet, and not even now with the issues out in the open. We no longer needed to debate over whether we are being wronged but over how to defend ourselves.

"For men of action, after making their plans, advance immediately against those who have not made up their minds. We know the way the Athenians encroach on their neighbors, how they proceed little by little. And when they think they are escaping notice because of your imperceptiveness, they are not so bold, but when they realize that you do know and are standing aside, they will press on vigorously. For you are the only Hellenes who are at peace, defending yourselves not by power but by procrastination, and the only ones who do not put an end to their enemies' growth when it is starting but when it has doubled. And yet you were said to be reliable: a case of reputation prevailing over actuality. For we ourselves know that the Mede came from the ends of the earth to the Peloponnesos before your forces offered real opposition, and that now you are passive spectators of the Athenians who are not distant but nearby, and instead of making your own attacks you prefer to ward off attackers and take your chances in the struggle when they are much more powerful even though you know that it was more the barbarian's own fault that he failed, and that in confrontation with the Athenians themselves there have been many cases of our surviving through their mistakes instead of your assistance; in fact, resting hopes on you has already ruined some who were unprepared because of that very trust. And let no one think that this is said out of hostility rather than as criticism; for criticism is directed toward friends who are in error, accusations toward enemies who are at fault.

[70] "In this connection, we think we have at least as much right as anyone else to censure our neighbors, especially when some major contrasts exist. We actually believe that you have never been aware of these, nor considered what sort of opponents you will have in the Athenians, how greatly, let us say totally they differ from you. They are definitely innovators and quick to form their plans and carry out whatever action they resolve. Your quickness, however, is to preserve the status quo, to make no further resolutions, and in your actions not even to complete what needs to be done. And again, they are bold even beyond their strength and risk-takers beyond their judgment and hopeful amidst dangers, but your way is to act short of your power and to mistrust your judgment even over certainties and to believe that you will never find an escape from dangers. And yet again, they are ready to act while you are delayers, and they are always abroad while you are the most home-bound of all. For they believe that by being away they are gaining; you, that by making any move you will damage even your present assets. And when they conquer their enemies they advance the farthest and when beaten fall back the least. What is more, they use their bodies as though not theirs at all on behalf of their city but their minds as their most personal resources for actions on her behalf. And any failure to carry out what they plan they regard as deprivation of their own property, and anything they set out after and achieve, as a small actual accomplishment compared with what remains to be done. And if they do fail in some attempt, they fill the need by their hopes of new alternatives. For they alone possess and hope as a single undertaking, on account of their speed in acting on their resolutions. In hardship and danger they toil throughout their lives for such ends, and least enjoy what they have on account of always acquiring and thinking that there is no holiday except in doing what the occasion demands, and that leisure without accomplishment is more of a misfortune than burdensome activity. And so, if someone were to sum them up

by saying that they were born to have no peace themselves and allow it to no one else, he would be right.

[71] "Yet with such a city confronting you, you keep on delaying and do not realize that peace is the most lasting for those who not only use their power justly but also show a clear determination not to submit to injustice, while you suppose that fair dealing means not harming others nor suffering injury even in self-defense. You would hardly have succeeded in this policy if you lived next to a state like your own. But as it is, everything we have just said shows that your ways are obsolete against theirs. Just as in technology, the most recent ideas must always prevail; for a city at peace, fixed customs are best, but those forced into full activity also need full development. This is exactly why Athenian institutions, because of the extent of their experience, have seen more innovation than yours.

"So let your slowness end at this point. Now, just as you promised, help your allies and especially the Potidaians by invading Attica at once, lest you betray friends and kinsmen to their worst enemies and drive us in despair to some other alliance. We would not be doing wrong in the sight of either the gods we swore by or men who take note. For those who break treaties are not the ones who go over to others because of their isolation but the ones who do not help those to whom they swore their oaths. If you are willing to show energy, we will stand by you; for we would then have no sanction for changing alliances, nor would we find others who are more congenial. After hearing us, make the right decision and strive to lead the Peloponnesos forward in its full greatness handed down to you by your fathers."

[72] This was the Corinthian speech. It so happened that Athenian representatives were already present in Lacedaemon on other business, and when they heard the speeches they decided to come before the Lacedaemonian assembly, not to make any defense against the charges brought against the city but to show that the whole case was not one for them to decide quickly but to consider over a longer period. At the same time, they wanted to reveal how great the power of their city was and to give the elder listeners a reminder of things they knew and the younger ones an account of things they were ignorant about, expecting that they would be led in the direction of peace rather than war by their words. So they approached the Lacedaemonians and said that they wanted to speak to their assembly, if nothing prevented it. The Lacedaemonians told them to speak, and the Athenians came forward and said the following:

[73] "Our mission was not intended for debating your allies but for the business on which our city sent us. Yet since we are aware of a considerable outcry against us, we have come before you, not with a reply to

charges made by the cities, since we would not be addressing you as either our judges or theirs, but to keep you from lightly allowing your allies to influence adversely your planning about important matters, and at the same time because we wish to show that it is not unreasonable for us to have what we have acquired, and that our city is one deserving consideration.

"Now as for the remote past, what need is there to speak when the audience would have the evidence of hearsay accounts rather than their personal experience? As for the Persian War, however, and all events of which you have knowledge of your own, even if it is rather tiresome for us to bring them up constantly, we are forced to speak. For when we took our actions, the risk was for the general good, and you shared in the results; do not deprive us of all the renown if it is of any benefit to us. The purpose of our speech will not be to make excuses but to present evidence and demonstrate what sort of city you will contend with if you do not plan sensibly. We claim that we alone dared battle against the barbarian at Marathon, and that when he came a second time, we as a people, unable to make our defense on land, embarked on our ships and joined the sea battle at Salamis; all that prevented the barbarian from sailing against the Peloponnesians and sacking their cities one by one, since they could not have helped one another against that number of ships. He himself provided the best proof of this; after defeat at sea, as though no longer enjoying his former power, he quickly withdrew with most of his army.

[74] "Now, given this outcome for the battle and a clear demonstration that the cause of the Hellenes rested on their ships, we provided three very important benefits: the greatest number of ships, the most intelligent general, and the staunchest courage. Toward the total of four hundred ships, our share was actually almost two-thirds, and the commander was Themistokles, the man most responsible for the sea battle's being fought in the strait, clearly the only thing that saved the situation; and on that account you yourselves honored him beyond all other foreigners who have visited you. And certainly we were the ones showing by far the most commitment and daring, because when no one came to help us on land, with everyone else up to our border already enslaved, we thought it our duty

---

1.73. There may be sardonic humor in the Athenians' rejection of the distant past as a topic (a pleasant surprise for the audience?) only to insist on the Athenian role in the Persian Wars; it is not clear whether this is expected to be tiresome for the listeners or the speakers (perhaps both). Ultimately, however, Spartan memory of that role saved Athens from destruction in 404 (Xenophon, *Hellenika* 2.2.19–20). See Tzifopoulos 1995.

that after abandoning our city and sacrificing our property we should neither desert the common cause of our remaining allies nor become useless
to them by dispersing, but embark on our ships, face the danger, and hold
no grudge against you for not helping us earlier. We therefore claim that
we gave you greater benefits than we received. For you were rising to the
defense from cities still populated, fighting to hold onto them in the
future, since your concern was more for your own sake than ours (at least,
you did not put in an appearance while our city was still intact); we, however, setting out from a city that no longer existed, facing danger for one
with small hope of existing, did our part to save you as well as ourselves. If
we had already gone over to the Mede fearing for our territory, as others
did, or had lacked the courage later to embark on our ships because we
considered ourselves lost, you would have had no further need to fight at
sea, since you would have lacked the sufficient number of ships, and the
barbarian would then have had the easy success he wanted.

[75] "Do we not deserve, then, Lacedaemonians, because of our commitment at that time and the intelligence of our policy, to rule the empire
we do in fact possess without such excessive resentment among the Hellenes? And this is an empire we did not take by using force, but because
you were unwilling to continue campaigning against what remained of the
barbarian's power, and because the allies came to us and of their own
accord begged us to be their leaders. We were compelled from the first by
the situation itself to expand the empire to its present state, especially out
of fear, then prestige as well, and later out of self-interest. And it no longer
seemed safe to risk letting it go when we were detested by most, some had
already revolted and been reduced, and you were by then not our friends
as you once were but a source of suspicion and contention (and allies who
left us would have gone over to you). All people are beyond reproach in
managing their own interests well when the greatest dangers are involved.

[76] "For example, Lacedaemonians, it is by directing the cities of the
Peloponnesos to your own advantage that you exercise your authority, and
if you had become detested, just like us, by continuing all along in the leadership of those days, we can be sure that you would have been no less severe
toward the allies and forced to rule with a strong hand or else come into
danger yourselves. On the same reasoning, we have done nothing remarkable, nor contrary to ordinary human behavior, if we not only accepted an
empire when it was offered but also did not let it go, submitting to the great
forces of prestige, fear, and self-interest—not as the originators of such
conduct, moreover, since the rule has always existed that the weaker is held
down by the stronger—and, beside, considering ourselves deserving and so

regarded by you as well, until now, when you calculate your own interests and use the argument about justice. It is an argument that never yet, when there was any opportunity to gain something by might, deterred anyone who propounded it from taking advantage. And all are entitled to praise whenever they follow human nature by ruling others and end up behaving more justly than their actual power dictated.

"We certainly think that anyone else taking over our position would make it clear whether we are moderate or not, but in our case even fairness has unreasonably resulted in more blame than praise. [77] For example, because our disadvantage in lawsuits against them in cases involving inter-state agreements caused us to bring these cases here among our impartial laws, we are considered addicted to courtrooms. And not one of them looks at the reason why others who rule and are less moderate toward their subjects do not encounter this reproach: it is that those who are in a posi-tion to use force have no need for legal procedures. Since our allies are used to associating with us on terms of equality, if they experience any deprivation, however small, either through a judgment or through the power inherent in our empire, compared with what they think is right, they are not thankful that no more was taken but angrier over the loss than they would be if we had set law aside from the start and taken advantage openly; that way, they would not have denied the necessity for the weaker to submit to the strong. Evidently men are more bitter when they are vic-timized by legalities than by force; for the first seems a case of taking advantage among equals, the second a case of compulsion by the stronger.

"Under the Mede, of course, they endured far more terrible sufferings, but for our rule to seem harsh is only natural; it is always the present situ-ation that is oppressive for subjects. You, in any case, if you became rulers after overthrowing us, would immediately forfeit the good will you have built up because of fear of us, if you are still going to follow anything like the same principles you disclosed before, when you briefly assumed the leadership against the Mede. For you have rules among yourselves which are incompatible with other people, and it may be added that each one of you when he gets abroad follows neither these nor the rules that the rest of Hellas observes.

[78] "Plan slowly, then, since these are important matters, and do not let the opinions and complaints of others persuade you to take on troubles of your own. Think first, before you get into war, about how much of it is

1.78. "Plan slowly" can hardly have been intended otherwise than as a taunt; cf. 1.84 with note.

beyond calculation. For as it goes on, it tends to end up mostly as a matter of chances that we have equal inability to control, and which way they will turn out is unforeseeable in our hour of danger. When men go to war, they begin by taking action, which they ought to do last, and only after they have suffered do they engage in discussion. Since neither we nor, apparently, you have made such a mistake yet, we tell you, as long as sound deliberation is still a free choice for both of us, do not break the treaty, do not transgress your oaths, but arbitrate our differences in accordance with our agreement. If you do not, we, with the gods we have sworn by as our witnesses, will attempt to defend ourselves against any move you initiate."

[79] This was the Athenian speech. And now that the Lacedaemonians had heard both their allies' complaints against the Athenians and what the Athenians said, they excluded everyone else and discussed the situation among themselves. While the opinions of most led to the single conclusion that the Athenians were already aggressors and that there must be war without delay, their king Archidamos, a man known as intelligent and prudent, came forward and spoke as follows.

[80] "Lacedaemonians, by this time I have experienced many wars myself, and I see some among you who are of my age, which means that you will not let inexperience make you enthusiastic about this business as others might be, nor think of it as good or safe. Any of you making prudent calculations about the operation we are now considering would find that it would not be on any limited scale. Whereas against the Peloponnesians and neighbors our strength is of a comparable sort and capable of being used swiftly at any point, against men who occupy a distant area, who are moreover extremely experienced at sea and well equipped in every other way—wealth both private and public, ships, horses, armaments, and a populace that no other single place in Hellas can match in size—and on top of this have many tributary allies, how should we lightly undertake a war with them, and where should we put our trust when we rush in unprepared? In our ships? We are inferior, and if we train ourselves and match their preparation, it will take time. In our funds? We are at a still greater disadvantage there and have neither money in a treasury nor readiness to pay it out of private sources.

[81] "Perhaps it is encouraging for some that we are superior in arms and numbers, so that we can plunder their land by repeated invasions. But they have much more territory in their empire, and they import what they need by sea. And then, if we attempt to cause revolt among their allies, it will be necessary to help them at sea, since most of them are islanders. What, then, will be our war? For unless we are able either to beat them at

sea or to deprive them of the revenues from which they support their navy, we will sustain the greater damage. And when that happens, there will also no longer be an honorable way to make terms, especially if we are considered the more responsible for beginning the quarrel. But let us never, under any circumstances, be carried away by the hope that the war will be settled quickly if we ravage their land, since it is my fear that we will pass it down to our children. So unlikely is it that the Athenians, in their pride, will either enslave themselves to their land or, like novices, be panic-stricken by the war.

[82] "Yet I certainly do not bid you to have the insensitivity to allow them to injure our allies, or to shut your eyes to their plotting. But instead of taking up arms yet, send to them and make complaints, not putting too much emphasis on either war or our willingness to accommodate, and during this time prepare our own resources, both by the acquisition of allies, Hellenic and barbarian alike, wherever we can add any source of either naval or financial strength (and no one who is the object of Athenian plots like ourselves can be blamed for saving himself by enlisting not only Hellenes but barbarians) and at the same time by developing our own.

"And if they pay some attention when we send embassies, that would be best. If not, by the time two or three years have passed, our position will have been strengthened if we decide to attack them. And it may be that when they look at us, now displaying both preparation and words to match it perfectly, they would tend to give way while they still have their land untouched and are making plans about material blessings that are in their possession, not yet destroyed. For you must think of their land purely as a hostage you hold, all the more so the better it is tended. We should spare it as long as possible and not make them more difficult opponents by driving them to desperation. If we plunder their land while we are unprepared because we are rushed into it by the charges of our allies, see that we do not make the situation more shameful and unmanageable for the Peloponnesos. For charges by cities and individual parties can be resolved; but a war that for the sake of individual interests we all undertake, one whose course there is no way of knowing, will not be easy to settle respectably.

[83] "And let no one think it cowardice that a multitude hesitates to attack a single city. For they have a comparable multitude who are allies and contribute money, and war is no more a matter of arms than of financial resources, by which arms are rendered usable, especially for land powers fighting sea powers. So let us first provide ourselves with these

1.81. "To our children": see 8.5n.

resources, without getting carried away in the meantime by the words of our allies, and since we will have the major responsibility for the consequences for better or worse, let us also be the ones to give them some forethought at our leisure. [84] And feel no shame over the slowness and hesitation for which they blame us most of all; by hurrying, you will delay the end because of starting unprepared. And besides, we live in a city that has always been free and of high reputation.

"It is very possible that true prudence is this quality of ours. It is the reason that we alone are not filled with insolence by our successes and give way less than others in misfortunes and are not swept away into perils against our better judgment because we are gratified by those who cheer us on nor again, if someone badgers us with contumely, are we the more likely to be overpersuaded in our chagrin. Through our orderliness we are rendered both warlike and wise: the former, because a sense of respect is the greater part of moderation, and courage is the greatest part of respect; and wise, because we are educated with too little learning to despise the laws and too sensibly, through our strictness, to disobey them, nor in such a way that after using too much useless cleverness to make a fine case against our enemies' preparations we proceed against them with quite contrasting results, but so as to consider our neighbors' designs comparable to ours and the chances that turn up as beyond determining by calculation. In practice, we always make our preparations against opponents on the assumption that they have planned well, and it is right to derive our hopes not from them, because of the mistakes they will make, but from ourselves, because of the secure provisions we are making, and to think that there is not much difference between man and man, but the strongest is the one brought up in the severest discipline.

[85] "Therefore, let us never abandon these practices that our fathers handed down to us and we ourselves to our benefit have kept all this time, let us not be hurried into deciding in the brief space of a day about many lives, possessions, cities, and reputations, let us decide calmly. More than any others, we have this choice because of our strength. Send to the Athenians about Potidaia, send to them about cases of aggression claimed by the allies, especially since the Athenians themselves are ready to accept judgment by arbitration; it is not lawful to move beforehand against one who makes this offer as one would against an aggressor. And at the same time,

---

1.84. "No shame over the slowness": probably responsive to both the Corinthian criticism (1.71) and the Athenian taunt (1.78).

make preparations for war. These plans will give you the most strength and make you the most formidable to your enemies."

This was Archidamos' speech; but Sthenelaïdas, one of the ephors at this time, came forward last and spoke to the Lacedaemonians in the following way: [86] "The Athenian speech was long, and I don't understand it. They praised themselves a good deal, but they nowhere denied that they are injuring our allies and the Peloponnesos. And yet if they were good then, against the Mede, they deserve double punishment for becoming bad instead of good. We are the same men now as then, and if we are prudent we will not look on while our allies are wronged or hesitate to help them; they are not hesitating to suffer. Others have a lot of money and ships and horses, but we have good allies who must not be betrayed to the Athenians, and judgments and speeches must not be used when we are not being injured in word alone, but help must be sent at once and in full strength. And let no one instruct us that it is fitting for us to deliberate while being wronged, but instead that it is fitting for those intending wrong to deliberate for a long time. Vote, then, in the way worthy of Sparta, Lacedaemonians, for war, and do not let the Athenians grow greater, nor let us betray the allies, but with the gods' help let us advance against the aggressors."

[87] After making this sort of speech, he himself as ephor put the question to the assembly of the Lacedaemonians. And he stated that he could not distinguish which shout was the louder (for they decide by acclamation, not by vote) but said, because he wanted them to become more eager for war by revealing their opinions openly, "Lacedaemonians, those of you who think that the treaty has been broken, and the Athenians are aggressors, stand over there," pointing out the place to them, "and those who do not think so, on the other side." They stood up and separated, and there were many more who thought the treaty had been broken. Recalling the allies, they told them that they believed that the Athenians had committed aggression but that they also wished to summon all the allies together and have them vote, so that they could conduct the war—if that was the decision—after making their plans in common. The allies departed for home after the realization of these objectives, and the Athenian representatives left later, after transacting the business on which they had come originally.

1.86. Despite his brevity, Sthenelaidas seems to allude to all three preceding speeches. On the nature and historical authenticity of his speech, cf. Allison 1984 and Bloedow 1987.

This decision of the assembly, that the treaty had been broken, took place in the fourteenth year of the thirty-year truce, which was made after the reduction of Euboia and had lasted until then. [88] The Lacedaemonians voted that the treaty had been broken and that they must go to war not so much because they were persuaded by the arguments of their allies as because they feared further increase in the power of the Athenians, seeing the greater part of Hellas already under their control.

[89] Now it was in the following way that the Athenians came into the situation that led to their expansion. After the Medes withdrew from Europe beaten by the Hellenes on both sea and land, and the contingent that took refuge at Mykale with its ships was destroyed, Leotychides, king of the Lacedaemonians and the man who led the Hellenes at Mykale, left for home with the allies from the Peloponnesos, but the Athenians and the allies from Ionia and the Hellespont, who had now revolted from the king, stayed and besieged Sestos, which was occupied by the Medes. They spent the winter there and captured it when it was abandoned by the barbarians, and after this they sailed away from the Hellespont to their own cities. And the people of Athens, after the barbarians had gotten out of their land, immediately brought back their children, women, and remaining property

1.88. It is illicit (even in light of 1.87) for Thucydides to indicate that the motion voted on included a declaration of war, see Badian 1993, pp. 147–48.

1.89–118. These chapters have been called the "Pentakontaetia" (the Fifty Years), a term first appearing in a scholion on 1.89 and presumably authorized by 1.118; "fifty" rounds off the period from 479 to 431. While acknowledging the restricted purpose of this digression as stated in the opening sentence, many scholars have been understandably critical of its brevity, chronological vagueness, and real or supposed omissions (especially after Thucydides' criticism of Hellanikos at 1.97); many of the dates I give below are in dispute. There is disagreement over whether Thucydides keeps events in chronological order (Pritchett 1995 argues this against Badian 1993). It is an account overall favoring the Athenians over the Spartans, and Badian, especially pp. 73–107, has powerfully stated the case that Thucydides, "writing as an impassioned Athenian patriot" (p. xi), distorted this account accordingly (cf. 88n.); Bradford 1994 discusses the Athenian context for Thucydides' attitude toward Sparta. For other revisionist discussion, cf. Schreiner 1976 and Robertson 1980; Pritchett disputes a number of Badian's arguments, see also Stadter 1993. Thucydides notoriously makes no mention of the "Peace of Kallias" between Athens and Persia, usually dated to 449, which a minority of scholars consider a fourth-century B.C.E. fiction, see Hornblower 1991, pp. 179–81; for its authenticity, see recently Badian, pp. 1–72 (convinced) and Pritchett, pp. 167–68 (skeptical) and cf. Stadter 1993, p. 66.

from the places where they had sent them for security and made provisions
to rebuild the city and its walls; little of the city wall was left standing, and
most houses were in ruins, the few that survived being the ones in which
the most important Persians had encamped.

[90] When the Lacedaemonians learned their intentions, they sent an
embassy, partly because they themselves would have preferred to see neither the Athenians nor anyone else having walls, but more because their
allies had spurred them on and were frightened by the size of their navy,
which had not existed before, and by the daring they showed in the war
with the Medes. The Lacedaemonians urged them, rather than building
walls of their own, to join them in pulling down all the city walls that had
been built outside the Peloponnesos, without disclosure to the Athenians
of any feelings of preference or suspicion but on the grounds that if the
barbarians came again, they would not have a strong base to operate from
as they had just done from Thebes, and they claimed that the Peloponnesos was adequate both as a refuge and as a base. On the advice of Themistokles, the Athenians replied to the Lacedaemonians who had made these
proposals that they would send an embassy to them about the subject they
had brought up and immediately dismissed them.

Themistokles told them to send him to Lacedaemon as quickly as possible but, instead of immediately sending out the other ambassadors
selected beside himself, to wait a long enough time for building the wall to
the minimal height that could possibly be used for defense, and to build it
using the whole population, including women and children, sparing no
private or public structure that might benefit the operation but tearing
everything down. After giving these instructions and adding that he would
take care of the rest himself in Lacedaemon, he departed. When he
arrived, he did not approach their officials but delayed and made excuses,
and whenever any of the authorities asked him why he did not come before
the public, he said that he was waiting for his colleagues, that they had
been left behind on some business, yet he expected them to come right
away and was surprised that they were not here already.

[91] When they heard Themistokles, they believed him because of
their friendship for him, but when others came and made the clear accusation that a wall was being built and already of considerable height, they
did not see how they could disbelieve them. Realizing this, he told them
not to be misled by stories but to send men of their own who were trust-

---

1.89. "Rebuild the city and its walls" implies that Athens had a city wall before 479
B.C.E.; for the debate over this, see Hornblower 1991, p. 135.

worthy and would give a reliable report after making an examination. So they sent off their men, and he secretly sent word to the Athenians regarding them, ordering that they be detained there, as unobtrusively as possible, and not let go until they themselves (for his colleagues Abronichos son of Lysikles and Aristeides son of Lysimachos were now here as well, with the news that the wall was high enough) came back; he was afraid that the Lacedaemonians, when they did hear the truth, would no longer let them leave. The Athenians detained the representatives just as instructed, and this was when Themistokles approached the Lacedaemonians and said that his city was now fortified well enough to protect her people, and that if the Lacedaemonians or their allies wanted to send any kind of embassy to them, in the future they were to come prepared to deal with men who thoroughly understood both their own exclusive interests and those they shared with others; when they had thought it best to abandon their city and embark on their ships, they had decided on this venture without involving the Lacedaemonians, and on the other hand, in any planning they had done with the Lacedaemonians, they had proved inferior to no one in judgment; and so now they thought it best that their city have a wall, and that this would be advantageous to their own citizens and even for the allies; for only from a position of equal preparedness was it possible to plan common policy in a fair and equal way; therefore, he said, either the alliance should be without walls or their actions should be considered right. [92] The Lacedaemonians heard this without showing open anger (for their embassy, supposedly, was not sent to be an obstacle but to recommend an idea to the assembly; and besides, at that time they were at their friendliest toward the Athenians on account of their zeal against the Mede), yet since they were not getting their way, they were secretly annoyed. And the embassies of both states left for home without recriminations.

[93] In this way the Athenians fortified their city in a short time. Even now, it is still obvious that the construction was done in a hurry. The lower courses are constructed of all sorts of stones, in some places not cut to fit but left the way various people brought them, and many gravestones and carved pieces were built in. For the enclosure of the city was extended in every direction, and for that reason they ransacked everything indiscriminately in their haste. Themistokles also persuaded them to build the rest of the wall around the Peiraeus (a start had been made on this earlier, when he was archon of Athens for a year), thinking that the site was a good one with its three natural harbors and gave the Athenians, now that they had become seafarers, a great advance toward obtaining power (he was in fact

the first person bold enough to tell them to take to the sea), and directly contributed to establishing the empire. And it was his idea that they build the wall around the Peiraeus to the width still visible today (two wagons would pass one another bringing in the stones), and in the interior there was not rubble or clay but great blocks cut square and laid in courses, their ends clamped together with iron and lead; the finished height was about half what he intended. By this size and thickness he hoped to frustrate all attempts by enemies, and he thought a garrison of a few soldiers, the least fit, would suffice while everyone else embarked on the ships. He concentrated on the ships, because he saw, in my opinion, that the approach was easier for the king's forces by sea than by land. He also considered the Peiraeus more valuable than the city above it and many times advised the Athenians, if they were ever truly hard pressed on land, to come down and use their ships to stand off the whole world.

So in this way the Athenians built their walls and strengthened themselves in other ways immediately after the withdrawal of the Medes. [94] Meanwhile, Pausanias son of Kleombrotos was sent out from Lacedaemon as commander of the Hellenes with twenty ships from the Peloponnesos. The Athenians joined them with thirty ships, as did a number of the other allies. They campaigned first against Cyprus and subjected most of it, later against Byzantion, which was held by the Medes, and forced its surrender, all under Pausanias' leadership. [95] But because of his violence the Hellenes already disliked him, especially the Ionians and those recently freed from the king. They went to the Athenians and asked them to become their leaders in view of their kinship and not to allow Pausanias to commit any acts of violence. The Athenians were receptive to what they said and resolved not to tolerate him, and also to arrange things in general the way it appeared best for themselves.

Meanwhile, the Lacedaemonians recalled Pausanias for an inquiry about what they had been hearing; extensive misconduct charged against him by Hellenes when they visited gave more the impression of an imitation tyranny than of a generalship. It happened that he was summoned just at the time when the allies, except for the troops from the Peloponnesos, had changed their allegiance over to the Athenians out of their hatred for him. On coming to Lacedaemon, he was rebuked for injustices committed against some individuals on a private basis but acquitted of the most serious charges of misconduct; medism was the most important accusation against him and appeared to be the least in doubt. They did not send him out again as a leader and instead sent Dorkis and a few others with a small force; but the allies would no longer accept them in command. When they realized this, they left and the Lacedaemonians sent no others subsequently, fearing that they would be corrupted away from home, just as they had observed in Pausanias, also wanting to be rid of the war against the Medes and considering the Athenians capable of leading it and close friends for the time.

[96] After assuming the leadership in this way, on the wishes of the allies because they hated Pausanias, the Athenians fixed the assessment both for the cities required to contribute money against the barbarian and the ones required to contribute ships; the ostensible purpose was to compensate for what they had suffered by ravaging the king's territory. And this was when the Hellenotamiai were first established as an office by the Athenians, and these received the tribute (for the contribution of money was given this name). The first tribute was assessed at four hundred sixty talents; their treasury was on Delos, and their meetings were held in the sanctuary.

[97] As leaders of allies who were at first autonomous and made decisions in general meetings, the Athenians proceeded to the following actions, both in warfare and in the direction of political affairs, between the war with the Medes and this war; some of these involved them against the barbarian, some against their own allies when they attempted revolutions, and some even against any Peloponnesians they encountered in the course of these various events. I have written about these and made a digression from my account because this period was omitted by my predecessors, who recounted either Hellenic events before the war with the Medes or the war itself; only one, Hellanikos, touched on them in his *Account of Attica*, and he recorded them briefly and without accuracy in dates. At the same time, the digression also supplies an explanation of the way the Athenian empire was established.

1.96. Rawlings 1977 argues that here, taken with 1.98, Thucydides indicates clearly that "*from the very first*, the Athenians used the Delian League [as the Athenian alliance is sometimes called] for their own hegemonial ends" (p. 5, his italics). Even though Thucydides insists throughout his work that the Athenian empire was unpopular among the subject states, Ste. Croix 1954 argues that his narrative frequently shows loyalty at least on the part of the general populace; this article not only generated a long debate (against Ste. Croix, see Bradeen 1960, recently cf. Hornblower 1991 *ad* 2.8.5) but also pioneered the practice of using Thucydides' "news columns" to refute his "editorials."

1.97. This unique reference to another, named historian dates the passage, and perhaps the Pentakontaetia, to 407–406 at the earliest, see *HCT* I, pp. 362–64 and Smart 1986, pp. 22–23.

[98] First, under the command of Kimon son of Miltiades, they besieged and captured Eion on the Strymon river, which was held by the Medes, and enslaved the inhabitants. Next, they enslaved the island of Skyros in the Aegean, occupied by Dolopians, and settled it themselves. There was a war between them and the Karystians, not involving the other Euboians, and the Karystians eventually surrendered on terms. After this they fought against the Naxians when they revolted and forced them back in by besieging them. And this was the first allied city subjected, a violation of what had been arranged, but afterward this also happened to the others according to individual circumstances. [99] Of the various causes for revolt, the main ones were failure to provide money or ships and all cases of desertion; for the Athenians were exacting and made themselves odious by putting severe pressure on people neither accustomed nor willing to exert themselves. In some other ways as well, the Athenians were no longer the popular leaders they had once been, and they did not participate in campaigns on a basis of equality and had no difficulty in forcing defectors back. The allies themselves were to blame for this; on account of shrinking from campaigns, most of them, in order to avoid going abroad, arranged to have themselves assessed to contribute the appropriate amount in money instead of ships, and the Athenian fleet was then expanded out of the funds they contributed, while they themselves went into each revolt without preparation or experience in war.

[100] Next, the land and sea battles on the Eurymedon river in Pamphylia were fought by the Athenians and their allies against the Medes, and the Athenians won both on the same day under the command of Kimon son of Miltiades and captured or destroyed the Phoenician triremes, about two hundred in all. Somewhat later occurred the revolt of the Thasians, who had quarreled with them over the markets on the coast of Thrace across from them and the mines they controlled. The Athenians not only sailed to Thasos with their fleet, won a sea battle, and made a landing but around the same time also sent ten thousand of their own cit-

---

1.98. The capture of Eion and Skyros is usually dated to 476, the war with Karystos to "perhaps 472" (Hornblower 1991 *ad* 1.98.3), the revolt of Naxos to the early 460s.

1.100. The battle of the Eurymedon is dated to the mid 460s, with much controversy, see Hornblower 1991 *ad* 1.100.1. The revolt of Thasos and foundation of Ennea Hodoi ("Nine Ways") took place in 465/4. Most scholars believe that the massacre at Drabeskos occurred soon after, but Badian 1993, pp. 80–86 dates it to 453/2 (contra, Pritchett 1995, pp. 94–121). Amphipolis was founded in 437.

izens and allies to the Strymon to settle what was then called Ennea Hodoi but later Amphipolis, and although they got control of Ennea Hodoi itself, which was occupied by the Edonians, when they advanced into the interior of Thrace, they were destroyed at Drabeskos, an Edonian town, by the united Thracians, to whom their occupation of the place was a hostile act.

[101] The Thasians, defeated in battle and under siege, appealed to the Lacedaemonians and asked them to rescue them by invading Attica. They promised to invade, keeping this from the Athenians, and intended to but were prevented by the occurrence of an earthquake, at which time the helots, also the Thouriatai and Aithaians among the perioikoi, revolted and fled to Ithome. Most of the helots were descendants of the Messenians of old who had been enslaved in the Messenian wars, and accordingly they all came to be called Messenians. So, with the Lacedaemonians involved in a war with the men in Ithome, the Thasians came to terms with the Athenians in the third year of the siege; they pulled down their walls and surrendered their ships, arranged to pay immediately as much money as demanded for reparations and pay tribute in the future, and gave up claims to the mainland and the mines.

[102] As for the Lacedaemonians, when the war with the men in Ithome grew prolonged, they appealed to their allies including the Athenians, who came with a considerable force commanded by Kimon. They called in the Athenians especially because they had a reputation for skill in capturing fortified places; after the long duration of the siege, their own weakness in this area was obvious, since otherwise they would have captured the place by assault. And the first open quarrel between the Lacedaemonians and the Athenians took place as a result of this campaign. When the place was not taken by assault, the Lacedaemonians, fearing that the daring and the revolutionary character of the Athenians, whose difference in nationality they were also conscious of, would lead them to revolutionary activities under the influence of the men in Ithome if they stayed there, dismissed only them among the allies, not revealing their suspicion but saying that they no longer had a need for them. The Athenians realized that they were not being dismissed for this comparatively acceptable reason but because some sort of suspicion had developed, and as soon as they returned home, in their anger and their conviction that they did not deserve this treatment from the Lacedaemonians, they broke off the alliance formed with them

1.101–3. Many scholars emend "tenth" to some other number to keep the fall of Ithome from occurring out of chronological order; cf. Badian 1993, pp. 89–96, Stadter 1993, n. 70, Pritchett 1995, pp. 5–61.

against the Mede and became allies of the Argives, enemies of the Lacedaemonians, and at the same time both parties undertook the same oaths and alliance with the Thessalians.

[103] The men in Ithome, unable to hold out any longer, in the tenth year reached an agreement with the Lacedaemonians by which they were to leave the Peloponnesos under truce and never set foot in it again; anyone caught there would be the slave of his captor. The Lacedaemonians also had an oracle from Delphi beforehand telling them to release the suppliant of Zeus at Ithome. They departed with their wives and children, and the Athenians, taking them in because of the hostility they now felt toward the Lacedaemonians, settled them at Naupaktos, which as it happened they had recently seized from the Ozolian Lokrians occupying it. The Megarians now also came over to the Athenians as allies, defecting from the Lacedaemonians because the Corinthians were pressing them in a war over boundaries, and the Athenians occupied Megara and Pagai, built the long walls for the Megarians extending from the city to Nisaia, and garrisoned these with their own men. And it was especially from this that the Corinthians first developed their bitter hatred for the Athenians.

[104] Inaros son of Psammetichos, a Libyan and king of the Libyans bordering Egypt, set out from Mareia, the city above Pharos, and brought about the revolt of most of Egypt from King Artaxerxes, and after making himself its leader he invited the Athenians in as helpers. The Athenians, who happened to be campaigning against Cyprus with two hundred ships of their own and the allies, abandoned Cyprus to go there, and sailing up the Nile from the sea and taking control of the river and two-thirds of Memphis they attacked the third part, called White Castle; within it were some Persians and Medes who had taken refuge there and the Egyptians who had not joined the revolt.

[105] There was a battle between the Athenians, who had landed at Haliai with their fleet, and the Corinthians and Epidaurians, and the Corinthians won. The Athenians later fought a sea battle against a Peloponnesian fleet at Kekryphaleia and won. After this, when the Athe-

---

1.105–6. These campaigns in Aigina and the Peloponnesos date to the beginning of the 450s. The massacre of the Corinthians is a notable example of Thucydides' use of understatement: within the selective and highly concentrated framework of the Pentakontaetia, he describes a relatively unimportant incident—yet briefly, without the fuller details and comments accompanying many of his other reports of disasters; he leaves it to the reader to conjecture the implications of the massacre—preceded by frustration and humiliation—for the Corinthians' "bitter hatred for the Athenians" (1.103).

nians became involved in a war with the Aiginetans, there was a great sea battle at Aigina between the Athenians and the Aiginetans with allies on both sides, and the Athenians won and after capturing seventy of their ships made a landing and besieged the place under the command of Leokrates son of Stroibos. In their desire to help the Aiginetans, the Peloponnesians then sent over to Aigina three hundred hoplites who had previously been supporting the Corinthians and Epidaurians, while the Corinthians seized the heights of Geraneia and descended into the Megarid, thinking that the Athenians would be unable to help the Megarians with much of their army away in Aigina and Egypt; if they did help, they would withdraw from Aigina.

The Athenians did not touch their forces against Aigina; both the elderly and the very young among those left in the city went out into the Megarid under the command of Myronides. After an indecisive battle against the Corinthians, the armies separated with each side thinking that it had been more successful in the fighting. The Athenians (who after all had had the better of it) set up a trophy after the Corinthians left; the Corinthians, after being subjected to taunts by their elders in the city and spending about twenty days in preparation, later came and retaliated by setting up their own trophy, and the Athenians sallied out of Megara, killed the men setting up the trophy, and then attacked and defeated the rest. [106] The defeated army withdrew, and a large contingent, under heavy pressure and completely off their route, plunged into the property of a private individual that happened to be enclosed by a great ditch and had no way out. When the Athenians realized this, they blocked them in front with hoplites, placed light-armed troops all around them in a circle, and stoned to death everyone who had gone in, and this was a major disaster suffered by the Corinthians. The main portion of their army made its retreat home.

[107] Around this time, the Athenians began to build their long walls to the sea, the one to Phaleron, the other to the Peiraeus. And when the Phokians campaigned against Doris, which was the mother-city of the

---

1.107–8. The battles in Boiotia date to 458/7. On the capitulation of Aigina in 457, see Figueira 1991, pp. 106–9. Plant 1994 has plausibly suggested that Thucydides has misinterpreted the main reason for the major battle at Tanagra (in the process emphasizing the national characteristics he attributes to the Athenians and Spartans in 1.70 and elsewhere); the Spartans were actually seeking such a battle hoping to offset recent Athenian gains in the Peloponnese, relieve the siege of Aigina, and undermine the democracy (in this event, they were unsuccessful despite their narrow victory in the field).

Lacedaemonians, Boion, Kytinion, and Erineon, and took one of these towns; the Lacedaemonians under Nikomedes son of Kleombrotos (commanding for king Pleistoanax, since he was still a youth) came to the defense of the Dorians with one thousand five hundred of their own hoplites and ten thousand from the allies, and after forcing the Phokians into an agreement to surrender the town, they left for home. And if they wanted to go by sea, crossing the Gulf of Krisa, the Athenians were ready to bring their fleet around and block them; yet going through Geraneia did not seem safe to them with the Athenians holding Megara and Pagai. Geraneia was difficult to cross and was always guarded by the Athenians, and on this occasion they had information that the Athenians were also ready to block them there. They decided to remain in Boiotia and determine the best way to get through. There was also the factor of Athenians making secret overtures to them in hopes of putting an end to the democracy and the construction of the long walls. The Athenians went to meet them in full force along with a thousand Argives and various contingents from the other allies; in all, they numbered fourteen thousand. They took the field against them because they believed that the Lacedaemonians were at a loss over how to make their way through, also suspecting something about the overthrow of the democracy. Some Thessalian cavalry also joined the Athenians in accordance with their alliance, and during the fighting they went over to the Lacedaemonian side.

[108] When the battle took place at Tanagra in Boiotia, the Lacedaemonians and their allies won, and there was great carnage on both sides. And the Lacedaemonians, after entering the Megarid and cutting down the orchards, made their way home across Geraneia and the isthmus; the Athenians marched into Boiotia sixty-two days after the battle under the command of Myronides, defeated the Boiotians at Oinophyta, and became supreme in the area of Boiotia and Phokis; and they pulled down the walls of Tanagra, took a hundred of the richest of the Opuntian Lokrians hostage, and also completed their long walls. After this, in addition, the Aiginetans submitted to Athenian demands that they tear down their walls, surrender their ships, and be assessed tribute in the future. The Athenians, under the command of Tolmides son of Tolmaios, sailed around the Peloponnesos, and they burned the shipyards of the Lacedaemonians, captured the Corinthian town of Chalkis, and defeated the Sikyonians after making a landing in their territory.

[109] Meanwhile, the Athenians and their allies in Egypt stayed on and experienced every variety of war. At first, they were masters of Egypt, and the king sent Megabazos, a Persian, to Lacedaemon with money to draw

the Athenians out of Egypt by inducing the Peloponnesians to invade Attica. Since he made no progress and the money was being spent uselessly, he recalled Megabazos to Asia with what was left and sent Megabyzos son of Zopyros, a Persian, with a large army. Arriving by land, he defeated the Egyptians and their allies in battle, drove the Hellenes out of Memphis, and finally shut them up on the island of Prosopitis; he besieged them there for a year and sixth months until, by draining the canal and diverting the water into another one, he left their ships on dry land and connected most of the island with the mainland and captured the island on foot. [110] So the project of the Hellenes was ruined after six years of fighting; out of their great numbers, a few survived by crossing through Libya into Cyrene, but most of them perished. Egypt came back under the control of the king except for Amyrtaios the king of the marshland; they were unable to capture him because of the size of the marshland, and besides the marsh-dwellers are the best fighters among the Egyptians. Inaros the king of the Libyans, the man who brought about all the events in Egypt, was betrayed, captured, and crucified. And fifty triremes sailing from Athens and the rest of the alliance as a relief force put in at the Mendesian mouth of the Nile with no knowledge of what had happened; infantry falling on them by land and the Phoenician navy by sea destroyed most of the ships, and only a few escaped and returned. Such was the final stage of the great Egyptian campaign of the Athenians and their allies.

[111] Orestes son of Echekratidas, king of the Thessalians, who was in exile from Thessaly, persuaded the Athenians to restore him. Taking with them the Boiotians and Phokians who were allies, the Athenians campaigned against Pharsalos in Thessaly. Their control of the area hardly extended beyond their camp (it was the Thessalian cavalry that limited their movements), and they did not take the town, nor was there any other kind of progress toward the objectives of the campaign, and they withdrew with Orestes and went back unsuccessful. Not much later, they embarked on their ships at Pagai, which was under their own control, and sailed along the coast to Sikyon under the command of Perikles son of Xanthippos, and they landed and won a battle against the Sikyonians who engaged them. They immediately crossed over, taking the Achaians with them, and

1.109–10. The Egyptian campaign ended in 454. On Thucydides' use of the phrase "every variety" in "emotional passages," see Flory 1988a; somewhat similar ideas about Thucydides' use of hyperbole, or at least superlatives, in connection with the unexpected were developed by Grene 1965, pp. 80–92.

attacked and besieged Oiniadai in Akarnania, and yet they were unable to take the place and returned home.

[112] Later, after an interval of three years, a truce was made between the Peloponnesians and the Athenians. The Athenians abstained from wars against Hellenes but campaigned against Cyprus with two hundred ships, both their own and allied, under the command of Kimon. While sixty of these left and sailed to Egypt on the summons of Amyrtaios the king of the marshlands, the rest besieged Kition. When Kimon died and provisions ran short, they withdrew from Kition; sailing off Salamis in Cyprus, they fought against the Phoenicians, Cyprians, and Cilicians on both sea and land, won both battles, and departed for home, and the ships returning from Egypt went with them. After this, the Lacedaemonians campaigned in what was called the sacred war, took control of the Delphic sanctuary, and handed it over to the Delphians; and later, after they left, the Athenians in turn made a campaign, took control, and handed it over to the Phokians.

[113] Some time after this, when the Boiotian exiles were in possession of Orchomenos, Chaironeia, and some other places in Boiotia, the Athenians campaigned against these places, which were hostile, with a thousand of their own hoplites along with allied contingents under the command of Tolmides son of Tolmaios; after capturing Chaironeia and enslaving its inhabitants, they left a garrison and started back. But while they were on their way, the Boiotian exiles from Orchomenos, along with Lokrians, Euboian exiles, and all others who supported their cause fell on them at Koroneia; they defeated the Athenians, killing some and taking others prisoner. And so the Athenians evacuated all of Boiotia after making a treaty through which they got their men back. The Boiotian exiles returned, and they and all the rest became independent once again.

[114] Not long after this, Euboia revolted from the Athenians. And after Perikles had already crossed to Euboia with Athenian forces, he

1.111. Thucydides' language seems tinged with sarcasm as he reports these unimpressive ventures following Athens' disasters in Egypt.

1.112. The five-year truce and the death of Kimon occurred in 451; the sacred war, in 449.

1.113–14. These events date to 446. Two notable Athenian casualties of Koroneia are mentioned by reliable later sources: Tolmides himself and Kleinias, the father of Alcibiades (on whom see 5.43 and frequently thereafter). There is considerable evidence that the Athenians marched into the Megarid after withdrawing from Euboia, see Hornblower 1991 *ad* 1.114.1; on Pleistoanax's withdrawal, see 2.21n and Hornblower *ad* 1.114.2.

received the news that Megara had revolted, the Peloponnesians were about to invade Attica, and the Athenian garrison had been slaughtered except for those who had escaped to Nisaia (in making their revolt the Megarians had called in the Corinthians, the Sikyonians, and the Epidaurians); Perikles quickly brought the army back from Euboia. After this the Peloponnesians invaded Attica as far as Eleusis and Thria and plundered them under the leadership of Pleistoanax son of Pausanias, king of the Lacedaemonians, and they left for home without advancing farther. And the Athenians, under the command of Perikles, crossed back over to Euboia and subdued the whole island, arranging everything under an agreement except at Hestiaia, where they expelled the people and occupied the land themselves. [115] They returned from Euboia and soon afterward concluded a thirty-year treaty with the Lacedaemonians and their allies, giving back Nisaia, Pagai, Troizen, and Achaia; these were the the places they held in the Peloponnesos. In the sixth year of the treaty, war broke out between the Samians and the Milesians over Priene, and the Milesians, getting the worst of it, came to Athens and raised an outcry against the Samians; they were supported by private individuals from Samos itself who wanted a revolution in the government. The Athenians accordingly sailed to Samos with forty ships and established a democracy, took fifty boys and an equal number of men from the Samians as hostages, depositing them on Lemnos, and returned after leaving a garrison on Samos. Some of the Samians, however, who had not stayed but fled to the mainland, made a compact with the most powerful men in the city and Pissouthnes son of Hystaspes, who controlled Sardis at that time, gathered about seven hundred mercenaries, and crossed over to Samos by night. First they staged an insurrection against the populace and overpowered most of them; then, after stealing the hostages away from Lemnos, they revolted, and they turned over to Pissouthnes the Athenian garrison and Athenian officials who had been left with them and immediately prepared to campaign against Miletos. The Byzantians revolted along with them.

[116] When the Athenians heard the news, they sailed against Samos with sixty ships, sixteen of which they did not use (what happened was that they sent some of them to Karia as a lookout for the Phoenician fleet, others to Chios and Lesbos to call up reinforcements), but with forty-four ships under ten commanders, including Perikles, engaged seventy Samian ships (twenty of them transports; all of these were sailing from Miletos) off

1.115–17. The Samian revolt of 440 (see 1.40–41) was put down in 439.

the island of Tragia, and the Athenians won. Forty ships from Athens and twenty-five from the Chians and the Lesbians subsequently reinforced them, and after landing and taking control on land they blockaded the city with a triple fortification as well as by sea. Perikles, however, taking sixty ships from the blockade, quickly went to Kaunos and Karia, since it was reported that Phoenician ships were sailing against the Athenians; for Stesagoras and others, leaving Samos in five ships, had indeed gone for the Phoenicians. [117] During this interval the Samians, sailing out suddenly and falling on the Athenian camp, which was not protected by a barricade, destroyed the ships on guard, defeated in battle the ships launched against them, and controlled their own waters for fourteen days and brought what they pleased in and out. But when Perikles returned, they were once again confined by the fleet. Later, as additional reinforcements, forty ships from Athens came with Thucydides, Hagnon, and Phormio; twenty with Tlepolemos and Antikles; and thirty from Chios and Lesbos. Although the Samians put up a brief fight at sea, they were unable to hold their own, and in the ninth month of the siege, they surrendered their city and agreed to terms, tearing down their walls, giving hostages, handing over their ships, and accepting an assessment to pay war retribution by installments. And the Byzantians also agreed to be subjects just as before.

[118] It was only a few years after this that the events already described took place, the Corcyrean and Potidaian affairs and everything else that constituted the cause of this war. All these actions of the Hellenes against one another and against the barbarian occurred within about fifty years, between the withdrawal of Xerxes and the beginning of this war. In this period the Athenians both made control over their empire more secure and made great advances in their own power. Although the Lacedaemonians were aware of this, they did not oppose it except in limited ways and remained inactive most of the time, slow as in the past to go to war unless they were forced to, also somewhat hampered by wars at home—until at last the power of the Athenians was understood with clarity and their actions were affecting the Lacedaemonian alliance. Then they no longer found the situation bearable, and it appeared that they had to put all their zeal into the attempt and destroy the might of the Athenians, if they could, by taking on this war. Now the Lacedaemonians themselves decided that the truce had been broken and the Athenians were aggressors, but they sent to Delphi and asked the god whether war was the best course. The god, it

1.117. "Thucydides": almost certainly not the author, see Hornblower 1991 *ad* 1.117.2.

is said, gave them the answer that if they fought with all their might, the victory would be theirs, and that he would assist them both at their request and without their bidding. [119] And they wanted to summon the allies and call once again for a vote as to whether they should go to war. After the allied representatives had arrived and the congress met, the others spoke as they pleased, most denouncing the Athenians and demanding that the war begin, and the Corinthians, who were also at the congress after previously, in their fear that Potidaia might fall, making their appeal in each individual city to vote for war, now came forward last and spoke as follows:

[120] "Allies, we can no longer find fault with the Lacedaemonians, after they have voted for war themselves and then convened us for this purpose; leaders, while duly taking care of their own affairs, must be first in considering the common interest, just as their public honors raise them above all others. Those of us who have already had dealings with the Athenians need no instructions to be on guard against them; but those who live farther inland and not on the trade routes need to know that if they do not defend the coastal states, bringing their produce down and exchanging it for the things the sea provides to the mainland will be difficult, and they must not be poor judges of what is being said now, as though this did not involve them, but acknowledge that if the coastal states were left to their fate, the danger would eventually reach them as well, and that they are now deliberating among themselves as much as about others. And they too must not hold back from exchanging peace for war. It is characteristic of prudent men that they are at rest if they are not wronged; yet characteristic of brave men, once they are wronged, that they leave peace for war and at the right opportunity leave war for reconciliation, and that they are neither carried away by good fortune in war nor victims of injustice because of enjoying the tranquillity of peace. For he who holds back for the sake of pleasure will very quickly, if he stays inactive, be deprived of that same blissful state that caused him to hold back, and he who goes too far because of success in war does not realize that he is being carried away by unwarranted confidence. Many poorly made plans have succeeded by chancing on opponents who have planned worse, and on the other hand a still greater number of excellent plans have turned out wretchedly. For no one forms a plan and carries it out with a uniform degree of confidence, rather, we form our opinions in a state of security and in action fall short in the presence of fear.

[121] "As matters stand, we are victims of aggression who are instigating the war with ample grievances and the ones who will put a timely end to it once we have chastised the Athenians. And it is probable on many grounds that we will be victorious, first because we surpass them in num-

bers and military experience, next because we all uniformly obey our orders, and we will also build up naval power, where their strength is, from both the resources available to each of us and the funds in Delphi and Olympia; borrowing will enable us to lure away their foreign sailors by higher pay. For the power of the Athenians is more purchased than homegrown, but ours would be less vulnerable there because of being based on manpower instead of money. One victory at sea, and with all probability they will fall into our hands. But if they hold out, we ourselves, given more time, will also get practice in naval warfare, and once we have drawn even in skill, there is no doubt whatsoever that we will surpass them in courage. For the good qualities we have by nature they cannot acquire by instruction, and what advantage they have in skill can be removed by practice. In order to have funds for this, we will pay contributions. Anything else would be monstrous, that their allies would never slacken in contributing for their own enslavement, whereas we would not even be spending for our own preservation along with chastising our enemies, not even to avoid being damaged by those very same funds after they take them away from us.

[122] "There are many other avenues of war open to us as well: revolt among their allies, which means above all deprivation of the revenues that make them strong, a fortified outpost in their territory, and all the other things one cannot now foresee. For war is the last thing to follow a prescribed course but draws on itself for a variety of means to meet each situation, leaving the man who approaches it with equanimity in relative security, while the one who deals with it in a passion gets into more trouble. Bear in mind also that if there were boundary disputes involving each of us against opponents of equal strength, this would be tolerable. But in actuality the Athenians are a match for all of us combined and even more powerful against us city by city. And if we do not make our defense against them with every people and every city united in a single purpose, they will have little difficulty overcoming us in our divided state. And never think that defeat, however terrible this is to hear, will bring anything short of outright slavery. For the Peloponnesians, it is shameful that this possibility exists even in word, and that so many cities should be brutalized by one; in the event, we would seem either to deserve our suffering or to put up with it out of cowardice and show ourselves lesser men than our fathers, who liberated Hellas, whereas we did not even secure freedom for our-

---

1.121. "Manpower instead of money": *HCT* I *ad* 1.121.3 notes the inconsistency of the Corinthian argument here.

selves but allowed a tyrant state to be set up and saw fit to put down monarchs within single cities. We do not see how all of this can be separated from the three greatest afflictions: stupidity, weakness, or negligence. For it cannot be that in avoiding these you have passed into that sense of superiority that has harmed so many, which from the numbers it has ruined has taken on the opposite name, senselessness.

[123] "Yet why is it necessary to criticize past actions any further than will benefit those of the present? And for the sake of the future, you must toil in reinforcing what you have on hand, with your heritage of building virtues through exertion, and not change your character even if you are now slightly to the better in wealth and resources, acquired amidst poverty and wrong to lose amidst abundance, but go to war with confidence on many grounds, since the god has ordained it and promised to support us, and all the rest of Hellas will join in the struggle, partly out of fear, partly out of self-interest. You will not be the first to break the treaty, which indeed the god, in bidding you go to war, regards as already transgressed; you will rather be supporting a treaty that has been outraged, for it is not those who defend themselves but those who attack first that break treaties.

[124] "Therefore, since there is every sort of justification for you to go to war, and since we recommend this for the general good (surely identical interests are the best safeguards for both states and individuals), do not hesitate to bring aid to the Potidaians, who are Dorians and besieged by Ionians, a reversal of the past, nor to seek freedom for others, since it is not acceptable that, by further waiting, some of us should be injured right now and others—if we are known to have met, but without daring to defend ourselves—will suffer this in the near future. Rather than this, allies, realizing that you have reached the point of necessity, and that what has been said here is right, vote for war, not with fear of the immediate danger but with longing for the lasting peace that will come of it; for after war, peace is more strongly confirmed, while refusal to leave inactivity and go to war is less free from risk. Understanding that the tyrant state that has been established in Hellas was established against all alike, spelling the domination extended over some already and projected against the rest, let us attack and overthrow it, and let us live in security for the future and free those now enslaved." Such was the Corinthian speech.

1.122. "Tyrant state": cf. 2.63, 3.37. The wordplay in Greek that I have indicated in "sense . . . senselessness" may be a regrettable reflection of contemporary rhetoric (see the discussion in *HCT* I *ad* 1.122.4) but must be translated, if only because Thucydides has (somewhat ponderously) called attention to the "renaming."

[125] When the Lacedaemonians had heard everyone's opinion, they put the vote to all the allies present in order, both the large and the small states, and the majority voted to go to war. After this resolution, it was not possible for them in their state of unpreparedness to attack immediately, but it was decided what contributions were to be provided by each and that there was to be no delay. Time was nevertheless spent in preparing what they needed, not a year but somewhat less, before they invaded Attica and openly began the war. [126] During this period they sent embassies to Athens and made charges, in order to have as good a reason as possible for going to war if the Athenians paid no attention. With the first embassy they sent, the Lacedaemonians ordered the Athenians to drive out the curse of the goddess; the curse was of the following sort. Kylon was an Olympic victor, an Athenian of former times, both well-born and influential. He was married to the daughter of Theagenes, a Megarian who was tyrant of Megara at that time. When Kylon was consulting the oracle at Delphi, the god responded that he should seize the acropolis of Athens during the greatest festival of Zeus. Kylon acquired an armed force from Theagenes and won over his friends, and when the Olympic festival was taking place in the Peloponnesos he seized the acropolis in an attempt at a tyranny, thinking that this was the greatest festival of Zeus and also rather appropriate to him as a victor at the Olympic games. Whether the greatest festival meant was in Athens or somewhere else (for the Athenians also have the Diasia, which is called the greatest festival of Zeus Meilichios and is outside the city, where they sacrifice as an entire people, many not with ordinary victims but with local offerings), he did not consider further but, thinking his was the right interpretation, made the attempt. When the Athenians found out, they came from the countryside to resist in full force,

1.125. "Voted to go to war": see 1.88n. "Not a year": Thucydides appears to be stressing the delay rather than the speed in preparation, but his language is confusing; cf. Hornblower 1991 *ad* 2.2.1 and Badian 1993, pp. 150–51.

1.126. See Hornblower 1991, pp. 202–10. Kylon's Olympic victory is usually dated to 640, but some would place his conspiracy in the early sixth century. The style (as opposed to the content) of this digression drew the comment from a scholiast, "Here the lion laughed"; Hornblower calls this chapter "discursive and Herodotean." We can compare the account in Herodotos (5.71, actually much sparer than Thucydides'), who indicates that Kylon was killed, and that officials other than the archons were responsible for the sacrilege, so Thucydides' apparent discursiveness may have a corrective function; it has been thought that he was also correcting a version in which the attempt occurred during the Diasia (this is at least more plausible than the idea that he was intent on vindicating the oracle).

took up settled positions, and besieged them. But as time passed, the Athenians were fatigued by the blockade and most departed, leaving it to the nine archons to keep watch and have sole authority to settle the matter as they judged best (at that time the nine archons handled most political duties). The group besieged with Kylon became weak through lack of food and water. Now Kylon and his brother escaped, but the others, since they were suffering and some even dying of famine, sat on the altar on the acropolis. When the Athenians entrusted with the guard saw them dying in the sanctuary, they raised them up on the understanding that they would do them no harm, led them away, and put them to death; on the way, they killed some who seated themselves in the sanctuary of the revered goddesses. And for this they were pronounced accursed and offenders against the goddess, they and their descendants. So the Athenians expelled these accursed men, and Kleomenes the Lacedaemonian, along with Athenian dissidents, also drove them out later and when they expelled the living also dug up the bones of the dead and cast them out. Nevertheless, they came back later, and their family is still in the city.

[127] This was the curse that the Lacedaemonians commanded them to drive out, in the first place honoring the gods, to be sure, but knowing that Perikles son of Xanthippos was connected with it through his mother and thinking that if he were exiled they would make easier headway with the Athenians. They did not anticipate so much that he would undergo this, however, as that they would prejudice him in the eyes of the citizens, inasmuch as war would come partly on account of his unfortunate association. The ablest man of his time and the leader of the state, he opposed the Lacedaemonians in everything and would not allow the Athenians to make concessions but was always urging them on to the war.

[128] In retaliation, the Athenians ordered the Lacedaemonians to expel the curse of Tainaron. For the Lacedaemonians at one time raised up helot suppliants from the sanctuary of Poseidon at Tainaron, led them away, and killed them, and they believe that they had the great earthquake

1.128–35. The medism of Pausanias, cited by Graf 1984 as the "classic illustration," is widely doubted by scholars, see Hornblower 1991, pp. 211–20 and Badian 1993, p. 131; this calls into question much of the Themistokles story as well. For Athenian use of Pausanias' medism as justification for Athenian hegemony, see Herodotos 5.32 and cf. Rawlings 1977, pp. 7–8. The letter from Xerxes undoubtedly reproduces an authentically Persian style, and his "delight" recalls his characterization in Herodotos; as presented by Thucydides, he and the Spartan are a fatuous, Willy-Nicky pair of intriguers, to whom Themistokles and Artaxerxes offer a sharp contrast.

in Sparta as a direct consequence. They also ordered them to expel the curse of the Bronze House. It came about in the following way. When Pausanias the Lacedaemonian was acquitted of wrongdoing after the first time the Spartiates recalled him, from his command in the Hellespont, and put him on trial, he was no longer sent out on public business, but in a private capacity he took a trireme from Hermione and went to the Hellespont without authorization from the Lacedaemonians, purportedly for the Hellenic war, in reality to intrigue with the king, just as he had attempted on the first occasion, aiming at rule over the Hellenes.

And the benefit he first conferred on the king, starting the whole affair, came out of the following situation. When he captured Byzantion during his previous campaign, after the return from Cyprus (the Medes held Byzantion, and some associates and relatives of the king were captured there at the time), he sent the prisoners he took to the king, without the knowledge of the allies, using the story that they had escaped from him. He did this with the assistance of Gongylos of Eretria, the same man he had entrusted with Byzantion and the captives. He also sent Gongylos with a letter to the king; its contents, as later discovered, were the following: "Pausanias the leader of Sparta, wishing to oblige you, sends these prisoners of his spear, and I propose, if you also approve, to marry your daughter and make both Sparta and the rest of Hellas subject to you. I consider myself capable of doing this if I plan it with your help. Therefore, if any of these things pleases you, send a trustworthy man to the coast through whom we may communicate in the future."

[129] This was as much as the message disclosed; Xerxes was delighted with the letter and sent Artabazos son of Pharnakes to the coast and ordered him to take over the Daskylitan satrapy replacing Megabates, who had previously governed it, and he gave him a letter to send as quickly as possible in reply to Pausanias at Byzantion, with instructions to show Pausanias his seal and, whatever Pausanias advised about the king's affairs, to attend to it with his full ability and trust. On his arrival he carried out his orders exactly and sent the letter. The following was written in reply: "Thus speaks King Xerxes to Pausanias. Your benefit to me in sending the men safely across the sea from Byzantion is recorded in our house forever, and I am also pleased with your words. Let neither night nor day cause you to slacken in carrying out your promises to me, nor let them be hindered for expenditure of gold or silver or for numbers of troops, wherever their presence is needed, but with the help of Artabazos, a good man I have sent to you, boldly act in both my interests and yours in any way that will be most honorable and best for both."

[130] On receiving this letter Pausanias, already held in high esteem by the Hellenes because of his leadership at Plataia, had then become much more conceited and could no longer bear to live in the conventional manner, but he would go forth from Byzantion wearing Median garb, Medes and Egyptians formed a bodyguard for him as he proceeded through Thrace, he had a Persian table set for himself, and he was unable to contain his pretensions but gave away by minor actions what he was resolved to do in the future on a grander scale. He made himself difficult of access and displayed such a harsh temper to everyone alike that no one could approach him. It was mainly for this very reason that the allies turned to the Athenians.

[131] On account of this conduct, the Lacedaemonians recalled him for the first time when they heard about it, and when, on going out a second time in the ship from Hermione without their orders, he was evidently behaving in the same way and, after being forcibly driven out of Byzantion by the Athenians, did not return to Sparta but was reported to be intriguing with the barbarians from a base at Kolonai in the Troad and using his stay for no good purpose; the Lacedaemonians then waited no longer, and the ephors sent a herald and a skytale ordering him not to let the herald leave without him; otherwise, he would be declared an enemy of the Spariates. Pausanias, wishing to avoid suspicion as much as possible and confident of overthrowing the accusation by means of money, returned to Sparta a second time. And at first he was thrown into prison by the ephors (it is in their power to do this to the king); then he subsequently contrived his release and presented himself for judgment by anyone who wanted to examine him.

[132] The Spartiates had no clear evidence, neither his enemies nor the entire state, on which they could sufficiently rely in punishing a man who was both of the royal family and in high rank at the time (for he was regent, as a cousin, for Pleistarchos son of Leonidas who was king and still under age), yet by his flouting of convention and his imitation of the barbarians he had furnished many reasons to suspect that he did not want to be limited to his existing circumstances. They reviewed both the various other ways in which he had changed his way of life from established customs and the fact that once, on the tripod at Delphi which the Hellenes dedicated as first fruits from the Medes, he presumed on his own initiative to have the following couplet inscribed:

Ruler of the Hellenes, when he destroyed the army of the Medes,
Pausanias dedicated this monument to Phoibos.

1.131. "A herald and a skytale": how this Spartan "message stick" actually worked now seems very uncertain; see Kelly 1985, cf. Russell 1994, pp. 189–91.

Now at the time the Lacedaemonians immediately erased the couplet from the tripod and inscribed by name all the cities that had joined in overthrowing the barbarian and set up the dedication; yet even then it seemed a crime on Pausanias' part, and now that the situation was as it was, it appeared an action consistent with his present behavior. They were also informed that he was intriguing with the helots, and this was the case; for he promised them freedom and citizenship if they joined his uprising and supported his future plans.

But not even then, not even trusting some informers among the helots, were they prepared to take extraordinary action against him, observing the practice so customary among them, slowness in planning anything irrevocable against a Spartan citizen without indisputable proof—until right now, so it is said, the man who was to bring Artabazos the latest letter for the king, a man from Argilos once Pausanias' beloved and in his full trust, turned informer because he became fearful on observing that none of the messengers before him had ever returned, and after counterfeiting the seal (so that if he was mistaken in his conjecture, or Pausanias needed to rewrite something, he would not be found out) he read the letter, where he found written as a postscript just what he had expected, that he was to be put to death.

[133] Certainly then, when he showed them the letter, the ephors were more convinced, yet since they still wanted to hear with their own ears when Pausanias himself said something, the man went to Tainaron as a suppliant by prearrangement and built a hut divided into two parts where he concealed some of the ephors, and when Pausanias came to him and asked the reason for his supplication, they heard everything plainly, because the man accused him over the letter about him and brought everything else out into the open in full detail, how he had never put Pausanias in jeopardy during his missions to the king yet had been given the distinction of dying like the common run of his emissaries, and the other admitted all this and begged him not to be angry over the situation but promised him a safe departure from the sanctuary and urged him to set out as quickly as possible and not hinder his activities.

[134] After listening carefully, the ephors then went away, but now that they knew with certainty, they began preparing for his arrest in the city. It is said that he was about to be arrested in the street and seeing the face of one of the advancing ephors realized what he was coming for, and when another gave him a covert nod and let him know out of kindness he went to the sanctuary of the Bronze House at a run and outstripped his pursuers; the precinct is nearby. Entering a chamber of modest size that was part of the temple, he kept still. The others, left behind in the moment of pur-

suit, then removed the roof, and when they had made sure he was inside and had trapped him there they walled up the doors and took up positions nearby and reduced him through starvation. When they learned that he was about to expire, right inside the chamber, they brought him out of the temple still breathing, and as soon as he was brought out he died. And they were going to throw him into the Kaidas ravine, but then it seemed best to bury him somewhere nearby. But the god in Delphi later ordained that they transfer his tomb to the place where he died (and he now lies in the area before the precinct, as recorded by inscribed stone markers) and, since what had been done was a curse on them, give back two bodies to the Bronze House in return for one. And they made two bronze statues and dedicated them in return for Pausanias.

[135] Since the god had pronounced the curse, the Athenians in retaliation ordered the Lacedaemonians to drive it out. As for the medism of Pausanias, the Lacedaemonians sent an embassy to Athens and accused Themistokles of involvement, which they discovered from the evidence about Pausanias, and demanded that they inflict the same punishment on him as well. They consented and—since he happened to be ostracized and was residing in Argos, frequenting the other parts of the Peloponnesos as well—sent men to accompany the Lacedaemonians, who were ready to help in the pursuit, with instructions to seize him wherever they found him. [136] Themistokles detected this first and fled the Peloponnesos for Corcyra, since he was a benefactor of the Corcyreans, but because they claimed that they were afraid to harbor him and incur the hatred of the Lacedaemonians and the Athenians, they had him sent from Corcyra across to the opposite mainland. Pursued by those assigned to trace his movements, he was forced in desperation to occupy the residence of Admetos, king of the Molossians, who was no friend of his. Admetos happened to be away, but when Themistokles supplicated his wife, he was instructed to take their son and sit at the hearth. And when Admetos arrived not much later, he revealed who he was and urged him, granted that he had spoken in opposition to his request of the Athenians, not to avenge himself on him when he was in exile; under the circumstances, he might be injured by one far weaker than Admetos, and vengeance on even terms against equals was the noble course; besides, he had opposed him over some need that did not involve his personal safety, but Admetos, if he gave him up (he told him who his pursuers were and why) would deprive his life of all salvation. [137] After listening, the other raised him up together with his son (since he was actually holding him as he sat, and that was the most important part of his supplication), and not much later, when

the Lacedaemonians and the Athenians came and said everything they could, he would not give him up, but since Themistokles wanted to make his way to the king, he sent him by land to Pydna on the opposite coast, which belonged to Alexandros.

Finding a merchant vessel there setting sail for Ionia and boarding it, he was carried by a storm to the Athenian fleet blockading Naxos. In his fear, despite not being recognized by anyone on the ship, he told the captain who he was and why he was in flight and said that if he did not save him he would claim that the other had been bribed to take him; their safety meant that no one was to disembark before sailing weather came, and if he obeyed he would remember him with a suitable reward. The captain acted accordingly, and after riding at anchor away from the squadron for a day and a half, he subsequently reached Ephesos. Themistokles rewarded him with a present of money (for he later received some from friends, in addition to what he had hidden away in Argos), proceeded inland with one of the coastal Persians, and sent a letter to Artaxerxes son of Xerxes, who had recently become king. The message declared: "I, Themistokles, have come to you, one who did your house the most harm of all the Hellenes, as long as I was forced to defend myself against your father's attack, but still more good, in a time of safety for me but of danger for him, when he was returning home. And the benefit is owed to me (he mentioned the warning about the retreat he sent from Salamis and the bridge left unbroken, which he falsely claimed as his doing), and now, able to do you great service, I have come here pursued by the Hellenes because of my friendship for you. I desire to wait one year before I in person reveal to you my purpose in coming." [138] The king, so it is said, was impressed by his intentions and told him to act accordingly.

In the year he kept his distance, he learned as much of the Persian language as he could and the customs of the land; and arriving after the one year, he became important in his court to a degree that no other Hellene ever had, both because of his established reputation and because of the hope he offered him of enslaving Hellas, but above all from demonstrations of his manifest intelligence. For Themistokles, displaying the very surest signs of natural ability, was far and away more worthy than anyone else of admiration for this quality. By native intelligence, without preparing or supplementing it by study, he was with the briefest deliberation the most effective in decisions about immediate situations and the best at conjecturing what would happen farthest into the future; whatever he was engaged in he was capable of explaining, over matters in which he had no experience he was not incapacitated from judging adequately, and in particular he foresaw what better or worse possibilities were still concealed in the future. To sum up, this man by natural ability, with rapid deliberation, was certainly supreme in his immediate grasp of what was necessary. His life ended through illness, but there are those who say he died of his own volition by poison, thinking that he was unable to carry out what he had promised the king. Now in the agora of Magnesia in Asia there is a monument to him; for he was ruler in that area, since the king gave him Magnesia for his bread, which brought in fifty talents each year, Lampsakos for his wine (since it had the reputation for surpassing all cities at that time in wine production), and Myous for his cuisine. They say that at his request his relatives brought his bones home and buried them in Attica, without the knowledge of the Athenians; for it was not allowed to bury anyone in exile for treason. Such were the ends of Pausanias the Lacedaemonian and Themistokles the Athenian, the most famous Hellenes of their time.

[139] In their first embassy, the Lacedaemonians made their demands as I have described and were ordered in return to drive out people under curse; in many later encounters they told the Athenians to lift the siege of Potidaia and leave Aigina autonomous, and they especially and with unmistakable clarity counseled them that there would not be war if they revoked the decree against the Megarians, in which it was stated that they could not use the ports of the Athenian empire or the market of Attica. The Athenians neither yielded on the other matters nor revoked the decree, accusing the Megarians of cultivation extending into consecrated land and unassigned land on their border, and of harboring runaway slaves. At last, when the final ambassadors from Lacedaemon arrived, Ramphias, Melesippos, and Agesandros, and said none of what they had repeatedly said before, but only this: "The Lacedaemonians wish there to be peace, and there would be if you leave the Hellenes autonomous," the Athenians called an assembly and exchanged opinions, and there was a decision to deliberate once and for all about everything and give an answer. A great variety of speakers came forward, taking both sides in their views, that they must go to war and that the decree must not stand in the way of peace but be revoked, and one of them was Perikles son of Xanthippos, the first man in Athens at that time, the ablest in both speaking and acting, who gave the following advice:

[140] "Athenians, I am of the same opinion as ever, against yielding to the Peloponnesians, but well aware that it is not with the same spirit that

1.140–44. For a notable critique of this speech revealing the thought underlying its confidence and intransigence, see Parry 1957, pp. 150–58.

men persuaded into war proceed with its execution, since their minds are swayed according to their encounters. And I see that now once more the same identical advice is required of me, and I charge those who stand persuaded that you support our common resolutions, even if there are setbacks, or else not to claim their intelligence as a contribution to our successes. For the outcome of situations can follow a course as absurd as the plans of man, which is just why we are accustomed to blame chance for whatever turns out contrary to calculation. It was clear in the past that the Lacedaemonians were plotting against us and is no less clear now. For although it was stipulated that we mutually offer and accept arbitration over our differences while each side keeps what it has, they have never yet asked for this nor accepted our offers of it but wish instead to resolve grievances by war rather than discussion and are at this point issuing commands, no longer making requests. They give orders to get out of Potidaia and leave Aigina autonomous and revoke the Megarian decree; and finally they are here with the ultimatum to leave the Hellenes autonomous. But let none of you think we would be going to war over an unimportant matter if we do not revoke the Megarian decree, since they particularly claim that there would not be war if it were revoked, nor let the accusation linger in your minds that you have gone to war for a trifle. This unimportant matter involves the confirmation and test of your entire policy; if you give way to them, you will immediately receive another command about something more serious, as though you would concede this as well out of fear. But a firm denial would show them clearly that they must deal with you on a more equal basis. [141] Here and now, resolve either to yield before coming to any harm or that if we go to war—which I for one think is the better course—we will not give way whether a major or a minor reason is advanced nor hold our possessions in fearfulness. For any requirement, of the greatest or the smallest importance, means the same subservience if it is a command issued by an equal to an equal before there is arbitration.

"As to the war, the resources on the two sides, listen to the particulars and understand that ours will not be the weaker side. For the Peloponnesians are farmers and have neither private nor public funds, and in addition they are inexperienced in prolonged and overseas wars because their incursions against one another are kept brief by poverty. Such people can neither man a fleet nor send out land armies with any frequency, because they would be simultaneously absent from their own property and spending out of their own resources, barred from the sea in addition. It is surplus wealth rather than forced contributions that supports wars; farmers are the type of men who are readier to go to war with their persons than their funds, with confidence that the former will survive the dangers but with no certainty that they will not expend the latter too soon, especially if the war is prolonged beyond their expectations, as is likely. The Peloponnesians are capable of withstanding all Hellas in a single battle but incapable of fighting against a power that confronts them with a different sort of preparation, as long as they fail to take any decisive action immediately by going to one single council house, and each of them, equal in voting and without common nationality, presses for its own concerns—a state of affairs in which it is normal for nothing to get accomplished; some want maximum redress against enemies, others the minimum damage to their property. Needing time to assemble, they spend a small fraction of it considering any public matter and the greater part acting on domestic interests; each thinks that his own negligence does no harm and it is someone else's business to use foresight on his behalf, so that when the same notion is entertained by everyone separately it goes unobserved that common interests are being destroyed collectively. [142] But the most important way in which they will be hindered is through shortage of money, so long as they waste time by its slow provision; military opportunities are not stationary.

"And neither a fortified outpost of theirs nor their navy is truly anything to fear. For regarding the former, it is difficult even during peace to found a rival city, surely no less so in hostile territory when their fortifications are countered by our own. If they build a small fort, they might harm the country somewhat by raids and by harboring runaways, yet it will certainly not be enough to keep us from sailing to their territory and building forts and retaliating with our navy, our real strength. For we have a greater advantage as to land warfare from our experience in seafaring than they have from their experience on land where naval matters are concerned. And becoming skilled at sea will not be an easy acquisition for them. Not even you, practicing right from the time of the Medes, have fully achieved it yet; how then would men who are agrarian and not seafaring, and furthermore will not be allowed to practice because they will be under our blockade, accomplish anything respectable? Against a small blockading fleet, they might risk an engagement, lending their ignorance the boldness of numbers; but if checked by a large fleet, they will stay quiet and through their lack of practice become more incompetent, and on that account more hesitant as well. Seamanship involves skill just like anything else, and there is no way to cultivate it as an outside activity when chance offers, but rather there can be no activities outside that. [143] And even if they try to lure away our foreign sailors by higher pay, taking money from Olympia or Delphi, that would be a threat only if we ourselves and the metics were not a match for them should we embark. This is in fact the case, and as our strongest asset of all we have citizens for pilots and other rowing specialists whose numbers and quality are superior to those of the rest of Hellas combined. And aside from the risk, none of our foreigners would accept a few days' high pay as the reward for exile from their countries and poorer prospects when fighting in their ranks.

"To me at least, it seems that this is very much the situation of the Peloponnesians, and that our situation is free of the specific problems I have found in theirs and has other features, important ones, they cannot match; if they move against our country on land, we will sail against theirs, and from then on there will be no comparison between devastating one part of the whole Peloponnesos and the whole of Attica; they will not be able to replace land without fighting battles, but for us there is abundant land on both the islands and the mainland. That is the greatness of sea power; and consider: if we were islanders, who would be more unassailable? As it is, thinking like them as nearly as possible, we must let go of the land and its houses and stand guard over the sea and the city, and not let rage over the former drive us to fight against the much greater numbers of the Peloponnesians (for if we win we will only fight again against the same superior numbers, and if we fail the loss of our allies—the source of our strength—will follow, since they will not stay quiet if we are not capable of campaigning against them), nor lament over houses and land, but over lives; those do not create men, men create them. If I thought I would persuade you, I would have told you to go out and lay waste your property yourselves and show the Peloponnesians that you would certainly not submit on that account.

[144] "I have many other grounds for the hope of prevailing, if you are willing not to add to the empire while at war and not to take on additional dangers of your own making; for I have come to fear our own mistakes more than the enemy's planning. But those other reasons will be revealed in another speech, depending on events; for now, send these men away with the answer that we will allow Megara to use our market and ports if the Lacedaemonians also cease directing their xenelasia against us and our allies (in the treaty, there is no provision against the one or the other); that we will leave the cities autonomous if we were allowing them autonomy when we made the treaty, and whenever they in turn permit their own cities to be autonomous in a way that suits not the Lacedaemonians' interests

1.144. "In another speech": an exceptional and certainly authorial statement; cf. 2.13 and see Rengakos 1996, p. 399.

but theirs, as they choose; and that we are willing to submit to arbitration on the terms of the treaty and will not begin war but defend ourselves against those who start it. This, as an answer, is both just and worthy of our city.

"And it must be known that war is inevitable, but that if we accept it more readily we will find our enemies less committed, and that out of the greatest dangers emerge the greatest honors for both city and individual. Remember that it was our fathers, standing against the Medes, not drawing on such resources but abandoning even what they had, more by their policies than by fortune, with greater daring than might, who drove out the barbarian and advanced our power to its present level. We must not fall short of them but resist our enemies by every means and attempt to hand it on undiminished to our descendants."

[145] Such was the speech of Perikles. And the Athenians, thinking that he had given the best advice, voted as he had told them and answered the Lacedaemonians with the answers of Perikles, both on individual points as he had stated them and overall, that they would do nothing under orders but were ready on the terms of the treaty to have complaints settled in an equal and fair way. [146] They left for home and sent no more embassies; these were the charges and differences on both sides before the war, arising immediately from the events in Epidamnos and Corcyra. They went on associating and dealing with each other without heralds, but not without suspicion; for things were taking place that meant the dissolution of the treaty and cause for war.

1.146. Both sides were ready for war but not at war; even after the final Spartan embassy was rebuffed, there was communication without heralds, see 2.1–2n. For the closing of a "great ring" here and ring composition as an organizational principle of book 1, see Katicic 1957.

BOOK TWO

INTRODUCTION

*The Peloponnesian War begins with a Theban attack on Plataia; in the first of
a series of excitingly written narratives involving the Plataians, the Thebans
fail and are harshly dealt with. Both sides now consider the Thirty-Year Peace
(dating from 445) at an end and mobilize. Led by the Spartan king Archidamos, the Peloponnesians invade and ravage Attica, whose evacuation causes the
Athenians great physical and emotional suffering; while offering only token resistance, they begin their own annual invasions of the neighboring territory of
Megara and also send a large Athenian and Corcyrean fleet to plunder the
Peloponnesian coast. Thucydides describes the elaborate public funeral for the
Athenian casualties of the first war year and records the eulogy by Perikles,
which commemorates the achievements and ideals of Athens as well as the cour-
age of the men themselves.*

*Early in the second year, Athens is devastated by a plague, whose terrible
symptoms Thucydides describes as one who was stricken and was fortunate
enough to survive. He does not mention the plague as the cause of Perikles'
death in the following year but uses the plague's aftermath as a setting for an
obituary before the event. The disease not only kills a great number of Athenians
but also leaves the surviving population in a mood of cynicism and lawlessness,
which provides the sharpest possible contrast with the Athens both described and
addressed in Perikles' funeral oration. The Athenians of this depressed city first
send ambassadors to Sparta to discuss peace, unsuccessfully, and then angrily
turn on Perikles; he responds with an uncompromising speech defending his war
policy, his qualities of leadership, and the necessity of making every personal
sacrifice to preserve an empire whose glory will outlast the hatred it now admittedly inspires. In response, the Athenians deposed and fined him. His speech is
his final appearance in Thucydides, who complements the speech with a long
chapter commending Perikles for his control over the people and the prudence of
his advice to them; the war was lost by his successors, self-serving demagogues
responsible for series of mistakes, notably the Sicilian expedition. This is the
most explicitly postwar passage in Thucydides and among the most vexed, be-*

cause the indictment of Athenian politicians is notoriously difficult to reconcile with his overall account.

Taken together, the sequence of Periklean speeches, especially the final one, juxtaposes Perikles' function of alternately encouraging and restraining the Athenians and the problem of imposing a relatively passive strategy, which demanded considerable patience and self-sacrifice on a dynamic and adventurous people. While Thucydides did not design book 2 as a unit, its subsequent events indicate a troubled period for Athens with Perikles first out of power and then, shortly after his re-election, dead. The Athenians successfully conclude the siege of Potidaia they had begun shortly before the war, but at the cost of some dissension among themselves and without ending revolts in the area. The Peloponnesians begin a siege of Plataia, a close ally to whom the Athenians can send only minimal help; even though this is in accordance with Perikles' strategy, the Athenians also demand resistance, brave and resourceful but ultimately doomed, on the part of the Plataians. Phormio wins a pair of important naval victories in the gulf of Corinth, but the second of these involves a last-minute reversal of impending and disastrous defeat in a situation created by Athenian mismanagement. Furthermore, a direct response on the part of the Peloponnesians is a surprise raid against Salamis; even though its failure is further indication of the inferiority of Peloponnesian seamanship, Thucydides insists both on its near-success and on the extreme panic it caused in Athens. The book ends on a note of anticlimax suggestive of missed Athenian opportunities. Sitalkes, a Thracian ally, who was not there to help when the Athenians suffered a sharp defeat by rebellious Greeks in the Chalkidike, campaigns against these same Greeks with almost grotesquely large forces (whose mustering from many local tribes Thucydides describes in detail) and at first strikes terror; but partly because of the difficulty of provisioning his huge army with winter approaching, partly because expected Athenian land and naval forces never materialize (because they in turn "did not believe he would come"), he withdraws before doing appreciable damage.

BOOK TWO

[1] And now, from this point, begins the war between the Athenians and the Peloponnesians and the allies on both sides, during which they no longer communicated with one another without heralds and, once they started, fought continuously. This has been written in the order that events occurred, divided into summers and winters. [2] The thirty-year truce made after the capture of Euboia lasted for fourteen years. In the fifteenth, when Chrysis had been priestess at Argos for forty-eight years, Ainesias was ephor at Sparta, and Pythodoros had two more months as archon at Athens, six months after the battle of Potidaia, at the beginning of spring, around the first watch, just over three hundred Thebans, led by the Boiotarchs Pythangelos son of Phyleides and Diemporos son of Onetorides, made an armed entry into Plataia, a city in Boiotia allied with Athens. Plataians called them in and opened the gates, Naukleides and his faction, who wanted to kill those in opposition and align their city with Thebes for the sake of their own personal power. They made these arrangements through Eurymachos son of Leontiades, a man of great importance in Thebes. For the Thebans, anticipating that there would be war, wanted to take the initiative in seizing Plataia, always at odds with them, while there was still peace and war had not broken out openly. Accordingly, they got in all the more easily without being detected, since no guard had been posted. After grounding their arms in the agora, they

2.1–2. I agree with much of Rawlings' valuable discussion (1981, pp. 18–36) but not his conclusion (accepted by Rusten 1989, pp. 95–96) that Thucydides regarded the war as beginning *not* with the attack on Plataia (occurring during peace [2.2, 2.7], elaborately dated and linked with the end of the treaty) but with the period following the final Athenian rejection of Spartan demands (1.145–46, where Thucydides describes both sides as ready for war—but not at war); Rawlings is in the process attempting to explain the problematic "difference of a few days" (5.20). It was not "arbitrary" (Hornblower 1991, p. 236, cf. Rawlings, p. 35) to choose the Theban attack as the beginning unless one radically questions Thucydides' record of events.

did not follow the advice of those who had called them in by getting into action immediately and going to the homes of their enemies but made a decision to use friendly proclamations, leading the city into an amicable understanding, and had their herald proclaim that anyone wishing to be an ally in accordance with the ancestral practice of all Boiotians was to ground his arms with them, since they thought that in this way the city would readily come over to them.

[3] When the Plataians realized that the Thebans were inside and the city had been taken over in an instant, filled with fear and thinking that a much larger number had entered (since they couldn't see them in the night), they came to an agreement and accepted the proposals without opposition, especially since the Thebans, for their part, had committed no violence against anyone. But at a certain point in their negotiations, they discovered that the Thebans were not numerous and felt that if they attacked they could easily overpower them; it was not the wish of the majority of Plataians to defect from Athens. So they decided that the attempt should be made, and they gathered together by cutting through the partitions between houses to avoid being noticed going through the streets, set up wagons without draft animals in the streets to serve as barriers, and made every other arrangement likely to be useful in this situation. And when their preparations were as ready as they could make them, they waited for the moment of dawn when it was still dark and moved out of the houses against the Thebans, so that they would not be attacking them when the daylight made them bolder and put them on an equal basis, but the Thebans would be more fearful at night and at a disadvantage against their own familiarity with the city. They attacked immediately and quickly came into close combat.

[4] When the Thebans realized that they had been completely fooled, they formed close ranks and pushed back the attackers wherever they struck. While they drove them off two or three times, after that, when their opponents assaulted them with loud commotion, and at the same time the women and slaves, with shouting and cheering, hurled stones and tiles from the houses, and on top of that there had been heavy rain during the night, they turned in fright and fled through the city, most of them ignorant of the passages that could lead them to safety through the darkness and mud (this was taking place at the end of the month), but with pursuers who had the knowledge to prevent their escape, and so many were killed. One

2.4. "The end of the month": there was no moon.

of the Plataians closed the gate where they had entered, the only one left open, using the butt of a spear in place of a pin, so that there was no longer a way out even there. As they were being pursued throughout the town, some climbed the wall, threw themselves over, and in most cases were killed, others got out undetected through a deserted gate when a woman gave them an axe and they cut through the bar (only a few, since discovery followed quickly), and others died scattered in various parts of the city. The largest and most concentrated group burst into a large building, which was part of the wall and whose doors happened to be open, under the impression that the doors were a gate and led directly outside. When the Plataians saw that they had been trapped, they deliberated whether to burn them just as they were by setting fire to the building or to make some other use of them. In the end, both these Thebans and all other survivors who were wandering throughout the city agreed to Plataian terms that they surrender themselves and their weapons, to be treated any way they wished.

This is how those inside Plataia fared; [5] the rest of the Thebans, who were supposed to arrive in full force while it was still night just in case anything went amiss for the men who had gone in and were given the news of what had happened while they were on the way, came to the rescue. Plataia is about seventy stades from Thebes, and the rain that fell during the night made their going slower, for the Asopos river was running high and not easy to cross. Making their way in the rain and crossing the river with difficulty, they arrived too late, since some of their men had already been killed and the others taken alive. When the Thebans realized what had happened, they formed designs against those Plataians who were outside the city (for there were men and equipment in the fields, since the trouble had come unexpectedly, during peace); they planned that anyone they caught should be available for them to exchange for the men inside, if any had in fact been taken prisoner. This was their intention; but while they were still making plans, the Plataians, suspecting that something of the sort would happen and fearing for those outside, sent a herald to the Thebans to tell them that they had acted impiously in attempting to seize their city during a truce, also that they were not to harm the men outside; otherwise, they in turn would kill their men whom they were holding alive; but if they withdrew from their land, they would give them back the men. This is what the Thebans say, and they claim that the Plataians swore an oath; the Plataians, however, say that they did not promise to give them back the men immediately, but if after discussion they reached some agreement, and they deny that they swore an oath. Now the Thebans withdrew from the territory without doing it any harm, but the Plataians, after quickly bringing in everything from the countryside, killed the men immediately. There were a hundred eighty who had been captured, and one of them was Eurymachos, with whom the traitors were intriguing. [6] After they did this, they sent word to Athens, gave the Thebans back their dead under truce, and organized things in the city as they thought best under the circumstances.

What happened at Plataia had been immediately reported to the Athenians, and they had at once arrested all Boiotians in Attica and sent a herald to Plataia with instructions to tell them not to take drastic action concerning the Thebans they were holding until they had made their own plans about them as well; it had not been reported to them that these had been killed; for the first messenger had gone out right at the time the Theban entry had occurred, the second just after they had been defeated and captured, and they knew nothing of later events. So the Athenians sent their instructions without full knowledge; when the herald arrived, he found that the men had been killed. After this the Athenians marched to Plataia, brought in food, and left a garrison, and they evacuated the least fit of the men as well as the women and children.

[7] After the action at Plataia occurred, flagrantly breaking the truce, the Athenians made their preparations to go to war, as did the Lacedaemonians and their allies, both sides also intending to send representatives to the king and to the barbarians in other areas, wherever they hoped they might acquire some additional help, and making allies of any cities outside their direct control. Orders were given by the Lacedaemonians to those in Italy and Sicily who had chosen to side with them to build ships in proportion to the size of their cities, adding to those available to the Lacedaemonians, so that the total number would be five hundred, and they were to make ready designated sums of money and were otherwise to remain at peace and receive the Athenians (but only in a single ship) until these preparations were complete. The Athenians for their part gave their existing

2.5. It is as uncharacteristic of Thucydides as it is characteristic of Herodotos to report conflicting accounts (cf. 1.22), and he does not attempt resolution here as Herodotos often does. The *immediate* murder of the prisoners, however, is a contravention in terms of the Plataians' own version.

2.7. As the beginning of Thucydides' war, the Plataian affair is paradigmatic. It involves allies of the major powers, and their long-standing hatreds, as well as internal dissension; there are unexpected factors (the rain) and blunders that frustrate hopes of accomplishing things "easily"; the final action is a savage one that will have an aftermath and grim finale (3.52–68).

alliance a thorough scrutiny and increased their representations to the regions beyond the Peloponnesos, such as Corcyra, Kephallenia, Akarnania, and Zakynthos, seeing that if their friendship were secure they would wear down the Peloponnesians by fighting them on all sides.

[8] Neither side planned anything on a small scale, and both were enthusiastic for war in a way that was not unnatural; everyone takes up a cause more eagerly at the beginning, and at that time there were also many young men in the Peloponnesos and many in Athens who, in their inexperience, took on the war with no unwillingness, and all the rest of Hellas was spellbound as the leading cities clashed. Many prophecies were declared, and interpreters of oracles made many recitations both among those making ready for war and in other cities. Moreover, just before all these events, Delos was shaken by an earthquake, where there had never been an earthquake as far back as the Hellenes remembered; it was both said and believed to have significance for the things about to happen, and if anything else of this sort occurred, it was always examined. Public opinion inclined by far in favor of the Lacedaemonians, especially since they proclaimed that they were liberating Hellas. Every individual and every city was eager to take part in their activities in any possible way, in both word and deed; each considered that the cause was held back at any point where he was not personally involved. Such was the anger most felt toward the Athenians, some wanting to be freed from their rule, others fearing that they would come under it.

[9] So they started out with preparations and attitudes of this sort, and the two leaders entered the war with the following cities as allies. These were the Lacedaemonian allies: all the Peloponnesians within the isthmus except for the Argives and the Achaians (these were friendly toward both sides; only Pellene of the Achaians fought with them from the first, then all of them did later), and outside the Peloponnesos the Megarians, Phokians, Lokrians, Boiotians, Ambraciots, Leukadians, and Anaktorians. The ones that supplied ships were the Corinthians, Megarians, Sikyonians, Pelleneans, Eleans, and Leukadians, and supplying cavalry were the Boiotians, Phokians, and Lokrians; the other cities supplied infantry. This

---

2.8. Herodotos 6.98 reports, as a great prodigy, an earthquake on Delos shortly before the battle of Marathon in 490, stressing that this was the first and last earthquake there. See Hornblower 1991 *ad* 2.8.3; I do not find it difficult to believe that Thucydides is both correcting Herodotos (who may, to be sure, have written "last" before 431) and competing with him over great-war atmosphere. "Public opinion . . . personally involved": for the idiosyncrasies of Thucydides' phrasing here, see Rusten 1989 *ad* 2.8.4 and cf. 4.12n and 4.14n; on the pro-Spartan bias attributed to the Greeks at the war's outset, see Hornblower *ad* 2.8.4.

was the Lacedaemonian alliance; the Athenian allies were the Chians, Lesbians, Plataeans, the Messenians in Naupaktos, most of the Akarnanians, the Corcyreans, Zakynthians, and other cities subject to them among all the following peoples, Karia along the coast, the Dorians next to the Karians, Ionia, the Hellespont, the area toward Thrace, all the islands to the east bounded by the Peloponnesos and Crete except Melos and Thera. Of these, the Chians, Lesbians, and Corcyreans supplied ships; the others, infantry and money.

[10] The two sides had these allies and preparations for the war, and after the events in Plataia, the Lacedaemonians immediately sent around instructions to the cities throughout the Peloponnesos and the alliance beyond to prepare an army and provisions of the sort regularly used for a foreign expedition, in order to invade Attica. And when they were all ready, forces of two-thirds strength from each city assembled at the isthmus at the designated time. When the whole army had gathered together, Archidamos king of the Lacedaemonians, the man who commanded this expedition, called together the generals from all the cities and those of highest rank and greatest importance and spoke as follows:

[11] "Peloponnesians and allies, not only did our fathers make many campaigns both in the Peloponnesos and beyond, but the older men among ourselves are not without experience of war. Even so, we have never yet gone forth with a greater force than this, but it is also against a most powerful city that we now march with our largest and finest army. It is right, therefore, that we show ourselves inferior to neither our fathers nor our own reputation. For all Hellas has been aroused by this undertaking and is paying close attention, motivated by hostility toward Athens to favor the accomplishment of our objectives. Accordingly, even if there are some who think that we are attacking with the advantage in numbers and that there is full assurance that the enemy will not meet us in battle, we must not on that account proceed with any less care in our preparations, but the commander and soldier of each city is to have constant expectations of encountering danger in his own right. For everything is uncertain in war, and attacks usually come at short notice, out of passion. And often an apprehensive smaller force is better able to fight off larger numbers caught off guard through overconfidence. When in enemy territory, it is

2. 11. "When in enemy territory . . . based on fear": Thucydides is almost certainly recasting the expression of a very similar sentiment in Herodotos 7.49.5, and the result is a strained, even paradoxical antithesis between planning and action; cf. *HCT* II and Rusten 1989 ad 2.11.5 and Allison 1989, pp. 55–56. The very size of

always necessary to fight with bold resolution, but after making thorough preparations based on fear; this is the way to combine the greatest courage in attacking with the greatest security in meeting attacks.

"Not that we are advancing on a city so incapable of defense, but one supremely prepared in every respect, so that we must have every expectation that they will engage in battle, even if they do not set out now, when we are not there yet, but rather when they see us in their land plundering it and destroying their possessions. For anger comes over men on seeing all of a sudden, before their eyes, that they are suffering something unaccustomed, and those who least employ calculation are most driven into action by passion. The Athenians, even more than others, are likely to do this, since they expect to rule others and to invade their neighbors' land and plunder it rather than seeing their own plundered. And so, since you are campaigning against a city of such greatness, and since you will make the greatest name for your ancestors and yourselves according to one outcome or the other, follow wherever you are led, giving discipline and watchfulness first importance and obeying commands quickly. For this is finest and the fullest security, that numerous as we are we show ourselves to be under a single discipline."

[12] After making this short speech and dismissing the meeting, Archidamos first sent Melesippos son of Diakritos, a Spartiate, to Athens in case the Athenians were more inclined to yield on seeing that they were already on the march. They, however, did not grant him admission to the city or access to the government, for a resolution by Perikles had been adopted earlier not to receive a herald or embassy from the Lacedaemonians once they were on the march. So they sent him away without hearing him and ordered that he be outside their borders that same day, and that in the future, if they wanted anything, they send embassies after withdrawing to their own territory. And they sent escorts with Melesippos to keep him from having contact with anyone. But when he reached the borders and was about to part from the escorts, he said this much before he continued on his way: "This day will be the beginning of great misfortunes for the Hellenes."

---

his army is Archidamos' chief concern, which he must express without undue pessimism: (1) the army's size has made the stakes extremely high, especially with respect to reputation and morale, (2) any setback resulting from overconfidence in turn caused by numbers will be the more catastrophic, (3) the army's size is contingent on its inclusion of many forces whose training is not up to Spartan standards. Taken as a whole, the Thucydidean speeches of field generals (on which, see Luschnat 1942, but cf. 1.22n) show great ingenuity in their various arguments from numbers.

When he reached the camp, and Archidamos understood that the Athenians were not yet making any concessions, this was when he now broke camp and advanced against their territory. The Boiotians, while supplying their own contingent and cavalry to the campaign, went to Plataia with their remaining forces and plundered the land. [13] At the time when the Peloponnesians were still assembling at the isthmus and making their march, before they had invaded Attica, Perikles son of Xanthippos and one of the ten Athenian generals, since he realized that the invasion was coming, suspecting the possibility that Archidamos, who happened to be his xenos, would spare his land and not plunder it because he personally wished to do him a favor, or that this would be done on the orders of the Lacedaemonians to discredit him (just as they had commanded that the curse be driven out on account of him), proclaimed to the assembly that Archidamos was his xenos, yet the intention had certainly not been to harm the city, and that he would give up his own fields and buildings to become public, in case the enemy did not burn them like all the others; let there be no suspicion against him on that account.

And regarding the current situation, he encouraged them, as in the past, to prepare for war and bring in their property from the fields, to make ready the fleet, their main strength, and to keep the allies under control, saying that their strength came from the financial income they paid and that, for the most part, success in war was a matter of judgment and abundant revenues. He told them they could take confidence, since six hundred talents in tribute usually came in every year from the allies apart from other revenue, and on the acropolis there was still six thousand talents in coined silver remaining at that time (the largest amount had been nine thousand seven hundred, from which they had made expenditures for the gateway of the acropolis and the other buildings as well as for Potidaia) and, apart from that, uncoined silver in private and public dedications, and there was all the sacred equipment for processions and contests and booty from the Mede and everything else of that sort, not less than five hundred talents; going further, he added the considerable amount from the other

2.13. "His xenos": the relationship is almost certainly hereditary "guest-friendship," see Rhodes 1988 and Hornblower 1991 *ad* 2.13.1. Nested within a very long sentence, the revelation at this time of the tie between the two very dissimilar leaders is striking and ironic; guest-friendship might epitomize tradition and civility in interstate relations. For a recent overview of the long controversy over the financial amounts recorded by Thucydides, see Hornblower *ad* 2.13.3 and Kallet-Marx 1993, pp. 96–108; the gold of the Athena Parthenos actually was removed, but in 296/5 B.C.E.

sanctuaries. They would use these and, if they were absolutely compelled, even the gold plating of the goddess herself; he pointed out that the statue had forty talents' worth of refined gold, and it was all removable. He said that if they used it for their safety they were bound to restore no less an amount. And there were thirteen thousand hoplites, not including the sixteen thousand in the garrisons and on the battlements (this was the number standing guard at the beginning of the enemy attacks, and they were from the oldest and youngest men and from all metics who were hoplites. For the Phaleron wall measured thirty-five stades to the circuit wall of the city, and the guarded section of the circuit itself was forty-three stades—there was an unguarded section as well, between the long wall and the Phaleron wall—and the long walls to the Peiraeus were forty stades, the outer one with sentries, and the overall system for the Peiraeus, including Munychia, was sixty stades, half of that under guard). He pointed out that there were twelve hundred cavalry including mounted archers, sixteen hundred archers, and three hundred seaworthy triremes. These resources, no less in each of these areas, were indeed available to the Athenians when the invasion of the Peloponnesians was about to take place for the first time, and they were entering the war. Perikles also said other things of the sort he regularly used to demonstrate their capability to prevail in the war.

[14] After listening to him, the Athenians were convinced, and they brought in from the country their children, their women, and the equipment they used in the home as well, and even the woodwork that they took out of their houses. They conveyed their livestock and draft animals over to Euboia and the outlying islands. The uprooting was a difficult process for them because the majority were always accustomed to living in the country. [15] This had been the case for the Athenians, more so than others, from very early times. For in the time of Kekrops and the first kings, down to Theseus, Attica always had its population distributed among cities with their own town halls and offices, and when they did not have something to fear they did not come together for deliberation before the king, but they each managed their own affairs and deliberated on their own. Some even went to war at times, as the Eleusinians did with Eumolpos against Erechtheus. But when Theseus became king, wielding this power combined with his intelligence, he not only organized the region in other ways but also unified the people in the present city, abolishing the

2.14. For an interesting note on the removal of woodwork, see Hornblower 1991 *ad* 2.14.1; in addition to preserving the furnishings, this left the houses less combustible (Spence 1990, p. 101).

council houses and offices of the other cities and designating a single council house and town hall, and he compelled them, even while they managed their own affairs just as before, to treat this as a single city, that, since everyone was now contributing, became the great one handed down by Theseus to later generations. And starting with him, even today the Athenians still hold the Synoikia as a publicly funded festival for the goddess.

Before that, what is now the acropolis was a city, along with the area below it, especially toward the south. And as proof: the sanctuaries of the other gods are also on the acropolis itself, and those outside it tend to be built toward that part of the city, the sanctuary of Zeus the Olympian, the Pythion, the sanctuary of Ge, and that of Dionysos in the Marshes, where the most ancient festival of Dionysos is held on the twelfth day of the month Anthesterion, just as the Ionians, who originate from the Athenians, also still observe it today. Other sanctuaries are also built in this area. Because of its proximity, they made special use of the fountain now called Enneakrounos, since the tyrants constructed it with this arrangement, but originally named Kallirhoe when the springs were left uncovered, and even today the ancient custom is preserved of using its water before weddings and for other religious ceremonies. Up to this day, because of the early occupation of this area, the acropolis is still called "the city" by the Athenians.

[16] For the most part, then, the Athenians lived in independent settlements throughout the region, and after they underwent unification most of them nevertheless, not only in antiquity but in later times up to this war, following custom, lived and dwelt in the countryside with their entire households and did not find it easy to move their homes, especially since they had only recently restored their furnishings after the Persian War. They were grieved and distressed at deserting their homes as well as what had been their ancestral shrines throughout going back to their ancient form of government, since not only were they about to change their way of life, but also each of them was doing nothing short of abandoning his own city. [17] When they arrived in Athens, a few had houses or places of shelter with some of their friends or relatives, but most occupied the uninhabited parts of the city and the sanctuaries and the shrines of heroes, except for the acropolis, the Eleusinion, and any other place firmly closed up. And the area called the Pelargikon, below the acropolis, which was under a curse against occupation, and the final part of some oracle from Delphi likewise banned this by saying, "The Pelargikon is better left unused," was

2.15. The fountain Kallirhoe ("Fair Flowing") was called Enneakrounos ("Nine Spouts") after its rebuilding.

occupied nevertheless under the pressure of the emergency. It seems to me that the oracle was fulfilled in the opposite way from what was expected, that disasters did not come to the city because of the unlawful occupation but the necessity for occupation came on account of the war, although it was without using that word that the oracle predicted that the place would never be settled in good circumstances. Many even made their homes in the towers of the city walls, and wherever each could manage. For the city was not adequate for them when they were all there, but later they divided up the long walls and most of the Peiraeus and settled there. At the same time, they were attending to measures for the war, collecting their allies together and outfitting an expedition of a hundred ships against the Peloponnesos. This was their state of preparation.

[18] Meanwhile the army of the Peloponnesians, moving ahead, first reached Attica at Oinoe, the point where they had planned to invade, and when they were settled there, they prepared to make assaults on the walls with siege machines and by other means; for Oinoe was fortified, since it is on the border between Attica and Boiotia, and the Athenians used it as an outpost whenever war broke out. So the Peloponnesians prepared to make assaults and otherwise lingered around there. It was especially on this account that there was criticism of Archidamos, who also seemed weak and sympathetic to the Athenians while the war was being instigated, since he did not enthusiastically recommend fighting, and when the army was assembled, both the wait that occurred at the isthmus and the additional slowness during the march made him unpopular, but above all the halt at Oinoe. During this time the Athenians were bringing their possessions inside, and the Peloponnesians thought that by attacking quickly they would have seized everything while it was still outside, if not for his delays. This was what angered the army against Archidamos while they were stopped; but he held them back, so it is said, because he had expectations that the Athenians would make some concession while their land was still untouched, unable to bear seeing it ravaged.

[19] Since, however, after attacking Oinoe and trying every means, the Peloponnesians were unable to take it and the Athenians sent no herald to negotiate, it was at this point that they set out from Oinoe and, on about the eightieth day after what happened at Plataea, when it was summer and the grain was becoming ripe, invaded Attica. Archidamos son of Zeuxidamos, king of Sparta, was the commander. They established a base and first ravaged Eleusis and the Thriasian plain, and they routed some Athenian cavalry at the place called Rheitoi. Then, keeping Mt. Aigaleos on the right, they advanced through Kropia until they reached Acharnai, the largest of

the places in Attica called demes. Establishing themselves there, they made camp and stayed a long time plundering. [20] It is said that Archidamos stayed around Acharnai drawn up for battle, not coming down into the plain during this invasion, with the following idea in mind. He expected that perhaps the Athenians, flourishing with an abundance of young men and prepared for war as never before, would come out against him and not watch their land being plundered. Accordingly, since they had not opposed him at Eleusis and the Thriasian plain, he established himself around Acharnai to see whether they would come out. His thinking was partly that Acharnai was a suitable place for a camp and partly that the Acharnians, who were a large part of the state (since they numbered three thousand hoplites), would not allow their property to be plundered but would even urge all the forces into battle. And if the Athenians did not even come out against them during this invasion, then there would be less cause for fear in later ravaging the plain and advancing against the city itself; deprived of their own property, the Acharnians would not feel a comparable eagerness to take risks on behalf of the others' land, and there would be dissension in Athenian policies. Archidamos was at Acharnai with this in mind.

[21] Meanwhile, as long as the army was around Eleusis and the Thriasian plain, the Athenians accordingly clung to hopes of their advancing no closer, since they remembered when Pleistoanax son of Pausanias, who had also invaded Attica at Eleusis and Thria with a Peloponnesian army, fourteen years before this war, had gone back again without advancing any farther (and for that very reason he suffered exile from Sparta, since it was thought that he was bribed to withdraw). But when they saw the army around Acharnai within sixty stades from the city, they no longer found it bearable, and when their land was being ravaged in full view, something the younger men had never seen before, nor the older ones except during the Persian Wars, it was naturally a terrible sight for them, and many, especially the young men, thought they should go out to attack instead of looking on. They formed groups in violent disagreement, some demanding that they go out, others opposing this, and prophets recited prophecies of every sort, which they were eager to hear according to individual inclination, and the Acharnians, who considered themselves the most important component of the Athenians, especially urged action.

2.20. The number of Acharnian hoplites is generally agreed to be impossibly large; on possible emendations, cf. recently Pritchett 1995, p. 47.

2.21. For the withdrawal of Pleistoanax, cf. 1.114n and 5.16.

The whole city was very aroused, and they felt rage against Perikles and recalled none of the advice he had given previously but abused him because he was a general yet did not lead them out, and they found him responsible for everything they were suffering.

[22] Perikles, since he saw that they were angry over the situation and not using their best judgment, and since he was confident that he was right about not going out, did not call them into an assembly or military meeting, lest they make mistakes by coming together in a passionate rather than reasonable state, but kept the city under guard and as calm as he could. He did, however, constantly send out cavalry to keep advance parties from attacking and damaging the fields close to the city. And one squadron of the Athenian cavalry and the Thessalians accompanying them had a minor battle at Phrygia against the Boiotian cavalry, and they had the advantage until the arrival of the hoplites in support of the Boiotians drove them back. A few of the Thessalians and Athenians were killed, but their bodies were recovered on the same day without a truce. The Peloponnesians set up a trophy on the following day. This assistance from the Thessalians came to the Athenians in accordance with their old alliance, and those present were from Larisa, Pharsalos, Peirasos, Krannon, Pyrasos, Gyrtone, and Pherai. Their commanders were Polymedes and Aristonous from Larisa, one from each party, and Menon from Pharsalos, and there were also leaders from the various cities.

[23] Since the Athenians did not come out against them in battle, the Peloponnesians left Acharnai and plundered some of the other demes between Parnes and Mt. Brilessos. While they were in their territory, the Athenians sent off the fleet of a hundred ships they had been preparing to sail around the Peloponnesos with a thousand hoplites and four hundred archers aboard; the generals were Karkinos son of Xenotimos, Proteas son of Epikles, and Sokrates son of Antigenes. They set out on the voyage with this preparation, while the Peloponnesians, after staying in Attica the length of time they had provisions for, withdrew through Boiotia rather than the same way they had invaded. Passing by Oropos, they plundered the land called Peraike, which is cultivated by the Oropians, subjects of the Athenians. When they reached the Peloponnesos, they disbanded to go to

2.22. It would appear that this use of cavalry, while neither without parallels nor militarily negligible, was partly intended to raise Athenian morale; Spence 1990, pp. 107–9 doubts that it was part of Perikles' original strategy.

2.23. "The land called Peraike": Peraike is often emended to Graike, but I have followed Hornblower 1991 *ad* 2.23.3.

their own cities. [24] After they withdrew, the Athenians established guardposts for land and sea, exactly as they would be doing throughout the war. And they voted to keep a thousand talents from the funds on the acropolis in reserve, setting it aside and not spending it, and to fight the war with their other funds. For anyone who proposed or put to the vote to touch this money for any purpose, unless the enemy sailed against the city with a naval force and there was need to repel them, they imposed the penalty of death. They made their hundred best triremes a corresponding reserve fleet for each year, with trierarchs for them, none of which was to be used for any purpose except along with the money for the same danger, if the need arrived. [25] The Athenians in the hundred ships off the Peloponnesos, together with the Corcyreans who had come to support them with fifty ships and some of the other allies in that region, damaged some places as they sailed around, and making a landing at Methone in Lakonian territory they attacked the wall, since it was weak and there were no men inside. It happened that Brasidas son of Tellis, a Spartiate, was in these parts with an expeditionary force, and when he heard he came with a hundred hoplites to support the locals. Passing through the Athenian forces, which were spread out over the area and had their attention directed toward the walls, he forced his way into Methone, and although he lost a few of his men in the onslaught, he not only secured the city but, a result of this act of daring, was the first in this war to be commended at Sparta.

The Athenians set out sailing along the coast, and putting in at Pheia in Elis they plundered the land for two days, and when three hundred picked men from Hollow Elis and some of the Eleans from the subject territory came to the defense they defeated them in battle. But when a great wind came up and they were caught by a storm in a place without harbors, most embarked on the ships and sailed around the cape called Ichthys into the harbor of Pheia, but during this time the Messenians and some others, unable to embark, proceeded by land and captured Pheia. Later the ships sailed around and picked them up, and they put out to sea, abandoning Pheia; by now the main army of the Eleans had come to the rescue. The Athenians sailed along the coast to other places and plundered them. [26] Around the same time, the Athenians dispatched thirty ships around Lokris, which were also to guard Euboia; Kleopompos son of Kleinias was the general. Landing at some places along the coast, he ravaged them and

2.25. "No men inside" cannot be literally true; for suggestions, cf. Classen/Steup II and *HCT* II *ad* 2.25.1. This chapter introduces Brasidas, one of the most striking individuals in Thucydides and indirectly responsible for his exile.

captured Thronion, taking hostages there, and at Alope he defeated the Lokrian defenders in battle.

[27] In this same summer the Athenians expelled the Aiginetans from Aigina, men, women, and children, charging that they were a major cause of the war against them; it also appeared safer to hold Aigina, which lies close to the Peloponnesos, by sending their own epoikoi. They sent out the settlers soon after. The Lacedaemonians gave Thyria to the Aiginetans expelled by the Athenians to settle and cultivate the land, both on account of their enmity with Athens and because these had been their benefactors at the time of the earthquake and the helot revolt. The land of Thyria is on the border between Argive and Lakonian territory, extending to the sea. Some of the Aiginetans settled there, while others were scattered throughout the rest of Hellas. [28] In this same summer, at the beginning of the lunar month, which appears to be the one and only time this can happen, the sun was eclipsed in the afternoon and became full again after it was crescent-shaped and some stars came out.

[29] Also in the same summer, the Athenians appointed as proxenos Nymphodoros son of Pythes, a man from Abdera whose sister was married to Sitalkes and had great influence with him, and invited him to Athens, someone they had previously considered an enemy, since they wanted Sitalkes son of Teres, king of the Thracians, to become their ally. This Teres, father of Sitalkes, was the first to make the Odrysians into the great kingdom, which is more extensive than the rest of Thrace; a large part of Thrace is also independent. This Teres has no connection with Tereus who had as his wife Prokne from Athens, daughter of Pandion, nor were they even from the same Thrace, since the one, Tereus, lived in Daulis in the land now called Phokis, which in his time was inhabited by Thracians,

---

2.27. For extensive discussion of the expulsion of the Aiginetans and their replacement by Athenian "reinforcing" settlers, see Figueira 1991, pp. 7–39.

2.29. This is probably the most unusual digression in Thucydides. Apparently he was among those who considered the Tereus-Prokne story among the most horrible in Greek mythology (he raped her sister Philomela and cut out her tongue to silence her; when she communicated this to her sister by weaving, Prokne killed her son Itys in revenge; she was transformed into a nightingale) and was writing about a personal matter, given his Thracian ties (although he refers to the bloodthirstiness of Thracians in 7.29), as well as a question of historical accuracy. See Hornblower 1991 *ad* 2.29.3 and La Rocca 1986, who suggests that the Tereus story was of current interest in Athens because of his associations with treacherously hostile Megara.

and it was here that the women carried out the deed involving Itys ("bird of Daulis" is the name used by many poets when mentioning the nightingale; and it is also likely that Pandion arranged his daughter's marriage for mutual assistance over the shorter distance rather than the many days' journey to the Odrysians). But Teres, who does not even have the same name, became the first powerful king of the Odrysians. It was the son of this man, Sitalkes, whom the Athenians were trying to get as an ally, wanting him to help them in getting control over the area around Thrace, and over Perdikkas. Nymphodoros came to Athens and arranged the alliance with Sitalkes and Athenian citizenship for his son Sadokos, and he promised to end the war with Thrace by persuading Sitalkes to send the Athenians a Thracian army of cavalry and peltasts. He also reconciled Perdikkas with the Athenians and persuaded them to restore Therme to him; Perdikkas immediately joined the Athenians and Phormio in a campaign against the Chalkidians. It was in this way that both Sitalkes, son of Teres, king of Thrace, and Perdikkas, son of Alexandros, king of the Macedonians, became allies of the Athenians.

[30] Meanwhile the Athenians in the hundred ships who were still around the Peloponnesos took Sollion, a Corinthian town, and they gave the Palairans of Akarnania exclusive rights to occupy the territory and the city. They overpowered Astakos, where Euarchos was tyrant, drove him out, and brought the place into their alliance. Sailing to the island of Kephallenia, they brought it over without a battle; Kephallenia lies across from Akarnania and Leukas and has four cities, those of the Paleans, Kranians, Samaians, and Pronnaians. Soon afterward they departed for Athens.

[31] In autumn of this year, the Athenians invaded the Megarid in full force, including metics, under the command of Perikles son of Xanthippos. As for the Athenians in the hundred ships around the Peloponnesos, when they heard that the men from the city were at Megara in full force, they sailed over and joined them. And this actually amounted to the largest single Athenian army, since the city was still at its peak and not yet stricken by the plague. There were no fewer than ten thousand hoplites from the Athenians themselves (they had the three thousand at Potidaia as well), no fewer than three thousand metics campaigned with them as hoplites, and in addition there were a considerable number of light-armed. After laying waste most of the territory, they returned. And later in the war there were other Athenian invasions of the Megarid every year, both with cavalry and in full force, until Nisaia was captured by the Athenians. [32] Also at the end of this summer, Atalante, the island lying off Opuntian Lokris and previously deserted, was fortified by the Athenians as an outpost to keep

pirates from sailing out of Opous and elsewhere in Lokris and causing damage to Euboia.

[33] These were the events during this summer after the Peloponnesian withdrawal from Attica. In the following winter Euarchos the Akarnanian, who wanted to return to Astakos, persuaded the Corinthians to sail with forty ships and fifteen hundred hoplites to restore him; he added mercenaries of his own. The leaders of the force were Euphamidas son of Aristonymos, Timoxenos son of Timokrates, and Eumachos son of Chrysis. They made the voyage and restored Euarchos. They wanted to take over some places elsewhere on the Akarnanian coast and made the attempt but were unsuccessful and started home. They kept to the coast and put in at Kephallenia; and making a landing in the territory of the Kranians, they were deceived by an agreement with them and lost some of their men when the Kranians caught them off guard by attacking; and after an embattled departure, they returned home.

[34] In this winter, following their traditional custom, the Athenians held burial rites at public expense for the first to die in this war, in the following manner. They lay out the bones of the dead two days beforehand, after setting up a tent, and each person brings whatever offerings he wishes to his own relatives. When the procession takes place, wagons carry cypress coffins, one for each tribe, and within are the bones of each man, according to tribe. One empty bier, fully decorated, is brought for the missing, all who were not found and recovered. Any man who wishes, citizen or foreigner, joins the procession, and female relatives are present at the grave as mourners. They bury them in the public tomb, which is in the most beautiful suburb of the city and in which they always bury those killed in war, except of course for the men who fought at Marathon; judging their virtue outstanding, they gave them burial right there. After they cover them with earth, a man chosen by the state, known for wise judgment and of high reputation, makes an appropriate speech of praise, and after this they depart. This is their burial practice, and throughout the whole war, whenever there was occasion, they followed the custom. Now for these first casualties, Perikles son of Xanthippos was chosen to speak. And when the moment arrived, coming forward from the tomb to a plat-

2.34. "Followed the custom": rather than "followed the law," see especially Ostwald 1969, p. 175; its antiquity has been much debated, see Hornblower 1991 *ad* 2.34.1. Marathon's casualties were not the only exception; Ostwald, followed by Hornblower among others, argues that Thucydides did not intend to exclude the other instances, but I do not find this very persuasive.

form that had been elevated so that he could be heard by as much of the crowd as possible, he spoke as follows:

[35] "Most of those who have already spoken here praise the man who made this speech part of the custom, saying that for this address to be made at the burial of those lost in war is a fine thing. I myself would have thought it sufficient that the honors for those who proved good in deed be bestowed by deed as well, just as you now see carried out at public expense for this burial, rather than that the virtues of many men depend for their credibility on whether a single man speaks well or badly. To speak in due proportion is difficult where grasp of the truth itself is hardly assured. For the man listening with understanding and good will may well consider what is set forth in some way inferior, measured against both his wishes and his knowledge, yet the one listening in ignorance may consider some things exaggerated, out of envy when he hears anything going beyond his natural endowments. Praise spoken of others can only be endured as long as each believes himself capable of doing something of what he hears about; toward what goes further, men feel envy and then actual disbelief. But since it was so judged by those of long ago, that this speech is a fine thing, I too must follow the custom and try to conform with the wishes and opinions of each one of you as far as is possible.

[36] "First of all, I will begin with our ancestors, since it is right and also appropriate on such an occasion as the present that the honor of this remembrance should be given to them. For it is the same men, always occupying the land through the succession of generations, who have handed it down in freedom until the present time because of their bravery. They are worthy of praise, and our fathers still more. In addition to what they received, they acquired through great effort the whole of the empire we now rule and left it to us in the present generation. Those of us here now who are still somewhere in the prime of life have expanded most areas of it and in all respects provided the city with the fullest resources for both war and peace. I will pass over the deeds in war that led to each of our acquisitions and every instance of stout resistance we or our fathers made against attacking enemies, whether barbarian or Hellene, since I do not wish to recount them at length among those who know of them. But I will

---

2.35. "Those who have already spoken" include Perikles himself; not all those chosen to deliver the funeral oration appear to have been "of high reputation," see *HCT* II *ad* 2.34.6. The eloquence and fame of the following oration should not blind us to possible political or partisan elements that may (1) refer to the immediate wartime context and (2) include misrepresentations in this context.

turn to praise of the dead after I have first set forth the principles by which we came into this position and the form of government from which its greatness resulted, since I believe that these are not inappropriate to mention in the present circumstances and are advantageous for the whole gathering, both citizens and foreigners, to hear about.

[37] "We have a form of government that does not emulate the practices of our neighbors, setting an example to some rather than imitating others. In name it is called a democracy on account of being administered in the interest not of the few but the many, yet even though there are equal rights for all in private disputes in accordance with the laws, wherever each man has earned recognition he is singled out for public service in accordance with the claims of distinction, not by rotation but by merit, nor when it comes to poverty, if a man has real ability to benefit the city, is he prevented by obscure renown. In public life we conduct ourselves with freedom and also, regarding that suspicion of others because of their everyday habits, without getting angry at a neighbor if he does something so as to suit himself, and without wearing expressions of vexation, that inflict no punishment yet cause distress. But while we associate in private without undue pressure, in public we are especially law abiding because of fear, in our obedience both to anyone holding office and to the laws, above all those established to aid people who are wronged and those which, although unwritten, bring down acknowledged shame. [38] Furthermore, we have provided for the spirit the most plentiful respites from labor by providing games and festivals throughout the year as well as attractive surroundings for private life, a source of daily delight, which drives away cares. Because of the importance of the city, everything is brought in from every land, and it is our fortune to enjoy good things from other people with as much familiarity as what comes from here.

[39] "In our approach to warfare, we also differ from our opponents, in the following ways. We leave our city accessible to all and do not, by xenelasia, prevent anyone from either listening or observing, although some enemy might benefit by seeing what we do not hide, because we do

2.37. "Called a democracy": see Hornblower 1991 *ad* 2.37.1. "Expressions of vexation": an irony of this attention to nuance is that Perikles' own aloof manner was cited by contemporaries as a major source of resentment.

2.39. The reference to xenelasia makes the comparison explicitly anti-Spartan, even if Thucydides' text did not originally include the term (see Hornblower 1991 *ad* 2.39.1), which Perikles also uses in 1.44. In 2.39 he is highly idiosyncratic in associating xenelasia with military security, as counterespionage, since other

not put more trust in contrivance and deception than in the courageous readiness for action that comes from within. As for education, starting as children they pursue manhood with laborious training, but with our more relaxed way of life we are no less willing to take on equivalent dangers. Here is proof: the Lacedaemonians do not invade our land alone but with all their allies, and we attack other lands by ourselves, and fighting in hostile territory against men defending their own possessions, we usually win easily. And no enemy has yet encountered our united forces, on account of our simultaneously maintaining the fleet and dispatching our own men to many points on land, but wherever our enemies meet a detachment, they flatter themselves that they have repelled all of us if they beat some of us and that they were defeated by all if they lose. And if we are willing to face danger with a mind at ease rather than with the habit of stress, with bravery owing no more to law than to character, surely it is our gain that we are not afflicted by hardships before they occur, that when we do encounter them we prove no less daring than those who are constantly straining, and that our city deserves admiration for these reasons and still others.

[40] "For we love beauty while practicing economy and we love wisdom without being enervated. We use wealth for opportune action rather than boastful speech, and there is no disgrace for one to admit poverty but much more in not avoiding it through activity. And it is within the capacity of some of us to manage private right along with public business and of the rest, while concentrating on their own occupations, to have no inferior understanding of public affairs; we are unique in considering the man who takes no part in these to be not apolitical but useless, and we ourselves either ratify or even propound successful policies, finding harm not in the

---

ancient sources explain it as a device for protecting Sparta from corrupting outside influences. The Periklean/Thucydidean usage is the more anomalous in that the passage does not clarify what it is that Spartans conceal and Athenians do not.

2.40. Any translation of this chapter, especially its first sentence, will be controversial. I agree with Rusten 1985 and 1989, pp. 151–57 and Hornblower 1991 *ad* 2.40.1–2 that the emphasis is on the Athenians as individuals; although I doubt their translation "lovers of what is noble" (rather than "beauty"), I do not think "beauty" refers to such public monuments as the Parthenon. The section on friendship, however, seems to begin a return to the whole city as a topic, and I would not draw the sharp line Rusten does between personal friendship and friendship among states.

effect of speeches on action but in failing to get instruction by speech
before proceeding to what must be done. For in that we are both especially
daring and especially thorough in calculating what we attempt, we can
truly be distinguished from other men, for whom ignorance is boldness
but calculation brings hesitancy. Rightly would they be judged strongest
in spirit who recognize both dangers and pleasures with utmost clarity
and are on neither count deterred from risks. In matters of goodness, we
also contrast with most people, since we acquire friends by conferring
rather than by receiving benefits. The giver is the more secure, through
preserving the feeling of gratitude by good will toward the recipient, who
is less fulfilled because he knows that he will repay the goodness not to
inspire gratitude but to return an obligation. We are unique in being benefactors not out of calculation of advantage but with the fearless confidence
of our freedom.

[41] "In summary I claim that our city as a whole is an education for
Hellas, and that it is among us as individuals, in my opinion, that a single
man would represent an individual self-sufficient for the most varied
forms of conduct, and with the most attractive qualities. And that this is
not boastful speaking for the occasion but factual truth our city's very
power, which we acquired because of these characteristics, proclaims
clearly. For she alone of existing cities surpasses her reputation when put
to the test, and only she brings neither chagrin to the attacking enemy as
to the sort of men by whom he has been worsted nor reproach to the subject that he is ruled by the unworthy. Through great proofs, and by exhib-
iting power in no way unwitnessed, we will be admired by this and future
generations, thus requiring no Homer to sing our praises nor any other
whose verses will charm for the moment and whose claims the factual
truth will destroy, since we have compelled every sea and land to become
open to our daring and populated every region with lasting monuments of
our acts of harm and good. It is for such a city, then, that these men nobly
died in battle, thinking it right not to be deprived of her, just as each of
their survivors should be willing to toil for her sake.

[42] "This above all is the reason I have lengthened my speech about
the city, to explain why our efforts have no equivalent among people who
do not share these values, and at the same time to give evidence for the

2.41. *Pace* Hornblower 1991 *ad* 2.41.1, "education for (or school of) Hellas" is not
a "tendentious" translation (reflecting Athens' later reputation as a cultural center), but well grounded both in contemporary usage of *paideusis* and in the overall
context of the funeral oration.

glory of those whom I am now eulogizing. The most important part of the eulogy has been said. For it is their virtues, and those of men like them, that have given honor to the qualities I have praised in the city, and for few other Hellenes would it be manifest, as it is for them, that reputation is equal to the deeds. It seems to me that this conclusion of these men's lives is what reveals a man's virtue, whether as the first indication or final confirmation. Even for those who were worse in other ways it is right that first place be given to valor against enemies on behalf of country; by effacing evil with good, they became public benefactors rather than individual malefactors. None of these men turned coward from preferring the further enjoyment of wealth, nor did any, from the poor man's hope that he might still escape poverty and grow rich, contrive a way to postpone the danger. Thinking defeat of the enemy more desirable than prosperity, just as they considered this the fairest of risks, they were willing to vanquish him at that risk and long for the rest, leaving to hope the uncertainty of prospering in the future but resolving to rely on their own actions in what confronted them now, and recognizing that it meant resisting and dying rather than surviving by submission, they fled disgrace in word but stood up to the deed with their lives and through the fortune of the briefest critical moment, at the height of glory rather than fear, departed.

[43] "So fared these men, worthy of their city; you their survivors must pray to meet the enemy at lesser cost but resolve to do so just as unflinchingly, not calculating the benefits by words alone—although one might recite at length to you who know them just as well all the rewards of resisting the enemy—but wondering at the city's power as you actually see it each day and becoming her lovers, reflecting whenever her fame appears great to you that men who were daring, who realized their duty, and who honored it in their actions acquired this, men who even when they failed in some

2.42. "Thinking defeat . . .": on the exceptional difficulty of this sentence, cf. Parry 1957, pp. 167–69, and Rusten 1986 and 1989 *ad* 2.42.4.

2.43. In a recent paper, Kathryn Morgan called attention to Thucydides' startling choice of words: "lover" is overtly sexual and denotes the aggressor in relationships, so that Athens (whose power has just been mentioned) becomes a passive object. Cf. Dover 1978 *passim* and Halperin 1990, esp. pp. 88–105. "Present in judgment alone": for another possible interpretation, cf. *HCT* II and Rusten 1989 *ad* 2.43.3. "For failures . . .": the language and logic have understandably baffled editors (cf. Classen/Steup II, *HCT* II, and Rusten *ad* 2.43.5); perhaps the best course short of emendation is to play down the antithesis, since *both* failures and successes have a reason for risking their lives.

attempt did not on that account think it right to deprive the city of their virtue, but to offer it to her as their finest contribution. For in giving their lives
in common cause, they individually gained imperishable praise and the
most distinctive tomb, not the one where they are buried but the one where
on every occasion for word and deed their glory is left after them eternally.
The whole earth is the tomb of famous men, and not only inscriptions set
up in their own country mark it but even in foreign lands an unwritten
memorial, present not in monument but in mind, abides within each man.
Emulate them now, judge that happiness is freedom and freedom courage,
and do not stand aside from the dangers of war. For failures, men bereft of
good expectations, have no more reason to be unstinting of their lives than
those for whom reversal is always a threat as long as they live, and in whose
sight the most important things are at stake if they come to grief. Indeed, for
a man of pride, misfortune associated with cowardice is more painful than
death coming imperceptibly in the midst of vigor along with shared hopes.

[44] "It is for this reason that I offer comfort, not pity, to all those
present as parents of these men. You know that you were reared among
ever-changing fortunes. It is happiness whenever men find the most glorious end, just like these men, even while you find sorrow, and for those
whose success in life has been measured out to the same limit as their mor-
tality. I know that it is difficult to persuade you in that you will often have
reminders of them through the happiness of others, which you once
enjoyed as well; for sorrow is not felt over the deprivation of good things
one has not experienced, but over the removal of what one was used to. But
those still of age to have children must take strength from hopes of other
sons. On the personal level, those who come later will be a means of forget-
ting those who are no more, and the city will benefit doubly, both in not
being left short and in security; for it is not possible for men to counsel anything fair or just if they are not at risk by staking their sons equally. All of
you who have passed beyond this, however, consider that the greater portion of your life, in which you were fortunate, is a gain, that this part will
be short, and that your heart will be lightened by the fame of these men.
For a love of honor is the only thing that has no old age, and it is not profit,
as some claim, but honor that brings delight in the period of uselessness.

[45] "For all those present who are sons or brothers of these men, however, I see that the effort will be a great one, since everyone tends to praise
those who are no longer, and it will be difficult for you to be judged not
equal, because of their surpassing merit, but only slightly inferior. For the

2.39. "You know that you": for the text, see *HCT* II *ad* 2.44.1.

living incur the envy toward a rival, but those who no longer offer opposition receive honor with a good will lacking in competitiveness. And if I should make any mention of the virtue of women, regarding all who will now be widows, I will express all of it in brief advice. Your renown is great through keeping up to the standard of your basic nature, and if your reputation has the least circulation among men, whether for virtue or in blame.

[46] "In words, as much as I in my turn could say suitably in accordance with the custom has been said, and in deed, these have been honored in burial now, and from this time the city will rear their sons at public expense until they are of age, conferring on both the dead and their survivors a beneficial crown for such contests as these. For it is among those who establish the greatest prizes for courage that men are the best citizens. And now, after each of you has made full lament for his own, you must depart."

[47] Such was the funeral that occurred in this winter, and when the winter was over, the first year of this war ended. And as soon as summer began, the Peloponnesians invaded Attica with a two-thirds force just as on the previous occasion, Archidamos son of Zeuxidamos, king of the Lacedaemonians was in command, and they established their position and plundered the land. When they had not yet stayed many days in Attica, the

2.45. "If I should make any mention": the comments of Rusten 1989 *ad* 2.45.2 about efforts to deny the coldness of these words are judicious and astringent; women are given a grudging (*pace* Hornblower 1991 *ad* 2.45.2) introduction and last-on-the-list placement. If Perikles' consolation to the other bereaved seems bleak, it is nevertheless based on the exhaustively argued idea that a fully lived Athenian life is the best possible life. For the most part, this life could only vicariously be experienced by Athenian women. Their dismissive treatment in the funeral oration is less consistent with what we know of Perikles than with Thucydides' general disregard, cf. Hornblower *ad* 2.4.2 and Crane 1996, pp. 75–92.

2.47–54. It is a truism that the juxtaposition of the funeral oration and the outbreak of plague is extraordinarily dramatic, also that Thucydides not only was fully aware of this but contrived the juxtaposition by recording no intervening events except—very briefly—the Peloponnesian invasion of Attica. Woodman 1988, pp. 34–35 develops the thesis that the plague, if not actually fictitious, was exaggerated beyond recognition and reality by Thucydides (who also refers to its long duration in 3.87, a passage Woodman notes and uses captiously). Woodman's arguments are adequately answered by Hornblower 1991, pp. 316–18 and many comments on specific passages of 2.47–54; while certainly not denying rhetorical or dramatic elements, he stresses the scientific validity of Thucydides' account. Morgan 1994 (writing as a physician as well as classicist) believes Thucydides misrepresented the symptoms because he took "dramatic license"; he particularly doubts the "head-to-toe sequence" (p. 204, see 2.49) and (like Woodman) gives little or no

plague first began to occur in Athens, said to have struck earlier in many other places, both around Lemnos and elsewhere, yet nowhere was so serious a disease or such destruction of human life recorded as taking place. In the first place doctors, who treated it in ignorance, had no effect (being themselves the ones who died in proportion to having the most contact with it), nor did any other human agency, and their supplications at sanctuaries and recourse to prophecies and the like were all of no avail. In the end they abandoned these, vanquished by the disaster. [48] Originally, it is said, it came from Ethiopia, south of Egypt, and then descended on Egypt, Libya, and much of the land of the king. It struck the city of Athens suddenly and first attacked the people in the Peiraeus, so that it was even claimed by them that the Peloponnesians had put poison in the wells (there were no fountains there yet). Later it reached the upper city as well, and then many more began to die. Now, let each man, doctor or layman, speak about it according to his understanding, what its origin is likely to have been and whatever causes of so great a change he thinks are sufficiently powerful to bring about disturbance. I will say what it was like in its course and describe here, as one who had the plague myself and saw others suffering from it myself, the symptoms by which anyone who studies it cannot possibly fail to recognize it with this foreknowledge, if it ever strikes again.

[49] That particular year, according to a consensus, happened to be especially free of disease with respect to other types of illness; but whatever sickness anyone had already was always subsumed in this. The others, when they were healthy, were suddenly, for no apparent reason, afflicted first in the head by high fever and redness and burning in the eyes, and internally both the throat and the tongue immediately became bloody and emitted an unnatural and foul-smelling breath. After these, sneezing and hoarseness ensued, and soon the trouble descended into the chest with violent coughing; when it settled in the stomach it brought disorder, and all the discharges of bile that doctors have names for ensued, and with extreme discomfort. For most, empty retching followed causing violent convulsions, in some cases after the discharges had abated, in other cases much later. On the outside, the body was neither especially hot to touch nor pallid but reddish, livid, and broken out in small blisters and sores. Internally, however,

---

weight to Thucydides' statement that he describes its "course" as one who had the plague himself. The plague's power to bring about "change" (2.48, cf. 2.53) was evidently Thucydides' main reason for giving it such a prominent place in his narrative. At the same time, the plague grimly provided the conditions he required for full accuracy in recording events (1.22). On the identification of the plague, see also Morens and Littman 1992.

there was such burning that they could not bear contact with even very light clothing or linen, nor anything other than going naked, and would have been happiest plunging into cold water. And many who were not watched actually did so in wells, seized by thirst which never ceased; and drinking a lot or a little came to the same thing. Inability to rest and sleeplessness were an affliction throughout. And the whole time the disease was at its height, the body did not waste away but held out surprisingly against its suffering, so that most either died from the internal burning on the ninth or seventh day, while they still had some strength, or if they survived and the disease descended into the belly, and severe ulceration occurred and completely liquid diarrhea set in at the same time, most perished later from the weakness this caused. For the illness first settled in the head and made its way through the entire body beginning at the top, and if anyone survived beyond the most serious effects, the attack on his extremities at least made a mark. For it struck the genitals and fingers and toes, and many survived with these lost, some their eyes as well. Total loss of memory also came over some as soon as they had recovered, and they could not identify either themselves or those closest to them. [50] The nature of the plague, as an occurrence beyond all accounting, not only in other respects affected each person more harshly than is humanly bearable but also showed itself in the following way above all to be something completely different from the familiar diseases: all the birds and animals that feed on man either did not approach, even though there were many unburied, or died if they tasted them. And as proof: the absence of birds of this type was unmistakable, and they were seen neither elsewhere nor in this context; dogs, on the other hand, made it more possible to notice the results because they live with men.

[51] The plague, then—to omit many other peculiarities in the way it happened to occur somewhat differently for one person compared with another—was like this in overall character. And during that time none of the usual diseases troubled them, or even if any did it ended in this. Some died in neglect; others, when they had been given a great deal of attention. And no single cure was established, practically speaking, whose application could bring relief; for what had helped one person actually harmed someone else. No constitution, as to strength or weakness, showed sufficiency against it, but it devastated every sort, cared for by every sort of regimen. What was most terrible in the whole affliction was the despair when some-

2.50. "All the birds": the argument is not quite clear; apparently, Thucydides means that the corpses were toxic enough to kill scavengers, which could be more directly observed of dogs, and inferred of birds by their absence—in which case it is strange that *none* were seen "in this context," i.e., eating the dead.

one realized he was sick (for immediately forming the judgment that there was no hope, they tended much more to give themselves up instead of holding out), and the fact that from tending one another they died like a flock of sheep; this brought on the most destruction. If they were unwilling, in their fear, to approach one another, they perished in isolation, and many homes were emptied for want of someone to give care; if they drew near, they were destroyed, especially those making some claim to virtue. For out of honor, they did not spare themselves in visiting friends, since even relatives, overcome by the prevailing misery, finally grew tired of the lamentations of the dying. Nevertheless, those who had survived felt the more pity for anyone dying or suffering because they had foreknowledge and were also now in a confident state as to themselves; for the disease did not attack the same person twice, at least not fatally. They were congratulated by the others, and they themselves, in their immediate joy, had some vain hope that in the future also they would never be killed by another disease.

[52] In addition to the prevailing misery, the crowding in from the country to the city oppressed them all the more, especially the new arrivals. Since they were without houses but lived in huts, which were stifling in that time of year, the devastation did not occur in an organized situation, but the dead and dying lay on top of one another, and half-dead men tumbled in the streets and around all the springs in their craving for water. The sanctuaries in which they had found shelter were filled with corpses, since they had died there on the spot; people, seeing nothing they could do as the disaster overwhelmed them, developed indifference toward sacred and profane alike. All the funeral customs they had previously observed were thrown into confusion, and they gave burial as each found the means. Many of them, in the absence of relatives because of the number who had already died, turned to shameless burial methods; some put a corpse of their own on the pyres of others and set fire to them before those who had built them could, while others put the body they were carrying on top of another that was being burned and went away.

[53] In other matters as well, the plague was the starting point for greater lawlessness in the city. Everyone was ready to be bolder about activities they had previously enjoyed only in secret, since they saw the sudden change for both those who were prosperous and suddenly died and

2.51. "No single cure": It is remarkable that no cure is *described* here. "Some vain hope": literally, "light" hope; the related verb-form appears in 2.44 ("your heart will be lightened"), and it is at least a striking coincidence that both references are to the future life of those who have survived catastrophe.

for those who previously owned nothing but immediately got their property. And so they thought it appropriate to use what they had quickly and
with a view to enjoyment, considering their persons and their possessions
equally ephemeral. No one was enthusiastic over additional hardship for
what seemed a noble objective, considering it uncertain whether he would
die before achieving it. Whatever was pleasant immediately and whatever
was conducive to that were deemed both noble and useful. Neither fear of
the gods nor law of man was a deterrent, since it was judged all the same
whether they were pious or not because of seeing everyone dying with no
difference, and since no one anticipated that he would live till trial and pay
the penalty for his crimes, but that the much greater penalty which had
already been pronounced was hanging over them, and it was reasonable to
get some satisfaction from life before that descended.

[54] The Athenians were afflicted by all this weight of suffering, with
people dying inside and the land plundered outside. During the misfortunes, as was natural, they also remembered the following verse, the old
men claiming that long ago it was recited: "A Dorian war will come, and
with it plague." Now there was the contention among people that those of
old did not use the word "plague" in the verse but "famine," but under the
circumstances, the opinion naturally prevailed that plague was mentioned;
men shaped their memories in accordance with what they experienced.
And yet, I suppose, if another Dorian war breaks out after this one, and it
happens there is famine, they will probably recite accordingly. Among
those who knew it, there was also mention of the oracle given to the
Lacedaemonians, who were told when they asked the god whether they
should go to war that, if they fought hard, victory would be theirs, and that
he himself would join them. So regarding the oracle they took the events
to correspond; after the Peloponnesians had invaded, the plague began
immediately, it did not reach the Peloponnesos to any significant extent,
but it made inroads in Athens most of all, and otherwise in the places most
thickly settled. These were the events in connection with the plague.

[55] Meanwhile, after they ravaged the plain, the Peloponnesians proceeded to the Parales or coastal area as far as Laureion, where the Athenians
have their silver mines. And they ravaged this first where it faces the
Peloponnesos, then where it is turned toward Euboia and Andros. Perikles,
who was general, had the same opinion as in the previous invasion, that the
Athenians should not go out. [56] When the Peloponnesians were still in
the plain, before they came to the coast, he prepared an expedition of a
hundred ships against the Peloponnesians, and when it was ready he set
sail. He brought four thousand Athenian hoplites on the ships and three

hundred cavalry in horse-transports, which were first built on that occasion, using old ships. The Chians and Lesbians campaigned along with them with fifty ships. When this Athenian force set sail, they left the Peloponnesians occupying the coast. When they reached Epidauros in the Peloponnesos, they ravaged most of its territory and after making an attack on the city they entertained hopes of capturing it, yet there was no success. Setting sail again from Epidauros, they ravaged the territory of Troizen, Halieis, and Hermione; these are all coastal areas of the Peloponnesos. After setting out from there, they reached Prasiai, a coastal town in Lakonian territory, ravaged the land, and captured and sacked the town. After they did this they returned home. They found that the Peloponnesians were no longer in Attica but had withdrawn. [57] The whole time that the Peloponnesians were in Athenian territory and the Athenians campaigning with their ships, the plague was destroying both the Athenians on the expedition and those in the city, so that it was even said that the Peloponnesians left the territory in fear of the plague, since they learned from deserters that it was in the city and were at the same time aware of the funerals. But it was during this invasion that they stayed longest and ravaged the whole territory, since they were in the land of Attica about forty days.

[58] That same summer Hagnon son of Nikias and Kleopompos son of Kleinias, who were generals along with Perikles, took the same forces he had used and immediately campaigned against the Chalkidians in the Thracian area and against Potidaia, which was still besieged, and tried in every way to capture it. But they had no success either in capturing the town or in any other way worthy of their expedition; for the plague broke out there and inflicted a very great amount of suffering on the Athenians, destroying the army, so that even the soldiers there earlier who had previously been healthy caught the plague from the troops with Hagnon. Phormio and his sixteen hundred were no longer in the Chalkidian area. Hagnon returned to Athens with his ships, having lost one thousand fifty hoplites out of four thousand to the plague in about forty days. The soldiers there earlier remained in place and continued to besiege Potidaia.

[59] After the second Peloponnesian invasion, the Athenians, since their land had been ravaged for the second time and in addition the plague had afflicted them along with the war, had undergone a change in their attitude, and they blamed Perikles as the one who persuaded them to go to war, and they had fallen into misfortunes because of him, and they were eager to reach terms with the Lacedaemonians. They sent ambassadors to them but without results. And with their minds reduced to despair on every count, they railed against Perikles. Seeing them incensed at the situation and in

every way acting just as he had expected, he called an assembly (since he was still general), wishing to encourage them and make them calmer by ridding their minds of anger. He came forward and spoke as follows:

[60] "Your anger at me has come with my full expectations, since I am aware of the reasons, and I have therefore called an assembly, to give you some reminders and condemn whatever may be misguided in either your anger against me or your surrender to your misfortunes. I believe that a city that is overall on the right course benefits individuals more than one that is prospering as far as each citizen is concerned but failing collectively. For if a man is well off in his own situation but his country is destroyed, he is ruined along with it nonetheless, but if he fares badly in one that is faring well, he is much more likely to come through safely. Since a city, then, is able to bear the misfortunes of individuals but each member is incapable of bearing those of the city, how should you not all come to its defense, instead of acting as you are now? In consternation at the afflictions of your households you are neglecting the salvation of the community, and you hold me to blame for advising you to go to war, and yourselves for joining in the decision.

"And yet I, the object of your anger, consider myself a man inferior to no one in judging what is necessary and explaining it; furthermore, a lover of my country and above money. For one who has ideas and does not instruct clearly is on the same level as if he had not thought of them; the man able to do both but ill-disposed toward his city cannot make any declaration with the comparable loyalty; and if he has that as well but he is conquered by money, for this alone he can be bought in entirety. And so, if in thinking that I rather than others was endowed with these qualities, however modestly, you were persuaded to go to war, I could not reasonably be charged now with misconduct. [61] For going to war is great folly for those whose general good fortune gave them a choice; but when it was necessary either to become the subjects of others by yielding or to prevail by taking risks, the one who shuns danger deserves condemnation more than the one confronting it. I am the same, my position unchanged; it is you who have shifted, because it developed that you were persuaded when unharmed and regretted it when injured, and in your weakened state of

---

2.60–64. For good recent discussion of this speech see Cogan 1981, pp. 42–44 and Hornblower 1991, pp. 331–32 (but I cannot agree with him that the speech "has received amazingly little attention").

2.61. "I am the same": Haslam 1990 and Lapini 1991, n. 19 recognize here *(pace* Hornblower 1991 *ad* 2.61.2) an iambic trimeter line undoubtedly echoing tragedy.

mind my policy appears wrong (because there is grief felt by each of you right now, but realization of the benefits is still a long way off for one and all), and since a great reversal has befallen you, and that with little warning, your attitude is too feeble to persevere in what you resolved. For that which is sudden and unexpected and which comes with least accountability is what enslaves the spirit; this has happened to you, especially, in addition to other reasons, on account of the plague. Nevertheless, since you inhabit a great city and were brought up with a way of life to match it, you must be willing to hold out even in the greatest misfortunes and not wipe out your fame (for men think it equally appropriate to blame whoever through slackness falls short of a reputation already established and to hate anyone who through arrogance grasps for one that is not deserved) but cease from private sorrow and take up the salvation of the community.

[62] "As for premonitions about the difficulty of the war, that it will be great and yet we may not prevail, let all that I have already done, a good many times, to demonstrate their lack of validity suffice for you now, yet I will also point out this, which I think you have never comprehended about your empire and the magnitude of its resources, and which I have not mentioned in previous speeches; nor would I make use of it now, since the claim it makes is quite boastful, if I did not see you discouraged beyond a reasonable point. You believe that you rule only over the allies, but I declare that of two realms available for use, land and sea, you are completely in control of one in its entirety, both as far as you occupy it now and as much farther as you wish. And there is no one, neither king nor any other people in existence, to prevent you from sailing with the naval forces you have at your disposal. Now then, the manifestation of this power is not related to the use of your houses and land, whose loss you consider serious; nor is it reasonable to be angry on their account, but rather to deprecate them by thinking of the latter as a garden and the former as ornaments of your wealth in comparison to this power and to understand that freedom, if we come through safely by taking up its cause, will recover them easily, but that for those who become subjects of others even what they have previously acquired is likely to be diminished. Show that you are not inferior to your fathers in either respect, since they secured what they possessed through their own efforts and not by receiving it from others and furthermore preserved it and handed it down to you (and it is more shameful to

2.62. "Not mentioned in previous speeches": this is hard to believe; cf. *HCT* II *ad* 2.62.1 and Hornblower 1991 *ad* 2.62.1. On the wordplay of "spirit/spirit of superiority" see *HCT* and Hornblower *ad* 2.62.3 and cf. 1.122.4.

lose possessions than to fail of acquisitions) and go into combat against the enemy not only with spirit but with a spirit of superiority. For boasting results from ignorant success and is an option even for a coward, whereas there is a sense of superiority whenever one trusts his judgment that he excels against his enemies, which is our situation. Where there is equality in fortune, intelligence resulting from feelings of superiority lends stability to boldness and puts less trust in hope, whose strength comes in desperate situations, than in judgment, which is a surer means of foresight.

[63] "It is right that you defend that which you all take delight in, the prestige that the city derives from ruling, and that you either not flee the hardships or not pursue the honors; and never think that the contest is over one issue alone, slavery instead of freedom, when it is over both loss of empire and danger from those whose hatred you incurred during your rule. You cannot abdicate from it, even if someone fearful under the immediate circumstances makes this upright display in his political indifference; for you now hold it like a tyranny that seems unjust to acquire but dangerous to let go. Men of that sort would very quickly destroy their city if they per- suaded others, or if they lived somewhere on their own in charge of their own affairs; for the politically indifferent element cannot survive unless it joins ranks with the active one and is useful not in a ruling city but in a sub- ject one, as a safe slave. [64] Do not be led astray by such citizens or be angry at me, whom you yourselves joined in the decision to go to war, even though the enemy has acted as was only natural in attacking when you were unwilling to submit, and even though, beyond what we were prepared for, this plague has occurred, the one thing that has happened with an impact beyond our expectations. And I know that it is largely on this account that I am hated more than ever, and unjustly, unless whenever you fare well in some incalculable way you are going to attribute that to me as well.

"One must bear what comes from heaven with resignation and what comes from enemies with courage; this was in character for our city before, and let it have no opposition from you now. Know that Athens has the greatest renown among all men because of not yielding to misfortune but expending the most lives and labor and has acquired certainly the greatest power known up to this time, of which it will be forever remembered by posterity, even if in the present we give way somewhere (for it is in the nature of all things to be diminished too), that we as Hellenes ruled over the most Hellenes, sustained the greatest wars against them both in com- bination and separately, and lived in a city that was in all ways the best pro- vided for and greatest. Admittedly the politically inactive might condemn this, but anyone who also wishes to accomplish something will be emulous, and whoever has not made such acquisitions will be envious. To be hated and disliked in season has been the situation for all alike, whenever any have claimed the right to rule over anyone else; but whoever gains unpopularity for the greatest ends is well advised. For hatred does not last long, but the brilliance of the moment and glory in the future remain in eternal memory. By your zeal at this time, already resolved on what is noble in the future and what is not shameful at the present, secure these both, and do not send heralds to the Lacedaemonians nor give any indication of being weighed down by your present hardships, since those who are least distressed in their minds confronting misfortunes but most hold out against them are the strongest of cities and the strongest of individuals."

[65] By speaking in this way Perikles attempted to relieve the Athenians of their anger against him and lead their minds away from the perils of the present. On a public basis they were won over by his words, and they no longer made approaches to the Lacedaemonians and were more actively committed to the war, but on a personal basis they were distressed by their suffering—the common people because they had owned less to begin with and had been stripped of even that, the leading men because they had lost fine possessions in the country with houses and expensive furnishings—and, what mattered most, by having war instead of peace. They did not actually cease their anger against him altogether until they had punished him with a fine. And then, not much later, as a multitude is apt to behave, they elected him general and entrusted all their affairs to him, since by now they were more inured to the pain that

---

2.65. The Athenians show a cognitive dissonance in their behavior, renewing their commitment to the war, yet (Thucydides is very emphatic) making this their chief grievance against Perikles. At the same time, this is ironically consistent with Perikles' idea of the relationship between public and private life (2.60). Note that both the common people and the leading men are involved, so Thucydides' priority is not criticism of democracy or the fickle masses; on this topic, also the "apt to" phrase, see 8.1n. It is probable, although not certain, that Thucydides meant that Perikles died two and a half years after the beginning of the war (not after the time of the speech just recorded): according to Plutarch, *Perikles* 38, a victim of lingering effects of the plague. After 2.65, he is not mentioned again in Thucydides except for a brief reference in 6.31. It is extremely frustrating that "other policies that seemed unrelated to the war" are not specified; for some possibilities, cf. Rhodes 1988 and Hornblower 1991 *ad* 2.65.7. "In their anger": see Romilly 1991, p. 101. At this point, space permits only the very general observation that scholars continue to find highly questionable, in light of Thucydides' own overall account, the distinction he draws here between Perikles and his unnamed successors. "Held out for three years": I follow Rusten 1989 *ad* 2.65.12 in accepting this manuscript reading, cf. Pritchett 1995, 48.

each felt over personal concerns and considered him the most valuable man for the needs of the whole city.

For as long as he presided over the city in peacetime he led it with moderation and preserved it in safety and it became greatest in his hands, and when war broke out it is clear that he foresaw the power it had at this time. He lived two years and six months longer, and after he died his foresight regarding the war was even more widely recognized. For he said that by keeping quiet, looking after the fleet, not extending the empire, and not endangering the city they would prevail; yet they managed all these affairs in the opposite way, and in accordance with personal ambition and personal gain they pursued other policies that seemed unrelated to the war, to the detriment of both themselves and the allies, since, when these succeeded, they brought honor and benefit more to individuals but, when they failed, they did damage to the city regarding the war. The reason was that he, influential through both reputation and judgment and notable for being most resistant to bribery, exercised free control over the people and was not led by them instead of leading them, because he did not speak to please in order to acquire power by improper means but, since he had this through his prestige, even contradicted them in their anger. Certainly, whenever he perceived that they were arrogantly confident in any way beyond what the situation justified, he shocked them into a state of fear by his speaking, and again, when they were unreasonably afraid, he restored them to confidence. And what was in name a democracy became in actuality rule by the first man.

Those who came later, in contrast, since they were more on an equal level with one another and each was striving to become first, even resorted to handing over affairs to the people's pleasure. As a result, many mistakes were made, since a great city ruling an empire was involved, especially the expedition to Sicily, which was a mistake not so much of judgment about those they were attacking as because the senders did not subsequently make decisions advantageous for the participants, but by engaging in personal attacks over the leading position among the common people they both reduced the vigor of the armed forces and for the first time fell into confusion in the administration of the city. And after they had failed in Sicily, not only with their other forces but also with the larger part of the fleet, and now had a revolutionary situation in the city, they nevertheless still held out for three years against both their previous enemies and those from Sicily along with them, and moreover the majority of their allies, who had revolted, and later against Cyrus the king's son in addition, who furnished the Peloponnesians with money for their fleet, and they did not give in until, coming to grief through individual disputes, they brought about their own overthrow. So great at this time was the abundance of resources at Perikles' disposal, through which he foresaw that the city would very easily prevail in the war over the Peloponnesians alone.

[66] In that same summer, the Lacedaemonians and their allies campaigned against the island of Zakynthos, which lies across from Elis; the people are Achaian colonists from the Peloponnesos and were allied with Athens. A thousand Lacedaemonian hoplites sailed on board, and Knemos, a Spartiate, was the admiral. They made a landing and plundered most of the island. When the Zakynthians would not come to terms with them, they left for home. [67] And at the end of that same summer, Aristeus the Corinthian, the Lacedaemonian envoys Aneristos, Nikolaos, and Pratodamos, the Tegeate Timagoras, and in a private capacity the Argive Pollis, who were making the crossing to see the king in Asia in case they could persuade him to provide money and join them in the war, first came to Sitalkes son of Teres in Thrace, wishing to persuade him, if possible, to abandon his alliance with the Athenians and go on a campaign to Potidaia, where there was a besieging Athenian army, and as their most urgent priority to cross the Hellespont with his help to Pharnakes son of Pharnabazos, who was to send them on to the king. The Athenian envoys Learchos son of Kallimachos and Amineiades son of Philemon happened to be with Sitalkes and persuaded Sitalkes' son Sadokos, the one who had become an Athenian, to deliver the men into their power to prevent them from going across to the king and doing their best to harm his own city. He agreed, and while they were passing through Thrace to the boat in which they were to cross the Hellespont, he arrested them before they could embark by sending men with Learchos and Amineiades, to whom they were instructed to hand over the envoys. They took the envoys and brought them to Athens. After they arrived, the Athenians, fearing that Aristeus would escape and do them still more harm, since it was obvious that he had previously been responsible for everything concerning Potidaia and the Thracian area, put them all to death that same day, although they had had no trial and had things they wished to say, and threw them into a pit, with the justification that they were defending themselves by the same methods that the Lacedaemonians had initiated when they put to death Athenian and allied traders that they caught sailing around the Peloponnesos in merchant ships and threw them into pits. For at the beginning of the war, the Lacedaemonians had indeed killed as enemies all whom they caught at sea, both those allied with the Athenians and those belonging to neither side.

[68] Around the same time, at the end of summer, the Ambraciots and many of the barbarians whom they had incited campaigned against Amphilochian Argos and the rest of Amphilochia. Their enmity against the Argives came from the following origins. Amphilochos the son of Amphiaraos founded Amphilochian Argos and the rest of Amphilochia on the Ambracian gulf after the Trojan War, when he returned home and was dissatisfied with the conditions in Argos, naming Amphilochian Argos after his own country, and this was the greatest city of Amphilochia and had the most powerful inhabitants, but many generations later, afflicted with misfortunes, they invited in as fellow-settlers the Ambraciots, who live on the borders of Amphilochia, and at that time they first became hellenized, regarding their present language, by their Ambraciot fellow-settlers; the rest of the Amphilochians are barbarians. Now in time the Ambraciots drove out the Argives and ruled the city themselves. After this had happened, the Amphilochians put themselves under the protection of the Akarnanians, and together they appealed to the Athenians, who sent Phormio as a general and thirty ships, and when Phormio arrived, they seized Argos by assault and enslaved the Ambraciots, and the Amphilochians and Akarnanians occupied Argos jointly. After this, the alliance was first concluded between the Athenians and the Akarnanians. The Ambraciots first developed their hostility against the Argives as a result of this enslavement of their people. Later, during the war, they made this campaign with their own men, the Chaonians, and some of the other neighboring barbarians. They came to Argos and got control of the countryside, but since they were unable to capture the city when they attacked it, they left for home and dispersed among their various peoples. All this took place during the summer.

[69] In the following winter, the Athenians sent twenty ships and Phormio as general, who used Naupaktos as a base for guarding against anyone sailing out of Corinth to the Gulf of Krisa or anyone sailing in, and sent six other ships to Karia and Lycia, with Melesandros as general, to raise money in that region and prevent Peloponnesian pirate raids from using it as a base for attacking merchant shipping from Phaselis, Phoenicia, and that part of the mainland. Melesandros went inland into Lycia with a force of Athenians from the ships as well as allies and was killed and lost part of his force after a defeat in battle. [70] In the same winter, since the Potidaians could no longer hold out against the siege, yet the Peloponnesian invasions of Attica did not make the Athenians any more inclined to withdraw, and their food had run out and already, in addition to many other forms of basic sustenance that had been found in the place, they had sometimes

eaten one another, under all these circumstances they made an offer to come to terms with the Athenian generals appointed against them, Xenophon son of Euripides, Hestiodoros son of Aristokleides, and Phanomachos son of Kallimachos. They accepted, seeing the army's hardships in a region of severe winters, also because the city had already expended two thousand talents on the siege. Now they made these terms with them, that they leave with their children, women, and the mercenaries, with one garment each—the women with two—and a fixed sum of money for the journey. They left under truce for Chalkidike or wherever each one could. The Athenians criticized the generals for making terms without their permission (since they thought they could have gotten control of the city in any way they wanted) and later sent their own epoikoi to Potidaia and occupied it. This occurred during the winter, and the second year of this war, which Thucydides recorded, came to an end.

[71] In the following summer, the Peloponnesians and their allies did not invade Attica but campaigned against Plataia; their leader was Archidamos son of Zeuxidamos, king of the Lacedaemonians. And after establishing his army's position, he was about to plunder the land, but the Plataians immediately sent envoys to him and said the following: "Archidamos and Lacedaemonians, you are committing an injustice worthy of neither yourselves nor your fathers in campaigning against the territory of Plataia, for after Pausanias son of Kleombrotos, a Lacedaemonian, freed Hellas from the Medes with the Hellenes who joined in facing the danger of the battle that took place in our land, he sacrificed to Zeus God of Freedom in the agora of the Plataians, summoned all the allies together, and conceded to the Plataians that they hold their own land and city and live there in independence, and that no one would ever campaign against them unjustly, nor to enslave them; and otherwise, the allies present would defend them with all their power. This your fathers granted us because of the courage and zeal we showed during those dangers, yet you are doing the opposite: you have come with the Thebans, our worst enemies, to enslave us. Making our witnesses the gods of the oaths sworn then and the gods of your ancestors and those of our country, we tell you not to wrong the land of Plataia nor to violate the oaths but to allow us to live in independence, just as Pausanias judged right."

[72] When the Plataians had said this, Archidamos spoke in reply. "What you say is right, Plataians, if you act in accordance with your words.

2.71. The pledge to the Plataians "is a rare allusion, in a Thucydidean speech, to an event otherwise unknown to us" (Hornblower 1991 *ad* 2.71.2).

Just as Pausanias granted you, live in independence yourselves and join also in freeing all the others who shared the dangers at that time and shared in the oaths to you, and who are now subject to the Athenians, and for the sake of their freedom and that of others this great force and this war have come about. Best of all, share in this and stand by your oaths in turn. But otherwise, just as we have already proposed to you before, remain inactive and tend to your own affairs, do not join others, receive both sides as friends but neither for purposes of war. Even this will satisfy us." This is all that Archidamos said, and when the Plataian envoys had heard it, they went into the city, and after communicating to the people what had been said, they replied that it was impossible to act as he had proposed without the permission of the Athenians (for their children and women were there) and that they also feared for the whole city, since after the Lacedaemonians withdrew the Athenians might come and not disallow the arrangement, or the Thebans, who would be included in the oath about receiving both sides, might again attempt to capture the city. And to reassure them over these concerns, he said, "Give over to us, the Lacedaemonians, your city and houses, and indicate the boundaries of your land and the number of your trees and whatever else can be numbered. You yourselves depart for any place you wish for as long as there is war; when it is over, we will give back to you whatever we have received. Until that time, we will hold it in trust, working the land and bringing you whatever revenue should be sufficient for you." [73] After hearing this, they went into the city again, and after consulting with the people, they said that they wished first to communicate his proposals to the Athenians and, if they consented, to accept. Until then, they urged them to make a truce and not plunder the land. He made a truce for the number of days reasonable for the journey and no longer plundered the land.

The envoys went to the Athenians, and after consulting them they returned and announced the following to the men in the city: "Men of Plataia, the Athenians claim that never in the past, from the time that we became allies, have they allowed you to be wronged by anyone, nor will they allow it now, and they command you by the oaths your fathers swore to commit no act against the alliance." [74] After the envoys made this announcement, the Plataians decided not to desert the Athenians but to hold out even while seeing their land ravaged, if they must, and suffering whatever else might happen to them; also that no one should go out again, but that they should reply from the walls that it was impossible to do as the Lacedaemonians proposed. When they had given their reply, King Archidamos first, at that precise moment, turned to invocation of the local gods and heroes, speaking in this way: "All gods and heroes who possess this land of Plataia, be my witnesses that, since these men were the first to break the oaths sworn by all, it was not unjustly that we first came against this land where our fathers who prayed to you defeated the Medes, and you made it auspicious for the Hellenes to contend in, nor will we be committing injustice if we take action now; for after we made many and fair proposals, they were not accepted. Grant that those who were the first to begin injustice be punished for it and that those lawfully seeking retribution obtain it."

[75] After making this appeal to the gods, he sent his army into action, and first they built a stockade around them with trees they cut down, so that no one could come out any longer, and then they piled up a ramp against the city, hoping that its capture would come very quickly with so large an army at work. So by cutting wood from Kithairon, they built a construction on both sides, setting up a lattice in place of walls, so that the ramp would not spread out over a great distance. They brought in wood, stones, and earth, and whatever else might be thrown in to further it. They built the ramp without interruption for seventy days and nights, dividing into relief parties so that some were carrying material and others sleeping or eating; the Lacedaemonian officers attached to each city to help supervise urged on the work. When the Plataians saw the ramp going up, they put together a wooden frame, set it on top of their wall where the ramp was being piled up, and built in bricks from nearby houses they had torn down; the wood was to bind them together to keep the structure from becoming weak as it gained height, and it had skins and hides in front so that the workmen and the timber would not be struck by flaming arrows but remain safe. The wall was raised to great height, and the ramp went up on the other side with the same urgency. And the Plataians also thought of this: making a breach in the wall where the ramp rested against it, they carried in the earth. [76] When the Peloponnesians noticed, they crammed clay into reed matting and thrust that into the cavity, so that it could not be loosened and carried away like the earth. The Plataians, consequently prevented from using this method, gave it up, but by digging a tunnel from the city and calculating its position under the ramp they once more kept taking earth away to their side. For a long time they were undetected by the men outside, so that as they piled up earth they made less progress, since their ramp was being removed from below and constantly settling into the area being emptied.

But the Plataians, fearing that even in this way, as a few men confronting many, they would not be able to hold out, contrived this in addition.

They stopped working on the large structure across from the ramp, but starting from either side of it from the inner face of the lower wall, they built a crescent-shaped wall toward the city, so that this would hold if the great wall was taken, and the enemy would once more have to pile up earth against that and have twice as much work as they advanced inward, increasingly caught in a crossfire. In addition to building the ramp, the Peloponnesians brought up machines against the city, one that was pulled up onto the ramp against the large structure, shook down a major part of it and frightened the Plataians, and put other machines against other parts of the wall, which the Plataians pulled aside by casting nooses around them, or they fastened long iron chains to both ends of large beams and to two poles that rested on top of the wall and overhung it, and, pulling the beam back at an angle whenever a machine was about to strike against any point, they let go their grip and released the beam with the chains slack, and the descending force snapped off the projecting part.

[77] After this, since their machines were bringing no advantage and there was also a counterwork against the ramp, the Peloponnesians, thinking that there was no way to capture the city with the devices at hand, made preparations to wall it off. But first they decided to try the possibility of setting fire to the city when a wind came up, since it was not large; for they thought of every way in which the city might somehow come under their control without the expense of a siege. They brought bundles of brushwood and threw them from the ramp, first into the space between the wall and the piled-up earth, and when that rapidly filled up because of the great number at work they also spread them over the rest of the city as far as they could reach from on top of the ramp and lighted the wood by throwing on fire with sulphur and pitch. And a blaze resulted that was the greatest that anyone had ever seen up to that time, of those intentionally set; for in the mountains wood rubbed together by the wind has sometimes started fire and flames by itself. But this was big and came very close to destroying the Plataians after they had survived the rest. A large area of the city inside was unapproachable, and if a wind had come up and carried the fire around it, they would not have escaped. But it is said that what happened now was this, that heavy rain came with thunder from heaven and put out the blaze, and so the danger ceased.

[78] When the Peloponnesians had failed in this as well, after leaving a portion of the army there and dismissing most of it, they built a wall around the city in a circle, dividing the area according to contingents from cities; there was a ditch on each side where they took material for bricks. And when all the work was completed, around the rising of Arktouros,

they left guards on half the wall (the Boiotians guarded the other half), departed with the army, and returned to their cities. The Plataians had previously sent to Athens their children, women, the oldest men, and the large number of men who were unfit, and the ones left behind under siege were four hundred of their own men, eighty Athenians, and one hundred ten women as bakers. They were the entire number when placed under siege, and there was no one else, slave or free, within the walls. These were the arrangements for the siege of Plataia.

[79] In the same summer and at the same time as the Plataian campaign, the Athenians campaigned against the Chalkidians in the Thracian area and the Bottiaians with two thousand of their own hoplites and two hundred cavalry, when the grain was beginning to ripen; Xenophon son of Euripides and two others were the generals. They came up in front of Spartolos in Bottika and destroyed the grain. It also appeared that the city would come over through certain men as agents from within. But after those not in favor of this sent to Olynthos, hoplites and other troops arrived in their defense. When they made a sally out of of Spartolos, the Athenians met them in battle right outside the city. The Chalkidian hoplites and some mercenaries were defeated by the Athenians and withdrew into Spartolos, but the cavalry and light-armed of the Chalkidians defeated the cavalry and light-armed of the Athenians; they had a few peltasts from the land called Krousis. Just after the battle had taken place more peltasts arrived from Olynthos to help. When the light-armed from Spartolos saw this, emboldened by the arrival of reinforcements and also because they had not been defeated previously, they attacked the Athenians again together with the Chalkidian cavalry and the reinforcements, and the Athenians withdrew toward the two contingents they had left by the baggage train. And whenever the Athenians attacked, the others gave ground, but when they retreated they pressed them hard and threw javelins. The Chalkidian cavalry also rode up and made assaults wherever they chose, and causing the most fear among the Athenians, they routed them and pursued them for a considerable distance. The Athenians took refuge in Potidaia, and afterward, when they had recovered their dead under truce, withdrew to Athens with the remainder of the force; four hundred thirty men and all the generals were killed. The Chalkidians and Bottiaians set up a trophy, and after taking up their own dead they dispersed to their own cities.

[80] In the same summer, not long after these events, the Ambraciots and Chaonians, wishing to subdue all of Akarnania and cause it to break away from Athens, persuaded the Lacedaemonians to prepare a fleet from their alliance as well as sending a thousand hoplites against Akarnania, say-

ing that if they went there with both ships and land forces along with the Lacedaemonians, after easily taking control of Akarnania because the Akarnanians would be unable to send help from the coast, they would conquer not only Zakynthos but Kephallenia, and the Athenians would no longer have the same capability of sailing around the Peloponnesos; there was even hope of taking Naupaktos. The Lacedaemonians were convinced and immediately despatched Knemos, who was still admiral, and the hoplites on board a few ships and sent orders around to the maritime allies to prepare as quickly as possible and sail to Leukas. The Corinthians were especially zealous in support of the Ambraciots, their colonists. The ships from Corinth, Sikyon, and places in that area were under preparation, and those from Leukas, Anaktorion, and Ambracia, which had already arrived, waited at Leukas. Knemos and the thousand hoplites with him, after making their crossing without being noticed by Phormio, in command of the twenty Athenian ships around Naupaktos, immediately made preparations for the campaign on land. With him from the Hellenes were the Ambraciots, Leukadians, and the thousand Peloponnesians he came with, and from the barbarians a thousand Chaonians, people with no king, who were led by Photyos and Nikanor from the ruling family by annual office. The Thesprotians, people with no king, also campaigned along with the Chaonians. Sabylinthos, as guardian of King Tharyps, who was still a boy, led the Molossians and Atintanians, and Oroidos as king led the Parauaians. A thousand Orestaians, whose king is Antiochos, campaigned along with the Parauaians, since Antiochos had entrusted them to Oroidos. And Perdikkas, without the knowledge of the Athenians, sent a thousand Macedonians, who arrived too late. With this army, Knemos began his march, not waiting for the ships from Corinth, and passing through Argive territory, they sacked Limnaia, an unwalled village. And they reached Stratos, the largest city in Akarnania, thinking that if they captured it first the rest of the country would easily come over to them.

[81] When the Akarnanians learned that a large army had invaded by land and enemies were also going to arrive by sea with a fleet, they did not join together for defense, but each city guarded its own property, and they sent to Phormio urging him to protect them. But he told them that since a fleet was about to sail out of Corinth he was unable to leave Naupaktos unguarded. The Peloponnesians and their allies formed themselves into three divisions and advanced against the city of the Stratians, so that after setting up camp nearby, if they did not persuade with words, they might use actions in an attempt on the walls. Occupying the center as they advanced were the Chaonians and the other barbarians, on their right the

Leukadians, Anaktorians, and those with them, and on the left Knemon and the Peloponnesians and the Ambraciots. They were widely separated from one another and sometimes out of sight. The Hellenes advanced in order and kept a lookout until they made camp in a suitable location. The Chaonians, however, self-confident and also known as the most warlike of the mainlanders in that area, had no intention of occupying their camp but advanced at a rush with the rest of the barbarians, thinking that they would take the city at one blow and the deed would be all theirs.

The Stratians realized that they were continuing to advance and, supposing that if they defeated them while they were isolated the Hellenes would be less inclined to attack, set up ambushes in the area around the city and when they were near came straight at them out of the city as well as falling on them from ambush. After they had been thrown into a panic, many of the Chaonians were killed, and when the other barbarians saw them giving way, they no longer held their ground but turned in flight. Neither camp of the Hellenes was aware of the battle because the others had gone far ahead, and they thought they were pressing on to occupy a camp. When the barbarians ran to them in flight, they took them in and combining their camps remained there inactive during the day, since the Stratians did not come to close quarters with them because the other Akarnanians had not yet sent aid, yet they used slings from a distance and put them at a loss; for it was impossible to move without armor. And the Akarnanians seem the most effective at doing this. [82] When night fell, Knemos quickly withdrew with the army to the Anapos river, which is eighty stades away from Stratos, and recovered the dead under truce on the next day, and since the people of Oiniadai were with him out of friendship, he withdrew to their country before the reinforcements arrived. From there they each returned home. The Stratians set up a trophy for the battle against the barbarians.

[83] The fleet from Corinth and the other allies on the Gulf of Krisa, which was supposed to join Knemos to keep the Akarnanians from sending aid inland did not do so but was compelled, around the same time as the battle at Stratos, to fight a sea battle against Phormio and the twenty Athenian ships on guard at Naupaktos. Phormio watched for them to sail along the coast and out of the gulf, since he wanted to attack in the open sea. The Corinthians and their allies were not sailing toward Akarnania with expectations of a sea battle but were equipped more as transports and did not believe that the Athenians, with their twenty ships against forty-seven, would dare to fight a sea battle; yet when they observed them sailing along the opposite coast while they were close to the land themselves and,

as they were crossing from Patrai in Achaia toward Akarnania on the oppo-site mainland, saw the Athenians sailing toward them from Chalkis and the Evenos river, and they did not elude them by setting sail at night, they were now indeed forced to fight a sea battle in the middle of the gulf. There were generals representing each city that made up the force, the Corinthians being Machaon, Isokrates, and Agatharchidas. And the Peloponnesians arranged their ships in as large a circle as possible without leaving spaces to sail through, the prows on the outside, sterns on the inside, and within it they put the small boats that were sailing with them and the five ships that were the best sailers, so that they were on hand a short distance away to sail out wherever the enemy attacked.

[84] The Athenians, by contrast, arranged in single file, sailed around them in a circle and kept drawing them closer together, always almost touching them as they sailed and making them think they would attack immediately; but there were orders from Phormio not to make the attempt until he himself signaled. For he expected that the enemy would not stay in formation, like infantry on land, but the ships would bump into each other and the boats would create confusion, and that if the wind blew out of the gulf, which was what he was waiting for as he sailed around and which usually happens during the morning, they would not stay still for any length of time. He considered that, since his ships were better sailers, the moment of attack was up to him whenever he wished and would be best at that time. And when the wind came up and the ships, already in a small space, became disordered by the impact from both sources simultaneously, the wind and the boats, and the ships ran into one another and were pushed apart with poles, and the crews, while shouting and fending one another off with abuse, listened to neither their orders nor their officers and, by lacking the ability in their inexperience to lift their oars in the ocean swell, made the ships less responsive to the helms-men, it was right then, in that state of affairs, that Phormio signaled, and falling on the enemy the Athenians first sank one of the generals' ships and then destroyed the others wherever they went, and their effect was that none turned to resist in their confusion but they fled to Patrai and Dyme in Achaia. The Athenians pursued them, captured twelve ships, seized most of the men from them, and sailed off to Molykreion, and after setting up a trophy at Rhion and dedicating a ship to Poseidon, they returned to Naupaktos.

And the Peloponnesians with their surviving ships immediately sailed around from Dyme and Patrai to Kyllene, the harbor of Elis; Knemos and the ships from the forces there, which were supposed to have joined those, arrived at Kyllene after the battle at Stratos. [85] The Lacedaemonians also sent Timokrates, Brasidas, and Lykophron to Knemos as advisors for the fleet, ordering them to prepare better for another sea battle and not be barred from the sea by a few ships. For especially since it was their first attempt at a sea battle, they found it very baffling to their expectations and did not believe that their own fleet was so greatly deficient, but that some kind of cowardice had occurred, not taking into consideration the long experience of the Athenians compared to their own brief training. So they sent out the advisors angrily. After they arrived, they joined Knemos in sending around to the cities for additional ships and equipped the ones they already had to fight a sea battle. And Phormio sent to Athens, both reporting their preparations and giving an account of the sea battle he had won, also urging them to send him quickly as many ships as possible, since every day there was constant expectation of fighting at sea. The Athenians sent him twenty ships, but they gave the man in charge of them additional instructions to go first to Crete. For Nikias, a Cretan from Gortyn who was proxenos, persuaded them to sail against Kydonia, claiming that he would win over this hostile city; but he called them in as a favor to the Polichnitans on the borders of Kydonia. He took the ships and went to Crete, and after he plundered the territory of Kydonia along with the Polichnitans, he was delayed for a considerable time by wind and bad sailing weather.

[86] Meanwhile, during the period when the Athenians were confined to Crete, the Peloponnesians at Kyllene, after making their preparations for a sea battle, sailed along the coast to Panormos in Achaia, which is where the land forces of the Peloponnesians joined them for support. Phormio also sailed along the coast toward Rhion in Molykria and anchored outside it with the same twenty ships in which he had fought. This was the Rhion friendly to Athens, and the other Rhion, the one in the Peloponnesos, is across from it; they are separated from each other by about seven stades of water, and this is the mouth of the Gulf of Krisa. The Peloponnesians, therefore, also anchored with seventy ships, at the Rhion in Achaia, which is not far from Panormos where the land forces were, when they saw the Athenians also at anchor. And for six or seven days they remained at anchor across from each other, practicing and preparing for a sea battle, one side resolved not to sail outside the two Rhions into open water, for fear of the earlier disaster; the other side, not to sail into the narrows, thinking that in a limited space the battle would be in the enemy's favor. Then Knemos, Brasidas, and the other Peloponnesian generals, wanting to bring about the sea battle quickly before any reinforcements

came from Athens, first called the troops together and, seeing most of them afraid because of the previous defeat and without eagerness, encouraged them and made the following speech:

[87] "There has been a sea battle, men of the Peloponnesos, but if any of you as a consequence now fears the one ahead, that fearfulness does not have a proper basis. For we were insufficiently prepared when the battle took place, as you know, since we were sailing not so much to fight a sea battle as to make an expedition. It also turned out that the elements of chance were very much against us, and perhaps even inexperience caused our failure to some extent, since it was the first time we were fighting at sea. So it was not through our cowardice that defeat came about, and it is not right, when the spirit was not overpowered but retains its power to respond, to let it be blunted by the turn of events, but to consider that men can fail through chance but it is always the same men who are truly brave in spirit, and that as long as they have their courage they would not have reason in any circumstances to use inexperience as an excuse for becoming cowards. And in your case the shortcoming of inexperience is not as great as your superiority in boldness; in their case, if their expertise, which you fear the the most, is accompanied by courage, it will also furnish, in the midst of peril, the powers of memory to carry out what it has learned, but without courage no skill can prevail against dangers. For fear drives out memory, and skill without heart is useless. Against their greater experience, then, set your greater boldness, and against the fear caused by the defeat set the fact that you happened to be unprepared. You have the advantage of a larger fleet, also of fighting close to your own shore with hoplites standing by; in most cases victory is with those who have greater numbers and better preparation. And so we cannot find a single reason for the possibility of our failure. And all our previous mistakes will now themselves be one more advantage by giving us a lesson. Have confidence, then, helmsmen and pilots, as each of you attends to your duties, and do not abandon the posts where each was stationed. We ourselves will prepare for the battle better than the previous commanders and furnish no one with a pretext for turning coward; and if anyone then is so inclined, he will be punished with suitable measures, while the brave will be honored with the rewards appropriate for courage."

2.87. "And perhaps even . . . to some extent": the same sequence of four two- and three letter words is also used by Antiphon (see 8.68n), *On the Murder of Herodes*, ch. 6 to introduce a painful admission.

[88] This was the exhortation the leaders made to the Peloponnesians. Phormio, meanwhile, since he himself had fears about a state of panic among his men and had noticed when they gathered in groups that they were frightened by the large number of ships, also wished to call a meeting both to encourage them and to give them advice for the present situation. In the past, he always told them, and conditioned them to think, that for them no naval force was so large that they could not withstand its attacks, and the crews had long since accepted this assessment among themselves, that as Athenians they did not give way before any horde of Peloponnesian ships; but on that occasion, seeing them disheartened by the sight confronting them, he wished to renew their confidence, and after calling the Athenians together, he said the following:

[89] "Men of the fleet, it is because I see you frightened by the number of enemy ships that I have called you together, and because I claim that with no cause for alarm you should not be afraid. For in the first place they prepared the large and disproportionate number of ships because they have been beaten before and even they themselves do not think they are a match for us. Next, regarding their chief reason for trusting in a confrontation, that it is normal for them to be brave, they have no reason for confidence except that they usually succeed because of their experience in land warfare, and they think that this will give them the same results in naval warfare. But by rights that will now stand more on our side, if it is indeed their advantage on land, since they are not at all superior in courage, but each is bolder to the extent that each side is in some way more experienced. And the Lacedaemonians who are leading the alliance because of their own reputation are forcing most of them into danger against their will, since they would never, after suffering a decisive defeat, have attempted another sea battle. Have no fear, then, of their boldness. You give them greater and more substantial reasons for fear, both through your previous victory and because they think you would not be opposing them if you did not intend to accomplish something worthy of its overwhelming decisiveness. For most opponents, like these, attack with more trust in might than resolve; but some with greatly inferior resources— who, moreover, are not forced into fighting—are bold in opposition because in the steadiness of their determination they have something great. In taking this into account, the enemy will fear us more for unexpectedness than for normal preparations. Many forces before now have fallen to smaller ones through inexperience, some also through lack of boldness; we have neither deficiency now.

"I will not willingly give battle in the gulf nor sail into it. I can see that, against many ships lacking in skill, the limited space is a disadvantage for a few experienced and better-sailing ships. For no one could sail up in the way ramming requires since he would not have a long view of the enemy, nor withdraw opportunely when coming under pressure; there are no breakthroughs or reverse turns, which are the function of the better-sailing ships, but the sea battle would necessarily turn into a land battle, and in that situation the more numerous ships are superior. I will accordingly take precautions against this as far as possible. For your part, stay by your ships in good order and obey commands promptly, especially since we are anchored not far apart. And in the fight make discipline and silence the most important qualities, since these are advantageous for most operations of war and especially in a sea battle, and confront these enemies in a manner worthy of your past achievements. We are in a great contest, either to end the Peloponnesians' hopes for their navy or to bring closer to the Athenians their fear for the sea. I remind you again that you have beaten most of these men; and it is not the way of men's spirits, after they have been defeated, to remain the same in facing the same dangers."

[90] With these words, Phormio also offered encouragement. And since the Athenians would not sail against them into the gulf and the narrows, the Peloponnesians, wanting to draw them in against their will, set out at dawn and sailed along their own shore into the gulf, arranging their ships in four columns, just as they had been when anchored, the right wing taking the lead; on this wing they stationed their twenty best sailers on this wing, so that now, if Phormio thought they were sailing against Naupaktos and sailed along the coast in that direction himself to defend it, the Athenians would not escape their attack beyond the reach of their wing, but these ships would close in on them. And just as they expected, Phormio, afraid for the position left unguarded when he saw them set sail, embarked reluctantly and in haste and sailed along the coast, and the Messenian infantry followed to provide support. The Peloponnesians, seeing them sailing in a single wing and now both inside the gulf and close to the land, exactly as they wanted, suddenly at one signal turned their ships to face the enemy and sailed against the Athenians, each at its best speed, and they were hoping to catch all their ships. Eleven of these which were in the lead outdistanced the Peloponnesian wing as it turned into open waters, but

2.90. The heroic actions of the Messenians are described with a rapidity and vigor that may reflect a Thucydidean partiality for these people (as extreme and long-term victims of Sparta?), cf. especially 4.1–41.

they overtook the others, drove them to shore as they were fleeing, disabled them, and killed all the Athenians who did not swim away. They lashed up some of the ships and towed them (and seized one with the men even still aboard), but the Messenians, coming to the rescue, going into the sea with their weapons, boarding the ships and fighting from the decks, took some away even as they were being towed.

[91] Here the Peloponnesians were winning and disabling the Athenian ships; meanwhile the twenty ships from the right wing pursued the eleven Athenian ships that had eluded their turn into open waters. These with one exception escaped to Naupaktos ahead of their pursuers and putting in near the Apollo temple with prows facing out they prepared to resist if the Peloponnesians sailed against them at the shore. And they subsequently arrived singing a paian as they sailed, as though they had won, and a single Leukadian ship far ahead of the others was pursuing the one Athenian ship that was left behind. A merchant ship happened to be anchored in the open water, and the Athenian ship, pulling ahead and sailing around it, rammed the pursuing Leukadian ship in the middle and sank it. As a consequence of this unexpected and unlikely event, fear gripped the Peloponnesians, who moreover were pursuing in disorder because they were winning and in some cases had put down their oars and stopped sailing, an inappropriate action considering the short distance from the enemy anchorage, wanting to wait for the main part of the fleet, while others, through ignorance of the area, had run aground in shallow waters. [92] When they saw all this happening, the Athenians were filled with confidence, and at a single command they charged against them with shouts. Because of their previous mistakes and present confusion, the enemy held out for a short time but were then driven to Panormos, their original starting place. The Athenians in their pursuit captured the six ships which were especially close to them and also recovered their own ships which the enemy had disabled and taken in tow at the beginning; they killed some of the men and took others prisoner. Timokrates the Lacedaemonian, on board the Leukadian ship sunk near the merchant vessel, killed himself when the ship was lost, and he was washed ashore in the harbor of Naupaktos.

After the Athenians returned, they set up a trophy right where they had set out for their victory, gathered all the bodies and wrecks on their shore, and gave back those of the enemy under truce. The Peloponnesians, as though they had won, set up a trophy as well for routing the ships that they had disabled near the shore, and they dedicated the one they captured at the Achaian Rhion next to the trophy. After this, fearing the reinforcements from Athens, all except the Leukadians set sail by night into the

Gulf of Krisa to Corinth. Soon after the withdrawal of the Peloponnesians, the Athenians arrived at Naupaktos from Crete with the twenty ships that were supposed to have reached Phormio before the battle. And the summer ended.

[93] Before disbanding the fleet, which had withdrawn to Corinth and the Gulf of Krisa, Knemos, Brasidas, and the other Peloponnesian commanders, at the beginning of winter, wanted to make an attempt on the Peiraeus, the harbor of the Athenians, at the suggestion of the Megarians; it was not guarded or closed, as was natural on account of their great superiority through their fleet. It was decided that each sailor should take his oar, cushion, and thong and go on foot from Corinth to the coast opposite Athens, and after reaching Megara as quickly as possible, they should launch from Nisaia, its harbor, forty ships, which happened to be there, and sail immediately against the Peiraeus. For there was no fleet there on guard and no apprehensiveness that the enemy would ever sail against it in this sudden way, since they would not dare this openly even at their leisure or, if they had the intention, fail to be found out in advance.

The Peloponnesians made this decision and proceeded immediately. Arriving at night and launching the ships they sailed, no longer against the Peiraeus as had been intended, since they feared the danger (and it is also said that there was a wind preventing them) but to the tip of Salamis facing Megara; there was a fort there and three ships to guard against anyone sailing into or out of Megara. They attacked the fort and captured the three ships without their equipment, and they fell on the rest of Salamis unexpectedly and plundered it. [94] Attack warnings were sent by torch to Athens, and the resulting consternation was as great as any during this war. For those in the city thought the enemy had already sailed into the Peiraeus, while those in the Peiraeus thought that Salamis had been captured and the enemy was just about to sail against them; this is just what might

2.93–94. "As great as any during this war": compare the superlatives 7.71, 8.1, and 8.96; *pace* Rusten 1989, p. 4, I agree with Hornblower 1991 *ad* 2.94.1 that 2.94 is not necessarily an early passage (i.e., Thucydides did not always keep exact account of his superlatives). Falkner 1992 persuasively argues that the raid was a success limited by practical problems, which Thucydides mentions but deprecates in judging the raid a failure due to loss of nerve. The rather ambiguous language of "no apprehensiveness . . . found out in advance" (cf. *HCT* II and Rusten 1989 *ad* 2.93.3) must then refer to the Athenian mistake of thinking that the Peloponnesians would not attack without enough preparation to make surprise impossible (presumably out of overcaution, in which case the Athenians were ultimately right after all?).

easily have happened, if they had been willing to keep their nerve, and a
wind would not have prevented them. At daybreak the Athenians went to
the Peiraeus in full force to defend it, launching and manning ships hastily
and with great commotion, and sailed on them to Salamis, while establishing a guard over the Peiraeus with their land troops. After the Peloponnesians had overrun most of Salamis and captured men and booty and the
three ships from Boudaron, the fort, they sailed back to Nisaia as quickly
as possible when they found out about the Athenian measures for defense.
Their ships were another factor to worry them, since they had been
launched after a long time and were not at all watertight. After they
reached Megara they went back on foot to Corinthian territory; when the
Athenians found that the enemy was no longer near Salamis they sailed
away in turn, and after this they kept the Peiraeus more under guard from
now on both by a closed harbor and by other precautions.

[95] Around the same time, at the beginning of this winter, Sitalkes the
Odrysian, son of Teres and king of the Thracians, campaigned against
Perdikkas son of Alexandros, king of the Macedonians, and the Chalkidians in the Thracian area, wishing to exact one of a pair of promises and ful-
fil the second himself. For although Perdikkas had made him a promise,
provided that Sitalkes reconciled him with the Athenians when he was
hard pressed at the beginning of the war and did not restore his brother
Philip, who was his enemy, to become king, he did not carry out what he
had promised; and his own undertaking had been to the Athenians when
he concluded the alliance, that he would put an end to the Thracian war.
So he made the expedition for the sake of both promises, and he brought
along both Philip's son Amyntas, in order to make him king of the Macedonians, and ambassadors of the Athenians who happened to be with him
for this purpose, and Hagnon as a leader; the Athenians were supposed to
join him against the Chalkidians.

[96] Setting out from the Odrysians, he first called to arms those Thracians between Mt. Haimos and Rhodope, all those he ruled as far as the sea

2.95–97. Thucydides insists, with considerable artificiality, on Sitalkes' involvement with "two promises"; accordingly, Sitalkes can at least emerge as a man of
rectitude (cf. 2.29n) from what was to be an unimpressive campaign, yet which
ended with a rare instance of Perdikkas *keeping* a promise (2.101). Badian 1993, pp.
178–85 argues that Thucydides' Athenian bias led him to misrepresent both
Sitalkes and Perdikkas; cf. the excellent discussion of Athens and Perdikkas in
Borza 1990, pp. 141–60. I find the comments of Cartledge (1993, pp. 54–55) on
Thucydides' ethnological observations unduly censorious and the claim that his
assessment of the Skythians was simply "lifted" from Herodotos unwarranted.

toward the Euxine Sea and the Hellespont, then the Getai beyond Haimos and all the other peoples dwelling this side of the Istros river more in the direction of the Euxine Sea; the Getai and the people in this area border on the Skythians and are armed like them, all mounted archers. He also sent for many of the mountain Thracians who are independent and carry knives and are called Dians, mostly living on Rhodope; he hired some as mercenaries, while others joined him as volunteers. He also called to arms the Agrianians and Laiaians and all other Paionian tribes he ruled, and these are the most distant people of his realm, for as far as the Laian Paionians and the Strymon river, which flows from Mt. Skombros through the land of the Agrianians and Laiaians, it is bounded from there on by the Paionians, who are independent. On the borders of the Triballoi, and these are also independent, are the Treres and Talataians; these are to the north of Mt. Skombros and extend westward as far as the Oskios river. This river flows from the same mountain as the Nestos and Hebros; it is a large one and deserted, an extension of Rhodope.

[97] In size, the kingdom of the Odrysians extended along the sea from the city of Abdera to the Euxine Sea as far as the Istros river; this land requires a voyage along the coast for four days and as many nights at a minimum for a regular merchant ship if the wind is always fair; by road a man in good condition will reach the Istros from Abdera on the eleventh day at the soonest. It extended this far along the coast, and inland it was thirteen days for a man in good condition to get from Byzantion to the Laiaians and the Strymon (for in this direction it extended farthest in from the sea). And the tribute from the whole barbarian territory and all the Hellenic cities that they ruled in the time of Seuthes, who as king after Sitalkes actually extended the kingdom farthest, was in value about four hundred talents of silver, which were paid in gold and silver, and gifts of both gold and silver worth just as much as that contributed, apart from all the embroidered and plain garments and other furnishings, not only to him but to the Odrysian chiefs and nobles. For they established the custom, opposite to that of the Persian kingdom, of taking rather than giving (and it was more disgraceful to be asked and not give than to ask and not get), which the other Thracians have as well, yet on account of their power they practiced it to a greater extent; it was not possible to accomplish anything without giving gifts. And so the kingdom achieved great strength. For of all the kingdoms in Europe between the Ionian Gulf and the Euxine Sea it was the greatest in material revenues and other kinds of prosperity, but in fighting strength and number of troops second by far to the kingdom of the Skythians. In the latter respect, it is not only impossible to equate the

states in Europe, but not even in Asia is there a single people that can be compared one against one with the Skythians if they were all united. Not that they are comparable, however, with others in wise planning and general intelligence concerning living conditions.

[98] As king of so great a country, then, Sitalkes prepared his army. When his preparations were finished, he began his march toward Macedon, first through his own realm and then through uninhabited Mt. Kerkina, which is on the border between the Sintians and Paionians. He proceeded through it by the road he himself had built previously by cutting down the forests when he campaigned against the Paionians. As they crossed the mountain from the kingdom of the Odrysians, they had the Paionians on their right and the Sintians and Maidians on their left. After traversing it, they arrived at Doberos in Paionian territory. During his march, no losses occurred in the army except to some extent through illness, but additions, instead; for many of the independent Thracians came with him for plunder as volunteers, so that the entire number is said to have become no less than one hundred fifty thousand. Although the majority of these were infantry, about a third were cavalry. The Odrysians themselves supplied most of the cavalry, and next to them the Getai. Of the infantry, the most warlike were the ones armed with knives, the independent men who had come down from Rhodope, whereas the rest of the crowd followed along as an undifferentiated mass mostly formidable for its numbers.

[99] So they assembled in Doberos and prepared to make an invasion from the heights into Lower Macedonia, which Perdikkas ruled. The Macedonians also include the Lynkestians, Elimiots, and other tribes of the upper region who are allies of the Lower Macedonians and subject to them yet have kings of their own. Alexandros the father of Perdikkas and his ancestors, who are Temenids of ancient Argive origins, first acquired what is now the coastal part of Macedonia and established themselves as kings by defeating and driving the Pierians from Pieria (they later settled Phagres and other places below Pangaion beyond the Strymon, and even today the area below Pangaion along the sea is still called the Perian gulf) and the Bottiaians from what is called Bottia (they now live on the borders of the Chalkidians). They acquired a narrow part of Paionia along the Axios river down to Pella and the sea, and they occupy the land called Mygdonia beyond the Axios as far as the Strymon after driving out the Edonians. They also drove the Eordians from what is now called Eordia (most of them were killed, but a scant few settled near Physka) and the Almopians from Almopia. These Macedonians also conquered other peo-

ples whom they still control even today, those in Anthemos, Grestonia, Bisaltia, and much of Macedonia itself. The whole is called Macedonia, and Perdikkas son of Alexandros was its king when Sitalkes attacked. [100] Unable to defend themselves against a large attacking army, these Macedonians moved to all the strong locations and forts in the country. These were few, but later when Archelaos son of Perdikkas became king, he built those that there are now in the country, made straight roads, and in other ways mustered resources for war with greater strength in horses, weapons, and general preparation than all the eight kings who had come before him.

From Doberos, the army of the Thracians first invaded what was formerly the kingdom of Philip and captured Eidomene by force, Gortynia, Atalante, and some other places when they came over out of their friendship with Amyntos son of Philip, who was present. Although they besieged Europos, they were unable to capture it. They then advanced into the rest of Macedonia on the left of Pella and Kyrrhos. They did not go past these to Bottia and Pieria but plundered Mygdonia, Grestonia, and Anthemos. The Macedonians did not even consider defending themselves with infantry, but after sending for more cavalry from their allies inland they made attacks on the Thracian army wherever they chose, despite being few against many. And where they charged, no one withstood them, since they were good horsemen and equipped with breastplates, but when they were surrounded by the main body, they placed themselves in danger from a crowd many times their number, and so in the end they stopped their activities, thinking that they were not strong enough against the odds.

[101] Sitalkes negotiated with Perdikkas over the objects of his campaign and, since the Athenians were not on hand with the ships because they did not believe he would come but sent him gifts and envoys, also sent part of his army against the Chalkidians and Bottiaians, and he plundered their territory, keeping them confined behind their walls. When he was established in this area, the people living to the south—the Thessalians, Magnetes, other subjects of the Thessalians, and the Hellenes as far as Thermopylai—were afraid that the army could proceed against them and were making preparations. Also frightened were the Thracians to the north beyond the Strymon and all who occupied the plains—Panaians, Odomantians, Droans, and Dersaians, who are all independent. Even as far away as the Hellenes, who were enemies of the Athenians, he gave reason to fear that his men, brought in by the Athenians in accordance with

---

2.100. It is generally believed that Thucydides writes as though summing up Archelaos after his death in 399; *HCT* II *ad* 2.100.1 is skeptical.

their alliance, would proceed against them as well. But he despoiled Chalkidike, Bottia, and Macedonia when he overran them, and since nothing of his purpose in invading was being accomplished, and his army was both without food and suffering from the winter, he was persuaded to make a rapid departure by Seuthes son of Sparadokos, his nephew and the man with the most power next to his own. Perdikkas secretly won over Seuthes by promising to give him his sister in marriage and a payment along with her. Sitalkes was persuaded, and after he had stayed for thirty days in all, eight of these in Chalkidike, he quickly returned home with his army. Perdikkas later gave his sister Stratonike to Seuthes just as he had promised. So this is what happened concerning Sitalkes' expedition.

[102] Meanwhile, in the same winter, after the Peloponnesian fleet had dispersed, the Athenians at Naupaktos sailed along the coast to Astakos under Phormio's command, landed, and made a campaign into the interior of Akarnania with four hundred Athenian hoplites from the ships and four hundred Messenians, and they expelled from Stratos, Koronta, and other places men they did not consider reliable, and after restoring Kynes son of Theolytos to Koronta, they went back to their ships. For they did not consider it possible to campaign against Oiniadai, which alone in Akarnania was always hostile to them, since it was winter; the Acheloos river, which flows from Mt. Pindos through Dolopian, Agraian, and Amphilochian territory, and the Akarnanian plain, near Stratos higher up and emptying into the sea near Oiniadai, surrounds their city with a lake and leaves no way to campaign in the winter because of the water. And most of the Echinades Islands lie opposite Oiniadai very close to the mouth of the Acheloos, so that the river, a strong one, is always forming deposits, and some of the islands have been joined to the mainland and there is reason to expect that this will happen to all of them within a short period. The current is strong, deep, and muddy, and the islands are closely spaced and together become a barrier against the dispersion of the deposits, lying not in rows but in alternating formations and giving the water no straight passages into the sea. They are uninhabited and not large. And it is said that the oracle of Apollo told Alkmeon son of Amphiaraos to live in this land, at the time when he was an exile after the murder of his mother, by instructing him that there was no release from his terrors until he found in this region somewhere to settle which had not yet been seen by the sun nor even existed as land when he killed his mother, since other land had been polluted by him. And he was at a loss, so they say, and at last discovered this deposit of the Acheloos, and it seemed to him that enough to sustain his life would have been deposited since he began his long wanderings after

killing his mother. After settling in the district around Oiniadai, he became its ruler and left the country its name from his son Akarnan. Such are the stories we have received about Alkmeon.

[103] As for Phormio and the Athenians, setting sail from Akarnania and arriving at Naupaktos, they sailed back to Athens at the beginning of spring, bringing both the free men among the prisoners from the sea battles, who were later released in a man-for-man exchange, and the ships they had captured. And this winter ended, and the third year ended of this war, which Thucydides recorded.

BOOK THREE

INTRODUCTION

Book 3 is written with a very high degree of finish. The most important events are, in the following order: the revolt of Mytilene from Athens; the escape of some of the Plataians from their besieged city; the end of the Mytilenean revolt and the ensuing debate, at Athens, over the punishment of the city's population; the surrender of the remaining Plataians, their trial, and, after a debate, their execution; civil war at Corcyra, ending in complete victory for the democrats; campaigns in the northwest, especially an Athenian debacle in Aitolia and sub-sequent Athenian and allied victories in Ambracia. Events in Sicily are inter-woven at a number of points.

This is arguably the darkest Thucydidean book. There are no brilliant vic-tories, and the emphasis is on the calamity of defeat. Even though the ingenuity and heroism of the escaping Plataians is the occasion for a very detailed and ex-citing narrative, the doom of the city hangs over it. The various shortcomings of the Spartans as liberators are increasingly developed, many of them personified in the contemptible commander Alkidas (who may in fact have been represented unfairly). Toward the beginning of the book, however, the speech of the Mytile-nean rebels seeking Spartan support argues eloquently that equitable treatment for allies within the Athenian empire is an impossibility. When the Athenians deliberate over destroying the captured city, the supporting and opposing speak-ers agree to disclaim considerations such as compassion, emphasizing expediency instead; both are sharply critical of the governing abilities of the Athenian as-sembly.

Demosthenes' campaigning in the northwest anticipates the first part of book 4, and these two books are almost as closely connected as 6 and 7; book 3 as an entity effectively culminates in the events at Corcyra. The atrocities committed by both sides, but especially by the pro-Athenian winners, are fully described; Thucydides adds an analysis of the psychology of civil war and its devastating effects on moral standards. To say that ideological passion is revealed here as an even more destructive force than national rivalry is still to give this passage less than its due. This is Thucydides' most sustained display of open emotion.

Perhaps as a sort of pendant, Thucydides uncharacteristically holds up a vignette of a brighter and more innocent past, and does so by an equally uncharacteristic means. With minimal pretext, and without reservations or deprecation, he quotes extensively from the Hymn to Apollo, which for Thucydides was as much "Homer" as the Iliad.

BOOK THREE

[1] In the following summer, just when the grain was ripening, the Peloponnesians and their allies campaigned against Attica, led by Archidamos son of Zeuxidamos, king of the Lacedaemonians, and they established their base and plundered the land. There were the usual attacks by the Athenian cavalry at every opportunity, and they prevented the main group of light-armed from going beyond the camp and damaging the areas near the city. After staying the length of time they had provisions for, the Peloponnesians withdrew and dispersed to their cities. [2] Immediately after the Peloponnesian invasion, all the Lesbians except for Methymna revolted from Athens, wanting to do so even before the war, except that the Lacedaemonians did not receive them, yet in the event compelled to act before they intended, when they were waiting for the completion of works in their harbors, wall-construction, and ship-building, and for the arrival of everything they needed from the Pontos, archers, grain, and other things they were requisitioning. For the Tenedians, who were at odds with them, the Methymnians, and some of the Mytileneans themselves who were personally in opposition, proxenoi of Athens, turned informer to the Athenians, saying that they were forcibly uniting Lesbos under Mytilene and pressing ahead with all their preparations, in collusion with the Lacedaemonians and their kinsmen the Boiotians, for the purpose of revolt; without preventive actions at once, the Athenians would lose Lesbos.

[3] Worn out both by the plague and by the war that had broken out recently and was at its height, the Athenians considered it a great hardship to fight against Lesbos as well, which had a fleet and intact resources, and at first did not credit the accusations, giving priority to wishing them untrue; when they were unable, however, even after sending representatives, to persuade the Mytileneans to abandon either the unification or their preparations, they became alarmed and were willing to strike first. They suddenly sent out forty ships, which had just been readied to sail around the Peloponnesos, under the command of Kleippides son of Dein-

ias and two others. They were advised that there was a festival of Malean Apollo outside the city in which the whole population of Mytilene took part, and that if they hurried there were hopes of making a surprise attack. If they succeeded, then they succeeded; otherwise, they were to tell the Mytileneans to hand over their ships and tear down their walls, declaring war if they did not obey.

The ships set off, while the Athenians detained the ten triremes from Mytilene that happened to be with them as auxiliaries in accordance with the alliance and put their crews under guard. But a man from Athens who crossed to Euboia, went to Geraistos on foot and, after finding a boat getting ready to sail, encountered good weather and reached Mytilene from Athens within three days, reported the expedition to the Mytileneans. And instead of going out to the Malean sanctuary, the Mytileneans kept a watch after putting stockades around the unfinished parts of the walls and harbors. [4] When the Athenians sailed in shortly afterward and saw this, the generals made their announcement as instructed and, since the Mytileneans did not comply, opened hostilities. The Mytileneans, forced to fight unprepared and at short notice, managed to send ships out for a battle just outside the harbor but then, after the Athenians ships chased them back, immediately began negotiating with the generals, wanting to get the ships sent away for the present on moderate terms if they could.

The Athenian generals accepted their offers, because of their own fears that they were incapable of fighting against all of Lesbos. After arranging an armistice, the Mytileneans sent to Athens one of the informants, now repentant, along with others, in case they could persuade the ships to leave on the understanding that they were doing nothing revolutionary. Meanwhile, they also sent envoys to Lacedaemon on a trireme, which eluded the Athenian ships anchored at Malea north of the city, since they did not count on the results from Athens to be favorable. After a difficult journey to Lacedaemon across the open sea, they negotiated with them for some sort of help; [5] and when the representatives came back from Athens unsuccessful, the Mytileneans and the rest of the Lesbians went to war, except for the Methymnians; these supported the Athenians, as did the Imbrians, Lemnians, and a few of the other allies.

3.3. "If they succeeded": the sentence is unusual in two ways. The result clause is suppressed (supply "then they succeeded—or "so much the better"); after this ellipsis, "the proposal to the assembly becomes a commission to the commander of the expedition" (Spratt 1905a *ad* 3.3.3).

The Mytileneans made a sortie against the Athenian camp with all their men but, despite an advantage in the fighting, did not bivouack nor did they feel confident, and they withdrew. After this, the Mytileneans kept quiet, wanting to risk action only in conjunction with whatever additional forces might come from the Peloponnesos, especially after the arrival of Meleas, a Lakonian, and Hermainondas, a Theban, who had been dispatched before the revolt but, unable to reach them before the Athenian expedition, sailed in secretly in a trireme after the battle and encouraged them to send another trireme with envoys back with them, which they did. [6] Meanwhile the Athenians, taking much fresh courage from the inaction of the Mytileneans, called on their allies, who arrived far more promptly for seeing no vigor on the part of the Lesbians, and they also sailed around to anchor south of the city and fortified two camps, one on each side of the city, and set up blockades of both harbors. While they cut the Mytileneans off from using the sea, the Mytileneans and the rest of the Lesbians who had come to their aid controlled almost all the land, and the Athenians held the limited area around their camps and made more use of Malea for their naval station and market.

This was how the war was going around Mytilene. [7] Meanwhile, during this same part of the summer, the Athenians also dispatched thirty ships to the Peloponnesos with Asopios son of Phormio as general, since the Akarnanians had urged that they send them a son of Phormio, or some other relative, as a commander. The ships sailed along the shore ravaging the coastal areas of Lakonia. Asopios then sent most of the ships home but went to Naupaktos with twelve and subsequently brought out the Akarnanians in full force and campaigned against Oiniadai. He sailed by way of the Acheloos with his ships, and his army on land plundered the countryside. Since Oiniadai would not come over, he dismissed the land forces but he himself, after sailing to Leukas and making a landing at Nerikos, was killed during his withdrawal along with a good portion of his force by the local people and a number of soldiers who had come to support them. After sailing away, the Athenians got their dead back from the Leukadians later under truce.

[8] Since the Lacedaemonians told the Mytilenean envoys sent out on the first ship to be at Olympia so that the rest of the allies as well could hear them and decide, they came to Olympia (it was the Olympiad in which Dorieus of Rhodes won for the second time), and when they were brought forward to speak after the festival they said the following:

[9] "We know, Lacedaemonians and allies, the convention prevailing among the Hellenes: when men revolt in wartime and desert their previous

alliance, those who receive them view them favorably to the extent that they are of service but think less of them for being traitors to their former friends. And this assessment is not unjust, as long as those who revolt and those they defect from are alike in their policies and loyalties and evenly matched in preparation and strength, and no reasonable excuse for revolt exists. This was not the case with us and the Athenians, and let no one think worse of us if we were honored by them during peace and revolted in dangerous times. [10] Especially since we are requesting an alliance, we will speak first about justice and honor, knowing that friendship between individuals and associations between states can in no way be permanent unless they are formed by those who recognize one another as honorable and have similar principles in general; for through discord in thinking, differences in conduct also come about.

"The alliance between ourselves and the Athenians first came about when you withdrew from the Median war and they stood by for the work that remained. We did not ally ourselves with the Athenians for enslavement of the Hellenes, however, but with the Hellenes for freedom from the Medes. As long as they led as equals, we followed with a will; but when we saw them not only relaxing their hostility toward the Mede but intent on enslaving their allies, we were no longer without misgivings. Unable to unite and defend themselves because of the large number voting, the allies were enslaved except for us and the Chians; supposedly autonomous and free in name, we joined in the campaigns. And yet we no longer considered the Athenians leaders we trusted, going by the example of what had already happened; it was not likely that they would have subjugated those they had bound themselves to by treaty and not have done that to us if it had ever been within their power.

[11] "If we had all still been autonomous, we would have had more assurance that they would attempt nothing extreme; but when they had most others in their power and were dealing with us on an equal basis, they were naturally bound to find this harder to tolerate by comparing the majority who were now submissive, since ours was the only remaining assertion of equality, especially inasmuch as they were becoming more powerful than ever, and we more isolated. Only a balance of mutual fear guarantees an alliance; the party that wants to overstep is deterred by not having the advantage if it attacks. And we were left autonomous entirely on the contingency that their goal of empire seemed attainable by specious

3.9–14. On this somewhat neglected speech, see Macleod 1978.

arguments and by political rather than armed assaults. On the one hand, they used us to support the claim that those who actually had an equal vote would not join campaigns willingly unless those they attacked were in the wrong. At the same time, they also led the strongest elements against the less powerful first, and by leaving the former to the last, with their other support stripped away, they were bound to find them weaker. But if they had begun with us, when all the others had both strength of their own and the circumstances needed for making a stand, they would not have taken control in the same fashion. Our fleet, as well, gave them grounds for fearing that in a future coalition, added to either yours or someone else's, it might represent a danger for them. And to some extent we survived by cultivating their public and its leaders at any given time. Nevertheless, we would not have expected to manage for very long at all if this war had not broken out, judging by what was done to the others.

[12] "What was there to trust, then, either in this friendship or in this freedom? These involved accepting each other against our inclinations, and while in war they cultivated us out of fear, we did the same to them during peace; and as to trust, what good will above all confirms for others, fear assured for us, and we were both bound as allies more by apprehension than by friendship. Whichever party, then, was first given courage by a position of safety was bound to commit a violation. And so, if anyone thinks we are doing wrong by revolting first, in view of their deferment of the dangers they present us with, rather than in turn waiting to learn with certainty which of these will come about, he is not considering things correctly. If we had the ability to plot against them in turn as equals, we would also have had some obligation to wait in turn as equals before being against them; but since attack is a possibility for them at any point, it is right that acting first in self-defense should be possible for us.

[13] "Lacedaemonians and allies, we have revolted because we had these reasons and grievances, both clear enough for our hearers to understand that we acted justifiably and substantial enough for us to be alarmed and turn to some form of security, as we wished to long ago when there was still peace, and we sent you suggestions about a revolt but were prevented by your refusal to receive us. Now, since the Boiotians proposed it, we immediately accepted, and we consider ourselves in a twofold revolt, from the Hellenes so as not to join the Athenians in injuring them but to take part in liberating them, from the Athenians so as not to be destroyed by them at a later time but to act first. Our revolt has nevertheless occurred suddenly and without preparation, which is reason for you to send us help immediately as your allies, in order to make it clear that you defend those

you ought to and in so doing harm your enemies. There is opportunity as never before. The Athenians have been weakened by both plague and financial expenditures, and their ships are either in your waters or stationed against us, so that if you invade them for a second time this summer by both land and sea, they are not likely to have any left in reserve, but either they will not prevent you from sailing against them or they will withdraw from both areas.

"And let no one suppose that he is risking his own land for someone else's. While he may think Lesbos is far away, the support it provides will be at close hand. The war does not depend on Attica, as some believe, but on the territory by which Attica is supported. Their revenues are from the allies and will be even greater if they subjugate us; for not only will our resources be added, but also no one else will revolt, and we would suffer more severely than those previously enslaved. But by actively helping us, you will add to your side a state with a large navy, exactly what you are in need of most, you will subdue the Athenians more easily by taking away their allies, who will all come over with greater boldness, and you will rid yourself of the reputation you have for not helping those in revolt. If you show yourselves as liberators, you will give your military strength a firmer basis. [14] Therefore, respecting the hopes the Hellenes place in you, and respecting Olympian Zeus in whose sanctuary we are tantamount to suppliants, defend the Mytileneans as allies and do not turn us away when we have staked our own lives and will bring about general good from our success, but still more general harm if we fail because you were not persuaded. Be the men the Hellenes expect you to be and that our fears desire."

[15] The Mytileneans spoke in this way; after the Lacedaemonians along with their allies heard them, they accepted their arguments and made the Lesbians their allies, and in order to carry out the invasion of Attica they told the allies while they were present to go to the isthmus as quickly as possible with two-thirds of their forces, arrived there first, and prepared machinery at the isthmus to haul ships over from Corinth to the waters around Attica and attack simultaneously with sea and land forces. Although they acted with zeal, the rest of the allies assembled slowly, involved in their harvests and sick of campaigning.

[16] The Athenians, aware that these preparations were based on contempt for their weakness, wished to show that this judgment was mistaken, and that without touching the fleet at Lesbos they were also able to defend themselves easily against the advance from the Peloponnesos, and they manned a hundred ships with both citizens (excluding the wealthiest class

and the cavalry) and metics and made a show of force around the isthmus and landings on the Peloponnesos wherever they chose. When the Lacedaemonians saw this, they thought there had been a complete miscalculation and the statements by the Lesbians untrue, and considering the situation hopeless, not only because their allies had not come but also because the thirty Athenian ships off the Peloponnesos were reported ravaging their territory, they departed for home; later, they prepared a fleet to send to Lesbos, sending orders around the cities for forty ships and appointing Alkidas as admiral to sail on board. But they departed, and after the Athenians saw this, they too departed with their hundred ships.

[17] And at the time these sailed they had one of their largest totals of ships in fine condition, but as many or even more when the war was beginning. For a hundred were guarding Attica, Euboia, and Salamis, and a hundred more were off the Peloponnesos, apart from those at Potidaia and elsewhere, so that the whole number in a single summer was two hundred fifty. And this along with Potidaia especially drained money away; for the hoplites were paid two drachmas for besieging Potidaia (each received a drachma a day for himself and one for his attendant), three thousand of them at the beginning, and the number continuing the siege was never smaller, as well as sixteen hundred with Phormio who left before it was over; and all the ships received the same rate. In this way money was drained away at the start, and this was the largest number of ships manned.

[18] At the same time that the Lacedaemonians were at the isthmus, the Mytileneans campaigned on land with both their own forces and auxiliaries against Methymna on the assumption that it would be betrayed. After they attacked the city and did not have the success they expected, they went away to Antissa, Pyrrha, and Eresos; when they had increased the security of these cities and strengthened their walls, they hurried home. After their withdrawal, the Methymnians made a campaign against Antissa as well; defeated when there was a sally by the Antissans and their auxiliaries, many of them were killed and the remainder hastened back. When the Athenians heard about the situation, that the Mytileneans controlled the countryside and their own soldiers were inadequate for holding them in check, they sent out Paches son of Epikouros as general and a thousand of their own hoplites, around the beginning of the fall. They arrived by serving as their own rowers and surrounded Mytilene by building a single wall all around it; forts were constructed at the stronger points. Mytilene was now forcibly cut off by both sea and land, and winter was beginning. [19] Since the Athenians needed more money for the siege even

though this was the first time they had taxed themselves, raising two hundred talents, they also sent twelve ships to the allies to collect money, with Lysikles and four others in command. Lysikles sailed to various places collecting money, and after going inland from Myous in Karia across the plain of the Maiandros as far as the hill of Sandios, he and many of his men were killed in an attack by the Karians and the Anaiitans.

[20] In this same winter, since the Plataians, still besieged by the Peloponnesians and the Boiotians, were suffering from insufficient provisions, and there was no hope of rescue by the Athenians nor was any other salvation in sight, they made plans with the Athenians besieged along with them, at first that they should all leave the city and go over the enemy wall if they could force their way, with Theainetos son of Tolmides, a soothsayer, and Eupompides son of Daimaches, one of the generals, suggesting the attempt; then half of them in one way or another drew back from the danger, considering it too great, but about two hundred twenty remained committed to escaping in the following manner. They built ladders to match the enemy wall; they measured them by the courses where the wall facing them happened not to be completely covered with plaster. Many of them counted at the same time, and inevitably, although some miscounted, most hit on the right number, especially since they counted repeatedly and besides were not far away, but at the point they wanted the wall was readily visible. So they got the measurement for the ladders in this way, estimating the unit of measure from the thickness of the bricks.

[21] The wall of the Peloponnesians was of the following construction. It had two circuits, one against the Plataians, one in case anyone from Athens attacked from the outside, and the circuits were about sixteen feet apart. Now the space in between was constructed as living quarters distributed among the guards, and these were joined together so that the wall had the configuration of a single thick one with battlements on both sides. At intervals of ten battlements were large towers the same breadth as the wall, extending both into the interior space and to the outside, so that there was no passageway next to the towers but the guards passed through the towers themselves. At night, accordingly, they left the battlements when-

3.19. "The first time they had taxed themselves": a disputed reading, cf. Hornblower 1991 *ad* 3.19.1 and Kallet-Marx 1993, pp. 134–38; there are implications regarding the chronology and writings of the Athenian politician Antiphon (see Sealey 1984, pp. 75–80) and hence his possible associations with Thucydides (see 8.68n).

ever there was a rainstorm and kept watch from the towers, since they were close together and covered. Such, then, was the wall that guarded the Plataians on all sides.

[22] When their preparations were made, waiting for a night with storms of rain and wind and with no moon, they went out; their leaders were the same men responsible for the attempt. First they crossed the ditch surrounding them, then they came up to the enemy wall undetected by the guards, who neither saw them in the darkness nor heard them because of the wind rushing over the noise they made by their approach; in addition, they were spaced far apart, so that their weapons would not give them away by banging together. They were lightly armed and wore shoes only on the left foot for insurance against the mud. They went up between towers to the battlements, knowing these would be unguarded; first the men carrying ladders, which they set in place. Then twelve men lightly armed with daggers and breastplates climbed up, led by Ammeas son of Koroibos who went up first, and following him six went up to the tower on each side. After these, more light-armed men with spears came next, whose shields were carried by men behind them so that they could get up more easily, and the others were to give them the shields the moment they encountered enemies.

When many of them were up, the guards in the towers detected them; for one of the Plataians in getting a grip knocked down a tile from the battlements, and it made a noise when it fell. There was an immediate outcry, and the soldiers rushed to the wall; they did not know what the trouble was, since it was a dark night and stormy, and at the same time the Plataians left in the city came out and made an attack on the enemy wall opposite the part where their men were crossing so that these would attract the least possible enemy attention. Accordingly, they were in confusion while they stayed where they were, yet no one dared to leave his post to help, and they were at a loss to guess what was happening. Their three hundred men with orders to come to the rescue if needed went outside the wall toward the shouting, and torch signals about enemy action were sent toward Thebes. But the Plataians on the walls of the city sent out many countersignals prepared earlier for the express purpose of making the meaning of the torch signals unclear to their enemies, so that they would think some-

3.22. "Only on the left foot": a religious rather than a practical precaution, which Thucydides rationalized unawares, as was first suggested by Evans 1974, p. 111; cf. Hornblower 1991 and Rhodes 1994 *ad* 3.22.2.

thing else was going on and not send help until their own men had gotten away and reached safety.

[23] Meanwhile, as for the progress of the Plataians in getting across, once the first of their men had gotten up and taken over the towers by killing the guards, they themselves occupied the passages through the towers and guarded against anyone coming to help by this route, and putting ladders up the towers from the wall and sending more men up there some of them held off rescuers by throwing missiles from both the tops and the bases of the towers, while the majority now set up many ladders, clearing away the battlements, and went over the section between the towers. Whenever each man got across, he took his stand at the edge of the ditch and from this point shot arrows and hurled javelins if anyone coming along the wall blocked the crossing. When all of them were over, the men from the towers—the last of them getting down with difficulty—proceeded to the ditch, and just then the three hundred men bore down on them carrying torches. Now the Plataians as they stood on the edge of the ditch saw them quite clearly out of the darkness and sent arrows and javelins toward their unprotected side, while they themselves were less visible because of the torches. And so even the last of the Plataians crossed the ditch without being caught, although hard pressed and with difficulty; for ice had formed on the surface, not firm enough to walk on but the watery sort, more from the east or north wind, and the night of snow brought on by the wind had made the water high, which they barely kept above as they crossed. Their escape as well resulted mainly from the storm.

[24] When they set out from the ditch, the Plataians stayed together along the road to Thebes, with the shrine of Androkrates on their right, since they thought this road, toward the enemy, was the last the others would suspect them of taking; as they went, they saw the Peloponnesians pursuing with torches along the road to Kithairon and Dryoskephalai, which led to Athens. For six or seven stades, the Plataians followed the road to Thebes, then turned and took the road toward the mountains to Erythrai and Hysiai, and after reaching the mountains they made their escape to Athens, two hundred and twelve out of the total number, since some turned back into the city before going across, and one man, an archer, was captured at the outer ditch. So the Peloponnesians went to their stations, giving up the pursuit; meanwhile, the Plataians in the city, who knew nothing about what had happened but got reports from the men who turned back that there were no survivors, sent a herald when day came and were negotiating a truce so that they could gather up their dead but stopped when they learned the truth.

[25] While the men from Plataia were in fact saved by getting across in this way, the Lacedaemonian Salaithos, as this same winter was ending, was sent out in a trireme from Lacedaemon to Mytilene and got in by sailing to Pyrrha and from there going on foot undetected along the bed of a torrent where it was possible to pass through the enclosure of fortifications, and he told the leaders that the attack on Attica would take place, that the forty ships that were supposed to help them would be coming as well, and that he had been sent ahead both as a messenger and to oversee the whole situation. The Mytileneans took courage and were no longer inclined to come to terms with the Athenians. And the winter ended, also the fourth year of the war which Thucydides recorded.

[26] In the following spring, after the Peloponnesians had sent the forty ships to Mytilene, putting their admiral Alkidas in charge, they and their allies invaded Attica, so that the Athenians would have trouble from both directions and less ability to attack the ships sailing to Mytilene. The leader of the invasion was Kleomenes for his nephew Pausanias son of Pleistoanax, since he was still a minor. They plundered both the part of Attica already ravaged, in case anything was still growing, and all that had been left alone in the previous invasions; this invasion was the most severe for the Athenians, after the second one. For they extended their ravages over most of the land, the whole time waiting to learn of some accomplishment by the fleet, since they thought it had gotten across by now. When they got none of the results they expected and their food had run out, they withdrew and dispersed to their cities.

[27] Meanwhile, the Mytileneans, since the ships did not arrive from the Peloponnesos but wasted time, and their food had run out as well, were forced to come to terms with the Athenians in the following way. Since Salaithos himself no longer expected the ships to come, he gave hoplite armor to the common people, previously light-armed, for an attack on the Athenians. After they were armed, however, the people would no longer listen to the authorities but gathered in groups and told those in power either to bring the provisions into plain sight and distribute them to everyone, or they would make their own agreement with the Athenians and surrender the city. [28] The authorities, realizing that they were both unable to prevent this and in danger if excluded from the arrangement, joined in

3.25. While the enterprise of Salaithos will form a contrast with the Peloponnesian lethargy described later, Thucydides also (not without a degree of artificiality) sets up a comparison nearer at hand: the Plataian escape from a besieged city and the Spartan's entrance into a besieged city.

making the agreement with Paches and his forces, on condition that, while the Athenians could make whatever plans they wished concerning the Mytileneans, and they would let the army into the city, the Mytileneans could send an embassy to the Athenians on their own behalf; until it returned, Paches was not to imprison, enslave, or kill any Mytilenean. These were the terms, but those working most closely with the Lacedaemonians were terrified nevertheless, and when the army entered, they gave way and sat on the altars. Paches raised them up on the understanding that they would not be harmed and deposited them on Tenedos until the Athenians made some decision. He sent triremes and captured Antissa in addition and in other ways deployed his forces as he thought best.

[29] The Peloponnesians in the forty ships, who were supposed to arrive quickly, wasted time even while sailing along the Peloponnesos and were leisurely in making the rest of their voyage, unnoticed by the Athenians in the city as they proceeded until they put in at Delos, and on reaching Ikaros and Mykonos from there they first learned that Mytilene had been captured. Wanting to know if it was certain, they sailed into Embaton in Erythrian territory; Mytilene had been in enemy hands for about seven days when they sailed into Embaton. On hearing that it was certain, they made their plans in light of the circumstances, and Teutiaplos, an Elean, told them this: [30] "Alkidas, and the rest of us who have led this army from the Peloponnesos, in my opinion we should sail to Mytilene just as we are, before being discovered. Probably we will catch them very much in the unguarded state of men who have just captured a city; all the more so by sea, where they have no expectation of an enemy attack and where we, as it happens, have our main strength. Their infantry as well is likely to be scattered among the houses, being less careful because in the midst of conquered people. Therefore, if we fell on them suddenly and in the night, with the help of anyone inside who might still be favorable to us, I expect that we would take control of the place. We must not shrink from

3.30–31. On the intractable problems of Teutiaplos' concluding sentence cf. Classen/Steup III, *HCT* II, and Hornblower 1991 *ad* 3.30.4. While his maxim would not necessarily be original or profound (comparison with Thucydides' other military speeches suggests that it might not be), it should be intelligible and reinforce his overall argument: here, that victorious soldiers do not expect attack. *Faute de mieux*, I have accepted Steup's emendation. In contrast to most scholars, Roisman 1987 argues persuasively that Teutiaplos' plan was unsound, also that Thucydides unfairly represents Alkidas throughout as a stereotypical timid and unenterprising Spartan leader—perhaps in part because he had received a malicious account from Brasidas (a consistent detractor of his associates?) or one of his followers.

the danger but understand that if there is any universal factor in war it is what I have described; if a general guards against it in his ranks and attacks when he observes it among the enemy, he will have the greatest success."

[31] He did not persuade Alkidas with this short speech, but others, some of the Ionian exiles and the Lesbians with the fleet, urged him, since he feared this risk, to seize one of the Ionian cities or Kyme in Aiolis, so that with a city as their base they could cause the revolt of Ionia (with grounds for hope, since their arrival was nowhere unwelcome) and remove this as the Athenians' greatest source of revenue, while the Athenians would incur expenses on their own if they blockaded them; and they thought they could persuade Pissouthnes to join the war. He would not accept this either, and his main idea, since he had been too late for Mytilene, was to arrive back in the Peloponnesos as quickly as possible. [32] He put out from Embaton and sailed along the coast. Putting in at Myonnesos in Teian territory, he slaughtered most of the prisoners he had taken on the voyage. And when he anchored at Ephesos, Samian envoys from Anaia came up and told him he was not liberating Hellas in the right way if he killed men who had neither taken up arms nor were enemies but were Athenian allies under duress; unless he stopped, he would convert few enemies to friends but make many more friends into enemies. He was convinced and released all the Chians he still held as well as some others (people did not flee when they saw his ships but came up to them in the belief that they were Attic, having not the slightest expectation that Peloponnesian ships would ever sail across to Ionia while the Athenians controlled the sea).

[33] Alkidas sailed quickly from Ephesos and broke into flight; for he had been sighted by the Salaminia and Paralos while he was still anchored off Klaros; they happened to be sailing from Athens. Fearing pursuit, Alkidas sailed across the open sea with no desire to touch any land but the Peloponnesos. The news reached Paches and the Athenians from Erythrai and then came in from every source (since Ionia was unfortified, there was growing fear that even if the Peloponnesians did not plan to stay on that account they would fall on the cities and plunder them as they sailed along the coast), and the Paralos and the Salaminia on their own evidence reported seeing Alkidas at Klaros. Paches hastened in pursuit, continuing as far as the island of Patmos, but when Alkidas was clearly no longer within reach he went back. He considered it a gain that, since he had not overtaken them in mid-ocean, they had not been caught where they would have been forced to set up a camp and make the Athenians guard them with a blockade.

[34] Sailing back along the coast, he stopped at Notion, part of Kolophon where the Kolophonians had settled after the upper town was seized by Itamenes and the barbarians, who had been called in as a result of private faction (this seizure was about the time when the second Peloponnesian invasion of Attica was taking place). Now the refugees who had occupied Notion were again divided by faction, and one group called in Arkadian as well as barbarian mercenaries serving with Pissouthnes and established them in a fort (and the medizers among the Kolophonians in the upper city came and joined them in forming a government), while the other group seceded and as exiles called in Paches. He invited Hippias, the leader of the Arkadians in the fort, to a parley on the understanding that he would let him return safe and sound if he rejected his proposals, then put him under guard although not in chains, made a sudden attack on the fort, and captured it by surprise, and he killed the Arkadians and all the barbarians inside; Hippias he brought in later, just as he had pledged, and, when he was inside, arrested him and killed him with a bowshot. He restored Notion to the Kolophonians, excluding the medizers. The Athenians sent founders later and colonized Notion under their own laws, gathering in any Kolophonians in the cities.

[35] When Paches arrived at Mytilene, he took over Pyrrha and Eresos, and after capturing the Lacedaemonian Salaithos who was hiding in the city he sent him to Athens, along with the Mytileneans he had left on Tenedos and anyone else he held responsible for the revolt. He also sent away most of the army, staying behind with the others and making arrangements for Mytilene and the rest of Lesbos as he saw fit. [36] When Salaithos and the others arrived, the Athenians put Salaithos to death immediately, although he offered among other things to arrange a Peloponnesian withdrawal from Plataia (which was still besieged). They debated over the others, and in a rage they voted to put to death not only the men there but also all Mytilenean adult males and to enslave the children and women, condemning the revolt both on general grounds and because they had acted without being subjects like the others, and it contributed most heavily to their rage that the Peloponnesian ships had dared to venture into Ionia to support them; it looked as though they had not revolted without long deliberation. Accordingly, they sent a trireme to Paches reporting their decision and instructed him to put an end to the Mytileneans without delay.

The next day they experienced immediate remorse and reconsideration about deciding on a savage and extreme resolution to destroy a whole city rather than the guilty ones. When the Mytilenean envoys present and their

Athenian sympathizers observed this, they prevailed on the authorities to open the matter again (they were easy to persuade, because it was also obvious to them that the majority of citizens wanted someone to make it possible for them to deliberate again). There was an assembly immediately, various individual opinions were voiced, and Kleon son of Kleainetos, the very man who had won over the previous assembly to the death sentence, and who was in general the most violent of the citizens and by far the most persuasive among the people at that time, came forward again and spoke as follows.

[37] "Many times before now, I have felt that a democracy is incapable of ruling others, and more than ever during your present change of heart over the Mytileneans. For because your daily lives are free of fears and conspiracies among yourselves, you have the same attitude toward the allies as well and do not understand that with any mistake you make because of heeding their words or in any concession you make through pity, your weakening brings danger to you and no gratitude from your allies, since you do not bear in mind that you hold your empire as a tyranny and, regarding men who are conspiring against you, ruled against their will, that their obedience does not result from the favors you bestow to your own detriment, but from the superiority you enjoy through might rather than good will. And the greatest danger of all is that we will not stand fast over anything that is decided and will not realize that by following worse laws without deviation a state is stronger than when it has good laws that are not binding, that ignorance combined with self-control is more beneficial than cleverness combined with intemperance, and that compared with more intelligent men the less gifted usually run their states better. For the former want to appear wiser than the laws and to prevail over what is said at any time in the common interest, as though they would not display their thoughts in other more important ways, and as a result of this they often ruin their cities; but those who mistrust their own intelligence find it proper to be less learned than the laws and less capable than the fine speakers in finding fault with arguments, and by acting as impartial judges rather than competitors they are more successful.

"This is what we should do as well, then, and not let cleverness or contests in intelligence incite us to advise your assembly against its judgment. [38] I myself am certainly of the same opinion, and I wonder at those who have proposed to speak again about the Mytileneans and have brought on

3.36–48. On Kleon, see Mitchell 1991; on the Mytilenean debate, see Cogan 1981, pp. 50–65, and Johnson 1990–1991.

a delay that is of more advantage to the guilty; for the sufferer proceeds against the perpetrator when his passion has been dulled, but revenge coming as soon after the injury as possible exacts the most equal repayment. I wonder also who will be the one to speak to the contrary and claim to reveal that the crimes of the Mytileneans are beneficial to us, whereas our misfortunes have done harm to the allies. It is clear that either he will be striving, out of confidence in his speaking, to demonstrate that what was absolutely decided was not resolved after all, or else he is motivated by profit when he fashions his attractive speech and attempts to mislead. In such contests as these, the state awards others the prizes yet bears the risks itself. You are the ones responsible; by mismanaging the games, you with your habit of approaching words as a spectacle and actions as a recitation, of considering future activities on the basis of fine speeches about their feasibility and events that have already happened on the basis of splendid words of criticism, instead of using your powers of sight to give greater credibility to what has been done than what has been heard; perfect at being tricked by novelty in speech and at not wishing to make sense of what has been scrutinized, slaves to everything outlandish in turn and detractors of the ordinary; each one wishing above all for speaking ability of his own, but if that fails racing everyone else to keep from appearing left behind in pursuing the argument, to be ready with instant approval when a point is made, and to be as keen in anticipating what is said as you are slow in foreseeing the consequences; seeking, I would say, something different from the life we lead without enough understanding of actual conditions; in short, overcome by the pleasure of listening, like men seated for entertainment by sophists rather than to deliberate for the city.

[39] "My way of transporting you from this is to reveal Mytilene as the single city that has done you the greatest harm. I can make allowance for any who revolt because they cannot bear our rule or were compelled by the enemy. But if they occupy an island with fortifications and fear our enemies only by sea, in which case, with their own force of triremes, they are not defenseless, and if they did this when they had their own government and were held in the highest honor by us, did they not plot against us and rise up against us rather than revolt (it is revolt when there is harsh treatment), and did they not attempt to destroy us by siding with our worst

3.39. "Compelled by the enemy" and "forced by enemies": allies forced into revolt by the Peloponnesians are hypothetical (see Hornblower 1991 *ad* 3.39.7), mentioned for rhetorical purposes; by implying that they would deserve milder punishment, Kleon makes it harder to accuse him of unreasoning severity.

enemies? The danger is even greater than if they had made war by them-selves in pursuit of power. The fate of their neighbors did not serve them as an example, nor did their prevailing prosperity make them hesitate to go into danger, but they grew bold about the future, went beyond their power in their hopes, although not beyond their desires, and started a war, think-ing they should set might above right; for when they thought they would prevail, then, without being injured by us, they attacked. It is the rule that those cities that encounter the greatest good fortune with the most surpris-ing suddenness are drawn toward insolence; in general, success is safer for men when in accordance with their calculations rather than contrary to their expectations, and it is easier, I would say, for them to fend off adver-sity than to hang on to prosperity. The Mytileneans should long since have gotten no more special treatment than we gave the rest, and they would not have gone this far in insolence; in all circumstances, it is natural to despise conciliation and admire firmness.

"As for now, let their punishment be everything their crime deserves, and do not let the blame fall on the few while you acquit the people. Just as surely as they could be in control of the city now if they had turned to us, they all without exception attacked us; they joined the revolt because they found the risks more acceptable on the side of the oligarchs. If you take account of the allies, once you give out identical punishment to those forced by enemies and those who revolt of their own accord, do you think that there is any who will not revolt on the slightest pretext when either success brings freedom or failure brings no fatal consequences? But our risks against every city will be extreme in both money and lives, and when we win, taking over a ruined city, you will not have future access to the revenue of former times, our source of strength, but when we fail we will have opponents added to the existing ones, and we will be at war with our own allies during the time we should be confronting the enemies that now exist.

[40] "No hope, then, whether relying on speeches or bought with bribes, should be held out for them to find pardon for human fallibility. For they did not do harm involuntarily but were conscious conspirators, and what is involuntary is what is pardonable. I am absolutely opposed, therefore, both on that first occasion and at present, to your reconsidering what was previously resolved and giving in to the three failings most incompatible with empire: pity, enjoyment of speeches, and evenhanded-ness. Compassion is a fair reaction toward one's own kind, not toward those who feel no pity in return and whose position is both inevitably and permanently hostile; the orators who charm by their words will carry on

the rest of their contests in less important situations but not where the city will pay a heavy penalty for brief enjoyment while the consequence for them is to be well treated for speaking well; and the gift of evenhandedness is more for those who are sure to be friendly even in the future than for those who will always be enemies just as surely.

"I will sum up with one statement: by following me, you will act both justly and expediently toward the Mytileneans, but if you decide otherwise you will not so much oblige them as condemn yourselves. For if they were right to revolt, you would be ruling when you should not. And if you then see fit to do so even when it is wrong, why, it stands to reason that you must also punish them in your own interests, or you must give up empire and be upright men in complete safety. Resolve to defend yourselves by this same penalty, and do not let it appear that you the survivors feel less sense of injury than the conspirators, keeping in mind what they are likely to have done if they had overcome you, especially since they acted first in their crimes. It is above all those who wrong someone for no reason who carry aggression to the point of annihilation, wary of anything left of the enemy; for after his escape, the victim of injury without cause is more ruthless than a regular enemy. Do not be traitors to yourselves, then, but try to return to your feelings during the ordeal and the urgency to overcome these people at all cost, and now pay them back, neither weakening in the face of the immediate circumstances nor losing sight of the danger once hanging over you. Punish them now as they deserve and show the other allies by a clear example that death will be the penalty for anyone who revolts. If they understand this, you will be less distracted from your enemies by fighting your own allies."

[41] Kleon spoke in this way. After him, Diodotos son of Eukrates, the very man who in the previous assembly had argued most against killing the

---

3.40. "This same penalty": presumably, the one previously voted; at least this is less "obscure" (*HCT* II *ad* 3.40.5) than any alternative interpretation. Kleon argues that the victim of even an unsuccessful plot has the fullest justification for outrage and then stokes the flames by pointing out how much worse it could have been (cf. the witty paraphrase by Winnington-Ingram 1965, p. 77: "Be beastly to the Mytileneans. Why? Because they would have been beastly to you. Why? Because you would have been beastly to them.").

3.41. Diodotos, Kleon's main opponent in the previous assembly as well, is otherwise unknown (cf. Ostwald 1979, Rhodes 1994 *ad* 3.41)—so perhaps obscure even by the end of the fifth century. Thucydides was showman enough to have calculated the dramatic effect his sudden emergence (cf. Kleon's ironic curiosity: "I wonder," 3.38) has always had on readers.

Mytileneans, came forward now as well and spoke as follows. [42] "I neither blame those who have again brought up the decision about the
Mytileneans nor commend those who find fault with frequent deliberation
over the most important matters, but I consider the greatest obstacles to
good counsel to be haste and anger, the latter usually involving folly, the
other ignorance and deficient reasoning. And as for speeches, whoever
maintains that they do not teach practicality is either stupid or has some
personal bias: stupid if he supposes that there is some other way the future
and its uncertainty can be considered; biased if he supposes, in his desire
to succeed with a disgraceful case, that he would not speak effectively in a
cause that is wrong yet by slandering effectively he would intimidate both
the opposing speakers and the listeners.

"The hardest to cope with are those who start out with accusations of
oratorical display for financial ends. For if they made ignorance the accusation, the unsuccessful speaker would step down looking less intelligent
but not less honest; but when dishonesty is brought in, he is made suspect
if he succeeds and dishonest on top of his incompetence if he fails. The city
does not benefit at all in such situations; because of fear, it is deprived of
its advisors. It would be best off if its citizens of that sort lacked the ability
to speak; the rest would be persuaded into the fewest mistakes. The good
citizen ought to prove the better speaker not by frightening his opponents
but on fair terms, and the wise city should not honor good advisors excessively (yet no less than is due) nor dishonor them, let alone penalize those
whose ideas do not prevail. In this way, it is least likely that the successful
ones, aiming at still higher esteem, would speak ingratiatingly against their
convictions, or that the unsuccessful, using the same means, would strive
by ingratiation of their own to win over the people.

[43] "Our behavior is the reverse, and what is more, if someone is even
suspected of financial motives for giving what is nevertheless the best
advice, in our envy over the unconfirmed impression of the rewards, we
deprive the city of the obvious benefit. The result is that straightforward
good advice is no less suspect than bad, so that it is equally necessary that
the man arguing for the most terrible proposals win over the people by
deceit and the man with better advice make himself trusted by lying. And
thanks to intellectual excess, the city is the only one that cannot be rendered service openly without guile; anyone making an obvious contribution is met with suspicion that in some obscure way he will profit. But it is
right to expect us the speakers, regarding the most important matters and
in a situation like this, to take a somewhat longer view than you whose
attention is brief, especially since we are accountable when we give advice,

while you are not accountable when you listen. If those who make proposals and those who accept them suffered equally, you would judge more carefully. But as it is, in accordance with whatever temper you fly into, there are times when you make mistakes and penalize the judgment of your advisor alone and not your own, however many have shared responsibility for the error.

[44] "But I have not come forward to speak in opposition, nor to bring charges as far as the Mytileneans are concerned. For the debate, if we are sensible, is not about their guilt but about the right planning for ourselves. And no matter how guilty I proclaim them, I will not on that account urge you to kill them if it is not expedient, nor that because there is some excuse they should keep their city, if it does not appear beneficial. I consider our deliberations to be more about the future than the present. And where Kleon is most insistent, that it will eventually be in the interest of fewer revolts if we set death as the penalty, I am equally insistent myself about what is best for the future, with the opposite conclusions. I beg you not to reject what is useful in my proposal because of what is attractive in his. His proposal might well have appeal as more just according to your present anger against the Mytileneans; but we are not taking them to court to get justice but deliberating as to how they might be of use to us.

[45] "Now then, states lay down the death penalty for many things, crimes that are not comparable to this but less important. Men take the risk nevertheless, led on by their hopes, and no one has ever yet faced the danger already resigned to failing in the attempt. And did any city in revolt ever undertake this with what seemed inferior resources, whether its own or through alliances? It is natural for all men, both individually and collectively, to make mistakes, and there is no law that will prevent this, seeing that people have truly used up all penalties in succession on the chance of lessening their injuries at the hands of criminals. It is likely that long ago milder ones were used for the worst offenses, and after a while, since these were disregarded, there were many elevations to the death penalty; yet this is disregarded too. This means that either something still more frightening must be discovered or there is this, which is no restraint at all, but either poverty, which brings about boldness through compulsion; abundance, which brings about ambition through insolence and pride; or other circumstances because of human passion, depending on how each of these is ruled by some irresistible force, will

3.44. "Nor that because there is some excuse": I have followed Spratt 1905a *ad* 3.44.2, cf. *HCT* II *ad* 3.44.2.

lead men into danger. And in every case, hope and desire—the one leading while the other follows, the one thinking up the scheme while the other holds out the full assistance of fortune—do the greatest damage, and although invisible, they have power over perils that can be seen. On top of these, fortune contributes no less incitement; for at times, by lending a hand unexpectedly, it leads men on to take risks even in unfavorable circumstances and especially whole cities, in proportion to the greatest consequences, freedom or rule over others, and together men irrationally have the individual impression of being greater. In short, it is impossible, and very foolish for anyone to believe, that when human nature is eagerly pressing toward some accomplishment, there is some deterrent to stop it by force of law or by any other threat.

[46] "Therefore, we must neither choose inferior policies by trusting in the death penalty as a safeguard nor make it hopeless for rebels to have any possibility of repenting and atoning for the mistake as soon as possible. Bear in mind that now, if some city in revolt realized that it was not going to prevail, it would come to terms while still able to repay the expenses and pay tribute in the future. In the other case, do you think any city would not prepare better than at present and hold out to the last in a siege, if to submit after a delay or right away meant the same thing? As for us, how is it not harmful to settle down to a siege and spend money because there is no surrender, and to take over a ruined city if we do take it and lose it as a future source of revenue? It is this that supplies us with strength against enemies. So we should not act as judges and harm ourselves by being strict toward sinners but should instead consider ways to use moderate punishment that will preserve the cities' strength in money matters for our use, and we should favor basing our security on the vigilance of our actions, not on the threat of our laws. Since our current practice is the reverse, we think that if we subdue free people ruled by force who understandably revolt in the cause of autonomy, they must be made to pay terribly. But we should not go to extremes in punishing free men when they are in revolt, we should go to extremes in watching them before they revolt and in taking precautions so that they never even approach such an idea, and when we have put down revolts, we should lay the blame on the smallest possible number.

[47] "And here too, bear in mind how misguided you would be by following Kleon. At present the common people in every city are friendly toward you and either do not join the oligarchs in revolt or, if they are forced to, they remain hostile to the rebels, and when a city becomes your opponent, you go to war with most of its people as your ally. But if you

destroy the people of Mytilene, who did not take part in the revolt and voluntarily surrendered the city after they got themselves arms, in the first
place you will be committing injustice by killing your benefactors, and in
the second place you will bring about what the men in power want most;
for when they start a revolt they will immediately have the people as an
ally, because you will already have demonstrated that the same penalty
applies without distinction to the guilty and to the innocent. Even if they
were guilty, you have to pretend they were not, so that your one remaining
ally does not become an enemy. And I consider this act of voluntarily submitting to injustice much more useful for the security of the empire than
justly destroying those you should not. Here, Kleon's punishment in
which justice and expediency are one is exposed as an impossible combination of both at the same time.

[48] "Understanding that this is the better course, and giving no priority to pity or evenhandedness, whose influence I would be the first to disallow, but simply on the basis of what has been advised, follow me by
judging at leisure the Mytileneans Paches sent over as the guilty ones, and
let the rest go on living. For this is both good for the future and fearsome
to your opponents right now; whoever plans well has a stronger position
against enemies than by attacking with actions of senseless force."

[49] Diodotos spoke in this way. And after these proposals were made
opposing one another with very even strength, the Athenians clashed in
their opinions after all, and in the show of hands the resolutions were
nearly equal, but that of Diodotos prevailed. They immediately sent off
another trireme in great haste, lest they find the city destroyed because the
first had already arrived; it was about a day and a night ahead. With the
Mytilenean envoys providing wine and barley for the ship and making
great promises if they arrived in time, the degree of zeal was so high during
the voyage that they ate barley kneaded with wine and oil as they rowed,
and while some rowed others slept in turns, and since by luck there was no
opposing wind, and the first ship was sailing without urgency for its horrible business while this one was pressing on as described, the one ship
arrived just far enough ahead that Paches had read the decree and was
about to carry out what had been decided, and the ship following it landed
and prevented the killings. Mytilene's danger came this close.

3.47. Connor 1984, pp. 87–88 argues that "the facts, as Thucydides reports them
in [Book 3] chapter 27, contradict Diodotos" [when he claims that the common
people took no part in the revolt]. But Thucydides—possibly deliberately—has
not provided enough "facts" to support decisively either Diodotos' version or
Kleon's in 3.39.

[50] On Kleon's motion, the Athenians killed those Paches had sent back as especially responsible for the revolt (these were slightly more than a thousand), and they tore down the walls of Mytilene and took over its ships. Later on, instead of imposing tribute on the Mytileneans, they divided the land, except for Methymna, into three thousand portions, selecting three hundred as sacred to the gods and sending out their own citizens to the rest as cleruchs according to lot. The Lesbians themselves worked the land after being assigned a payment to them in silver, two minas a year for each allotment. The Athenians also took over all towns that the Mytileneans had ruled on the mainland, and in the future they were subjects of Athens. This was how things turned out regarding Lesbos.

[51] In the same summer after the capture of Lesbos, the Athenians made an expedition under the command of Nikias son of Nikeratos against the island of Minoa, which lies off Megara and which the Megarians used as a fort after they had built towers there. Nikias wanted the Athenians to have their blockade at that closer location, not from Boudoron and Salamis, both to keep the Peloponnesians from secretly sailing out of the area either in triremes, as had actually happened previously, or by sending out privateers, and at the same time so that nothing would come in to the Megarians by sea. Accordingly, after he had first used siege equipment from the sea to capture two towers projecting from the side facing Nisaia and freed the entrance to the space between the island and the mainland, he also walled off the side facing the mainland, where the island had a means of reinforcement by a bridge across the shallow water, since the mainland is not far away. Since they accomplished this in a few days, he later left a fort and garrison on the island itself and departed with his forces.

[52] And around the same time in this summer, the Plataians, with no more food and unable to hold out in the siege, came to terms with the Peloponnesians in the following way. The enemy attacked their wall, and

3.50. The number of Mytileneans put to death has been questioned, cf. *HCT* II, Hornblower 1991, and Rhodes 1994 *ad* 3.50.1, also Connor 1984, p. 87. On the cleruchs at Lesbos, see Figueira 1991, especially pp. 8–11, 251–53; he argues convincingly, against most previous scholarship, that cleruchies did not function as Athenian garrisons (see especially pp. 172–74).

3.51. See especially *HCT* II *ad* 3.51 for both the coastal topography of Megara and the remarkably awkward and obscure language of this chapter. This is Thucydides' first mention of Nikias (see Hornblower 1991 *ad* 2.85.5), now in mid-career but most fully known by Thucydides' extensive references in books 4–7. What had "happened previously" was the surprise attack on the Peiraeus, see 2.93.

they were unable to defend themselves. The Lacedaemonian commander, aware of their weakness, had no wish to take them by force (he had been told not to by Sparta, so that if there was ever a treaty with the Athenians, and they agreed that all the places that each side occupied by fighting be returned, Plataia would not be subject to return, on the grounds that they had come over of their own accord) but sent them a herald saying that if they were willing to give up the city to the Lacedaemonians of their own accord and accept them as judges, they would punish the guilty but no one illegally. The herald said only this much, but the Plataians, now in the furthest stage of weakness, surrendered the city. The Peloponnesians fed them for several days until the judges from Lacedaemon, five in number, were present. On their arrival, no accusation was brought forward, but they summoned the Plataians and asked just this, whether in the present war they had done any service to the Lacedaemonians and their allies. They replied after requesting to speak at greater length and making Astymachos son of Asopolaos and Lakon son of Aeimnestos, the Lacedaemonian proxenos, their representatives. They came forward and spoke as follows:

[53] "When we surrendered our city, Lacedaemonians, we thought, because we trusted you, that we would undergo no such trial as this but a more normal one, and we supposed, because we had consented to face no other judges, the way we do now, that we would receive the most certain justice. But now we fear that we have been wrong on both counts. For we have reason to suspect that the trial involves the most terrible of all possibilities, and that you will not prove impartial, and we infer this both because no accusation was brought against us first so that we could answer it, but instead we were the ones who asked to speak, and because the question is a limited one, so that a truthful one brings adverse consequences yet a false answer can be refuted. We are forced from every direction into a desperate position, and it seems safer to say something in our danger. For in our situation, words left unsaid would lead to the reproach that if spoken they would have been our salvation. But persuasion is a difficulty added to the others we have. If we were unknown to one another, we might have benefited by bringing in additional evidence of which you were

3.52. The first hint that the Spartan liberators might consider a negotiated settlement; Hornblower 1991 *ad* 3.52.2 suspects Thucydidean hindsight. Badian 1993, pp. 109–123 discusses the status of Plataia, with pronounced skepticism about Thucydides' objectivity and accuracy.

3.53–67. On the Plataian debate, see Macleod 1977 and Debnar 1996; I am grateful to Professor Debnar for letting me see this article before publication.

unaware; as it is, everything said will be what you know, and our fear is not that you, having already condemned us for being inferior to you in merit, are making this the charge, but that we are being made to face a predetermined judgment to gratify others.

[54] "Nevertheless, by bringing forward what justification we have both concerning the quarrel with the Thebans and in relation to you and the other Hellenes, we will offer a reminder of our good deeds and attempt to persuade you. We state, in response to the limited question, whether we have done any service for the Lacedaemonians and their allies in this war, that if you ask us as enemies you were not wronged if you received no benefits, but that if you consider us friends it is you rather who are in the wrong, since it is you who campaigned against us. During the peace and against the Mede, we were upright in our actions; we were not the first peace-breakers now, in the past we were the only Boiotians to join the attack for Hellenic freedom. We even fought at Artemision, although we are landsmen, and in the battle taking place in our own land we stood by you and Pausanias, and whatever further dangers confronted the Hellenes at that time, we shared in all of them beyond our strength, and to help you in particular, Lacedaemonians, at just that time after the earthquake when fear most overwhelmed Sparta because of the helots' secession to Ithome, we sent a third of our own men. These are things that should not be lost from memory.

[55] "In past events of the highest importance, it was thus that we resolved to act, yet later we became enemies. You are to blame; when we asked for an alliance at the time the Thebans were pressing us hard, you sent us away and told us to turn to the Athenians because they were nearby, whereas you lived far away. Nevertheless, you neither have encountered nor will encounter any incorrectness on our part during the war. And if we were not willing to desert the Athenians at your bidding, we did not do wrong. For it was they who helped us against the Thebans when you held back, and it was not honorable now to betray them, especially when there had been good treatment, alliance at our own request, and a share of their citizenship, but it was right to follow their orders readily. And wherever the leadership on either side takes its allies, the followers are not to blame if some wrong was done, but those who direct them on an improper course.

[56] "While the Thebans have committed many other wrongs against us, you have your own knowledge of the last one, which is the very reason we are reduced to this condition. When they were seizing our city during peace, and moreover in a sacred period, we retaliated rightfully in accor-

dance with the rule observed by all, that defense against an attacking enemy is lawful. And we should not be harmed now on their account. For if you define justice by your immediate advantage along with their hostility, you will not appear true judges of what is right but minions of expediency instead. And yet if the Thebans seem useful to you now, we and the other Hellenes were much more so at a time when you were in greater danger. For now you are in yourselves formidable to others on the attack, but in that crisis, when the barbarian was threatening to enslave all, these Thebans were with him.

"It is just to offset our present error, if we have actually committed one, with our zeal at that time, and you will see that it was greater compared with smaller, and also in circumstances where it was rare for Hellenic courage to resist the power of Xerxes, and greater praise than now was given to those who did not respond to the invasion by acting safely in their own interests but were willing to dare the noblest actions in the midst of danger. We who were among these and held in the highest honor now fear that we will be destroyed by the same conduct, by choosing the Athenians out of justice rather than yourselves for gain. And yet consistency ought to be prominent when you make comparable decisions about comparable situations, and you ought to believe that there is no expediency except when what is perhaps to your immediate advantage is also established by continuing to keep firm your gratitude for the courage of those who were good allies.

[57] "And reflect further that at present you are regarded by most Hellenes as an example of upright qualities; but if you reach a decision about us that is not right (for you will not be judging this case in obscurity, men of renown judging us, ourselves not contemptible), beware of their abhorrence that an unseemly decision about good men was upheld by you, their betters, and that spoils from us, benefactors of Hellas, were dedicated in the national shrines. And it will seem monstrous for the Lacedaemonians to destroy Plataia, that your father recorded the city on the tripod at Delphi for its bravery while you will erase it in its entirety from Hellenic civilization for the sake of the Thebans. To these very depths of misfortune have we fallen, ruined after Persian victories and now ranked below Thebans among those you cherish and subjected to two extreme ordeals, first destruction by famine if we did not surrender our city and now judgment over life and death. We Plataians, ardent for Hellas beyond our power, have been thrust aside by all, deserted and unprotected; none of our former allies will help, and, Lacedaemonians, we fear that you, our only hope, may not be relied on.

[58] "Even so, we do beg you, for the sake of the gods who once made us allies and our courage on behalf of the Hellenes, be swayed and relent wherever the Thebans have prevailed on you, ask them to grant that you not kill those you should not, a concession to you in return, and see yourselves thanked for virtuous instead of disgraceful conduct. Do not let your gratification of others make you share in wickedness. The brief action of destroying our lives brings the laborious one of wiping out the infamy; for we are not foes whom you will punish rightly but friends, made enemies by necessity. And so, if you pardon our lives, you would be righteous in your decision, remembering that we became your prisoners voluntarily with hands outstretched, such men as are not killed under Hellenic law, and that beyond that we were always benefactors. See where your fathers lie, killed by the Medes and buried in our land, whom we honored publicly every year with raiment and the other customary gifts, offering also first fruits of all our land produced with best wishes from a friendly country, as allies to our old comrades in arms. You would be doing the opposite if you decide wrongly. Just consider: Pausanias buried them thinking that he was placing them in a friendly land and among friends as well; but if you kill us and make the country of Plataia Theban, what is this but to abandon your ancestors and kinsmen in hostile territory among their murderers, deprived of the honors they now enjoy? And you will enslave the land in which the Hellenes gained freedom, leave desolate the shrines of the gods to whom they prayed before they defeated the Medes, and take away the ancestral sacrifices by those who founded and established them

[59] "There is no glory for you there, Lacedaemonians, neither in offending against the common laws of the Hellenes and against your ancestors nor in destroying us your benefactors for the sake of another people's hatred without suffering wrong yourselves, but in sparing us and letting your thoughts be softened by awareness of pity and restraint, looking not only at the horror of what we are to suffer but at the sort of men who would suffer and at the unpredictability of misfortunes that may some day descend even on the undeserving. As is right for us and as our need urges, we beg you, calling aloud on the gods whose altars we share and who are those of all Hellas that we may be heard, invoking the oaths your fathers swore we supplicate you on your ancestral tombs, we appeal to the departed that we not fall under the Thebans, that their best friends not be handed over to their worst enemies, and recall for them now, on the day when we risk the most terrible fate, that day when together we accomplished the most glorious deeds. But as must be and is also hardest for men in our situation, ending our speech, since the danger to our lives is there

too, we will stop now by saying that we did not surrender our city to the Thebans, we would have chosen well before that the extreme disgrace of death by starvation, it was you we trusted and approached, and what is just, if we do not persuade you, is to restore us to the same circumstances and let us make our own choice of the risks involved. And at the same time we charge you: do not let the Plataians, the most zealous on behalf of the Hellenes, be given up to the Thebans, our worst enemies, from your hands, Lacedaemonians, when we were your trusting suppliants, but become our saviors, and do not in freeing the other Hellenes destroy us utterly."

[60] The Plataians spoke in this way. But now the Thebans, fearing that the Lacedaemonians would make some concession in response to their speech, came up and said that they also wanted to speak, since contrary to their understanding the others had been allowed a longer speech than an answer to the question. When the Lacedaemonians assented, they spoke as follows.

[61] "We would not have requested to make a speech if they had been brief themselves in answering the question and had they not directed an accusation against us, defended themselves at length over matters outside the issue as well as against charges never made, and praised what no one has blamed. But now we have to answer the case against ourselves and refute theirs, so that neither our dishonor nor the glory of their deeds will help them, and you will hear the truth about both and decide.

"We first came into conflict with them because, after we had founded Plataia at a later time than the rest of Boiotia, along with other places we held after driving out a mixture of peoples, these men did not see fit to accept our leadership, as had originally been arranged, but broke away from the other Boiotians in disregard of their ancestry, and when they were constrained they went over to the Athenians. And in association with them they did us much harm, for which they also suffered in return.

[62] "They also claim that when the barbarian attacked Hellas they were the only Boiotians who did not medize, and they use this above all to glorify themselves and abuse us. We claim that while they did not medize, simply because the Athenians did not, then by the same principle they were the only Boiotians to atticize when the Athenians attacked the Hellenes. Then again, consider the government under which each of us took these actions. For in our case, as it happened, the city was at that time run neither by an oligarchy providing equality nor by a democracy; it was that government most opposed to law and to all that is moderate, also closest to tyranny, that held power: domination by a few men. Hoping to hold still

greater personal power if the cause of the Mede prevailed, these kept the people down by force and invited him in. And yet the city as a whole was not independent when it took these action, and neither should it be reproached for wrongs it committed when lacking a constitution. In any case, after the Mede withdrew, and the city regained its constitution, this is what must be considered: when the Athenians subsequently attacked the rest of the Hellenes, attempted to subjugate our country, and already held most of it because of faction, did we not liberate Boiotia by fighting at Koroneia and beating them and are we not now helping zealously to liberate the others, supplying cavalry as well as larger forces than any other ally?

[63] "This much we say in our defense against medism. On the other hand, we will attempt to show that it is you who did the Hellenes greater wrong and are more deserving of full punishment. It was for protection against us, you say, that you became allies and citizens of Athens. In that case, should you not simply have called them in where we were involved instead of joining them in attacking others, which was entirely possible for you if you were actually led anywhere by the Athenians against your will, since you already had an alliance with these very Lacedaemonians against the Mede, which you yourself mention as your main excuse? It was certainly adequate to keep us away from you and, the most important point, to give you security in planning your course. But voluntarily, and not under compulsion now, you chose in favor of Athens. And you say that it would have been shameful to betray your benefactors; yes, but far more shameful and unjust the greater betrayal of all the Hellenes, sworn allies, rather than merely the Athenians, the enslavers of Hellas whereas the others were its liberators. And the way you repaid the Athenians was neither in due proportion nor free of disgrace. For you claim that you called them in because you were being wronged, but you became their accomplices when they were wronging others. And yet it is declining to repay favors in kind that is shameful, not declining when favors are just obligations but their repayment leads to injustice.

[64] "Clearly, then, it was not for the sake of the Hellenes that you alone did not medize, it was because the Athenians did not, and you did not because you wanted to be on their side and opposed to the others. And now

---

3.64–67. The first sentence of 3.64 is problematic because the balancing phrase "opposed to the others" is vague: the other Boiotians (omitted from the "you alone" phrase above)? The other Greeks who medized? In making the Plataians compulsively contrary as well as pro–Athenian the Thebans almost imply that it was unpatriotic *not* to medize. More overtly, they use the dubious yet successful argument throughout that the consideration of atticism overrides medism, cf. Cogan

you expect to benefit from your good behavior when this was at the behest of others. But this is unreasonable; since you chose the Athenians, share the risks with them. Do not plead the alliance sworn to in the past as something that should save you now. You deserted the alliance, and in violation of it you did not hinder but assisted in the enslavement of the Aiginetans and other members, and that not unwillingly, under the same constitution you have maintained until now, and without being forced as we were. And the final proposal before you were besieged, for you to be left in peace on condition you helped neither side, you rejected. So who would be more justly hated by all the Hellenes than you who used the pretext of upright conduct toward their ruin? You have demonstrated that what once gave you the nobility you claim was not ingrained, while what your nature long desired has been exposed as the truth; for you went along with the Athenians when

---

1981, 69–72. Atticize is probably not a Theban (or Thucydidean) coinage, see Hornblower 1991 *ad* 3.62.2. In 3.65–66, the tone of the Thebans becomes noticeably less aggressive. They are not only vulnerable to charges of breaking the peace but risk the recoil on themselves of their argument in 62 (cf. Hornblower *ad* 3.62.3 and 3.65.1), and the concept of "good" Plataians is a very sudden departure. *HCT* II *ad* 3 66.3 comments that murder of the prisoners is the best Theban case, "but . . . it still does not take up much of their argument—for it would not appeal to the Spartans." Here we have a notable opportunity to compare the author's narrative (2.2–5) with an account in a speech. There are enough verbal similarities to indicate authorial responsibility for the latter passage (although the actual Theban speech must have included such an account) and enough similarities in content to spotlight the discrepancies: the Thebans exaggerate initial Plataian acceptance of their proposal and, even while making the broken promise a separate "crime," drop the mention of an oath (possibly because oaths are so important an element in the Plataian speech). "The leaders break the law": a mocking paraphrase of the Plataians in 3.55. "Double punishment": cf. 1.86. "Adequate punishment": the argument is both sophistic (*HCT* II *ad* 3.67.5) and somewhat obscure. The Plataians did represent themselves as men who called for quarter (3.58) and imply that their status is effectively unchanged; the Thebans would apparently reverse this by contrasting the Plataians with their own men who (although they did surrender unconditionally) never received a trial. See Hornblower 1991 *ad* 3.67.5–6 for the heavy Theban emphasis on "law." The Theban speech, even without its sarcasm, would inevitably have alienated the reader, both because of the circumstances, and because the debate follows the one over Mytilene; Debnar 1996 points out numerous shortcomings. Yet Thucydides shows that the Thebans did have a case against the Plataians, and his real condemnation is of the Spartans, who were uninterested in that case. The final Theban sentence, however, leads into this by flattering the Spartans that their single-question procedure has set new standards of justice.

they took the unjust road. We therefore declare that this was the character of our involuntary medism and your voluntary atticism.

[65] "As for the last wrong you claim to have suffered, because we lawlessly entered your city during peace and at a time of religious festival, we do not think that even here we were more at fault than you. If we on our own initiative entered your city as combatants and plundered your land, we did wrong; but if the foremost among you by wealth and birth, wishing both to rid you of the alien alliance and to restore you to the ancestral traditions of Boiotia, invited us of their own accord, how did we do wrong? After all, the leaders break the law, not their followers. But they did not break the law, in our judgment, any more than we did. Just as much citizens as yourselves and with more at stake, opening up their own walls and admitting us with friendly, not hostile intentions, they wanted to keep your worst elements from becoming still worse and let the better elements have their due, bringing moderation to your policies, not depriving the city of your persons, but reconciling you with your kinsmen, making you enemies of no one but at peace with all.

[66] "Here is proof that we were not behaving in hostile fashion: we harmed no one and announced that anyone wishing to live under the ancestral government of Boiotia should join us. At first you kept quiet after gladly coming up and making an agreement, but what you did later when you noticed how few we were, even if it appeared that we were doing something not quite correct in entering without the consent of your common people, was not to repay us in kind by taking no drastic action and persuading us to leave, but when you attacked in violation of the agreement, we are not so much troubled about those you killed in the fighting (for their fate was not altogether unwarranted), but those who stretched out their hands, whom you took prisoner and later promised us you would not kill, and you lawlessly slaughtered them, how did you not treat them atrociously? And then, after committing three crimes in quick succession, the broken agreement, the later execution of the men, and the betrayal of the promise to us about not killing them if we did not harm you through your property in the country, you still claim that we are the lawbreakers and expect to escape punishment yourselves. No, if the men here indeed judge with righteousness, you will be punished for each and all.

[67] "Lacedaemonians, our reason for dealing with all these matters, for both your sake and ours, is this, for you to know that you condemn these men justly and we that our vengeance has been sanctioned still further. And do not be softened on hearing about past virtues, whatever there actually were, which should save those who are being wronged but mean dou-

ble punishment for those acting shamefully, because it was not innate behavior for them to sin. Nor let them benefit by wails and lamentation or by calling aloud over the tombs of your fathers and their own isolation. For in answer we point to the far more terrible suffering of our own youth whom these men slaughtered, and whose fathers, whether they died at Koroneia bringing Boiotia over to you or have been left as old men with isolation in their homes, much more justly supplicate you for the punishment of these men. And whoever suffers at all improperly has a better claim to receive pity, but whoever like these suffers justly is, on the contrary, fit to rejoice over. Their isolation now is also of their own making; for by their own choice they rejected the better allies. They acted lawlessly without previous injury by us, but judging by hatred rather than by right, and without repaying us now with adequate punishment. For they will suffer under law, not stretching out their hands on the battlefield, as they tell it, but after an agreement to give themselves up for trial.

"Uphold the law of Hellas, then, which they have broken, Lacedaemonians, and repay us, victims of this illegality, by just reward for the zeal we have shown, do not let us be thrust from our relationship with you by their words, but show the Hellenes that the contests you set before them involve not words but actions, of which a brief recital suffices when they are good ones, while artfully adorned speeches serve as screens for wrongs committed. But if leading powers act as you are doing now and come straight to the point with all alike when forming resolutions, men will hardly look for fine words in connection with their unjust actions."

[68] The Thebans spoke in this way. And the Lacedaemonian judges, who thought that the question as to whether they had received any service from the Plataians during the war would be a rightful one for them, because they had in former times, to be sure, requested them to stay inactive in accordance with the old treaty of Pausanias after the Persian war, also when they later offered them, before the siege, the chance to be neutral on those same terms, and who supposed that, since the others did not accept, they themselves, released from treaty obligations by the very justice of their intentions, had suffered wrong at their hands, again brought them in one by one and asked them the same question, whether they had done the Lacedaemonians and their allies any service during the war, taking each one out and executing him when he said that he had not, and they made no exceptions. They killed no fewer than two hundred of the Plataians themselves and twenty-five Athenians who were with them in the siege; they enslaved the women. For about a year they made occupation of the city available to some Megarians driven out by faction and to any Plataians who

had survived as their collaborators. Later, after destroying the whole city to the ground right from its foundations, next to the Hera sanctuary they built a hostel two hundred feet on each side with upper and lower rooms around its circuit, using the roofs and doors of the Plataians, with the rest of the material, bronze and iron, within the walls they fashioned couches and dedicated them to Hera, and they built a hundred-foot stone temple for her. Confiscating the land, they rented it out for ten-year periods, and Thebans cultivated it. In virtually every respect, it was on account of the Thebans that the Lacedaemonians were as unfeeling as they were about the Plataians, since they thought the Thebans were useful to them in the war which had recently broken out. This was how matters ended for Plataia, in the ninety-third year after it became the ally of Athens.

[69] As for the forty Peloponnesian ships that had gone to help Lesbos and were at that time in flight across the sea with the Athenians in pursuit, at Kyllene, after they were caught by a storm off Crete and driven to the Peloponnesos in scattered fashion as a result, they found thirteen Leukadian and Ambraciot triremes and Brasidas son of Tellis, who had just arrived as an advisor to Alkidas. Since the Lacedaemonians had failed at Lesbos, they wanted to enlarge their fleet and sail to Corcyra, where there was a civil war, in order to get there first while the Athenians had only twelve ships at Naupaktos and before a larger fleet came from Athens to reinforce them. Brasidas and Alkidas began making preparations for this.

[70] And this Corcyrean civil war occurred after the prisoners from the sea battles over Epidamnos arrived following their release by the Corinthians, supposedly on the pledge of eight hundred talents by their proxenoi, in actuality because they had been suborned to win over Corcyra. By soliciting each citizen, these men intrigued to cause the city's defection from Athens. When an Athenian ship and a Corinthian ship both arrived with envoys, the Corcyreans held a discussion and voted to be Athenian allies according to their agreement, yet friends of the Peloponnesians just as before. These same men, since Peithias was voluntary proxenos of Athens and leader of the common people, now brought him to trial, saying that he was enslaving Corcyra to Athens. On his acquittal, he in turn brought

3.68. The physical details of the reuse of the site, especially the cannibalization of material, serve as a sad epilogue to the technical ingenuity displayed by the Plataians (as well as the Thebans; a Boiotian trait, cf. 4.100?) and extensively described by Thucydides on three separate occasions (2.3, 2.75–76, 3.20).

3.70. "The prisoners from the sea battles": see 1.55. "Fine of one stater": for the uncertainty about this amount, see *HCT* II and Hornblower 1991 *ad* 3.70.4.

their five richest men to trial, alleging that they made a practice of cutting vine-poles in the sanctuaries of Zeus and Alkinoos; a fine of one stater was imposed for each vine-pole. When they were convicted and, because of the size of the fine, seated themselves in the sanctuaries as suppliants in order to pay by installments, Peithias, who happened to be a member of the council, convinced it to enforce the law. After they were held to the law and also learned that Peithias, as long as he was still on the council, intended to persuade the people to have the same friends and enemies as Athens, these men banded together, took daggers, and suddenly entered the council and killed Peithias as well as about sixty others, both councillors and private citizens; some who shared Peithias' views, but only a few, escaped to the Athenian trireme, which was still there.

[71] After they had committed this deed and called the Corcyreans to an assembly, they said that what had happened was for the best and the Corcyreans would now be at the farthest remove from enslavement to the Athenians, and henceforth they were to receive neither side in peace except for single ships, treating any larger number as hostile. After this speech, they forced ratification of their proposal. They also sent envoys to Athens immediately to provide a self-serving explanation of what had been done and to persuade refugees there not to engage in any controversial activities, so that there would not be countermeasures. [72] On their arrival, the Athenians arrested the envoys as revolutionaries, along with anyone influenced by them, and deposited them on Aigina. Meanwhile, when a Corinthian trireme arrived with Lacedaemonian envoys, the Corcyreans in power attacked the democrats and defeated them in a battle. When night came, the democrats took refuge on the acropolis and the higher parts of the city and settled there in a body, and they held the Hyllaic harbor; the others seized the agora, which was where most of them lived, and the harbor next to it facing the mainland. [73] On the following day there were a few skirmishes, and both sides sent around the countryside inviting the slaves to join them and promising them freedom; most household slaves sided with the democrats, while eight hundred mercenaries from the mainland reinforced their opponents.

[74] After a day passed, there was fighting again, and the democrats won through their advantages of strong position and numbers, and the women also assisted them actively by throwing tiles from the houses and facing the turmoil with a boldness beyond their sex. After a rout developed late in the afternoon, for fear that the democrats at a single blow would not only attack and capture the arsenal but also slaughter them, the oligarchs set fire to the houses surrounding the agora and to the apartment buildings

to keep them from advancing, sparing neither their own nor others' houses, so that much merchandise was burned up, and the city risked total destruction if a wind had come up to carry the flames in that direction. Now, after they stopped fighting and kept quiet on both sides, they spent the night on guard, the Corinthian ship stole out to sea after the victory of the democrats, and most of the mercenaries secretly crossed over to the mainland.

[75] The next day Nikostratos son of Dieitrephes, an Athenian general, came to help from Naupaktos with twelve ships and five hundred Messenian hoplites. He arranged a settlement and persuaded them into a mutual agreement that they try the ten men most responsible (who immediately fled trial), that the rest make a truce and live together, and that they deal with the Athenians by having the same friends and enemies. After arranging this, he was about to sail away, but the leading democrats persuaded him to leave five of his ships with them, so that their opponents would be less inclined to make trouble, and they would man the same number of their own ships to sail with him. After he agreed, they enlisted their opponents for the ships. Fearing that they might be sent to Athens, these men took up suppliants' positions in the sanctuary of the Dioskouroi. Nikostratos tried to raise them up and reassure them. After he failed to persuade them, the democrats, using this excuse to arm themselves, that because of their mistrust of embarking they had no wholesome intentions, removed the weapons from their houses and would have killed some they encountered if Nikostratos had not stopped them. When the rest saw what was happening, they sat in the sanctuary of Hera as suppliants; there were no fewer than four hundred. Fearing that they would do something drastic, the democrats employed persuasion to raise them up and conveyed them to the island in front of the temple of Hera, and provisions were sent to them there.

[76] During this stage of the civil war, four or five days after the men were sent to the island, the Peloponnesian ships that had been at anchor since the voyage from Ionia arrived from Kyllene, numbering fifty-three; in command was Alkidas just as before, and Brasidas was on board as his advisor. After anchoring at Sybota, a harbor on the mainland, they sailed into Corcyra at dawn. [77] The democrats, in great confusion and frightened by both the events in the city and the arrival of the ships, got sixty ships ready all at once and sent them against the enemy whenever they

3.75. On the activities of Nikostratos, see the important note in Hornblower 1991 *ad* 3.75.2

were manned, although the Athenians advised them to let themselves sail out first and to come up behind them later with all their ships at the same time. When their scattered ships approached the enemy, two immediately deserted; on others the crews were fighting among themselves; and there was no organization in anything they did. Seeing their disarray, the Peloponnesians went into formation with twenty of their ships against the Corcyreans and the rest against the twelve Athenian ships, two of which were the Salaminia and the Paralos.

[78] While the Corcyreans made a wretched fragmented attack and were in difficulty in their area, the Athenians, fearing superior numbers and a flank attack, did not attack the center of the ships concentrated against them but fell on the wing and sank one ship. After this they sailed around the enemy, who had formed a circle, and tried to throw them into confusion. The Peloponnesians facing the Corcyreans noticed this and came to the rescue, afraid that the same thing would happen as at Naupaktos; gathering all their ships into a single formation, they advanced against the Athenians. These now backed water, retreating and at the same time wanting the Corcyreans to get away first as well as they could while they themselves were withdrawing at their leisure and the enemy was occupied with them. So there was this sort of sea battle, lasting till sunset. [79] And the Corcyreans, afraid that their victorious opponents would sail against the city, pick up the men from the island, or take other decisive action, brought the men back from the island to the sanctuary of Hera and kept the city under guard. But the enemy, even though they had won the sea battle, did not venture an attack on the city but sailed away with thirteen captured Corcyrean ships to the same place on the mainland where they had set out. The next day they were no more willing to sail against the city, even when its people were in complete disorder and panic and although Brasidas is said to have advised this to Alkidas, but without having an equal voice, and instead disembarked at the promontory of Leukimme and plundered the countryside.

[80] During this time the Corcyrean democrats, who were terrified that the ships would sail against them, had a parley with the suppliants and the

---

3.77–81. The account, especially in 3.78, is extremely flattering to Athenian seamanship (for possible bias, see Hornblower 1991 *ad* 3.71.1); the Corcyrean navy is impressive only in numbers, mocking Corcyrean claims in book 1 (as for the Peloponnesians, it would be hard to find more indications of caution packed into a single sentence than in "accordingly . . . to be seen sailing around").

3.78. "As at Naupaktos": see 2.83–84.

others over some way to save the city and persuaded some of them to board the ships; they even launched thirty. The Peloponnesians ravaged the land until midday and then sailed away. And toward night they learned through torch signals from Leukas that sixty Athenian ships were approaching, which the Athenians had sent, under the command of Eurymedon son of Thoukles, when they found out about the civil war and that the ships with Alkidas were going to sail to Corcyra. [81] Accordingly, the Peloponnesians made a hurried voyage home in the dark, keeping close to the shore, and arrived after dragging their ships across the isthmus of Leukas to avoid being seen sailing around. When the Corcyreans realized that the Athenian ships were arriving and the Peloponnesian ships leaving, they brought in the Messenians, who had previously been outside the city, gave the ships that they had manned instructions to sail around into the Hyllaic harbor, and while the ships were coming around they killed any of their enemies they caught. Then they took off the ships all the men they had persuaded to embark and did away with them, and going into the sanctuary of Hera, they persuaded about fifty of the suppliants to stand trial and condemned them all to death. As for the majority, the entire number of suppliants who had refused to stand trial, when they saw what was happening, they killed each other right in the sanctuary, and some hanged themselves from trees, but any way they could they ended their lives. For the seven days that Eurymedon stayed there after his arrival, the Corcyreans butchered those fellow-citizens they regarded as enemies, charging them with putting down the democracy, but some also died because of personal hatred and others at the hands of those who owed them money. Every form of death prevailed, and whatever is likely in such situations happened—and still worse. Fathers killed sons, men were dragged from the sanctuaries and killed beside them, and some were even walled up in the sanctuary of Dionysos and died there.

[82] With this savagery, the civil war progressed, and it seemed all the more savage because it was the first, while later the rest of Hellas, almost without exception, was also in turmoil, with rival efforts everywhere by

---

3.82–83. See especially Macleod 1979.
3.82. Probably "it was the first" rather than "among the first," but cf. Connor 1984, p. 103, n. 61. On the relationship between war and civil war, see especially Cogan 1981, pp. 149–54 and Loraux 1986b. "Inverted the usual": on the complexities of interpreting this sentence, cf. especially Hogan 1980, pp. 139–40, also Wilson 1982a, pp. 18–20, Loraux 1986b, pp. 103–24, and Swain 1993, pp. 36–38. "Deliberation . . . dereliction": the Greek is strained, but even more so if we translate

the popular leaders to bring in the Athenians and the oligarchs, the Lacedaemonians. In peacetime they had neither the pretext nor the willingness to call them in, but during war, with alliances available to both factions for damaging their opponents and at the same time strengthening themselves, occasions for bringing in outsiders were readily found by those wishing to make any change in government. And during the civil wars the cities suffered many cruelties that occur and will always occur as long as men have the same nature, sometimes more terribly and sometimes less, varying in their forms as each change of fortune dictates. For in peace and good circumstances, both states and individuals have better inclinations through not falling into involuntary necessities; but war, stripping away the easy access to daily needs, is a violent teacher and brings most men's passions into line with the present situations.

So the condition of the cities was civil war, and where it came later, awareness of earlier events pushed to extremes the revolution in thinking, both in extraordinarily ingenious attempts to seize power and in outlandish retaliations. And in self-justification men inverted the usual verbal evaluations of actions. Irrational recklessness was now considered courageous commitment, hesitation while looking to the future was high-styled cowardice, moderation was a cover for lack of manhood, and circumspection meant inaction, while senseless anger now helped to define a true man, and deliberation for security was a specious excuse for dereliction. The man of violent temper was always credible, anyone opposing him was suspect. The intriguer who succeeded was intelligent, anyone who detected a plot was still more clever, but a man who made provisions to avoid both alternatives was undermining his party and letting the opposition terrorize him. Quite simply, one was praised for outracing everyone else to commit a crime—and for encouraging a crime by someone who had never before considered one.

---

alternatively, "plotting in security (i.e., without being threatened) was a legitimate form of self-defense"; admittedly this would add a new idea rather than near repetition of "hesitation while looking." "As a rule, men": this aphoristic sentence is too clever by half and has been a source of puzzlement since antiquity. Apparently, the equation of brains with unscrupulousness is so prevalent as to imply occasionally the corollary that simpletons are virtuous; in a culture valuing intellectual over moral qualities, the compliment is necessarily backhanded, as both deserving and undeserving recipients are well aware. "Most men prefer to be called clever knaves rather than honest fools" (cf. Marchant 1918, p. 192) is not only impossible without emendation but leaves the latter part of the sentence meaningless.

Kinship became alien compared with party affiliation, because the latter led to drastic action with less hesitation. For party meetings did not take place to use the benefits of existing laws, but to find any advantage in breaking them. They strengthened their trust in one another less by religious law than by association in committing some illegal act. Men responded to reasonable words from their opponents with defensive actions, if they had the advantage, and not with magnanimity. Revenge mattered more than not being harmed in the first place. And if there were actually reconciliations under oath, they occurred because of both sides' lack of alternatives and lasted only as long as neither found some other source of power. The one who first recovered his confidence at the right moment, when he saw the other off guard, enjoyed vengeance more in a situation of trust than if accomplished openly; the element of safety was an asset, and because of prevailing through deception he also won the prize for intelligence. As a rule, men are more easily called clever when they are scoundrels than virtuous when ignorant—and are as ashamed of the second description as they are exultant in the first.

All this was caused by leadership based on greed and ambition and led in turn to fanaticism once men were committed to the power struggle. For the leading men in the cities, through their emphasis on an attractive slogan for each side—political equality for the masses, the moderation of aristocracy—treated as their prize the public interest to which they paid lip service and, competing by every means to get the better of one another, boldly committed atrocities and proceeded to still worse acts of revenge, stopping at limits set by neither justice nor the city's interest but by the gratification of their parties at every stage, and whether by condemnations through unjust voting or by acquiring superiority in brute force, both sides were ready to satisfy to the utmost their immediate hopes of victory. And so neither side acted with piety, but those who managed to accomplish something hateful by using honorable arguments were more highly regarded. The citizens in the middle, either because they had not taken sides or because begrudged their survival, were destroyed by both factions.

[83] In this way, every form of viciousness was established in the Hellenic world on account of the civil wars, and the simplicity that is especially found in noble natures disappeared because it became ridiculous. The division into distrustful groups opposed in their thinking was very extensive. To reconcile them, there was no secure principle, no oath that was feared, but those who were stronger, in contemplation of the impossibility of security, all took measures to avoid suffering rather than allowing them-

selves to feel trust. The weaker in intellect were more often the survivors; out of fear of their own deficiency and their enemies' craft, lest they be defeated in debate and become the first victims of plots as a result of the others' resourceful intellects, they went straight into action. And those who contemptuously supposed that they would know all in advance, and that there was no need to seize by force what would come to them through intellect, were instead caught off guard and destroyed.

[84] In Corcyra, then, most of these atrocities were first committed: all that men do in resisting those who, after ruling them abusively rather than moderately, provide opportunity for revenge; all that men resolve unjustly when, wishing to escape their usual poverty—especially if pressed by disaster—they desire their neighbors' possessions; all that others, attacking not for gain but on clearly equal terms, impelled most by raw fury, carry out savagely and without mercy. With public life confused to the critical point, human nature, always ready to act unjustly even in violation of laws, overthrew the laws themselves and gladly showed itself powerless over passion but stronger than justice and hostile to any kind of superiority. For men would not have placed revenge above pity, gain above justice, if not for the destructive power of envy. And the universal laws about such things, laws that offer hope of salvation to all in adversity, men see fit to do

3.83. "Weaker in intellect . . . destroyed": far from being "a somewhat lame conclusion to the whole of 82–83" (*HCT* II *ad* 3.83.4), these sections powerfully demonstrate the self-destructiveness of civil war by paralleling the fate of the more "moderate" partisans with that of the real moderates; in the Greek word-order, "destroyed" (constantly used by Thucydides to describe one-sided slaughter in war) is also the final word of 3.82.

3.84. Most scholars consider 3.84 spurious—rightly, I think. Christ 1989, who makes many excellent points in defending its authenticity (and convinces Maurer 1995, p. 77), is certainly correct in doubting that it is "an attempt to clarify what precedes it" (p. 148); the difficulty of the language has a more rhetorical character, the criticism of human nature is less nuanced than in 3.82, the sentence about envy is anticlimactically simplistic. Connor 1984, p. 102, n. 60, in arguing that 3.84 is a remnant of an *early* draft asks the hard questions: who else would have or could have written such a passage, how did it become part of our text? I can only respond here that Thucydides' mind is ultimately at least more accessible to us than the procedures of unknown editors. Does any other passage in Thucydides, representing whatever stage of composition, add so little sense with so much strain? And could the Thucydides who in 3.82–83 saw the development of civil-war mentality as a macabre perversion of progress have evolved from a Thucydides who in 3.84 viewed mankind as depraved from the outset?

away with at the outset in taking revenge instead of letting them stand until they actually run into danger and find need of them.

[85] The Corcyreans, then, treated one another with such fury, the first of its kind, and Eurymedon and the Athenian ships sailed away. Later, however, the exiled Corcyraeans (for about five hundred escaped) seized some forts located on the mainland, gained control of the Corcyrean territory across from the city, and did considerable damage by using it as a base for raiding those on the island, and a severe famine in the city resulted. They also sent representatives to Lacedaemon and Corinth concerning their restoration; since they accomplished nothing, they provided themselves with boats and mercenaries and crossed over to the island at a later time, about six hundred in all, and after burning the boats to leave themselves no hopes short of controlling the countryside they went up to Mt. Istone, and they built a fort and proceeded to harass those in the city and control the countryside.

[86] At the end of this summer, the Athenian ships sent twenty ships to Sicily with Laches son of Melanopos and Charoiades son of Euphiletos as commanders. For the Syracusans and the Leontines were at war with one another. As allies, the Syracusans had all the Dorian cities except Kamarina, the same ones that had been enrolled in the Lacedaemonian alliance from the very beginning of the war yet had taken no part in it at all, while the Leontines had the Chalkidian cities and Kamarina; in Italy, the Lokrians sided with the Syracusans and the Rhegians with the Leontines, because of kinship. The Leontine alliance, then, in accordance with an old alliance and also because they were Ionians, sent to Athens and persuaded them to send a fleet; they were under Syracusan blockade by both land and sea. The Athenians sent the ships on the pretext of common nationality, but wishing to prevent grain from that area from reaching the Peloponnesos and also testing the possibility that Sicilian affairs might be brought under their control. They accordingly established themselves at Rhegion in Italy and carried on the war with the allies, and the summer ended.

3.85. "First of its kind": Hornblower 1991 *ad* 3.85.1 paraphrases "they were the first to do so" (see also *HCT* II *ad* 3.85.1), but there may be deliberate ambiguity: a dubious first for the Corcyreans (cf. 4.46–48) and the Greeks. Cf. 3.82n.

3.86. The Leontine representatives included the rhetorician Gorgias, whose prose style created a sensation in Athens; Thucydides is silent about the man often cited since antiquity as a major influence on his own style.

[87] In the following winter the plague struck the Athenians for the second time, not that it had ever entirely disappeared, yet there had been a certain respite. The later outbreak lasted no less than a year, the first fully two years, so that nothing afflicted and damaged Athenian strength more than this. No fewer than four thousand four hundred from the hoplite ranks and three hundred cavalrymen died, and an untold number of the general population. Many earthquakes also occurred at that time in Athenian territory, and in Euboia, Boiotia, and especially Boiotian Orchomenos.

[88] In this same winter, the Athenians in Sicily and the Rhegians campaigned with thirty ships against the islands that are called Aiolian; it was impossible to campaign in summer because of lack of water. The Liparians, colonists of the Knidians, inhabit these. They live on one of the islands called Lipara, of no great size; from this one they go out and farm the others, Didyme, Strongyle, and Hiera. People there believe that Hephaistos has his smithy on Hiera, because great flames at night and smoke during the day can be seen pouring forth. These islands lie off the coast of the Sikels and Messenians, and they were allies of Syracuse. The Athenians plundered their land and, when they did not come over to them, sailed back to Rhegion. And the winter ended, also the fifth year of this war, which Thucydides recorded.

[89] In the following summer, the Peloponnesians and their allies went as far as the isthmus intending to invade Attica under the leadership of Agis son of Archidamos, king of the Lacedaemonians, but because there were many earthquakes they turned back, and there was no invasion. During this period when earthquakes were prevalent, the sea at Orobiai on Euboia retreated from what was then the coastline, and forming a wave it returned over much of the city, flooding here and receding there, and what was once land is now sea; the wave destroyed everyone who was unable to run up to higher ground in time. A similar flooding occurred around Atalante, the island off the coast of the Opuntian Lokrians, and it carried away part of the Athenian fort and wrecked one of two beached ships. On Peparethos there was also some recession of the waters, yet they did not rise again; an earthquake knocked down part of the wall, the town hall, and a few other buildings. As the cause for such flooding, I think that at that point where the earthquake had the most impact the sea withdraws, and when it suddenly returns with greater force it causes the flooding; without earthquakes I do not think something like this would happen.

[90] During the same summer there was various fighting in Sicily, according to individual situations, both by the Sikeliots themselves against one another and by the Athenians along with their allies; but what I will

mention is what was most notable among the Athenian and allied actions or counteractions against the Athenians. After the Athenian general Charoiades had already been killed in battle by the Syracusans, Laches in command of the entire fleet campaigned against Mylai, which belonged to Messena. And it turned out that two Messenian tribes were on garrison duty at Mylai and had even set up some sort of ambush against the men landing. The Athenians and their allies routed the men lying in ambush and killed a great number, and when they assaulted their defensive works, they forced them to agree to the surrender of their acropolis and to participation in the campaign against Messena. After this the Messenians themselves went over to the Athenians when they approached with their allies, and they gave hostages as well as furnishing other forms of security.

[91] In the same summer, the Athenian sent thirty ships around the Peloponnesos under the command of Demosthenes son of Alkisthenes and Prokles son of Theodoros and sixty ships and two thousand hoplites against Melos; Nikias son of Nikeratos was their commander. This was because the Melians were islanders, yet unwilling to be their subjects or join their alliance, and they wanted to bring them over by force. When the Melians did not come over to them after their land was ravaged, they left Melos and sailed to Oropos on the mainland, and landing at night the hoplites immediately left the ships and proceeded by land to Tanagra in Boiotia; the Athenians from the city under the command of Hipponikos son of Kallias and Eurymedon son of Thoukles joined them there in full force as arranged by signals. Setting up camp at Tanagra that same day, they plundered and spent the night there. The next day they won a battle against the Tanagrans who went out to meet them and some Thebans who had come to help, captured some weapons, set up a trophy, and then went back either to the city or to the ships. Sailing near the shore with his sixty ships, Nikias plundered the coastal area of Lokris and returned home.

[92] Around the same time, the Lacedaemonians founded Herakleia, their colony in Trachis, for the following purpose. The Malians overall consist of three separate groups, the Paralians, the Hieraians, and the Trachinians; it was the Trachinians, hard pressed in a war with the Oitaians and at first on the point of attaching themselves to the Athenians but afraid

---

3.90. "What I will mention": it is astonishing that Thucydides, who obviously and inevitably practiced selectivity, should have stipulated this only once, in this trivial context, cf. Hornblower 1991 *ad* 3.90.1; possibly he was signaling that only a stern sense of duty prevented him from passing over these events entirely.

3.91. "Oropos on the mainland": see Hornblower 1991 *ad* 2.23.3, 3.91.3.

to trust them, who applied to Lacedaemon, choosing Teisamenos as their ambassador. The Dorians, from the mother-city of the Lacedaemonians, came on the embassy as well, with the same requests, for they also were under pressure from the Oitaians. After the Lacedaemonians heard them, they were determined to send out the colony, since they wanted to help both the Trachinians and the Dorians, and at the same time the city seemed well placed regarding the war with Athens; a fleet could be prepared against Euboia and have a short distance to cross, and it would also be useful for access to Thrace. Altogether, they were eager to found the place. Accordingly they first consulted the god at Delphi, and when told to proceed, they sent out colonists from both their own citizens and the perioikoi and invited volunteers from the rest of Hellas to accompany them, except for Ionians, Achaians, and certain other nationalities. The leaders were three of the Lacedaemonians as founders, Leon, Alkidas, and Damagon. They established and fortified anew the city now called Herakleia, which is about forty stades from Thermopylai and twenty from the sea, and began construction of shipyards and blocked off the side toward Thermopylai right at the pass, so that it would be easy for them to keep guard. [93] The Athenians were alarmed at first when the city was being founded and considered it primarily an establishment against Euboia, because the passage across to Kenaion on Euboia is a short distance. Eventually, however, things turned out contrary to their expectations; no danger at all resulted from the colony. The reason was that both the Thessalians, who held the power in that areas, and the people in whose territory it was settled, fearing that the new settlers would constitute very powerful neighbors, continuously harassed them and made war on them until they wore them out, even though they were very numerous at first, since everyone came with confidence in the Lacedaemonians as colonizers, assuming that the city was secure; and yet it was very much the leaders who arrived from Lacedaemon who ruined the situation and brought the city to depopulation, frightening the majority by governing harshly and at times incompetently, so that their neighbors then overpowered them more easily.

[94] In this same summer, around the time the Athenians were occupied at Melos, the Athenians who were off the Peloponnesos in thirty ships first ambushed and killed some guards at Hellomenos in Leukadian territory

3.92–93. Teisamenos: "Why is the name recorded?" (Hornblower 1991 *ad* 3.92.2 in an interesting note). Alkidas is almost certainly the admiral; that Thucydides does not explicitly associate him with the harshness and incompetence may be because he was not at Herakleia very long, see Hornblower *ad* 3.92.5.

and then moved against Leukas with a larger expedition: all the Akarnanians, who joined in full force except for Oiniadai, the Zakynthians, the Kephallenians, and fifteen Corcyrean ships. The Leukadians, while their land was being devastated both beyond and within the isthmus on which Leukas and the Apollo sanctuary are situated, were compelled by numbers to stay inactive, and the Akarnanians urged Demosthenes, the Athenian general, to wall them off, thinking that they would easily capture and be rid of a city that had always been their enemy. But Demosthenes at this point had been won over by the Messenians to the excellent prospects, with such a large force gathered under him, for attacking the Aitolians, since not only were they hostile to Naupaktos, but if he conquered them he would easily bring the rest of that part of the mainland over to Athens. Since the people of Aitolia, although numerous and warlike, live in unwalled villages which are also far apart and are armed with light equipment, they argued that it would not be hard to conquer them before they could help one another. They advised attacking the Apodotians first, then the Ophonians, and after these the Eurytanians, the largest contingent of the Aitolians, who are the most unintelligible in speech and are said to eat raw meat; for after these were conquered, the rest would come over without trouble.

[95] Demosthenes was persuaded out of gratitude to the Messenians, but above all because he supposed that by using the mainlanders as allies without support from Athens he, along with the Aitolians, could go against the Boiotians by land, through the Ozolian Lokrians to Kytinion in Doris, keeping Parnassos on his right until he descended to the Phokians, who in his opinion would eagerly join the campaign on account of their longstanding friendship with Athens or could also be brought over by force (and Boiotia is right on the Phokian border), and accordingly he set out from Leukas over the objections of the Akarnanians and sailed along the coast to Sollion. He communicated his plans to the Akarnanians and, since they rejected them because of the failure to blockade Leukas, made the campaign against the Aitolians himself with the rest of the army: the Kephallenians, Messenians, Zakynthians, and three hundred Athenians as marines from their own ships (as for the Corcyreans, their fifteen ships had left). He made Oineon in Lokris his base. These Lokrians, the Ozolians, were allies and were supposed to meet the Athenians inland with all their forces; as neighbors of the Aitolians and armed in the same way, they were

---

3.94. The Messenians enter the narrative with abruptness; cf. 2.90n and 4.9n. "Out of gratitude" (see Spratt 1905a *ad* 3.95.1); the words could also mean "to gratify," the more common translation.

expected to be of great value as members of the expedition because of their familiarity with Aitolian warfare and topography.

[96] After bivouacking with his army in the sanctuary of Nemean Zeus (where it is said that the poet Hesiod was killed by the local people, after receiving an oracle that this would befall him at Nemea), he set out at dawn and marched into Aitolia. He took Potidania on the first day, Krokyleion on the second, and Teichion on the third, and he remained there and sent back the booty to Eupalion in Lokris. His intention was to subdue the other areas in this way as far as the Ophonians and, if they did not come to terms, withdraw to Naupaktos and make a later campaign. The Aitolians had not been unaware of these preparations even from the first designs against them, and when the army invaded, they all came to the defense in such great strength that even the most distant of the Ophonians as far away as the Malian gulf, the Bomians and Kallians, rose up. [97] But the Messenians advised Demosthenes with the same arguments they had first used in persuading him that the conquest of Aitolia would be easy; they told him to advance on the villages as quickly as possible and not wait until they had all banded together and organized against him but seize each one that stood in his path. He was convinced and besides hopeful because of his good luck in meeting no opposition, and without waiting for the Lokrians who were supposed to reinforce him (and it was light-armed javelin throwers he needed most), he advanced on Aigition, attacked it, and took it by assault; actually, the inhabitants had evacuated the town, which was on high ground about eighty stades from the sea, and taken up positions on the hills above it. The Aitolians, who had by now come to help Aigition, attacked the Athenians and their allies, running down from the hills on all sides hurling javelins, and they gave ground when the Athenians advanced and fell on them when they withdrew. And for a long time the fighting was of this sort, pursuit and retreat, with the Athenians at a disadvantage in both.

[98] Now as long as their archers had arrows and were able to use them, they held out; the Aitolians in their light armor were kept in check by their volleys. But when the archers scattered after their leader was killed, and the men themselves were worn out by the repeated efforts they were forced to make, with the Aitolians bearing down and hurling javelins, now they turned and fled, and as they plunged into dry streambeds with no exit

---

3.96. I agree with Hornblower 1991 *ad* 3.96.1 that this chapter does not intend an authorial statement about the truth of oracles. The anecdote may be more than "spice" or "color," however, since the unseemly occupation of the sanctuary is already an ominous note at the outset of the expedition.

and unfamiliar terrain, they were cut down; it happened that their path-
finder, Chromon the Messenian, had been killed. And the Aitolians, light-
armed and fleet runners, overtook many on foot in the rout itself and cut
them down with their javelins, and when a still greater number got into an
impassable woods by losing their way, they set it on fire and burned it
down around them. The Athenian forces experienced flight and ruin in
every form, and those who survived barely managed to escape to the sea
and Oineon in Lokris, right where they had started out. Many of the allies
died, and about as many as one hundred twenty of the Athenians, in this
number and just in their prime; they were surely the finest men from the
city of Athens to die in this war. Prokles, the other general, was killed as
well. After getting back their dead from the Aitolians under truce and
withdrawing to Naupaktos, they subsequently made their way back to
Athens on their ships. Demosthenes stayed behind in Naupaktos and the
area, afraid of the Athenians after what had happened. [99] Around the
same time, the Athenians off Sicily sailed to Lokris and in a landing
defeated the Lokrians who came out against them, also capturing a fort on
the Halex river.

[100] During this same summer, the Aitolians, who had already sent
Tolophos the Ophonian, Boriades the Eurytanian, and Teisandros the
Apodotian on an embassy to Corinth and Lacedaemon, won support for
their request to send an expedition against Naupaktos for calling in the
Athenians. Toward autumn, the Lacedaemonians sent out three thousand
hoplites from their allies (these included five hundred from Herakleia in
Trachis, the city, which was newly founded at the time); the Spartiate
Eurylochos led the expedition, and his associates were the Spartiates
Makaraios and Menedaios. [101] When the army had assembled at Delphi,
Eurylochos sent a herald to the Ozolian Lokrians; the route ran through
their territory, and besides he wanted to detach them from the Athenians.
The Amphissans of Lokris were very much his collaborators, fearful
because of the hostility of the Phokians; the first to give hostages themselves, they also persuaded the others to do so in fear of the approaching
army, and so their neighbors the Myonians (whose terrain is the most difficult in Lokris) were the first, and then the Ipnians, Messapians, Trita-
ians, Chalaians, Tolophonians, Hessians, and Oianthians. All these also
joined the expedition. The Olpians gave hostages, but without coming
along; the Hyaians did not give hostages until after the seizure of a village
of theirs called Polis.

[102] When preparations were complete and he had left the hostages at
Kytinion in Doris, he advanced against Naupaktos through the territory of

the Lokrians and on his march captured Oineon and Eupalion, since they did not come over to him. In the territory of Naupaktos, they plundered along with the Aitolians who had already arrived to support them, and they captured the unfortified suburbs; they attacked and captured Molykreion, a Corinthian colony but subject to Athens. Demosthenes the Athenian, who happened to be still around Naupaktos after the outcome in Aitolia, had already learned about the expedition, and fearing for Naupaktos he went to the Akarnanians and persuaded them (with difficulty, because of his withdrawal from Leukas) to send help there. They sent a thousand hoplites with him on his ships, who entered and secured the site; it had been in danger of not holding out, since the walls were extensive and the defenders few. When Eurylochos and his associates learned that the hoplites had gone in and the place was impossible to capture by assault, they withdrew, not to the Peloponnesos but to what is now called Aiolis, to Kalydon and Pleuron, to places in that area, and to Proschion in Aitolia. For the Ambraciots had come and persuaded them to make an attack along with themselves against Amphilochian Argos and the rest of Amphilochia, and against Akarnania as well, maintaining that if they subdued these the entire mainland would be secured for the Lacedaemonian alliance. Eurylochos was convinced, and after dismissing the Aitolians he and his army stayed inactive in the area until they were to help the Ambraciots when they had taken the field around Argos. And the summer ended.

[103] In the approach following winter, the Athenians in Sicily, along with their Hellenic allies and those Sikels who were Syracusan allies through forcible subjection defected to join their campaign, came up to Inessa, a Sikel town whose acropolis was held by the Syracusans, made an attack, and went away unable to capture it. During their withdrawal, the Syracusans made an attack on the allies who were withdrawing after the Athenians, fell on them, and routed a considerable part of their army and killed a large number. After this, Laches and the Athenians from the ships made some landings in Lokris, defeated the Lokrians, about three hundred, who came out against them with Proxenos son of Kapaton on the Kaikos river, and departed after capturing arms.

[104] In the same winter, the Athenians purified Delos, certainly in accordance with an oracle of some sort. To be sure, the tyrant Peisistratos had purified it previously, only not the whole island but the part that was visible from the sanctuary; this time the whole island was purified, in the

---

3.102. "The entire mainland": the near repetition from 3.94 does not bode well for the Lacedaemonian undertaking.

following way. They dug up the burials of all those who had died on Delos and proclaimed that in the future no one was to die or give birth on the island, but be conveyed to Rheneia; and Rheneia is such a short distance from Delos that Polykrates, who had a powerful navy for a time, ruled over the islands, and seized Rheneia, dedicated it to Delian Apollo by attaching it to Delos with a chain. At this time also, after the purification, the Athenians first established the Delian festival, which is held every four years. Formerly, long ago, there was also a great gathering of the Ionians and the neighboring islanders on Delos; they held the festival with wives and children, just as the Ionians now do at the Ephesia, both athletic and poetic contests were held there, and the cities brought groups of dancers. Homer, above all, shows that this took place by the following verses, from the *Hymn to Apollo*:

When Delos has delighted most your heart, Phoibos,
There the long-robed Ionians with their children and wives
Gathered on your sacred way.
There, calling your praises, they delight you with boxing and dancing
and song as they hold the contests.

And again, in these verses from the same hymn, he shows that there were poetic contests, and they frequented them to contend; for when he sang of the Delian dance for women, he ended his tribute with the following verses, where he also praises himself:

Now, maidens, may Apollo and Artemis be gracious,
And all farewell. But remember me even hereafter,
Whenever some other of men on earth
Comes here weary and inquires:
"Maidens, which man comes here sweetest to you of all bards,
And you delight most in him?"
Answer him well, all of you, not saying my name:
"A blind man, and he lives on rocky Chios."

3.104. On the purification of Delos and its relation to Thucydides' views on religion, see Hornblower 1991, pp. 517–29 and Brock 1996 (with the suggestion that Kleon was responsible for the purification). This is the first known mention of the "Homeric Hymn to Apollo," no longer attributed to Homer and probably dating from the sixth century. "Not saying my name": for this translation (of Thucydides' variant reading), cf. Hornblower *ad* 3.104.5 and Rhodes 1994 *ad* 3.104.1.

Homer has given all this evidence that long ago there was also a great assembly and festival on Delos; later the islanders and Athenians would send the dancers with offerings, but the arrangements for games and most of the festival were discontinued because of misfortunes, as is natural, up to this time when the Athenians established contests and equestrian races, something not held previously.

[105] In the same winter, the Ambraciots, just as they promised Eury-lochos in detaining his army, took the field against Amphilochian Argos with three thousand hoplites, and invading Argive territory they seized Olpai, a strong fort on a hill near the sea, which the Akarnanians had for-tified and at one time used for their common court of law; it is about twenty-five stades from the city of Argos on the coast. Some of the Akar-nanians went to the defense of Argos, while others set up camp at the place in Amphilochia called Krenai, standing guard against the Peloponnesians with Eurylochos lest they slip past to meet with the Ambraciots. They also sent word to Demosthenes, who had commanded the Athenians against Aitolia, with the idea of making him their leader, and to the twenty Athe-nian ships that happened to be off the Peloponnesos, commanded by Aris-toteles son of Timokrates and Hierophon son of Antimnestos. The Ambraciots around Olpai also sent a message to their city asking them to bring help in full force, fearing that the men with Eurylochos would not be able to get by the Akarnanians and that they themselves would be either in a battle without assistance or in danger if they wanted to withdraw.

[106] Now the Peloponnesians with Eurylochos, when they learned that the Ambraciots had reached Olpai, set out and hurried to support them, and after they had crossed the Acheloos they proceeded through Akarnania, deserted because of the defense of Argos, and kept the city of the Stratians on the right with its garrison and the rest of Akarnania on the left. After crossing the territory of the Stratians, they proceeded through Phytia, around the edges of Medeon next, and then through Limnaia and entered the land of the Agraians, no longer Akarnania and friendly. Reach-ing Mt. Thyamos, which is part of Agraia, they crossed it and descended into Argive territory after darkness, and in passing between the city of Argos and the Akarnanians on guard at Krenai they got through unnoticed and joined the Ambraciots at Olpai. [107] With their forces combining at dawn, they took up a position at the place called Metropolis and made camp. Not much later, the Athenians on the twenty ships arrived in the Gulf of Ambracia in support of the Argives, and Demosthenes arrived with two hundred Messenian hoplites and sixty Athenian archers. The ships off Olpai blockaded the hill by sea, and the Akarnanians and a few

Amphilochians (most were forcibly held back by the Ambraciots) who had by now met at Argos prepared for battle with the enemy and chose Demosthenes as leader of the whole allied force along with their own generals. He brought his forces up close to Olpai and set up camp; a great ravine separated the armies.

They stayed inactive for five days, and on the sixth both formed their lines for battle. Demosthenes, since the Peloponnesian army proved the larger and outflanked him, feared encirclement, and in a hollow roadway overgrown with bushes he placed hoplites and light-armed in ambush, about four hundred men altogether, so that at the moment of contact these could spring out where the enemy flank projected and come from the rear. When both sides were prepared, they engaged in close combat, with Demosthenes holding the right wing with the Messenians and the few Athenians, while the various Akarnanian contingents and javelin-throwers who came from Amphilochia formed the rest of the line; the Peloponnesians and Ambraciots were drawn up mixed together except for the Mantineans, who were grouped toward the left but not on the farthest part of the left wing, where Eurylochos and his men faced Demosthenes and the Messenians. [108] When the Peloponnesians on the projecting wing were fully engaged and beginning to encircle the enemy right, the Akarnanians coming out of ambush at their rear fell on them and caused such a rout that they both failed to fight back and in their terror sent most of their own soldiers into flight as well; for when these saw the contingent around Eurylochos, their strongest, destroyed, their own terror became much greater. The Messenians there with Demosthenes did most of the work. The Ambraciots and those on the right defeated their opponents and pursued them to Argos; they happen to be the best fighters in that region. But returning and seeing most of their army defeated and the Akarnanians bearing down on them, they escaped to Olpai with difficulty, and many were killed. The onrush was undisciplined and disorderly except for the Mantineans; out of the whole army, they made the most organized retreat. The battle ended late in the day.

[109] On the next day Menedaios, who had taken over the command after the death of Eurylochos as well as Makarios and was at a loss, after the severe defeat, as to how he could either stand a siege cut off on land and also by sea by the Athenian ships or reach safety by retreating, negotiated with Demosthenes and the Akarnanian generals about a truce and withdrawal in addition to recovery of the dead. They gave back the dead and set up a trophy, and they also recovered their own men who had died, about three hundred. As for the withdrawal, they gave a public refusal to

all alike, but secretly Demosthenes along with the Akarnanian generals gave permission for a quick departure to the Mantineans, to Menedaios and the other Peloponnesian leaders, and to any Peloponnesians of high standing, since they wanted to strip support from the Ambraciots and the crowd of foreign mercenaries, and especially to discredit the Lacedaemonians and Peloponnesians among the people of the area for serving their own interests by betraying their own side. They took up their dead and quickly buried them as well as they could, and those who had received permission secretly planned their retreat. [110] Meanwhile, Demosthenes and the Akarnanians received the news that the full force of Ambraciots from the city were coming to the defense through Amphilochia in response to the first message from Olpai, knowing nothing of what had happened, and he immediately sent part of the army ahead to line the roads with ambushes and occupy the strong positions, and at the same time he prepared to march against them with the rest.

[111] In the meantime, the Mantineans and the others involved in the arrangement went out pretending to gather herbs and firewood and stole away in small groups, at the same time gathering what they had supposedly gone out for; once they had advanced well outside Olpai, they would quicken their departure. The Ambraciots and whoever else happened to come into contact with them realized that they were leaving, and they too hurried and broke into a run hoping to catch up. At first, the Akarnanians thought that they were in all cases leaving without permission and pursued the Peloponnesians; one threw a javelin at the generals themselves for hindering them and saying that the men had permission, thinking they were being betrayed. After this, however, they let the Mantineans and Peloponnesians get away and killed the Ambraciots. And there were plenty of arguments and mistakes over distinguishing between an Ambraciot and a Peloponnesian. They killed about two hundred Ambraciots; the rest escaped to the Agraian border, and Salynthos the king of the Agraians, who was friendly to them, took them in.

[112] The Ambraciots from the city reached Idomene. Idomene consists of two high hills; at nightfall the men sent ahead from the camp by Demosthenes occupied the larger one ahead of them without being noticed, and it turned out that the Ambraciots ascended the smaller one first and bivouacked. After supper, just after dark, Demosthenes with half the rest of the army went into the defile, while the others went into the Amphilochian mountains. Right at dawn, he fell on the Ambraciots while they were still in their beds and had no suspicion of what had happened but quite to the contrary thought that these were their own men. Demos-

thenes had deliberately stationed the Messenians in front and with orders
to address them, speaking the Doric dialect and inspiring trust in their
sentries while still invisible in the darkness. This was how they fell on the
Ambraciot army and put it to flight, and they killed most on the spot, and
the rest rushed into the mountains to escape. But the roads were already
occupied, and besides the Amphilochians were familiar with their own terrain and were light-armed against hoplites, while they lacked experience
and knowledge of which way to turn and were killed by falling into ravines
or the ambushes set in advance. Taking every form of escape, some even
turned to the sea, which is not far off, and when they saw the Attic ships
moving along the shore at the same time the action took place, they swam
over to them, thinking in the moment of panic that it was better to be killed
if need be by the Athenians instead of the Amphilochians, barbarians and
their worst enemies. So few out of many Ambraciots escaped to their city
after this sort of devastation, and the Akarnanians stripped the dead, set
up a trophy, and went back to Argos.

[113] The next day a herald came to them from the Ambraciots who
had fled from Olpai to the Agraians to request recovery of the men they
had killed following the first battle, when those without permission were
leaving along with the Mantineans and those given permission. When the
herald saw the arms of those from the Ambraciot city, he was amazed,
since he did not know about the disaster and thought they belonged to
those in his own group. Someone asked him why he was amazed and how
many of them had died, the questioner thinking in turn that the herald was
from those at Idomene. Close to two hundred, he said. And the questioner
put in again, "But those don't look like the arms of two hundred, but more
than a thousand." The herald now asked, "So these are not from the men
who were fighting along with us?" The other answered, "They are, if you
were fighting at Idomene yesterday." "But we fought no one yesterday,
but during the retreat the day before." "Very well, but we certainly fought
against your reinforcements from the city of the Ambraciots yesterday."
When the herald heard this and realized that the reinforcements from the

3.113. The unique rapid dialogue (despite Hornblower 1991 *ad* 3.113.1, 5.87–111
is hardly comparable) makes this chapter tragic in style as well as content; see Lapini 1991, who stresses the historical implausibility of the dialogue and the incident
itself. I agree with *HCT* II *ad* 3.113.4 that "it is the appearance of agreeing which
makes the Akarnanian's answer so harsh," but not with the implication that "an
unsympathetic, harsh answer" was intended; as in many recognition scenes in
tragedy, the horror of the truth is ironically juxtaposed with the collaborative spirit
of the investigators.

city had been destroyed, he cried out in grief and, stunned by the magnitude of the misfortunes all around him, immediately went off without his objective and did not ask for the bodies again. For this was certainly the greatest disaster in this war for a single Hellenic city within so few days. I have left the number of the dead unrecorded because the total reported was unbelievable in proportion to the city's size. I know, however, that if the Akarnanians and the Amphilochians had been willing to destroy Ambracia, as Demosthenes and the Athenians urged, they would have taken it without resistance; but now they feared that if the Athenians occupied it they would be more troublesome as their neighbors. [114] After these events, allocating a third of the spoils to the Athenians, they distributed the rest among the cities. Those of the Athenians were captured at sea, and the ones now dedicated in the Attic sanctuaries are three hundred sets of armor especially picked out for Demosthenes, which he brought with him when he sailed back. And returning after the calamity in Aitolia was less fearsome for him as well because of this exploit.

The Athenians on the twenty ships sailed off to Naupaktos, and after the departure of Demosthenes and the Athenians the Akarnanians and the Amphilochians gave the Ambraciots and the Peloponnesians who had taken refuge with Salynthos and the Agraians permission to withdraw from Oiniadai, where they had moved after leaving Salynthos. For the future, the Akarnanians and Amphilochians made a treaty and a hundred-year alliance with the Ambraciots on these terms, that the Ambraciots were not to campaign with the Akarnanians against the Peloponnesians nor the Akarnanians with the Ambraciots against the Athenians but were to defend each others' territory, and the Ambraciots were to give back all Amphilochian places and hostages they held and not send help to Anaktorion, which was at war with the Akarnanians. In fixing these terms, they ended the war. After this, the Corinthians sent out about three hundred of their own men as a garrison for Ambracia, commanded by Xenokleides son of Euthykles; they arrived by a difficult journey overland.

[115] This was how events turned out in Ambracia. In the same winter the Athenians in Sicily made a landing from their ships in the territory of Himera, joined by the Sikels who had invaded the edges of Himera's territory from the interior, and they sailed to the Aiolian islands. When they returned to Rhegion, they encountered the Athenian general Pythodoros

---

3.114. "Captured at sea": it is frustrating that Thucydides does not explain; perhaps not all the Athenian spoils were lost, see *HCT* II, Hornblower 1991, and Rhodes 1994 *ad* 3.114.1.

son of Isolochos as successor for the ships Laches commanded. This was because the allies in Sicily had sailed to Athens and persuaded them to send more ships to help. For the Syracusans not only controlled their territory but were assembling a fleet, preparing to cease looking on while kept off the sea by a few ships. The Athenians manned forty ships to send, thinking that the war in Sicily would be finished more quickly and at the same time wishing to give their navy practice. Accordingly, they dispatched Pythodoros, one of their generals, with a few ships and intended to send out Sophokles son of Sostratides and Eurymedon son of Thoukles with the rest. At the end of the winter, Pythodoros, already in command of Laches' ships, sailed to the Lokrian fort that Laches had captured earlier, and after a defeat in battle by the Lokrians he returned.

[116] At the very beginning of this spring, the fire streamed out of Aitna, just as it had before. It ruined some of the land of the Katanaians, who live on Mt. Aitna, the highest mountain in Sicily. They say that this eruption came fifty years after the previous one, and that there have been three eruptions since Sicily was settled by the Hellenes. These were the events of this winter, and the sixth year ended of this war that Thucydides recorded.

3.116. It is almost certain that this chapter was written before the eruption of 396 B.C.E., although this is not evidence that Thucydides had died by then; cf. *HCT* II, Hornblower 1991, and Rhodes 1994 *ad* 3.116.2.

BOOK FOUR

INTRODUCTION

*While book 3 is somber in its emphasis on military frustration and resulting
stalemate, book 4 is a suitably spectacular setting for "the most unexpected thing
in the war": with these words, Thucydides sums up the surrender of nearly three
hundred Spartan hoplites, concluding an Athenian campaign in Spartan territory. The book begins with an update on the affairs of the West Greeks, which
had already motivated the expedition to Sicily, which the Athenians now dispatch. The Athenian ships are soon diverted to the Peloponnesos, however, because of the scheme of Demosthenes (at this point, not a general but a private
citizen) to occupy Pylos as a beachhead against Sparta. After both sides concen-
trate large forces here (the Spartans withdrawing theirs from the usual invasion
of Attica), the Athenians not only succeed in holding Pylos but in trapping
Spartan citizen-soldiers on a small island; the Spartans consequently send an
embassy to Athens proposing a general peace. Because the Athenians look for
greater gains, they reject this proposal, and fighting is renewed. Although their
prize almost eludes the Athenians, they eventually make the capture.*

*There is neither space nor need to list here the paradoxes and role reversals
in which the Pylos campaign abounds; the most gigantic of these is the descent
of the Spartans into military impotence. Their subsequent embassies to Athens
accomplish nothing, and the Athenians use their hostages to deter further invasions of Attica; meanwhile, they successfully carry the war against the Peloponnesos, including Spartan territory. In Sicily, however, they suffer a setback
when the Syracusan leader Hermokrates persuades the Greek cities there to end
their wars and unite against the common danger of Athenian intervention. The
Athenians react as though deprived of an easy conquest. Immediately after this,
their string of military successes ends when their takeover of Megara is thwarted
by the Spartan general Brasidas.*

*It is Brasidas who, with little backing from the Spartan state, begins to re-
store the balance of power. Leading an army of helots and Peloponnesian mercenaries into the Thracian area, he brings about the revolt of several Athenian
allies. He succeeds by what Thucydides stresses are un-Spartan qualities: ini-*

tiative, boldness, personal charm, and speaking ability. Meanwhile, the Athenians are occupied by their campaign against the Boiotians, which ends in their decisive defeat. They do not give priority to events farther north until Brasidas captures their important colony of Amphipolis. After the additional loss of Torone, they accept Spartan proposals for a one-year armistice, joined by most Peloponnesians. The armistice is effectively ignored by Brasidas, who accepts the revolt of two more Athenian allies; the Athenians recover one and are besieging the other as book 4 ends.

While much appreciated for its literary qualities, this book has been extensively criticized as a historical account. In recording the Pylos campaign, the author has made it extremely difficult to assess the relative roles played by planning and by the factor of luck, and scholars have advanced various theories to explain Thucydides' neglect of the former element. His interpretation of history has been further called into question by his account of the battle for Amphipolis; Thucydides himself, as a general, was involved in the Athenian defeat, and there is some reason to believe that he attempted to minimize his share of the responsibility.

BOOK FOUR

[1] In the following spring, around the time the grain was shooting up, ten Syracusan ships set sail and with an equal number of Lokrian ships took over Messena in Sicily on the invitation of the Messenians, and Messena revolted from Athens. The Syracusans brought this about especially because they saw that the place provided an approach to Sicily and feared that the Athenians, using it as a base, would some day attack them with a larger force, and the Lokrians, out of hatred for the Rhegians and wanting to make war on them from both sides. The Lokrians at the same time had invaded the territory of the Rhegians in full force to keep them from sending help to the Messenians, and because Rhegian exiles among them added their invitation. The Rhegians had long been in a state of faction, and it was impossible under the circumstances for them to defend themselves against the Lokrians, who accordingly attacked them all the more. After devastating their land, the Lokrians withdrew with their infantry, while the ships guarded Messena; other ships being manned were to come to the harbor there and carry on the war from that point. [2] Around the same time in the spring, before the grain was ripe, the Peloponnesians and their allies invaded Attica led by Agis son of Archidamos, king of the Lacedaemonians, and after establishing their position they ravaged the land.

The Athenians dispatched their forty ships to Sicily according to plan, with Eurymedon and Sophokles as generals to join Pythodoros, who was already there. They also told them that, on the course of their voyage, they were to look after the Corcyreans in the city, who were being harassed by the exiles in the mountains. Sixty Peloponnesian ships had already sailed there to help those in the mountains on the assumption that, with a serious famine in the city, it would be easy to take control of the situation there. The Athenians also complied with a request by Demosthenes, a private citizen after his return from Akarnania, telling him to use these ships around the Peloponnesos if he wished.

[3] When they were sailing off Lakonia and learned that the Peloponnesian ships were already at Corcyra, Eurymedon and Sophokles were for hurrying to Corcyra, but Demosthenes urged them to make the voyage

only after putting in at Pylos and doing what needed to be done. While they were objecting, it happened that a storm came up and forced them into Pylos. Demosthenes immediately asked them to fortify the place (this was why he had sailed with them) and pointed out that there was a good supply of timber and stones around, that the place was naturally strong and, like the surrounding countryside, uninhabited (for Pylos is about four hundred stades from Sparta in the land that was once Messenia; the Lacedaemonians call the site Koryphasion). They said that there were plenty of deserted promontories in the Peloponnesos if he wanted to spend up the city by occupying them. To Demosthenes, however, this place seemed somewhat different from any other, with a harbor nearby, and because the Messenians, the original natives of the region who spoke the same dialect as the Lacedaemonians, would do them the most harm by using it as a base of operations as well as constituting a reliable garrison. [4] Since he convinced neither the generals nor the soldiers, even after communicating with the taxiarchs, Demosthenes fell in with the general inactivity caused by the bad sailing weather: inactivity that ended when the soldiers themselves, with nothing to do, suddenly got the impulse to go around and fortify the place from start to finish. They went to work with their hands, with no stone-working tools, bringing stones they had picked out and setting them where they happened to fit; since they had no hods, they carried mortar on their backs wherever they needed it, bending forward to make it stay on as well as possible and clasping their hands behind their backs to keep it from falling off. They hurried by every means to frustrate the Lacedaemonians by finishing work on the most vulnerable parts before they could attack, since most of the place was strong enough without walls.

[5] The Lacedaemonians happened to be celebrating a festival. They heard the news without concern, thinking that whenever they marched out the Athenians would either withdraw or be easily overcome. To some extent, the absence of part of their army in Athenian territory also held them back. The Athenians fortified the part facing inland and other crucial

4.3. "This was why he had sailed": certainly Thucydides' comment and a reference to prior planning. The obscurity of this element in Thucydides' account has drawn heavy criticism from scholars, along with a variety of explanations: e.g., Demosthenes' need for tight security, Thucydides' overemphasis on chance, his hostility toward Kleon, or both Demosthenes and Kleon. Cf. especially Hunter 1973, pp. 63–83, Connor 1984, pp. 108–21 (his opening statement, "To the historian, the fourth book of the *Histories* is perhaps the least convincing of the entire work," is directed mainly at the Pylos account), Babut 1986, and Strassler 1990. "Spend the city": possibly an idiom (note the sarcastic context), cf. Maurer 1995, pp. 55–56.

points in six days, left five ships with Demosthenes as a garrison, and pushed on to Corcyra and Sicily with the rest of the fleet. [6] When the Peloponnesians in Attica heard that Pylos had been occupied, they hurried back home, the Lacedaemonians and King Agis thinking that the business of Pylos affected them directly. Besides, the Peloponnesians, invading early and before the grain was ripe, were short of food for the majority, and the army suffered from unusually severe weather for the time of year. To sum up, there were many reasons why they withdrew quickly, and this turned out to be the shortest invasion: they stayed in Attica fifteen days.

[7] Around the same time, the Athenian general Simonides seized Eion, a Thracian colony of the Mendaians but hostile to Athens, by collecting a few Athenians from the garrisons and a number of allies in the region and by instigating treachery within. When the Chalkidians and Bottiaians came to Eion's rescue, he was immediately booted out and lost most of his men.

[8] When the Peloponnesians had returned from Attica, the Spartiates themselves and the nearest of the perioikoi went directly to the defense of Pylos, but the approach of the other Lacedaemonians was slower, since they had just returned from other campaigning. They also issued a call around the Peloponnesos to come to the aid of Pylos as quickly as possible, and they sent for their sixty ships at Corcyra, which were dragged across the isthmus at Leukas, eluded the Athenian ships at Zakynthos, and arrived at Pylos; the land troops were already there. While the ships were still on the way, Demosthenes succeeded in secretly sending two ships to tell Eurymedon and the Athenians on the ships at Zakynthos to come and help, since the site was in danger. In response to his orders, they sailed without delay.

The Lacedaemonians meanwhile prepared to attack the fort by land and sea, expecting no problems in capturing a construction built in a hurry

---

4.5–6. While the Spartans at home are complacent (this is emphasized by juxtaposition with bursts of Athenian activity), those in the field react very differently, realizing that the Athenians may do to them in some measure what they have become accustomed to doing to Attica.

4.7. "This Eion is otherwise unknown. The whole episode is of the smallest importance; Thucydides had it among his 'notes'" (*HCT* III *ad loc*); I would take this chapter as an example of Thucydides' skill in using digressions as the *Iliad* does, to deepen resonance and build suspense. Briefly leaving one Athenian commander in extreme danger, we hear about another Athenian who showed initiative, and the unceremonious verb translated as "booted out" (later used by the orator Demosthenes of an actor hissed off the stage) emphasizes Simonides' discomfiture; the terseness of the account, which gives us no opportunity to assess his chances, is all very much to the point.

and held by a small force. At the same time, they anticipated the Athenian reinforcements from Zakynthos and planned—unless they captured the fort first—to block the harbor entrances to prevent the Athenians from anchoring. The island called Sphakteria extends directly across the front of the harbor, sheltering it and leaving two narrow entrances: one, toward the fort and Pylos, wide enough for two ships to pass; the other, toward the rest of the mainland, wide enough for eight or nine. The island itself was entirely wooded and trackless because uninhabited, and about fifteen stades long. They intended to block the entrances with ships close together, prows toward the enemy. Concerned about the island, since the Athenians might use it for fighting them, they transported some hoplites over to the island and stationed others along the mainland. This way, the Athenians would have the island hostile to them as well as the mainland, where there is no place to land; the whole coast of Pylos, without a harbor except the one with two entrances, would give them no base for supporting their troops, and they would probably besiege the place successfully without a sea battle or other risk, since there was no food inside the fort, and it had been occupied with little preparation. Since these considerations seemed best to them, they transported the hoplites to the island, picking them by lot from all the companies. The ones finally trapped there, after other hoplites had previously crossed over in relays, were four hundred twenty, with their helots, under the command of Epitadas son of Molobros.

[9] Demosthenes, seeing that the Lacedaemonians were going to attack with both ships and infantry, made his own preparations. He hauled the ships he still had up under the fort and protected them with a stockade, and he armed their crews with shields of inferior quality, most of them wicker; it was impossible to find weapons in a deserted place, and even the shields they got from a Messenian thirty-oared pirate ship and boat that had just arrived. About forty of these Messenians were hoplites, which he

4.8. "About fifteen stades": a considerable and surprising underestimation of the actual length of twenty-four or twenty-five stades; the text may be corrupt. On the topographical problems of the Pylos account, cf. *HCT* III, pp. 482–86, Bauslaugh 1979, Wilson 1979, and Strassler 1988.

4.9. Demosthenes' prior close collaboration with the Messenians as well as their central role in his project make it impossible to doubt that they had responded to a hasty summons by Demosthenes. As *HCT* III *ad* 4.9.3 inquires, "Why had Demosthenes never imagined that he would be so much weaker at sea?" This is one of the clearest indications of prior arrangements (here gone wrong) not reported by Thucydides.

used along with the others. He stationed most of his men, both armed and unarmed, at the best fortified and strongest points, facing the mainland, and ordered them to ward off any attacks by the land army. He himself, after picking sixty hoplites and a few archers out of the whole force, went outside the wall to the sea, to the area where he thought the Lacedaemonians were mostly likely to try to land. Although it was rough and rocky ground facing the open sea, he thought they would be drawn there irresistibly by the weakest point in the wall. The Athenians had not strengthened this part thoroughly because they had never expected to be inferior at sea; and the position seemed easy to capture once the Lacedaemonians forced a landing.

So it was there that Demosthenes, going right down to the sea, stationed his hoplites to block a landing, if possible, and encouraged his soldiers in this way. [10] "Since we all share the same risks, men, let no one in a desperate situation like this try to show cleverness by figuring out all the dangers that surround us, but instead, without deliberation, come to grips with the enemy confidently, expecting to survive even this. Every situation that has become as desperate as this one calls for confronting the risks with the least calculation and the least delay. But I also see that most of the advantages are ours if we are willing to stand fast and not let their numbers panic us into throwing away the elements in our favor. I consider the difficulty of landing here one of these factors, but it helps us only if we stand fast, while once we have given way, the terrain, rugged as it is, will be easy to cross with no one in the way, and we will have an enemy more formidable by having no easy retreat, even under pressure from us; they are easiest to defend against when aboard their ships but on equal terms as soon as they land. Next, we should not be too afraid of their numbers, since their large forces will be fighting in small installments because there is no way of mooring, and they are not an army on land, on an equal basis and outnumbering us, but an army, fighting from ships, which need many things to turn out right in the water. So I believe that their difficulties compensate for our smaller numbers, and at the same time I call on you as Athenians, men who know from experience about landing from ships against opposition that if they stand their ground and do not retreat out of fear of the surf and the terrifying approach of the ships they will never be

4.10. "Without deliberation . . . with the least calculation": while Thucydides does not, to say the least, normally endorse such sentiments, this speech is the exception that proves the rule; Demosthenes proceeds to a subtle, even sophistic assessment of the situation: "Leave the thinking to me."

overpowered: now stand fast yourselves, make your defense right where the waves hit the shore, and save both yourselves and the place."

[11] With Demosthenes offering this encouragement the Athenians felt more confident, and they went down and took up their position right by the sea. And the Lacedaemonians set out and simultaneously attacked the fort with their land army and with forty-three ships, their commander Thrasymelidas son of Kratesikles, a Spartiate, on board. He attacked exactly where Demosthenes expected. The Athenians were defending themselves from both directions, land and sea; the enemy made their attacks a few ships at a time (because it was not possible to get in with more), resting in turns and using the utmost effort as well as exhortation to drive out the Athenians by any means and take the fort.

In this, Brasidas was especially prominent. Serving as a trierarch and seeing that the other trierarchs and the helmsmen, because of the difficult terrain, were holding back even where it seemed possible to land and taking care not to wreck their ships, he shouted that it was not right to spare timber while tolerating an enemy fort built in their land; he urged them instead to smash their ships in forcing a landing and—addressing the allies—not to shrink at this time from giving their ships for the Lacedaemonians in return for great past benefits; to run aground, land in any way possible, and overpower the men and their position. [12] In this way he urged everyone else on and advanced to the gangway after compelling his own helmsman to run the ship ashore. In the attempt to land, he was beaten back by the Athenians and fainted after receiving many wounds, and when he fell into the outrigger his shield slipped off into the sea, and after it was cast up on land the Athenians picked it up and later used it for the trophy they set up over this engagement. The other attackers made every effort but were unable to land because the terrain was difficult and the Athenians stood their ground, yielding nowhere. And this remarkable turn of events came about, the Athenians warding off Lacedaemonians attacking their own land by sea, with Lacedaemonians attacking Athenians from ships and trying to land on enemy territory, which was actually their own: remarkable in that the latter at that time particularly prided themselves on being a land power supreme in infantry, the former on being seafarers who excelled in fighting with ships.

4.12. "In the attempt to land": this very paratactic sentence functions like a cinematic tracking shot, vividly placing the action before our eyes. It also foreshadows as well as announces the doom of the Spartans: their bravest is unwittingly compelled to commit the ultimate un-Spartan act of surrendering his shield. See 4.14n.

[13] So, after making attacks during this day and part of the next, the Lacedaemonians held off. The following day they sent to Asine for timber to make siege machinery, expecting that they would find the wall high where it faced the harbor but, since landing was easiest there, that they would take it with machines. At this time, the Athenian fleet arrived from Zakynthos numbering fifty ships, since some ships left their guard duty at Naupaktos to reinforce them along with four Chian vessels. When they saw that both the mainland and the island were filled with hoplites, and that the fleet was in the harbor with no sign of sailing out, the Athenians, at a loss where to anchor, then sailed to Prote, which is a deserted island not far away, bivouacked, and on the next day set out prepared for a sea battle, in the open water if the enemy was willing to come out against them, otherwise sailing into the harbor to attack.

The Lacedaemonians neither came out against them nor, as it happened, carried out their intention of blocking the entrances but instead, with no activity on land, manned their ships and prepared to fight in the harbor (which is not small) in the event of an attack. [14] When the Athenians realized this, they rushed out against them through both entrances and, falling upon the main part of the fleet, which was by now at sea and in formation, they put it to flight; pursuing the whole of the short distance to shore, they disabled many and captured five, one together with its crew, and fell upon the others, which had taken refuge on the shore. Of those still being manned, some were battered before they could put out to sea, and some the Athenians towed away empty, since their crews had rapidly taken flight. The Lacedaemonians, seeing what was happening and agonized by the disaster, nothing less than the isolation of their men on the island, came to the rescue, plunging into the water in armor, taking hold of the ships, and trying to drag them back. And in this action each man felt nullified if at any point he was not present in person. There was great turmoil with a reversal on each side of the usual naval tactics. For the Lacedaemo-

---

4.13. "Not small": it is in fact by far the largest in Greek waters. The theory of Strassler 1988 that the "cove harbor" is actually meant is unconvincing because Thucydides emphasizes the island's *length* (4.8).

4.14. "Each man felt nullified": *HCT* III *ad* 4.14.2 comments (comparing 2.8.4), "The phrase is not one a good writer would repeat." An equally idiosyncratic phrase from 2.8 (same section), however, has been repeated just previously, where I have translated "particularly prided themselves" (4.12); this occurs nowhere else in Greek. The double repetition of unusual constructions is purposeful; whereas 2.8 describes the mood of the Lacedaemonian alliance at the beginning of the war,

nians in their zeal and consternation were, one could say, fighting a sea battle on land, while the Athenians, victorious and wishing to follow up their success to the utmost, were fighting a land battle from ships.

After inflicting great suffering on each other and with many wounded, they drew apart, and the Lacedaemonians rescued their empty ships except for the ones seized at first. After both sides made camp, the Athenians set up a trophy, gave back the dead, and took possession of the wrecks, and they immediately began to sail around the island and kept it under guard on account of the men who were trapped. The Peloponnesians on the mainland, now including those who had come from all over to help, remained in place.

[15] When the news about Pylos was announced at Sparta, it was decided in view of the seriousness of the disaster that the authorities should go to the camp and as observers on the spot make whatever seemed the best decision. And since they saw that it was impossible to aid their men and were unwilling for them to risk either dying of hunger or being defeated by the strength of numbers, they decided that after making a truce regarding Pylos with the Athenian generals, provided they agreed, they should send ambassadors to Athens to reach an understanding and to try to get the men back as quickly as possible. [16] Since the generals accepted their proposals, the following truce went into effect. The Lacedaemonians were to bring to Pylos the ships used in the battle and all those in Lakonia, which were warships, and hand them over to the Athenians, and they were to make no attack on the fort by land or sea. The Athenians were to allow the Lacedaemonians on the mainland to send out daily to the men on the island grain, which was measured and kneaded, two Attic liters of barley for each, along with two cups of wine and some meat, and half the amount for servants; the food was to be sent out under the scrutiny of the Athenians, and no boat was to sail in secretly. And the Athenians were to keep guarding the island but refrain from landing, and to make no attack against the Peloponnesian forces by land or sea. If either side broke any of the terms in any way, the truce was ended. Otherwise, it was to be observed until the Lacedaemonian ambassadors returned from Athens; the Athenians were to send them and bring them back in a

---

the battle in the harbor (the context of 4.12 and 4.14) came close to ending that war. "Sea battle on land" and "land battle from ships" are forced and not strictly accurate descriptions; possibly an imitator has elaborated on the theme of role reversals (*HCT ad* 4.14.3: "I should be glad to believe that Thucydides did not write this").

trireme. When they returned, the truce was to end, and the Athenians were to give back exactly as many ships as they received, and in the same condition. The truce was made on these terms. The approximately sixty ships were handed over, and the ambassadors dispatched. After arriving in Athens, they spoke as follows.

[17] "Athenians, the Lacedaemonians have sent us to make an arrangement concerning the men on the island, whatever we convince you is to your advantage and, regarding the disaster, will at the same time bring us as much credit as possible under the circumstances. In taking the time to speak at greater length, we will not be contradicting but conforming with our practice, since it is characteristic for us not to use many words when few will suffice but to use more when it is opportune to explain something important in order to accomplish what must be done. Understand them neither in a hostile spirit nor as though dullards were to receive instruction, but regard them as a reminder about good planning for the knowledgeable. For it is possible for you to make good use of your current success, keeping your domain and adding honor and reputation, without experiencing the same problem as men who uncharacteristically get an advantage: invariably, they reach out in hope of more, because they enjoy even their present success unexpectedly. Those who have encountered the most vicissitudes of good and bad also have every reason to be the most distrustful of success. This would in all probability be the result of experience both for your city and for us. [18] And you can be sure of this by observing our present predicament, involving men of the highest standing in Hellas who have come to you with the very requests that we formerly considered ourselves better empowered to grant. And yet we have not been brought to this by decreased strength, nor because we became insolent as a result of increased strength, but by miscalculating on the basis of unchanged resources, a situation which is possible for all alike.

4.17–20. The Spartan speech has drawn an interesting variety of reactions: "A tone of somewhat arrogant superiority" (Graves 1888, p. 141); "elaborately tactful; and they had need of tact, for in fact they have nothing but a sermon to offer" (*HCT* III *ad* 4.17.2); "an extremely decent speech" which is too "cool and rational" to succeed in these circumstances (Cogan 1981, p. 75); "patently unrealistic" (Rusten 1989, p. 156). The Spartans both flatter and patronize the Athenians, by stressing their similarity to themselves, while they put the best face on their humiliation. But they are also trying to put the best face on something else: for their own immediate advantage, they are prepared to betray the original allied war aims, which they brazenly suggest have been forgotten. But there is no missing the *Realpolitik* of the closing sentence.

"Accordingly, it is not reasonable for you to suppose that, on account of the present flourishing of your city and its acquisitions, the same degree of fortune will always be with you. The prudent are those who secure their gains looking toward the element of uncertainty (and the same men would most capably deal with setbacks), those who suppose that war does not always attend a man in just the measure that he wishes to pursue it, but as the ways of fortune control him. And such men, the last to stumble because of being carried away by trust in good progress, would be the first to come to terms in fortunate situations. The time is right, Athenians, for you to do this with us, and not later—if you in fact reject our advice and fail—be thought to have enjoyed even your present success through chance, when it was possible for you to leave behind a secure and lasting reputation for strength and intelligence.

[19] "The Lacedaemonians invite you to a truce that will end the war, offering peace, alliance, and every other sort of friendship and closeness to exist between us, and ask in return for the men from the island, thinking it better for both sides that the ultimate risk not be run, whether they force their way out when some chance of salvation comes along or instead are reduced by the blockade. And we do not believe that great enmities are most likely to have a lasting termination if one side, getting the better in war in its defense, makes an unequal agreement by holding the other side to enforced oaths, but if, when it is quite possible to do this, that party makes peace on moderate terms, conquering the other also in generosity contrary to his expectations. For the other side, under obligation not to defend itself against force but to return the generosity, will be the readier to abide by the terms. And men tend to do this toward their leading enemies rather than those with whom they have lesser differences, and it is in their nature to make concessions in return towards those who willingly yield, but to undergo risks against their own judgment in opposing arrogance.

[20] "Now, if ever, is the right time for both sides to reconcile, before something irremediable befalls us in the meantime, in which case it will be necessary for you to have our undying hostility, personal as well as public, and you will be deprived of what we are now offering. While matters are still undecided, while you have reputation and the gain of our friendship, and with our problems resolved on moderate terms before some disgrace, let us come to terms and choose peace instead of war for ourselves and give the rest of Hellas a respite from suffering, which they will attribute mainly

---

4.20. "In which case it will be necessary": an extremely vexed passage; for other possible readings, see *HCT* III *ad* 4.20.1.

to you. For they are at war without certainty as to which side began it, but if there is peace, which is more in your power than in ours, it is you who will receive their gratitude. So if you make this sensible decision, you can become firm friends of the Lacedaemonians at their invitation, bringing them gratification rather than compelling them. And observe what important benefits this is sure to entail; for if we speak the same language, you can be certain that the rest of Hellas will be most respectful in its subordinate position."

[21] Now the Lacedaemonians said this much keeping in mind that the Athenians had previously been eager for a truce but were thwarted by their opposition, and supposing that they would gladly accept peace when it was offered and give back the men. But the Athenians considered that, since they held the men on the island, the truce was now available at any time they wanted to arrange it with the Lacedaemonians, and they grasped at more. In particular, Kleon son of Kleainetos urged them on, a popular leader at that time and most influential with the people. And he persuaded them to answer first that the men on the island must be taken to Athens after surrendering themselves and their arms and that on their arrival the Lacedaemonians must return Nisaia, Pagai, Troizen, and Achaia—places that they did not take by fighting but under the earlier agreement, which the Athenians accepted at a time of misfortune when they were in considerably greater need of a truce—before getting back their men and making a truce for as long as both sides should agree.

[22] The Lacedaemonians responded, without commenting on the Athenian reply, that they should choose commissioners for themselves, to discuss each point and, in an atmosphere of calm, decide on what was mutually acceptable. Whereupon Kleon descended on them in full force, saying that he had known even before that they had no just intentions, and it was clear now as well, men who were unwilling to speak at all to the people but wanted to go into council with a small group; if they had anything proper in mind, he called on them to say it to everyone. And the Lacedaemonians, aware both that it was not possible for them to speak in public if it seemed best to them to make some concession in view of the disaster, lest they be maligned to their allies after making unsuccessful proposals, and that the Athenians would not do on moderate terms what they proposed, returned from Athens with nothing accomplished.

4.21. "A popular leader": Lang 1972 has argued persuasively that Kleon may have been more an oligarch than a democrat (the usual view).

[23] With their arrival, the truce regarding Pylos was immediately ended, and the Lacedaemonians asked for their ships back, just as had been agreed. The Athenians, however, using as grievances an attack on the fort in violation of the truce and other things that did not seem important, refused to give them back, insisting that it had been expressly stated that the truce was broken if there were any infraction whatsoever. The Lacedaemonians denied the accusations and branded the matter of the ships an injustice; they left and got ready for fighting. And hostilities around Pylos were carried on actively by both sides, the Athenians sending two ships around the island in opposite directions during the day; at night they were all at anchor around the island except on the side of the open sea whenever it was windy (since twenty ships had joined them from Athens for the blockade, they numbered seventy in all). The Peloponnesians camped on the mainland and made attacks on the fort, watching for any chance opportunity to rescue the men.

[24] At this time, the Syracusans and their allies in Sicily, adding to the ships guarding Messena the rest of the fleet they had been preparing, carried on the war from Messena (the Lokrians, who had invaded Rhegian territory in full force, especially urged them on out of their hatred of Rhegion). They wanted to venture a sea battle, seeing that the Athenians had few ships on the spot and learning that the larger naval force that had been intended for this campaign was blockading Sphakteria. They hoped that, with a victory by their fleet, they would easily conquer Rhegion by blockading it with both land and naval forces and immediately put themselves in a strong position, since with the promontories of Rhegion in Italy and Messena in Sicily very close to each other it would be impossible for the Athenians to moor there and control the strait. This strait is the water between Rhegion and Sicily where Sicily is the shortest distance from the mainland, also the place called Charybdis where Odysseus is said to have sailed through. Because of its narrowness, and with strong currents from the two great seas, the Tyrrhenian and the Sicilian, rushing in, it is understandably known as dangerous. [25] And it was here that the Sicilians and their allies, late in the day, were forced to fight a sea battle over the passage of a ship, putting out to sea with a little over thirty ships against sixteen Athenian and eight Rhegion ships. Beaten by the Athenians, they hurried back to any friendly camp they could find in either Messenian or Rhegian territory, after losing one ship; the action was interrupted by nightfall.

4.23. Garner 1987, pp. 77–78 argues for the greater efficiency of sending both guard-ships in the *same* direction.

Subsequently, the Lokrians withdrew from Rhegian territory, while the Sicilians and allied ships reunited and anchored at Peloris in Messenian territory, where their land forces joined them. The Athenians and Rhegians, sailing in and seeing the ships left unmanned, attacked them; they in turn lost one ship when a grappling hook was thrown against it, the crew swimming to safety. After this, the Athenians attacked again when the Syracusans had manned their ships and were sailing on a tow rope along the shore to Messena; when the Syracusans countered by backing hard into them, they lost another ship. Holding their own in this type of running sea battle, the Syracusans sailed along into the harbor of Messena. When the Athenians got word that Kamarina was going to be betrayed to the Syracusans by Archias and his supporters, they sailed there. At this point, the Messenians attacked Naxos, their Chalkidian neighbor, in full force, with ships as well as on land. On the first day, they confined the Naxians behind their walls and plundered their territory, and sailing around on the next day they plundered their land along the Arkesinas river while making an attack on the city with their infantry.

Meanwhile, the Sikels came down from the hills in large numbers against the Messenians. When the Naxians saw this, gaining confidence and encouraging one another with the expected arrival of help from the Leontines and other Hellenic allies, they suddenly rushed out of the city against the Messenians and routed them, killing over a thousand; the rest had a terrible retreat home, since the barbarians attacked them on the roads and slaughtered most. The allies put into Messena and afterward dispersed to their respective homes. Immediately, the Leontines and their allies along with the Athenians moved against Messena in its weakened condition and attacked, the Athenians making their attempt against the harbor with the ships, the land forces against the city. But the Messenians and some Lokrians with Demoteles who had been left in the city after the disaster made a sally, all of a sudden falling on the Leontine army, routing most of it and killing a large number. When the Athenians saw this, they disembarked and came to the rescue, and finding the Messenians in disarray, they chased them back into the city. After setting up a trophy, they withdrew to Rhegion. After this, the Hellenes in Sicily campaigned on land against one another without Athenian involvement.

[26] And in Pylos the Athenians were still besieging the Lacedaemonians on the island, and the Peloponnesian camp on the mainland remained in place. The guard was troublesome for the Athenians because of the shortage of food and water. There was just a single spring, right on the acropolis of Pylos and not large; most of the men drank the kind of water

they scraped from the gravel along the shore. Camping in a small place proved restrictive, and since the ships could not be moored, some crews took their meals on shore while others were anchored out at sea. And the greatest discouragement resulted from the lapse of time beyond the few days in which they calculated they would capture men on a deserted island drinking brackish water. The Lacedaemonians were responsible for this by calling for volunteers to send in ground grain, wine, cheese, and any other food that might help in a siege, offering high pay and promising freedom to any helot bringing in food. And helots in particular, along with others, successfully took the risk, setting sail from any point on the Peloponnesos and coming in when it was still night, on the side of the island facing the sea. Mostly, they waited for a wind to carry them in, since they eluded the triremes on guard more easily when there was a wind from the sea and the ships had trouble mooring, and they landed without hesitating to run aground; they had their boats evaluated, and the hoplites were watching for them at the island's landing places. All who took their chances in calm weather were caught. There were also divers who swam the harbor under water, using cords to tow skins filled with poppyseed mixed with honey and ground linseed. After the first escaped notice, there was later a guard against them. Both sides exercised every ingenuity—the one in sending food in, the other in not letting it past.

[27] When they learned in Athens that the troops were undergoing hardships and food was getting in to the men on the island, they were at a loss and fearful of winter overtaking their blockade, since they saw that it would become impossible to send provisions around the Peloponnesos, when they were in a place without resources and unable even in summer to send in enough, and that there could be no continuing blockade of a region without harbors; the men on the island would either survive because they had abandoned their guard or would watch for winter storms

4.27–28. "In a place without resources and unable": I adopt the suggestion that Thucydides has identified the Athenians at Pylos with those at home, cf. Graves 1888 *ad* 4.27.1; I think this is supported by 7.14, see note there. Connor 1984, pp. 113–18 is perhaps the most recent to suggest that Kleon, already collaborating with Demosthenes, manipulated both the assembly and Nikias throughout and intentionally provoked the latter's resignation in his favor; this must be rejected, if only because the controversy with the messengers would have been an unnecessary and possibly counterproductive preliminary. More plausibly, Flower 1992 argues that the Athenians, in a previous assembly not recorded by Thucydides, had discussed a relief force in detail and elected Nikias to command it. Cf. Small 1995, pp. 164–65.

and sail out in the boats that brought in food. Most of all, they were alarmed about the Lacedaemonians, supposing that it was because they had some source of security that they were no longer negotiating with them; and they regretted not having accepted the truce.

Kleon, realizing that their misgivings over the refusal of the agreement were directed toward himself, said that the reports were not truthful. When the messengers from Pylos recommended that, if the Athenians did not believe them, they send official inspectors, Kleon himself was chosen, along with Theagenes. Realizing that he would be forced either to agree with those he had been denouncing or to face exposure as a liar when he said anything to the contrary, Kleon advised the Athenians, since he saw them also pretty much inclined to take military action, that they should not send inspectors and let the opportunity slip by delaying but, if they thought the reports were true, sail against the Lacedaemonians. He pointed to Nikias, one of the generals, putting personal hostility into the criticism that with the right preparation it was easy—if the generals were men—to sail and capture the troops on the island, and that he himself would certainly do it if he were in command. [28] And Nikias, since the Athenians were doing some clamoring at Kleon because he was not sailing right now if it seemed so easy, and since he saw himself under criticism, told him that, as far as the generals were concerned, he could try it with any force he wanted.

Kleon was ready at first, thinking that he was quitting in word only, but realizing that Nikias wanted to turn things over to him in actuality he backpedalled and said that he was not the general, Nikias was, by now terrified and not thinking that Nikias would have the audacity to withdraw in his favor. Nikias again told him to sail, and he made the Athenian people his witness that he resigned from the Pylos command. As a crowd is apt to do, the more Kleon continued to shun the expedition and take back what he had said, the more the Athenians exhorted Nikias to give up his command and shouted at Kleon to sail. And so Kleon, no longer having any escape from his words, took on the expedition and, addressing the assembly, said that he had no fear of the Lacedaemonians and would sail taking no forces from the city, but the Lemnians and Imbrians who were there, peltasts who had come to help from Ainos, and four hundred archers from other places. With these in addition to the troops at Pylos, he said, within twenty days he would either bring back the Lacedaemonians alive or kill them there. The Athenians now actually gave in to some laughter at his fatuous talk, while the more prudent among them also calculated with satisfaction that they would have one of two benefits: either they would get rid of Kleon, which they considered more likely, or, if their judgment was wrong, he would make the Lacedaemonians their prisoners.

[29] After Kleon had made all the arrangements in the assembly, and the Athenians had voted to entrust the expedition to him, he chose Demosthenes, one of the generals at Pylos, as his colleague and prepared for a quick departure. He chose Demosthenes on learning that he had his own intentions of making the landing on the island; the soldiers, in great difficulty because of the area's poor resources and more blockaded than blockading, were eager to risk the attempt, and the burning of the island gave Demosthenes additional keenness as well. Previously, the island's mostly overgrown state and lack of paths from remaining uninhabited had alarmed him, and he counted this more in the enemy's favor; if he landed with a large army, they would inflict damage by falling on him from an unseen position. Their mistakes and preparations would not be so visible to his men because of the woods, whereas all his own army's mistakes would be fully apparent, so they would be attacking him unexpectedly wherever they chose; the initiative would be with them. Conversely, if he was forced to go into a wooded area in close combat, he thought that a smaller force that knew the terrain would be superior to a larger one without that knowledge; his own army, large as it was, would be slaughtered before they realized it, since there was no way to see where they needed to help one another.

[30] These thoughts struck him especially because of the Aitolian disaster, which happened partly on account of the woods. But since his men were compelled by the shortage of space to land on the edges of the island and eat meals with an advance guard posted, and one of them accidentally set fire to a small part of the woods, and after this a wind came up, most of the woods burned down before they knew it. Seeing as a result that the Lacedaemonians were more numerous than he had thought (previously suspecting that they were sending in food for a smaller number) and that the Athenians were pursuing a more worthwhile object, also that the island was more accessible, he sent for forces from the nearby allies and made everything else ready.

Kleon, having sent word to Demosthenes that he was coming, arrived at Pylos with the forces he had requested. On meeting, they first sent a herald

---

4.30. It is very hard to believe that the fire was accidental; see Hunter 1973, pp. 71–72 and Wilson 1979, p. 103. "He had requested": probably Kleon rather than Demosthenes, but the idea of light-armed forces is just as probably Demosthenes' (this does not necessitate believing that the two men had long been in collusion, cf. 4.27–28n). See Flower 1992.

to the camp on the mainland, inviting them, if they wished, to tell the men on the island to surrender themselves and their arms, on the condition that they would be kept under the moderate sort of guard until some more extensive agreement was made. [31] When they refused, the Athenians waited one day, and on the next they set sail after embarking all their hoplites on a few ships during the night, landed a little before dawn on both sides of the island (toward the sea and toward the harbor), about eight hundred hoplites, and advanced at a run against the first guardpost on the island.

Now these were the Lacedaemonian positions: in the first guardpost were about thirty hoplites; most of the troops, with the commander Epitadas, held the middle and the most level part, which was also near the water supply; a detachment, which was not very large guarded the very end of the island near Pylos, which drops sheer to the sea and is also the hardest to attack from the side toward the land, since there was an old fort there built simply out of picked stones, which they thought would be useful if they had to retreat under severe pressure.

So they were stationed in this way; [32] and the Athenians with their charge against the first guards, immediately slaughtered them while they were still in their beds or in the process of arming, the Athenians having landed undetected because the Lacedaemonians thought that the ships were sailing in to the usual nighttime mooring. Right at dawn, the rest of the forces landed, the entire crews of slightly more than seventy ships (except for the lowest bank of rowers) equipped in whatever possible way, the Messenian reinforcements, and all others occupying Pylos except the guards of the fort. According to Demosthenes' organization, they were divided into groups of two hundred, sometimes more, sometimes less, seizing the highest areas so that the enemy would be in the greatest possible difficulty, surrounded on all sides and not knowing in which direction to form ranks, would then be struck from all sides by great numbers: hit by those from behind if they attacked those in front and by those on one side if they attacked on the opposite side. Whichever way they advanced, their enemies were always bound to be at their back, light-armed, and the most difficult opponents with their long-range strength through archery, javelins, stones, and slings, and immune to attack; for they would prevail by fleeing and fall on them when they withdrew.

4.31. The fortuitous old fort on an uninhabited island was built in the same primitive way as the Athenian fort (4.4).

4.32. Thucydides resumes the Athenian charge interrupted at mid-run by a "Homeric digression"; cf. 4.7n.

[33] With all this in mind, Demosthenes both first planned the landing and then organized it in actuality. And when the troops with Epitadas, the largest contingent on the island, saw that their first guard was destroyed and the enemy advancing, they formed their line and moved against the Athenian hoplites hoping to come to grips with them; for these were the ones standing in front of them, the light-armed on their flanks and rear. But, of course, they were unable to engage them or use their expertise, since the light-armed checked them by striking from both sides, and at the same time the hoplites did not move out to meet their advance but stayed still. Where the light-armed ran up and particularly pressed them, the Lacedaemonians would rout them, but the light-armed would turn around and fight back, being men with light equipment, who easily got the advantage in flight, and on difficult terrain, also rough on account of its previous deserted state, where the Lacedaemonians in their full armor could not pursue.

[34] So for a while they fought each other in this way, from a distance. But when the Lacedaemonians were no longer able to run out quickly where they were attacked, the light-armed, who realized that they were now slower in defending themselves, gaining the highest degree of confidence by seeing that they appeared much more numerous and getting used to the enemy's no longer appearing as formidable as before, since they had not immediately suffered in proportion to their expectations—especially compared with their mental subjugation when they first landed, going against Lacedaemonians—rushed them as one man, shouting their disdain, and struck them with stones, arrows, and javelins, depending on what each had at hand. And the shouting along with the attack struck consternation in men unused to this sort of battle, and the thick dust from the recently burned woods rose up, and it was difficult to see anything before one's eyes because of the arrows and stones hurled by many men, mixed with the dust.

At this point, the action settled into an ordeal for the Lacedaemonians. For their armor did not keep out the arrows, and the javelin points broke off as they were hit, and they were of no use to themselves, cut off from using their vision to see ahead, not hearing the orders they gave each other because of the louder shouting of their enemies, and, with danger threatening from every side, having no hope in any way of defending themselves and surviving. [35] Finally, with many casualties by now because all their manoeuvres were confined in the same space, they closed ranks and moved to the furthest point of the island, not far away, where their guards were. As they gave ground, right then the light-armed closed in with even louder shouting than before. All the Lacedaemonians caught during the retreat died, but most of them made their escape to the fort and stationed themselves along with the guards there at every point that could be attacked. The pursuing Athenians, unable to surround and encircle them because of the strength of the position, attacked frontally and tried to overpower them.

For a long time, in fact most of the day, both sides held out despite the hardships of fighting, thirst and hot sun, the one trying to drive the other from the high ground, the other trying not to give way. The Lacedaemonians defended themselves more easily than before, since they were not surrounded on their flanks. [36] After this went on endlessly, the Messenian commander came up to Kleon and Demosthenes and told them that they were wasting their efforts; if they were willing to give him some archers and light-armed to go around in back of the enemy wherever he could find a path, he thought they could force their way through. After he got what he requested, starting from a point out of sight to avoid detection and proceeding along the island's sheer side as long as it afforded some footing and where the Lacedaemonians, trusting in strength of position, had not set guards, he managed with extreme difficulty to get around them undetected and suddenly appeared on the high ground behind them, threw the one side into consternation by his unexpectedness, and gave the other much more vigor when they saw what they had been waiting for. And the Lacedaemonians, now being hit from both sides and in the same situation as at Thermopylai, to compare small things with great—there they were slaughtered when the Persians came around on the path, and these, now that they were struck from both sides, did not hold out, but fighting few against many and physically weakened by lack of food they gave way, and the Athenians were in control of every approach.

[37] Kleon and Demosthenes, realizing that if the Lacedaemonians continued to give way even in the slightest they would be slaughtered by their troops, stopped the battle and held their men back, wanting to bring the Lacedaemonians back to the Athenians alive, in case on hearing a her-

---

4.36. "And the Lacedaemonians . . . they gave way": I have tried to convey the way Thucydides strains syntax (*pace HCT* III *ad* 4.36.3, the text can stand) for the sake of a comparison that turns into a reiterated contrast disparaging the Spartans on Sphakteria. "To compare small things with great" is a phrase taken from Herodotos (2.10, 4.99: used to make purely physical comparisons), the definitive historian of the Persian War; the mock-tribute suggests a sceptical stance toward Thermopylai as well. Cf. 4.40n.

ald they might weaken in their resolve and succumb to the imminent danger. And they called on them to give up their arms and themselves, if they were willing, for the Athenians to deal with as they thought best. [38] When they heard this, most of them put down their shields and waved their hands, showing that they agreed to what was announced. After this, with a ceasefire established, Kleon and Demosthenes met to talk with Styphon, son of Pharax, from the other side, since of those previously in command Epitadas was dead; Hippagretos, who had been chosen as his successor, was still alive but lying among the corpses and believed dead; and Styphon had been chosen third in command according to their laws, in case anything happened to the others. Styphon and those with him said that they wanted to send a herald to the Lacedaemonians on the mainland to ask what they should do. Letting none of them leave, the Athenians summoned heralds from the mainland themselves, and after two or three consultations, the last man crossing over to them from the Lacedaemonians on the mainland announced, "The Lacedaemonians instruct you to make your own decision about yourselves, provided you do nothing dishonorable." After consulting one another, they surrendered their arms and themselves.

That day and the following night, the Athenians kept them under guard; the next day, after setting up a trophy on the island, they made other preparations to sail and handed over the men to the trierarchs under guard. The Lacedaemonians sent a herald and took back their dead. These were the numbers of the men who died on the island and those taken alive: four hundred twenty hoplites in all crossed over; two hundred ninety-two of these were brought back alive; and the rest died. Of those who lived, about one hundred twenty were Spartiates. Few of the Athenians were killed, since the fight was not a set battle. [39] The whole time the men were blockaded on the island, from the sea battle to the fight on the island, was seventy-two days. For about twenty of these, while the ambassadors were away seeing about the truce, they had food delivered, but the rest of the time they were provisioned by what came in secretly. There was actually grain on the island, and other food was recovered, since the commander Epitadas gave each man less than his resources would have permitted.

The Athenians and the Peloponnesians now each went home from Pylos with their forces, and Kleon's promise, crazy though it had seemed, was fulfilled: he brought back the men within twenty days, just as he undertook. [40] And indeed the Hellenes found this to be the most unexpected thing in the war, for they thought that the Lacedaemonians were not supposed to give up their arms because of hunger or compulsion but to keep them and die fighting any way they could. In this disinclination to believe that those who gave up were the equals of those who died, when an Athenian ally later asked one of the prisoners offensively whether their men who died were gallant gentlemen, he answered that it would be a valuable spindle (meaning the arrow) that distinguished the brave, making it clear that chance decided who was destroyed by stones and arrows. [41] After the men were brought in, the Athenians planned to keep them in fetters until some agreement was reached but, if the Peloponnesians invaded their land before then, to lead them out and kill them. They established a garrison at Pylos, and the Messenians from Naupaktos, sending their best-qualified troops to the land they considered their country (Pylos is what was once called Messenia), plundered Lakonia and caused the most damage because they spoke the same dialect. The Lacedaemonians, both because they had no previous experience of plundering and warfare of this sort and because, since the helots were deserting, they feared they would have some more extensive uprising throughout the territory, found this unbearable and, even though they did not want the Athenians aware of their desperation, sent embassies to them and tried to get back both Pylos and their men. But the Athenians were intent on larger gains and sent them away unsuccessful as often as they came.

This was the outcome regarding Pylos. [42] During the same summer, right after these events, the Athenians campaigned against Corinth with eighty ships, two thousand citizen hoplites, and two hundred cavalry on horse-transport ships. From their allies, the Milesians, Andrians, and Karystians joined them, and Nikias son of Nikeratos was one of the generals. They made their voyage and at dawn landed between Chersonesos and Rheitos on the beach of the region below the Solygeian hill, on which the Dorians of old camped and made war on the Corinthians in the city, who were Aiolians, and a village called Solygeia is there now. From this beach where the ships put in, this village is twelve stades, the city of Corinth sixty stades, and the Isthmus twenty. The Corinthians, who had learned previously from Argos that the Athenian forces would be coming, had all gathered in advance for defense at the isthmus, except for those who lived beyond; five hundred of their men were also absent for garrisons in

---

4.40. "Gallant gentlemen": on the phrase (more literally, "fine brave men") see Bourriot 1995 (vol. 1, pp. 167–78 on 4.40), more briefly Dover 1974, pp. 41–45, and cf. 8.48. "A valuable spindle": Herodotos' account of Thermopylai also includes a Spartan witticism disparaging archery (7.226).

Ambracia and Leukas. But the rest kept a watch in full force for the Athenians to land. Since the Athenians, by sailing at night, escaped their guard, and signals sent them warning, they left half their men at Kenchreai in case the Athenians moved against Krommyon and hurried to the defense. [43] And Battos, one of the generals (there were two in the field), took part of them and went to Solygeia to defend the village, which was unfortified, while Lykophron went into battle with the rest.

The Corinthians first advanced against the Athenian right wing, which had just disembarked in front of Chersonesos, and then against the rest of the army. The battle was hard fought and completely hand-to-hand. The right wing of the Athenians and the Karystians (these had been stationed on the end) stood their ground and with an effort drove the Corinthians back; after they had retreated to a stone wall, since the whole area was very steep, they threw stones from their position above and after singing the paian they attacked again, and once more the fighting was hand-to-hand as the Athenians stood their ground. A Corinthian detachment that had come to help their left wing routed the Athenian right and pursued it to the sea; but at the ships the Athenians and the Karystians rallied in turn. The other troops on both sides fought stubbornly, especially the Corinthian right where Lykophron, opposing the Athenian left, was holding them off; for they expected them to make an attempt on the village of Solygeia. [44] So for a long time both sides stood their ground without giving way. Then, since the cavalry gave the Athenians valuable help in the fighting when the other side had none, the Corinthians were routed and after withdrawing to the hill took up their position there and remained inactive instead of coming back down. And during this rout most of those on the right wing were killed along with the general Lykophron. The rest of the army, since they were not pursued far, and there was no hurried flight when they were forced back, had a settled position when they retreated to the high ground in this way. But the Athenians, since the others no longer took the field against them, stripped the bodies, took up their own dead, and immediately set up a trophy.

For the half of the Corinthian army stationed at Kenchreai as guards lest they sail against Krommyon, the battle was invisible because of Mt. Oneion, but when they saw the dust and understood, they immediately came to help. The older Corinthians also came to the rescue from the city when they realized what had happened. The Athenians, since they saw all these men advancing and thought reinforcements were advancing from nearby neighbors in the Peloponnesos, withdrew hastily to their ships with the spoils and their own dead except for two they could not find and left behind. They embarked and crossed to the islands off shore, and after sending a herald from this position they took up under truce the bodies they had left behind. Two hundred twelve Corinthians and slightly under fifty Athenians died in the battle. [45] Putting out from the islands, the Athenians sailed on the same day to Krommyon in Corinthian territory, about one hundred twenty stades from the city, and after dropping anchor they plundered the land and bivouacked for the night. The next day, after first sailing along the coast to Epidauros and making a landing, they reached Methana between Epidauros and Troizen, and they built a wall cutting off the isthmus that Methana occupies, and after they installed a garrison they subsequently raided the land of Troizen, Haliai, and Epidauros. When they had fortified the place, they returned home with their ships.

[46] Around the same time this was happening, Eurymedon and Sophokles, after setting out from Pylos for Sicily with the Athenian ships, reached Corcyra and campaigned along with the people from the city against the Corcyreans entrenched on Mt. Istone, who had crossed over in that time after the revolution and were controlling the countryside and doing great damage. They attacked their fort and captured it, and the occupants, after escaping together to the high ground, agreed to terms by which they were to give up their foreign mercenaries and were themselves to lay down their arms and let the Athenian people decide about them. The generals conveyed them under a truce to the island of Ptychia to guard them until they were sent to Athens, on the condition that, if anyone was caught running away, the truce was broken for all. Fearing that the Athenians would not execute them on arrival, the Corcyrean popular leaders used the following scheme. They convinced a number of the men on the island by secretly sending friends over and, as though out of actual good will, instructing them to tell the men that the best thing for them was to escape as quickly as possible, and they had a boat ready; for the Athenian generals were going to hand them over to the Corcyrean people. [47] In this way they convinced them, and after they provided the boat those sailing out were caught, and the truce was broken and all handed over to the Corcyreans. Largely responsible for this, in rendering the pretext valid and the schemers bolder in their attempt, were the Athenian generals, who unmistakably did not want the men to be brought back by others, since they themselves were sailing to Sicily, and transfer the honor to their escorts.

The Corcyreans took control of the men and shut them up in a large building, and later they brought them out in groups of twenty and sent them between two rows of hoplites lined up on either side, and while bound together they were beaten and stabbed by anyone in the lines who saw a personal enemy; men with whips went beside them and hurried the progress of those who passed too slowly. [48] And they led out and killed up to sixty without the knowledge of those in the building (who thought they were taking the men to move them somewhere else). But when they understood, and someone made it clear to them, they called on the Athenians, urging that they kill them themselves if they wished, and they were no longer willing to go out of the building but said that as far as it was in their power they would let no one in. The Corcyreans were equally disinclined to use force at the doors but, after going onto the top of the building and piercing through the roof, threw down the tiles and shot arrows. While protecting themselves as well as they could, most of them killed themselves, either by plunging into their throats the arrows fired down or by hanging themselves with cords from some beds they happened to have inside and with strips taken from their clothing. And for much of the night that descended on their suffering they did away with themselves by any means or were hit by the men above them. When day came, the Corcyreans piled them in wagons like lumber and hauled them out of the city. They enslaved all the women they captured in the fort. In this way the Corcyreans from the mountain were destroyed by the common people, and the civil war, which had been so extensive, ended here, at least as far as this war is concerned; for on one side there was nothing left to speak of. Sailing off to Sicily, their original destination, the Athenians carried on the war with their allies there.

[49] Just as the summer was ending, the Athenians at Naupaktos and the Akarnanians campaigned against Anaktorion, the Corinthian town that lies at the mouth of the Ambracian gulf and took it with the help of traitors. Expelling the Corinthians, the Akarnanians occupied the place with their own settlers from all over. And the summer ended. [50] In the following winter, Aristeides son of Archippos, one of the commanders of the Athenian ships sent out to the allies to collect money, arrested Artaphernes, a Persian, at Eion on the Strymon when he was on his way from the king to Lacedaemon. After he was brought to Athens, the Athenians had his correspondence transcribed from Assyrian writing and read it, where the main topic among the many things recorded was that the king did not know what the Lacedaemonians wanted, for many ambassadors had come, and none said the same thing; now if they were willing to speak plainly, they were to send men to him with the Persian. The Athenians later sent Artaphernes to Ephesos in a trireme along with ambassadors. After learning there that King Artaxerxes son of Xerxes had recently died (it happened around this time), they returned home. [51] During this same

winter, the Chians pulled down their new wall on orders from the Athenians, who were suspicious of them, but only after getting the best pledges and security they could on the part of the Athenians that they were planning nothing drastic toward them. And the winter ended, also the seventh year of this war, which Thucydides recorded.

[52] At the beginning of the next summer, there was an eclipse of the sun at the time of the new moon, and early in the same month there was an earthquake. Also, Mytilenean and other Lesbian exiles, setting out in most cases from the mainland with mercenaries they had hired from the Peloponnesos and gathered locally, captured Rhoiteion. After receiving two thousand Phokaian staters, they returned it without doing damage. After this they campaigned against Antandros and captured the city when treachery occurred. And it was their intention to free the other Aktaian cities as well, which were once held by the Mytileneans and now occupied by the Athenians, but above all Antandros, and with it in their possession (for it was convenient there for building ships, with timber at hand and Mt. Ida nearby, and for other preparations) to make easy expeditions from there to ravage Lesbos nearby and subdue the Aiolian towns on the mainland.

[53] They planned these preparations, and meanwhile, in the same summer, the Athenians campaigned against Kythera with sixty ships, two thousand hoplites, and a few cavalry, bringing Milesians and some other allies; they were commanded by Nikias son of Nikeratos, Nikostratos son of Dieitrephes, and Autokles son of Tolmaios. Kythera is an island lying off Lakonia opposite Malea; the people are Lacedaemonians from the perioikoi; an official called the Judge of Kythera went over to it every year, and they also kept a garrison of hoplites over there at all times and paid the place considerable attention; it was the point of approach for merchant ships from Egypt and Libya, and in addition pirates were then less able to harm Lakonia from the sea, the only area where from which there was a possibility of doing damage (the whole area extends out into the Sicilian and Cretan seas). [54] Now the Athenians put in with their forces and captured the town called Skandeia on the sea with ten ships and two thousand Milesian hoplites, and landing with the rest of the army on the side toward Malea, they advanced on the city of the Kytherians and discovered that they had all immediately turned it into a camp. When a battle ensued, the Kytherians held their ground for a short time and then turned and fled to the upper city, and afterward they accepted terms from Nikias and his colleagues to entrust themselves to the Athenians provided they were not killed. There had been some correspondence between Nikias and some of the Kytherians previously as well, and on that account both the immediate

terms and those of the subsequent agreement were arranged more favorably as well as more quickly; otherwise, the Athenians would have expelled the Kytherians, both because they were Lacedaemonian and because of the position the island had off Lakonia. After the agreement, the Athenians took over the town of Skandeia near the harbor and installed a garrison for Kythera, then sailed to Asine, Elos, and most of the places on the coast, and after landing and bivouacking in convenient locations they ravaged the land for about seven days.

[55] The Lacedaemonians, seeing the Athenians in control of Kythera and expecting them to make these landings on their own territory, did not oppose them anywhere with a concentration of strength but distributed throughout their land garrisons of hoplites in the numbers each place required and in general were in a very protective position, fearing some kind of revolution in the established order, both because the disaster on the island had been unexpected and severe and because Pylos and Kythera were occupied, and on all sides a rapid and unpredictable war encompassed them; and so, contrary to their usual practice, they organized four hundred cavalry and some archers. And in military activity, although hesitant before, they became very much more so, engaged in a naval struggle that was outside the settled pattern of their methods, a struggle against the Athenians for whom whatever was not attempted was a gap in their expected accomplishments. And at the same time, many turns of fortune within a short period and beyond calculation had brought them into a complete state of shock, and they were afraid that once again they would encounter some catastrophe just like the one on the island, and this made them less bold in giving battle, and they thought any action they took would go wrong, owing to their loss of self-confidence in place of their previous unfamiliarity with failure. [56] For the most part, they acquiesced now as the Athenians ravaged the coastal area, every time a garrison was faced with a landing, every garrison thinking its numbers too few for such a situation. One garrison that actually did make a stand, near Kotyrta and Aphroditia, terrified the unorganized mob of light-armed by charging, but faced with hoplites they drew back again after the loss of a few of their men and the capture of some of their weapons, and the Athenians set up a trophy and sailed away to Kythera. They sailed from there around to Limeran Epidauros and after plundering part of the territory reached Thyrea, which is in the territory called Kynouria and on the border between Argive and Lakonian land; its owners, the Lacedaemonians, had given it to the Aiginetans to live in after they were expelled, for their good service to them at the time of the earthquake and helot revolt, also

because the Aiginetans had always taken their side despite being subject to the Athenians.

[57] Now the Aiginetans, while the Athenians were still approaching at sea, abandoned the fort that they were just building on the coast and withdrew to the upper town where they lived, about ten stades from the sea. Their Lacedaemonian garrison, one of those sent all over which was helping them build the fort, had no wish to join them inside, as the Aiginetans pleaded, when being shut up in the fort seemed an obvious danger to them; withdrawing to the high ground, since they did not consider themselves evenly matched, they stayed inactive. At this point, the Athenians landed, advanced immediately with all their forces, and captured Thyrea. They burned the town and sacked its possessions; any Aiginetans not killed in action, they took with them to Athens as well as the Lacedaemonian leader among them, Tantalos son of Patroklos, taken prisoner after he was wounded. They also took a few men from Kythera whom it seemed best to remove for reasons of security. The Athenians decided to deposit them on the islands, to let the other Kytherians occupy their own lands and pay four talents in tribute, to kill all the Aiginetans that they had captured on account of the hostility already long in existence, and to imprison Tantalos with the other Lacedaemonians on the island.

[58] In Sicily, during the same summer, there was first an armistice between the Kamarinaians and Geloans; then the other Sikeliots also gathered at Gela in delegations from all the cities and conferred with one another about some way to end the fighting. After much was said in favor and in opposition as they advanced their arguments and their claims of their own supposed deprivations, Hermokrates son of Hermon and also the man who had done the most to persuade them to come to the meeting, spoke in much these words: [59] "It is not because I come from the most insignificant city, Sikeliots, nor from one that has suffered most in the war that I address you, but because I am declaring in public what I think is the best policy for all of Sicily. Regarding war and how terrible it is, why

---

4.57. The withering indictment of Spartan military ineptitude and the contrast with past complacence (4.55) are dramatized by the fate of the Aiginetans. The Spartans had given them a refuge that they must have thought unassailable for all time; they are now pusillanimous as protectors.

4.59. "Not . . . from the most insignificant city": striking and masterful opening. Syracuse is powerful, and Hermokrates acknowledges this at the outset; concomitantly, he breaks away from the parochial and querulous tone which, according to Thucydides, has dominated the conference.

would anyone rehearse everything it involves in a long speech among men
who know this? For no one is forced into it out of ignorance any more than
he is deterred by fear if he believes he will gain an advantage. The situation
of the former is that the gains appear greater than the risks, while the latter
is willing to face the danger before accepting any momentary deprivation.
But if both parties happen to have chosen the wrong circumstances for
even this behavior, advice about accommodation is invaluable. For us to
see this in the present situation would be a great benefit. Each of us
planned the right way to deal with our own affairs when we first went to
war, no doubt, and now we are attempting reconciliation by debating one
another, and if each of us does not then manage to leave here with his fair
share, we will go back to fighting.

[60] "Yet we must realize that if we are sensible our conference will not
be only about individual concerns but also about whether we can still save
Sicily, the whole of which, in my judgment, is being plotted against by the
Athenians, and we must understand that my words do not mediate these
individual concerns nearly so insistently as the Athenians do, who have
the greatest power in Hellas, who are here with a few ships watching for
our mistakes, who are speciously using the respectable concept of alliance
to take advantage of normal hostilities. For if we choose war and call them
in, men who of their own accord join the campaigns of others without
invitation, and we use our own resources to damage one another, and in
so doing carve a path for their domination, it is likely that, when they see
us worn out, they will one day come in person with a larger armada and
try to bring whatever we have under their control. [61] If we are prudent,
however, it should be for adding to our own states what is not yet available, rather than ruining what is already on hand, that we call in allies and
take on risks, and we should understand that faction is the greatest
destroyer of cities and of Sicily, where the inhabitants are assuredly all in
one group regarding the plots against us, but as cities we are disparate.
Understanding this should make us reconcile individual with individual
and city with city and not leave anyone with the notion that, while those
of us who are Dorians are enemies of Athens, the Chalkidian element is
safe through Ionian kinship. For it is not against races that they attack,
because there are two here and they hate one of them, but out of longing
for the good things in Sicily, which we possess in common. They have
demonstrated this now in the case of the appeal from the Chalkidian people; for to those who never once sent help to them in accordance with their
alliance they have eagerly offered on their part a measure beyond their
agreement.

"For the Athenians to reach for more and lay plans in this way, one can make every allowance, and I do not blame those who wish to rule but those who are too willing to be subjects; for it is ever part of human nature to rule those who yield, just as it is to resist those who encroach. But any of us who realize this and have not made the right provisions, or have not come here with the decision to give priority to this, a common resolution of the threat against all, are misguided. The quickest way of dealing with this would be to settle with one another; for the Athenians are not launching their onslaught from their own land but from that of the people who have called them in. And this will not be ending war through war, but disputes through peace without interference, and those whose invitation gives them a good excuse for coming unjustly will have a good reason for going away unfulfilled.

[62] "Regarding the Athenians, all this benefit may be found by those making the right plans; but as to what is universally acknowledged as the greatest benefit, how should we not in this case make peace among ourselves? Or is it your opinion that, where one party enjoys good things and another their opposite, war instead of peace would end the latter situation and confirm the former, that peace does not involve honor and splendor of a less dangerous kind, and all the other qualities that would take as long to describe as would talking about war? Keeping these in mind, you should not overlook my words but look beyond them to the safety they offer each. And if there is anything someone feels assured of accomplishing, either because he is right or because he is powerful, let him not be embittered by failing against his hopes, but realize that many men before now have pursued wrongdoers with vengeance, or in other cases strength has given hopes of aggrandizement, and then so totally failed to settle accounts that they did not survive, or it turned out that instead of making gains they lost even what they had. For vengeance does not succeed as a matter of justice, for all that wrong is committed, and might is not security, for all that it is accompanied by hope. But the uncertain side of the future holds the widest domain and has proved the most baffling thing of all, yet also the most useful; for the fear that we all feel alike makes us more circumspect about attacking one another.

[63] "And now, in our undefined fears of this lack of certainty, as well as in alarm at the immediate presence of the Athenians, since we are unnerved on both counts, let us suppose that if there was inadequate fulfillment of what each of us expected to accomplish, we were adequately blocked by these obstacles, and let us arrange for the enemies who have presented themselves to leave the country, and ideally let us reconcile for

all time, but if not, let us make a truce for as long as possible and put off our individual quarrels until later. And let us have the most total understanding that by taking my advice each of us will have a free city giving us sovereign power to act as equals in making rightful redress for good actions and bad. But if we fail to believe this and submit to others, there will be no question of our punishing anyone, but even at our most successful, we may have enemies as our friends, but we are being forced into alienation where we should not be.

[64] "As for myself, even though, as I said straightaway, I represent a very great city and have the initiative rather than a defensive role, foresight makes me capable of concessions in the situation here, in not damaging my enemies in such a way that will do me the greater harm nor supposing that I am equally master of my own policies and of chances beyond my control, rather than yielding whatever is within reason. I call on the rest of you to act as I do, letting this be your own choice, not one made by enemies. For there is nothing disgraceful in kinsmen yielding to kinsmen, as Dorian does to Dorian or Chalkidian to his relatives, and when we are all finally neighbors living together in the same land and surrounded by the same waters and given the single name of Sikeliot. And as such we will go to war when it suits us, I suppose, and come to terms among ourselves again, no doubt, through common debates. But we will always be united in defense against foreign invaders if we are sensible, since we are all truly endangered when any one of us is harmed, and never in the future will we import allies or mediators. By these actions we will not deprive Sicily of two benefits, release both from the Athenians and from domestic war, and in the future we will live in freedom among ourselves with fewer threats from others."

[65] After Hermokrates spoke in this way, the Sikeliots were convinced and reached an agreement among themselves with a resolution that they end their wars, each of them keeping what they held, and that the Kamarinaians were to have Morgantina after paying the Syracusans a specified sum. The allies of the Athenians sent for the Athenians in charge and told them they were going to make peace, and that the terms would include them. After these gave their approval, they concluded their agreement, and afterward the Athenian ships sailed away from Sicily. On the arrival of the generals, the Athenians in the city exiled two of them, Pythodoros and Sophokles, and fined the third, Eurymedon, because when it had been possible for them to take over Sicily, they took bribes and left. So extreme, in the midst of their current good fortune, was their conviction that nothing would stand in their way, that they would accomplish the practicable and the more problematic alike, whether with a great force or a weaker one.

The cause was their extraordinary success in most respects, lending strength to their hopes.

[66] In the same summer, the Megarians in the city, hard pressed in the war by the Athenians, who invaded their land twice every year in full force, and also by their own exiles based at Pagai, troublesome as raiders after the popular party had exiled them during a revolution, began suggesting to one another the need to let the exiles return so that the city would not be ruined from both quarters. When the friends of the outsiders heard about this talk, they became more open in their own insistence on this proposal. The democratic leaders, knowing that the people would not be capable of standing firm with them in these difficulties, were frightened into making approaches to the Athenian generals, Hippokrates son of Ariphron and Demosthenes son of Alkisthenes, and were willing to betray the city because they considered this a lesser danger to themselves than the return of those they had driven out. And so they arranged that first the Athenians were to take the long walls (these extended about eight stades, from the city to the port of Nisaia), to keep the Peloponnesians from bringing help from Nisaia, of which they were the sole occupants as a garrison for keeping the Megarians on their side, and then they would attempt to turn over the upper city; by that time, after what had already been done, the people were expected to come over with less trouble. [67] Accordingly, after they had finished arranging what they would do and say, the Athenians sailed in the night to the Megarian island of Minoa with six hundred hoplites commanded by Hippokrates and took up a position in a nearby pit used to make bricks for the walls. A group with Demosthenes, the other general, some light-armed Plataians and other special forces, lay in ambush at the sanctuary of Enyalios, which is somewhat closer. No one was aware of this except, on that night, those intended to know.

When dawn approached, it was the Megarian traitors who acted, in the following way. As a long-standing provision for getting the gates opened, they had been bringing a small boat on a wagon through the moat down to the sea at nighttime like privateers, with the commander's permission, and sailing out; before day, bringing it back to the wall on the wagon, they went in through the gates, supposedly so that the Athenian guards off Minoa would have nothing to see, since there was no boat visible in the harbor. And this time the wagon was already at the gates, and when they were opened for the boat, as usual, the Athenians (since all this was pre-arranged) saw this and ran from the ambush at top speed, since they wanted to get there before the gates were shut, and while the wagon was still there blocking their closing; meanwhile, their Megarian collaborators were helping them by killing the guards at the gates. The Plataians and special forces with Demosthenes rushed in first, where the trophy now stands, and as soon as they were inside the gates the Plataians met and defeated the Peloponnesians who came to the rescue (since those closest had learned what was happening) and kept the gates ready for the attack of the Athenian hoplites. [68] Then each of the Athenians went to the wall as soon as he was inside. At first a few Peloponnesians made a stand and fought back, and some of them were killed, while most were put to flight, terrified because the enemy had fallen on them at night and also thinking, since the Megarian traitors were fighting against them, that all the Megarians had betrayed them. It also happened that the Athenian herald on his own initiative proclaimed that any Megarian who wished should go to fight along with the Athenians. And when they heard this, they no longer stayed but fled to Nisaia, thinking that they were unquestionably facing a concerted attack.

At dawn, when the walls had been captured, and the Megarians in the city were in turmoil, those working with the Athenians, along with a number of others in on the plot, said that they should open the gates and march out for battle. Their arrangement was that when the gates were opened the Athenians would rush in, but they themselves were to be marked (by anointment with oil) to avoid being harmed. There was additional safety in opening the gates; as part of the arrangements, four thousand Athenian hoplites from Eleusis and six hundred cavalry had arrived after a night march. But when they were anointed and already at the gates, one of the conspirators denounced the plot to the other side. These drew themselves into a compact group and said that they should neither march out, which they had never been bold enough to do even when their strength was greater, nor put the city in obvious danger; and if anyone objected, the battle would be here and now. They did not reveal what they knew about what was going on, but they insisted that their advice was best and at the same time stayed around the gates guarding them, and it was impossible for the plotters to carry out their intentions.

[69] The Athenian generals realized that there had been some setback, and that they would not be able to capture the city by force, and they immediately began walling off Nisaia, thinking that, if they took it before reinforcements came, Megara would come over sooner as well. Iron, stoneworkers, and other necessities were quickly brought from Athens. Starting from the wall, which they held, and building a cross wall at the part toward Megara, from that point to the sea on either side of Nisaia, the army divided up the work on both the ditch and the walls, using stones and

bricks from the suburbs, and they cut down orchards and woods and built a palisade wherever it was needed; even the suburban houses became defenses by acquiring battlements. They worked for this entire day; the next afternoon the wall was all but finished, and the men in Nisaia, alarmed because of the lack of food (they were being provisioned day by day from the upper city) and since they did not expect the Peloponnesians to reinforce them soon and considered the Megarians hostile, reached an agreement with the Athenians that each would be ransomed for a stated sum after laying down his arms, and that the Athenians would deal as they chose with the Lacedaemonians, both the commander and all others inside. They agreed to these terms and came out, and the Athenians broke the long walls away from the city of Megara, took over Nisaia, and made their other preparations.

[70] Brasidas son of Tellis, the Lacedaemonian, happened to be around Sikyon and Corinth at this time, preparing an army to go to Thrace. When he heard about the capture of the walls, he feared for the Peloponnesians in Nisaia and that Megara would be captured, and he sent to the Boiotians urging them to meet him as quickly as possible at Tripodiskos (a village in the Megarid by that name which is under Mt. Geraneia) and went himself with twenty-seven hundred Corinthian hoplites, four hundred Phleiasians, six hundred Sikyonians, and all those of his own men already collected, thinking that he would reach Nisaia while it was still uncaptured. When he found out, before possible discovery (as it happened, he had gone out to Tripodiskos at nighttime), he picked out three hundred men and came up to Megara without being detected by the Athenians down by the sea, wishing, as he claimed and intended if possible, to make an attempt on Nisaia but above all to enter the city of Megara and keep it loyal. [71] He told them they should admit him, since he had hopes of recovering Nisaia, but the factions in Megara were afraid—one of them that he would bring in the exiles and drive them out, the other that the common people would fear this very thing and fall upon them, and that with a battle inside and the Athenians lying in wait nearby the city would be destroyed—and did not admit him, and both sides decided instead to stay quiet and wait for the outcome. For they each expected a battle between the Athenians and the rescue forces as well, so that it would be safer to join whichever of these each side favored once they had won. And Brasidas, since he had not persuaded them, returned to the rest of his army.

[72] Just at dawn, the Boiotians, having intended to help Megara even before Brasidas sent for them, arrived since there was nothing remote about the danger, and they were already at Plataia in full force; but when

the messenger came, they were far more urgent even than before and sent off twenty-two hundred hoplites and six hundred cavalry, returning home with the rest. Once the whole army was present, no fewer than six thousand hoplites, and the Athenian hoplites were in formation near Nisaia and the sea, while their light-armed were scattered over the plain, the Boiotian cavalry drove the light-armed to the sea by falling on them unexpectedly (for in the past, no sort of help had ever been sent to Megara from any source). The Athenian cavalry in turn charged out and engaged them, and there was a cavalry battle for a long time, in which both sides claimed to be the winners. The Athenians killed and stripped the Boiotian cavalry commander and a few others who had charged on Nisaia itself, and with these dead in their possession they gave back the bodies under truce and set up a trophy; yet in the overall action, neither side had by any means accomplished anything definite when they separated and retired, the Boiotians to their army, the others to Nisaia.

[73] After this, Brasidas and the army came closer to the sea and the city of Megara, and finding the terrain advantageous, they stayed inactive after forming their ranks, not believing that the Athenians would attack and understanding that the Megarians were watching to see which would be the victor. And they thought that both factors were in their favor, first by their not taking the initiative of beginning the battle or willingly undertaking the risk, since they had made their readiness to defend themselves very apparent, and the victory would justly be attributed to them, like that of an unchallenged athlete, and also in their success regarding the Megarians; for if they had not come and showed themselves, there would have been no chance at all, but clearly they would have lost the city right away, just as though they had been defeated; but now it might even happen that the Athenians were unwilling to contend with them, so that what they wanted would result without a fight.

This was exactly what happened. Since the Athenians, after coming out and forming their ranks beside the long walls, stayed inactive as well when they were not attacked, their generals in turn thinking that, with most of their objectives realized, there was too heavy a risk in starting a battle against superior numbers and either capturing Megara by winning or crippling their strength in hoplites by losing, but on the opposite side each contingent of the whole army and the forces on hand would naturally be inclined toward bold risks, and waited for a while, and since neither side ever

---

4.73. "Not believing": I believe that this passage requires emendation as in Classen/Steup IV *ad* 4.73.1 (contra, *HCT* III *ad* 4.73.2–3).

attacked, but the Athenians made their withdrawal to Nisaia first, and then the Peloponnesians to where they came from, what finally occurred was that the Megarians friendly to the exiles, as though Brasidas had won because the Athenians were no longer willing to fight, were confident enough to open the gates and admit him and the leaders from the other cities and confer with them, while the partisans of the Athenians stood by dumbfounded.

[74] Afterward, when the allies had dispersed to their cities, Brasidas himself went back to Corinth and prepared for his expedition to Thrace, which was actually his destination in the first place. Meanwhile, after the Athenians had also left for home, the Megarians who had been especially involved on the Athenian side, knowing that they had been found out, immediately slipped away, while the others, after consultation with the friends of the exiles, restored them from Pagai and bound them by the most solemn oaths not to hold grudges but counsel what was best for the city. But for their part, after they were in office and held a review of the hoplites, in separating the companies they picked out their enemies and those who seemed especially partial to the Athenians, about a hundred, and after compelling the people to make an open vote on them, resulting in their conviction, they put them to death and they turned the city into an extreme oligarchy. And this result of political strife, the work of so few, was a very lasting political change.

[75] In the same summer, when Antandros was about to be equipped by the Mytileneans in accordance with their plans, Demodokos and Aristeides, the commanders of the Athenian money-collecting ships, heard about the preparations for the place while they were near the Hellespont (Lamachos, the third commander, had sailed into the Pontos with ten ships) and thought there was a danger of its becoming what Anaia was for Samos (this was where the Samian exiles established themselves, helped the Peloponnesians by sending pilots for their ships, and kept the Samians in the city in turmoil and took in defectors), so they then gathered together a force from the allies, and setting sail and defeating in battle those who came out against them from Antandros, they took the place back. Not long after, Lamachos, who had sailed into the Pontos and anchored on the Kalex river in the territory of Herakleia, lost his ships when rain fell, and the flood suddenly descended. He and his forces went on foot through the Bithynian Thracians, who are over in Asia, to Chalkedon, the Megarian colony at the mouth of the Pontos.

[76] Also in the same summer, Demosthenes, the Athenian general, arrived at Naupaktos with forty ships, right after the withdrawal from the Megarid. For he and Hippokrates were involved in a Boiotian intrigue on

the part of certain men in the cities, who wanted to change the government and turn it toward democracy just as in Athens. And these preparations were being made with Ptoiodoros, a Thespian exile, as the chief instigator. Some were to betray Siphai (a coastal town on the Gulf of Krisa, in Thespian territory); others, from Orchomenos, were to turn over Chaironeia, which belongs to what was once called Minyan, but now Boiotian Orchomenos, and exiles from Orchomenos were especially active in the conspiracy and hiring mercenaries from the Peloponnesos (Chaironeia is on the border of Boiotia near Phanotis in Phokis, and some Phokians were involved). The Athenians were supposed to seize Delion, the sanctuary of Apollo in Tanagran territory across from Euboia. All this was supposed to happen at the same time on the designated day, so that the Boiotians would not defend themselves by uniting at Delion but separately, where each had their own troubles. And if the attempt succeeded, and Delion was fortified, they fully expected, even if there was no immediate revolution in Boiotian government, that once these places were captured, the land was plundered, and a refuge for any defector was close at hand, the situation would not remain as it had been but after a while, with the Athenians supporting the rebels and the opposing forces divided, would be settled in a favorable way. [77] The plot was designed in this way; Hippokrates himself was to march against the Boiotians with a force from the city when the right time came, and he sent Demosthenes ahead to Naupaktos with the forty ships to form an army in those parts from the Akarnanians and the other allies and sail to Siphai when it had been betrayed; a day was decided between them for doing these simultaneously. Demosthenes, reaching Oiniadai and finding it had been forced into the Athenian alliance by the Akarnanians, for his part raised all the allied forces in the area, campaigned against Salynthios and the Agraians and brought them over, and then made his preparations to appear at Siphai at the right time.

[78] Around the same time in the summer, Brasidas marched to the Thracian area with seventeen hundred hoplites. When he arrived at Herakleia in Trachis, he sent a message to his friends in Pharsalos asking them to escort him and his army; only after Panairos, Doros, Hippolochidas, Torylaos, and Striophokos, the Chalkidian proxenos joined him at Meliteia did he continue his march. Other Thessalians also accompanied him, including Nikonidas, a friend of Perdikkas. For in general it was not easy to pass through Thessaly without an escort, and of course among all

4.76. "A Thespian exile": see *HCT* III *ad* 4.76.3.

the Hellenes alike suspicion definitely existed concerning an armed force crossing a neighbor's territory without permission. Besides, the majority of Thessalians felt long-standing good will toward the Athenians; if the Thessalians had been ruled not by a narrow oligarchy of their traditional sort but by constitutional government, Brasidas would never have been able to proceed, since even then other Thessalians of the opposition confronted him and blocked his way, saying that he was acting illegally in marching without unanimous consent. His escorts said that they would not take him through against their will but were acting as his hosts, attending to an unexpected visitor. Brasidas himself stated that he came as a friend to Thessaly, themselves included, and was in arms against the Athenians, who were at war with him, not against them; although he knew of no hostility between Thessaly and the Lacedaemonians to prevent access to each others' land, he would not now proceed against their wishes, since this was impossible, but nevertheless requested them not to stop him. They listened and went away; on the advice of his escorts, he moved on rapidly without a halt before a larger group could gather to block him. And on the day he set out from Melitia, he reached Pharsalos and camped on the Apidanos river, reached Phakion next and then Perrhaibia. His Thessalian escorts left him at this point, and the Perrhaibians, who are subjects of the Thessalians, brought him to Dion, a Macedonian town in the kingdom of Perdikkas, under Mt. Olympos, toward Thessaly.

[79] In this way, Brasidas hurried through Thessaly quickly enough to anticipate any preparation to stop him, and he reached Perdikkas and the Chalkidike. For Perdikkas as well as those in Thrace who had revolted from Athens, fearful because of the Athenians' success, instigated the expedition from the Peloponnesos: the Chalkidians because they thought that it was against them the Athenians would advance first (at the same time, neighboring cities that had not revolted had secretly sent to the Peloponnesians); Perdikkas because, without being openly at war with the Athenians, he had his own fears about their long-standing differences, and especially because he wanted to subdue Arrhabaios, king of the Lynkestians.

The current predicament of the Lacedaemonians made it relatively easy for these to get an army from the Peloponnesos. [80] For the Lacedaemonians, since the Athenians were attacking the Peloponnesos and especially their own land, saw their best chance of diverting them in harassing them in return by sending an army to their allies, especially since these were willing to support it and were calling it in to help their revolt. At the same time, the Lacedaemonians were glad for the pretext to send some helots away, lest with Pylos captured the present situation might lead them to start an insurrection. Indeed, in their fear of the intransigence and numerical strength of the helots (for at all times most of the Lacedaemonians' relations with the helots were based mainly on security), they also did the following. They proclaimed that as many as claimed to have done best against the enemies of the Lacedaemonians should be chosen in order to receive their freedom, making a test on the assumption that those who first claimed their freedom would in each case also be the ones who would rise against them, on account of their high spirit. And with the selection of about two thousand, these put on garlands and went around the temples thinking that they had been freed; but the Lacedaemonians soon after did away with them, and no one knew how each was murdered. And now they eagerly sent seven hundred of them as hoplites with Brasidas, who brought the rest of his men from the Peloponnesos by hiring them as mercenaries.

[81] The Lacedaemonians sent out Brasidas mainly at his own wish but also with the enthusiasm of the Chalkidians, a man who in Sparta was considered energetic in every way and also, outside the country, was of the greatest value to the Lacedaemonians. For right away, by behaving justly and moderately toward the cities, he caused many to revolt and took other places with the help of treachery, with the result that the Lacedaemonians had the possibility of places to give in exchange when they wanted to make peace—as they eventually did—and also got a respite from warfare based in the Peloponnesos. In the later part of the war after the Sicilian expedition, the courage and intelligence of Brasidas in earlier times, known to some by experience and assumed by others from hearsay, especially inspired enthusiasm for the Lacedaemonians among the Athenian allies. For by being the first to go out, and by showing himself a good man in all respects, he left behind the lasting conviction that the others were of the same sort as well.

[82] Meanwhile, when the Athenians learned of his arrival in Thracian territory, they declared war against Perdikkas, whom they considered responsible for the expedition, and kept a closer guard on the allies there. [83] Perdikkas, immediately taking Brasidas and his army along with his own forces, marched against Arrhabaios son of Bromeros, king of the Lynkestians and his neighbor, whom he had a dispute with and wished to subdue. But when he and Brasidas reached the entrance to Lynkos with his army, Brasidas said that before fighting he wished, if possible, to persuade Arrhabaios to become a Lacedaemonian ally. For Arrhabaios had in fact sent word to him by herald that he was willing to accept Brasidas as an

4.80. For recent suggestions about the murder of the helots, see Jordan 1990; some (e.g., Whitby 1994, pp. 98–99) doubt that the incident ever took place.

arbitrator, and the Chalkidian envoys accompanying them warned Brasidas not to start by removing Perdikkas' grounds for concern, so that they could enjoy his more committed support for their own aims as well. In addition, the representatives of Perdikkas in Lacedaemon had spoken to the effect that he would bring many of the places around him into their alliance. And on this basis Brasidas thought himself more generally justified in dealing with Arrhabaios. Perdikkas stated first that he had not brought in Brasidas as an arbitrator of their quarrel but as the destroyer of those he himself designated as enemies; next, that since he was supporting half his army Brasidas would be acting unjustly by dealing with Arrhabaios. After an unresolved quarrel with Perdikkas, Brasidas negotiated and was persuaded to lead away his army without invading. Perdikkas consequently paid a third of his support instead of half, considering himself wronged.

[84] Without delay, Brasidas campaigned against Akanthos, the colony of Andros, in the same summer, a little before vintage. The inhabitants divided into two factions over whether to let him in; there were those who had joined the Chalkidians in inviting him in, and there were the common people. Nevertheless, when the common people were persuaded by Brasidas—on account of their fear for the fruit that was still outside the city—to let him in before deciding, he was admitted, and coming before the people (he was not an unskilled speaker for a Lacedaemonian) he spoke as follows:

[85] "Akanthians, the purpose of the Lacedaemonians in sending me out with my army was to uphold the cause we proclaimed in beginning the war, that we would go to war against the Athenians as liberators of Hellas. If we have come belatedly, mistaken in our idea based on the war in our area, which led us to hope that we by ourselves, without risk to you, would quickly clear out the Athenians, let no one blame us. For now, when it became possible, we have arrived and with your help will try to overthrow them. And I am amazed not only by the gates closed against me but that I have not arrived to your welcome. For we Lacedaemonians, thinking both that we would be arriving among allies in spirit even before we were here in fact and that we would be wanted, have taken on this great risk in making a march for many days through foreign country and have exhibited the utmost enthusiasm.

"If you have any different intentions or are going to stand in the way of freedom for yourselves and the other Hellenes, it would be a terrible thing. It is not only that you yourselves oppose me, but also anyone I approach will be less likely to join me, raising the difficulty that you, those I came to first, and men who have an important city and a reputation for intelligence, did not admit me; I will succeed in giving the impression that my cause is not one to trust in, but that either I bring a freedom that is unjust or I come in weakness and without the capability of providing defense against the Athenians if they attack. And yet when I went to help Nisaia with this army that I have now, the Athenians were not willing to engage me, although they were more numerous, so that it is not likely that they will actually send against you a maritime force equal in numbers to the one there. [86] And I myself have come not for harm to the Hellenes but for their freedom, after binding the authorities of the Lacedaemonians to the most solemn oaths that the allies I bring over will be autonomous, and not in order for us to acquire you as allies by force or deception but to ally ourselves with you who have been enslaved by the Athenians. Accordingly, I claim that I should neither be suspected personally, after giving you what are certainly the greatest pledges, nor regarded as an inadequate defender, and that you should take courage and join me.

"And if anyone is perhaps hanging back fearing someone for private reasons, lest I hand the city over to a certain element, that person should feel the most trustful of all. I have not come to side with factions, nor is it my practice to bring a dubious freedom, as I would if I disregarded ancestral institutions and enslaved the majority to the few or the minority to everyone. That would be harsher than alien rule, and for us Lacedaemonians it would not bring about thanks in return for toil, but blame instead of honor and glory; as for the charges we used in going to war with the Athenians, we would garner these ourselves in more hateful form than anyone who did not profess virtue. For it is more shameful for those held in honor to take advantage by deceit, with fine pretexts, than by open force; the one advances by the justification of strength, which fortune gives; the other, by the plotting of an unjust mind. [87] And so we give all circumspection to matters of the greatest importance to us, and you could have no greater assurance, in addition to sworn oaths, than by dealing with men whose words, examined in light of their deeds, lead only to the conviction that it is actually in our interest to act as I have said.

"But if you maintain, even after I have advanced these arguments, that you cannot act accordingly, yet claim that as friends you should not be harmed by this refusal, that freedom is not without its obvious dangers, and it is right to offer it to those in a position to accept but not to force it on anyone against his wishes, I will call on the gods and heroes of this land

---

4.85. "When I went to help Nisaia": as noted in *HCT* III *ad* 4.85.7, this sentence contains two lies and a misleading statement; see 4.108n. "So that it is not likely": the logic is probably obscure because of textual problems, see *HCT loc. cit.*

to witness that I came here as a benefactor but was rejected, I will try to compel you by ravaging your territory, and I will consider that this is no longer wrong, but that I have furthermore been given every justification by two constraints, not only to keep the Lacedaemonians from being damaged by this friendship of yours because of the money you will contribute to the Athenians unless you join us, but also lest the Hellenes be hindered by you in breaking out of slavery. This would certainly not be reasonable behavior on our part, and we Lacedaemonians are not obligated to liberate the unwilling except by reason of some general benefit. And again, we do not desire empire, but since we are eager to end it for others, we would wrong all the rest if in offering universal independence we overlooked your opposition. After hearing me, decide wisely and strive to be the first in beginning the liberation of Hellas and in winning undying fame, while avoiding harm to yourself and gaining for your whole city the finest of reputations."

[88] Brasidas said this much; and the Akanthians, voting by ballot, after a great deal was said on both sides, decided by a majority to revolt from Athens, partly because of what was appealing in Brasidas' speech, partly out of fear for their fruit, and after they had bound him to the oaths sworn by the Lacedaemonian officials when they sent him out, that the allies he brought over would be truly independent, they then admitted the army. And not much later, Stagiros, a colony of Andros, joined the revolt.

[89] Now these were the events of this summer. Right after the start of the following winter, when the places in Boiotia were going to be turned over to Hippokrates and Demosthenes, the Athenian generals, and Demosthenes was to appear before Siphai with his ships, and the other before Delion, there was a mistake about the days on which each was supposed to begin his campaign, and Demosthenes, setting sail to Siphai with the Akarnanians and many of the allies from the region on board, did not accomplish anything, because Nikomachos, a Phokian from Phanotis, informed to the Lacedaemonians about the plot, and they told the Boiotians. Help came from all over Boiotia, and (with Hippokrates not there yet to create difficulties on land) both Siphai and Chaironeia were occupied in advance. Since the conspirators found out about the mistake, they caused no disturbances in their cities. [90] As for Hippokrates, he brought out the Athenians in full force, including the metics and all foreigners

---

4.87. "We Lacedaemonians are not obligated": an extremely problematic sentence, see especially Classen/Steup IV *ad* 4.87.4. I have found attempts at emendation implausible and offered a translation that avoids them and refers to the "constraints" (one practical and one moral) in the preceding sentence.

present, and reached Delion later, when the Boiotians had already returned from Siphai. And after settling the army in camp, he fortified Delion, the sanctuary of Apollo, in the following way. They dug a trench around the temple and sanctuary, and in place of a wall they piled up earth from the excavation, adding a palisade of stakes, and threw in the vines cut down around the sanctuary and robbed stones and bricks from the nearby houses as well and did everything possible to build up the bulwark. They also set up wooden towers at the important points and where nothing remained of the sanctuary's buildings; the portico itself had collapsed. Starting on the third day after they left home, they worked that day, the fourth, and until supper on the fifth. Then, when most of it had been completed, the army now went perhaps ten stades in the direction of home, and while most of the light-armed immediately went on, the hoplites grounded their arms and rested; meanwhile, Hippokrates stayed behind longer to arrange the guards and the way any remaining portions of the outworks were to be completed.

[91] During this period, the Boiotians were gathering at Tanagra. And when they had arrived from all the cities and learned that the Athenians had by now left for home, while the rest of the eleven Boiotarchs were not in favor of fighting a battle, since they were no longer on Boiotia (the Athenians, when they grounded their arms, were around the border, at Oropos), Pagondas son of Aioladas, Boiotarch from Thebes along with Arianthides son of Lysimachidas and in overall command, wanted to force a battle and preferred to take this risk, and calling forward every man by company, so that they would not all leave their arms at once, he tried to persuade the Boiotians to attack the Athenians and force the issue, speaking as follows: [92] "Men of Boiotia, the notion that it is not right to meet the Athenians in battle unless we actually encounter them still in Boiotia should not even have occurred to any of us in command. For it is Boiotia they mean to ruin by coming over the border and installing a fort, and I would say they are enemies in any land they are found in, and wherever they have advanced from to commit enemy acts. And if anyone sees a safer course now, think again. When someone is attacked by another, with his own land involved, the same prudence in calculation is not allowable in the way it is for those who are invading others by their own choice, secure in what they hold and grasping for more. Your tradition is to defend yourselves against an alien army invading, in your own country and just as much in any country around. And against Athenians, living on your borders at that, all the more need. For when it comes to neighboring states, holding one's own always constitutes freedom, and above all, when it

comes to these neighbors, who attempt to enslave even those who do not live near them, even those far away, how can we do anything but combat them to the end (we can use Euboia across from us as an example, or the position in which they have put most other Hellenes), understanding that for other people battles are fought over territorial boundaries, but for us, if we are beaten, one boundary for all the land will be recognized, without dispute? They will come and take what we have by force. This is how much more dangerous to us their proximity is than that of any others.

"It is characteristic of those whose strength gives them the boldness to attack neighbors, which is what the Athenians are doing now, that they are more confident when attacking those who are inactive and only defend themselves in their own land, less ready to dominate those who confront them first, beyond their borders, and, with the right opportunity, take the initiative in war. We have experience of this regarding the Athenians. For by beating them at Koroneia, at the time when they dominated our land because of our internal strife, we brought notable freedom from fear to Boiotia up to this day. Remembering this, those of us who are older must equal their earlier deeds and the younger, as sons of brave fathers at that time, must endeavor not to cast shame on the virtues of their heritage, and trusting in the support of the god whose sanctuary they impiously occupy as a fort, and in the favorable signs from the victims we have sacrificed, we must go forth together against these men and show them that they can go ahead and conquer when those they attack do not defend themselves, but if they attack those whose birthright is to keep their own land always free by their arms and never to enslave that of others unjustly, they will not leave before facing their challenge."

[93] With this exhortation, Pagondas persuaded the Boiotians to attack the Athenians; and breaking camp quickly (it was now late in the day), he led on the army; and when he drew near the enemy forces, he halted at a point from which the armies were concealed from each other by a hill in between, formed ranks, and prepared for battle. When Hippokrates, who was at Delion, was informed that the Boiotians were attacking, he sent orders to the army to form ranks, and not long after he arrived himself, leaving about three hundred cavalry behind at Delion, both to guard it in case anyone attacked and to watch for the opportunity to help against the Boiotians during the battle. The Boiotians positioned men to defend against them and, when their arrangements were satisfactory, they appeared over the hill and grounded their arms, drawn up in the formation they intended to use, about seven thousand hoplites, more than ten thousand light-armed, a thousand cavalry, and five hundred peltasts. The Thebans and those of

their division held the right wing; in the middle were the Haliartians, the Koroneians, the Kopaians, and the others from around the lake; the Thespians, Tanagrans, and Orchomenians held the left. The cavalry and light-armed were on both wings. The Thebans were drawn up twenty-five shields deep, and the rest, as each was accustomed. [94] These were the Boiotian forces and their order of battle. The Athenians, their whole army, were drawn up eight hoplites deep, equal in number to the enemy, and the cavalry were on each wing. There were no regular light-armed troops, nor did the city have any; what light-armed joined the invasion, who were many times more numerous than the enemy's, followed unarmed in most cases, as in an army including foreigners and citizens from the city, and since they had been the first to leave for home, only a few were present.

When the armies were in their formations and about to engage, Hippokrates the general moved along the front ranks of the Athenian army to encourage them by speaking as follows. [95] "Athenians, this address is a brief one, just as good for men with real courage, and it is more a reminder than than a reassurance. None of you should believe that we are taking this risk on alien land without good cause. For we will be contending in their country on behalf of our own; and if we win, the Peloponnesians, with no cavalry from here, will never invade our land, and by a single battle you gain the one country and make the other more free. Go to meet them, then, in a manner worthy of both your city, which gives each of you the glory of belonging to the foremost nation of Hellas, and of your fathers, who once held Boiotia by beating these men with Myronides at Oinophyta."

[96] When Hippokrates was halfway through the army with this exhortation and had gone no further, the Boiotians, after Pagondas also had encouraged his men in a hurried way here as well, sang the paian and advanced over the hill; the Athenians advanced to meet them and engaged at a run. And the extreme wings of both armies were not involved in the action but experienced the same problem: streams were in their way. The rest engaged in a fierce battle, shoving with their shields. The left wing of the Boiotians as far as the center was defeated by the Athenians, and here they pressed them hard, especially the Thespians. When the men stationed next to them gave way, and they themselves were surrounded in a small space, all the Thespians who were killed were cut down defending them-

---

4.96. Some recent scholarship has doubted the central importance of "shoving" in hoplite battles, but their objections are convincingly addressed by Luginbill 1994; Pagondas was the first but not the last Theban general to exploit this by using an unusually deep formation.

selves at close quarters; even some of the Athenians, confused by encircling, killed their own men without recognizing them. On this wing, then,
the Boiotians were beaten and fled toward the middle of the fighting, but
the right wing, where the Thebans were, defeated the Athenians, and they
were shoved back and pursued, gradually at first. And what happened,
when Pagondas sent two squadrons of cavalry from out of sight around the
hill because his left wing was in difficulty, was that these suddenly appeared
and struck panic into the victorious Athenian wing, who thought that
another army was attacking, and now on both counts, because of this and
because of the Thebans pressing in and breaking their ranks, a rout began
throughout the Athenian army. Some rushed to Delion and the sea, some
to Oropos, and others to Mt. Parnes, and wherever each saw a chance of
safety. The Boiotians, especially the cavalry, both Boiotians and Lokrians
who had come up to help just as the rout began, pursued and killed them;
because night interrupted the action, the main portion of the fugitives got
away more easily than they would have otherwise. The next day, after leaving a garrison at Delion (which they still occupied despite everything), both
the men from Oropos and those from Delion were brought home by ship.

[97] The Boiotians set up a trophy, and after they gathered their dead
and stripped those of the enemy they left guards, withdrew to Tanagra,
and planned an attack on Delion. A herald coming over from the Athenians encountered a Boiotian herald who told him that he would achieve
nothing before his own return, and when he came before the Athenians, he
gave the Boiotian message, saying that they had done wrong by transgress-
ing the laws of the Hellenes; for it had been the custom among them all
that when invading the lands of one another they would keep away from
the sanctuaries there, but the Athenians had fortified Delion and were living there, and all that people do in an unhallowed place was occurring
within, and water that was untouched by themselves except for purification at sacrifices was being drawn and carried. And so the Boiotians, on
behalf of both the gods and themselves, invoking the other gods dwelling
in the temple and Apollo, served notice on them to leave the sanctuary
before taking away what was theirs.

[98] After the herald had said this, the Athenians sent their own herald
to the Boiotians and stated that they had done no injury to the sanctuary,
nor would they willingly harm it in the future. For it was not with this purpose that they had entered to begin with, but rather to defend themselves
there against their own injuries from others. The law of the Hellenes was
that whoever held the power in any land, whether of greater or lesser
extent, the sanctuaries were theirs as well, which were cared for in every

way practiced before this, as far as they could. For the Boiotians and almost everyone else, whenever they drove someone out and occupied the land by force, first came to sanctuaries as the property of others and now possess them as their own. And if the Athenians had been able to conquer more of Boiotia, it would have been theirs; but as it was, they were in a portion of it and, as though it was their own, not willing to leave it. The water was something they had touched in an emergency, but not one imposed on them by their own insolence, since they had been forced to use it in defense against those who had invaded their land first, the Boiotians. It was reasonable for all actions committed in war or any kind of danger to be excusable, even in the god's sight (for altars were a refuge applying to involuntary crimes), and transgressor was a term for men who were evil and not under compulsion, rather than men who acted somewhat unusually in the midst of disaster. Giving back bodies in exchange for shrines made the Boiotians far more impious than anyone unwilling to recover what was rightfully theirs by using shrines. And they directed the Boiotians to tell them unambiguously to take up their dead, not by evacuating Boiotian land (for they were in land that was no longer Boiotian but spear-won), but by making a truce according to ancestral custom. [99] The Boiotians told them in reply, if they were in Boiotia, to evacuate their land and carry off what was their own, but if they were in their own land, to make their own decision about what to do, and their thinking was that Oropos, where the dead actually were after the battle on the frontier, was subject to the Athenians, who could not claim them by force (and the Boiotians, of course, were not going to apply a truce to Athenian land), while "let them take back what they are requesting after evacuating our land" was a plausible answer. The Athenian herald listened and returned unsuccessful.

[100] The Boiotians immediately campaigned against the fort, after sending for javelin-throwers and slingers from the Malian gulf and with reinforcements after the battle from two thousand Corinthian hoplites, the

4.98. "'Whenever they drove someone out": i.e., the Boiotians were not the original occupants either, see 1.12 (!) but also 3.61.

4.99. *HCT* III *ad loc.*, after a good discussion of the obscurities here, makes the Boiotian refusal, justified by sophistry, the main point, as further wartime brutalization. The Athenians, however, are so egregious in claiming their mini-conquest that the Boiotians eventually appear to give them their deserved comeuppance (cf. also 4.101). The Athenians have attempted a second Pylos, and their failure foreshadows their losses in Thrace; on similarities between the Pylos and Delion campaigns, see Strassler 1990, p. 112.

Peloponnesian garrison that had left Nisaia, and Megarians along with them. They used a variety of methods and brought in the following device, which enabled them to take the fort. They sawed a large beam into two halves, completely hollowed out each, fitted them back together tightly like a pipe, and fastened a caldron to one end with chains, and an iron tube for a nozzle, projecting out of the beam, was bent down into it; a large portion of the wood was covered with iron as well. Using wagons, they brought it from a considerable distance up to the wall where it was built mostly of vines and wood; when it was close, they put a large bellows to their end of the beam and blew. The blast passed through the narrow space into the cauldron, which contained lighted coals, sulphur, and pitch, and started a great blaze, setting the wall on fire, so that no one could stay near it any longer, but all were forced to run out to escape; in this way they captured the fort. Some of the garrison were killed, and about two hundred were captured; most of the others got on board the ships and were taken home. [101] When the Athenian herald, knowing nothing of what had happened, came again for the dead soon after Delion was captured, which was seventeen days from the battle, the Boiotians gave them back instead of continuing to make the same reply. Slightly under five hundred Boiotians died in the battle and slightly under a thousand Athenians along with the general Hippokrates, also a large number of light-armed and baggage-carriers.

Soon after this battle, Demosthenes, since the project of betraying Siphai had gone wrong when he made his voyage, took the force of Akarnanians and Agraians and four hundred Athenian hoplites and made a landing in Sikyonian territory. Before all the ships had gotten to the shore, the Sikyonian defenders came up, routed the men who had already landed, and chased them back to the ships, killing some and taking others prisoner. After setting up a trophy, they gave back the dead under truce. During the same period as the events at Delion, Sitalkes the king of the Odrysians died when he campaigned against the Triballians and was defeated in battle. Seuthes son of Sparadokos, as his nephew, became king of the Odrysians and everywhere else in Thrace Sitalkes had ruled.

[102] During the same winter, Brasidas campaigned with the allies in Thrace against Amphipolis, the Athenian colony on the Strymon river. On the site where the city now stands, Aristagoras the Milesian, when in flight from King Dareios, attempted to start a settlement earlier but was pushed out by the Edonians, and then, thirty-two years later, the Athe-

4.102. For the Athenian colonies, cf. 1.100n.

nians sent ten thousand of their own settlers and anyone else who wanted to go, and they were massacred at Drabeskos by Thracians. Twenty-nine years later, the Athenians came again when Hagnon son of Nikias was sent out as founder, and they drove out the Edonians and settled the site, which was formerly called Ennea Hodoi. They started out from Eion, using it as their coastal market at the river mouth, twenty-five stades from the present city, which Hagnon named Amphipolis because the Strymon flows on both sides of it, and he walled it off between the river courses and built it to be conspicuous from both sea and land.

[103] Against this city, then, Brasidas with his forces set out from Arne in Chalkidike. Arriving toward evening at Aulon and Bormiskos, where the lake of Bolbe empties into the sea, he stopped for a meal and went on during the night. It was stormy and snowing a little, which made him hurry all the more, wanting to escape detection by the people in Amphipolis, except for the traitors. These were residents from Argilos (the Argilians are Andrian colonists) and others involved in their plot, some won over by Perdikkas and others by the Chalkidians. Above all, the Argilians, people who lived nearby and were always under suspicion from the Athenians and had designs against the place, had intrigued with their compatriots there well before this to find a way to betray the city, and now, since the opportunity had appeared and Brasidas had arrived, they let him into their city and revolted from Athens, and during that night they brought the army before dawn to the bridge across the river. The town is some distance from this crossing, and the walls did not go down to it as they do now, and only a minimal guard was stationed. Easily overpowering them, partly because treachery occurred, partly because it was stormy and his attack unexpected, Brasidas crossed the bridge and immediately held what the Amphipolitans living over the whole area owned outside the walls.

[104] Since his crossing caught people in the city unawares, and some of those outside were captured, while others fled inside the walls, the Amphipolitans were thrown into complete confusion, especially because

---

4.103–7. For the Amphipolis campaign, Thucydides' role, and his account, cf. *HCT* III, pp. 584–88 and Ellis 1978; the latter argues that Thucydides consistently and subtly disguises his share of responsibility for the fall of the city. The author was certainly capable of calculating the favorable effect on readers of withholding explicit blame (for Eukles) or praise (for his own defense of Eion), although in 4.107 a certain satisfaction at his showing against the wondrous Brasidas is apparent. The whole account is suspiciously flat; where Thucydides had exceptional opportunities as an eye-witness, he includes few of the vivid details that characterize other narratives (e.g. 4.110–16).

they were suspicious of one another. And it is said that if Brasidas, instead of letting the army pillage, had immediately advanced against the city, he seemed likely to capture it. But as it was, he kept his army there and overran the area outside, and since he had none of the results he expected from the people inside, he stayed inactive.

Meanwhile, those opposed to the traitors, using their superior numbers to take control, prevented the gates from being opened immediately, and acting with the general Eukles, who had come from Athens to guard the place, they sent to the other general in the Thracian area, Thucydides son of Oloros, the man who recorded all these events and was then around Thasos (this island is a colony of Paros and about a half day's voyage away), urging him to come to their defense. When he heard this, he sailed at once with seven ships he happened to have, and he wanted above all, of course, to get to Amphipolis before its surrender, but otherwise to occupy Eion in advance. [105] Brasidas, meanwhile, fearing the help coming from the ships from Thasos, also because he had learned that Thucydides owned the right of working the gold mines in that part of Thrace and accordingly had influence among the leading men on the mainland, redoubled his efforts to take over the city first, before the common people of Amphipolis, in their hopes that Thucydides would assemble an alliance from maritime people and from Thrace and preserve them, lost all inclination to come over. He offered a moderate settlement, issuing this proclamation, that any Amphipolitan or Athenian inside might keep his property and stay with full and equal rights if he wished, or leave within five days if he was unwilling, taking his property along. [106] When the majority heard this, there was a shift in their thinking, especially since the citizens included few Athenians and were mainly a mixture, and a large number of those within were related to those captured outside. They found the proclamation a fair one compared with what they had feared—the Athenians because they were glad that they might leave, since they hardly saw their peril as only the general one and besides did not expect help soon, and the rest of the masses because they were not losing equal rights of citizenship and were being unexpectedly freed from danger. And so, with the partisans of Brasidas now openly endorsing the settlement, since they saw that the common people had changed and were no longer heeding the general who was present, the surrender was effected, and they admitted Brasidas on the terms he had proclaimed. In this way they handed over the city, while late on the same day Thucydides and his ships sailed into Eion. Brasidas had just taken Amphipolis and came within a night of taking Eion; if the ships had not come to the rescue quickly, it would have been his at dawn.

[107] After this, the one commander made arrangements in Eion to keep it secure for both the moment, in case Brasidas attacked, and in the future, receiving those who had submitted to leaving the inland area in accordance with the treaty. The other, suddenly sailing down the river to Eion with a number of boats to see if he could control the entrance by seizing a projecting portion of the walls and making a simultaneous attempt by land, was beaten off on both fronts, and he attended to conditions around Amphipolis. Myrkinos, an Edonian city, also came over to him after Pittakos, the king of the Edonians, had died at the hands of Goaxis' sons and his own wife Brauro, and shortly after, so did Galepsos and Oisyme; these are Thasian colonies. Perdikkas was on hand as well immediately after the capture and involved himself in these events.

[108] With Amphipolis taken, the Athenians were in a state of great alarm, especially because the city was valuable to them both for its provision of ship timber and for its revenues, also because the Lacedaemonians, with Thessalian escorts, had access to Athenian allies as far as the Strymon, yet without controlling the bridge, since for a long way toward the interior the river was a lake, and from the side toward Eion they were watched by triremes, they would not have been able to proceed; but they thought this had now become easy. They were also afraid that the allies would revolt. For Brasidas not only behaved moderately in general but was spreading the word everywhere that he was sent out in order to liberate Hellas. When the cities subject to Athens learned about the capture of Amphipolis and what the terms were, also about his gentleness, they were strongly motivated toward revolutionary action and secretly sent proposals to him, urging him to make the rounds among them, each wanting to start the first revolt. It was obvious to them that they could do so with impunity, a mistake about Athenian power as great as the obviousness of that power later on, but their decisions were based more on vague wishes than on secure foresight, following the human habit of entrusting desires to heedless hopes, while using arbitrary reasons to dismiss what is unacceptable. Besides, since the Athenians had recently been trounced in Boiotia, and since Brasidas made the appealing and untrue assertion that the Athenians had been unwilling to engage his single army, they were encouraged and convinced that no relief forces would be sent against them. Most of all,

---

4.108. "Unwilling to engage": the manuscripts include the words "him at Nisaia," but following Classen/Steup IV *ad* 4.108.5, I believe this to be a gloss (*contra*, cf. *HCT* III *ad* 4.108.5). The comment "untrue" about a previous speech is exceptional.

because of the immediate pleasure involved, and because they were to act when the Lacedaemonians, for the first time, were enthusiastic, they were ready to take any sort of risk. Aware of this, the Athenians sent garrisons to the cities as short notice and the winter season permitted, while Brasidas urgently sent to Lacedaemon for additional forces and made preparations for building triremes on the Strymon. But the Lacedaemonians did not support him, partly because of the envy of the leading men, partly because they wanted to get the men back from the island and end the war.

[109] In the same winter, the Megarians captured their long walls, which had been occupied by the Athenians, and razed them to the foundations, and Brasidas, after the capture of Amphipolis, campaigned against the peninsula called Akte. This is the one projecting from the King's excavation, and the high mountain of Athos is at the end toward the Aegean sea. It contains Sane, a colony of Andros right by the canal, facing the sea toward Euboia, and in addition Thyssos, Kleone, Akrothoi, Olophyxos, and Dion, which are inhabited by a mixture of bilingual barbarian people. There is also a Chalkidian element, but small, and the majority are Pelasgian, part of the Tyrrhenians who also once occupied Lemnos and Athens, in addition to Bisaltians, Krestonians, and Edonians; they are distributed among very small cities. Most of these came over to Brasidas, but Sane and Dion resisted, and he stayed in their territory with his army and plundered it. [110] When they did not yield, he immediately campaigned against Torone in Chalkidike, which was occupied by the Athenians; a few men ready to betray the city had called him in. Arriving while it was still night, just before dawn, he and his army took up a position near the sanctuary of the Dioskouroi, which is about three stades from the city.

Now the Toronians in general and the Athenians were unaware of him; but since his collaborators knew he was coming, and some had secretly gone ahead a short way to watch for his approach, on learning of his arrival they admitted into their number men with daggers, seven light-armed (out of twenty originally assigned, only this number were not terrified of entering; their leader was Lysistratos from Olynthos), and these slipped through an opening in the wall on the seaward side, and without being seen they climbed up to the highest guardpost in the city, which is built against a hill, killed its sentries, and began breaking through the Kanastraion gate. [111] And moving slightly forward and halting with his main force, Brasidas sent a hundred peltasts ahead to rush in first as soon as gates were

4.109. The "king's excavation" is the canal dug by King Xerxes in 480 B.C.E.; see Herodotos 7.22–25.

opened and a beacon lighted as arranged. Although some time passed, and they were puzzled by this, the men were meanwhile edging closer to the city; and on the inside, after some Toronians along with the light-armed had managed to break through the gate, and the gates to the agora were being opened once the bar was cut, they first took some of the peltasts around to the gate and let them in, so that they could frighten the townspeople who had remained ignorant by surprising them from behind and from both sides, and then they lit the fire signal as arranged and at this point admitted the rest of the peltasts through the gates to the agora. [112] On seeing the expected signal, Brasidas came on at a run and incited every part of his army to shout and strike consternation among the townspeople. Some burst in through the gates and others over planks, which happened to be placed against the wall for hauling up stones where it had collapsed and was being rebuilt. As for Brasidas, he and the main group immediately headed upward toward the heights of the city, wanting to capture it decisively, from the top down; the rest all swarmed in every direction. [113] Among the Toronians, the unsuspecting majority were in confusion as the capture took place, but the conspirators and those in sympathy with them immediately joined the invaders. And when the Athenians found out (and there happened to be about fifty hoplites in the agora, sleeping), a few of them were killed in fighting, while the rest escaped either on foot or on the two ships on guard and took refuge at Lekythos, the fort which they seized and occupied in a part of the city projecting into the sea, joined only by a narrow isthmus. And all the Toronians on their side joined their refuge.

[114] Once it was day, and the city was securely in his possession, Brasidas proclaimed to the Toronians who had taken refuge with the Athenians that any who wished could come back out to their own property and claim their rights with safety, and he sent a herald to the Athenians asking them to leave Lekythos under truce, keeping their possessions, since it was Chalkidian territory. They refused to leave but asked for a day of truce to take up their dead; he gave them two. During this time, he bolstered the strength of the nearby buildings, and the Athenians strengthened their own position.

And he called a meeting of the Toronians and told them very much what he had told the Akanthians, that it was not right either that they regard as base or treacherous those who had arranged the capture of the city with him (for they had not acted to enslave or because of bribes, but for the good and freedom of the city) nor for those who had not taken part to suppose that they would not get the same advantages (for he had not come to destroy either city or individuals). This was why he had made the proclamation to those in refuge with the Athenians, since he thought none the worse of them for their friendship with them; he believed that after becoming acquainted with his own side, they would not find the Lacedaemonians less to their liking but much more, in proportion to their more upright conduct, since it was through lack of acquaintance that they were frightened now. And he told them all that they must prepare to be firm allies and, from this time on, to be held responsible for any misconduct; in their past actions, they had not wronged the Lacedaemonians, they had been wronged by others who were too strong for them, and any opposition to him could be pardoned.

[115] After he offered these reassurances and the truce expired, he began assaults on Lekythos; the Athenians defended themselves behind a weak wall and from houses and battlements and drove him off for a day. On the following day, when a device of the enemy designed to throw fire on the wooden breastworks was about to be brought up against them, and the army was already advancing on the point where they thought they could best position the device, and where it was easiest to attack, the Athenians set a wooden tower on top of a house and carried up many jugs and casks of water and large stones, and many men climbed up as well. Under the added weight, the house suddenly collapsed with a loud noise, annoying rather than scaring those Athenians close enough to see, but those not as near, especially the farthest off, thought that now the position had been captured at this spot and ran in flight to the sea and the ships. [116] When Brasidas realized that they were leaving the battlements and saw what was happening, he charged with the army and took the fort immediately, killing all he caught inside. And the Athenians, evacuating the place in this way, traveled to Pallene in boats and the ships; meanwhile, since there is a sanctuary of Athena in Lekythos, and since it happened that Brasidas, when about to attack, had announced that he would give thirty silver minai to the first to scale the wall, he decided that the capture was caused by more than human means and paid the thirty minai to Athena for her temple, and clearing Lekythos by removing all buildings, he dedicated the whole place to her as sacred ground. During the rest of the winter, he organized the places he occupied and made plans against the rest. And when the winter was over, the eighth year of the war ended.

[117] In the following summer, as soon as it was spring, the Lacedaemonians and the Athenians made an armistice for a year: the Athenians because they thought that it would keep Brasidas from going on causing revolts before they had ample time for their preparations and also, if it was to their advantage, that they could make a more general agreement; the

Lacedaemonians because they believed that the Athenians were afraid for this reason, which was exactly why they did fear, and that after a respite from hardships and suffering this experience would make them more eager to reach an agreement and, after giving their men back, to make a more lasting peace as well. To be sure, they gave higher priority to getting their men back, since Brasidas was still meeting with success, and since, if he made further gains and brought about a balance, they were likely to lose the men yet, in defending themselves, to run their risks on equal terms, through Brasidas' doing, and prevail. Accordingly, they and their allies agreed to the following armistice:

[118] "Concerning the shrine and oracle of Pythian Apollo, we resolve that whoever desires is to consult without fraud or fear according to ancestral practice. This is resolved by the Lacedaemonians and their allies present; they declare that they will send heralds to the Boiotians and Phokians and persuade them if it is within their power. Concerning the treasures of the god, we resolve to attend to the discovery of criminals, rightly and justly following ancestral practice, yourselves, ourselves, and all others who wish, following ancestral practice. Concerning these matters, then, the Lacedaemonians as well as their allies have resolved this. And the Lacedaemonians as well as their allies have resolved the following, if the Athenians agree to the truce. Each side is to remain in its own territory, keeping whatever it now holds: those in Koryphasion within Bouphades and Tomeus, those in Kythera not communicating with the alliance, neither we with them nor they with us, those in Nisaia and Minoa not crossing the road from the gates by the shrine of Nisos to the temple of Poseidon, and from the temple of Poseidon directly to the bridge to Minoa, nor are the Megarians and their allies to cross this road, the Athenians holding the island they have captured, but neither side communicating with the other, and keeping the places in Troizen, which they now hold and as the Troizenians have agreed on with the Athenians. And in use of the sea, in all parts along

---

4.117. "To be sure": in other words, the Spartans were now less eager for peace, because of Brasidas' victories; if after this point the men were killed, it would presumably be because of Brasidas' further successes (and Athenian vengefulness), which would enable them to win (or simply, bearing in mind their preoccupation with the helots, prevail). Thucydides is at his most cryptic in this crucial passage, and the text may well be corrupt in addition, cf. the exhaustive discussions of Classen/Steup IV, Graves 1888, and *HCT* III *ad* 4.117.2; I offer a translation without emendation but also without great confidence.

4.118. Koryphasion: i.e., Pylos, see 4.3.

their own territory and that of their allies, the Lacedaemonians and their allies are to sail in no warship but in any other oared boat carrying up to five hundred talents in weight. Heralds, embassies, and as many attendants as they choose, concerning the settlement of the war and of claims, are to travel under truce to and from the Peloponnese and Athens, by both land and sea. During this time, neither you nor we are to receive deserters, whether free or slave. You are to submit claims against us to arbitration, and we are to do the same, according to ancestral practice, and to settle disputes by arbitration without fighting. These are the resolutions of the Lacedaemonians and their allies. And if anything seems to you more fair or just than these, come to Lacedaemon and inform us; for neither the Lacedaemonians nor their allies will decline whatever you say that is just. And let those who come have the same full authority you request of us. And the truce shall be for one year. This has been resolved by the people. The Akamantid tribe was prytanizing, Phainippos was secretary, and Nikiades was treasurer. Laches moved, to the good fortune of the Athenians, to accept the armistice according to the terms agreed on by the Lacedaemonians and their allies, since it was approved in the assembly that there be a truce for one year. It is to begin on this day, the fourteenth of the month of Elaphebolion. During this time, ambassadors and heralds are to go from the two sides and discuss the terms on which the war will be ended. The generals and the prytanies are to call an assembly first, and the Athenian people, to decide whatever the embassy will propose concerning the ending of the war. And the embassies present are to agree forthwith to abide by the truce in full for one year. [119] The Lacedaemonians and their allies arranged these terms with the Athenians and their allies and swore to them on the twelfth day of the Lacedaemonian month of Gerastios. Those of the Lacedaemonians making the arrangement and pouring libations were Tauros son of Echetimidas, Athenaios son of Perikleidas, and Philocharidas son of Eryxilaidas; of the Corinthians, Aineas son of Okytos, and Euphamidas son of Aristonymos; of the Sikyonians, Damotimos son of Naukrates and Onasimos son of Megakles; of the Megarians, Nikasos son of Kekalos and Menekrates son of Amphidoros; of the Epidaurians, Amphias son of Eupaiidas; of the Athenians, the generals Nikostratos son of Dieitrephes, Nikias son of Nikeratos, and Autokles son of Tolmaios." This was the armistice, and during the whole time it was in effect they met to discuss a more general truce.

[120] During the period when they were concluding the arrangements, Skione, a city in Pallene, revolted from Athens in favor of Brasidas. The Skionians say that they are Pallenians from the Peloponnese, and that when

their founders were sailing from Troy they were forced into this place by the storm the Achaians encountered and settled it. In support of their revolt, Brasidas accomplished the voyage to Skione by night with a friendly trireme sailing ahead, and he himself followed some distance behind in a boat, so that if he encountered a vessel larger than the boat the trireme would protect him, and thinking that if another comparable trireme came up, it would turn not to the smaller boat but toward the trireme, and meanwhile he would escape. After his crossing, he held a meeting of the Skionians and said the same things as at Akanthos and Torone, stating in addition that they deserved the highest praise as men who were virtually islanders, since Pallene was cut off by the Athenians occupying Potidaia, and yet had taken the stride toward freedom of their own will, rather than abjectly waiting for the factor of compulsion concerning their own obvious good; this was a sign of their courage to endure anything else, however severe, and if he were to arrange matters according to his own thinking, he would consider them in truth the most reliable friends of the Lacedaemonians and honor them in all other ways. [121] The Skionians were elated by his words, and all alike were emboldened, even those who had not previously supported the plot, and, in addition to resolving to support the war enthusiastically they gave Brasidas a warm reception in every respect, publicly by setting a gold crown on his head as liberator of Hellas, personally by covering him with wreaths and fillets and approaching him as though he were an athlete. And he, after leaving a garrison for the time being, went back across and not much later sent over a larger force, planning to use them to make attempts on Mende and Potidaia, since he supposed that the Athenians would send help to Skione, as the equivalent of an island, and wanted to act first; there were also dealings between him and these cities to bring about betrayals.

[122] While he was getting ready for these attempts, Aristonymos circulating word of the armistice for the Athenians and Athenaios for the Lacedaemonians sailed up to him in a trireme. The army crossed back to Torone, these two announced the agreement to Brasidas, and all the Lacedaemonian allies in Thrace accepted the situation. While Aristonymos gave his consent in the other cases, he discovered by calculating the days that the Skionians had revolted afterward, and he said that they were not included in the truce. Brasidas argued very much to the contrary, that they had revolted beforehand, and would not give up the city. When Aristonymos reported this to the Athenians, they were immediately prepared to campaign against Skione. The Lacedaemonians sent envoys and claimed that they would be breaking the truce, and they contested the claim to the city because they believed Brasidas but were also ready to have

the case judged by arbitration. But the Athenians chose not to risk arbitration but to campaign as soon as possible, angered that even the islanders now had the audacity to revolt through trusting in Lacedaemonian land strength, which was useless to them (the truth about the revolt was more in accordance with Athenian claims, since the Skionians had revolted two days later), and they immediately passed a decree, following the motion of Kleon, to seize and kill the Skionians. They suspended other activities as they prepared for this.

[123] At this point, Mende, a city in Pallene and a colony of Eretria, revolted from them, and Brasidas supported the revolt without regarding this as wrong in that Mende had obviously come over during the armistice; for he in turn charged the Athenians with certain infractions of the truce. The Mendaians were bolder as a consequence of seeing the resolute attitude of Brasidas and because they used the example of Skione, which he had not given up, and in addition because of their agents, who were few and, once they had set their course, did not slacken but fearing for themselves in the event of discovery forced the majority against its inclinations. As soon as the Athenians found out, they were even more enraged and made preparations against both cities. Expecting their arrival by sea, Brasidas moved the children and women of Skione and Mende to Olynthos in the Chalkidike, and he sent over to them five hundred Peloponnesian hoplites and three hundred Chalkidian peltasts, all under the command of Polydamidas. They worked together in preparing for the situation facing them, expecting the Athenians in a short time.

[124] Brasidas and Perdikkas meanwhile campaigned together for the second time against Arrhabaios in Lynkos. The latter led the forces of the Macedonians he ruled over and hoplites from the Hellenes residing there, while the former, in addition to the remaining Peloponnesians in the area, led the Chalkidians, Akanthians, and any forces the others could contribute. The overall force of Hellenic hoplites was about three thousand, and all the Macedonian cavalry along with Chalkidian accompanied them, almost a thousand, as well as a large crowd of the other barbarians. Invading the territory of Arrhabaios and finding the Lynkestians encamped against them, they took up their own position confronting them. With the infantry of each side on a hill and a plain lying in between, the cavalry of both armies galloped down to it and began the fighting. And then, after the Lynkestian hoplites were the first to advance from the hill ready to fight along within the cavalry, Brasidas and Perdikkas responded by leading their own troops out and attacked and routed the Lynkestians, killing many, while the rest fled to higher ground and stayed inactive. After this,

they set up a trophy and stayed two or three days, waiting for the Illyrians who were just about to join Perdikkas for pay. Perdikkas then wanted to proceed against the villages of Arrhabaios instead of staying where they were, but Brasidas, worrying about Mende, in case it ran into trouble when the Athenians sailed up in the meantime, also over the failure of the Illyrians to appear, was less interested in this than in returning.

[125] While they were arguing, a message came that the Illyrians had actually gone over to Arrhabaios, betraying Perdikkas. With both men now thinking it best to withdraw out of fear of the Illyrians, since they were warlike men, yet with nothing determined about when to set out because of their quarrel, as night came on the Macedonians and the crowd of barbarians, suddenly frightened in the way that large armies are apt to be panic-stricken without an apparent reason, and thinking that many times more than had come were not only approaching but almost there, suddenly broke into flight and ran for home, and this forced Perdikkas, when he realized what was happening after not at first understanding, to leave without contacting Brasidas first (the two camps were far apart). At daybreak, when Brasidas saw that the Macedonians had gone elsewhere, and the Illyrians as well as Arrhabaios were about to attack, he made his own preparations to withdraw by putting the hoplites into a square formation with the mass of light-armed in the center. For sallies at any point where they might be attacked, he positioned the youngest men, and he himself intended to retreat last with three hundred picked men and stand off the front ranks of enemy attackers. And before the enemy came close, he managed to offer his soldiers this brief speech of encouragement.

[126] "Peloponnesians, if I did not suspect that you feel shock at being abandoned, and because barbarians are attacking and in large numbers, I would not have given you this sort of instruction along with encouragement. But as it is, in the face of the desertion of our allies and the the number of our enemies, I will try to convince you of what matters most by briefly giving you advice and a reminder. I say that bravery in war is characteristic of you, not because of allies present on every occasion but because of native courage, just as it is characteristic for you to fear no one's numbers, any more than you have come here from states where the many rule the few, but instead small groups rule the majority, acquiring domi-

---

4.126. "Where the many rule the few": I agree with *HCT* III *ad* 4.126.2 that it is incredible that Brasidas, addressing troops from states with a variety of political systems, should give unqualified praise to the narrowest and harshest sort of oligarchy; Gomme argues that Brasidas actually praises the rule of the many and

nation purely through fighting and conquering. As to the barbarians you
now fear because of your inexperience, you need to understand, both from
what you have already learned by fighting the Macedonian variety and
from what I can conjecture and am told by others, that they will not be formidable. For whenever what gives the impression of strength in an enemy
is actually weakness, a timely reference to the truth always encourages his
opponents; but whenever his capabilities are not in question, it will take
someone uninformed to engage him with increased boldness. And what
these enemies have is an aspect that terrifies the inexperienced; for the size
of their presence is formidable and the noise of their shouting unbearable,
and waving their weapons in the air gives an impression of menace. But
none of this sustains them in encounters with opponents who stand their
ground; since they do not form ranks, they would feel no shame on leaving
a position under pressure, and since running away and pressing ahead
bring them equally high credit, neither says anything about their manhood
(free-lance fighting will always accommodate a credible excuse for saving
one's self), and they count less heavily on coming to grips than on frightening you without risk to themselves; otherwise, they would not have tried
the second before the first. And you can see plainly that all their prelimi-
naries are short on substance, however imposing in sight and sound. By
standing your ground against this sort of attack and then, at the right
opportunity, withdrawing in order and formation to a place of safety, you
will get there sooner and also know in the future that rabble of this sort will
make threats from long range against those who resist their initial charge
and will show off their manhood by their intentions, although, in a safe
demonstration of their spirit, they will be immediately on the heels of anyone who gives way."

[127] After giving this advice, Brasidas led the army off, and the barbarians saw this and came on with much shouting and commotion, since
they thought he was in flight, and that they would overtake and kill them.
And when they were met by sallies wherever they closed in, and Brasidas
with his picked men resisted their attacks, and so these men both with-

criticizes that of the few (which is a more straightforward understanding of the
Greek). The barbarians, then, would be cowed subjects, permanently "conquered." But this would make nonsense of Brasidas' argument about the relationship between power and numerical strength. He is unmistakably dealing with two
different factors: numbers and barbarians. His military address, "not for publication," must be held up against his moderate and "appealing" speeches to people
like the Amphipolitans.

stood their first onrush, to their surprise and from then on met and warded them off as they attacked and then continued their retreat when the attacks stopped, most of the barbarians left the Hellenes with Brasidas alone while they were in open country, and one portion stayed behind to keep after them, but the others ran after the fleeing Macedonians, killing all they caught, and then went ahead and were the first to occupy the narrow pass between two hills which leads into the territory of Arrhabaios, since they knew that there was no other line of retreat for Brasidas. Just as he was approaching the difficult part of the route, they surrounded him to cut him off. [128] Brasidas discovered and forestalled this by telling his three hundred to break ranks and run, each as fast as he could, to the hill he considered easiest to take, and to try to expel the barbarians who had already gone up, before the main force encircling him could get into the action. These men attacked and overpowered the enemy on the hill, and the way there was now made easier for the rest of the Hellenes; for the barbarians were terrified once their men had been driven off the high ground, and they stopped following the main army, thinking that now they were at the border they had escaped.

Brasidas, meanwhile, after he took the high ground, went on with little danger and on the same day reached Arnisa, the first place under Perdikkas' rule. And the soldiers, in their anger at the premature withdrawal of the Macedonians, of their own accord, every time they encountered one of their oxcarts on the road, or any baggage that had fallen off as would normally happen during a a panic-stricken retreat at night, they unyoked and slaughtered the oxen while helping themselves to the belongings. And it was in consequence of this that Perdikkas began to consider Brasidas an enemy, and in the future, although thanks to the Athenians his attitude toward the Peloponnesians was not one of fixed hostility, he disregarded the constraints of his natural interests and looked for the quickest way to come to terms with the former and detach himself from the latter.

[129] After withdrawing from Macedon to Torone, Brasidas found the Athenians already in control of Mende and stayed inactive where he was, thinking that he was now unable to cross over and help in Pallene and keeping watch over Torone. For around the same time as the events in

---

4.128. "In consequence of this": Thucydides strains language considerably here to show the paradoxical effects of emotion, even on the wiliest. The hostility of Perdikkas toward Brasidas had long been growing (4.83, 4.124); now, while frustration at the Illyrians' treachery and shame at his soldiers' panic must have contributed, the catalyst is the impulsive action of Brasidas' troops.

Lyngkos, the Athenians sailed out to Mende and Skione, just as they had
planned, with fifty ships including ten from Chios, a thousand of their
own hoplites, six hundred archers, a thousand Thracian mercenaries, and
other peltasts from their allies in the area; Nikias son of Nikeratos and
Nikostratos son of Dieitrephes were in command. Setting sail from
Poteidaia and putting in at Poseidonion, they advanced against the Mendaians. These, along with three hundred Skionian reinforcements and
their Peloponnesian auxiliaries, seven hundred hoplites in all, and Polydamidas in command, camped, as it happened, in a strong hilltop position
outside the city. Nikias, trying to push his way in by a path up the hill with
one hundred twenty Methonian light-armed, sixty Athenian hoplites, and
all the archers, was wounded and could not force his way through; meanwhile, Nikostratos and the rest of the army took a different and longer
approach to the inaccessible hill and were thrown into confusion, and the
whole Athenian army came close to defeat. On that day, since the Mendaians did not yield, the Athenians fell back and set up camp, and when night
approached, the Mendaians went back into the city.

[130] On the next day, sailing around to the side toward Skione, the
Athenians seized the outskirts and spent the day plundering the countryside without anyone attacking them (for there was division inside the city),
and the following night the three hundred Skionians returned home. The
following day, while Nikias advanced with half the army to the Skionian
border and plundered the land, Nikostratos and the rest occupied a position in front of the city at the gate leading to Poteidaia. Polydamidas (for
this happened to be where the Mendaians and their allies had their arms
stacked) began organizing them for a battle and encouraged the Mendaians
to go out. And when someone from the popular party made the partisan
retort that he would not go out and saw no need for fighting and, as he
spoke, was pulled by the arm and shaken up by Polydamidas, the common
people immediately picked up their arms and in extreme anger flew at the
Peloponnesians and those who were dealing with them and in opposition
to themselves. And they charged and immediately routed them, partly
because of the suddenness of the fight, partly because of their fear that the
gates would be opened for the Athenians. For they believed that the attack
occurred only after these had received some sort of notification. All who
were not killed outright took refuge in the citadel, which had also been the
previous stronghold of the Peloponnesians. And the Athenians (for Nikias
had by this time returned to the front and was next to the city) fell on the
city, which had been opened but without any agreement, and pillaged it in
full force as though they had taken it by assault, and the generals barely

stopped them from killing the people as well. And after this, they told the Mendaians to govern themselves according to their regular practice, deciding among themselves which were responsible for the revolt. Meanwhile, they blockaded those in the citadel by walls to the sea on each side and left guards. After they had secured their position at Mende, they advanced on Skione. [131] The Skionians and the Peloponnesians came out against them and stationed themselves in front of the city on a strong hill, making the enemy's attempt at surrounding them futile without capturing it. Attacking in force and taking it by assault, the Athenians drove out the men holding it and set up their camp there, and after they set up a trophy they prepared the circumvallation. And not much later, when they were already at work, the auxiliaries besieged in the citadel of Mende forced their way past the guards along the sea and arrived in the night, and most of them avoided the army at Skione and came in.

[132] During the circumvallation of Skione, Perdikkas sent a herald to the Athenian generals and reached an understanding with the Athenians on account of his hatred of Brasidas since the retreat from Lynkos, the time when he had immediately begun his negotiations. Just then, as it happened, the Lacedaemonian Ischagoras was about to lead an army to Brasidas on foot, and Perdikkas, both because Nikias, after their agreement, ordered him to give the Athenians some evidence of his trustworthiness and because he himself no longer wanted Peloponnesians coming into his land, mobilized his associates in Thessaly, where he had always been on close terms with the leading men, and blocked the army at the preparation stage, so that there was not even an approach to the Thessalians. Ischagoras himself, however, along with Ameinias and Aristeus reached Brasidas, since the Lacedaemonians had sent him to inspect the situation, and in violation of all agreements they brought him some of the young men from Sparta to appoint as governors in the cities instead of leaving this to those on hand. And he appointed Klearidas son of Kleonymos at Amphipolis and Pasitelidas son of Hegesandros at Torone.

[133] During the same summer, the Thebans tore down the walls of the Thespians on the charge of atticism, since they had always wanted to do this, and now that it had been made easier after what had been the flower of their youth had perished in the battle against the Athenians. And in the same summer the temple of Hera at Argos burned down, because Chrysis, the priestess, placed a lighted lamp next to the garlands and fell asleep, so that they all caught fire and burned before she noticed. Chrysis immediately fled in the night to Phleious in fear of the Argives, while they, following their regular laws, appointed another priestess, whose name was

Phaeinis. Chrysis, when she fled, had served through eight years of this war and half of the ninth. By the very end of the summer, Skione was completely walled off, and the Athenians left troops on guard and returned home with the rest of the army.

[134] In the following winter, there was little Athenian or Lacedaemonian activity because of the armistice, but the Mantineans and Tegeans and allies on both sides clashed at Laodokeion in Oresthis, and victory was disputed; for each city routed the opposing wing, and both set up a trophy and then sent spoils to Delphi, yet the Tegeans, after both sides lost heavily with no clear outcome, bivouacked when night stopped the action, and they set up their trophy immediately, while the Mantineans withdrew to Boukolion and set theirs up later.

[135] At the end of this winter, Brasidas, when it was almost spring, made an attempt on Poteidaia. He arrived at night and set up ladders, getting that far without detection (for when the alarm bell was being passed along, he acted in the interval before the man who handed it over came back), yet right after discovery, before anyone climbed up, he quickly led his army away and did not wait for day. And the winter ended, also the ninth year of this war, which Thucydides recorded.

BOOK FIVE

INTRODUCTION

The first few chapters conclude the fighting in Thrace. Both Brasidas and Kleon are killed, and their deaths facilitate the conclusion of a general truce, the "Peace of Nikias," badly needed by both sides. From the outset, Thucydides emphasizes the fragility of this peace, and the other treaties and alliances that are made subsequently and also makes the case, in his "Second Preface (5.25–26)," for dealing with the entire period of 431–404 B.C.E. as one continuing war. The bulk of book 5 relates the confused and confusing negotiations and realignments of both major and minor Greek states, along with the actual fighting these entail. This is a natural setting for the introduction of Alcibiades, the ambitious, unscrupulous, and able Athenian politician and general who is the dominant personality in books 6 and 8. Ultimately, without constituting a formal breaking of the peace, a large-scale hoplite battle is fought at Mantinea, where an Athenian-Argive coalition is decisively defeated by the Spartan alliance; as one consequence, Thucydides states, the Spartans regain the military reputation they had lost because of the Pylos disaster and a variety of shortcomings as war leaders.

It is in the context of Sparta's rehabilitation that Thucydides describes the Athenian campaign against the Melians, islanders who fall into the rare category of Spartan colonists; during the war, they have refused to pay tribute assessed by Athens and have not completely honored their self-proclaimed neutrality. Before opening hostilities, the Athenians send representatives to persuade the Melian oligarchs to submit peacefully, insisting that the matter be discussed solely in terms of Realpolitik. Formally, the Athenians lose the debate, the "Melian Dialogue"; citing their trust in both divine and Spartan assistance, the Melians refuse to become tributary allies. After a siege, they surrender; adult males are executed, the others are sold into slavery.

Apart from the Thracian campaign at the beginning and the Melian Dialogue at the end, book 5 is normally regarded as a relatively unfinished work (or, according to one theory, composed by Xenophon). There are no speeches, whereas the entire texts of treaties and alliances are quoted (in non-Thucydide-

an language and Doric dialect); *the reverse might have been expected. In addition, the narrative is commonly criticized as disjointed and obscure in expression, as well as for its many loose ends and omissions. Other explanations, however, have been advanced for many of these peculiarities. Whatever stages of composition produced book 5, the incessant realignments of the Greek states, in which deliberate deception is overshadowed by miscalculation and misunderstanding, constitute a tragicomedy often richly detailed and always inimitably Thucydidean. Similarly, Mantinea, Thucydides' set-piece among hoplite battles, is notoriously full of surprises; if this is a battle the Athenians and Argives should have won, it is preceded by a narrow (and wholly unwitting) Argive escape from a more crushing defeat.*

BOOK FIVE

[1] In the following summer, the one-year armistice expired at the time of the Pythian games, and during the truce the Athenians expelled the Delians from Delos, supposing that because of some old crime they had been impure when they were consecrated, and that this had also been an oversight on their own part in the purification, which they thought they had properly carried out by removing the graves of the dead, as I have described previously. And the Delians, after Pharnakes gave them Atramyttion in Asia, settled there according to individual inclination.

[2] After getting the consent of the Athenians, Kleon sailed out to the Thracian area after the armistice, taking twelve hundred Athenian hoplites, three hundred cavalry as well as a larger number of allies, and thirty ships. Putting in first at Skione, which was still under siege, and taking additional hoplites from the garrison, he sailed into the harbor of Kophos in Toronian territory, not far from the city. When he learned from deserters there that Brasidas was not in Torone and that those who were had inadequate strength, he advanced on the city with the land army and sent ten ships to sail around to the harbor. He came first to the surrounding wall, which Brasidas had built in front of the city with the intention of putting the suburbs within it, and by breaching the old wall he had made the whole into a single city. [3] Pasitelidas, the Lacedaemonian commander, and the garrison on hand went to defend in this area and resisted when the Athenians attacked. Since they were being overpowered and the ships were sailing into the harbor, Pasitelidas, afraid that the forces from the ships would reach the city first and capture it while it was undefended, also that he would be taken prisoner when the fortification was seized,

---

5.1. "At the time of the Pythian games": for the obscurity in meaning and chronology, see *HCT* III *ad* 5.1.1, but the reference to the Pythian festival leads neatly into the desire to placate Apollo. "Described previously": 3.104 (a rare cross-reference). Pharnakes was the Persian satrap in the area.

5.3. According to 4.132, the commander was Epitelidas.

abandoned this location and ran for the city. But the Athenians were too quick, the men from the ships taking Torone and their infantry meeting no resistance as they rushed in right behind him through the breach in the old wall. In the fighting, some of the Peloponnesians and Toronians were killed immediately and others taken prisoner, including Pasitelidas the commander.

Brasidas was coming to support the forces in Torone but when he found out on the way that the city had been captured, he went back, stopping after he had come within forty stades of getting there in time. Kleon and the Athenians set up two trophies, one down at the harbor and one by the wall, and enslaved the Toronian women and children but sent to Athens the Toronians themselves, the Peloponnesians, and any Chalkidians there, seven hundred overall; they were able to return, the Peloponnesians in the peace that was made afterward, the rest when the Olynthians brought them back by man-for-man exchanges. And it was around this same time that the Boiotians, through treachery, captured Panakton, an Athenian fort on the border. After leaving a garrison in Torone, Kleon set out and sailed around Athos going toward Amphipolis.

[4] Around the same time, Phaiax son of Erisistratos and two other ambassadors sent out by the Athenians in two ships sailed to Italy and Sicily. For the Leontines, when the Athenians had left Sicily after the settlement, enrolled many new citizens, and the common people had intentions of redividing the land; when the leading men found out, they called in the Syracusans and expelled the common people. These became wanderers without ties to one another, while the leading men, by an agreement with the Syracusans, left the city deserted and lived at Syracuse as citizens. And later some of them left again in dissatisfaction and occupied Phokaia, as a certain part of the city of Leontini is called, and Brikinniai, which is a stronghold in the countryside. Many of the common people who were in exile at the time came to them, and they settled there and took up the war from these forts. It was this news that caused the Athenians to send Phaiax in case they could find a way of saving the Leontine common people by persuading their allies there and, if possible, the other Sikeliots to join in a united campaign because of the power the Syracusans were acquiring.

On his arrival, Phaiax persuaded the Kamarinaians and the Akragantians, but when there were hostile developments in Gela, he did not go on to any others, realizing that he would not persuade them, and after he went back through Sikel territory to Katana, passing by Brikinniai and encouraging the inhabitants, he sailed home. [5] During his travels to and from Sicily, he also approached some of the cities in Italy about friendship with

Athens, and he encountered the Lokrian refugees from Messena, who had been sent there as epoikoi when there was faction among the Messenians after the Sikeliots reached an agreement, and one party called in the Lokrians, so that for a while Messina belonged to the Lokrians. Now when Phaiax encountered those who were on their way home, he did them no harm; the Lokrians had made an agreement with him to reconcile with the Athenians. For out of the allied cities, these alone did not make peace with Athens when the Sikeliots reconciled with one another and would not have done so now except for the pressure from a war with the Hipponians and the Medmaians, who were their neighbors and also their colonists.

[6] So Phaiax returned a while later. This was when Kleon sailed from Torone toward Amphipolis, and using Eion as a base he attacked Stagiros, an Andrian colony, without taking it but captured the Thasian colony Galepsos by assault. After he sent envoys to Perdikkas to get him to come with an army, in accordance with the alliance, and others into Thrace, to Polles, king of the Odomantians, so as to hire as many Thracians as possible, he himself remained inactive and waited at Eion. When Brasidas learned about this, he took up his own position at Kerdylion; this is a place on high ground across the river not far from Amphipolis, belonging to the Argilians, and it gave him a full view so that Kleon and his army could not proceed without being seen; he had every expectation that Kleon, contemptuous of the enemy numbers, would do so, advancing on the Amphipolis with the army on hand. At the same time, he made his preparations, calling up fifteen hundred Thracian mercenaries and all the Edonians, both peltasts and cavalry, and he had a thousand Myrkinian and Chalkidian peltasts in addition to those in Amphipolis. Overall, about two thousand hoplites were assembled, and three hundred cavalry. Brasidas took up his position at Kerdylion with fifteen hundred of these, while the rest were stationed in Amphipolis with Klearidas.

[7] Kleon stayed inactive for a while and then was forced to act exactly as Brasidas anticipated. Since the soldiers were not only irritated by the inactivity but airing their feelings about his leadership and the degree of incompetence and cowardice he was matching against a like degree of expertise and daring, also about their reluctance to follow him from the very start, Kleon, aware of the murmurs and not wanting the men to be demoralized by staying in the same place, roused them and set out. He assumed the same attitude whose success regarding Pylos assured him that he had some sort of ability; far from expecting anyone to come out and meet him in battle, he said that he was going out to look over the situation and was not waiting for his full forces in order to have the edge in safety,

in case of difficulty, but in order to surround the city and take it by storm. Moving the army to a strong hill before Amphipolis and taking up a position there, he viewed the marshy area by the Strymon and the position of the city toward Thrace, and he assumed he could leave at any time without a fight; there was no one to be seen on the walls, nor was anyone emerging from the gates, which were all closed. Accordingly, it even seemed a mistake that he had not come with siege machinery; for he could have taken the city in its deserted state.

[8] As soon as Brasidas saw the Athenians stirring, he came down from Kerdylion and entered Amphipolis. He did not consider marching out in regular formation, doubtful about his forces and considering them overmatched, not in numbers (these were about equal) but in quality (for the whole Athenian contingent in the expedition was first-class, along with the best of the Lemnians and Imbrians), but prepared to attack with guile. If he were to reveal his numbers to the enemy and also the barely adequate way his men were armed, he doubted that he would be more successful than by giving the other side no prior opportunity to see them and not using their contempt for his actual situation. He accordingly selected one hundred fifty hoplites for himself and assigned the rest to Klearidas, wanting to make a sudden attack before the Athenians moved away, since he thought he would not catch them by themselves again if they ever got rein-

5.7–11. On the battle of Amphipolis, cf. *HCT* III, pp. 635–57, Hunter 1973, pp. 30–41, Ellis 1978, Jones 1978, Boeghold 1979, Westlake 1980, Daverio Rocchi 1985, Nikolaidis 1990, and Mitchell 1991, pp. 182–92. Thucydides has not previously indicated any defects in Kleon's leadership in the north; in 5.3, he even mentions gratuitously the realization of Pasitelidas' worst fears (and there could hardly have been a more unfortunate time for the Spartans to have a commander captured). There has accordingly been much controversy over what is meant by Kleon's "attitude" (or, some believe, "plan"); "regarding Pylos" is general enough to include reference to Kleon's behavior in 4.27–28. What is clear is that all his following conduct is to be understood as combining enough incompetence, overconfidence, and cowardice to offset his superior troops and lose the battle in advance. Brasidas can read his thinking and its consequences (however illogically, see *HCT ad* 5.7.1, Hunter, p. 40) and shrewdly weigh the advantages of an over-confident enemy and of one caught completely by surprise (in emphasizing the choice to use surprise, Thucydides severely strains language with "not using their contempt"); see Boeghold. The most magnetic character in Thucydides, Brasidas emerges as impressive even in an avowedly debunking article (Wylie 1992; perhaps more damaging is Roisman 1987, not cited by Wylie, cf. 3.30–31n), but the Amphipolis account in particular calls Thucydides' objectivity into question; exalting the man who effectively ended his public career not only was in his own interest but gave him an effective stick to beat other Spartans with.

forcements. After summoning all his forces with the intention of encouraging them and also telling them his plan, he spoke as follows:

[9] "About your country, men of the Peloponnese, that courage has always kept it free, or that as Dorians you are about to fight Ionians, whom you are accustomed to beating, let this brief mention suffice. What I will explain is how I have devised the attack, so that it will not reduce your boldness by the apparent disadvantage of attempting it in small detachments rather than combined. My assessment of the enemy is that they have gone up there and are now ignoring us, carelessly occupied with the view, out of contempt for us and with no expectation that anyone will come out to meet them in battle. Whoever launches his attack by taking the closest possible look at such mistakes by his opponents in conjunction with his own strengths as well will always be the most successful, not so much by open countermeasures rather than by any means suitable to the circumstances; these are the tricks that bring the most glory when they benefit friends the most by most completely fooling the enemy.

"So, then, while they are still confident and unprepared and, by the look of them, more interested in slipping away than in standing their ground, when they are slack in their attitude, before they can marshall their resolve instead, I and my men will fall on the center of their army at a run and do our best to take them by surprise; and then you, Klearidas, after you see me pressing them hard and in all probability causing a panic, take your own men, open the gates all of a sudden, run out, hurry to engage them as quickly as possible. This is our best hope of causing them to panic; for a contingent attacking later is more terrifying to the enemy than the one in action on the field. And show your own courage, as you should, being a Spartiate, and you allies follow him bravely too and understand that fighting well involves three things, willingness, a sense of shame, and obedience to leaders, and that this day brings you either freedom, if you are brave, and the name of Lacedaemonian allies, or that of Athenian slaves, with escape from bondage or extermination the best you can hope for, and a slavery harsher than you already know, along with halting the liberation of the other Hellenes. But there must be no weakening, since you understand the high stakes of this contest, and I will show that I am not the man to encourage those around me rather than following through in action."

[10] After this short speech, Brasidas prepared for his own sortie and stationed the others with Klearidas by the Thracian gates, as they are

5.9. "A sense of shame": see *HCT* III *ad* 5.111.3.

called, so that they could go out just as they had been ordered. After he had been seen coming down from Kerdylion and when he was in the city (which can be observed from outside) sacrificing at the sanctuary of Athena and making these preparations, it was announced to Kleon (who at just that moment had gone ahead for his view) that the whole army was clearly inside the city, and that the feet of many horses and men showed under the gates as though ready to come out. He came over when he heard this, and after a look, since he did not want to risk a battle before his reinforcements arrived and believed that he could withdraw first, he ordered the signal for retreat and at the same time gave those moving on the left wing instructions to retire toward Eion, the only possible way. But when this seemed slow to him, he wheeled the right wing around and, giving the enemy his unshielded side, led the army away himself. And when Brasidas saw his opportunity here, with the Athenian army on the move, he told his men and the others, "They won't stand up to us; it shows in the way they keep moving their spears and their heads. After men get like this, they are not likely to stand up to attackers. So come on, someone open the gates for me where I said, and let us get out right away and rush them with complete confidence."

Coming out at the gates of the stockade and the first one in the long wall that existed at that time, he advanced at a fast run where the road goes straight (right where now, as you come to the steepest part of the place, a trophy has been set up), and he struck at the middle of the Athenian army, where there was panic caused by disorder as well as astonishment at his daring, and routed it, and at the same time Klearidas, following his orders to come through the Thracian gates with his forces, was attacking. The overall result was that the Athenians, taken by surprise, were thrown into sudden confusion on both sides. Their left wing, which was toward Eion and had already moved ahead, was cut off immediately and fled. And Brasidas, moving along to the right wing as soon as the left was in retreat, was wounded; and the Athenians did not notice that he had fallen, but those at his side lifted him up and carried him away. The Athenian right wing was more resistant, and while Kleon, since he had not intended to stand his ground in the first place, immediately fled and was run down and killed by a Myrkinian peltast, the hoplites with him drew their ranks close together and fought off the attacks of Klearidas two or three times and only gave way when Myrkinian and Chalkidian cavalry and peltasts surrounded

5.10. "This seemed slow": more plausible Greek than reading along the lines of "there seemed ample time" (e.g., Mitchell 1991, p. 185), see *HCT* III *ad* 5.10.4.

them throwing javelins, and then they were routed. So the whole Athenian army was now in a disastrous flight, and the remnant, after the others were killed either in the fighting or by the Chalkidian cavalry and peltasts, took different routes through the hills and got away to Eion. Those who had borne Brasidas from the fighting and rescued him brought him into the city while he was still alive; he heard that his men were the winners and died not long afterward. The rest of the army, returning from the pursuit with Klearidas, stripped the dead and set up a trophy.

[11] After this, all the allies, in attendance under arms, gave Brasidas public burial in the city in front of what is now the agora (and since then, the Amphipolitans, who have built an enclosure around the tomb, sacrifice to him as a hero and have given him the honor of games and annual offerings, and they attributed the colony to him as founder, tearing down the buildings associated with Hagnon and obliterating any possible surviving reminder of a foundation by him, believing along with their timely cultivation of the Lacedaemonian alliance in their fear of the Athenians that Brasidas had been their savior, and that honors to Hagnon, considering their hostility to Athens, could not benefit themselves or gratify him as before). They also gave the Athenians back their dead. About six hundred Athenians were killed and seven of their opponents, which was because of the sort of battle it was, not in formations but haphazard and filled with panic. After they received their dead, they sailed home, and those with Klearidas organized matters around Amphipolis. [12] Around the same time, at the end of the summer, the Lacedaemonians Ramphias, Autokratidas, and Epikydides led nine hundred hoplites to the Thracian area as reinforcements, and when they reached Herakleia in Trachis they attended to whatever they thought had gone wrong there. While they were spending time there, this battle took place, and then the summer ended.

[13] At the beginning of the following winter, Ramphias and his associates proceeded as far as Pierion in Thessaly, but since the Thessalians were obstructing them, and besides Brasidas, for whom they were bringing the troops, was dead, they turned back for home, thinking that there was no longer any point, since the Athenians had left in defeat, and they themselves did not have the capability to carry out his objectives. Above all, they went back because they knew that the Lacedaemonians, when they sent them out, were inclined toward a peace.

[14] The development right after the battle of Amphipolis and Ramphias' return from Thessaly was that neither side resumed the war, since both were more inclined toward peace: the Athenians because they had been badly beaten at Delion and again, shortly afterward, at Amphipolis

and no longer trusted in their strength with the same confidence that made them reject a settlement earlier, when their current success gave them the impression that they would emerge superior, and there was also the fear that, because of their setbacks, their allies would be more likely to revolt, and they were sorry that they had not settled in the favorable circumstances after Pylos; in the case of the Lacedaemonians, because the war had not gone according to their expectation, which was that a few years would be enough for them to destroy the power of the Athenians by ravaging their land, and instead they met with the disaster on the island, unlike anything that had ever happened to Sparta before, and because their country was being raided from Pylos and Kythera, the helots were deserting, and there was always the possibility that even the ones who stayed, abetted by those on the outside, might react to circumstances as they had done in the past, by starting a revolution. At the same time, their thirty-year truce with the Argives was expiring, and the Argives were unwilling to make another unless Kynouria was returned to them; so there was the obvious impossibility of fighting the Argives and Athenians at once. And they suspected that some Peloponnesian cities would go over to the Argives, which actually happened.

[15] Both sides, then, when they weighed these considerations, felt that they had to reach an agreement, especially the Lacedaemonians, because of their eagerness to get the men back from the island; the ones who were Spartiates were of high rank, and by the same token their relatives. They therefore began to negotiate immediately after their capture, but the Athenians had no desire to resolve anything on a moderate basis when they were doing well. But after they were humbled at Delion, the Lacedaemonians realized that they would now be more accommodating and immediately concluded the one-year armistice, during which they were to meet to consider a longer period. [16] And after the Athenian defeat at Amphipolis and the deaths of Kleon and Brasidas, certainly the main opponents of peace on each side—one of them because of the success and honor derived from the war, the other because he thought that in calmer times he would

5.15. "By the same token their relatives": the text is probably corrupt here, see Classen/Steup and *HCT* III *ad* 5.15.1.

5.16. The interminable first sentence is as unsatisfactory as any in Thucydides. There has very probably been considerable interpolation, as some of the vocabulary suggests, see *HCT* III *ad* 5.16.1; the difficulties, however, evidently began with the elaborateness of his four-way comparison among the two Athenians and two Spartans.

be recognized as a rogue, and his slanders would lack credibility—at this time the men in each city particularly eager for leadership, Pleistoanax son of Pausanias, king of the Lacedaemonians, and Nikias son of Nikeratos, more successful in his commands than anyone else at the time, expended a great deal more effort toward the peace: Nikias because he wished to safeguard his good fortune where he had been undamaged and held in honor, and to end his own labors and put an end to those of his fellow-citizens immediately and leave to posterity the claim that throughout his life he had never brought harm to the state, thinking that this is what resulted from avoiding risk, every time a man relies on luck as little as possible, and that peace was the way to avoid risk; Pleistoanax because his enemies abused him over his restoration and represented him to the Lacedaemonians as the problem every time they had a reverse, saying that it was because of him and his unlawful restoration. Their charge was that he, along with his brother Aristokles, had persuaded the priestess at Delphi to keep giving this response to the Lacedaemonians when their delegations came to consult her: bring the seed of the demigod, son of Zeus, back from foreign lands to his own, or plow with a silver plow; and after a while she prevailed on the Lacedaemonians to restore him in the nineteenth year of his exile in Lykaion, where, in his fear of the Lacedaemonians, he had a house built halfway inside the sanctuary of Zeus (this was because his withdrawal from Attica at one time was supposedly due to bribery) and celebrate with the same dances and ceremonies as when they first set up their kings on founding Lacedaemon. [17] Accordingly, vexed by these attacks and thinking that, if there were no setbacks, because it was peacetime, and in addition the Lacedaemonians got back their men, this would also put him beyond the reach of his enemies, whereas under wartime conditions it was inevitable for those in high places to be blamed for disasters, he was eager for a settlement.

They held talks during this winter, and when it was close to spring, on the Lacedaemonian side there were preparations for a fortified outpost, with a call sent around to the cities, intended to make the Athenians more amenable; and when the meetings, after all the claims against one another, meanwhile resulted in agreement to make peace by giving back what each had taken in war, but with the Athenians keeping Nisaia (when the Athenians in due course demanded Plataia, the Thebans claimed that they did not hold the place by force but because the Plataians had come over by agreement, without treachery; and the Athenians claimed the same process for Nisaia), the Lacedaemonians then summoned their allies, and when they all voted to end the war, except for those who disliked the arrangements, the Boiotians, Corinthians, Eleans, and Megarians, they made the treaty. These were the terms on which they gave their oath to the Athenians, and the Athenians to the Lacedaemonians:

[18] "The Athenians and the Peloponnesians and their allies made a treaty on the following terms and swore to them city by city. Concerning the national sanctuaries, anyone who wishes is to sacrifice, consult oracles, and attend festivals according to ancestral custom and to have secure passage by land and by sea. The sanctuary and temple of Apollo at Delphi and the Delphians are to be independent and to have their own taxation and law courts for themselves and their land, according to ancestral custom. The treaty is to bind the Athenians and their allies and the Lacedaemonians and their allies for fifty years without deception or injury. Let no one have the right to take up arms to bring woe, neither the Lacedaemonians and their allies against the Athenians and their allies nor the Athenians and their allies against the Lacedaemonians and their allies, by any contrivance or device. If there is any dispute, let them use law and oaths in any way they agree upon.

"The Lacedaemonians and their allies are to give back Amphipolis to the Athenians. In all the cities that the Lacedaemonians have turned over to the Athenians, let it be allowed for the people themselves to go wherever they wish with their own property. The cities are to be independent, paying the tribute of Aristeides, and once the treaty is in force let neither the Athenians nor their allies take up arms to harm them if they have provided the tribute; they are Argilos, Stagiros, Akanthos, Skolos, Olynthos, and Spartolos. Let them be allies of neither side, Lacedaemonian or Athenian. If the Athenians convince the cities, and they wish it, let it be possible for the Athenians to make them allies. The Mekybernians, Sanaians, and Singaians are to inhabit their own cities, just like the Olynthians and Akanthians. The Lacedaemonians and their allies are to give back Panakton to the Athenians.

"The Athenians are to give back to the Lacedaemonians Koryphasion, Kythera, Methone, Pteleon, and Atalante. They are also to release all Lacedaemonians who are in Athenian custody or in custody anywhere else

---

5.18–19. On the terms of the treaty, see *HCT* III, pp. 666–78, where Gomme puts considerable emphasis on the discreditable treatment of Spartan adherents in Thrace (for Skione, cf. 4.122.6 and 5.32.1). Connor 1984, pp. 144–47, has persuasively argued that this and several other documents are cited in book 5 to point up the "ironic . . . discrepancy between professions of enduring stability and the rapidly shifting reality of events." "Give back . . . Koryphasion": see 4.3.

under Athenian control and the Peloponnesians besieged in Skione, as well as all others in Skione who are Lacedaemonian allies and all those Brasidas sent there and any other Lacedaemonian ally in Athenian custody or in custody anywhere else under Athenian control. The Lacedaemonians and their allies are likewise to give back any Athenians or Athenian allies in their possession. As for the Skionians, Toronians, and Sermylians, and any other city in Athenian possession, the Athenians are to make such plans as they see fit concerning these and the other cities.

"The Athenians are to swear an oath to the Lacedaemonians and their allies, city by city. Let the seventeen men from each city swear his strongest native oath. Let this be the oath: I will abide by this agreement and treaty rightly and without deceit. For the Lacedaemonians and their allies, let their oath to the Athenians be in the same fashion. Both parties are to renew the oath every year. Inscribed pillars are to be set up at Olympia, Pytho, and Isthmus, at Athens on the Acropolis and in Lacedaemon at Amyklai. If they overlook anything, either party concerning any matter, the oath is to allow for both to give just cause and make alterations as they think best, both the Athenians and the Lacedaemonians. [19] The treaty begins in the ephorate of Pleistolas on the twenty-seventh day of Artemision and in the archonship of Alkaios on the twenty-fifth day of the month of Elaphabolion. The following swore the oath and poured the libations: from the Lacedaemonians, Pleistoanax, Agis, Pleistolas, Damagetos, Chionis, Metagenes, Akanthos, Daithos, Ischagoras, Philochoridas, Zeuxidas, Antippos, Tellis, Alkinadas, Empedias, Menas, Laphilos; and the following from the Athenians: Lampon, Isthmionikes, Nikias, Laches, Euthydemos, Prokles, Pythodoros, Hagnon, Myrtilos, Thrasykles, Theogenes, Aristokrates, Iolkios, Timokrates, Leon, Lamachos, Demosthenes."

[20] This treaty was made at the end of the winter when spring came, immediately after the City Dionysia, when ten years had passed, with a difference of a few days, since the first invasion of Attica and the beginning of the war took place. One must make observations according to time of year, rather than trusting in the enumeration of names from here and there to mark events, whether they were officials or because of some title: for there is no clear indication whether an event took place when they were beginning, in the middle, or somewhere else in their term. Counting by summers and winters, as recorded here, one will find that ten summers

5.20. "With a difference of a few days": see Konishi 1983 and cf. 2.1–2n.

and an equal number of winters, with each of these half the length of a year, comprised this first war.

[21] Since the Lacedaemonians were designated by lot as the first to give back what they had taken, they immediately released all the prisoners in their possession and, sending Ischagoras, Menas, and Philocharidas as envoys to the Thracian area, ordered Klearidas to hand over Amphipolis to the Athenians and the others to observe the treaty as it applied to each of them. They were unwilling, since they did not think the terms were to their advantage; and Klearidas, showing favor to the Chalkidians, did not hand over the city but said that he had no power to hand it over against the will of the Amphipolitans. With envoys from the region, he hurried to Lacedaemon to defend himself if Ischagoras and his associates blamed him for not complying, also because he wanted to know whether the agreement was still flexible, and when he learned that they were committed he hurried on his way back, since the Lacedaemonians sent him with instructions to hand over the place if at all possible, but otherwise to bring out any Peloponnesians who were there.

[22] The allies happened to be still in Lacedaemon in person, and the Lacedaemonians asked those who had not accepted the treaty to do so. With the very same grounds for rejection as before, they refused to accept the treaty if no fairer one than this could be made. Since they would not give in, the Lacedaemonians dismissed them and concluded their own alliance with the Athenians thinking, after the Argives had been unwilling to make a treaty when Ampelidas and Lichas were there, that they were least formidable by themselves, without the Athenians, and that there would be the most stability in the rest of the Peloponnesos, which would have gone over to the Athenians if that had been possible. Accordingly, when envoys from Athens were on hand, and there had been conferences, they reached terms, and the following oaths of alliance were sworn:

[23] "The Lacedaemonians and the Athenians shall be allies for fifty years, on the following terms. If any enemies attack the land of the Lacedaemonians and do harm to the Lacedaemonians, the Athenians are to aid the Lacedaemonians in whatever way they can with all their strength according to their power; if they depart after pillaging, that city is to be the enemy of the Lacedaemonians and the Athenians and is to be dealt with severely by both, and the two cities are to end the war together. This is to be just, earnest, and without deceit. And if any enemies attack the land of the Athenians and do harm to the Athenians, the Lacedaemonians are to help the Athenians in whatever way they can with all their strength according to their power; if they depart after pillaging, that city is to be an

enemy of the Lacedaemonians and the Athenians and is to be dealt with severely by both, and the two cities are to end the war together. This is to be just, earnest, and without deceit. If there is a slave uprising, the Athenians are to assist the Lacedaemonians in full force according to their power. On each side, those who swore to the other treaty shall swear this. It is to be renewed annually by the Lacedaemonians going to Athens at the Dionysia and by the Athenians going to Lacedaemon at the Hyakinthia. Each are to set up an inscribed pillar, in Lacedaemon by the Apollo statue at Amyklai, in Athens on the Acropolis by the Athena statue. If it seems best to add or delete anything regarding the alliance, the oath is to allow this to both parties as they see fit. [24] From the Lacedaemonians, the following swore the oath: Pleistoanax, Agis, Pleistolas, Damagetos, Chionis, Metagenes, Akanthos, Daithos, Ischagoras, Philocharidas, Zeuxidas, Antippos, Alkinadas, Tellis, Empedias, Menas, Laphilos; from the Athenians: Lampon, Isthmionikes, Laches, Nikias, Euthydemos, Prokles, Pythodoros, Hagnon, Myrtilos, Thrasykles, Theogenes, Aristokrates, Iolkios, Timokrates, Leon, Lamachos, Demosthenes." This alliance was made soon after the treaty; the Athenians gave the men back to the Lacedaemonians, and with the summer the eleventh year began. The first war, which was continuous during the ten-year period, has been recorded.

[25] After the treaty and the alliance which occurred after the ten-year war, when Pleistolas was ephor in Lacedaemon and Alkaios was archon in Athens, those accepting them had peace, but the Corinthians and some of the cities of the Peloponnese tried to unsettle the arrangements, and right away relations between the allies and the Lacedaemonians were thrown into further disorder. As time passed, the Lacedaemonians came under suspicion from the Athenians as well, since on some occasions they did not do what was stated in the terms. While for six years and ten months they stopped short of invading one another's land, they harmed each other as much as possible elsewhere under the unstable truce. Then, however, forced into actually breaking the truce that followed the ten-year period, they went back to open war.

[26] The same Thucydides, an Athenian, has recorded these events as well, in the order that they occurred according to summers and winters, up to the point when the Lacedaemonians and their allies overthrew the empire of the Athenians and captured the long walls and the Peiraeus. For the war overall, to that time, there were twenty-seven years in total. As for the agreement in the middle part, if anyone ventures to think it was not wartime, his claim will be incorrect. Let him look at it, and he will find it unreasonable for this to be called a peace, during which they neither

returned nor received everything they agreed on, and aside from this there were wrongs on both sides in connection with the Mantinean and Epidaurian wars and in other cases, and the allies in Thrace were no less hostile, and the Boiotians had ten-day armistices. Therefore, what with the ten-year war, the questionable truce after this, and the war that followed from that, anyone who calculates by seasons will find that this was the number of years, with a few days in addition, and that for those who have any faith in oracles this alone was what actually happened in clear accordance. I certainly remember that all along, when the war began and until it ended, there were many who prophesied that it must last thrice nine years. I lived through all of it when I was of an age to comprehend and had my mind engaged, in order to know with some exactness; it also happened that I was exiled from my city for twenty years after the command at Amphipolis and, being present at the activities of both sides, especially the Peloponnesians, unoccupied because of my exile, I understood these all the more. Accordingly, I will relate the disagreement after the ten years and violation of the truce and how the war was fought from then on.

[27] After the truce was made, followed by the alliance, all the representatives from the Peloponnese who had been summoned there for the purpose returned from Lacedaemon, and while the others left for home, the Corinthians first turned aside to Argos and declared to some of the Argives in power the necessity for the Argives (since the Lacedaemonians, not for any good ends but for enslaving the Peloponnesos, had made a truce with their worst enemies until now, the Athenians) to see how the Peloponnesos could be saved, and for a decree that every Hellenic city

---

5.25–26. It is difficult to see Thucydides' remark about oracles as anything but disparaging, see Dover 1988, pp. 71–72. It is quite possible that Kleon was responsible for Thucydides' exile, but there is no evidence, see Westlake 1968, pp. 60–61. By making a series of procrustean revisions of the text at 5.26.5, L. Canfora has argued that the exile referred to was actually that of Xenophon, not only Thucydides' continuator but his editor; see (e.g.) Canfora 1980, and for his other publications on this topic and some sensible criticism of them, see Piccirilli 1986. Untenable as well is the claim by Konishi 1987 that Thucydides had not intended to extend his account beyond the present book 8. For a useful list of "troublesome passages" in 5.27–84 and 5.114–16 supporting arguments that book 5 was left in unfinished state, see *HCT* V, pp. 376–77. Connor 1984, p. 143, argues that the "Second Preface" (which itself was evidently composed at different times, see *HCT* IV *ad* 5.26.2, Westlake 1972) is an indication less of Thucydides' changing views of the war during different stages of composition than of his desire to convince contemporaries that there was a single war lasting twenty-seven years (for the religious significance of "thrice nine years," see Rawlings 1981, p. 10).

willing, if it was independent and dealt in fair and equal judgments, should make an alliance with the Argives based on the mutual defense of territory and designate a few men as having complete authority, with no speaking before the people, to avoid exposure for those who failed to convince the populace; they said that many would come over out of hatred of the Lacedaemonians. The Corinthians made these recommendations and went home.

[28] And after the Argives who heard them referred the proposals to their officials and people, Argos passed a decree and chose twelve men with whom any Hellenes who wished were to negotiate an alliance, except for the Athenians and Lacedaemonians; neither of these were permitted to make peace without the consent of the Argive people. The Argives gave this readier acceptance because they saw that they were going to be at war with the Lacedaemonians, since the treaty with them was reaching an end, and in addition hoped to become the leaders of the Peloponnesos. For at that time the Lacedaemonian state was very poorly regarded and despised because of its misfortunes, and the Argives were also in their best situation all around, since they had not taken part in the war with Attica but had instead enjoyed the profits of peace with both sides. So the Argives accordingly undertook to receive as allies any Hellenes who were willing.

[29] The Mantineans and their allies were the first to come over, since they were afraid of the Lacedaemonians. For part of Arcadia had become subject to the Mantineans, taken over while the war with Athens was still going on, and they thought that the Lacedaemonians, especially now that they had an easy situation, would not look the other way while they ruled there; so they were glad to turn to Argos, which impressed them as a great city always at odds with the Lacedaemonians and governed by a democracy like their own. After the Mantineans broke away, the rest of the Peloponnesians fell to murmuring about needing to do this themselves, since they thought that the Mantineans had changed sides because of some special knowledge, and since they had their own reasons for anger toward Lacedaemon, including the statement in the treaty with Attica that it was in accordance with the oath for the two states, Lacedaemon and Athens, to add or remove whatever they chose. This clause in particular caused consternation among the Peloponnesians and led them to suspect the Lacedaemonians of planning to enslave them with the complicity of Athens; for the right wording would have left changes up to all the allies. So most of them were frightened and eager to make individual alliances with Argos.

[30] When the Lacedaemonians found out that these murmurs had gotten started in the Peloponnesos, and that the Corinthians were the instiga-

tors and about to make an alliance with Argos themselves, they sent ambassadors to Corinth, since they wanted to forestall what was imminent, and they accused them of masterminding the whole thing and said that if they left them to become allies of the Argives they would be breaking their oaths, and that they were already in the wrong for not accepting the treaty with the Athenians, since it had been stated that whatever the majority of the allies voted was decisive, unless there was obstruction from gods or heroes. The Corinthians, in the presence of all their allies who had likewise rejected the treaty (whom the Corinthians had summoned previously), replied to the Lacedaemonians without directly revealing how they had been injured by not recovering Sollion or Anaktorion from the Athenians or any other way in which they felt deprived, but instead using the excuse that they would not betray the people in Thrace; they had sworn a separate oath of their own when they first joined the Potidaians in revolt, as well as on later occasions. Therefore, they claimed that they were not breaking their oaths to the allies when they did not enter into the treaty with the Athenians; since they had given the others pledges before the gods, they would not be true to their solemn oath if they betrayed them. It was stated, "unless there was obstruction from gods or heroes"; now here, as far as they could see, was divine obstruction. This was as much as they said about their past oaths; concerning the Argive alliance, they would deliberate with their friends and do what was right.

The Lacedaemonian ambassadors left for home. But there were also Argive ambassadors present, and they urged the Corinthians to enter into the alliance without delay; the Corinthians directed them to come to the next meeting held among themselves. [31] An embassy of Eleans arrived right away and first made an alliance with the Corinthians and went from there to Argos, just as instructed, and became Argive allies. For they happened to be at odds with the Lacedaemonians over Lepreon. The Lepreates had once been at war with some of the Arkadians, when the Eleans were called in as allies by the Lepreates for a half-share of their territory, and after putting a stop to the war the Eleans assigned a talent for the Lepreates to pay Olympian Zeus as tribute for cultivating the land themselves. And they paid it up until the war with Attica, and then, when they stopped and used the war as an excuse, the Eleans began coercing them, and they turned to the Lacedaemonians. When the case was given to the Lacedaemonians to arbitrate, the Eleans, since they suspected that they would not be treated fairly, rejected the arbitration and ravaged the land of the Lepreates. The Lacedaemonians, nevertheless, made a judgment, that the Lepreates were autonomous and the Eleans in the wrong, and when the latter did not abide by their arbitration they sent a hoplite garrison to Lepreon. Since the Eleans regarded the Lacedaemonians as receiving a city that had revolted from them and referred to the statement in the compact that the possessions all parties had when they undertook the war with Attica should also be theirs when they left it, they defected to the Argives on grounds of unjust treatment, and they too made an alliance with them in accordance with prior instructions. Immediately after them, the Corinthians and the Thracian Chalkidians also became allies of Argos. The Boiotians and the Megarians, acting together, remained inactive, since they were left alone by the Lacedaemonians and considered the Argive democracy less favorable to them as oligarchs than the Lacedaemonian constitution. [32] Around the same time during this summer, the Athenians captured Skione by siege and killed the adult males, enslaving the children and women and giving the land to the Plataeans to occupy. They brought the Delians back to Delos, mindful of their failures in battle, and also because the god at Delphi delivered an oracle. And the Phokaians and the Lokrians began their war.

The Corinthians and the Argives, on becoming allies, went to Tegea to detach it from the Lacedaemonians, noting that it was a large area and thinking that if this part came over to their side they would have the entire Peloponnese. But since the Tegeates said that they would do nothing to oppose the Lacedaemonians, the Corinthians, who until then had acted very vigorously, moderated their contentiousness, in dread that none of the others would come over to them now. Nevertheless, they went to the Boiotians and begged them to become allies of themselves and the Argives and to act in common with them overall; the Corinthians also asked the Boiotians to accompany them to Athens and bring about an additional truce for them of the same kind the Boiotians had, the one arranged for ten days between the Athenians and the Boiotians soon after the fifty-year treaty, and to renounce their armistice if the Athenians refused and make no future truce without including them. The Boiotians, in response to the Corinthian pleas about the Argive alliance, told them to wait but went with them to Athens, failing to obtain the ten-day truce, however, since the Athenians replied that the Corinthians had a truce through being allies of the Lacedaemonians. Now the Boiotians still did not renounce their ten-day truce, although the Corinthians were insistent and claimed the others had agreed to this; they got a working armistice with Athens.

5.32. On the problem of ten-day truces, see Arnush 1992.

[33] During the same summer, the Lacedaemonians campaigned in full force under the leadership of Pleistoanax son of Pausanias, king of the Lacedaemonians, against the Parrhasians in Arcadia, subjects of the Mantineans, since a factional party had called them in, and in addition they intended, if possible, to tear down the fort at Kypseloi which the Mantineans had built and garrisoned themselves as an outpost in Parrhasian territory against Skiritis in Lakonia. The Lacedaemonians plundered the territory of the Parrhasians, and the Mantineans handed over their city to Argive guards while they themselves kept watch over the territory of their alliance; unable to save the fort at Kypseloi or the Parrhasian towns, they went back. After making the Parrhasians independent and destroying the fort, the Lacedaemonians returned home.

[34] Also during the same summer, on the arrival from Thrace of the soldiers who had gone out with Brasidas and been brought back by Klearidas after the treaty, the Lacedaemonians voted that the helots who had fought with Brasidas were to be free and to live wherever they chose (not long afterward, they settled them, along with the neodamodeis, at Lepreon, which is situated next to Lakonian and Elean territory, since they were by now unfriendly toward the Eleans); as for their men from the island who had been captured and surrendered their arms, they were afraid that these might expect to be reduced in status because of the disaster and start revolutionary activity while they had citizen rights, and they now deprived them of rights, even though some were in office, to the extent that they could not hold office or have authority to buy or sell anything. At a later time, their rights were restored.

[35] During this same summer, also, the Dians seized Thyssos on the peninsula of Athos, which was allied with Athens. Throughout this summer there were regular communications between the Athenians and the Lacedaemonians, but they became suspicious of each other immediately after the treaty over places not restored to one another. The Lacedaemonians, the first according to lot to give back Amphipolis and other places, had not given them back, nor were they getting their allies in Thrace, the Boiotians, or the Corinthians to accept the treaty, although they said constantly that they would act in common with the Athenians to force them if they were unwilling, and they also set up times, which were not written down, when those who did not include themselves were to be enemies of both sides. The Athenians, seeing none of this occurring in actuality, began to suspect the Lacedaemonians of having no rightful intentions, and so they did not restore Pylos as the Lacedaemonians demanded (instead, they even began to regret that they had given back the prisoners from the

island) and held on to the rest, waiting until the others had done what was promised. The Lacedaemonians claimed that they had done what they could; they had given back the Athenian prisoners in their possession, withdrawn their soldiers in Thrace, and done whatever else was in their power. They claimed that the surrender of Amphipolis was beyond their control, but they would bring back all Athenian captives in Boiotia. They still called on them to return Pylos; but failing that, to withdraw both the Messenians and the helots, just as they had withdrawn their men from Thrace, and garrison the place with Athenians if they wished. After much talking on many occasions during the summer, they persuaded the Athenians to withdraw the Messenians and the rest, who were either helots or other deserters from Lakonia. The Athenians settled them in Kranioi on Kephallenia. So during this summer there was peace and regular communication between the two sides.

[36] In the following winter, however, when there were different ephors now in office, not those serving when the treaty was made, and some of them were even hostile to it, embassies came from the allies, the Athenians, Boiotians, and Corinthians were present, and there was a great deal said among them without any agreement, and when they were leaving for home Kleoboulos and Xenares, the very ephors who especially wanted to do away with the treaty, held private talks with the Boiotians and Corinthians, advising that they coordinate their policies as closely as possible, and that the Boiotians, first becoming Argive allies themselves, attempt with the help of Corinth to make the Argives allies of the Lacedaemonians; this way there would be the least pressure on the Boiotians to enter into the Attic treaty; the Lacedaemonians would attribute more importance to having the Argives as friends and allies than to the enmity of Athens and the end of the treaty. The two ephors were sure that the Lacedaemonians, because they thought it would make the war outside the Peloponnese easier, were always eager for an honorable friendship with Argos. They urged that the Boiotians turn over Panakton to the Lacedaemonians, however, so that by possibly getting Pylos in exchange they would be in a better position for war with Athens.

[37] After the Boiotians and Corinthians got these instructions to give to their respective governments from Xenares and Kleoboulos and any friends they had among the Lacedaemonians, they departed. But two Argives in very high office, who were watching the road for them as they went, joined them and opened discussion about a way that the Boiotians might become their allies, like the Corinthians, Eleans, and Mantineans; they thought that this would open the way to a unified policy that would

then simplify making war or peace against the Lacedaemonians, if that was their choice, or against anyone else as necessary. The Boiotian representatives were pleased to hear this; by good luck, what was requested was also what their friends from Lacedaemon had directed. Since the men from Argos found them receptive, they told them on parting that they would send ambassadors to Boiotia. When the Boiotians returned, they reported to the Boiotarchs what had been said to them at Lacedaemon and also by the Argives who fell in with them; the Boiotians were not only pleased but especially enthusiastic over the coincidence that Argives were coming from a different direction for ends very similar to the requests of their Lacedaemonian friends. Before long ambassadors arrived from Argos with the proposals that had been indicated, and the Boiotarchs, after approving what they had to say, sent them back with the promise to send their own ambassadors to Argos to arrange the alliance.

[38] Meanwhile, it was agreed among the Boiotarchs, the Corinthians, the Megarians, and the representatives from Thrace that they first exchange solemn oaths to defend whoever needed help on any occasion and not to make war or peace with anyone except by decision in common, and that once this was done the Boiotians and the Megarians (who were acting jointly) make the treaty with Argos. Before the oaths were sworn, the Boiotarchs shared these plans with the four councils of the Boiotians, which are the supreme authority, and advised that oaths be exchanged with any cities willing to form a defensive league. But the members of the Boiotian councils rejected the proposal, afraid of acting in opposition to the Lacedaemonians by joining a league with the Corinthians, who had defected from them; for the Boiotarchs had not told them what happened at Lacedaemon, that the ephors Kleoboulos and Xenares and friends of the Boiotians had advised them first to become allies of the Argives and the Corinthians and subsequently to join with the Lacedaemonians, since they did not believe that the council, even if it had not been told, could vote any other way than advised by the Boiotarchs, who had considered the question in advance. After the project had been frustrated, the Corinthians and the representatives from Thrace departed with nothing accomplished, while the Boiotarchs, who had previously intended to try to arrange the Argive alliance once their proposals had been accepted, made no proposals to the council about Argos now, nor did they send ambassadors to Argos as promised, and there was a certain apathy and delay about the whole business.

[39] During this same winter, the Olynthians overran Mekyberna and captured it with an Athenian garrison inside. After this, the Lacedaemonians, hoping that if the Athenians got Panakton back they themselves

would recover Pylos (for talks had continued between the Athenians and the Lacedaemonians about places they had captured from one another), sent envoys to the Boiotians and begged them to hand over Panakton as well as their Athenian prisoners so that they could exchange them for Pylos. But the Boiotians refused to give them back unless they made a separate alliance with them like the one with the Athenians. The Lacedaemonians knew that they would be wronging the Athenians because of the provision against going to war or making peace anywhere without each others' consent, yet they wanted to get Panakton to exchange it for Pylos, and since, in addition, those bent on nullifying the treaty were promoting the relationship with Boiotia, they made the alliance just as winter was ending and it was almost spring, and Panakton was immediately demolished. And the eleventh year of this war ended.

[40] In the following summer, as soon as it was spring, the Argives, since the ambassadors the Boiotians promised to send did not arrive, and they were also aware that Panakton was being demolished, and that the Boiotians had gotten a separate alliance with the Lacedaemonians, became fearful that they would be isolated, and the entire alliance would go over to the Lacedaemonians. For they believed that the Boiotians had been persuaded by the Lacedaemonians to demolish Panakton and to be included in the treaty with Athens, and that the Athenians knew all this, so it was no longer possible for themselves to make an alliance even with the Athenians, despite previous expectations that if their treaty with the Lacedaemonians were discontinued they would at least have the Athenians as allies, considering the problems between the two. Accordingly, in this dilemma and afraid of being at war against the Lacedaemonians at the same time as against the Tegeates, Boiotians, and Athenians, the Argives, who had once rejected the treaty and even had high hopes of becoming the leaders of the Peloponnesos, sent Eustrophos and Aison to Lacedaemon as quickly as possible, the ambassadors they thought had the most popularity there, with the idea of making the best possible treaty under the circumstances, whatever could be agreed on, and staying neutral.

[41] After their ambassadors arrived, they began discussing terms on which they could obtain the treaty. And at first the Argives demanded the right of arbitration by a city or a private individual over the territory of Kynouria, which is a place on their borders that the two cities are constantly disputing (the cities of Thyrea and Anthene are there, and the Lacedaemonians are in possession); but then, since the Lacedaemonians were not willing to have it brought up but indicated readiness if the Argives wanted to make a treaty on the previous terms, the Argive ambas-

sadors got this concession from the Lacedaemonians, that for the present there should be a truce for fifty years, but with the possibility for either party, as long as there was neither plague nor war in Lacedaemon or Argos, to give formal challenge and contest this territory by combat, just as on one earlier occasion when both sides claimed victory, and with no pursuit allowed beyond the Argive or Lacedaemonian borders. At first the Lacedaemonians thought this was foolishness, but eventually, since they wanted desperately to have Argos friendly, they gave in to the demands and had the terms written down. But the Lacedaemonians told them that before any of the terms took effect they were to return to Argos and proclaim them to their assembly and, if they were approved, come to the festival of Hyakinthia to swear the oaths. [42] The Argives returned, but while they were involved in this business the Lacedaemonian ambassadors Andromedes, Phaidimos, and Antimenidas, who were supposed to recover Panakton and the prisoners in Boiotia to give back to the Athenians, found that Panakton had been demolished by the Boiotians on their own initiative (with the justification that long ago, after disputing it, they and the Athenians had sworn an oath that neither was to occupy it but both were to share its use), but Andromedes and the others received the Athenians held prisoner in Boiotia and gave them back, also informing them of Panakton's destruction with the notion that they were giving this back as well; for it would no longer be occupied by an enemy of Athens.

When the Athenians heard this, they took violent exception, considering themselves abused by the Lacedaemonians, both because of the destruction of Panakton, which was supposed to be returned in proper condition, and because they had learned that they had made a separate alliance with the Boiotians after their earlier promise to unite in coercing anyone who did not accept the treaty. When they had reviewed every other part of the agreement that the Lacedaemonians had not fulfilled, they felt they had been cheated and therefore gave the ambassadors an angry reply and dismissed them.

[43] When differences between the Lacedaemonians and the Athenians reached this state, those in Athens who wanted to get rid of the treaty immediately went into action. One of them was Alcibiades son of Kleinias, a man at that time still young in point of years for any other city but highly esteemed for his ancestry. He saw advantage in turning to Argos, which is not to say that his competitive spirit had not been affronted in addition after the Lacedaemonians negotiated the treaty through Nikias and

5.41. "One earlier occasion": for this battle ca. 550 B.C.E., see Herodotos 1.82.

Laches, overlooking him because of his age while failing to show him respect because of the ties of one-time proxenia, which his grandfather had renounced but he himself had meant to renew by solicitousness toward their prisoners from the island. And since he considered himself slighted on all counts, he had initially spoken in opposition, claiming that the Lacedaemonians could not be trusted but had made a treaty in order to get rid of Argos and then move upon Athens by itself, and now, after the disagreement, he immediately sent a personal message to Argos telling them to come as quickly as possible, along with the Mantineans and the Eleans, to invite the Athenians into an alliance, since the moment was right, and he would give them full support.

[44] When the Argives received the message, now that they also realized that the Athenians had no complicity in the Boiotian alliance but were themselves involved in a major disagreement with the Lacedaemonians, they became unconcerned with their own ambassadors who happened to be away in Lacedaemon negotiating a treaty and tended to favor the Athenians, on the theory that if they were involved in a war they would be fighting alongside a city whose friendship was of long standing, whose government was democratic like their own, and whose power at sea was great. Accordingly they sent ambassadors to Athens immediately to seek an alliance; they were joined by the Eleans and the Mantineans.

Philocharidas, Leon, and Endios, Lacedaemonian ambassadors considered to be on friendly terms with the Athenians, also arrived hurriedly out of fear that the enraged Athenians would make an alliance with Argos, also to demand Pylos in return for Panakton and defend the Boiotian alliance on the grounds that it had not been concluded with the intention of harming Athens. [45] Their statement to the council that they had come with authorization to resolve this and all other differences prompted Alcibiades' concern that if they said this to the assembly they would win over the people, and the Argive alliance would be rejected. Alcibiades' scheme for preventing this was as follows. Giving the Lacedaemonians his every assurance, he persuaded them that, if they did not disclose their authorization to the assembly, he would restore Pylos to them, persuading the Athenians as effectively as he now opposed this, and bring about an overall reconciliation. These actions were intended both to detach them from Nikias and to enable him, once he had discredited them in the assembly for concealing their motives and never speaking consistently, to make the Argives, Eleans, and Mantineans allies. And that was what happened.

5.43–45. Kebric 1976 argues that Alcibiades and Endios were acting in collusion.

They came before the assembly and faced questioning, and when they did not say, as they had in the council, that they came with authorization, the Athenians ran out of patience, heard Alcibiades out as his denunciations of the Lacedaemonians became much more strident, and were ready to bring in the Argives and their companions immediately and make them allies. But the whole meeting was adjourned when an earthquake occurred before any formal action was taken.

[46] In the next assembly, Nikias, despite the fact that because the Lacedaemonians had been tricked he in turn was tricked over the disavowal of their authorization, persisted in claiming that they ought rather to be friends with the Lacedaemonians and should pause in their dealings with the Argives and send a further mission to the Lacedaemonians to learn their intentions, and he said that staying out of war was an honorable situation for themselves, although a disgraceful one for the other side; their own affairs were flourishing, and it was best for them to preserve this prosperity as long as they could but a blessing for the others, in their misfortune, to stake everything as soon as possible. He persuaded them to send him and other ambassadors to tell the Lacedaemonians that they could prove the justice of their intentions if they returned both Panakton in proper condition and Amphipolis and gave up the Boiotian alliance if the Boiotians refused to enter into the treaty, in strict accordance with the requirement that neither of them make agreements without the other's consent. He also told them to say that if their own state had chosen the course of injustice it would already have made the Argives its allies, since the Argives were present, and for just that purpose.

With full instructions covering every other cause for complaint, Nikias and his embassy were sent off. After they arrived and reported their message, saying at the end that unless the Lacedaemonians dropped the Boiotians as allies if they did not comply with the treaty they themselves would take the Argives and their associates as allies, the Lacedaemonians said that they would not drop the Boiotians as allies, an outcome dictated by the ephor Xenares and his group along with all others who agreed with them, although they renewed the oaths at the request of Nikias; he was afraid of coming back with all his aims unaccomplished and facing attacks as the one considered responsible for the treaty with the Lacedaemonians, which was exactly what happened. And when he returned, and the Athenians heard that no results had been brought back from Lacedaemon, they flew into a rage at him and, thinking themselves wronged, made a treaty and alliance with the Argives (they and their allies happened to be on hand, with Alcibiades to bring them in), as follows:

[47] "The Athenians and the Argives, Mantineans, and Eleans, acting on behalf of themselves and of the allies subject to each of the two parties, made a treaty with each other for a hundred years, without deceit or harm, on land and sea. Let it be forbidden for the Argives, Eleans, and Mantineans and their allies to bear arms to bring woe to the Athenians and the allies the Athenians rule, or for the Athenians and their allies to the Argives, Eleans, Mantineans, and their allies, by any contrivance or by any device. The Athenians, Argives, Eleans, and Mantineans are to be allies for a hundred years, on the following terms. If enemies attack the land of the Athenians, the Argives, Eleans, and Mantineans are to come to Athens and help, in accordance with any request from Athens, in whatever way they can with all the strength in their power; if they depart after pillaging, that city is to be the enemy of the Argives, Mantineans, Eleans, and Athenians and dealt with severely by all these cities; none of the cities is to be able to end the war against that city unless it is resolved by all. The Athenians are to send help to Argos, Mantinea, and Elis, if enemies attack the territory of the Eleans or Mantineans or Argives, in accordance with any request from these cities, in whatever way they can with all the strength in their power; if they depart after pillaging, that city is to be the enemy of the Athenians, Argives, Mantineans, and Eleans and dealt with severely by all these cities; none of the cities is to be able to end the war unless it is resolved by all the cities.

"No one under arms is to pass for warlike purpose through the territory of these parties or the allies they severally rule, nor by sea, unless all the cities, Athens, Argos, Mantinea, and Elis vote that passage is allowed. To those cities coming in support, let the city provide sustenance for thirty days from their arrival in the city that summoned them in support, and including their return; if it wishes to employ them for a longer period, let the city that sent for them furnish sustenance at three Aiginetan obols a day for each hoplite, light-armed, and archer, and an Aiginetan drachma for each cavalryman. Let the city that sent for the army have the leadership when the war is in their territory; if it is resolved by all cities to make a joint campaign, leadership is to be shared by all the cities on an equal basis.

"The Athenians are to swear to the treaty on their own behalf and that of their allies, and the Argives, Mantineans, and Eleans and their allies by each city separately. Each is to swear the most solemn oath according to local custom over full-grown victims. And let this be the oath: 'I will abide by the alliance in accordance with its provisions with justice and without harm and without deceit, and I will not transgress it by any contrivance or device.' At Athens, let the council and the domestic officials swear, and let the prytanies administer the oath; at Argos, the council, the Eighty, and the Artynai, and let the Eighty administer the oath; at Mantinea, the Damiourgoi, the council, and the Theoroi, and let the Theoroi and the military officials administer the oath; at Elis, the Damiourgoi, the officials, and the Six Hundred, and let the Six Hundred and the Thesmophylakes administer the oath. The Athenians are to renew the oaths by going to Elis, to Mantinea, and to Argos thirty days before the Olympic festival, and the Argives, the Eleans, and the Mantineans by going to Athens ten days before the Great Panathenaic festival. The Athenians are to inscribe the provisions of the treaty, the oaths, and the alliance on a stone pillar on the Acropolis; the Argives, in the shrine of Apollo in the marketplace; the Mantineans, in the shrine of Zeus in the marketplace; let them also jointly set up a bronze pillar at Olympia during the approaching Olympic festival. If it seems better to these cities to add anything to the terms, whatever is resolved by all the cities in common deliberation is to be binding."

[48] In this way, the treaty and alliance were made; even then, those between the Lacedaemonians and the Athenians were not renounced by either. The Corinthians, on the other hand, although allies of Argos, did not enter into these, nor indeed had they sworn to the alliance between the Eleans, the Argives, and the Mantineans before this one, whereby they would be at war or peace with the same states, but said that they were satisfied with the earliest defensive alliance, whereby they assisted each other but made no joint campaigns against anyone. The Corinthians stood apart from their allies in this fashion and turned their thinking back toward Lacedaemon.

[49] During this summer, the Olympic festival was held, where the Arkadian Androsthenes won the pankration for the first time; and the Lacedaemonians were barred from the sanctuary by the Eleans, which prevented them from sacrificing or taking part in the games, since they would not pay the fine the Eleans had assessed against them by Olympic law, alleging that they had taken up arms against them at the fort of Phyrkos and sent their hoplites into Lepreon during the Olympic truce. The assessment was two thousand minai, at the rate of two minai for each hoplite, in full accordance with the law. The Lacedaemonians sent envoys and argued that they had been fined unjustly, claiming that the truce had not been proclaimed at Lacedaemon when they sent in the hoplites. The Eleans claimed that they were already observing the truce (for they proclaim it first among themselves) and that the aggression had taken them by surprise while they were in a tranquil and unsuspecting state, as in time of peace. The Lacedaemonians retorted that there was no longer any point in

making the proclamation in Lacedaemon if they already believed them to be aggressors, and that the Eleans had proceeded as though they did not believe this; yet the Lacedaemonians had taken no further military action. But the Eleans kept to the same argument, that they would not allow that there had been no aggression, but said that if the Lacedaemonians were willing to restore Lepreon to them, they would give up their share of the money and would themselves pay on behalf of the Lacedaemonians what was due to the god. [50] Since this was not accepted, their next request was that instead of restoring Lepreon, if they were unwilling, the Lacedaemonians ascend the altar of Olympian Zeus, since they were keen on having their rights in the sanctuary, and swear before the Hellenes that they would later make good on the assessment without fail.

Since the Lacedaemonians would not agree to this either, they were barred from the sanctuary, the sacrifices, and the games, and they conducted sacrifices at home, while the other Hellenes took part in the festival, except for the Lepreans. Nevertheless, the Eleans were afraid that the Lacedaemonians would make sacrifice by force and maintained a guard of young men under arms; these were supported by Argives and Mantineans, a thousand apiece, and Athenian cavalry who had been waiting at Argos for the festival. And there was fear among the celebrants of an armed entry by the Lacedaemonians, especially after Lichas son of Arkesilaos, a Lacedaemonian, was flogged by officials during the games because, when his team won and was announced as a communal entry of the Boiotians on account of his ineligibility, he came up to the track and crowned the charioteer to make it clear that the chariot belonged to him. This made them much more afraid, and they expected a disturbance. The Lacedaemonians, however, made no move, and so they saw the festival through. After the Olympic games, the Argives came to Corinth to urge the Corinthians to join their number, and it happened that envoys from Lacedaemon were there. And after long discussions nothing final was settled, but after an earthquake they all went home, and the summer ended.

[51] In the following winter, there was a battle between the Herakleiots in Trachis and the Ainianians, the Dolopians, the Malians, and some of the Thessalians. These nations that lived nearby were hostile to the city; for it was unmistakably against their region that the place had been established and fortified. They opposed it from its very foundation, doing all they could to ruin it, and then defeated the Herakleiots in this battle, and Xenares son of Knidis, a Lacedaemonian and their leader, died, and there

5.51. For Herakleia, see 3.92–93.

were other Herakleiots killed as well. And the winter ended, as did the twelfth year of the war.

[52] As soon as the summer began, the Boiotians took over Herakleia, since it was completely ruined after the battle, and dismissed the Lacedaemonian Agesippidas for his poor leadership. They took over the place out of fear that the Athenians would seize it while the Lacedaemonians were in disarray over the situation in the Peloponnesos; the Lacedaemonians were angry at them all the same. In the same summer, Alcibiades son of Kleinias, one of the Athenian generals, acting with support from the Argives and the allies, took a few Athenian hoplites and archers into the Peloponnese, adding allies from the region, settled various business of the alliance as he passed through the Peloponnesos with his forces, and persuaded the Patraians to build their walls all the way to the sea, with intentions of building fortifications of his own at Rhion in Achaia. But the Corinthians, the Sikyonians, and all others who would have been harmed by their construction came up and prevented this.

[53] In the same summer, there was a war between the Epidaurians and the Argives, beginning over the sacrifice to Apollo Pythaieus (the Argives had the final authority over his sanctuary), which the Epidaurians failed to send although they were obligated to fulfill it for the castration of the bulls; but aside from this grievance it was also a priority for both Alcibiades and the Argives to annex Epidauros if possible, to keep Corinth inactive and so that the Athenians would have a shorter route for reinforcements from Aigina than the voyage around Skyllaion. The Argives accordingly prepared to invade Epidauros by themselves to enforce the sacrifice.

[54] Around the same time, the Lacedaemonians campaigned in full force against Leuktra on their border opposite Lykaion, led by Agis son of Archidamos, the king; no one, even in the cities contributing soldiers, knew the destination of the campaign. Since the sacrifices for crossing the border were not favorable, they returned home and sent word around the allies to prepare for a campaign after the coming month, which was Karneios, a sacred month for Dorians. When they withdrew, the Argives went out with three days left before Karneios and, stopping the calendar for the entire period, attacked Epidauros and plundered it. The Epidaurians called for their allies; some used the month as an excuse, and the others came up to their border and stayed inactive.

[55] During the time the Argives were around Epidauros, delegations from the cities met at Mantinea on invitation from the Athenians. When deliberations began, Euphamidas the Corinthian said that their words did

not accord with their actions; while they were assembled to discuss peace, the Epidaurians and their allies and the Argives were in the field against each other, so first they needed to go to each side and separate the armies, then go back to talking about peace. They agreed and went out and led the Argives away from the Epidaurians. Later, when they met at the same place and could not reach agreement, the Argives went back and plundered Epidauros. The Lacedaemonians also went out for a campaign against Karyai, but since there too their sacrifices for crossing were not successful, they withdrew again. The Argives ravaged about a third of the territory of Epidauros and went home. They were supported by a thousand Athenian hoplites and Alcibiades in command, who had learned about the Lacedaemonian campaign, but they left when they were no longer needed. And this was how the summer ran its course.

[56] In the following winter, the Lacedaemonians sent into Epidauros a garrison of three hundred men commanded by Agesippidas who got past the Athenians by sea. The Argives went to the Athenians and blamed them for allowing a move by sea when it had been stated in the treaty that none of them was to let the enemy cross his territory; they would be suffering an injustice if the Athenians did not set the Messenians and the helots against the Lacedaemonians at Pylos. The Athenians were persuaded by Alcibiades to add to the inscription on the Lakonian pillar that the Lacedaemonians had not honored their oaths, and they brought the helots from Kranioi to Pylos to plunder but otherwise kept inactive. During this winter there was no organized battle in the fighting between the Argives and the Epidaurians but ambushes and raids with some casualties on both sides. At the close of winter, with spring now approaching, the Argives took ladders to Epidauros to seize it by force, with the idea that it would be left unoccupied because of the war, and they returned home without success. And the winter ended, as did the thirteenth year of the war.

[57] In the middle of the following summer, the Lacedaemonians, whose allies the Epidaurians were in difficulty, with the rest of the Peloponnese either alienated or in disarray, thought that unless they took immediate countermeasures there would be further problems and campaigned against Argos with their own soldiers and the helots in full force; their leader was Agis son of Archidamos, king of the Lacedaemonians. The Tegeates and all the other Arkadian allies of the Lacedaemonians took the field with them. The allies from the rest of the Peloponnesos and beyond assembled at Phleious: the Boiotians with fifteen hundred hoplites, an equal number of light-armed, five hundred cavalry, and an equal number of cavalry supporters; the Corinthians with two thousand hop-

lites; the others in what numbers each had managed; and the Phleiasians with their entire army, since the campaign was in their territory. [58] The Argives had advance knowledge of their operations from the start, and when the Lacedaemonians were on the way to Phleious intending to make contact with the others, they took the field themselves. They had the support of the Mantineans, who brought their allies, and three thousand Elean hoplites. They advanced and confronted the Lacedaemonians at Methydrion in Arkadia.

Each army took up a position on a hill. The Argives prepared to engage the Lacedaemonians while they were isolated, but Agis eluded them by moving his army during the night and got through to Phleious and the rest of the allies. The Argives discovered this at dawn and proceeded first to Argos and then along the Nemea road, which they expected the Lacedaemonians to take into the plain. Agis did not take this expected direction but gave the Lacedaemonians, Arkadians, and Epidaurians instructions and took another and difficult road down into the Argive plain; the Corinthians, Pellenians, and Phleiasians came by another steep road. The Boiotians, Megarians, and Sikyonians, however, were told to go down the Nemea road, where the Argives had taken up their position, so that if the Argive defenders attacked them in the plain those could use cavalry against their rear. After making these arrangements and invading the plain, Agis plundered Saminthos and other areas.

[59] Now that it was day, and the Argives realized what was happening, they came from Nemea to put up a defense and, encountering the army of the Phleiasians and the Corinthians, they killed a few of the Phleiasians and lost a slightly larger number at the hands of the Corinthians. The Boiotians, the Megarians, and the Sikyonians, as instructed, proceeded to Nemea and found the Argives no longer there, since they had come down when they saw their land plundered and formed their line of battle; and the Lacedaemonians formed opposite them. The Argives were caught in the middle; for the Lacedaemonians and their allies cut them off from Argos by the plain, the Corinthians, Phleiasians, and Pellenians from above, and the Boiotians, Sikyonians, and Megarians from the direction of Nemea. And they had no cavalry with them; for the Athenians were the only allies who had not yet arrived.

Now the main army of the Argives and their allies did not consider the situation this dangerous but thought it would be favorable for battle, and that they had intercepted the Lacedaemonians in their own territory and close to their city. But two Argives, Thrasyllos, one of the five generals, and Alkiphron, the Lacedaemonian proxenos, coming forward just as the battle was about to begin, held a parley with Agis and kept him from engaging, saying that the Argives were ready to make or accept a fair and equal settlement if the Lacedaemonians had complaints against the Argives, and to make a treaty and live in peace in the future. [60] They said this for the Argives on their own initiative and did not speak at the bidding of the people, and Agis, accepting the offer, also without the consent of the majority and without consulting anyone except a high official accompanying the army, whom he informed, granted a truce for four months during which they were to fulfill the terms they had stated; he immediately led the army away without giving word to any of the allies. The Lacedaemonians and the allies followed him as their lawful leader but talked very critically about Agis among themselves, since they felt that although they had encountered circumstances favorable to themselves, with the enemy cut off on all sides by both infantry and cavalry, their army had gone away without accomplishing anything worthy of its quality. For this was the most superb army assembled up to this time and looked it especially when still united around Nemea, comprising the Lacedaemonians in full force, the Arkadians, the Boiotians, the Corinthians, the Sikyonians, the Pellenians, the Phleiasians, and the Megarians, picked units all, and appearing not only a match for the Argive alliance but another like it in addition.

So this was the way the army withdrew blaming Agis, and the contingents all dispersed to their homes. But on the Argive side as well there was criticism, and far more of it, against those who negotiated the truce without consulting the people, since in their opinion the Lacedaemonians had gotten away when there would never be a more favorable opportunity for themselves; for the issue would have been contested next to their own city when they had many and good allies. And after they fell back they began to stone Thrasyllos in the Charadros, where they judge cases involving campaigns before entering the city, and he saved his life by escaping to the altar; but they confiscated his property.

[61] After this, when a thousand Athenian hoplites and three hundred cavalry arrived as reinforcements under Laches and Nikostratos, the Argives, who despite everything shrank from breaking the truce with the Lacedaemonians, asked them to leave and would not give them access to the people when they wanted to consult with them until the Mantineans and the Eleans, who were still there, pleaded and prevailed on them. The Athenians, with Alcibiades there to represent them, said in the presence of both the Argives and the allies that the truce, without the consent of the allies, had not even been concluded legally, and now, since they had come at the right time, there was need for a determined war effort. Since the

allies were convinced by these arguments, they all immediately marched on Orchomenos in Arkadia, except for the Argives; they were convinced as well but at first stayed behind anyway, and then they came along later. After taking up a position in front of Orchomenos, they all laid siege to it and made assaults, since hostages from Arkadia had been deposited there by the Lacedaemonians, and they wanted the place in their possession in any case. The Orchomenians, afraid that the inadequacy of their walls and the number of attackers would result in their annihilation before any help arrived, accepted terms by which they became allies, gave the Mantineans hostages of their own, and handed over the ones the Lacedaemonians had deposited. [62] After this, with Orchomenos now under their control, the allies considered where to attack first among the other enemy cities. The Eleans argued for Lepreon, the Mantineans for Tegea, and the Argives and the Athenians sided with the Mantineans. The Eleans, in a rage because they had not voted for Lepreon, left for home; the other allies made preparations at Mantinea for going against Tegea. And there were some Tegeates inside the city who were ready to turn it over to them.

[63] When the Lacedaemonians came back from Argos after making the four-month truce, they were extremely critical of Agis for not having brought Argos under their control when there was a better opportunity than ever before, as they thought; for it was not easy to bring together so many allies of such quality. But when the news came about Orchomenos, its capture, they were a good deal angrier still, and in their rage they made an immediate decision, uncharacteristically, that they ought to demolish his house and fine him ten thousand drachmas. He begged them not to take either of these actions; he would redeem his faults after good service in campaigns, and then they could do as they pleased. They put off the fine and the demolition but made a law for the time being which they had never had before; they assigned ten Spartiates to him as advisors, without whose consent he had no authority to lead an army out of the city.

[64] Meanwhile, word arrived from their partisans in Tegea that unless they arrived quickly Tegea would defect from them to the Argives and their allies and had just about done so. Right then, help came in full force from the Lacedaemonians themselves and the helots, with speed such as never before; they proceeded to Orestheion in Mainalia. They instructed their allies among the Arkadians to form one group and keep right behind them to Tegea, while they themselves all went as far as Orestheion, sent home from there one-sixth of their citizens made up of the oldest and youngest to stand guard at home, and reached Tegea with the rest of the army. Not much later, the allies from Arkadia arrived. They also sent word

to Corinth and the Boiotians, the Phokians, and the Lokrians, telling them to support them at Mantinea as quickly as possible. These, however, got word at short notice, and it was not easy for them to cross enemy territory, which lay between them, without banding together by waiting for one another, but they hurried nevertheless.

The Lacedaemonians, meanwhile, adding the Arkadian allies on hand, entered the territory of Mantinea, and after setting up camp near the sanctuary of Herakles they plundered the land. [65] When the Argives and their allies saw them, they took up a strong, unapproachable position and formed ranks for battle; the Lacedaemonians advanced against them immediately. And they came within range of stones and javelins. Then one of the older men who saw them advancing on a strong position shouted to Agis that he was trying to cure one evil with another, meaning that his present untimely zeal was intended as redemption for his censured withdrawal from Argos. And Agis, whether because of the shout or because he also had second thoughts, suddenly led the army back at a rapid rate before it engaged. He went into Tegeate territory and began diverting into Mantinean territory the water that causes most of the fighting between the Mantineans and the Tegeates, since it damages whichever territory it runs into. His intention was to make the Argives and their allies descend from the hill toward the diversion of the water, whenever they found out and came to the defense, and to have the battle on level ground. And he spent this day here by the water, diverting it.

Meanwhile, the Argives and their allies were at first astounded by the sudden withdrawal from close quarters and did not know what to think; then, when the others disappeared after their withdrawal, and they themselves were keeping still and not pursuing, they began blaming their generals all over again, both for letting the Lacedaemonians get away the earlier time when they were nicely trapped near Argos and now because they were running away, and no one was pursuing, but there was plenty of time for them to escape and themselves to be betrayed. Confounded for the moment, the generals eventually led them down from the hill and moved on into the plain, where they set up camp with the intention of attacking the enemy. [66] The next day, the Argives and their allies went into the formation they meant to fight in if they met the enemy, and the Lacedaemonians, coming back from the water to the same camp near the sanctuary of Herakles, saw their opponents just ahead, not only positioned in advance of the hill but all in ranks already. At that moment, the Lacedaemonians were fully as startled as at any time within memory; for they had little time to waste in preparing. Immediately and in haste they went into their own formation with Agis the king directing everything in accordance with the law. For when a king is the leader, all are under his command, and he tells the polemarchs what to do, they tell the lochagoi, they tell the pentekostyes, and then these tell the enomotarchs, who tell the enomatia. In the Lacedaemonian army practically all are leaders of leaders, and the oversight of execution is the responsibility of many. [67] On this occasion, the Skiritai made up their left wing, the Lacedaemonians who always have this place to themselves alone; next to them, Brasidas' men of Thrace and the neodamodeis along with them; then the Lacedaemonians themselves next stationed their companies in order, and the Arkadians from Heraia beside them; and after these, the Mainalians; on the right wing, the Tegeates and a few Lacedaemonians, on the end; and the cavalry on both wings. Thus was the disposition of the Lacedaemonians; opposing them, the Mantineans held the right wing, because the action was taking place in their territory, and next to them were the Arkadian allies, then the thousand picked Argives, whom the city had been giving training in warfare for a long time at public expense, and the other Argives close beside them, and next to them their allies, the Kleonians and the Orneates, then the Athenians occupying the extreme left wing, and their own cavalry along with them.

[68] These were the forces and their disposition on both sides, and the Lacedaemonian army appeared larger. But as for recording the numbers, either for contingents on each side or overall, I could not do this with precision; for the total number of Lacedaemonians was unknown through the secrecy of their government, and conversely the numbers of the others were made known through the human habit of boasting about one's own share. By calculating as follows, however, one can study the number of Lacedaemonians employed on this occasion. For apart from the Skiritai, who num-

---

5.66–68. On the Spartan military terminology here, see *HCT* IV *ad* 5.68.3. It would seem that Agis' ruse worked perfectly; yet the Spartans were caught off guard. *HCT ad* 66.1 provides full discussion of this problem and its possible solutions, e.g. that the Argives marched at night (Gomme) or were concealed by a wood (Andrewes). Neither of these is very convincing, nor is there any evidence for them in Thucydides; the crux of the problem is that he shows no awareness that the reader might be baffled, and this is inexplicable even in a rough draft. The Spartans were apparently more surprised by the enemy's state of readiness than by his position, yet this should not have escaped Agis' observation. Overall, Thucydides represents Agis as an erratic commander, full of bright ideas but faulty in his timing; the Spartans will win despite his generalship, not because of it (see especially 5.72).

bered six hundred, there were seven companies with four pentekostyes, and there are four enotomiai in a pentekosty; in an enotomia, four fought in the front row. In depth, they were arranged as each lochagos chose rather than all alike, but generally they were fixed at eight. The front rank along their whole army was four hundred forty-eight without the Skiritai.

[69] And as they were just about to engage, now came the following words of encouragement for each nation from their own leaders: for the Mantineans, that the battle would be for their country and for its dominion or servitude, to keep from losing the former after they had once experienced it and from experiencing the second all over again; the Argives, for their leadership of old and their former equality in the Peloponnesos, to avoid lasting deprivation of those and moreover to take vengeance on these enemies and neighbors for many wrongs; the Athenians, because it was noble to be second to none when there were many and brave allies beside them in the fray, and because by beating the Lacedaemonians in the Peloponnesos they would make their empire both more secure and more extensive, and no one else would ever invade their land. So the Argives and their allies had this sort of encouragement. As for the Lacedaemonians, man to man and singing war songs, they cheered one another on to remember what they knew as brave men, aware that long-time training in action gives more assurance than brief encouragement in fine speeches.

[70] After this came the clash, as the Argives advanced with excitement and fury, the Lacedaemonians slowly and to the tune of many flutes as their law provides, not for religious reasons but so that they proceed evenly as they march to the music, and their formations do not break apart, as large armies tend to do when engaging. [71] And while they were still coming together Agis the king planned the following. What every army does is this: when engaging, they are extended on their right wing, each overlapping the enemy's left wing with its own right, because of the way each man in his fear presses his unprotected side as close as possible to the shield of the man posted to his right, supposing that the close contact means the best protection; and this problem is initiated by the far man on the right wing, eager to keep his vulnerability away from the enemy at all times, and the others follow out of the same fear. Now on this occasion the Mantineans overlapped the wing with the Skiritai by a wide margin, and the Lacedaemonians and the Tegeates overlapped the Athenians by even more, in proportion to their larger forces. Agis, fearing that his left would be outflanked and considering the Mantinean projection too great, gave

5.69. The translation "war songs" is debatable, see *HCT* IV *ad* 5.69.2.

the Skiritai and the Brasidians the signal to move in from their position and draw up even with the Mantineans, and to fill this gap he ordered the polemarchs Hipponoidas and Aristokles to move over with two companies from the Lacedaemonian right and rush in, thinking that his right would still have superior strength, and the part opposite the Mantineans would have a more solid formation.

[72] Now what resulted from his order given at short notice right during the attack was that Aristokles and Hipponoidas refused to move over (but for this misdeed were later exiled from Sparta, declared guilty of cowardice), and the enemy onrush, even though Agis told the Skiritai to come back in again (since the companies had not moved over), came when these could no longer close up the ranks. But on this occasion the Lacedaemonians, absolutely worsted in skill on all counts, showed their superiority in bravery to the same degree. For when combat began, the Mantinean right wing routed their Skiritai and Brasidians, and the Mantineans, their allies, and the thousand picked Argives burst into the unclosed gap and did damage to the Lacedaemonians as they surrounded them, and they routed them and drove them back to the wagons, killing some of the older men stationed there. Here the Lacedaemonians were defeated, but elsewhere in their army, especially in the center, which was the position of King Agis in the midst of the so-called Three Hundred Horsemen, they fell on the older Argives and those named the Five Companies, and the Kleonians, the Orneates, and the Athenians stationed next to them and caused a rout in which most did not even stand and fight but immediately gave way and in some cases were actually trampled in trying to avoid being caught.

[73] When the Argive and allied troops gave way here, their line was now broken at each end, and at the same time the Lacedaemonians and the Tegeates on the right began to use their projecting flank to encircle the Athenians, who were engulfed by danger because where they were not being encircled they had already been defeated. And their suffering would probably have been the worst in the army if their cavalry had not been on hand to help.

Another development was that Agis, seeing his left wing in difficulty opposite the Mantineans and the thousand Argives, gave the entire army orders to go toward the defeated sector. And when this happened, in that the army came over and angled away from the Athenians, they escaped unhindered along with the beaten portion of the Argives. As for the Mantineans, their allies, and the picked Argives, they were no longer intent on pressing their opponents but turned in flight when they saw their own men defeated and the Lacedaemonians bearing down on them. Many of the

Mantineans were killed, while most of the picked Argives got away. There was neither flight under pressure nor prolonged retreat, however; the Lacedaemonians fight long and steadfastly in standing their ground until a rout, but after the rout their pursuit is brief and over no great distance.

[74] Such was the battle, and this is very much the way it took place, the greatest among the Hellenes in a very long time, involving the most important cities. The Lacedaemonians, grounding their arms in front of the enemy dead, immediately set up a trophy and stripped the bodies, gathering up their own dead and taking them to Tegea, where they buried them, and they gave back the enemy dead under truce. Seven hundred of the Argives, Orneates, and Kleonians died, two hundred of the Mantineans, and two hundred of the Athenians, including the Aeginetans and both generals. On the Lacedaemonian side, the allies suffered losses but not enough to require mention; for the Lacedaemonians themselves, it was difficult to learn the truth, but about three hundred were said to have died.

[75] When the battle was imminent, Pleistoanax, the other king, set out also with the older and younger men as reinforcements; when he reached Tegea and learned of the victory, he returned. The Lacedaemonians also sent back the allies they had summoned from Corinth and beyond the Isthmus, and after they themselves had returned and dismissed their allies, they observed the holiday, since it happened to be during Karneia. And the blame that they had incurred among the Hellenes, both for cowardice because of the disaster on the island and otherwise for indecision and slowness, was wiped away by this single deed, since it appeared that they had been humiliated because of luck while still the same men in spirit.

The day before this battle, when Argive territory was deserted, there was an invasion by the Epidaurians in full force, who killed many of the guards the Argives left when they went off. After the battle, when three thousand Elean hoplites came to help the Mantineans, and a thousand Athenian hoplites reinforced the other Athenians, these allies all campaigned immediately against Epidauros while the Lacedaemonians were celebrating Karneia, and they divided up the work of walling off the city. Although the rest of them quit, the Athenians promptly completed their assigned portion, the Heraion promontory. And after each had contributed to the garrison for this fortification, they went back to their own cities. And the summer ended.

[76] As soon as the following winter began, the Lacedaemonians went out on campaign after they had celebrated the Karneian festival, and on reaching Tegea they sent ahead to Argos with conciliatory proposals. They already had supporters who wanted to overthrow the democracy in Argos,

and after the battle took place they had much more ability to influence the people in the direction of oligarchy. They intended to make a truce with the Lacedaemonians first, then an alliance, and as soon as this was accomplished to launch an attack on the democracy. Lichas son of Arkesilaos, the Argive proxenos, arrived with two Lacedaemonian proposals for Argos, one if they wanted war, one if they wanted to make peace. And after considerable debate (since Alcibiades happened to be present), the partisans of the Lacedaemonians, now daring to act openly, persuaded the Argives to accept the proposal for accommodation. This is it:

[77] "It was resolved by the assembly of the Lacedaemonians to make an agreement with the Argives on the following terms: that they give back to the Orchomenians their children, and to the Mainalians their men, and to the Lacedaemonians their men among those in Mantinea, and that they depart from Epidauros and raze their fortifications; that the Athenians, if they do not withdraw from Epidauros, be enemies of the Argives and the Lacedaemonians and the allies of the Argives and the allies of the Lacedaemonians; and if the Lacedaemonians hold any children, that they restore them to every city; concerning the sacred victim, that they administer an oath to the Epidaurians, and these swear to provide it; that the cities in the Peloponnese, small and large, all be independent in accordance with their ancestral governments; and that if anyone outside the Peloponnese enters Peloponnesian land as aggressors, they repel him after determining together what is resolved best for the Peloponnesians; that all allies of the Lacedaemonians outside the Peloponnese shall have the same status as themselves, and those of the Argives shall have the same status as themselves, keeping their own possessions; that they make the agreement after they show this to the allies, if they approve. And if the allies approve anything else, they send it back."

[78] The Argives accepted this proposal first, and the Lacedaemonian army left Tegea for home. And next, now that there was association between them, the same people soon afterward arranged in addition for the Argives to abandon the treaty with the Mantineans, the Eleans, and the Athenians and make an alliance with the Lacedaemonians. The terms were the following:

[79] "On the following terms, it was resolved by the Lacedaemonians and the Argives that there be a treaty and alliance for fifty years with settlement of disputes on a fair and equal basis in accordance with ancestral custom; and that the other cities in the Peloponnesos participate in the treaty and alliance as independent and self-governing states on an equal basis with themselves, settling disputes on a fair and equal basis; that

whichever states outside the Peloponnese are allies of the Lacedaemonians shall be on the same basis as the Lacedaemonians; and that those who are allies of the Argives shall be on the same basis as the Argives, keeping their own possessions; and that if a joint campaign is necessary, the Lacedaemonians and the Argives plan what they decide is the most just for the allies; and that if any of the cities has a dispute either within or outside the Peloponnesos, whether over borders or anything else, they will resolve it; but if any allied city quarrels with another, they are to come to any city which seems fair to both cities; citizens are to be judged according to ancestral custom."

[80] This treaty and alliance were concluded, and they relinquished whatever they had taken from one another in war or otherwise. And managing their affairs in common now, they voted not to receive heralds or representatives from the Athenians unless they left the Peloponnesos, evacuating their forts, and not to make peace or war with anyone except jointly. Acting energetically in everything they undertook, both cities sent representatives to the Thracian region and to Perdikkas. They persuaded Perdikkas to join them, although he did not immediately break with the Athenians, but this was his intention after observing the Argives; he himself was of distant Argive origins. They also renewed their old oaths to the Chalkidians and swore additional ones. The Argives also sent representatives to the Athenians ordering them to evacuate the fort at Epidauros, and the Athenians, since they saw that their men were far outnumbered by the others in the garrison, sent Demosthenes to bring them out. On his arrival, he organized some sort of athletic competition outside the fort as a pretext, and when the rest of the garrison went out, he shut the gates. Later, after renewing their treaty with the Epidaurians, the Athenians gave back the fort of their own accord. [81] After the Argives' departure from the alliance, then the Mantineans, who held out at first but lacked power without the Argives, came to their own agreement with the Lacedaemonians and gave up their control over other cities. The Lacedaemonians and the Argives, each numbering a thousand, went on campaign, and the Lacedaemonians went to Sikyon by themselves and put matters there on a more oligarchic basis, and after that both armies together finally put down the democracy at Argos, and an oligarchy friendly to the Lacedaemonians was established. These events took place very close to spring, when winter was fading, and the fourteenth year of the war came to an end.

[82] In the following summer, the Dians defected from the Athenians to the Chalkidians, and the Lacedaemonians rearranged what had been an unfavorable situation in Achaia. The people of Argos, gradually banding

together and recovering their courage, fell upon the oligarchs after timing this exactly with the Lacedaemonian athletic festival for youth. A battle was fought in the city, which the people won, and they killed some and exiled others. The Lacedaemonians, after long unwillingness while their friends were calling on them, postponed the festival and came to their aid. When they found out at Tegea that the oligarchs had been defeated, they were then unwilling to go any further, although the exiles pleaded with them, and they returned home and held the festival. Afterward, when representatives came from the city and messengers from those outside Argos, and the allies were also present, and a lot was said on both sides, they determined that those in the city were in the wrong and resolved to campaign against Argos, but delays and procrastination followed. Meanwhile the Argive common people were afraid of the Lacedaemonians and sought the return of the Athenian alliance in the opinion that this would help them the most, and they built long walls to the sea so that if they were cut off by land they would have the advantage of importing necessities with Athenian assistance. Some of the Peloponnesian cities also had complicity in building the walls. The Argives turned out in full for the work, including women and household slaves, and carpenters and stone-workers joined them from Athens. And the summer ended.

[83] In the following winter, since the Lacedaemonians were aware of the construction of the wall, they campaigned against Argos with the allies, except for the Corinthians; there was also an element working with them in Argos itself. Agis son of Archidamos, king of the Lacedaemonians, commanded the army. The expected developments in the city went no further, but they seized and tore down the walls under construction, and after capturing Hysiai, a place in Argive territory, and killing all the free men they caught, they returned and dispersed to their cities. After this, the Argives campaigned against Phleious and returned after plundering it for receiving their exiles; most of them had settled there. In the same winter, the Athenians set up a blockade in Macedonia, blaming Perdikkas for the alliance with the Argives and the Lacedaemonians, also in that when they were preparing to lead an expedition against the Chalkidians in Thrace under the command of Nikias son of Nikeratos he betrayed their alliance, and the

5.82. Connor 1984, p. 147, notes that the Athenians and Argives now made an enduring alliance (an inscription preserves part of the agreement), yet Thucydides does not cite a document, as he does in the case of the Peace of Nikias and other ephemeral agreements recorded in book 5; on the "ironic" citation of documents, see 5.18–19n.

campaign was disbanded primarily because of his absence; he was therefore an enemy. And the winter ended, and the fifteenth year of the war.

[84] In the following spring, Alcibiades sailed to Argos with twenty
ships and seized the remaining Argives who seemed untrustworthy and
sympathetic to the Lacedaemonians, numbering three hundred, and the
Athenians deposited them on nearby islands under their rule. The Athenians also campaigned against the island of Melos with thirty of their ships,
six Chian, two Lesbian, twelve hundred of their hoplites, three hundred
archers, twenty mounted bowmen, and about fifteen hundred hoplites
from their allies, who were islanders. The Melians are Lacedaemonian colonists, and unlike the rest of the islanders they had been unwilling to submit to Athens, at first taking neither side and staying inactive, but after the
Athenians applied pressure by plundering their land they became openly
hostile. Campaigning against their land with these forces, then, the generals Kleomedes son of Lykomedes and Teisias son of Teisamachos, before
they did any damage to the land, sent representatives to speak to them. The
Melians did not bring them before the common people but told them to
speak to the officials and a small group about their reasons for coming. The
Athenian representatives spoke as follows:

[85] "As long as discussion is not open to the public, clearly in order to
avoid a continuous presentation by which the people would be taken in
after hearing us say things that appealed to them and with no chance for
rebuttal (which we know is the purpose of bringing us before a small
group), give yourselves even more insurance as you sit here: do not decide
on every aspect by an overall statement but by responding immediately to
whatever is said that sounds unfavorable. To begin with, if what we suggest suits you, say so."

[86] The Melian commissioners answered: "The fairness of instructing
one another peacefully cannot be faulted, but a readiness for war right now
instead of eventually is obviously inconsistent. We see that you have come
as the judges of all that is said, also that this will presumably have the outcome of war if we make the better case and accordingly do not give in, or
of servitude if we are won over."

5.85–113. For useful summaries of various opinions about the Melian Dialogue, see
HCT IV, pp. 181–88, and Kagan 1981, pp. 149–53. Both are convincingly skeptical
of the widely held theory that Thucydides intended here to dramatize the moral
decline of the Athenians; too much accords with what they have said on previous
occasions. Their intolerance of neutrality, however, is new, as Cogan 1981, pp. 91–
92 has noted. On the dialogue, see also Stahl 1966, pp. 158–71 and Amit 1968.

[87] Athenians: "As to that, if you have met to weigh your suspicions about the future or for anything else besides planning your city's survival on the basis of the present circumstances as you see them, we can stop; but if that is the reason, we can speak."

[88] Melians: "It is natural and understandable for men placed in this situation to look in many directions as they speak and reflect. Nevertheless, this is a meeting concerned with survival, so if you think it best, let discussion proceed as you propose."

[89] Athenians: "In that case, we will neither use noble phrases to furnish a lengthy and unconvincing speech ourselves, about having the right to rule because we put down the Mede or attacking now because we were wronged, nor expect you to think that you can convince us by saying that you are colonists of the Lacedaemonians and did not campaign with them, or that you have done us no injury, but to deal with the possibilities defined by what both parties really believe, understanding as well as we do that in human considerations justice is what is decided when equal forces are opposed, while possibilities are what superiors impose and the weak acquiesce to."

[90] Melians: "In our opinion, at least, there is every advantage (a necessary term, because of the way you require us to speak of expediency apart from justice) in your not destroying a universal benefit, but that at all times there be fairness and justice for those in danger, and that even without satisfying strict accountability one might find help by persuading. This is especially relevant in your case, to the degree that on your downfall you would set the example for the heaviest retribution."

[91] Athenians: "As for the termination of our empire, if it ever were to end, we are undaunted. For those who rule others, as the Lacedaemonians do (not that we are contending against the Lacedaemonians), are not the

5.87. The entire situation is the result of *Athenian* "suspicions about the future," as the dialogue will inevitably reflect.

5.89. The Athenians state that they will not claim (a) that they deserve their empire because they defeated the Persians, and (b) that the Melians have injured them, provided the Melians do not claim that (c) they did not join the Spartans against Athens (here I follow Andrewes against Gomme, see *HCT* IV, p. 162), and (d) they have done the Athenians no injury. Since (c) is true, (d) should be also; (b) is then false, implying that (a) is also false. The statement that "The speakers do not renounce in principle the claim arising from Athens' conduct in the Persian Wars" (*HCT*, p. 161) is therefore called into question; cf. Tzifopoulos 1995, pp. 97–98.

5.90. Cf. the last sentence of (probably spurious) 3.84.

danger for the vanquished that subjects are by themselves when they attack and overpower the rulers. And let it be our own affair that we have this risk; what we will demonstrate is that we are here to help our empire, also that there is salvation for your city in what we are now about to say, since we hope to rule over you without trouble and let both parties benefit as you are saved."

[92] Melians: "Just how might becoming subjects bring us as much benefit as ruling would to you?"

[93] Athenians: "Because it would involve your submitting before suffering the worst fate, and we would profit from not destroying you."

[94] Melians: "Then you would not tolerate our staying neutral, friends not enemies, but allies of neither side?"

[95] Athenians: "No, since your hostility does us less damage than your friendship: to our subjects, as clear proof of weakness as hatred is of strength."

[96] Melians: "Is this what your subjects consider reasonable, that people who have no connection with you be placed in the category made up mainly of colonists and partly of rebels who were subdued?"

[97] Athenians: "They suppose that there is no shortage of legal arguments on either side, that some stay clear by strength, and we do not attack because of fear; accordingly, aside from adding to the number we rule, you would offer us security by succumbing, especially since as islanders, and the weakest of these, you would not have prevailed over masters of the sea."

[98] Melians: "But do you see no security the other way? For here, just as you have diverted us from claiming rights and persuade us to defer to your interests, is where we must again attempt to persuade you by explaining what is to our advantage, which may prove to be to yours as well. Insofar as there are any who now belong to neither alliance, how will you not turn them into enemies, when after what they have seen they assume that you will some day attack them as well? What is this but expanding the number of enemies you have already and forcing this on those who had no such intentions?"

[99] Athenians: "The ones we consider a threat are not those whose precautions against us will be long in coming because of their liberty as mainlanders, but rather islanders wherever outside the empire, like your-

5.93. The Athenians, in returning their complacent answer, fail to realize that they have turned the rhetorical initiative over to the Melians and from now on will respond to Melian arguments.

5.96. "Colonists," i.e., Ionians.

selves, and those already exasperated by the empire's constraints. It is they who would indulge most fully in unreason and subject both themselves and us to foreseeable dangers."

[100] Melians: "Surely then, if you take such desperate action to keep from losing your empire, and those already in thrall do so to be delivered, it is complete baseness and cowardice for us, still free, not to go to every length before being enslaved."

[101] Athenians: "No, provided you consider sensibly. For this is not an evenly matched contest over your manliness, lest you incur disgrace, but planning for your survival, lest you stand up to those who are much stronger."

[102] Melians: "But it is our understanding that warfare sometimes admits of more impartial fortune than accords with the numerical disparity of two sides. For us, to yield is immediately hopelessness, but in action there is still hope of bearing up."

[103] Athenians: "An incitement to danger, hope does not destroy, although it may damage, the richly endowed who resort to it, but for those risking everything they have (and it is intrinsically extravagant) it is recognized at the moment they fail and allows no means of detection while one could still be on guard. Since you are weak and depend on a single turn of the scale, do not choose to undergo this fate nor emulate the common run of men who, when human means of saving themselves are still available, in times when tangible hopes desert them in their afflictions turn to intangible ones, to prophecy, oracles, and whatever else of this sort combines with hope to bring ruin."

[104] Melians: "Rest assured that we ourselves see the difficulty of contending against your might, or against fortune if it is not to be impartial. Nevertheless, we have faith that we will not go without our share of fortune from the gods, as righteous men who stand in opposition to unjust ones, and that the Lacedaemonians and their allies will redress our deficiency in power, compelled, if for no other reason, to help us because of honor, on account of our kinship. Our confidence is not completely irrational after all."

5.99. The Athenians here give a muddled answer to the last Melian point and depart from their main line of argument: that the terror of others is their own best protection. The text has often been questioned, but see Radt 1976, p. 37.

5.104. The dialogue overall indicates that the Melians are not included in the alliance and have only their colonial status as a claim; for kinship as one of the less powerful forms of "compulsion," see Ostwald 1988, pp. 8, 9.

[105] Athenians: "Now, when it is a question of standing in divine favor, we do not expect to be denied our share of it. For nothing in what we assert or in what we are going to do is a departure from men's concept of god and attitude toward themselves. According to our understanding, divinity, it would seem, and mankind, as has always been obvious, are under an innate compulsion to rule wherever empowered. Without being either the ones who made this law or the first to apply it after it was laid down, we applied it as one in existence when we took it up and one that we will leave behind to endure for all time, since we know that you and anyone else who attained power like ours would act accordingly. As far as the gods are concerned, then, we do not fear the likelihood of being at a disadvantage. But in your beliefs about the Lacedaemonians, which lead to your faith that they will help you out of honor, we find a touching naivety yet do not envy your folly. For in dealing with their own affairs and their local institutions, the Lacedaemonians are the greatest practitioners of virtue; where others are involved, one could speak extensively about their conduct but summarize it just as clearly by the statement that they are the most striking example we know of men who regard what is agreeable as noble and what is expedient as just. Such an outlook surely does not further your present interest of irrational salvation."

[106] Melians: "For us, these are just the considerations making it most credible that in their own interests they will not be willing to betray the Melians, their colonists, and sow distrust among friendly Hellenes while benefiting their enemies."

[107] Athenians: "You do not believe, then, that self-interest involves safety, while justice and nobility involve risks to be run? The Lacedaemonians are the last to venture very far in that direction."

[108] Melians: "But in our opinion they will be the more inclined even to take risks on our behalf and consider them safer than in other cases, in that from the practical standpoint we are situated near the Peloponnesos, and in that our kindred spirit will make us more reliable than others."

[109] Athenians: "Come now, when men are about to take up another's struggle, they do not see their safeguard in the good will of those calling them in, but wherever there is more than enough strength from a practical standpoint; the Lacedaemonians pay much more attention to this even

5.105. In the closing sentence, very compressed and idiosyncratic (see Radt 1976, p. 38), "irrational" is certainly a derogatory reference to the close of 5.104.

5.109. The Athenians adroitly give a single response to two disparate Melian arguments, mocking their tenuous "practicality" in the process.

than others. At any rate, in their lack of confidence in their national forces they attack their neighbors in the company of many allies, so that there is no probability of their crossing over to an island by themselves when we control the sea."

[110] Melians: "They could send others as well. The Cretan sea is wide, an expanse where interception is more problematic for those who control it than escape for those who want to get through. And if the Lacedaemonians fail in this, they would turn on your own land and every remaining ally Brasidas did not approach, and your efforts will not involve alien territory but rather your own and that of your allies."

[111] Athenians: "As to that, you would not be unaware, after your turn to experience it, that never once have the Athenians withdrawn from a siege out of fear of others. But we reflect that you, who asserted that you would give thought to your survival, have said a great deal without mentioning anything that would give human beings the confidence to think that they will be saved, but in your case your main source of strength is what you hope lies in the future, whereas your actual resources are inconsequential for prevailing against the resources now confronting you. So the attitude you evince is fully irrational, unless after you send us out you can still decide on something else, more sensible than any of this. Surely you will not be led into that sense of shame that is man's chief ruin amidst shameful and manifest dangers. For in many instances, the name of disgrace, by the power of the word's fascination, induces men still able to foresee what is in store for them to fall knowingly into irremediable disasters, their actions overcome by a phrase, and earn for themselves shame more shameful in folly than in misfortune. You, on proper consideration, will look to this and suppose that it is not unseemly to give in when the greatest of cities invites you on moderate terms, keeping your own territory as tributary allies, not, when a

5.110. Although it is natural enough that the Melians should raise the bogey of Brasidas, the name of an individual is nevertheless startling in so generalized a context. MacKay 1953 has suggested that the reader should recall the cheerfully brutal praise of oligarchy attributed to Brasidas (see 4.126n.) and appreciate that the Melian speakers, as oligarchs, oppress their own people in the same way the Athenians do their subjects. This is ingenious but too allusive even for Thucydides, especially since he has hardly made indictment of oligarchy a *leitmotif.*

5.111. I have followed a new interpretation by Radt 1976, pp. 38–39, of the first sentence, which has elsewhere been approached very differently (see *HCT* IV *ad* 5.111.1); for the Melians' previous "experience," see 3.91. Neither Radt, pp. 39–41, nor anyone else to my knowledge has resolved the difficulties of the final sentence, however, and my translation is an approximation.

choice between war and security is offered, contentiously choose for the worse; after all, those who do not yield to equals but comport themselves well toward superiors and treat inferiors with moderation are the most successful. Think it over then, even while we are absent, and remind yourselves continually that you are deliberating about your country, concerning which a single country will depend on a single judgment for success or failure."

[112] The Athenians absented themselves from the conference, and the Melians, since on being left to themselves they upheld the same objections they had put forward, gave this reply: "Athenians, our thinking is unchanged since the beginning, and we will not in a matter of minutes do away with the freedom of a city whose habitation has lasted seven hundred years, but by trusting in the favor from the gods, which has preserved it up till now, and in the help of men as represented by the Lacedaemonians, we will try to save ourselves. We ask of you that we be friends, enemies of neither side, and that you leave our territory after the conclusion of whatever treaty both parties find suitable."

[113] This was the sum of the Melian reply. The Athenians, now finished with the conference, said, "But in that case, at least to judge from these resolutions, you are unique in considering the future clearer than what is before your eyes and in using wishful thinking to look on the unforeseeable as already taking place, and in the full measure of what you have risked by your trust in Lacedaemonians, fortune, and hope, in that measure you will be undone."

[114] The Athenian representatives returned to the army. And their generals, since the Melians were not submitting, immediately directed themselves toward war, and after making assignments among the cities they built a wall completely around the Melians. After this, leaving men of their own and from the allies to stand guard on both land and sea, the Athenians departed with most of the army, but those left behind stayed on and besieged the place. [115] Around the same time, the Argives invaded Phleiasian territory and lost about eighty men in an ambush by the Phleiasians and their own exiles. And the Athenians from Pylos took a lot of plunder from the Lacedaemonians; in consequence, the Lacedaemonians, although even now they did not break the truce and go to war, made a proclamation that anyone from their side might plunder the Athenians at will. And the Corinthians went to war with the Athenians because of differences of their own; the other Peloponnesians stayed inactive. The Melians, attacking at night, captured the portion of the walls across from the Athenian market, killing some men, and after bringing in grain and as much useful material as they could they withdrew and stayed inactive; the

Athenians made preparations to keep a closer watch in the future. And the summer ended.

[116] During the following winter, the Lacedaemonians, after planning to campaign against Argive territory, went back at the border when their sacrifices for crossing were unfavorable. Because they had had these intentions, the Argives became suspicious of persons inside the city and arrested some, while there were others who escaped. And around the same time, the Melians once again seized part of the wall in a different area, since there were few on guard. And afterward, when because of these occurrences more forces arrived from Athens commanded by Philokrates son of Demeas, and they were now under heavy siege, also after a certain amount of treachery in their midst, they surrendered to the Athenians to be dealt with as they wished. They killed all the grown men they captured, enslaved the children and women, and settled the place themselves by sending out five hundred colonists later.

5.116. It must be chance that the name of the Athenian commander suggests "Lover of Might, Son of Populace (or Democracy)," but this possibly motivated Thucydides to supply the detail. Far less likely to be coincidental is the mention of the Spartan withdrawal after the failure of "crossing-sacrifices," especially since this detail is inserted between descriptions of successful actions taken by the Melians themselves; the practice was apparently peculiar to the Spartans (see 5.54 and 5.55 with *HCT* IV *ad* 54.2). It is not necessary to deny the genuineness of their piety in order to see some confirmation for the Athenian comments on their limitations as allies (see especially 5.105). For an argument that not all Melian men were killed, see Seaman 1995; I am grateful to Mr. Seaman for letting me read his paper, which is forthcoming in *Historia*.

BOOKS SIX AND SEVEN

INTRODUCTION

Books 6 and 7 are Thucydides' account, with very little digression, of the great expedition the Athenians sent out to Sicily in the summer of 415. Their ostensible purpose is to help several allies there, but most Athenians think in terms of conquest from the start (as they had even in 424), recognizing Syracuse as their main opponent. To indicate the magnitude of the enterprise and emphasize Athenian ignorance of this, Thucydides begins book 6 with a lengthy summary of the history of human settlement in Sicily; in the process he establishes a formal parallelism with book 1, whose "Archaeology" prefaces the outbreak of war in 431. The Athenians are generally aware that the scale of their expedition would put an end to the shaky Peace of Nikias.

Nikias himself persistently opposes the expedition, and two of his speeches in the assembly are reported, bracketing one by Alcibiades, the most enthusiastic and influential proponent. The Athenians find both speakers impressive and respond by reaffirming their prior decision to sail; by expanding their preparations to the titanic size that Nikias (hoping to deter them) had recommended; and by appointing both Nikias and Alcibiades to the command (as Alcibiades had sardonically suggested) along with Lamachos.

While the Athenians are in the middle of their preparations, they are horrified by the mysterious mutilation of most of the city's traditional statues of Hermes, and their attempts to find the perpetrators (modern scholars have renewed the search, with no conclusive results) lead to an open-ended investigation of recent acts of sacrilege. Alcibiades is soon implicated, but his trial is postponed to avoid delaying the expedition (Alcibiades inveighs against this bizarre decision).

And the expedition sails. The description of its physical splendor and emotional atmosphere, as striking as any passage in Thucydides, sets the scene for a debate at Syracuse between Hermokrates, who urges resistance to the utmost but has difficulty even convincing the Syracusans that invasion was imminent, and Athenagoras, the spokesman for the doubters who blames the rumors of invasion on sinister political plotting inside the city. Thucydides has already indicated that Syracuse might be acquiring a position in the west comparable to that of Athens in the Aegean; here he begins to show that the two cities were analogous in character.

On their arrival at the tip of Italy, the Athenians receive a sharp disappointment over the degree of support forthcoming from the locals, and in this context the generals discuss how to proceed, each offering a different plan. Alcibiades, steering a middle course by proposing that attack on Syracuse be postponed until after the Athenians have used diplomacy to win over as many allies as possible, prevails. Soon after, however, he is summoned to return to Athens for trial; rather than face the Athenians in their current mood of fear and suspicion, Alcibiades bolts and defects to the Spartans. Thucydides uses this occasion to analyze (as he did much more briefly in book 1) the events that brought down the Athenian tyrants at the end of the sixth century.

The remaining generals, after a number of indecisive operations, finally advance on Syracuse and win a land battle near the city, but the courage of their disorganized and inexperienced opponents and the effectiveness of the Syracusan cavalry has ominous implications. The winter season then brings a hiatus to fighting; the Syracusans reorganize their military, starting with the structure of command, and both sides actively seek more allies. Thucydides devotes considerable attention to the example of Kamarina, where Hermokrates debates the Athenian envoy Euphemos, whose speech is often cited as particularly mendacious in its insistence on the limited nature of Athenian aims in Sicily and the defensive character of the Athenian empire. Hermokrates is the effective winner; Kamarina, initially inclined toward Athens, is impressed by Hermokrates' prediction of a victorious and vengeful Syracuse and adopts a neutrality that eventually tilted toward Syracuse.

The Syracusans also ask the Spartans and Corinthians to send direct aid as well as reopening the war on the Greek mainland. The Corinthians need little persuading and appeal to the Spartans as they had in 432 (the close relations between Corinth and its Syracusan colonists form a pendant to the bitter hostility between Corinth and its Corcyrean colonists in book 1). Their appeals are successful mainly because of a speech by the renegade Alcibiades, who characterizes the expedition in terms of such Athenian aims at world conquest as only he is likely to have envisioned; he also urges that the Spartans send one of their generals to take command at Syracuse and galvanize the defense, and that they fortify Dekeleia as an outpost in Attica (which was ultimately to have a more damaging effect than its analogue at Pylos).

The vigorous Athenian offensive in the spring of 414 threatens to preempt these developments. Defeated in battle, almost cut off by Athenian circumvallation, the Syracusans consider surrender; Nikias, in frequent contact with the pro–Athenian party, pays little attention to the unprepossessing arrival of the Spartan Gylippos at the end of book 6. But not only is Gylippos able to revive Syracusan energy and morale, but he has also arrived before the Athenians had completed their circumvallation; thanks to his prompt actions, they are never to complete it.

Nikias, in sole command (Lamachos had been killed in the spring offensive), sends a dispatch to the Athenians disavowing the generals' responsibility for the worsened situation and advising them either to recall their forces or reinforce them on the same scale as the initial expedition, while relieving him of command (he is seriously ill). Thucydides now records no debates at Athens but simply the decision to send a second enormous armada; the Athenians do not relieve Nikias but send him colleagues, one of them Demosthenes. He arrives to find a situation further deteriorated; at sea, the Syracusans have progressed from a narrow defeat (for which gains on land more than compensate) to a draw to a victory, and additional support was coming in from both Sicily and Greece. Nevertheless, the arrival of massive reinforcements in the summer of 413 dismays the Syracusan side, and Demosthenes immediately seeks to take full advantage by making a night attack on the Syracusan wall that had forestalled circumvallation. Very nearly succeeding, the attack ends in Athenian defeat with heavy losses.

Demosthenes' contingency plan, should the attack on the wall fail, had been withdrawal, and he now presses for this; Nikias resists, partly because he expects harsh punishment on returning to Athens unsuccessful, partly because he believes that the Syracusans are worn out and close to surrender. He is persuaded when more enemy reinforcements arrive, but the Athenian departure is now delayed by superstitious responses to an eclipse of the moon. The Syracusan side reacts to Athenian defeatism by attacking the reinforced fleet and defeating it decisively. They now intend to capture the invaders rather than expelling them; the Athenians see no option but to fight their way out of the harbor. These contrasting aims are emphasized in starkly contrasting speeches by Nikias and by the Syracusans (and nominally Gylippos) to their forces before the Athenian attempt. Thucydides' designation of the ensuing battle as the fiercest yet is borne out by his long and vivid account, with emphasis on the reactions of the Athenian infantry as they watch. At length, to their unparalleled horror, the Athenian ships are routed.

The final attempt to escape by land is an increasingly miserable affair, all of which Thucydides describes unflinchingly; the men are not only demoralized but weak from lack of sustenance, and attacks from cavalry and javelin-throwers are constant. Finally, the contingent led by Demosthenes surrenders. That of Nikias struggles on slightly longer, only to be massacred when crossing a river.

Nikias stops the slaughter by surrendering, but he and Demosthenes are both put to death. The survivors are kept for months in inhumanly harsh conditions.

Thucydides calls this debacle, not the final Athenian defeat in 404, the greatest event known in Greek history. Books 6 and 7 are very highly finished (suggestions of incomplete revision have generally been directed toward the digressions on the tyrant-slayers and Dekeleia) and may have been the first portions of the book to reach this state, before the end of the war; whether this would have remained the final emphasis is almost impossible to say. It might be argued that Thucydides lived long enough to know of the revival of Athens and its empire, without the brilliant and arrogant idealism of the Periklean period, and therefore 413 represented a kind of closure that 404 did not. As it is, the preceding books often read as though intended to lead up to 6 and 7, and this is especially true of book 4, with its interweaving of Sicilian events into the main theaters of the war, its dynamic speech by Hermokrates, and its presentations of Nikias, who escaped from the Pylos campaign with indecent ease, and Demosthenes, whose Pylos campaign ended triumphantly.

Books 6 and 7 are pervaded by the comparison of the expedition to a city, which originated as a gigantic colonizing enterprise; in the closing sentence of book 5, Thucydides records that the Athenians replaced the exterminated Melians with their own colonists. For the past century, arguments have been made that Thucydides cast the Peloponnesian War as a tragedy of pride, overreaching, and retribution, perhaps subscribing to the theodicy conventionally attributed to many surviving Athenian tragic plays; the reversals and the emphasis on the emotional vicissitudes of both groups and individuals have encouraged such speculation. This, I believe, is to misunderstand Thucydides' mission. He intended to show how historical events, even from the remote past, might be exhaustively analyzed so as to result in a literary account as compelling and moving as any invention of poets.

BOOK SIX

[1] During the same winter, the Athenians wanted to sail to Sicily again with a larger force than the one under Laches and Eurymedon and subjugate it if possible, most of them unaware of the size of the island and the number of its inhabitants, both Hellenic and barbarian, and that they would be taking on a war just about as great as the one against the Peloponnesians. For the voyage around Sicily in a merchant ship is not very much under eight days, and yet for all its size it is kept from being mainland by about twenty stades of water.

[2] Here is how it was originally settled, and these are all the people who occupied it all told. The earliest mentioned as living in some part of the area are the Kyklopes and Laistrygones, but I have no idea what their race was, where they came from, or where they went; what has been said by the poets and what any person may know of them must suffice. The Sikans were clearly the first settlers after these, even earlier according to their own account, by virtue of being indigenous, but Iberians according to what has proved to be the truth, driven by the Ligurians from the Sikanos river in Iberia. And in those days the island, formerly called Trinakria, was called

6.1. There was actually no expedition "under Laches and Eurymedon"; Thucydides has telescoped those of 427 and 425, see *HCT* IV *ad* 6.1.1. For an excellent thematic analysis of both the Athenian operations in Sicily and the Syracusan defense, see Allison 1989, pp. 66–120.

6.2–5. The account of the renewed war, like that of the original one, begins with an "archaeology." Rawlings 1981, pp. 65–67 points out many similarities to 1.1–19, also noting differences; book 1 is "far more analytical." The different functions might be stressed. In book 1, Thucydides seeks to deprecate the magnitude of past events, while here he emphasizes Sicily's size and importance by showing the complexity of its history; not incidentally, his display of knowledge accentuates Athenian ignorance. At the same time, he shows some basis for Athenian beliefs that Sicily was always available to "colonists"; Avery 1973, pp. 8–13 points out that the expedition is constantly compared to a settlement. On the foundation dates (e.g., Syracuse 733/2 B.C.E.), their reliability, and the possible sources for Thucydides' information, see *HCT* IV, pp. 198–210.

Sikania after them; they live in Sicily even in the present time, in the west. After Ilion was captured, some of the Trojans who escaped the Achaians reached Sicily by boat, and settling next to the Sikans they were collectively called the Elymians and their cities were called Eryx and Egesta. Some Phrygians also joined them as settlers, carried from Troy at that time by a storm, first to Libya and then on to Sicily. And the Sikels, in flight from the Opikians, crossed over from Italy, which was their home, to Sicily on rafts, as has been maintained and is plausible, watching the straits when the wind was coming down, but probably sailing in by other means as well. There are still Sikels in Italy even today, and from Italos, a certain Sikel king who had that name, the country was accordingly named Italy. Coming to Sicily as a large army, they defeated the Sikans in battle, forcing them into the southern and western parts and causing it to be called Sicily instead of Sikania, and after they crossed over and settled they occupied the best land for nearly three hundred years before Hellenes came to Sicily; even today, they still hold the central and northern parts of the island. The Phoenicians also settled all around Sicily, seizing the coastal promontories and outlying islands for commerce with the Sikels. But they left most areas when the Hellenes began to come in by sea in large numbers, and concentrating their settlements near the Elymians they occupied Motya, Soloeis, and Panormos, trusting in their alliance with the Elymians and because these are the points in Sicily with the shortest voyage from Carthage. All these barbarians, then, settled in Sicily in this fashion.

[3] Of the Hellenes, the first were Chalkidians from Euboia who sailed with their leader Thoukles, founded Naxos, and built the altar of Apollo Leader of Colonies, which is now outside the city, where religious delegations sacrifice first whenever they sail from Sicily. In the following year, Archias of the Herakleidai in Corinth founded Syracuse, first driving the Sikels from the island, today no longer surrounded by water, which contains the city; afterward, over time, the city outside it was also included within the walls and became populous. Thoukles and the Chalkidians, setting out from Naxos five years after the foundation of Syracuse, expelled the Sikels in a war and founded Leontinoi, and then Katana; the Katanaians themselves chose Euarchos as their founder.

6.2. For "Phrygians" rather than "Phokians," see Rigsby 1987.

6.3. "Now outside the city": archaeological evidence presented by Magnelli 1991 indicates that this observation was made between 403 and 395 B.C.E. "No longer surrounded by water": a causeway built long before Thucydides' time connected the original city on the island with the rest of Syracuse.

[4] Around the same time, Lamis also arrived in Sicily, leading a colony from Megara, and after he founded a place called Trotilos beyond the Pantakyas river and then left to occupy Leontinoi jointly with the Chalkidians for a short period and was driven out by them and founded Thapsos, he died, and the others were driven out of Thapsos and, since Hyblon, a Sikel king, gave them the land and conducted them there, founded Megara known as Hyblaian. After living there for two hundred forty-five years, they were expelled from the city and territory by Gelon, the tyrant of Syracuse. Before their expulsion, they sent out Pamillos and founded Selinous; he took part in the settlement after coming to them from Megara as the mother city.

Antiphemos from Rhodes and Entimos from Crete joined together in leading settlers and founding Gela in the forty-fifth year after the colonization of Syracuse. Although the city took its name from the Gela river, the site where the city is now and the first part fortified is called Lindioi. And they were provided with Dorian institutions. Close to one hundred eight years after their own colony, the Geloans settled Akragas, and they named the city after the Akragas river, appointed Aristonous and Pystilos as founders, and gave it Geloan institutions.

Zankle was originally settled when pirates came from Kyme, the Chalkidian city in Opikia, but later large numbers came from Chalkis and elsewhere in Euboia and occupied the area along with them; the founders were Perieres and Krataimenes, the first from Chalkis, the second from Kyme. At first it was called Zankle, a name given by the Sikels because the place is sickle-shaped, and the Sikels call a sickle a zanklos; but later these were driven out by Samians and other Ionians who landed in Sicily fleeing the Medes, and not long afterward Anaxilas the tyrant of Rhegion, after expelling the Ionians, colonized the city himself with a mixture of people and renamed it Messene after his original homeland. [5] Himera was colonized from Zankle by Eukleides, Simos, and Sakon, and, although mostly Chalkidians came to the colony, Syracusan exiles called the Myletidai joined them after being defeated in a civil war. Their speech was a cross between Chalkidian and Dorian, but Chalkidian institutions prevailed. Akrai and Kasmenai were colonized by Syracusans, Akrai in the seventieth year after the foundation of Syracuse and Kasmenai nearly twenty years after Akrai. And Kamarina was first colonized by Syracusans close to one hundred thirty-five years after the foundation of Syracuse; its founders were Daskon and Menekolos. But since the Kamarinaians were made homeless by the Syracusans in a war because of a revolt, at a later time Hippokrates, the tyrant of Gela, who had received the territory of Kamarina as ransom for Syracusan prisoners, resettled Kamarina as founder. After it was once more depopulated, by Gelon, it was settled for a third time by Geloans.

[6] So many Hellenic and barbarian peoples occupy Sicily, and against a place of this size the Athenians were bent on campaigning, their eagerness for complete conquest the truest cause but with a reasonable pretext as well in wanting to help their kinsmen and the allies they had acquired. In particular, the presence of Egestaian envoys and the increased urgency of their invitations spurred them on. The Egestaians, neighbors of the Selinountines, had gone to war with them over marriage rights and disputed territory, and the Selinountines, by bringing in the Syracusans as allies, were pressing them hard in the war on both land and sea. So the Egestaians reminded the Athenians of the alliance formed with the Leontines in the time of Laches and the earlier war and begged them to send ships in their defense, using many arguments toward their main point that, if the Syracusans were allowed to go unpunished after driving out the Leontines and, by destroying the remaining Athenian allies, to hold all the power in Sicily by themselves, there was the danger that some day, with a large force, they as Dorians would help the Dorian Peloponnesians, colonists helping those who had sent them out, and join them in overthrowing the power of the Athenians as well; the prudent course was resistance to the Syracusans in association with their remaining allies, especially when the Egestaians themselves would furnish enough funding for the war. The Athenians listened to them in assemblies and, after the Egestaians and their supporters had repeated their arguments many times, voted to send envoys first, to investigate as to whether the money existed as claimed, in their treasury and sanctuaries, and at the same time to see what stage the war with the Selinountines had reached.

[7] So the Athenian envoys were dispatched to Sicily. And during the same winter the Lacedaemonians and their allies, except for the Corinthians, campaigned against Argive territory, ravaging a small part, and brought in wagons and carried off some grain, and after they settled the Argive exiles at Orneai, leaving them a few soldiers from the army, and arranged a truce for a period in which the Orneates and the Argives would not injure each others' land, they went home with their army. Not long

6.6. "Truest cause": at the outset, Thucydides establishes the dual motivation for invading Sicily, a theme recurring frequently; at the same time, by using the same (otherwise unique) phrase as in 1.23, he links the events beginning in 415 with the outbreak of war in 431; see Rawlings 1981, p. 68.

after this, when the Athenians arrived with thirty ships and six hundred hoplites, the Argives went out with them in full force and besieged the men in Orneai for one day; during the night, since the army had bivouacked at a distance, the men escaped from Orneai. The next day, when the Argives found out, they razed Orneai and left, and afterward the Athenians left for home with their ships. The Athenians also took some of their cavalry and some from the Macedonian exiles they had with them by sea to Methone on the Macedonian border and ravaged the country of Perdikkas. The Lacedaemonians, sending to the Chalkidians in Thrace who were observing ten-day truces with the Athenians, urged them to join Perdikkas in the war, but they refused. The winter ended, as did the sixteenth year of this war recorded by Thucydides.

[8] In the following summer, as soon as it was spring, the Athenian envoys arrived from Sicily along with the Egestans, who brought sixty talents of uncoined silver as a month's pay for sixty ships, which they were going to ask the Athenians to send. After the Athenians called an assembly and heard from the Egestaians and their own envoys much else that was attractive and untrue and that, as for the money, there was a good deal in the shrines and the treasury, they voted to send sixty ships to Sicily and Alcibiades son of Kleinias, Nikias son of Nikeratos, and Lamachos son of Xenophanes as commanders with full power, in support of the Egestaians against the Selinountines, and to join in reestablishing the Leontines if their success in the war provided for this and manage everything else in Sicily in whatever way they judged best for Athens. Five days after this, there was an assembly again about getting the ships ready in the quickest way and voting anything else the generals needed for the voyage. Nikias, chosen against his will, and of the belief that the city was not making the right decision but on a slight and specious pretext aiming at all of Sicily, a large task, came forward wishing to dissuade them and gave the Athenians the following advice:

[9] "This assembly has met about preparations, about how we should sail to Sicily. In my opinion, however, we should still also consider the very idea, whether it would be well to send the ships, instead of undertaking in this way, with little deliberation, after listening to foreigners, a war

6.9–14. Tompkins 1972 has shown conclusively that the cautious Nikias is characterized by his speaking style (for later references, see Mader 1993a, n. 5), which abounds in qualifications and subordination of clauses; this does not result in obscurity, as in some other Thucydidean speeches (Nikias was not a deep or original thinker).

that does not concern us. And yet I myself derive honor from such actions and am less fearful than most about my own person, although I think that he who takes his person and property into account is just as good a citizen; it is exactly such a man who would wish for his own sake that the affairs of his city prosper as well. Nevertheless, neither in the past have I said what was contrary to my judgment to earn esteem nor do I now, but I will speak in whatever way I judge best. In dealing with that characteristic which is yours, arguments of mine would be powerless if I were to advise you to preserve your assets and not risk what is at hand for what is uncertain and off in the future; but what I will show you is that your haste is inopportune, and that what you are striving for is not easily secured.

[10] "I tell you that you are leaving many enemies here even while spoiling to sail over there and bring more back here. Perhaps you believe that you have some security from the treaty in effect, which will exist in name (since this is what men from both here and the other side have contrived) while you are inactive, whereas if you stumble anywhere with appreciable forces, the attack from our enemies will come swiftly, since in the first place they were forced into the treaty in disastrous circumstances and on a less honorable basis than ourselves, and then in the treaty itself we have many points in dispute. There are those who have never accepted even this agreement, and they are not the weakest; while some are engaged in outright hostilities, there are also those who, because the Lacedaemonians are still inactive, are themselves checked as well by ten-day truces. In all probability, if they found our forces divided, just the situation we are rushing into now, they would attack right along with the Sikeliots, since in past times they would have prized them highly as allies. So, then, one ought to consider things and not presume to take chances with a city in mid-voyage and grasp at another empire before we have secured the one we have, given that the Chalkidians in Thrace, who have been in revolt for so many years, are still unpunished, and there are others on the mainland whose allegiance is questionable, but we are keen to help the Egestans, our allies of course, because they have been wronged, and against those rebels by whom we ourselves have been wronged long since we are still waiting to retaliate. [11] And yet if we subdued them, we would subjugate them, whereas these people, even if we conquered them, would be ruled with difficulty, thanks to their being a long way off and a

---

6.9–10. "Whether it would be well" and "I tell you" give Nikias' warning a prophetic sound, see Classen-Steup and *HCT* IV *ad* 6.9.1, Spratt 1905b *ad* 6.10.1. "Uncertain and off in the future"; cf. 1.42.

lot. It is senseless to move against men if they can not be subjugated when conquered, and if after failure there will not be circumstances comparable to those before the attempt.

"The Sikeliots, in my opinion, based on the way they are now, would be even less a threat to us if the Syracusans ruled over them, which is just what the Egestans use to scare us most. For as it is, they might perhaps come separately, from good will toward the Lacedaemonians, while in the latter case it is not natural for an empire to campaign against an empire. Whatever their means of taking ours away with the help of the Peloponnesians, it would be natural for theirs to be destroyed that way by the same people.

"The Hellenes there would be most terrified of us if we never came, and then if we displayed our power for a short time and went away; for we all know that what is farthest off and puts reputation to the fewest tests is held in awe. But if we were foiled in any way, they would immediately despise us and join attackers from here. You have reached this state of mind now regarding the Lacedaemonians and their allies, Athenians; in your contempt for them, because of prevailing unexpectedly in comparison with your fears at first, you are aiming now at Sicily. You should not be elated by enemies' misfortunes but encouraged when your designs overcome theirs and should not believe that the Lacedaemonians in their disgrace are considering anything except ways to trip us up and even now, if possible, make the best of their loss of face, the more so in that a reputation for courage is their greatest and most enduring concern. And so, if we are prudent, our efforts do not involve the Egestaians in Sicily, who are barbarians, but keeping an alert watch against a city making oligarchic plots. [12] We must also remember that we have only recently had a little respite from a great plague and from war, so as to build up both property and manpower; it is appropriate to expend these here on our own behalf, not on behalf of these exiles begging for auxiliaries, men in whose interest it is to lie nicely and, by endangering someone else while they themselves supply only words, either to feel no proper gratitude if they succeed or to ruin their friends along with themselves if they fail.

6.11. See *HCT* IV *ad* 6.11.2 for defense of the text and *ad* 6.11.3 on the dubious argument that one empire would not attack another.

6.12. Nikias' first target is a blend of the Egestaians, who are "begging" (he implies that they seek to hire the Athenians as mercenaries), and the Leontines, who are exiles; his second, unnamed but unmistakable, Alcibiades. For his captiousness and distortions, cf. Classen/Steup VI and *HCT* IV *ad* 6.12.1.

"And if there is anyone pleased at being chosen to command who advises you to sail, thinking only of himself, especially since he is still too young for a command, so that he can not only be admired for his stable of horses but, since they are expensive, also get some benefit from the command, do not allow this person to show off as an individual by endangering the city but understand that such men damage public resources as they spend their own, also that the matter is important and not one to be deliberated or implemented hastily by younger men. [13] When I see them sitting here, rallied around this same man, I am alarmed, and I call on their elders to rally against them without feeling shame, even if they are sitting next to some of them, at being thought cowards for not voting for war, to avoid sharing the fatal desire for the faraway that afflicts the young by understanding that there is very little success won by craving but a great deal by foresight, and, for the sake of their country, which is risking greater danger than ever before, to raise their hands in opposition, voting that the Sikeliots, separated from us by the same existing boundaries that are hard to fault, the Ionian Sea for coastal voyages and the Sicilian for direct voyages, are to be left alone to enjoy their own possessions and come to terms; that the Egestaians in particular be told that since they originally took up the war against the Selinountines without Athenian consent, they may also end it on their own; and finally, that in the future we not continue the habit of making allies whom we defend when they are in trouble but from whom we get no benefits when we are in need ourselves.

[14] "And you, president of the council, if you consider it among your duties to care about the city and wish to be a good citizen, call another vote and put the question before the Athenians once more, with the understanding, if you are afraid of re-voting, that with so many witnesses in your support you would not be charged with breaking the law, that you would be the healer of your city's counsels, and that this is governing well, whenever a man helps his city as much as possible or does it no harm intentionally."

[15] Nikias spoke in this way. Most of the Athenians who came forward argued for making the expedition and not canceling the vote, although a few also spoke in opposition. Most passionately urging on the expedition

---

6.13. In an extremely long and complex sentence, Thucydides appears to have intentionally left it ambiguous whether "that the Egestans in particular be told" is part of the vote or, like the final advice about future alliances, a separate injunction dependent on "rally against them"; see Classen/Steup VI and *HCT* IV *ad* 6.13.2.

6.14. "Healer": on the echo of medical writing in Nikias' following words, see *HCT* IV *ad* 6.14.

was Alcibiades son of Kleinias, who wanted to counter Nikias, because he was at odds with him politically in other respects and Nikias had mentioned him critically, and who was above all eager to take command and hoped that this would enable him to conquer both Sicily and Carthage, and that by succeeding he would at the same time add to his personal wealth as well as prestige. For he was held in such esteem among the citizens that he indulged himself in expenditures beyond his actual resources, both for horse-breeding and for other luxuries; and to a great extent it was this which destroyed the Athenian city. The masses, frightened by the magnitude of his license in conducting his personal life and of his aims in absolutely everything he did, whatever it was, developed hostility toward him as an aspiring tyrant, and while he as a public person managed the war with the utmost skill, they as private individuals detested him for his behavior, and by entrusting the city to others they ruined it in short order. So now he came before the Athenians and advised them as follows:

[16] "Athenians, I more than others am entitled to command, which must be my first point because of Nikias' attack on me, and I consider myself deserving as well. For the outcry against me involves things that bring glory to my ancestors and myself but also benefit the country. The Hellenes, who had previously expected our city to be exhausted by warfare, believed it to be even greater than its real power because of the splendor of my representation at Olympia, where I entered seven chariots, more than any individual ever had before, and won the prize and also finished second and fourth, and I arranged everything else as my victory warranted. There is honor in this by tradition, and from the accomplishments comes the further inference of might. And again, any brilliance I display in the city by providing choruses or in some other way is only naturally a cause for envy among the citizens, yet for foreigners this too points to strength.

6.15–18. Thucydides' overall treatment of Alcibiades is notably complex, perhaps partly, as many scholars believe, because his account involves at least one reassessment, in the course of writing, of Alcibiades' role in the war. A recent good, perhaps too admiring overview of Alcibiades is Ellis 1989, cf. Bloedow 1991a. It does not appear that Thucydides, like many modern scholars, fell under the spell of Alcibiades' famous charm (from his presentation, one would hardly guess that it existed); rather, he insists on Alcibiades' superior ability and therefore shows marked partiality for him in the context of Athenian politics, distinguishing Alcibiades from other leaders jockeying for power (6.28–29, 6.61). On Alcibiades' speech, see Bloedow 1990.

6.16. "Even greater than its real power": cf. 1.10. Alcibiades is referring to the Olympic games of 416.

This is not useless folly, if a man benefits not only himself but his city through personal expenditure, let alone unfairness for the man to take pride in himself and to be on a different level, since failures do not share their adversity evenly with others; so just as we are not hailed when we are unfortunate, let all submit to the arrogance of the successful, then, or let them demand equality when that is what they bestow. I observe that such men, indeed all men who stand out with any brilliance, are resented during their lifetimes, especially by their peers, then by all who come in contact with them, but afterward they leave behind claimants of kinship, even without validity, and, wherever they lived, a country that prides itself on men who were no aliens or failures but belonged to it and excelled.

"When I with these aspirations am personally assailed for them, consider whether my public management can be matched by anyone. For I brought together the strongest powers in the Peloponnesos with little risk or cost to you and made the Lacedaemonians contest everything in a single day at Mantinea; and as a consequence, even though they prevailed in the battle, their confidence is still not restored to this very day. [17] Here we see the way my youth and supposed extraordinary folly encountered Peloponnesian might with the appropriate arguments and endowed these with credibility through ardor. Do not fear this quality now but, as long as I possess it in my prime, and Nikias appears fortunate, make full use of the services of both men.

"And do not reconsider sailing to Sicily as though it would be against a great power. Its cities swarm with people of every sort and readily exchange and take in citizens. In consequence, there is no one equipped with arms for his person or the usual property on his land as though he had his own country; what each man keeps in readiness is this, anything he thinks he can take out of public goods, either by persuasive speaking or by faction, and, if things go wrong, settle in another land. It is not likely that a mob like that will either listen to proposals with a single purpose or go into action in a common cause; probably each would come over to us separately on hearing anything attractive, especially if they are in faction, as we are informed. And they do not have as many hoplites as they boast, any more than the other Hellenes turned out to be as numerous as the individual assessments by each state, but Hellas, deceiving itself to the highest degree, has hardly had sufficient forces during this war.

6.17. If the sentence about hoplite numbers is genuine (and this has been questioned because it includes a reference to "this war," see *HCT* IV *ad* 6.17.5), it is revealing that Alcibiades implicitly represents "Hellas" as an opponent.

"This, then, is the situation over there, as I understand it, one that will be even more favorable in that hatred of the Syracusans will bring in many barbarians to join us in attacking them, and the situation here will be no obstacle if you consider it correctly. For our fathers, with the same enemies whom we are now told we would leave behind us if we sail, and furthermore with the Mede as an opponent, acquired the empire, without any advantage other than naval strength. And the Peloponnesians have never had fewer hopes against us than now, but if they had all the confidence in the world, their forces would be adequate when it comes to attacking our land whether we sailed or not, yet incapable of harming us with their navy; the one we left behind would be a match for them.

[18] "So on what plausible pretext could we ourselves shrink back or excuse ourselves to our allies there for not helping them? There is an obligation to support them, since that was the oath we swore, rather than protesting that they have not supported us. We did not make them associates to take their turn helping us here, but to harass our enemies there enough to keep them from attacking us here. This is the way we built our empire, in exactly the same way as anyone else might, by our energetic response to every appeal, whether from barbarians or Hellenes, whereas if we were to stay inactive or let race determine whom we should help, the insignificance of our additions to the empire would put its very existence in danger. For when there is a superior power, one does not simply ward off its attacks but takes the steps that will keep them from occurring. And there is no possibility for us to regulate the amount of empire we want but a need, now that we have reached this stage, to make aggressive plans while allowing no defections, because of the danger of being ruled by someone else if we do not rule others. And inaction must not mean for you what it does for others, unless you are also going to change your ways to conform.

"So then, counting on improving the situation here all the more if we venture there, let us sail on the expedition, so that we may lay the pride of the Peloponnesians in the dust when we show our contempt for the prevail-

---

6.18. "Lay . . . in the dust" (literally, "spread"): a unique and "colorful metaphor," which might reflect Alcibiades' actual speaking (*HCT* IV *ad* 6.18.4); alternatively, it could possibly be a Thucydidean allusion to the carpet-treading scene in Aeschylus, *Agamemnon*, which uses this same verb twice (909, 921). "Now to Sicily"; cf. Nikias in 6.11, with Spratt 1905b *ad* 6.18.4. With his inclusion of the "lowly" and "average," Alcibiades again parallels Nikias by using medical language in his concluding remarks, see *HCT* IV *ad* 6.18.6; there may also be some foreshadowing of his willingness to credit the "acknowledged folly" of democracy with mitigating features (6.89). See also Forde 1989, p. 90.

ing peace by sailing now to Sicily, and on top of that, either we will quite probably be the rulers of all Hellas if those elements take our side, or at least we will ruin the Syracusans, in which case we and our allies will benefit. Our ships will provide safe prospects of staying, if all goes well, and of leaving; for we will sweep the seas of the Siceliots, even all of them together.

"And do not be deterred by this apathy in Nikias' speech and this division of young against old, but in our well-tried order, just as our fathers as young men took counsel with their elders and raised our power to this level, in the same fashion strive now to lead it on, with the understanding that youth and age can do nothing without each other, but the lowly, the average, and the extremely gifted are most potent when they are all combined, and that the city, like anything else, will cause its own deterioration if left idle, and internally all its skills will age, but when engaged it will keep adding to its experience and become further accustomed to defending itself, not by words but by actions. I have no doubt whatsoever in my mind that a city never inactive would be soonest ruined by change to inaction, and that men who conduct their affairs with the least violence to their normal character and customs, even if these are less than ideal, are the ones who live in greatest security."

[19] Alcibiades spoke in this way; when the Athenians had listened to him, as well as the Egestaians and Leontine exiles who came forward and begged them to help and supplicated them with reminders of their oaths, they were far more eager than before to make the expedition. And Nikias, after deciding that he could no longer dissuade them with the same arguments but could probably change their minds by the magnitude of preparations if he made them considerable, came before them again and spoke as follows:

[20] "Athenians, since I can see that you are intent on making the expedition at all events, may it turn out as we hope, but I will disclose my sentiments in the present circumstances. For the cities we are to proceed against, according to what I have heard, are great ones that are not subject to one another or in need of change as a welcome progression from some harsh servitude to easier conditions, also unlikely to accept our rule in place of their freedom, and very numerous, the Hellenic ones, for a single island. Aside from Naxos and Katana, which I expect to join us in accordance with their kinship to the Leontines, there are seven more cities equipped very much in the same fashion as our forces in every aspect, and especially the ones that are the main object of our expedition, Selinous and Syracuse. Not only are there large numbers of hoplites, archers, and javelin-throwers but also of triremes with the population to man them; they

have funds, privately and also what is in the Selinountine sanctuaries; in addition, the Syracusans are offered first fruits by certain barbarians. But their main superiority over us is in possessing many horses and using their own rather than imported grain.

[21] "Against a power of this sort, then, there is need not simply of a fleet and a meager army, but for a large land force to accompany the sailing, if we really want to accomplish something worthy of our ambitions rather than being kept out of the countryside by a lot of cavalry, especially if the cities become frightened enough to band together, and aside from the Egestans no one becomes friendly enough to compensate us by furnishing the means of defending against cavalry (if we are forced to leave or send for reinforcements later because we planned carelessly to start with, that is disgraceful), and for us to advance with substantial forces straight from here, understanding that we are to sail a long way from our own territory, not on a campaign comparable to any time when you made some attack in alliance with your subjects here, where in friendly territory provisions for additional needs were easy to get, but isolating ourselves in an entire hostile country, from which it is not easy to get a messenger out within even four months during winter.

[22] "In my opinion, then, we must bring plenty of hoplites, our own and allied, both from our subjects and anyone from the Peloponnese we can either persuade or attract with pay, as well as plenty of archers and slingers, in order to hold our own against the other side's cavalry, and we must also have great superiority in ships, so as to bring in supplies more easily, and take grain from here, wheat and roasted barley, and paid bakers conscripted from the mills in due proportions, so that if we are caught anywhere in poor sailing weather the army will have its provisions (for with its size it will not find every city able to take it on), we must get everything else ready as far as possible and not depend on others, and above all bring as much money as possible from here; as to what is said to be available among the Egestaians, consider that mainly available in talk. [23] My point is that if we arrive with our own forces, all taken from here, not simply

---

6.20. According to a scholiast *ad* 6.20.3, the seven cities were Syracuse, Selinous, Gela, Akragas, Messena, Himera, and Kamarina; Berger 1992 argues that Nikias names only the first two because the others were questionable enough as Athenian opponents to strengthen Alcibiades' case rather than his own.

6.21–22. Extreme examples of Nikias' tortuous sentence construction (see 6.9–14n); it is poignantly ironic that he should comment on the disgrace of requesting reinforcements (see 7.10–15).

brought up to equal strength (except, of course, in hoplites, their most formidable contingent) but actually superior in all respects, we will still have difficulty in conquering and in surviving alike. We must assume that we are going there to found a city in an alien and hostile land, when it behooves men to control the country from the same day they land or, if they fail, to know that they will find every element hostile. Since the latter is what I fear, and since I know that we are greatly in need of good planning and still more of good fortune, a problem because we are human, I want to depend as little as possible on fortune throughout the expedition and to sail with the assurance of preparation for all eventualities. This is what I consider both the fullest security for the whole city and the safe course for us, the ones who are going to make the expedition. If anyone thinks otherwise, I yield the command to him."

[24] This was as much as Nikias said, with the idea that by raising a large number of difficulties he would either dissuade the Athenians or, if he were compelled to make the expedition, they would set out under the safest conditions. Yet they lost none of their eagerness for the voyage because of all the trouble of preparing but were much more urgent about it, and he ended up with the opposite result; it appeared that he had given good advice, and that there would certainly be full security now. And a passion for the expedition afflicted everyone alike, the older men satisfied that either they would get control of the places they were sailing against or a great force could meet with no harm, others with the longing of youth for faraway sights and experiences and as confident of surviving as the masses were of earning money in the military for now and acquiring dominion that would provide unending service for pay. And so, because of the extremes of eagerness among the majority, if anyone felt at all unhappy he was afraid of seeming unpatriotic by an opposing vote, and he kept quiet.

[25] Finally, one Athenian came forward and appealed to Nikias by telling him that he should not give them excuses or delays but say in front of everyone right now what forces they were to vote to him. With reluctance, he said that he would deliberate with his colleagues in quieter circum-

6.24. "The opposite result" refers both backward, emphasizing his strong preference for the first alternative, and well forward, since fulfillment of the second alternative is only apparent. This should not detract from the basic shrewdness of his tactics (although they are hardly original, see Connor 1984, pp. 166–67); there is too much hindsight in calling the demand for a large force an outright "mistake" (*HCT* IV *ad* 6.19.2). The sentence beginning "And a passion" literally and no doubt deliberately lacks structure but flows irresistibly, indicating to the reader that Athenian emotions were irresistible and irrational.

stances, but, as far as he could see right now, they had to sail with no fewer than a hundred triremes (and as many from Athens as they saw fit would be troop-transports, and more had to be sent for from the allies), and a total of no fewer than five thousand Athenian and allied hoplites, and more if at all possible; and the generals would have the other contingents prepared in due proportion, taking archers from there and from Crete and slingers and whatever else seemed appropriate. [26] When the Athenians had heard this, they immediately voted that the generals be given full authority over the size of the army and over the expedition overall, and that they were to do whatever they thought was best for Athens. After that, the preparations began, and they sent word to the allies and mustered the forces at home. The city, because of the armistice, had made a recent recovery from the plague and continuous warfare in respect to both the number of young men who had grown up since then and the accumulation of funds, so that everything was easier to procure.

[27] Their preparations were under way, but then, of all the stone herms in the city of Athens (the square-cut type, following local custom), most had their faces mutilated during a single night. No one knew who the perpetrators were, but there was a search for them with large rewards out of public funds, and they voted in addition that whoever wished, if he knew of any other sacrilege that had occurred, was to give information with impunity, citizen, foreigner, or slave. They took the matter seriously; it looked like an omen for the voyage, and furthermore as though it had been done as part of a conspiracy for revolution and the overthrow of the democracy. [28] So information came in from certain metics and servants, not about the herms but concerning mutilation of some other statues as acts of drunken sport on the part of young men, and, in addition to this, that scurrilous celebrations of the Mysteries were being held in private homes; they accused Alcibiades. Taking up the charges were those who especially resented Alcibiades for standing in the way of their assured ascendancy over the people, and in the belief that by removing him they would rise to the top they exaggerated them and raised the cry that both the Mysteries and the mutilation of the herms were connected with the overthrow of the democracy, and that none of this had been done without his complicity, adducing as evidence the undemocratic licentiousness of his conduct in general.

6.27. "Most had their faces mutilated": their phalloi as well, see Aristophanes, *Lysistrata*, 1093–1094. Scholars continue to debate over the perpetrators; Keuls 1985, pp. 387–95 has made an intriguing case for the women of Athens. See also 6.60n.

[29] He defended himself against the informers then and there and was ready to stand trial before the voyage (for by now everything needed in the preparations had been supplied) over whether he had done any of these things, and pay the penalty if he had, but to take command after being acquitted. He appealed to them not to entertain slanders in his absence but put him to death immediately if he was guilty, pointing out that it was more sensible not to send him on so great an expedition, facing such an accusation, before he was judged. But his enemies, fearing that he would have the army partial to him if tried right away, and that the populace would be lenient, showing favoritism because it was his doing that the Argives and some of the Mantineans made up part of the force, were opposed and put up an active resistance, bringing to bear additional speakers who urged that he sail now and not delay the departure but come back and stand trial within a specified period, wanting him to go on trial when recalled under heavier incrimination, which they expected to bring about more easily in his absence. And it was resolved that Alcibiades should sail.

[30] After this, when it was already the middle of the summer, the departure for Sicily took place. Now it had been prearranged for most of the allies, the grain transports and smaller boats, and everything else that would be used on the expedition to be assembled at Corcyra, so that from that point the entire host would cross the Ionian sea to the tip of Iapygia; the Athenian forces and the allies who were with them went down to the Peiraeus at dawn on the appointed day and manned the ships for departing. The rest of the populace, virtually in its entirety, went down with them, both citizens and foreigners, the local people in every case escorting those close to them, whether comrades, relatives, or sons, and combining hope with lamentations as they did so, the possibility of acquisitions against whether they would see these men once more, taking to heart how far from home the voyage was taking them. [31] And now that they had reached the moment of parting with all its uncertainty, the danger had a greater impact than when they voted to sail; nevertheless, their courage was restored by the strength close at hand because of the quantities of every component they saw when they looked around. As for the foreigners and the general public, they came to view a notable and even incredible endeavor.

For taken as a force launched from a single city from the might of Hellas, this was indeed the first to be more costly and splendid than any up to that

6.31. "For taken as a force": the translation reflects the strained Greek (see *HCT* IV *ad* 6.31.1), the most difficult word being "first." The sense is certainly not "the first expedition" (see 7.16); Thucydides would never have undercut this set-piece

time. In number of ships and hoplites, the one against Epidauros under Perikles and then against Potidaia under Hagnon was not inferior; four thousand hoplites from Athens alone, three hundred cavalry, a hundred triremes and fifty from Lesbos and Chios, and many additional allies sailed with it. But it set out for a short voyage with limited equipment, and this expedition sailed with expectations of a long campaign and furnished with both ships and men, to use either resource as needed, its naval component fitted out at great expense to the trierarchs as well as the city, since the treasury was paying a drachma a day to each sailor and providing the hulls for sixty warships and forty transports and the best personnel to go with them, while the trierarchs were giving bonuses on top of their state pay to the lead rowers and the rest of the staff, adding expensive ornaments and furnishings, each one going to the greatest lengths to make his own ship preeminent for both good looks and fast sailing, while the land troops were picked from the best register and enthusiastic in their competition regarding their weapons and personal equipment. And what resulted, along with their own rivalry at each assigned position, was something resembling an exhibition of might and wealth, so far as the rest of Hellas was concerned, rather than an army directed against enemies. For if someone had calculated both public expenditures of the city and the personal expenditures of the men taking part, all that the city had already paid out and what it was giving the generals to take along and, as a separate matter, what individuals had spent on their personal equipment and on their ships as trierarchs, and all that they were still to spend in addition, and everything besides that every one of them was likely to have gotten together as travel money for a long campaign, even apart from their state pay, and all that each, whether soldier or merchant, brought on board for trade, these overall calculations would have revealed an enormous removal of talents from the city. And the expedition became no less celebrated for the miraculousness of its daring and for its splendor to look upon than for its military superiority over those in its path, and because it was the longest voyage from home ever attempted, with the highest hopes for the future compared with the actual circumstances.

---

by alluding to the future relief force. I believe "first" is motivated by the following comparison, a very ominous one. The expedition assembled by Perikles (2.56) accomplished little under Hagnon (2.58), suggesting Athens' decline without Perikles; it failed because the plague followed it from the city, so that in this ghastly sense the expedition of 430 was a city on the move (cf. 6.23, 6.37). "An enormous removal of talents": cf. Alcibiades' reference to Sikeliot movable wealth (6.17).

[32] When the ships were manned and everything they intended to take along was now on board, the trumpet gave the signal for silence, and they offered the prayers that are made before setting sail, not separately on each ship this time but following a herald in unison, sending bowls of wine around the whole army as the marines and commanders poured a libation from gold and silver cups. The rest of the crowd on land also joined in the prayers, both citizens and everyone else on hand who wished them well. After they sang the paian and finished the libation, they put to sea, and sailing out at first in a column they then raced as far as Aigina, and while they hurried to reach Corcyra, the place where their additional allied forces were gathering, word of their approach was reaching the Syracusans from every quarter, not that anything was believed for a long period. Even after an assembly was called, this was reflected in further speeches by those who believed what they had heard about the Athenian expedition and others who spoke to the contrary, and Hermokrates son of Hermon, coming forward in the belief that his knowledge about this was certain, spoke to give the following advice:

[33] "I suppose that I, just like the others, will have no credibility when I tell you the truth about the invasion, and I am aware that those who say or report what seems incredible not only fail to persuade but are also taken for fools; nevertheless, I will not be cowed into restraint when the city is in danger, since I am sure in my own mind that I am speaking with clearer knowledge than the next person. The Athenians, for all your astonishment, have indeed set out against us with a great force of both ships and soldiers, ostensibly because of an alliance with the Egestaians and in order to resettle the Leontines, in reality with Sicily as their object and our city in particular, on the assumption that once they capture it they will have no trouble taking the rest as well. Since this means that they will soon be here, look to your available resources for the best way to defend against them rather than being caught with your guard down because of your complacence or neglecting everything you have because of your incredulity.

"But anyone who finds me at all credible must not feel consternation because of their daring or their might. For they will not be able to do us more damage than they will suffer, nor by attacking in great force are they doing us a disservice when this is a great advantage regarding the rest of the Sikeliots, whose own consternation will make them more willing to join us, and whether we go on to defeat them or send them away without achieving their objective (for I have no fear whatsoever that they will actually carry out their purpose), the outcome will provide us with a most glorious feat, and I see nothing unlikely about this. Few indeed are the great expeditions, Hellenic or barbarian, that succeed when they have ventured a long way from their own land. For the invaders cannot outnumber the inhabitants and their neighbors, since fear drives every element to unite, and if the lack of supplies in a foreign country is their undoing, they still leave the renown with the people they plotted against even when it is more their own fault that they failed. It was in just this way that these same Athenians, when the Mede suffered a great and unexpected fall, came into glory based on the idea that he came to attack Athens, and it is no vain hope that we will experience the like.

[34] "Let us be bold, then, as we make our preparations here, as we send word among the Sikels to make more certain of some and try to promote friendship and alliance with the others, and as we send envoys to the rest of Sicily, showing that the danger is to all, and to Italy, in order for us either to have it as an ally or keep it from receiving the Athenians. It seems to me that it would be well to send to Carthage in addition. For it will come as no surprise to them, rather they are in constant fear that the Athenians may attack their own city, and so it looks likely that they will consider themselves in trouble if they forfeit everything here and will want to back us, at least secretly if not openly, or in one fashion anyway. Once they are willing, they have greater means than anyone else at present; they possess the most gold and silver, by which war like everything else is sustained. And let us also send to Lacedaemon and Corinth urging them to send help here immediately and activate the war there.

"And what I consider the most opportune measure is also the last one you would give quick assent because of your habit of inactivity, but let it be said. If all the Sikeliots, or the greatest number that could join us, were willing to launch our entire available navy with two months' provisions and meet the Athenians at Taras and the tip of Iapygia and make it clear that there will be no struggle for Sicily before they have one over crossing the Ionian Sea, we would cause them the greatest consternation and reduce them to considering that we are based in friendly territory as its guardians (for Taras is receptive toward us), whereas they have a wide sea to cross with their whole armament and the difficulty of keeping it in formation because of the length of the voyage, and by confronting us gradually in small detachments it would be wide open to our attack; then again, if they lightened their loads and struck with faster ships in a unit, either we would fall on them when they were exhausted if they used their oars, or if we chose not to we also have the possibility of falling back on Taras, but they, short on provisions after crossing for a sea battle, would be at a loss in deserted surroundings, and they would either stay and be blockaded, or they would try sailing along the coast, with the rest of the fleet left behind, and be disheartened by having no certainty about which of the cities might receive them.

"And so, I fully believe, they would be deterred by these factors from even leaving Corcyra, but instead, after full consideration and with intelligence reports about our numerical strength and its disposition, they would either be pushed into the winter because of the time of year or, with the shock to their expectations, disband the expedition, especially since their most experienced general, I hear, is in command against his will and would gladly seize the excuse if anything of significance was detected in our quarter. Our numbers would be exaggerated in reports, I am sure. With men, what is said is also what shapes their thinking, and they have greater fear of those who start by attacking or at least showing that they will defend against an attack, supposing them a match for the danger. This is just how the Athenians would feel at this point. For they are attacking on the assumption that we will not defend ourselves, justified in their low opinion of us because we did not join the Lacedaemonians to destroy them; but if they saw us showing unexpected daring, they would be more shocked by the surprise than by our power in actuality. Let me persuade you, then, to show this daring, or short of that to make the rest of your preparations for war as quickly as possible, and each one take it to heart that contempt for invaders shows up in deeds of resistance, and that to act now as though facing the danger, understanding that preparations made in the presence of fear are the safest, would bring the most advantageous results. They are attacking, I am sure of this, and that they are on the sea and all but here."

[35] Hermokrates said this much, and the people of Syracuse were considerably at odds among themselves, some because there was no possible way the Athenians could be coming, and what he said was untrue, others arguing that, if they did come, what could they accomplish that would not cost themselves more heavily, and still others in complete contempt turned it into a laughing matter; there were few who believed Hermokrates and feared what would happen. And Athenagoras, the popular leader and

6.35–40. Athenagoras is otherwise unknown. By giving him an intolerably self-laudatory as well as aggressive and wrong-headed speech and then never mentioning him again, Thucydides emphasizes that, although there were political power-struggles in Syracuse as well as Athens, at this time the Syracusans, unlike the Athenians, would not let them impede their war effort (see also 7.86n). Cf. Mader 1993b and Bloedow 1996.

the most influential among the common people, came before them and
spoke as follows:

[36] "Anyone who would not wish for the Athenians to be this senseless
and put themselves in our hands by coming here is either a coward or no
friend of his country; as for those who are reporting such things and
throwing you into a panic, I am less amazed at their audacity than their
stupidity if they think they are not obvious. It is because they have their
own reasons for fear that they want to put the city into a state of panic, so
that they can use the general alarm to disguise their own concern. This is
what these stories are good for, since they were not manufactured by
themselves but by men, the same ones who are always agitating here. For
your part, if you give due consideration you will judge probabilities by
looking at them not on the basis of what these men report but on the basis
of what clever and experienced people, which is how I regard the Athenians, might do. When they would be leaving behind the Peloponnesians
before they have put a secure end to the war back there, they are not likely
to enter into another equally serious war of their own free will, since, as I
believe, they are happy that we, who have so many great cities, are not the
ones attacking them.

[37] "But if they did come, just as in the reports, I consider Sicily more
competent than the Peloponnesos to see the war through to the finish, by
virtue of being better equipped in every respect, and our city much stronger by itself than the army they claim is now invading, even if twice as
many were to come. I am at least certain that horses will not accompany
them and cannot be acquired here other than a few from the Egestaians,
nor will hoplites in numbers to match ours, because of their coming by
ship along with all other equipment, hardly a small amount, that must be
supplied against a city of this size, when it is a major undertaking just to
be brought here on such a long voyage even on ships that have not been
loaded down. I have therefore reached the point of thinking that if they
took along a city as large as Syracuse, set it down on our border, and carried on the war, they would hardly escape complete destruction, and certainly not with all Sicily at war with them (for it will unite), having a camp
sustained by ships and huts and minimal supplies while unable to get any
distance away because of our cavalry. All told, I think they would not even
control their own area; so superior do I consider our own preparations.

[38] "But just as I have been saying, the Athenians, I am certain, know
all this and are looking after their own sphere of influence, and people here
are making up stories, which are not true and never could be, people I am
aware of all along, not on this as the first occasion, as wishing to panic your

populace, whether by stories just like these and even more iniquitous or by actions, and rule the city themselves. And indeed I am concerned that by making constant attempts they may actually succeed; we are equally bad at taking precautions before coming to grief and at taking action when we find out. Right there is the reason we have a city that is seldom untroubled but takes on at least as much strife and confrontation within itself as with its enemies, along with occasional tyrannies and lawless dynasties. I, however, provided you are willing to follow me, will make an effort to let none of this happen in our time and, with you the people in support, to punish the authors of all such schemes, not only when they are caught red-handed, a difficult achievement, but also for their aspirations when they lack the means (that is, we must forestall not only what the enemy does but his intentions as well, just as surely as anyone who is not the first with defensive actions will be the first ruined), while as for the oligarchs I will do some accusing, some guarding, even some instructing—for I think this is the best way for me to dissuade them from chicanery.

"Now then, as I have often asked myself, just what is it you want, young men? To hold office right now? That is unlawful; the law was established in view of your incapacity, not to disgrace you if qualified. Is it rather to avoid sharing the same rights as the majority? Now how is it right that the same people not enjoy the same status? [39] It will be said that democracy is neither wise nor fair, that those with property are also the best qualified to rule best. What I say is, first, that the people means everyone, oligarchy a segment; next, that the rich are the best guardians of property while the wise give the best advice, but for hearing and then judging the people are supreme; and that in a democracy these, individually and collectively, have a fair share. Oligarchy offers the many a portion of the dangers and is not simply greedy over the benefits but takes them all away and keeps them. Those among you who are powerful or young are eager for this, but it cannot be attained in a major city.

[40] "But even at this hour, most senseless of all the Hellenes I know if you do not understand that you are aiming at evil, or the most villainous if your boldness takes this into account, advance the cause of your city, the concern of all alike, whether you have been enlightened or have felt remorse, once you have realized that here your best element can take the same share as the city's masses, even a greater one, but that by other intentions you risk a total deprivation. And bring no more of these reports to men who are cognizant and out of patience. Even if the Athenians are coming, the city will offer a defense worthy of itself (indeed, we have generals who will look after that), and if none of this is true, and I believe none of it

is, the city will not impose elective slavery on itself by going into a panic over your reports and choosing you as leaders, but of and by itself, after inspecting your words as though they stood for deeds, it will judge them and not let current freedom be stripped away because of what it hears but will attempt to preserve it, resisting by exercising vigilance."

[41] After Athenagoras spoke in this way, one of the generals got up and prevented anyone else from coming forward, while he himself directed the following words toward the situation: "It is not sensible either to utter slanders against one another or for those listening to accept them, but instead, with a view to the reports coming in, to consider how we, both as individuals and as an overall city, can prepare to make an excellent defense against the invaders. If that turns out to be unnecessary, there is no harm in a public mobilization of weapons and horses and all the other accoutrements of war, the supervision of which will be in our hands, and in embassies to the cities in the meantime for reconnaissance and any other useful purpose. There are still other matters that we have already attended to, and whatever we find out we will put before you." After this short speech by the general, the Syracusans dismissed the gathering.

[42] By this time, the Athenians were at Corcyra along with all their allies. First the generals carried out a further review of the forces and an exact arrangement of the way they were to anchor and make camp, forming three divisions and assigning one to each of themselves, so that they would not sail together and have difficulties with water, anchorages, and supplies at their landing places, and also so that through their assignment to a commander by divisions they would in other respects be better organized and easier to lead. Next, they sent ahead three ships to Italy and Sicily to learn which cities might receive them. And they gave instructions to meet them ahead of time, so that landings would be made with full knowledge.

[43] After this, the Athenians set sail from Corcyra and began the passage to Sicily with a force that now numbered as follows: one hundred thirty-four triremes in all and two Rhodian pentekonters (a hundred were Attic, sixty of these fighting ships and forty troop ships, and the rest of the fleet from Chios and the other allies), five thousand one hundred hoplites altogether (fifteen hundred of these were Athenians from the register, seven hundred were thetes on board as marines, and the others were allies joining the campaign, some of them Athenian subjects as well as five hundred Argives and two hundred fifty Mantineans and other mercenaries), four hundred eighty archers altogether (the eighty were Cretan), seven hundred Rhodian slingers, one hundred twenty Megarian exiles as light-armed, and

one horse transport carrying thirty cavalry. [44] This was the size of the first force that sailed over in the war, and bringing supplies for it were thirty cargo ships as grain transports, also carrying bakers, stone-masons, workmen, and all the tools for wall building, and a hundred small boats, which likewise joined the voyage by constraint; but many additional boats and cargo ships went along with the expedition voluntarily for commercial purposes, all of them at this time joining in the passage from Corcyra across the Ionian gulf. Touching land with all forces at both the Iapygian promontory and Taras, wherever each found the best approach, they sailed along the Italian coast, where the cities did not allow access to their markets or urban centers but only water and anchorage, and at Taras and Lokroi not even these, until they reached Rhegion at the tip of Italy. This was where they now combined their forces, and outside the city, since they were not allowed in, they established a camp in the precinct of Artemis, where they were also provided with a market, drew their ships up on land, and stayed inactive, and they also conferred with the Rhegians, demanding that as Chalkidians they support the Leontines who were Chalkidian; the Rhegians told them that they would not side with one or the other, but in all that was agreed on by the other Italiots they would act accordingly.

The Athenians deliberated over the best way to proceed regarding the situation in Sicily; at the same time, they waited for the ships sent ahead to come from Egesta, since they wanted to know whether the money was there, as the messengers had said in Athens. [45] In the meantime, from many sources, including intelligence agents, clear reports that the ships were at Rhegion were now reaching Syracuse, and the Syracusans accordingly began to get ready for them with a full commitment that no longer included any doubts. And they sent guards around to some of the Sikels and embassies to the others, installed garrisons in the outposts of the countryside, inspected the city forces by checking weapons and horses for full readiness, and arranged everything else for an immediate war that was almost upon them.

[46] From Egesta, the three ships sent in advance rejoined the Athenians at Rhegion with the news that the rest of the promised money was not there, and thirty talents were all that was in evidence. The generals were immediately despondent, since at the start they had encountered this setback, and in addition the Rhegians were unwilling to join in the campaign, the first of their prospects for persuasion and very likely ones, since they were kinsmen of the Leontines and had always been friendly toward Athens. And while the business with the Egestaians only accorded with Nikias' expectations, it was far from what the other two had calculated.

The Egestans had in fact concocted the following sort of arrangement when the first Athenian envoys came to check up on the money. They brought them to the sanctuary of Aphrodite at Eryx and displayed the dedications, the bowls, jugs, incense burners, and a lot of other trappings, all of which were silver and so, with scant financial resources behind them, presented a much more impressive appearance, and when they offered the ships' crews entertainment, they collected gold and silver cups from both Egesta itself and the cities nearby, both Phoenician and Hellenic, and at each banquet used as their own what they had borrowed. And since everyone used pretty much the same items, and a lot was on display all over, the astonishment among the Athenians from the triremes was pronounced, and when they returned to Athens they made it known that they had seen enormous wealth. When word got around that the money was not in Egesta, these men who let themselves be tricked and convinced everyone else at the time were severely faulted by the members of the expedition, while the generals began making plans in response to the situation.

[47] Nikias' proposal was that they sail with the entire force against Selinous, where they had been most expressly sent, and, if the Egestaians provided money for the whole army, plan accordingly, and if not, require them to give sustenance for sixty ships, exactly the number they had requested, and that they stay and bring the Selinountines to terms with them either by force or by agreement and then, after sailing past the other cities and displaying the might of the Athenian state, demonstrating their resolve to friends and allies, set sail for home, unless they had a sudden and unexpected opportunity to help the Leontines or bring over some of the other cities, and not endanger the city by expending domestic resources. [48] Alcibiades said that after setting out with such a large force they should not go away disgraced by lack of accomplishment but send heralds to all the other cities, excluding the Selinountines and Syracusans, and also try to detach some of the Sikels from Syracuse and make the rest their friends, in order to get grain and troops, but first win over Messena (for it was on the straits and the landing point for Sicily and would constitute the perfect observation post and harbor), and then, after winning over cities and knowing who would be fighting on their side, finally attack the Syracusans and the Selinountines, unless the former came to terms with the Egestaians and the latter allowed the restoration of the Leontines.

6.46–50. Note the irony of movable wealth in Sicily—among Athenian allies (cf. 6.17, 6.31n). For an excellent analysis of the "Potemkin" episode at Egesta, see Mader 1993a; on the rather surprising conference that ensues, Liebeschuetz 1968.

[49] But Lamachos said that they should sail directly against Syracuse and bring the fight to the city as soon as possible, while they were still unprepared and in the greatest state of alarm. For all armies were most terrifying at the beginning; if they wasted time before coming into sight, as men recovered their courage in their minds they tended to feel contempt even at the sight of them. If they suddenly descended while the Syracusans were still awaiting them, they would have the greatest success and throw them into the most complete panic, through their appearance (since now was when they would appear the most numerous), through the Syracusans' anticipation of their sufferings, and especially through the immediate danger of battle. And it was likely that many would be caught out in the fields because of not believing that they would come, and while they were moving everything inside the army would not lack for supplies if it took a position in front of the city while in full control. This way, in addition, the other Sikeliots would now tend to avoid alliance with the Syracusans and come over to their side and not wait around to see which would win. He said that if they were forced back and blockaded they should make Megara, which was deserted, their naval base, since it was neither a long voyage nor a long march from Syracuse.

[50] After he said this, Lamachos nevertheless threw his support to Alcibiades' ideas. When Alcibiades subsequently sailed over to Messena in his own ship and proposed alliance, it was refused, and he was told that they would not admit him to the city but provide a market outside it, so he sailed back to Rhegion. The generals immediately manned and provisioned sixty ships out of the whole and sailed along the coast to Naxos, leaving the rest of the force at Rhegion with one general. After the Naxians admitted them to the city, they sailed along to Katana. When the Katanaians did not receive them (there were people inside who favored the Syracusans), they made their way to the Terias river, bivouacked, and sailed on the following day to Syracuse with most of their ships in line but sent ten ahead to sail into the Great Harbor and detect whether any fleet had been launched, also, when they had drawn close, to issue a proclamation from the ships that the Athenians had come, in accordance with their alliance and kinship, to restore the Leontines to their own territory; any Leontines in Syracuse were therefore to leave without fear in the presence of Athenian friends and benefactors. After this had been proclaimed, and they had reconnoitered the city, the harbors, and the features of the countryside that would have to be their base in the fighting, they sailed back to Katana.

[51] After holding an assembly, the Katanaians would not admit the army but invited the generals to enter and say what it was they wanted.

While Alcibiades was speaking, and the people in the city were occupied by the assembly, the soldiers secretly broke through a poorly installed gate, came in, and gathered in the marketplace. When the Katanaians who had Syracusan sympathies saw the army inside, these few were immediately alarmed and withdrew, while the others voted for an alliance with the Athenians and invited them to bring the rest of the army from Rhegion. After this, the Athenians sailed over to Rhegion and now with all their forces set out for Katana and established their camp on arrival.

[52] They had reports from Kamarina that it would come over to them if they went there, also that the Syracusans were manning a fleet. Accordingly, they sailed ahead, first to Syracuse; since they saw no fleet being manned, they made their way to Kamarina in turn, and after putting in on the shore they sent their heralds. But the Kamarinaians did not admit them, saying that they were under oath to receive the Athenians only if they entered with a single ship, unless they themselves sent for more. After this failure, they sailed away; they made a landing somewhere in Syracusan territory and carried off plunder, and after the Syracusan cavalry and light-armed met them and killed a few stragglers, they made their way back to Katana. [53] At this point they discovered the Salaminia here from Athens to get Alcibiades, with orders that he sail back and defend himself against charges by the city, also to get those soldiers who, like him, had been named by informers for impiety in connection with the Mysteries, some also in connection with the herms.

After the fleet sailed, the Athenians in fact had not slackened in their investigation of the acts committed regarding both the Mysteries and the herms, and instead of testing the informers they found everything grounds for suspicion, arresting some very upright citizens because of their own trust in scoundrels and putting them in prison, since they felt it more essential to investigate the affair exhaustively and find out than to let any-one accused, however worthy he seemed, escape examination on account of the informer's vileness. For the people, understanding through hearsay that the tyranny of Peisistratos and his sons had become harsh in its last stage, and furthermore that it had been overthrown not by themselves and Harmodios but by the Lacedaemonians, were in constant fear and saw everything as suspicious.

[54] For the exploit of Aristogeiton and Harmodios was undertaken because of a love affair, and by describing it in full I will show that neither other sources nor the Athenians themselves say anything accurate about their own tyrants or about the incident. For after Peisistratos died at an advanced age while holding the tyranny, it was not Hipparchos, as widely

believed, but Hippias as the oldest who took his place. When Harmodios was conspicuous in his youthful prime, Aristogeiton, an Athenian and a citizen of the middle class, possessed him as a lover. Harmodios, after he was propositioned by Hipparchos and refused him, denounced him to Aristogeiton. And he, with a lover's outrage, fearing Hipparchos' rank and a possible abduction by force, immediately plotted, as far as one of his class could, to overthrow the tyranny. Meanwhile, Hipparchos, after he had again propositioned Harmodios with no greater success, was unwilling to use force yet arranged to insult him in a surreptitious way, as though it were quite unconnected. He was in fact not oppressive toward the people in his use of power but managed it without arousing resentment; these tyrants actually operated with principles and good sense to a very great extent, and by exacting from the Athenians only a twentieth of their income they adorned the city beautifully, carried on its wars, and con-

6.54–59. After a thorough discussion of this digression and its problems, *HCT* IV, pp. 317–29 concludes that Thucydides "succumbed here to the temptation before which all historians and commentators are by their very nature weak, the temptation to correct historical error wherever they find it, regardless of its relevance to their immediate purpose." This will also provide a reason for Thucydides to revisit a topic dealt with in 1.20; he did not want to risk his lesson being taken only by readers who "finished the book." There is space here to address only a few aspects. Thucydides begins by stating that neither the Athenians nor other sources say *anything* accurate about the tyrants ("other sources" are probably Hellanikos and perhaps other writers, with whom he emphatically contrasts himself by "*I* will show"); yet he is at least in violent agreement, as it were, with current Athenian belief that the tyrannicides did *not* end the tyranny (6.53). While insisting that Hipparchos was *not* a tyrant, he also states that "He . . . was not oppressive . . . in his use of power" (more literally, "in his rule"). I suspect that the problem is less severe than *HCT* concludes. Thucydides, using the term "rule" with characteristic flexibility, saw a way to lead into a major point, that "these tyrants" (note also the change in number in 6.56: "he besmirched . . . they expelled") ruled moderately, by making the related point that Hipparchos was even moderate in indulging his personal spite. It is again characteristic that Thucydides was more sensitive to his own awareness of the connecting thread (and the overarching irony that even these tyrants effectively failed in their programmatic attempt to avoid displaying the arrogance of power) than to any reader's confusion over the inconsistency in presentation. The tyrannicides digression is a kind of play within a play; the tyrants, like Alcibiades highly competent in public life, were brought down by extreme reactions to personal conduct; that memories of the episode now contribute to reactions against Alcibiades serves to discredit *those* reactions further. Cf. Kirby 1983, p. 200. The style of the digression is ostentatiously clear, perhaps both to show that Thucydides could tell a story nicely and to leave the readers no excuse for misunderstanding.

ducted its ceremonies in the sanctuaries. In all respects, this city in its own right followed the laws previously in force, except that the tyrants saw to it that one of their number held office. Among those who held the annual archonship of Athens was Peisistratos, son of the Hippias who became tyrant and bearing his grandfather's name, who during his term dedicated the Altar of the Twelve Gods in the agora and the Altar of Apollo in the Pythian sanctuary. When the people of Athens later built onto the altar in the agora and lengthened it, they erased the inscription, but even now the one in the Pythian sanctuary is still legible as saying the following, in faint letters: "Peisistratos son of Hippias set up this monument of his archonship in the precinct of Apollo Pythias."

[55] That Hippias ruled as the eldest, as I insist with more accurate knowledge than others through what I have heard, might also be understood simply from the following: in his case alone, among the legitimate brothers, do there appear to have been children, as the altar indicates and also the pillar about the injustice of the tyrants set up on the Athenian acropolis, on which no child of either Thessalos or Hipparchos is mentioned, but five of Hippias, whom Myrrine daughter of Kallias son of Hyperochides bore him; now it was natural for the eldest to marry first. And on this same pillar he is the first one recorded after the father, not improbably because of being the senior next to him as well as being the tyrant. Nor again do I think it would have been easy for Hippias to seize the tyranny on the spot if Hipparchos had died while in power, and he himself had come into it on that very day; but also because of earlier familiarity with intimidation of citizens and firmness toward mercenaries he took over with a great preponderance of security and was not at a loss like a younger brother whose position would have involved no previous association with leadership. It was the lot of Hipparchos that in making his name by the sadness of his fate he also acquired for posterity the status of tyrant.

[56] Harmodios, then, who had refused his advances, he insulted just as he had planned; after enlisting his sister, a maiden, to carry a basket in a certain procession, they expelled her saying that they had not enlisted her in the first place because of her unworthiness. While Harmodios was resentful, Aristogeiton on his account became very much more enraged as well, and after they had made their other arrangements with those taking part in the deed, they awaited the Great Panathenaia, which was the only day that those citizens who escorted the procession assembled in arms without becoming suspect. They themselves were to begin, and the others

6.54–55. On the younger Peisistratos, see Arnush 1995.

were supposed to join in the attack immediately by attending to the mercenaries. The members of the conspiracy were not many, for reasons of security; they hoped that if even a few acted boldly, those with no advance knowledge, since they even had weapons, would want to take part in their own liberation then and there.

[57] And when the festival came around, Hippias was outside with the bodyguard in what is known as the Kerameikos arranging how each part of the procession was to go forth; and Harmodios and Aristogeiton, with their daggers now, were advancing for the deed. And when they saw a member of their own conspiracy talking informally with Hippias (who was approachable to everyone), they were alarmed and thought that they had been informed on and were just on the point of being arrested. Accordingly, they hoped that if possible their revenge would come first, against their tormenter who had caused them to risk everything, and in this state they rushed inside the gates, encountered Hipparchos near what is called the Leokoreion, and falling on him immediately, with no hesitation, in all the fury that a man in love and a man humiliated could feel, they stabbed until they killed him. The one, Aristogeiton, escaped the bodyguard for the moment when the crowd was milling around and later, after capture, was dealt with in no gentle way; Harmodios was killed right on the spot.

[58] When the news reached Hippias in the Kerameikos, he immediately proceeded not toward the incident but toward the hoplites in the parade before they found out, since they were some way off, and making his face inscrutable in the presence of the calamity he ordered them to go where he had pointed to a certain spot, without their weapons. They went off, thinking that he was going to tell them something, but he, after a signal to the bodyguard to remove the weapons, picked out those he held responsible, along with anyone caught carrying a dagger; for their practice was to parade with shields and spears.

[59] It was in this way, because of a lover's grievance, that both the original plot and the heedless daring of Harmodios and Aristogeiton, in the alarm of the moment, came about. After this, the tyranny took on a harsher form for the Athenians, and Hippias, now more under the influence of fear, put many citizens to death and at the same time looked around in foreign parts to see where he could find some place providing him with security if a revolution occurred. After all, he, an Athenian, gave his daughter Archedike to one of the Lampsakenes, Aiantides son of Hippoklos the tyrant of Lampsakos, aware that they had great influence with King Dareios. Her tomb in Lampsakos carries this inscription: "This dust covers Archedike daughter of Hippias, the finest man of Hellas in his time;

although father, husband, brothers, and sons were tyrants, presumption never stirred in her mind." After he continued as tyrant in Athens for three years and was deposed in the fourth by the Lacedaemonians and the Alkmeonid exiles, he went under truce to Sigeion and Aiantides at Lampsakos, and from there to King Dareios, and forth to Marathon twenty years later, when he set out, by now an old man, and campaigned with the Medes.

[60] Taking all this to heart and recalling everything they knew about it from hearsay, the people of Athens were at this time bitter and suspicious of anyone who stood accused over the Mysteries, and it seemed to them that it had all been done to further oligarchic and tyrannical conspiracies. And during their rage over this, when many highly esteemed men were already in prison and there appeared to be no end of it, but each day brought them to greater savagery and the arrest of still more men, at this point one prisoner, and a man who seemed especially guilty, was persuaded by a fellow-prisoner to give information, whether it was actually true or even if it was not; there is conjecture in both directions, and no one then or later could say anything definite about the perpetrators. And this argument convinced him that it was necessary, even if he had done nothing, to save himself by gaining immunity and rid the city of the prevailing suspicion; his safety would be more certain if he confessed with immunity than if he denied all and went to trial. He informed against both himself and others in the matter of the herms; and the people of Athens, pleased at getting hold of the facts, so they thought, and horrified up till now over never being able to know who was plotting against their people, immediately set the informer free and all those with him who had not been accused, and putting the accused on trial they executed all those they had arrested, while they sentenced to death the ones who had fled and added a reward for the slayers. In these circumstances, although there was a question over whether the victims had been punished unjustly, it was at least unmistakable that for the time the rest of the city was better off.

6.60. The man who seemed "especially guilty" was Andocides, whose own account has survived in the speech *On the Mysteries*; in addition to *HCT* IV, pp. 271–88, see especially MacDowell 1962, who argues (pp. 173–76) that Andocides was actually guilty in the affair of the Mysteries, not that of the herms, and that Thucydides (who was not in Athens at the time) misunderstood the events of 415 B.C.E.; *contra*, Marr 1971. Classen/Steup VI *ad* 6.60.1 believe that after "accused over the Mysteries" a reference to the herms must have fallen out of the text, but for Thucydides to proceed from an outcry over the Mysteries to the arrest of a man who "seemed especially guilty" to a revelation about the herms is thoroughly in keeping with his jaundiced view of the investigations.

[61] Where Alcibiades was concerned, since his enemies were active, the very same people who had previously made him sail, the Athenians had a harsh attitude; and since they thought they had certainty in the matter of the herms, the affair of the Mysteries looked all the more like the work of Alcibiades, for the same purpose of conspiracy against the democracy. As a matter of fact, right in the midst of this commotion, it happened that a modest force of Lacedaemonians had advanced as far as the isthmus for some dealings with the Boiotians. As a result, it appeared that their arrival was prearranged and Alcibiades' doing, unconnected with the Boiotians, and that it was entirely because they themselves had used their information to make arrests that the city had not been betrayed. There was even one night when they slept under arms in the Theseion of the city. In addition, the friends of Alcibiades at Argos were suspected during this period of having designs against the democracy, and at this time the Athenians handed over to the democracy of Argos the Argive hostages who had been deposited on the islands, so that they could be put to death for this.

From every direction suspicion surrounded Alcibiades. So, intending to bring him to trial and execute him, they accordingly sent the Salaminia to Sicily for both him and others named by informers. They gave instructions to order him to follow it back to make his defense, but without arresting him, since they were concerned not to stir up reactions among either their own men in Sicily or the enemy, and especially since they wanted the Mantineans and the Argives to stay, who they believed had joined their expedition thanks to him. Alcibiades and the others who were incriminated, using his ship, accompanied the Salaminia in sailing from Sicily, seemingly for Athens; when they reached Thouria, they stopped following, left the ship, and disappeared, because they were afraid to sail back for a trial amidst prejudice. For a while, the men on the Salaminia searched for Alcibiades and his companions; since they were nowhere to be found, they left and sailed home. Not much later, Alcibiades, now a fugitive, crossed over from Thouria to the Peloponnese in a boat; the Athenians sentenced him and those with him to death in absentia.

[62] After this, the remaining Athenian generals in Sicily divided the army into two sections, each taking one of them by lot, and sailed with the combined forces toward Selinous and Egesta, since they wanted to know whether the Egestans were going to give them the money and also to know how matters stood among the Selinountines and where they differed with the Egestans. Sailing along with the coast of Sicily on their left, where it faces the Tyrrhenian Gulf, they stopped at Himera, the only city in this part of Sicily that belong to Hellas; when it did not receive them they kept

going. On the way, they captured Hykkara, a Sikan town but hostile to Egesta; this was on the coast. They enslaved the population and handed the town over to the Egestans, whose cavalry had joined them, and with their own infantry they marched back through Sikel country until they reached Katana, while their ships came around bringing the captives. But Nikias sailed straight from Hykkara to Egesta, and after he had taken care of other business and collected thirty talents he met the army. They sold the captives, and one hundred twenty talents came in from these. They sent around to their allies among the Sikels asking for troops and with half of their own men attacked Hybla in the territory of Gela without taking it, and the summer ended.

[63] In the following winter, the Athenians immediately began preparing to advance on Syracuse and the Syracusans likewise to move against them. For when the Athenians did not attack them immediately, in conformity with their initial fears and expectations, they increasingly recovered their courage with each passing day, and when the Athenians were observed sailing to parts of Sicily far removed from their own, going to Hybla and trying without success to take it by assault, the Syracusans thought still less of them and, just as a mob is apt to do when its courage is up, demanded that their generals lead them to Katana, since the enemy would not come to them. And the Syracusan cavalry who kept riding up to the Athenian army as scouts asked, among their other taunts, whether they had come to join the Syracusans in a settlement abroad instead of resettling the Leontines in their own land. [64] The Athenian generals noticed this and wanted to draw them out in full force as far away from the city as possible, while they themselves used this time to bring their ships along the coast by night and occupy a convenient place for camp without being disturbed, since they knew that they would have quite different possibilities compared with disembarking against prepared opposition or being detected as they moved by land (for the Syracusans, with plentiful cavalry while they had none, would severely damage their light-armed and noncombatants; but now they would seize a position that would not be seriously harmed by cavalry; and the position that they occupied near the Olympieion sanctuary was one that Syracusan exiles in their company told them about), and accordingly they devised the following scheme to further their plans. They sent a man who was well disposed toward themselves but gave the Syracusan generals the impression of being equally well disposed; a Katanaian, he claimed that he was coming from men in Katana familiar by name to the Syracusans and known to be among their remaining friends in the city. He said that the Athenians stayed overnight inside the city, far

from their arms, and that if the Syracusans on a given day were willing to attack the enemy lines at dawn, they would do their part by shutting in the occupiers and setting fire to the ships, while the Syracusans would easily take the camp by rushing the stockade; there were many Katanaians who would join in and were already prepared for this, he had come from them.

[65] The Syracusan generals, full of confidence on other grounds as well and intentions of moving against Katana regardless, believed the fellow all the more uncritically and immediately set a day to arrive and sent him off, and since the Selinountines and other allies had now arrived, they commanded all the Syracusans to come out in full force. When the details of their preparations were complete, and the time they set for their approach had come around, they marched to Katana, bivouacking on the Symaithos river in Leontine territory. When the Athenians learned that they were on their way, they broke camp, and boarding the ships and boats with their entire army and all Sikels and others who had joined them, they sailed in the night to Syracuse. At daybreak the Athenians were disembarking across from the Olympieion to occupy the camp, and the Syracusan cavalry, who rode ahead to Katana and discovered that the whole army had put out to sea, wheeled around and gave word to the infantry, and they all then turned around and went to the defense of the city. [66] Since they had a long way to go, the Athenians during this time brought the army to a leisurely halt in a convenient spot where they might offer battle whenever they chose, and the Syracusan cavalry would do them the least damage either during the fighting or before; for there were walls and houses, trees, and a marsh in the way on one side and cliffs across from them. Cutting down the nearby trees and hauling them down to the sea, they planted a stockade for the ships, put up a hasty barricade of random stones and timber at Daskon, where access was easiest for the enemy, and broke up the bridge over the Anapos. During their preparations, no one came out of the city and tried to stop them, the Syracusan cavalry being the first to confront them, and then the infantry all gathered as well. Initially they advanced close to the Athenian army, but after this, when it did not take the field against them, they withdrew, crossed the Helorine road, and bivouacked.

[67] The next day, the Athenians and their allies prepared for battle and formed their ranks as follows. The Argives and the Mantineans held the right wing, the Athenians the center, and the rest of the allies the other

6.65. The Olympieion was not only a sanctuary of Olympian Zeus (see 6.70) but apparently an area of the city as well; see 7.4 and *HCT* IV, p. 480.

wing. Half the army was in front, eight men deep, and half next to the tents, also eight deep; these had orders to watch where the army was in any particular difficulty and assist there. They put the baggage train inside this formation. The Syracusans formed hoplite ranks sixteen deep, the full Syracusan force and whatever allies had joined them (the Selinountines were the main helpers, and then Geloan cavalry totalling two hundred, and up to twenty cavalry and about fifty archers from Kamarina), and stationed the cavalry, no fewer than twelve hundred, on the right wing and the javelin-throwers next to them. And when the Athenians were about to start the battle, Nikias went along the ranks and encouraged them both as national contingents and as a united army, with the following words:

[68] "Men, when we have come here facing the same task, what need is there for any long exhortation? It seems to me that this army provides a more substantial basis for courage than a lot of fine speeches to go with a weak force. For considering that we are Argives and Mantineans and Athenians and the foremost islanders, how can each fail to hold hopes of victory high in the presence of such comrades in such numbers, especially against men who are defending as an all-inclusive force, not an elite like ourselves, and Sikeliots, moreover, who can disdain us but not withstand us, on account of not matching their boldness with their skill? Impress this on your minds as well, that we are far from our own countries and upon no friendly ground except for whatever we win for ourselves in battle. And my reminder to you, the reverse of the appeal that the enemy is sure to be making on their side, that the battle will be for their own country, is that it will be in a country not our own, from which withdrawal will not be easy if we do not conquer, since their cavalry will descend on us in force. Remembering your renown, then, attack your opponents with a will and consider the present constraints and difficulties a greater threat than the enemy."

[69] After this exhortation, Nikias immediately led on the army. At this moment, the Syracusans were not expecting that they would be in battle so soon, and some had even gone inside, since the city was close by (they came up belatedly at a run, in a hurry to help, and took up their positions where each encountered the main group; they were certainly not lacking in zeal or daring in either this or the other battles, but while they matched up in bravery as long as their skill held good, it was through deficiencies in the latter that despite themselves they lost their resolve as well); nevertheless, even though they did not think that the Athenians would engage first and were compelled to make a hurried defense, they seized their arms and immediately took the field. The stone-throwers, slingers, and archers of

both sides did the preliminary fighting, routing one another as is normal for light-armed, and then the soothsayers offered the customary sacrifices, and trumpeters sounded the call for the hoplite clash. They advanced, the Syracusans about to fight for their homeland and for each man's individual preservation at the moment and freedom in the future; among their opponents, the Athenians, for making an alien country their own possession and to avoid harming their own country by defeat; the Argives and independent allies, to help them gain what they had come for and, by winning, to see once more the country belonging to them; and the subjects among the allies had their strongest motivation in the immediate survival they could expect only by conquering, and then, as a further consideration, that if they joined in making a further conquest their subjection might be of another and easier sort.

[70] When the battle became hand-to-hand, they held out against one another for a long while, and some thunder and lightning with heavy rain occurred at the same time, so that for those in their first fight and very little acquainted with war this too played a part in their fear, while it seemed to the more experienced that what was happening was simply following the time of year, and their opponents caused them much more concern by not going down to defeat. Finally, when first the Argives drove back the left wing of the Syracusans, and then the Athenians those opposing them, the rest of the Syracusan line was broken as well and put to flight. The Athenians did not pursue them far (the Syracusan cavalry, numerous and unvanquished, held them in check and, by charging any hoplites they saw leading the pursuit drove them back), but after following in a body as far as was safe they fell back and set up a trophy. The Syracusans, gathering at the Helorine road and doing what they could to regroup, nevertheless also sent some of their men to the Olympieion as a guard, out of fear that the Athenians might touch some of the treasures there, while the rest went back to the city.

[71] The Athenians did not go to the sanctuary but bivouacked after gathering their dead and putting them on a pyre. The following day, they gave the Syracusans back their dead under truce (about two hundred sixty of their men and the allies had died), collected the bones of their own dead (about fifty of their men and the allies had died), and sailed back to Katana with the enemy spoils. Not only had winter come, but it also did not yet seem possible to sustain the war over there until they had sent for cavalry from Athens and gathered some from the local allies, to keep from being completely overmatched in cavalry, and meanwhile collected money from the locals, some also to arrive from Athens, and also won over some of the

cities that they hoped would be more responsive to them after the battle, and gotten everything else ready, grain and anything else needed, in order to attack Syracuse in the spring. With all this in mind, they sailed away to Naxos and Katana to spend the winter.

Meanwhile, the Syracusans buried their dead and called an assembly. Hermokrates son of Hermon, a man who was second to none in overall intelligence and had shown competent skill and notable bravery in war, came forward and encouraged them, conceding nothing to the course of events; it was not that their spirit had been vanquished, but their disorder had been harmful. All the same, they had not been as greatly overmatched as would seem likely, especially when they had been contending against the foremost Hellenes with respect to experience, amateurs against professionals, one might say. But the number of generals and the fragmentation of authority (since they had fifteen generals) had also done great harm, along with the disorganized disunity of their whole force. But if the generals were to be few and experienced, and if they were to train the hoplite force during the present winter, providing arms for those who lack them so as to make it as large as possible and maintain strictness in drilling, it was likely, he stated, that they would overcome their enemies, since bravery was already there and orderliness in action would be acquired; for both would see a development, the latter through discipline amidst dangers, while their valor would be more confident than ever before through the assurance of skill. They should choose a few generals and give them full powers, swearing an oath that they would indeed allow them to command in accordance with their own judgments; in this way, what had to be kept secret would be under a tighter seal, and preparations overall would be made more efficiently and straightforwardly.

[73] After listening to Hermokrates, the Syracusans voted for everything he had advised and elected Hermokrates himself, Herakleides son of Lysimachos, and Sikanos son of Exekestes as generals, just these three, and sent envoys to Corinth and Lacedaemon with the intention of bringing over allied troops and persuading the Lacedaemonians to conduct the war in a more definitely open fashion on their behalf, so that either they would draw the Athenians away from Sicily or the Athenians would be less able to send further reinforcements to the army in Sicily. [74] The Athenian forces at Katana immediately sailed for Messena, whose betrayal was expected. The plans had been made but did not succeed; when Alcibiades left Sicily once he was recalled from his command, realizing that he would become an exile he gave information to the Syracusans' friends in Messena, since he knew what was in store; these had already killed the men,

and now their partisans, forming an armed faction and prevailed against letting the Athenians in. The Athenians stayed about thirteen days, and since they suffered from the weather, lacked supplies, and were making no progress, they sailed off to Naxos, and after laying out their camp and building a stockade they wintered there. They also sent a trireme to Athens for money and cavalry, to have them there in the spring.

[75] Also during the winter, the Syracusans built a wall onto the city, keeping the Temenites temple inside, all along the area facing Epipolai, so that they would not be as vulnerable to a counter-wall close up after a possible defeat, and built a fort at Megara and another at the Olympieion. They also put up fences off the coast wherever there were landing places. And since they knew that the Athenians were wintering at Naxos, they marched to Katana, ravaged the land, burned the huts and campsite of the Athenians, and then went home. In addition, when they found out that the Athenians were sending envoys to the Kamarinaians in accordance with the alliance concluded under Laches, on the chance that they could win them over, they sent envoys of their own; their suspicions were that the Kamarinaians had not been eager to send them even what they had sent for the first battle and in the future, noting that the Athenians had been successful in the battle, would refuse them all further assistance and join the other side, won over by the earlier friendship. Accordingly, when Hermokrates and others from Syracuse had arrived at Kamarina as well as Euphemos and his associates from the Athenians, Hermokrates spoke as follows in the meeting held by the Kamarinaians, since he wanted to discredit the Athenians in advance.

[76] "Kamarinaians, we have sent this embassy out of concern not that the clear and present might of the Athenians may terrify you, but rather that the speeches still to come from them may convince you before you have heard us as well. Now then, they have come to Sicily with the pretexts you know about and the intentions we all suspect; if you ask my opinion, they are interested not so much in bringing the Leontines home as in evicting us. For it hardly makes sense to uproot cities over there but restore them here, or to cherish the Leontines because of kinship, since they are Chalkidians, but hold in servitude the Chalkidians on Euboia, when the former are the colonists of the latter. No, with the self-same policy they got control there and are making the attempt here. For once they were granted the leadership of the Ionians and any other allies from their own stock, for the purpose of punishing the Mede, they subjected them by charging some with desertion, some with campaigning against one another, and others with whatever plausible claim they could find in each case. So it was not

on behalf of freedom, then, that they resisted the Mede, neither Athenians for Hellenes nor Hellenes for themselves, but the Athenians did so on behalf of enslavement, to themselves instead of the Mede, and the others to get by the exchange a more capable master, capable of worse.

[77] "But of course we are not here now to expose to a knowledgeable audience the many crimes of a city so open to censure as Athens, but much rather to bring forward the charge against each one of ourselves that despite having the example of the Hellenes over there, enslaved because they did not support one another, and the reality of the same tricks confronting us now, resettlement of Leontine kinfolk and assistance for Egestaian allies, we are unwilling to rally together and let them know with a greater will that here we are no Ionians nor Hellespontines and islanders, who serve as master either the Mede or one such anyway through all their changes, but free Dorians from an independent Peloponnese who inhabit Sicily. Or will we wait until each city is taken, one after the other, knowing that only in this way are we open to attack and seeing them turning to this course, of dividing some of us by speeches, involving some in wars among themselves by raising hopes of alliance, and doing others what damage they can by a smooth word in each case? And do we suppose, when a distant compatriot is the first to perish, that the danger will not come home to ourselves, that every prior victim keeps misfortune to himself?

[78] "And now, if it strikes anyone that it is the Syracusan and not himself who is the enemy of Athens, and he finds it appalling to take risks where my country is involved, let that person reflect that he will be fighting in my country for his own in the process, just as much as for mine, and with all the more security in that I was not already destroyed, but he will enter the struggle with me as an ally, not in isolation; also that the Athenian intention is not to chastise the hostility of the Syracusan but much rather, by using me as a pretext, to secure the friendship of that person. And if anyone feels envy or even fear (for great powers encounter both) and accordingly wishes Syracuse to be brought low so that we may learn moderation, but to survive for his own security, he harbors a wish beyond human capabilities. There is no way that the same man who regulates his desires can regulate fate in like fashion. And if he were to err in his judgment, he would probably, as he was listening to lamentations over his own misfortunes, also wish for another chance to envy my blessings. It is impos-

6.78. Having frankly acknowledged Syracuse's intimidating power in 4.59 (see note there) and 4.64, Hermokrates now uses it as a central—and, in the event, decisive—argument.

sible for him to sacrifice me unless he is also willing to take on risks, which are the same when it comes to reality rather than labels; for it would be preserving our power in name but his own salvation in actuality. And it was especially appropriate for you, Kamarinaians, on our borders and the next to be in danger, to have looked this far ahead and not been the faint allies you are now but instead, coming to us of your own accord, made it plain that exactly what you would have told us as an appeal if you had called us in because the Athenians had come to Kamarina first, which is that we should never yield, you were now telling us as encouragement in like terms. But as it is, neither you nor the others have roused yourself to this.

[79] "Perhaps, out of cowardice, you will devote yourselves to fairness toward both ourselves and the invaders, saying that you have an alliance with the Athenians; yes, and you did not enter into it against friends but in case someone attacked you, and to help the Athenians of course, if the wrongs were against them, not theirs against neighbors with no provocation, as now. In fact, even the Chalkidian Rhegians are unwilling to help restore the Chalkidian Leontines. It is remarkable that they, suspecting the real basis of the noble cause, have implausibly checked themselves, while you, because of a plausible pretext, are willing to help those naturally hostile to you and ruin those even more naturally akin, joining their worst enemies. No fairness there, rather in defending kin, do it without fearing the opposing forces; they are not formidable if we are all united but if we are separated, which is exactly what they are working for. After all, even when they attacked us by ourselves and won a battle, they did not carry out their plans but immediately went away.

[80] "As long as we stay together, then, there is no reason to despair, but to join together with a greater will, especially since help will be on hand from the Peloponnese, where they are completely superior in warfare. And as for the common sense of helping neither since actually allies of both, no one should think this fair to us while safe for yourselves. In actuality, it is not as fair as is claimed. For if it is through your failure to join that the victim succumbs and the winner prevails, could there be any doubt that because of this very abstinence you neither gave one side the help to survive nor stopped the other from doing evil? It is indeed the nobler course to safeguard the common benefit for Sicily by adherence to the victims of injustice who are also your kin and not allow the Athenians, those friends, to go astray. To sum up, we Syracusans say that there is clearly no need to instruct either you or the others in matters you understand just as well by yourselves; but we appeal to you and at the same time bear witness, if you do not heed us, that we are being plotted against by Ionians, our constant

enemies, and betrayed by you, Dorians by Dorians. And if the Athenians subdue us, they will conquer because of your policies, but the honors they receive will be in their own name, and the prize they take away will be none other than he who handed them the victory. And if we, on the other hand, are the ones who prevail, it will be you who suffer reprisals for causing our dangers. Consider, then, and choose now between immediate servitude without risk and the possibility that by prevailing with us you will not have the disgrace of these masters and will avoid no slight hostility on our part."

[81] While Hermokrates spoke in this way, after him the Athenian envoy Euphemos spoke as follows. [82] "We came here for renewal of the previous alliance, but after the Syracusan calumnies we also have a need to speak about the empire and our right to hold it. Now the best proof is what he said himself, that the Ionians are the eternal enemies of the Dorians. Just so; and we as Ionians considered how we might be least subject to Peloponnesians who are Dorians, more numerous, and live beside us. After the Persian Wars, when we had acquired a fleet, we got rid of the rule and leadership of the Lacedaemonians, since it was no more their place to dictate to us than ours to dictate to them, except to the extent that they were stronger at the time, and we ourselves govern after our establishment as leaders of those formerly subject to the king, considering that this way we would be least under Peloponnesian control, with power to defend ourselves, and that strictly speaking we had not been unjust in subjecting the Ionians and islanders, whom the Syracusans say we enslaved, although they were kinsmen. For they came with the Mede against their mother

6.81–87. Scholars often refer to Euphemos ("Good Speaker"? cf. Forde 1989, p. 61), introduced without even a patronym, as otherwise unknown (e.g., *HCT* IV *ad* 6.75.4; Orwin 1994, p. 131, n. 26 is one of the most recent to doubt his historical existence), but he almost certainly is the same Euphemos who served on the Athenian council in 420/419, added a rider to a treaty with Egesta in 418/17 (?), and served as *archon* in 417/416; cf. Green 1970, pp. 175–76 and Smart 1972, nn. 55, 125, who offer additional biographical speculations. He has been characterized as uniquely duplicitous among Thucydidean speakers (see especially Strasburger 1958, who sees him as "using unmasking as a mask"); it is also possible that he reflects the ambivalence of Athenian aims in Sicily, especially in the wake of Alcibiades' departure (see 6.83n). It is significant that Alcibiades will soon (6.90) give a diametrically opposed account of the purpose of the expedition. Technically, Euphemos' speech is a *tour de force*, as he stands Hermokrates' arguments on their head (see especially de Romilly 1956, pp. 186–96); no other Thucydidean speech is so completely an answer to another. Yet Euphemos' cleverness is his undoing, since in exploiting Hermokrates' emphasis on Syracusan power he actually loses the Kamarinaians, whose partiality to Athens might have been reinforced by a more assertive tone.

city, against us, and did not dare to revolt and destroy their property, as we did in abandoning our city, but willed their own slavery and to impose the like on us.

[83] "We rule both because we deserve to on these counts, that we furnished the Hellenes with the largest navy and most unwavering zeal, and they harmed us by readily doing as much for the Mede, and at the same time because we have been seeking strength to counter the Peloponnesians. We will not use fine phrases about our right to rule because we overthrew the barbarian by ourselves or ran our risks for the freedom of the Ionians and islanders rather than that of everyone including ourselves. No one can be begrudged due provision for his own protection. And now, while our presence here is again for our own safety, we observe that you share the same interests. We will show this both by what the other side alleges and by what you yourselves suspect much too fearfully, since we know that men in a state of fear because of some suspicion are momentarily charmed by speeches but follow their own interests later on when it is time to act.

"Now we have said that we hold our empire over there because of fear and because of it also have come with our friends to put matters here on a safe basis, intending not to enslave but rather to prevent this from befalling anyone. [84] And no one should have the idea that we are concerning ourselves about you to no purpose, once he understands that if you are kept safe, and through your providing more than weak resistance to the Syracusans, less harm would come to us by their sending a force to the Peloponnesians. In this connection, you are immediately of the greatest importance to us. This is exactly what also makes it reasonable to restore the Leontines, in no subject condition like their kinsmen on Euboia but as strong as possible, so that on our behalf they might present problems for the Syracusans from the borders of their own land. For back there, we are a match for our enemies just by ourselves, and the Chalkidian, whose enslavement they say makes it implausible for us to free those here, has his uses for us when he is unequipped and simply supplying money, but, over here, the Leontines and other friends when they are as independent as possible.

[85] "When a man is a tyrant, or a city rules an empire, no factor is unreasonable if advantageous, nor akin if not trustworthy; in each case,

6.83. For the problem of "Now we have said," see Classen/Steup VI, Spratt 1905b, and *HCT* IV *ad* 6.83.4; "this [the reasons for coming to Sicily] Euphemos has not yet said; he is going to say it" (*HCT*). I suggest that Euphemos is taking the line that the purpose of the expedition has already been fully declared (cf. 6.6n, 6.33, and 6.76) but now needs to be more fully explained.

hostility or friendship must suit the situation. And this is how we are benefited here, not if we weaken friends but if enemies are powerless because of the vigor of our friends. This should not be doubted, for our charge to the allies there is in accordance with the utility of each, that the Chians and Methymnians stay independent by contributing ships, that the majority be on harsher terms by contributing money, and that still others be allies in complete freedom, even though islanders and easy to take over, because they occupy strategic places around the Peloponnesos. It is natural therefore to arrange matters here as well in terms of self-interest and, as we say, fears about Syracuse. For their aim is rule over you, and their intention, after uniting you in suspicion of us, is to rule Sicily themselves, either forcibly or in isolation following our fruitless departure. It is inevitable, if you unite in their favor; for so great a force in a single combination will no longer be one we can deal with, yet in our absence their strength would not be inadequate to confront you.

[86] "Anyone thinking differently is refuted by the plain facts, for when you called us in earlier, it was exactly this fear you brandished before us, that if we watched while you fell to Syracuse we would ourselves be endangered. It is not right at this point to be incredulous about the very same argument you thought would convince us, nor that we should be suspect because we are here with a more substantial force to confront their power, but much rather that you should disbelieve them. We ourselves are unable to stay here without your support and not able to subjugate you even if we turned rogue and subdued you, on account of the distance to sail and the difficulty of guarding large cities equipped like mainlanders. They, however, confronting you with no encampment but a city of greater size than anything we have assembled here, are constantly plotting and let no opportunity pass once they find it. They have already demonstrated this in other ways as well as in their dealings with Leontini and now, as though you were fools, have the audacity to call you in against the men who have been preventing this and up to now keeping Sicily from falling into their power. For our part, we beckon you toward a security certainly far more genuine in urging you not to throw away the kind that each party provides for the other, and to understand that for them, even without allies, the path against you is always an open one because of their numbers, while for you there will not often be possibilities of defending yourselves with auxiliary forces of this magnitude; if in your suspicion you allow these to leave after frustration or even reverse, there will come a day when you wish to see even a small fraction of them, a day when its arrival will be of no use to you.

[87] "But let their slanders win no support, Kamarinaians, either among you or among the others; we have told you the whole truth about what has placed us under suspicion, and by making additional mention of the main points we expect to convince you. For we maintain that we rule back there to avoid being another's subjects and are liberators here lest we be harmed from here, that we are forced to take many measures because we are also on guard in many directions, and that we have come, now as previously, not unbidden but invited as allies to those of you who have suffered from aggression here. And let there be no attempt on your part at changing our course by acting to judge our conduct or correct it, a difficult matter by now, but as far as any aspect of our forwardness and our character also benefits you, seize and make use of it in the understanding that our ways are not injurious to all alike but even benefit the great majority of Hellenes. For in all lands, even without our presence, all men, anyone believing himself wronged and anyone plotting to commit wrong, when the one lives in the prevailing expectation of getting aid from us to compensate, the other of making no venture without danger whenever we arrive, are equally constrained to behave moderately without wishing to in the latter case and to come through safely without exertion in the former. Therefore, do not reject this security, which is open to anyone requesting it and now made available to you, but at last, putting yourselves on the same basis as the others through our assistance, exchange your constant watchfulness against the Syracusans for the countermeasures of an equal."

[88] Euphemos spoke in this way. And the Kamarinaians went through the following reactions. They were well disposed toward the Athenians, except for the one reservation that they might enslave Sicily, while always at odds with the Syracusans as neighbors. Since their proximity made them all the more afraid in the event that the Syracusans prevailed even without their help, they sent them the few cavalry in the first instance and also resolved that in the future it should be the Syracusans who received their effective support, in the most modest possible amounts, but that in the present situation, lest they seem to have a lesser regard for the Athenians, who after all had been superior in the battle, they should give both sides the same formal answer. In accordance with this plan, they answered that, since it happened that there was war between two parties who were

---

6.87. The argument resembles Alcibiades' in both 6.17 and 6.92: "Once you use me, you will trust me well enough." "Equally constrained": unusual use of language, perhaps with a touch of irony; cf. *HCT* IV *ad* 6.87.4 and Ostwald 1988, p. 58.

both allies of theirs, it seemed consistent with their oaths to side with neither. Then both embassies left.

The Syracusans finished equipping their side for the war, while the
Athenians negotiated with the Sikels from their camp at Naxos to get as
many as possible to come over. The ones toward the plain, subjects of the
Syracusans, did not revolt in large numbers, but the communities of those
occupying the interior, which had been continuously independent long
before this, immediately joined the Athenians with few exceptions, and
they sent down grain for the army and even, in some cases, money. As for
those who would not come over, the Athenians campaigned against them
and compelled some but were kept away where the Syracusans sent garrisons to help. After moving their quarters from Naxos to Katana and recon-
structing their former camp, which had been burned by the Syracusans,
they settled in for the winter. They also sent a trireme to Carthage to propose friendship, in case they could offer any help, and sent one to Tyrrhenia, where some of the cities were even volunteering to join them in the
war. And by a proclamation among the Sikels and a request transmitted to
Egesta they asked them to send as many horses as possible and got everything else ready for a blockading wall, bricks, iron, and whatever was
required, in order to carry on the war when spring began.

The Syracusan envoys dispatched to Corinth and Lacedaemon also,
during their voyage along the coast, tried to persuade the Italiots not to
ignore the activities of the Athenians, on the grounds that these were
aimed just as much against themselves, and when they reached Corinth
they made a speech urging them to help in accordance with their kinship.
The Corinthians, after first passing an immediate vote to aid them whole-
heartedly, also dispatched envoys to accompany the mission to Lacedaemon, so that they could help persuade the Lacedaemonians to take up the
war against the Athenians more openly over there as well as sending some
sort of aid to Sicily. There were the envoys from Corinth at Lacedaemon
and also Alcibiades with his fellow-exiles, since he had originally crossed
from Thouria right away on a cargo ship, first to Kyllene in Elean territory
and then later on to Lacedaemon, arriving under official protection when
the Lacedaemonians themselves invited him; for he was afraid of them
because of his activities in the Mantinean affair. What happened in the
Lacedaemonian assembly was that the Corinthians and the Syracusans
impressed the Lacedaemonians because they were urging the same things
as Alcibiades. And Alcibiades, when it was the intention of the ephors and
officials to send envoys to Syracuse forbidding capitulation to the Athe-

nians, but with no eagerness to help, came forward and inflamed and inspired the Lacedaemonians by the following speech.

[89] "I must speak to you first about the prejudice against me, so that you will not give public concerns a diminished hearing because of suspicions about me. The position as your proxenos, renounced by my ancestors because of some complaint, I personally revived, and I served you in various matters, especially the disaster of Pylos. But although I remained committed, you, when reconciling with the Athenians, conferred power on my enemies and disgrace on me by working through them. On that account, you rightfully suffered at my hands when I favored the cause of the Mantineans and Argives, and anywhere else I opposed you. And now, if at that time there was indeed anyone unreasonably angry at me during the trouble, let looking at the truth alter his opinion; and if anyone thought the worse of me for the additional reason that I was more aligned with the popular side, he must conclude that not even for this is he right in hating me. For all resistance to absolute rule is called popular, and we were at all times the opponents of tyrants; originating from this, the championship of the people has abided with us. At the same time, when the city had a democratic government, it was necessary to adapt to the situation in most respects. But in our political activity we attempted to be more moderate than the prevailing intemperance. There were those in early times and present who steered the crowd in evil directions, the same men who banished me. We were leaders of the whole, choosing to do our part in preserving the same system, just as it was handed down, under which it so happened that the city was greatest and freest; for certainly those of us with sense understood democracy, I better than anyone else, measured by what I might say to abuse it; but nothing new can be said about acknowledged folly. Meanwhile, we did not think changing it was safe while you were entrenched as enemies.

[90] Such were the factors in the prejudice against me; now, be informed about matters which are for you to consider but for me to expound wherever my knowledge is superior. We sailed to Sicily to subju-

6.89. Just before condemning what he explicitly calls democracy, Alcibiades justifies a career of supporting a system that not only opposed tyranny but was at least concurrent ("it so happened") with the rise of Athens. The word translated "system" is very rare in Thucydides; cf. 8.89, where it is understood to mean a political smokescreen (see *HCT* V *ad* 8.93.3). Yet Alcibiades gives it a context suggesting something more: a delicately balanced partnership (i.e., "the whole," cf. 6.18), which has now become unbalanced.

gate the Sikeliots first, if we could, the Italiots next, and then to go after the empire of the Carthaginians and the Carthaginians themselves. If all or most of this went well, we were going to attack the Peloponnesos, not only bringing the entire force of Hellenes acquired over there but hiring many barbarians, Iberians and others currently acknowledged as the most war-like of the barbarians in those parts, and building many triremes in addition to the ones we have, since Italy has no shortage of timber. By imposing a complete blockade with these and by an infantry onslaught on land, we hoped that after we took some of the cities by assault and invested the others we would easily overwhelm the Peloponnesos and rule all that is Hellenic. As for money and provisions to make all this come about more conveniently, the territories added over there were to provide more than enough by themselves, without revenues from here.

[91] "You have heard this about the expedition now in progress from the man with the most accurate knowledge about our intentions; and every remaining general will still carry them out if he can. What you must now understand is that nothing will be left over there if you do not help. For even at this point the Sikeliots, although at a disadvantage in experience, could survive if they were closely united. But the Syracusans alone, already defeated in battle and at the same time hemmed in by ships, will not be able to hold out against the forces Athens has there now. And when this city is captured, all Sicily is taken, and also Italy forthwith; and the danger from that direction which I just finished declaring would descend on you without delay. So let no one think that he is deciding about Sicily alone rather than the Peloponnesos as well, if you are not quick to take these actions: send over an army on ships, one with the capability of rowing itself there and immediately fighting as hoplites, and, even more useful than that army in my opinion, a Spartiate as a commander who can bring some discipline to all who have made themselves available and coerce anyone who has not; this way, the friends you already have will feel more confident, and the doubters will be less fearful about joining.

"At the same time, you must fight a more open war here, so that the Syracusans will be more resistant when they see you as committed, and the Athenians less able to send their side more reinforcements. And you must fortify Dekeleia in Attica, which has always been the Athenians' worst fear and to their mind the only wartime experience they have been spared. This is the surest way to damage an enemy, when you take your ideas about what worries him most, confirm them, and strike; for it is only natural for each to fear what he himself is acutely aware means danger for him. Passing over most of the benefits you will gain for yourselves and deny the enemy through this fortification, I will summarize the most important. Any commodities around the countryside will come into your possession, most by seizure, some running to meet you; they will be deprived at once of the income from the Laureion silver mines, all the current profits from the land and from jurors' pay, above all by reduction in revenues handed over by the allies, who will become less punctilious after concluding that there is now to be serious fighting on your part.

[92] "It is up to you, Lacedaemonians, whether any of this gets done quickly and energetically, since I have complete confidence, surely not misplaced, that it is entirely possible. And I do not expect any of you to think the less of me if I, once considered a patriot, vigorously attack my own city along with its worst enemies, nor to have my words distrusted as the exile's type of zeal. For exile takes me away from the villainy of those who expelled me, not from serving you if you listen to me, and you who harm your enemies as you find them are not so hostile as those who compel friends to become enemies. And furthermore, my patriotism does not apply where I am wronged but where I was secure in exercising my rights; nor do I think of myself as attacking a homeland that still exists, but as recovering one that does not; and this is the real patriot, not the one who loses his country to injustice without attacking it but the one whose desire brings him to every means of regaining it. I tell you in consequence to use me without hesitation in every dangerous or arduous situation, Lacedaemonians, appreciating what is after all the argument you can hear from any source, that if I did you serious harm as an enemy I would certainly be of adequate service as a friend, given that I know the situation in Athens but was guessing about yours, and I tell you, since you will understand that the matters under consideration are of the utmost importance, that you must not shrink from campaigning in both Sicily and Attica, so that you can preserve your interests overseas by participating with a fraction of your forces and destroy any power Athens has or hopes to have and thereafter live in security yourselves and take the supremacy that all Hellas offers you, not under duress but out of good will."

6.91. "Running to meet you" presumably refers to runaway slaves (see 7.27), in which case the wording is unusual: perhaps facetious, and I have translated accordingly. For the suggestion that Alcibiades has outrageously and deliberately exaggerated the importance of jurors' pay, see *HCT* IV *ad* 6.91.7.

6.92. Cf. Shakespeare, *Henry V*, act 5, scene 2: "I love France so well that I will not part with a village of it; I will have it all mine." On Alcibiades' speech, see Pouncey 1980, pp. 110–16.

[93] Alcibiades spoke in this way; the Lacedaemonians, who already had their own motives for campaigning against Athens but were still hesitating and looking around, were far more enthusiastic after this man had given them this specific information, which they believed they had heard from the man with the most accurate knowledge. Accordingly, they now gave their attention to fortifying Dekeleia and also sending aid to people in Sicily right away. Assigning Gylippos son of Kleandridas to the Syracusans as a commander, they instructed him to implement, in consultation with them and the Corinthians, the best and quickest means under the circumstances for some kind of help to reach people there. He told the Corinthians to send two ships for him to Asine at once, equip all others they intended to send, and at the right time have them ready to sail. With this agreed on, they left Lacedaemon. And the Athenian trireme, which the generals had dispatched to get money and cavalry arrived from Sicily. After they were informed, the Athenians voted to send the cavalry and the subsistence for the army. And the winter ended, as did the seventeenth year of this war, which Thucydides recorded.

[94] As soon as spring began in the following summer, the Athenians in Sicily set out from Katana and sailed along the coast against Megara in Sicily, which the Syracusans, just as mentioned by me previously, depopulated in the time of the tyrant Gelon, and they occupy the territory themselves. They made a landing and plundered the fields, and after they attacked a Syracusan post without taking it they then proceeded by both land and sea to the Terias river and made a landing on the plain, plundering it and burning the grain, and after they encountered a few Syracusans, killed some, and set up a trophy, they went back to their ships. After they sailed back to Katana, they got provisions and advanced from there with all their forces against Kentoripa, a Sikel town, took it over when it surrendered, and left, burning the grain of the Inessians and Hyblaians as they went. On their arrival in Katana, they found the cavalry sent from Athens, two hundred fifty with no horses but their equipment, on the assumption that horses would be provided locally, also thirty mounted archers and three hundred silver talents.

[95] Also in this same spring, the Lacedaemonians campaigned against Argos as far as Kleonai, but when there was an earthquake they went back. After this, the Argives invaded Thyrea on their border and took a lot of booty from the Lacedaemonians, which was sold for not less than twenty-five talents. Not much later in the same summer, the people of Thespiai moved against their government but without prevailing, and when it got help from Thebes some were arrested, while others bolted to Athens.

[96] During this summer, the Syracusans learned that the Athenian cavalry had come and that they were now about to move against them, and because they believed that unless the Athenians secured Epipolai, which is hilly terrain lying directly above the city, they would not easily wall them off even if they prevailed in battle, they were determined to guard the approaches so that the enemy would not take them unawares when he came up these; for he had no other possible route. The place is steep everywhere else, it slopes down clear to the city, and everything on it is in plain sight; it is called Epipolai by the Syracusans because it is "up above." They went out at dawn in full force to the meadow along the Anapos river and conducted an inspection of weapons (as generals they had Hermokrates and his group who had recently taken up their commands) and before doing so set aside six hundred hoplites as a picked group under the command of Diomilos, an exile from Andros, to be guards for Epipolai and present themselves immediately in a body if needed for anything else.

[97] And during this night the Athenians, now with their entire force, went undetected as they landed from Katana at the place called Leon, six or seven stades from Epipolai, brought the infantry ashore, and moored the ships at Thapsos; this is a peninsula running out into the sea after a narrow isthmus, and it is not a long way from the city of Syracuse by either sailing or going overland. The Athenian naval forces stayed inactive at Thapsos after putting a stockade across the isthmus, while the army immediately advanced on Epipolai at a run and was able to get up by way of Euryelos before the Syracusans found out and came away from their inspection in the meadow. In addition to the six hundred with Diomilos, each of the other defenders came with all possible speed; they had a full twenty-five stades to go before engaging. With the circumstances making their charge so much more disorderly, then, the Syracusans were defeated in battle on Epipolai and withdrew to the city, and Diomilos was killed with about three hundred others. Subsequently the Athenians, going right down to the city on the following day after they had set up a trophy and given back the Syracusan dead under truce, and withdrawing when no one came out to oppose them, built a fort at Labdalon on the edge of the cliffs of Epipolai, facing Megara, so that they would have a storehouse for their equipment and money whenever they went forward while in combat or while building walls.

6.97. I have followed *HCT* IV *ad* 6.97.1 in dealing with the textual problems.

[98] And not much later, three hundred cavalry came to them from the Egestans and about a hundred from the Sikels, Naxians, and some others; two hundred fifty cavalry from Athens were also there, for whom they received horses from the Egestaians and Kamarinaians and bought more. Altogether, then, they mustered six hundred fifty cavalry. After installing a garrison at Labdalon, the Athenians proceeded to Syka, which was where they quickly built their circular fort. They startled the Syracusans by the speed of its construction; the latter came out determined to give battle instead of looking on. Just when the formations were facing one another, the Syracusan generals, who observed that the ranks of their army were broken and having trouble coming together, took them back into the city, except for a portion of the cavalry. These stayed in the field and tried to prevent the Athenians from gathering stones or going any distance in different directions. One tribe of Athenian hoplites, together with all the cavalry, charged and routed the Syracusan cavalry, killed some, and set up a trophy for the cavalry battle.

[99] The next day, while some of the Athenians were building the wall north of the circular fort, others constantly gathered stones and wood and set them down as far as the cove called Trogilos, which left them the shortest line from the Great Harbor to the sea on the other side. The Syracusans, at the suggestion of their generals and especially Hermokrates, were no longer prepared to risk mass battles with the Athenians but decided in favor of building a counterwall, where the enemy were going to extend their wall and where enclosure would result if they got there first, and sending part of their own forces, in case the enemy opposed their operations, to be the first to occupy the land ahead, planting a stockade there, and divert everyone in their direction and away from continuing their work. Accordingly, they came out and began building their wall starting from their own city, making a perpendicular south of the Athenian circular fort, and cut down the olive trees in the sanctuary and installed wooden towers. The Athenian ships had not yet sailed over from Thapsos into the Great Harbor, and instead the Syracusans still held the coastal positions, and the Athenians brought in supplies overland from Thapsos.

[100] When the Syracusans thought that their stockades and wall-construction were far enough along, and the Athenians had not come to hinder them because they feared that they would be easier to fight with their forces divided and at the same time were intent on completing the circuit of their own wall, the Syracusans went back into the city, leaving one tribe on guard at the wall. The Athenians destroyed the pipes for bringing drinking water into the city subterraneously, and, after watching until most of the Syracu-

sans had gone into shelters at midday, some even back into the city, and those in the stockade were negligent in their guard, they sent ahead a select three hundred of their own hoplites and some light-armed who were picked out and given heavy equipment, with orders to attack the counter-wall suddenly at a full run, and the rest of the army advanced in two sections, toward the city under one general, in case there were reinforcements, toward the stockade in the Pyramid area under the other general. The three hundred attacked and took the stockade, and the guards abandoned it and fled into the fort built around the Temenites sanctuary. Their pursuers rushed in with them got inside but were vigorously ejected by the Syracusans, and some Argives and a few Athenians were killed here. The whole army drew back, and they tore down the wall, broke up the stockade, carried off the stakes for themselves, and set up a trophy.

[101] The next day, starting from the circular fort, the Athenians began building a wall toward the cliffs above the marsh, which on this side of Epipolai faces the Great Harbor, which made the line of their surrounding wall shortest once they had brought it down through level ground and the marsh to the Great Harbor. At this point, the Syracusans came out and began building another stockade starting from the city and through the marsh, also digging a trench alongside, to make it impossible for the Athenians to build their wall all the way to the sea.

After the Athenians had completed their fortifications toward the cliffs, they made another attack on the Syracusan stockade and trench, telling the fleet to sail from Thapsos over to the Great Harbor of Syracuse and making their descent from Epipolai onto level ground at predawn, and after crossing where the marsh was claylike and almost solid by laying down doors and planks to step on, they captured most of the stockade with its trench just at dawn and later took the remaining parts. A battle also occurred, and there the Athenians were victorious. The Syracusans on the right wing fled to the city, those on the left along the river, and the three hundred picked Athenians, who wanted to cut them off from crossing, hurried to the bridge at a run. In their fear, the Syracusans, who also had most of their cavalry in the area, came to close quarters with these three hundred, routed them, and drove on into the Athenian right wing; and with this onslaught the front line of the right wing joined in the panic as well. Lamachos saw this, and when he came from the left wing to help with

---

6.100. For a good overall discussion of Thucydides' inconsistent familiarity with Syracusan topography and inconsistency in assuming familiarity on the part of the reader, see *HCT* IV, pp. 466–84 ("Pyramid area" p. 467).

just a few archers, adding the Argives, went across some sort of ditch in pursuit, and he and a few with him were isolated, he was killed with five or six of his men. The Syracusans were quick enough to make off with their bodies right away to a place out of reach beyond the river, and once the rest of the Athenian army advanced, they made good their own withdrawal. [102] And they seized and demolished the thousand feet of outer circuit, but Nikias, who happened to have been left there because of illness, prevented this at the fort itself. He ordered the servants to set fire to all the timber and siege equipment left in front of the walls, since he realized that with no men he could not survive in any other way. And it turned out just as he thought. Because of the fire, the Syracusans did not continue their advance but fell back; besides, by then relief for the fort was coming from the Athenians lower down, who had chased away their opponents there, and at the same time their fleet from Thapsos, following orders, was sailing into the Great Harbor. When they saw all this, the men up above left quickly, and the entire Syracusan army went into the city, in the belief that with their present strength they would not be capable of stopping the fortifications to the sea.

[103] After this, the Athenians set up a trophy, gave the Syracusans back their dead under truce, and recovered their men and Lamachos himself. With all their forces on land and sea now present, they began to surround the Syracusans with a double wall down to the sea, starting from Epipolai and the cliffs. And provisions for the army were coming in from every part of Italy. Also, many of the Sikels who had previously looked on were coming to the Athenians as allies, as well as three pentekonters from Tyrrhenia. Everything was furthering their hopes. And the Syracusans even stopped believing that they could survive by fighting, since no help at all was arriving from the Peloponnese, and coming to terms was what they talked about, among themselves and also with Nikias; for with Lamachos dead he was now in sole command. There were no definite results, but, as was natural for men who were desperate and besieged more than ever, a great deal was said to him and still more around the city. For because of their present plight they even became suspicious of one another and deposed the generals under whom this had come about, with the idea that they were being harmed by bad luck or treachery on their part, and replaced them with others, Herakleides, Eukles, and Tellias.

[104] Meanwhile, the Lacedaemonian Gylippos and the ships from Corinth, intent on bringing aid to Sicily as quickly as possible, had reached Leukas. And because the news coming in was grim and in every case contained the same falsehood, that Syracuse was already completely walled

off, Gylippos had no further hopes for Sicily but, since he wanted to preserve Italy, crossed the Ionian Sea to Taras as quickly as possible with
Pythen the Corinthian and two Lakonian and two Corinthian ships, and
the Corinthians were to cross later after manning two Leukadian and three
Ambraciot ships in addition to their own ten. From Taras, Gylippos first
sent an embassy to Thouria, in keeping with his father's former citizenship, and when he failed to win them over he set sail following the Italian
coast, was caught off the Terinaian Gulf by the wind from the north that
blows there with great force, and carried out to sea, and he landed back at
Taras after experiencing the worst possible weather. Beaching all the ships
that had suffered from the storm, he made repairs. Nikias learned that he
had landed and was scornful of his few ships, which had also been the reaction of the Thourians, considered them primarily equipped for pirate voyages, and did not yet station any guard.

[105] Around the same part of this summer, the Lacedaemonians with
their allies attacked Argos and ravaged much of its territory. The Athenians supported the Argives with thirty ships, and by sending them they
committed the most flagrant breach of the treaty with the Lacedaemonians
on their side. For previously they helped the Argives and the Mantineans
in war by raids from Pylos and against every other part of the Peloponnese
rather than by descending in Lakonian territory, and although the Argives
repeatedly urged them just to land in Laconian territory, join them in ravaging a minimal area, and leave, they were unwilling; but this time, under
the command of Pythodoros, Laispodias, and Demaratos, they made a
descent and ravaged the land at Epidauros Limera, Prasiai, and wherever
else they landed and now gave the Lacedaemonians a far more plausible
claim of self-defense against the Athenians. After the Athenians withdrew
from Argos with their ships, and the Lacedaemonians withdrew, the
Argives attacked the territory of the Phleiasians, plundered it, killed some
of them, and then returned home.

6.104. Thouria (usually called Thourioi) was a Panhellenic colony founded by the
Athenians in 443 on the site of the destroyed city of Sybaris; it experienced faction
from the start (see 6.33) and was often anti-Athenian. "In keeping with his father's
former citizenship": cf. *HCT* IV *ad* 6.104.2.

BOOK SEVEN

[1] As for Gylippos and Pythen, after repairing their ships they sailed from Taras along the coast to Epizephyrian Lokroi and, now with the more accurate information that Syracuse was not yet completely walled off, and that it was still possible to approach by Epipolai and come in with an army, deliberated over whether to keep Sicily on their right and take the all-out risk of sailing in or keep it on their left and sail to Himera first, pick up the Himeraians themselves and any other forces they could enlist, and come by land. It seemed best to them to sail to Himera, especially since the four Attic ships, which Nikias had dispatched after all were not yet at Rhegion. They crossed the strait ahead of these guards, and after putting in at Rhegion and Messene they reached Himera. While there, they persuaded the Himeraians to take part in the campaign both by joining in person and by supplying weapons to those of their ships' crews who lacked them (their ships they had beached at Himera), and they sent word to the Selinountines to meet them in full force at a certain spot. The Geloans also promised to send a force, although a small one, as did some of the Sikels, who were ready to come over with much greater enthusiasm both because Archonides, ruler of some of the Sikels in the area and a friend of the Athenians with considerable power, had recently died and because Gylippos had arrived from Lacedaemon and appeared enthusiastic. Taking those of his sailors and marines who were armed, about seven hundred, a total of a thousand Himeraian hoplites and light-armed combined and a hundred cavalry, a few Geloans, and about a thousand Sikels altogether, he marched on Syracuse; [2] with the rest of the ships, the Corinthians came to help from Leukas as quickly as they could, and Gongylos, one of the Corinthian commanders, started last with a single ship yet reached Syracuse first, just ahead of Gylippos, and when he found them on the point of holding an assembly about putting an end to the war, he stopped them and encouraged them by saying that there were more ships still approaching and Gylippos son of Kleandridas, a commander sent by the Lacedaemonians. The Syracusans regained their courage and immediately went out in full force to

meet Gylippos; for they found out that he was now very near. Gylippos, who was at that time seizing Ietai, a Sikel fort on his route, and forming for battle, arrived at Epipolai, and after ascending by way of Euryelos, exactly as the Athenians had at the start, he advanced on the Athenian fortifications along with the Syracusans. It happened that he came at that decisive moment when the double wall to the Great Harbor, seven or eight stades, had already been completed by the Athenians, except for a short part at the sea (they were still constructing this), and along the rest of the circuit toward Trogilos on the other shore, stones had already been set down for the major portion, and it had been left with some parts half-finished and others wholly finished. Syracuse came within this degree of danger.

[3] The Athenians were at first thrown into confusion when Gylippos and the Syracusans suddenly moved against them, but they formed ranks in opposition. After grounding his arms nearby, he sent over a herald who told them that if they were willing to leave Sicily within five days, taking their belongings, he was ready to make a truce. But they reacted contemptuously and sent him back without an answer. After this, they began preparing to fight against one another. And when Gylippos saw that the Syracusans were disorganized and not easily reorganized, he led the army back to the more level area. Nikias did not lead the Athenians against them but stayed inactive by his own wall. Since Gylippos realized that they were not advancing, he led his force off to the height called Temenites, and they bivouacked there. The following day, he brought most of his forces and stationed them across from the wall of the Athenians, to keep them from reinforcing other positions, and sent one contingent against the fort of Labdalon, seized it, and killed all those he caught inside; the place was not within view of the Athenians. And that same day an Athenian trireme blockading the Great Harbor was captured by the Syracusans.

[4] After these events, the Syracusans and their allies began building a single wall up from the city across Epipolai at a right angle, so that the Athenians, if unable to stop them, would have no further possibility of walling them off. At this point, the Athenians had gone up after finishing their wall to the sea, and Gylippos, since one part of the Athenian wall was weak, brought his forces up at night and advanced on it. Since the Athenians happened to be bivouacking outside it, they detected this and advanced on him; when he saw this, he quickly led his own men back

---

7.2. "Within this degree of danger": the sentence is certainly dramatic (cf. 3.49), but Connor 1984, pp. 187–88, exaggerates its implications and, consequently, its function of "jolting the reader" through foreknowledge.

again. After building that part higher, the Athenians themselves stood guard there and now assigned each place where the other allies were to guard the rest of the wall.

Nikias decided to fortify the place called Plemmyrion; this is a promontory opposite the city, whose projection makes the mouth of the Great Harbor narrow, and he had the impression that if it were fortified the importing of supplies would be easier; they would be blockading the harbor of the Syracusans at closer range and would not, as at present, make their naval attacks from the far corner of the harbor if the other fleet made any move. And he now gave his attention more to the war on the sea, since he saw that what was developing on land was less hopeful for them after Gylippos arrived. Accordingly, he brought over troops and the fleet and built three forts; most of the supplies were put inside, and the large boats and warships were now moored there as well. And then and there the condition of the crews first began to deteriorate; in addition to using scant sources of water which were not close by, whenever the sailors went out to collect firewood they were devastated by the Syracusan cavalry who controlled the countryside; for a third of their cavalry had been stationed at the town near the Olympieion because of the men on Plemmyrion, to keep them from marauding. Nikias also learned that the rest of the Corinthian ships were sailing up and sent twenty ships to watch for them, with orders to lie in wait at Lokroi, Rhegion, and the passage to Sicily.

[5] Gylippos continued both to build the wall across Epipolai, using the stones the Athenians had set in position for their own future use, and to lead out the Syracusans and their allies, constantly forming ranks in front of their wall; the Athenians would form ranks against them. When the opportunity seemed right to Gylippos, he began his onslaught; and they engaged and fought a battle in between the walls, where there was no way of using the Syracusan cavalry. After the Syracusans had been defeated and collected their dead under truce, and the Athenians had set up a trophy, Gylippos called the soldiers together and told them that the failure was not theirs but his: because of his battle formation, which he had placed too far within the walls, he had lost the benefit of their cavalry and javelin-throwers; accordingly, he would now lead them on again, and he urged them to adopt the attitude that they were not overmatched as to resources, while as to morale, if they as Peloponnesians and Dorians expected any-

---

7.4. "And then and there": Thucydides' evident belief that Plemmyrion was a bad decision is probably justified, see especially Green 1970, pp. 224–25. For the Olympieion, see 6.65n.

thing less than to vanquish Ionians, islanders, and assorted rabble and drive them out of the country, that would be intolerable.

[6] After this, when the opportunity came, he led them on again. As for Nikias and the Athenians, since they felt that even if the other side was unwilling to begin the fighting, it was not possible for them to look on as the wall was catching up with their own (for by now the other wall had all but passed the end of the Athenian wall, and once it did it was all one if they fought over and over and won or never fought), they accordingly went to meet the Syracusans. When Gylippos engaged with them, he led his hoplites farther from the walls than the last time, while placing his cavalry and javelin-throwers on the flank of the Athenians in the open area, where construction of both walls left off. And when the battle started, the cavalry attacked and routed the Athenian left wing, which was facing them; because of this, the rest of the army was beaten by the Syracusans as well and driven to the wall in disarray. During the following night, they overtook the construction of the Athenians and got beyond, so they themselves were no longer impeded by the Athenians and had also deprived them of any further possibility whatsoever, even if they won battles, of walling them off. [7] After this, the remaining twelve ships of the Corinthians, Ambraciots, and Leukadians, eluding the guard of the Athenians, sailed in under the command of Erasinides the Corinthian and helped the Syracusans with the rest of the cross-wall. And Gylippos traveled everywhere else in Sicily to raise forces by gathering them for service on both land and sea and at the same time winning over any city that was not zealous or had abstained from the war entirely. And more envoys, Syracusans and Corinthians, were dispatched to Lacedaemon and Corinth to get more men coming across in merchant ships, boats, or any other possible means, since the Athenians were also sending reinforcements. The Syracusans were manning their fleet and practicing so that they could also engage that way, and in general they were very encouraged.

[8] As for Nikias, since he was aware of this and saw a daily increase in enemy strength and his own difficulties, he sent to Athens, on many other occasions reporting events in detail and now in particular, since he thought they were in danger, and that unless they were either recalled or reinforced in no small way, as quickly as possible, there was no salvation. Because he was afraid that the men he sent would not report the facts, whether because of incompetence in speaking, failure of memory, or speaking to please the crowd, he wrote a letter in the belief that this was the best way for the Athenians, with their knowledge of his opinion nowhere obscured in transmission, to deliberate about the true situation. The emissaries left

to deliver the letter along with whatever they needed to say in person; around the camp, keeping watch now concerned him more than running avoidable risks. [9] At the end of the same summer, Euetos, an Athenian general, combined with Perdikkas to campaign against Amphipolis with numerous Thracians and did not capture the city but brought triremes around to the Strymon and blockaded it from the river, making Himeraion his base. And this summer ended.

[10] In the following winter, when the men from Nikias reached Athens, they stated what they had been told orally, answered any questions they were asked, and delivered the letter. The secretary of the city came forward and read it to the Athenians, divulging the following: [11] "Athenians, you know from many other letters what has been done previously; it is no less important now for you to deliberate with knowledge of our situation. For although we won most of the battles against the Syracusans, whom we were sent against, and built the fortifications where we are now, Gylippos the Lacedaemonian has come with forces from the Peloponnese, also from some cities in Sicily. He was beaten by us in the first battle, but on the next day, under pressure from numerous cavalry and javelin-throwers, we withdrew to the walls. Accordingly, after stopping the circumvallation we are now inactive because of enemy numbers, since we would not be able to use all our forces when guarding the walls is absorbing a good portion of the hoplites, and they have built a single wall past us, so that it is no longer possible for us to invest them unless someone were to attack this counterwall with a large force and seize it. And the result is that while supposedly besieging others, we are more in that situation ourselves, at least on land; for because of their cavalry, we cannot go any distance into the countryside either. [12] They have also sent envoys to the Peloponnesos for more troops, and Gylippos is going to the cities in Sicily to persuade any which are now neutral to join the war and bring still more land

7.8–15. There must have been such a letter, but its language is Thucydidean (as tailored for Nikias, see 6.9–14n), and so we have the same question of accuracy as with the speeches. Thucydides indicates that it was unusual for Nikias to write one; the phrase "many other *letters*" (7.11) might then use the term loosely (Classen/Steup VII *ad* 7.11.1). But Thucydides clearly wanted to describe the reasons for this particular letter—yet did he do so fully and credibly in 7.8? The document he presents seldom mentions a difficulty (actual or exaggerated) without attaching some form of self-justification; this was presumably what Nikias was afraid a messenger might omit. *Pace* Dover 1965 *ad* 7.14.4, "I considered it safer" clearly refers to safety for Nikias, not Athens; in light of 6.104 and 7.1, the effrontery of "without detection . . . before you act" is amazing.

and naval forces from the others if he can. For I am informed of their intention to make a combined attempt with land and naval forces, against our walls and on the sea.

"Let no one find it so strange that I say 'on the sea.' As they are fully informed, our fleet was in its prime, both for soundness of ships and well-being of crews, at the beginning; now the ships are soaked through, since they have already been in the sea for so long, and the crews have deteriorated. It is impossible to beach the ships and dry them out because of the enemy fleet, in numbers a match for us and even more, which keeps us in constant expectation that it will sail against us. They are maneuvering in full sight, the initiative to attack is theirs, and they have better possibilities of drying their ships; for they are not blockading anyone. [13] This would hardly be the case for us if we had a great numerical superiority in ships and were not, as now, compelled to use them all to stand guard; for if we let up on our vigilance even to the slightest degree, we will not have the supplies that even now we have difficulty in bringing in past their city. Our crews were and still are being devastated now, with the sailors being killed by cavalry, and this is why, because of gathering wood and pillaging and going a long way for water, while now that we have become evenly matched with our opponents the servants are deserting, and the mercenaries who came on board under duress are promptly going off to their cities, and the ones who were inspired in the first place by high pay and expected to make money rather than fight are going away after getting the unexpected sight of actual enemy resistance from the fleet and otherwise, some of them using the servants' desertion as a pretext, others any way they can (there is a lot of Sicily), and there are also those who go into business for themselves, send Hykkarian slaves on board in their stead by persuading the trierarchs, and deprive the fleet of its efficiency. [14] I am writing to men well aware that a crew's prime is brief and sailors who get the ship going and synchronize their rowing are few. And the most frustrating part is that I, the general, cannot prevent these things (for you are difficult types to govern), and that we have no source of additional ships' crews while many sources are available to our enemies, but what is in service and what has been expended both have to come out of what we arrived with; the cities now allied with us, Naxos and Katana, cannot help. And if there

7.13. "Using the servants' desertion as a pretext": i.e., pretending to pursue them, see Graham 1992, especially pp. 260–61.
7.14. "You are difficult": there is a degree of identification between the Athenians in the field and those at home, cf. 4.27 with note.

is one additional gain for our enemies, that the places in Italy which supply us, when they see our situation and your failure to send reinforcements, go over to their side, the war will have been ended by them without a battle, after we are reduced by siege.

"I might have been able to send you a different and pleasanter message but certainly not a more useful one, if you need full knowledge of the situation here to deliberate. At the same time, since I know your nature, which is to wish to hear what is the most pleasant but to make accusations later, if you get any outcome that is inconsistent with it, I considered it safer to reveal the truth. [15] And now make up your minds to this, that your soldiers and commanders merit no criticism from you regarding the original objectives of our expedition; but since all Sicily is united, and an additional army from the Peloponnesos is anticipated, decide right now, inasmuch as the forces here are not even capable of withstanding those already facing them and it is necessary either to recall them or send over just as many to reinforce them, both land and naval forces, also a considerable amount of money, and someone to succeed me, since I am unable to remain because of kidney disease. I claim a right to your forbearance; when I was fit, I served you well in many commands. But whatever you intend, do it immediately at the beginning of spring with no postponements, since the enemy will get some provisions in Sicily straightaway and more from the Peloponnesos less promptly but still, unless you pay attention, without detection, as in the past, or before you act."

[16] This was as much as Nikias' letter disclosed. When the Athenians heard it, they did not release Nikias from his command, but so that he would not face hardship alone in his bad health until other elected generals joined him they chose two additional men from those in the field, Menandros and Euthydemos, and they voted to send another land and naval force from both the Athenians on the register and the allies. And as his co-commanders they chose Demosthenes son of Alkisthenes and Eurymedon son of Thoukles. They sent Eurymedon to Sicily with ten ships immediately, around the winter solstice, bringing one hundred twenty silver talents and announcing that help would come, and that they would be attended to; [17] meanwhile Demosthenes stayed behind and prepared to make his voyage at the beginning of the spring, sending to the allies for forces and getting money, ships, and hoplites ready from home.

The Athenians also sent twenty ships around the Peloponnese to guard against anyone crossing from Corinth and the Peloponnesos to Sicily. For the Corinthians, thinking after their envoys arrived and reported the better situation in Sicily that they had not been untimely in their earlier dispatch of ships, were greatly encouraged and they were preparing to send off hoplites to Sicily in merchant ships, as were the Lacedaemonians from the rest of the Peloponnesos in the same fashion. The Corinthians were also manning twenty-five ships so that they might attempt a sea battle against the ships on guard at Naupaktos, and the Athenians would be less able to prevent their merchant ships from setting sail because of keeping guard against the triremes confronting them. [18] The Lacedaemonians were also preparing for an invasion of Attica, as they had already resolved and also with the Syracusans and Corinthians urging them on, after they had found out about the Athenian reinforcements for Sicily, so that these might actually be forestalled when an invasion took place. And Alcibiades was insistent in arguing that they fortify Dekeleia and not slacken in the war.

But above all something of vigor had gotten into the Lacedaemonians, because they thought that the Athenians, if involved in a double war, against themselves and the Sikeliots, would be easier to overthrow, and because they considered them the first to break the truce; in the previous war, the transgression had been more their own, both because the Thebans had entered Plataia during a truce and because, although it was stated in the previous agreements that no one was to take up arms if others were willing to go to arbitration, they themselves did not respond when the Athenians invited them to arbitrate. And therefore they considered that they had deservedly suffered misfortune, and they reflected on the disaster at Pylos and any others they had experienced. But now that the Athenians had set out from Argos and plundered parts of Epidauros and Prasiai and other places and were at the same time raiding from Pylos, and every time there were disagreements about any of the disputed points in the treaty they were unwilling to submit to arbitration when the Lacedaemonians invited them, at this point the Lacedaemonians considered that the very same unlawful conduct of which they had been guilty previously had turned around to implicate the Athenians in turn, and they were zealous about the war. And during this winter they sent around to the allies for iron and got ready the other tools for the fortification. At the same time, they were making their own provisions for dispatching reinforcements in merchant ships as well as requiring this of the rest of the Peloponnesians. And the winter ended, as did the eighteenth year of this war, which Thucydides recorded.

[19] As soon as the following spring began, the Lacedaemonians and their allies made their very earliest invasion of Attica; Agis son of Archidamos, king of the Lacedaemonians, was in command. They first plundered

the area of the plain, and then fortified Dekeleia, dividing up the work among the cities. Dekeleia is about one hundred twenty stades from the city of Athens and about the same distance or not much more from Boiotia. Visible as far as the city of Athens, the fort was built looking toward the plain and the best parts of the land, with the idea of despoiling them. The Peloponnesians and their allies, then, were building the fort; meanwhile, those in the Peloponnesos were dispatching the hoplites to Sicily in merchant ships during the same period, the Lacedaemonians selecting the best of the helots and the neodamodeis, six hundred hoplites combined and Ekkritos, a Spartiate, in command, and the Boiotians selecting three hundred hoplites, whose commanders were the Thebans Xenon and Nikon and the Thespian Hegesandros. Now these were the first to sail from Tainaron in Lakonia into the open sea; not long after them, the Corinthians sent out five hundred hoplites, some from Corinth itself, some Arkadians they had hired in addition, appointing Alexarchos, a Corinthian, as commander. The Sikyonians also, at the same time as the Corinthians, dispatched two hundred hoplites, whose commander was Sargeus, a Sikyonian. The twenty-five Corinthian ships manned during the winter stayed facing the twenty Athenian ships at Naupaktos up to the moment they got their hoplites in merchant ships clear of the Peloponnese; this was exactly why they were manned in the first place, so that the Athenians would not give their attention to the merchant ships rather than the triremes.

[20] Meanwhile the Athenians, at the time of the fortification of Dekeleia, as soon as spring began, sent thirty ships around the Peloponnese under the command of Charikles son of Apollodoros with instructions, when he arrived at Argos, to summon Argive hoplites to the ships in accordance with the alliance, and they dispatched Demosthenes to Sicily, just as they had intended, with fifty Athenian and five Chian ships, twelve hundred Athenian hoplites from the register, and as many islanders as it was possible to employ, helping themselves from the other allies, the subjects, wherever they found any items useful for war. His orders were first, while he was sailing over, to join Charikles in campaigning off Lakonia. And Demosthenes, after sailing ahead to Aegina, waited for any part of the force that had been left behind and also for Charikles to pick up the Argives.

[21] In Sicily, around the same part of the spring, Gylippos reached Syracuse bringing from the cities he won over the largest force he could get from each. And he called the Syracusans together and said that they should man as many ships as possible and brave a sea battle; as a result,

he hoped to accomplish something worth the risk to further the war. Hermokrates in particular backed him in persuading them not to lack the heart to attack with their ships, saying of the Athenians that their skill at sea was neither inherent nor permanent, but despite being more the landsmen than the Syracusans they had become seafarers because they were forced to by the Medes, and those who matched daring against daring men, such as the Athenians, appeared most troublesome to them. And now they themselves, just as the Athenians terrorized their neighbors, sometimes with no advantage in strength but attacking with boldness, would have the same effect on their opponents. He said that he was certain that the Syracusans, by unexpectedly daring to stand up to the Athenian navy, would gain out of their consternation over this to a greater extent than the Athenians would damage Syracusan inexperience with their skill; they must come to the test of their fleet, then, and not shrink from it. So the Syracusans, persuaded by Gylippos, Hermokrates, and whoever else, were eager for the sea battle and began manning their ships.

[22] When the fleet was prepared, Gylippos led out the entire army by night, intending to make a land attack on the forts at Plemmyrion, while at the same time, by a prearranged signal, thirty-five Syracusan triremes sailed to attack from the Great Harbor and forty-five sailed around from the smaller one where the shipyard was, wanting to join forces with those inside and at the same time sail against Plemmyrion, so that the Athenians would be thrown into confusion on both fronts. The Athenians, hurriedly manning sixty ships to meet them, began a battle with twenty-five ships against the thirty-five ships in the Great Harbor while going to meet those sailing around from the shipyard with the remainder. And they immediately fought a sea battle in front of the mouth of the Great Harbor and for a long time held out against each other, one side wishing to force the entrance and the other to block it. [23] Meanwhile Gylippos, since the Athenians had gone down to the sea and turned their attention toward the sea battle, took the initiative by suddenly assaulting the forts at dawn, seized the biggest one first, and then the two smaller ones, whose garrisons did not stay when they saw the biggest one captured easily. And as many men as escaped from the first one that was captured to the boats and a merchant ship were brought back to the camp, with some difficulty; for they were pursued by a single trireme, a good sailer, since the Syracusans in the harbor were winning at sea; but when the two smaller forts were captured, it happened that now the Syracusans were already losing, and the men who were escaping sailed past more easily. For after the Syracusan ships that

were fighting in front of the harbor mouth had overpowered the Athenians ships, they sailed into the harbor in no sort of order, and by getting tangled up with one another they handed over the victory to the Athenians. They routed both these and the ones whom they were losing to in the harbor at first. And they sank eleven Syracusan ships and killed most of their men, except those from three ships, whom they took prisoner; of their own ships, three were destroyed. After beaching the Syracusan ships and setting up a trophy on the little island opposite Plemmyrion, they withdrew to their camp.

[24] While this was how the Syracusans fared in the sea battle, they held the forts at Plemmyrion and set up three trophies for these; they destroyed one of the two captured later but repaired and garrisoned the other two. In the capture of the forts, many men were killed or taken prisoner, and many goods were seized overall; for since the Athenians were using the forts as a storage place, there were many goods belonging to the merchants and food inside, also many belongings of the trierarchs, since even the sails and other equipment of forty triremes had been left there as well as three beached ships. But the capture of Plemmyrion did the Athenians the greatest and very major damage; sailing in to bring provisions was no longer safe (for the Syracusans hindered this by lying in wait with their ships, and it was now by fighting that shipments came in), and in other respects too it brought consternation and despondency to the army.

[25] After this the Syracusans sent out twelve ships with Agatharchos, a Syracusan, in command. One went to the Peloponnesos, carrying envoys to state that they were hopeful about their own situation and urge that even more warfare be carried on over there; the eleven ships sailed to Italy, since they found out that boats full of goods for the Athenians were sailing there. They encountered them, destroyed most, and in Kaulonian territory also burned timber for building ships, which had been in readiness for the Athenians. After this they went to Lokroi, and while they were at anchor, one of the merchant ships from the Peloponnese sailed in carrying Thespian hoplites; after taking them on board their ships, the Syracusans sailed along the coast toward home. The Athenians, watching for them at Megara with twenty ships, captured one ship with its men but could not take the rest, who instead escaped to Syracuse.

There was also skirmishing around the stakes which the Syracusans had planted in the sea in front of the old shipyards, so that they could have their ships moored within, and the Athenians could not sail up and damage them by ramming. The Athenians had brought a ship up to them weighing ten thousand talents, with wooden towers and bulwarks, and from small boats they attached them to winches and pulled them up or broke them, or they sawed them off by diving down. The Syracusans threw missiles from the shipyards, the Athenians threw them from the merchant ship in return, and finally the Athenians removed most of the stakes. The hidden part of the stockade was the most troublesome; for there were some stakes that they had planted with no projection above the water, so that sailing up was perilous, in case someone punctured his ship, as on a rock, without seeing them first. But hired divers descended and sawed off these as well. Nevertheless, the Syracusans planted stakes again. And they devised many other things against one another, such as was natural with the camps close together and in confrontation, and skirmished and used stratagems of all sort. The Syracusans also sent Corinthian, Ambracian, and Lacedaemonian envoys to the cities to report the capture of Plemmyrion, and that concerning the sea battle they had not been beaten by the might of the enemy as much as by their own disarray, and to declare that they were hopeful and ask them to help with ships and troops, since the Athenians were expected with more forces as well, and if they could anticipate these by destroying the army on hand first, they would have finished off the war. And these were the things they were doing in Sicily.

[26] Demosthenes meanwhile, after the army of reinforcements he was to bring to Sicily was assembled, put out from Aigina, sailed to the Peloponnesos, and joined forces with Charikles and the thirty Athenian ships. And after bringing Argive hoplites on board them, they sailed against Lakonian territory. First they ravaged part of Epidauros Limara, and then, after landing at an area in Lakonian territory opposite Kythera, where the sanctuary of Apollo is, they ravaged parts of the land and fortified a certain isthmus-like place, so that the helots of the Lacedaemonians could desert to it and at the same time raids for plunder could be made from there, just as from Pylos. And Demosthenes, immediately after he had helped to occupy the place, sailed along the coast to Corcyra so that after picking up allies there as well he could make the voyage to Sicily as quickly as possible; but Charikles, after waiting until he had completed the fortifications and leaving a garrison, then went home along with his thirty ships at the same time as the Argives.

7.25. On the obscurity of some points in the account of Athenian efforts against the stakes, see *HCT* IV *ad* 25.6; the enormous weight of the (merchant) ship must have served somehow to assist the winching operation.

[27] Also during this same summer, there arrived at Athens thirteen hundred peltasts from the Dian tribe of knife-wearing Thracians who were supposed to sail with Demosthenes to Sicily. Since they arrived too late, the Athenians were inclined to send them back to where they had come from in Thrace. To keep them for the war out of Dekeleia seemed expensive; each was receiving a drachma a day. For after Dekeleia was used as a fort, first by the entire army during this summer, and later occupied by garrisons from the cities over successive periods, it did the Athenians much harm and by the destruction of property and the ruin of the population was foremost in damaging their affairs. For previously, because the invasions were short, they did not prevent their benefiting from the land the rest of the time. But since at this time they became a continuous occupation, sometimes also with superior forces invading and sometimes with the garrison, a match for themselves, overrunning the land out of need and pillaging, also with Agis the king of the Lacedaemonians present, who did not consider the war an incidental matter, the Athenians were suffering great damage. They were deprived of all the land, more than twenty thousand slaves, most of them artisans, had run away, and all their herds and draft animals were lost. And since the cavalry sallied forth every day making raids on Dekeleia and keeping watch throughout the country, the horses also were going lame on the hard ground and because they were constantly worn out, and some were getting wounded. [28] Also, the shipment of provisions from Euboia, which had previously been quicker over land from Oropos by way of Dekeleia became expensive by sea around Sounion by sea. The city needed to have everything alike imported, and instead of being a city it existed as a fortress.

For on the battlements the Athenians were becoming exhausted by standing guard, in relays by day, all except the cavalry by night, some

7.27–30. It is very Thucydidean that a digression should suspensefully separate the arrival of the Thracians from the ghastly account of their actions in 7.29–30. Dover (*HCT* IV, pp. 400–4) discusses the confusing chronological shifts within the digression (which add much to its rhetorical effectiveness) and considers—but doubts—the possibility of interpolation. In 7.27, the translation of "sometimes also with superior forces . . . out of need" is conjectural; according to *HCT* IV *ad* 7.27.4, "the text is certainly corrupt," but at least, unlike Dover, I do not find Thucydides' brief shift to the garrison's "need" (an example of *anangke* apparently missed by Ostwald 1988, who discusses similar passages on p. 10) strange. Thucydides has enclosed one set piece within another (see preceding note); juxtaposing the sufferings of Athens with those of Mykalessos, he indicates the ultimate Athenian responsibility for both. "Every form . . . prevailed": see 1.109n.

under arms somewhere, others on the wall, summer and winter. And it afflicted them most that they had two wars at the same time and had developed such a passion for victory as anyone who heard about it would have disbelieved before it happened, that when they themselves were under siege because of a Peloponnesian encampment they did not even pull out of Sicily but were in turn, in the same fashion, laying siege to Syracuse, a city that all by itself was no smaller than Athens, that in their strength and daring they did something so astounding for the Hellenes—inasmuch as some of these thought they would survive a year, some two, and no one more than three if the Peloponnesians invaded their land—as coming to Sicily in the seventeenth year after the first invasion, already worn out by the war, and taking on another war no smaller than the one facing them from the Peloponnesos. For these reasons, and because of Dekeleia's doing them heavy damage, and since other great expenditures were besetting them, they became crippled financially and at this time, instead of tribute, they exacted from their subjects a twentieth of everything that went by sea, supposing that this way they would have more revenues coming in. For their expenses were not what they were in the past but became greater to the same extent that the war was greater and revenues were disappearing.

[29] As for the Thracians who were too late for Demosthenes, they then, unwilling to spend money because of their current lack, immediately sent them away, adding Dieitrephes as an escort and giving instructions that, as part of his voyage along the coast (they went by the Euripos), he get them to harm the enemy if at all possible. He disembarked them at Tanagra and did some quick pillaging, sailed from Chalkis in Euboea across the Euripos at nightfall, and after landing them in Boiotia he led them against Mykalessos. During the night, he bivouacked undetected near the shrine of Hermes, about sixteen stades from Mykalessos, and at daybreak he assaulted the city, which is not large, and captured it by falling upon people who were off guard and without suspicion that anyone would come so far in from the sea and attack them, with their wall negligible, partly fallen down, partly built low, and their gates open in addition because of their absence of fear. Rushing into Mykalessos, the Thracians plundered the houses and shrines and butchered the people, sparing neither the eldest nor the youngest, but all in their turn, anyone they encountered, killing children and women and, for good measure, the pack-animals and anything else they saw with life in it. For the Thracians, in keeping with barbarians of that particular stripe, are most murderous in times of confidence. And on this occasion general turmoil and every form of destruction prevailed, and falling on a school for boys, the largest

around and one the boys had just entered, they cut them all down; this disaster, both unimagined and terrible beyond any other, was second to none befalling the whole city.

[30] When the Thebans found out, they came to the rescue, and catching the Thracians when they had moved on without going far they stripped them of their booty and pursued them in a panic to the Euripos, where the boats that brought them were anchored. Most of those they killed were in the act of embarking, since they were unversed in swimming, and the men in the boats anchored them out of reach of bowshot when they saw what was happening on land; for at other points in their withdrawal, by running out and regrouping in their native fashion, they actually made a decent defense against the Theban cavalry, their first attackers, and few of them were killed while doing this. A fair number, caught in the act of pillaging, were also killed in the town itself. In all, two hundred and fifty of the Thracians were killed out of thirteen hundred. Of the Thebans and others who came with them to help, about twenty of the cavalry and hoplites combined were killed as well as Skirphondas, one of the Theban Boiotarchs; a fair number of the Mykalessians were gone. This was the way events turned out at Mykalessos, which in proportion to its size experienced a fate as pitiable as any in the war.

[31] As for Demosthenes, now sailing off to Corcyra after building the fort in Lakonia, he destroyed a boat anchored at Pheia in Elis, which had on board Corinthian hoplites to be brought over to Sicily, but the men got away and sailed later, after obtaining another boat. And after this Demosthenes, on his arrival at Zakynthos and Kephallenia, took hoplites on board, sent for some from the Messenians of Naupaktos, and crossed over to Akarnania on the opposite mainland at Alyzeia and Anaktorion, which was in their possession. In the course of these activities he encountered Eurymedon, who had been sent to Sicily back during the winter with the money for the army and was now on his return voyage, and who reported among other things that he learned about after he had already set sail, the capture of Plemmyrion by the Syracusans. Konon, who was in command at Naupaktos, joined them as well, reporting that the twenty-five Corinthian ships stationed opposite his were not backing down but ready to fight a sea battle; accordingly, he asked them to send ships, since his eighteen

7.31. Konon had a distinguished, even spectacular career as an admiral after this war but is only mentioned here by Thucydides; it is ironic that a request symptomatic of the relative decline of the Athenian navy should come from this man (and apparently there was good reason for the request, see 7.34).

were incapable of fighting the opposing twenty-five. Demosthenes and Eurymedon accordingly sent Konon ten ships, the best sailers they had among their own ships, to add to those at Naupaktos, and gathered their own forces in readiness for the expedition, Eurymedon sailing to Corcyra, where he ordered fifteen ships manned and enlisted hoplites (for, in full accordance with his election to the joint command with Demosthenes, he now reversed his course), and Demosthenes gathering slingers and javelin-throwers from the area of Akarnania.

[32] As for the envoys from Syracuse who had gone to the cities after the capture of Plemmyrion, successfully made their case, and were about to bring back the army they had collected, Nikias got word of them in advance and sent to the Sikels who controlled the routes and were allies, the Kentoripes, Alikyaians, and others, to tell them not to let the enemy past but join forces and prevent them from getting through; they would not attempt it anywhere else, since the Akragantines had not allowed passage through their land. And when the Sikeliots were already on their way, the Sikels, just as the Athenians requested, set an ambush at three points, suddenly attacked them off guard, and killed about eight hundred and all the envoys except one, the Corinthian; he escorted those who escaped, about fifteen hundred, into Syracuse.

[33] Around the same time, the Kamarinaians also arrived with five hundred hoplites, three hundred javelin-throwers, and three hundred archers as reinforcements. Also the Geloans sent a fleet numbering five ships and four hundred javelin-throwers and two hundred cavalry. For by now almost all Sicily, not the Akragantines (they took neither side) but all the others who had previously looked on, united with the Syracusans and were sending help. As for the Syracusans, since they had had a disaster among the Sikels they held off from attacking the Athenians immediately, while Demosthenes and Eurymedon, with their army from Corcyra and the mainland now ready, crossed the Ionian Sea to the tip of Iapygia with all their forces. Setting out from there, they put in at the Choirades Islands of Iapygia and took on board around one hundred fifty Iapygian javelin-throwers of the Messapian tribe, and after renewing the old friendship with Artas, the local chief who had furnished them with the javelin-throwers, they arrived at Metapontion in Italy. After they persuaded the Metapontines to send along three hundred javelin-throwers in accordance with their alliance and took these on board, they sailed along the coast to Thouria. And they found that those hostile to the Athenians had recently been driven out in civil war; since they wanted to assemble the whole army there and review it, in case anyone had been left behind, and persuade the

Thourians to join the campaign as enthusiastically as possible, even, since they had had this sort of luck, to have the same enemies and friends as the Athenians, they waited at Thouria and attended to this.

[34] Around the same time, the Peloponnesians in the twenty-five ships that had been at anchor facing the Athenians at Naupaktos on account of the transports to Sicily by merchant ships, after preparing for battle and manning still more ships so that they were only a little fewer than the Attic ships, anchored off Erineos in Achaia in Rhypaian territory. And since the place where they were anchored was crescent-shaped, the land army of both Corinthians and local allies, which had come for support, was drawn up on each end, and the ships occupied the center to block it off; the commander of the fleet was Polyanthes, a Corinthian. The Athenians sailed out of Naupaktos to meet them with thirty-three ships, whose commander was Diphilos. The Corinthians stayed inactive at first, then, when their signal was raised at what seemed the right moment, they sailed at the Athenians and began the battle. For a long time, they held out against each other. Three of the Corinthian ships were sunk, and none of the Athenians was sunk outright, but about seven were put out of commission, rammed head-on and shattered in the bow by the Corinthian ships, which had their prows thickened for just this purpose. After a battle indecisive enough that both sides claimed victory, but the Athenians still got control of the wrecks because of a wind driving them out to sea and no further advance by the Corinthians, they separated, and there was no pursuit nor prisoners taken on either side; for the Corinthians and Peloponnesians easily got to safety because they were fighting next to shore, and no Athenian ship was sunk. After the Athenians sailed back to Naupaktos, the Corinthians immediately set up a trophy as though they were the winners, because they had disabled more enemy ships, and since they thought they had not been beaten for the same reason that the Athenians thought they had not won; the Corinthians supposed themselves victorious if not decisively beaten, and the Athenians thought themselves beaten if not decisively victorious. When the Peloponnesians had sailed away, and the land army had dispersed, the Athenians also set up their own trophy in Achaia, about twenty stades from Erineos, where the Corinthians had been anchored, as though they had won. And this was how the sea battle ended.

[35] After the Thourians had been prevailed on to join the campaign with seven hundred hoplites and three hundred javelin-throwers, Demosthenes and Eurymedon ordered the fleet to sail along the coast to the territory of Kroton, and they themselves, after a review of the whole army at the Sybaris river, advanced through the territory of Thouria. And when

they reached the Hylias river and the Krotoniates sent word that if the army went through their land it would be without their consent, they came down and bivouacked by the sea and the mouth of the Hylias; their ships met them at that spot. The next day, they embarked and sailed along the coast, putting in at the cities, apart from Lokroi, until they reached Petra in the territory of Rhegion.

[36] Meanwhile, when the Syracusans found out about their approach, they wanted to put their ships to another test as well as the rest of their forces on land, which they had been gathering together for just this purpose, wanting to take the initiative before their arrival. And they prepared the rest of their fleet in ways that they observed, in light of the previous sea battle, would give them an advantage, and while shortening their prows they made them more solid, attached thick anchor-blocks to the prows, and ran braces underneath from these to the sides, up to six cubits long on both the inside and outside; in just this way the Corinthians had re-equipped their ships at the prows when they fought the Athenian ships at Naupaktos. For the Syracusans thought that they, when facing Athenian ships that had not been similarly rebuilt but were light in the prow on account of their making less use of head-on ramming than ramming by sailing round, would be at no disadvantage, and that in the Great Harbor the sea battle, involving many ships in little room, would be in their favor; in head-on ramming, they would shatter them at the prows by striking with thick solid rams against weak, hollow ones. For the Athenians would have no possibility of either sailing round or sailing through, and these were the skills they relied on most; they themselves would do their best to deny them sailing through, while the close quarters would prevent them sailing round. And they themselves would make the fullest use of what had formerly appeared incompetence on their pilots' part, crashing head-on; for if the Athenians were shoved out of position, they would have no possibility of backing water anywhere except toward the shore, a short distance to a short part of it, where this camp was; the Syracusans would control the rest of the harbor. And if forced back anywhere, they would be crowded into a small space, the same space for all of them, and thrown into confusion as they ran into one another (which was just what hurt the Athenians most in all the sea fighting, since unlike the Syracusans they did not have the whole harbor for backing water); sailing round into open water

7.36. Just as Thucydides (4.32) previews the tactics that will lead to the startling Spartan surrender at Pylos, here he previews those that will result in disaster for the Athenians.

would be impossible, since they themselves controlled both their entrance from the sea and also their backing out, especially since Plemmyrion would be hostile to them and the mouth of the harbor was not large.

[37] After making these innovations to favor their own skills and strengths, and at the same time with increased confidence now as a result of the previous sea battle, the Syracusans began their simultaneous attacks on land and sea. Gylippos, a little in advance, brought out the land forces in the city and led them up to the wall of the Athenians all along the part facing the city; and from the Olympian sanctuary, all the hoplites there and the Syracusan cavalry and light-armed advanced on the wall from the other side; after this, the Syracusan and allied ships immediately sailed out to attack. When the Athenians, who at first thought that they were going to make an attempt with their land forces alone, saw the ships bearing down as well, they were in a state of confusion, some stationing themselves on the walls and in front of the walls to face the attackers there, some going out to meet the large cavalry force and the javelin-throwers rapidly advancing from the Olympian sanctuary, others manning the ships and coming down to the beach to help, and once they were manned seventy-five ships met the attack; there were about eighty Syracusan ships. [38] After they had tested one another for much of the day by sailing ahead and backing water, and neither was able to make any gains worth mentioning, except for the Syracusans sinking one or two Athenian ships, they separated; the land forces withdrew from the walls at the same time.

The next day, the Syracusans stayed inactive, giving no indication of what they would do next; Nikias, seeing that the fighting at sea had become evenly balanced and expecting the other side to attack again, compelled the trierarchs to repair their ships wherever there was damage, and he anchored merchant ships in front of the stockade, which he had planted in the sea in front of their ships in place of a closed harbor. In positioning the merchant ships, he left intervals of up to two hundred feet between them so that if any ship came under pressure it would have a safe refuge and a way to sail back out without interference. In making these preparations the Athenians spent the whole day until nightfall.

[39] The next day, at an earlier hour but with the same form of attack on both land and sea, the Syracusans engaged the Athenians, and facing

7.39. See Marchant 1919, p. 157 and Powell 1937, p. 103 (contra, Hornblower 1987, p. 94, Stroud 1994, p. 270, n. 6) for the possible wordplay on Aríston and "best" (*áristos*); the word for "midday meal" (*áriston*) should then be involved as well.

each other with their ships in the same manner they again continued to test one another far into the day, right up until Ariston son of Pyrrhichos, a Corinthian, who was the best pilot on the Syracusan side, persuaded their commanders to send word to those in charge in the city asking them to move the commercial market down to the shore as quickly as possible and compel everyone to bring whatever edible provisions they had and sell them there, so that the sailors, after disembarking among them, could have their midday meal right beside the ships and after a short time, against all expectations, attack the Athenians again on the same day. [40] They were convinced and sent a messenger, the market was set up, and the Syracusans, suddenly backing up, sailed back to the city, immediately disembarked, and ate their midday meal right there; as for the Athenians, believing that the others had acknowledged their inferiority by backing up to the city, they disembarked at their leisure and began to occupy themselves in various ways as well as over their meal, certain that they would have no more fighting that day. But the Syracusans suddenly manned their ships and sailed against them again; in total confusion, most of them without food, they embarked in complete disorder and finally just got under way. For a certain time they stayed apart, watching one another; then the Athenian decision was not to delay and burden themselves with fatigue of their own making but attack as quickly as possible, and amid cheers they bore down and started the battle.

The Syracusans, meeting their charge and using their ships for ramming just as they had planned, shattered extensive areas of the outriggers on the Athenian ships with their ramming equipment, and javelin-throwers from their decks inflicted serious damage on the Athenians, but it was the Syracusans sailing around in small boats who did much heavier damage still by slipping in among the banks of oars, coming next to the ships, and throwing javelins at the crews from their boats. [41] Finally, by putting all their effort into this style of fighting, the Syracusans were victorious, and the routed Athenians went past the merchant ships into their own anchorage for refuge. The Syracusan ships pursued them as far as the merchant ships. At that point, the dolphin-bearing spars over the channels, suspended from the merchant ships, halted them; two Syracusan ships, elated by victory, came right up to the merchant ships and were destroyed, and one was captured with its crew. After sinking seven Athenian ships, crippling a large number, taking many of the men prisoner, and killing the others, the Syracusans withdrew, and they set up a trophy for both sea battles and now felt complete confidence that they were by far the stronger at sea, and it was their opinion that they would also overpower the forces on land.

So they made preparations to renew the attack once more on both elements; [42] but at this point, Demosthenes and Eurymedon arrived with the reinforcements from Athens, about seventy-three ships including the foreign ones, around five thousand hoplites, both their own and from the allies, no few javelin-throwers, slingers, and archers, both barbarians and Hellenes, and sufficient equipment in all other respects. And the instantaneous result among the Syracusans and their allies was no little consternation over whether they would ever reach the point of deliverance from danger when they saw that a force as large or almost as large as the first, the fortification of Dekeleia not withstanding, had come as reinforcements, and that the power of the Athenians was obviously great in every respect; among the original Athenian forces, considering their troubles, a certain degree of vigor resulted.

Demosthenes, seeing how matters stood and considering it out of the question to waste time and have the same experience as Nikias (for although Nikias was terrifying when he first arrived, when he did not immediately attack Syracuse but spent the winter at Katana he was despised, and Gylippos took the initiative away from him by arriving from the Peloponnesos with forces that the Syracusans would not even have sent for if he had attacked right away; for believing in their own adequacy, they would only have learned their inferiority when they had been completely walled, so that even if they had sent for such forces these would no longer have been as helpful), accordingly took this all into account and recognized that, in the present situation as well, he himself was most of all formidable to his opponents on the very first day, and he wanted to exploit the shock that prevailed because of his army as quickly as possible. Since he also saw that the cross-wall of the Syracusans, which was how they had

7.42. The long parenthesis presents interesting and perhaps unique difficulties. The switch to finite verbs within indirect statement should mark it as an authorial interjection (Donini 1964 and *HCT* IV *ad* 7.42.3); but why should Thucydides insert an observation notoriously hard to reconcile both with his overall account and with 2.65 (see *HCT, loc. cit*) and at the same time make this observation essential to Demosthenes' plan of action? The parenthesis is in fact wholly appropriate to Demosthenes as he quickly surveys an alarming situation and single-mindedly (and ironically, see 7.86) wishes to avoid having "the same experience as Nikias"; Schneider 1974, pp. 55–56 and Connor 1984, pp. 191–92 believe that Thucydides has blended his own and his character's judgment. Since this seems to me illogical, I venture the suggestion that Thucydides used finite verbs in the parenthesis for emphasis, not expecting the contents to be attributed to the author accordingly: an extreme example of Thucydides' confidence that the reader will follow his train of thought? Possibly comparable boldness within indirect statement occurs in 8.48,

prevented the Athenians from walling them off, was a single wall and, once anyone got control first of the ascent of Epipolai and then of the camp on top, easy to capture (since there would be no resistance), he felt impelled to try the attack and considered this his most direct means of settling the campaign; either, by succeeding, he would capture Syracuse or he would bring the army home and not needlessly wear out the Athenians on the expedition as well as the entire city.

Accordingly, the Athenians first went out and ravaged the land of the Syracusans as far as the Anapos, dominating with their forces just as at the beginning, on both land and sea (for except from the cavalry and javelin-throwers in the Olympieion, the Syracusans presented no opposition on either element). [43] Demosthenes next decided to make an initial attempt on the cross-fortifications with siege engines. But after he saw his engines burned as he brought them up by the enemy defending from the wall, and they were also driven back at every point in attacking with the rest of their army, he resolved to waste no more time, and after getting the consent of Nikias and the others who shared the command he did as he had intended and made the attempt on Epipolai.

Since it seemed impossible to make both the approach and the ascent without detection during the day, he ordered rations for five days, took all the stone-workers and carpenters, the remaining force of archers, and everything else needed for building walls in case of success, and after the first night watch he along with Eurymedon and Menandros led out the entire army and proceeded to Epipolai, while Nikias remained behind in the fortifications. After they reached it by Euryelos, exactly where the earlier army had first made its ascent, they passed the Syracusan guards undetected and advanced on the Syracusan fort in that area, captured it, and killed some of the garrison; but most of the men immediately fled to the camps, the three on Epipolai below the walls (one for the Syracusans, one for the other Sikeliots, one for the allies), and brought news of the incursion, and they also warned the six hundred Syracusans who were the

---

where the nominative *akritoi* is a drastic anacoluthon, apparently for emphasis (see Classen/Steup VIII and *HCT* V *ad* 8.48.6). Cf. 8.43n. For consideration and convincing refutation of the ingenious theory that the "parenthesis" is actually a fragment of the fourth-century historian Philistos incorporated into Thucydides' text, see *HCT* V, p. 425, n. 1.

7.43. "He did as he had intended": cf. the first sentence of 4.33. "The remaining force of bowmen (?)": a very puzzling phrase, cf. Marchant 1919, p. 161, *HCT* IV *ad* 7.43.2, Allison 1989, p. 115.

advance guards on that part of Epipolai. They came right to the defense, and Demosthenes and the Athenians met them and routed them, although they made a spirited resistance. These men immediately advanced straight ahead, to let the impulse that filled them set the pace for accomplishing their mission; others at the outset were seizing the Syracusan cross-wall, whose guards did not make a stand, and tearing off the battlements. The Syracusans and their allies and Gylippos and his men came to the defense from the outposts, attacked the Athenians while in a state of shock over this bold action at night, and at first gave way under their pressure. And as the Athenians drove forward, now in increased disorder since they had the upper hand and wanted to push through all the forces of the enemy that had not yet been engaged, lest these in turn rally if their own momentum faltered, the Boiotians were the first to stand up to them, and when they charged they routed the Athenians and put them to flight.

[44] And it was at this point that the Athenians fell into great disorder and difficulty, in a sequence of events whose details were not easy to learn from either side. For things are clearer in the daytime, yet each person present is limited to what he barely knows of them in his immediate area; and in a night battle, the only one in this war at least that actually took place between two large armies, how could anyone know anything clearly? There was bright moonlight, but they saw one another as is normal by moonlight, catching sight of a form in front of them and not trusting the recognition of a friend. In a limited space, a good many hoplites from both sides were milling around. And the Athenians included those already defeated and those who were still advancing unbeaten in their first onrush; and in addition a large part of the rest of their army had either just gotten up or was still on the way up to join in, and so did not know which contingent to move toward. For by now, because of the rout that had occurred, all their front ranks were in a state of confusion and difficult to distinguish among the shouts. The Syracusans and their allies were both cheering each other on in victory and doing a great deal of yelling, since there was no other way to give orders in the night, and at the same time they were confronting attackers. And the Athenians were looking for their own men and

---

7.44. Although Thucydides' complaint about the difficulty of getting information is undoubtedly genuine, what follows emphasizes instead the terrible circumstances for the Athenians; the problems of seeing and hearing are, once again, reminiscent of Sphakteria (which began as a night attack). A final irony is the confusion caused by "friendly" Dorian speech; cf. Demosthenes' *exploitation* of this in 3.112, 4.3, and 4.41.

regarding whatever came from the opposite direction as hostile, even a friend from among those now turning around in flight, and by making constant demands for the password, since they had no other means of recognition, they caused a great uproar among themselves when they all demanded it at the same time, and moreover they disclosed it to their enemies; but they were not likewise getting to know that of their opponents, who less often failed to know one another, because they were winning and had not gotten scattered; and consequently, if a superior force on the one side encountered enemies, these got away from them by virtue of knowing their password, but when they themselves had no answer they were cut down. And the singing of the paian harmed them, first and last; for it confounded them by sounding much the same coming from either side. When the Argives or the Corcyreans or any Dorian contingent among the Athenians sang the paian it brought terror to the Athenians, just as the enemy did. And so in the end, colliding with their own men once they had fallen into disorder, friend against friend and citizen against fellow-citizen, they not only got into a panic but came to blows with one another and were separated with difficulty. And as they were pursued, many threw themselves from the heights and died, since the way down from Epipolai was narrow, and after others made their escape and got down to level ground the majority, especially those from the earlier expedition, got through to the camp safely because of greater familiarity with the countryside, while some of those who came later missed the roads and wandered over the countryside; the Syracusan cavalry rode around and killed them when it was daytime.

[45] The next day the Syracusans set up two trophies, at the approach to Epipolai and also on the spot where the Boiotians first made their stand, and the Athenians recovered their dead under truce. No few were killed, both their own men and allies, yet the arms captured were even more than accounted for by the bodies; for some of those driven to leap from the heights without their armor died, but others survived. [46] After this the Syracusans, with their confidence restored once more to its former level because of their unexpected success, sent Sikanos with fifteen ships to Akragas, where there was civil war, to bring over the city if he could, while Gylippos went again to the other parts of Sicily to raise more troops, since he was hopeful about taking the Athenian walls by storm after events on Epipolai had turned out as they did.

[47] Meanwhile, the Athenian generals deliberated regarding the disaster that had occurred and the complete debilitation that prevailed in the army. They saw that they were not succeeding in their undertakings, and also that the soldiers were oppressed by the prolonged stay; for they were

afflicted by disease from a double cause, since the time of year was the one when people particularly fall sick, and at the same time the location of the camp was marshy and difficult to live in, and it was clear to them in general that there was absolutely no hope. Demosthenes' opinion, therefore, was that they should not stay any longer, and just as he had intended in risking the attack on Epipolai, since that had failed he voted to depart and not waste time while it was still possible to cross the sea and use at least the superiority from the ships of the later expedition. He said that it was also more beneficial to the city to wage war against opponents building a fort in their own country than against the Syracusans, who were no longer easy to conquer; moreover, it was not reasonable to spend a lot of money to no purpose by prolonging the siege.

[48] So these were the sentiments of Demosthenes, but Nikias, although he also thought their situation was terrible, did not want either that their weakness be revealed by an announcement or that they be reported to the enemy as plainly and publicly voting to withdraw; whenever they wanted to do so, they would be much less likely to avoid detection. There was also the fact that the situation of the enemy, according to the information he possessed more abundantly than anyone else, gave hopeful signs of becoming worse than their own if they went on with the siege. For they would wear them out through shortage of supplies, especially since with their present fleet they now had fuller control of the sea, and owing to a party in Syracuse that wanted to put the Athenians in control he had received messages urging him not to pull out. With this information, he still in actuality considered both alternatives and kept weighing them, but in his open declaration at that time he said that he would not lead the army away; for he knew very well that the Athenians would find this action on their part unacceptable, that they had left without their vote; and those voting over their fate would not be men who would judge the situation by seeing it firsthand, like themselves, rather than hearing about it in

7.47. In 425, it had been Demosthenes whom Athenian generals accused of wasting money on an encampment in enemy territory (4.3); his reference to Dekeleia now is reminiscent of Spartan reactions then (4.6).

7.48. To his succinct condemnation of Nikias' self-serving priorities, Dover (1965 *ad* 7.48.4) added the comment (omitted from *HCT* IV) that the aristocratic Thucydides "took a more lenient view of Nikias . . . than we ought to take." If Thucydides expresses no criticism, neither does he indicate that Nikias' fears of a biased Athenian public are justified, as he does in Alcibiades' case (note the odd parallelism between Nikias and Alcibiades).

castigations by others, but who instead, whatever slanders any fine speaker might bring forward, would be persuaded accordingly. And many of those who were present as soldiers, in fact, he said, the majority, who were now raising the cry that they were in an awful plight, would raise the opposite cry when they got home, that the generals left because they turned traitor for money. Therefore, he at least, knowing the Athenian character, had no wish to die unjustly, on a shameful charge, at the hands of the Athenians, rather than taking his chances as an individual and meeting his end, if he must, at the hands of the enemy. He also said that, despite all, the situation of the Syracusans was even worse than theirs; for since they were paying to support mercenaries spending at the same time on guardposts, and furthermore had already been maintaining a fleet for a year, they were in difficulty and would be at a loss yet; they had already spent two thousand talents and were in debt for still more, and if they lost anything at all from their present forces, their cause would be ruined, since it was upheld by pay rather than by obligation to serve, as theirs was. Therefore, he said, they should wear them down by continuing the siege and not go away defeated because of money, in which they had marked superiority.

[49] Nikias said this much with firmness, since he had accurate information about the situation in Syracuse, their lack of money and the fact that a large element there wanted the Athenians in control and was communicating with him to keep him from pulling out, and at the same time he had more confidence of victory than previously, at least at sea. Demosthenes, however, would not even hear of continuing the siege; if they were obliged not to bring the army away without a vote of the Athenians but to wear down the enemy, he said that they must do so after moving to Thapsos or Katana, from which they could attack large areas of the country with their land forces, supporting themselves by plundering their enemies' property as they damaged them as well, and there would be the open sea for their fleet, which would not fight its battles in a restricted space, something more in favor of the enemy, but an unrestricted one, where they would have the benefits of their skill and their retreats and attacks would not consist of setting out from a limited enclosure and sailing back into it. In summary, he said that to stay in the same place, rather than getting themselves out as quickly as possible, now, with no delay, was in no way acceptable to him. Eurymedon supported these arguments. But when Nikias disagreed, a tendency to hesitate and wait set in, together with apprehensions that Nikias was being firm because he had some extra knowledge. And in this way the Athenians procrastinated and stayed where they were.

[50] Meanwhile, Gylippos and Sikanos had returned to Syracuse, and Sikanos had failed to gain Akragas (the faction friendly to Syracuse had been driven out while he was still in Gela); but Gylippos returned with a large additional force from Sicily as well as the hoplites sent out from the Peloponnesos in merchant ships during the spring, who had reached Selinous from Libya. After they had been driven off course to Libya and the Kyrenians had given them two triremes and guides for the voyage, and then, as they sailed along the coast, they had joined forces with Euespiritai besieged by Libyans and defeated the Libyans, then sailed along the coast from there to Neapolis, a Carthaginian trading station from which the distance to Sicily is the shortest, two days and a night, and then crossed over to Sicily from there, they reached Selinous. As soon as they arrived, the Syracusans began preparing to attack the Athenians again on both elements, on sea and land; the Athenian generals, in contrast, since they saw that the other side had been reinforced by an additional army, and that at the same time their own situation had not made progress but was becoming worse every day in all respects and was especially handicapped by the sickness of the soldiers, regretted not moving away earlier and, since not even Nikias was still as much opposed except for requiring that there be at least no open vote, they gave everyone advance instructions, as secretly as possible, for departure from the camp by sea and to be prepared whenever the order was given. And when they were about to sail away, since everything was ready, there was an eclipse of the moon; for the moon happened to be full. Most of the Athenians, deeply impressed, urged the generals to stop, and besides Nikias (who was indeed somewhat over-credulous about divination and everything of the sort) said that until he had waited thrice nine days, as the seers dictated, he would not even deliberate about moving first. So after this reason for delay the Athenians stayed on.

[51] As for the Syracusans, when they in turn found out about this, they were much more motivated not to relax their concentration on the Athenians, since now they themselves had acknowledged that they were no longer superior either on sea or on land (or they would not have made plans for departure) and, in addition, because they did not want to let them become more difficult opponents by settling somewhere else in Sicily but to force them to fight a sea battle right there, as soon as possible, where cir-

---

7.50. On the eclipse, see *HCT* IV *ad* 7.50.4; for the religious reactions ("over-credulous" is a slightly free translation to indicate that the criticism is aimed at Nikias rather than at religion in general), cf. also Powell 1979, pp. 47–48, Marinatos 1981, pp. 63–64, and Jordan 1986, pp. 135–36.

cumstances were in their own favor. They accordingly manned their ships and practiced as many days as they considered sufficient. When the time was right, one day ahead they attacked the walls of the Athenians, and, when a small number of hoplites and cavalry came out against them at one of the gates, they cut off some of the hoplites, routed them, and gave pursuit; since the entrance was narrow, the Athenians lost seventy horses and a few hoplites.

[52] That day the Syracusans withdrew; but on the following day they sailed out with their ships, numbering seventy-six, and at the same time advanced against the walls with their land forces. The Athenians put out to sea against them with eighty-six ships, engaged, and began the sea battle. Eurymedon, who held the Athenian right wing and wanted to encircle the ships of the enemy, steered a course too close to the shore, and the Syracusans, first defeating the Athenian center, then cut him off in the bay deep in the harbor and destroyed him along with the ships that had followed him; and then, after this, they pursued all the Athenians ships closely and drove them onto the land. [53] When Gylippos saw the enemy ships being defeated and driven onto a part of the shore outside the stockade and their camp, he came down to the mole with part of the army intending to kill the men disembarking and make it easier for the Syracusans to drag away the ships, after the shore was occupied by friends. The Tyrrhenians (they were standing guard for the Athenians) saw them coming on in disorder, and when they rushed out in defense and fell on those in front, they routed them and drove them into the marsh called Lysimeleia. Later, after larger Syracusan and allied forces arrived, the Athenians came to the defense as well and engaged them in battle, in fear for their ships, and after they won they pursued them and killed a few hoplites and also rescued most of their ships and gathered them together at their camp, but the Syracusans and their allies captured eighteen, killing their crews in every case. With the intention of burning the rest, they filled an old merchant ship with branches and pine torches, set it on fire, and sent it adrift (the wind was toward the Athenians). And the Athenians, fearing for their ships, countered with devices for fire prevention and avoided the danger by putting out fires and keeping the merchant ship from approaching too close.

[54] After this, the Syracusans set up a trophy both for the sea battle and for cutting off the hoplites up above by the wall, where they also captured the horses, while the Athenians set up a trophy both for the rout by the Tyrrhenians, which drove the infantry into the marsh, and for their own with the rest of the army. [55] But since the Syracusans now had also

had a decisive victory at sea (they had previously feared the additional ships that came with Demosthenes), the Athenians were in a completely dejected state, and their astonishment was great, their misgivings about the expedition much greater still. For since these cities, alone among the ones they attacked, were similar to them in their institutions, democratically ruled and possessing the resources of ships, cavalry, and size as well, and there was nothing they could apply to break the stalemate, either a change of government, their method of bringing cities over, or great military superiority, and they had been mainly unsuccessful, they were at a loss even in their previous circumstances and very much more so after they had even been defeated with their fleet, something they could never have believed.

[56] The Syracusans, in contrast, immediately began sailing up and down the harbor as they pleased and intended to close off its mouth, so that even if the Athenians wanted to they could no longer sail out undetected. For they were no longer concentrating merely on survival for themselves but also on ways of denying it to the enemy, thinking that in the present circumstances their own position was far superior, which it was, and that if they could defeat the Athenians and their allies both on land and at sea, their feat would appear glorious in the eyes of the Hellenes; immediately, the other Hellenes would be either set free or delivered from fear (for the remaining power of the Athenians would be incapable of bearing up under the war that would subsequently be brought against them), and they themselves, credited with responsibility for this, would be greatly admired both by the rest of mankind and by men thereafter. And indeed the contest was a worthy one, both on these counts and because they were surpassing not only the Athenians but also many others allied with them, not that they themselves were alone and unaided rather than combining with those who came to their assistance, since they had become leaders

7.55. Only Syracuse can really sustain the comparison (and for the more limited comparison cf. 8.96), but by including other Sicilian cities Thucydides is able to refer back to 6.17 and 6.20; and the overall resources of the island had actually been a factor (see especially 7.50).

7.56. "And indeed": here Thucydides switches to an authorial statement, which concludes with a comparison serving as a bridge between recognition for the Syracusan achievement and an unconventional "catalogue" (see next note). The comparison, like many in Thucydides, is forced and problematic, and he seems to betray uneasiness by very vague language, see especially Marchant 1919, p. 176 (on line 31).

along with the Corinthians and Lacedaemonians and had also been the ones to put their own city in the path of impending danger and to make the decisive advance in seafaring. For the number of nationalities converging on this one city was actually the largest, with, of course, the single exception of the overall total for the cities of the Athenians and the Lacedaemonians during this war.

[57] And on the two sides, against Sicily or for it, coming either to join in taking over the country or in preserving it, these were all the nationalities who fought at Syracuse, aligning themselves not out of principle or kinship so much as in accordance with the degree of advantage or compulsion each found in its lot. The Athenians themselves, as Ionians, went voluntarily against the Dorian Syracusans, and joining the campaign as their colonists who still shared their dialect and customs were the Lemnians, the Imbrians, the Aiginetans who held Aigina at that time, and in addition the Hestiaians who inhabited Hestiaia in Euboia. Of the rest, some joined the campaign as subjects, others independently because of alliances, and there were also mercenaries. Comprising the subjects who paid tribute were the Eretrians, Chalkidians, Styreans, and Karystians from Euboia, the Keians, Andrians, and Tenians from the islands, the Milesians, Samians, and Chians from Ionia; out of these, the Chians came along as subjects with autonomy who contributed ships instead of paying tribute. These, the most numerous contingent, all Ionians and of Athenian origins except for the Karystians (who are Dryopes) followed as subjects and under constraint but at least as Ionians against Dorians nonetheless.

In addition to these were Aiolians, the Methymnians, whose service was in ships, not tribute, and the Tenedians and Ainians, who paid tribute. These were Aiolians forced to fight Aiolians, their Boiotian founders on the Syracusan side, but only the Plataians, not surprisingly considering their hatred, fought directly as Boiotians against Boiotians. As for the Rhodians and Kytherians, both Dorian, the latter, colonists of the Lacedaemonians, bore arms along with the Athenians against the Lacedaemonians with Gylippos, while the former, Argives by descent,

7.57–59. On Thucydides' innovative reuse of the catalogue genre, see Dover 1965, pp. 47–52, *HCT* IV, pp. 432–40, and Connor 1984, pp. 195–96; these chapters were almost certainly written between 405 and 400 B.C.E., see *HCT*, pp. 435–36, and cf. Hunter 1977, pp. 292–94. On the Athenian colonists, see Figueira 1991, pp. 8, 12–13, 36–37. Thucydides is noticeably more perfunctory in accounting for Syracusan allies (the Leukadians and Ambraciots were also Corinthian colonists; for the Sikyonians, see *HCT ad* 7.58.3) but concludes by emphasizing once again the size of the Sicilian cities.

were compelled to go to war not only against the Dorian Syracusans but also against the Geloans, who were their own colonists campaigning with the Syracusans. Among the islanders off the Peloponnesos, the Kephallenians and Zakynthians who came along were autonomous yet more than half coerced because of their islander status, since the Athenians ruled the sea; the Corcyreans, on the other hand, not simply Dorians but outright Corinthians, came against the Corinthians and Syracusans when they were colonists of the one and kinsmen of the other, allegedly out of compulsion but no less by choice, in accordance with their hatred of the Corinthians. And the Messenians, as they are now called, were brought into the campaign from Naupaktos and from Pylos, which was then held by the Athenians. In addition, a few Megarian exiles, in their unfortunate situation, fought against the Megarian Selinountines.

When it came to the others, the expedition was of a more voluntary nature. The Argives came along with the Athenians, who were Ionians, as Dorians against Dorians, not on account of their alliance as much as on account of their enmity toward the Lacedaemonians as well as the immediate benefits for each of them individually, whereas the Mantineans and other Arkadians came as mercenaries, accustomed to march against anyone designated to them as an enemy at a given time and on this occasion, to make a profit, regarding the Arkadians with the Corinthians as enemies like any other, and the Cretans and Aitolians also came with pay as their motivation; for the Cretans, the result was that they, having joined with the Rhodians in founding Gela, did not go with their colonists but against their colonists, freely and on a paid basis. And some of the Akarnanians served for profit but also and much more because of their friendship for Demosthenes and good will toward the Athenians as allies. These were within the boundary of the Ionic gulf; of the Italiots, the Thourians and Metapontines joined the campaign, so severe was the crisis of civil strife it found them caught up in at the time; of the Sikeliots, the Naxians and Katanaians; of the barbarians, those same Egestaians who had called in the Athenians, also the majority of the Sikels; of those outside Sicily, some of the Tyrrhenians, in consequence of disputes with the Syracusans, and Iapygians as mercenaries. All these nationalities joined the Athenian campaign.

[58] Opposing them and aiding the Syracusans were the Kamarinaians, who lived next to them, the Geloans, who lived next to these, and then, since the Akragantines were neutral, the Selinountines, who had settled in the area next to them. Now these inhabit the part of Sicily looking toward Libya, while the Himeraians are from the section facing the Tyrrhenian Sea, also the only Hellenes living there; and they alone brought support

from there. These comprised the Hellenic peoples, all Dorian as well as autonomous, who fought on this side; among the barbarians, only the Sikels who had not gone over to the Athenians. From the Hellenes outside Sicily, there were the Lacedaemonians, who furnished a Spartiate as the leader and otherwise neodamodeis and helots; the Corinthians, the only ones on hand with both ships and a land force, and the Leukadians and Ambraciots for reasons of kinship; mercenaries from Arkadia sent over by the Corinthians; the Sikyonians, serving under compulsion; and from those outside the Peloponnese, the Boiotians. In comparison with those who were coming in, the Sikeliots themselves furnished greater quantities all around inasmuch as they had large cities; numerous hoplites, ships, and horses and a huge host of other soldiers had been assembled. And, once again in comparison with all the rest, practically speaking, the Syracusans themselves provided the larger numbers, because of both the size of their cities and the fact that they were in the greatest danger.

[59] Those were the forces that had been brought together to support each side, and by this time all were already present on both sides, and nothing further was added to either. The Syracusans, then, understandably considering it a glorious feat on their part if they followed up the victory they had already won in the sea battle by capturing the entire Athenian force, vast as it was, and the Athenians had no escape in either way, either across the sea or overland. Accordingly, they immediately began closing off the Great Harbor, whose mouth is about eight stades in width, using triremes, boats, and small craft positioned sideways at anchor, and made every other preparation in case the Athenians still dared to fight at sea, and nothing they thought of was on a small scale.

[60] The Athenians, as they saw the closing of the harbor and became aware of their overall intentions, thought it essential to hold a council. And when the generals and taxiarchs met over both the other difficulties of their present condition and the fact that they had no more supplies for immediate use (for on the assumption that they would be sailing out they had sent ahead to Katana and cancelled their provisioning) and were not likely to have any in the future unless they got control of the sea, they decided to vacate the upper walls and use a cross-wall to close off, right next to the ships, the smallest space that would suffice for both their supplies and the sick, and to put a garrison there and, with the rest of the land forces, man all their ships, the serviceable and the less seaworthy, embarking every single man, and fight it out on the sea, making their way to Katana if they won and, if they did not, form ranks after burning their ships and retreat on land in whichever direction they were likely to find

themselves some friendly place, whether Hellenic or barbarian, as quickly as possible. And on making these decisions they put them into effect; they came down gradually from the upper walls and manned all the ships, forcing everyone from the right age group to embark if he seemed in any way fit. Altogether, about one hundred ten ships were manned; they put on board a large number of archers and javelin-throwers, from both the Akarnanians and the other foreigners, and made such other provisions as they could in light of their constraints and their consequent planning. When most of this was done, Nikias, for his part, seeing that the soldiers were demoralized because of being badly beaten at sea, contrary to their usual experience, and also wanting to risk battle as soon as possible on account of the shortage of supplies, called them all together and exhorted them first, speaking as follows:

[61] "Soldiers of Athens and of our allies as well, for all of us alike no less than for our enemies, the coming contest will be for salvation and homeland; for if we win at sea now, it is possible for us to live to see our native cities, wherever they are. And we should not lose heart, nor experience the same thing as the most untested men who after failure in their first contests then hold lasting expectations originating in the fear that accords with their memories. Remember instead, all those present who are Athenians and have already experienced many wars, and all those who are allies and have always taken part in our campaigns, what is unpredictable in war, and make your preparations hoping that the element of fortune may stand by us and expecting to renew the fight in a manner worthy of your own numbers, whose magnitude you see here before your eyes. [62] And whatever we saw as helpful, considering the restricted space of the harbor, to use against the mass of ships that are going to be packed in and the forces on the enemy decks, all of which harmed us in the past, this too, after consultation with the helmsmen, has been implemented as far as existing circumstances allow. That means there will be many archers and javelin-throwers going on board in a concentration, which we would not permit when fighting a sea battle in open waters because of what it would do to our skill by weighing down the ships, but which will be an asset in the land battle from ships forced on us here. All necessary countermeasures in equipping our ships have been seen to by us, and, to offset the thickness in their anchor-blocks, undoubtedly what did us the most dam-

---

7.60. "Made such other provisions . . .": see *HCT* IV *ad* 7.60.4. The Athenians were making a virtue of necessity, at least in crowding their decks with combatants (see 7.62).

age, these include grappling irons to hurl, which will keep any ship ramming us from backing away again, provided the marines take care of the next part. For we have been forced to do just this, fight a land battle from ships, and it is clearly in our interest neither to back water ourselves or let them do it, especially since the shore, except for the amount our land forces occupy, is in enemy hands.

[63] "With all this in mind, you must stand your ground, fighting to the limits of your ability, not getting pushed back to the shore, resolved that when two ships meet you must not be separated before you have swept the enemy deck clear of hoplites. Here my exhortation is more for hoplites than for sailors, inasmuch as this is more the work of those on deck; and even now it is still within our capabilities to get the upper hand with our land forces for the most part. As for the sailors, I urge, even with an element of pleading, that you not be overly alarmed because of our misfortunes, since your forces up on deck are now stronger and your number of ships greater, and that you reflect on your satisfaction and the importance of maintaining it, you who the whole time were regarded as Athenians even though you were not, admired throughout Hellas thanks to knowledge of our language and imitation of our ways, also sharing fully in the empire, even though it was ours, when it came to benefiting by the intimidation of our subjects and to escaping aggression. Therefore, since you alone are free as our partners in empire, be just by not betraying it now, but with scorn for both the Corinthians, whom you have defeated many times, and the Sikeliots, not one of whom thought of standing up to us when our fleet was at its best, defend yourselves and show them that even amidst weakness and misfortune your skill is superior to the strength good luck brings to anyone else.

[64] "The Athenians among you I remind once again that you left no other ships in the docks to compare with these nor hoplites in the prime of life, and that if the outcome for you is anything other than victory your enemies here are going to sail immediately against what remains back there, and the men we left will be unable to hold off attackers added to the ones on the spot. So while you would immediately fall into the hands of the Syracusans, knowing what your own intentions were when you attacked them, those back there would fall into the hands of the Lacedaemonians. Therefore, in this single contest for a double cause, be steadfast as never before, and be mindful each and every one that, for the Athenians, those who will be on the ships now are the army and navy and the extant city and the great name of Athens, on whose behalf no one, if in skill or heart he exceeds anyone else, would ever at any better time display this in coming to his own aid and the rescue of all."

[65] After making this exhortation, Nikias immediately ordered them to man the ships. As for Gylippos and the Syracusans, while what they could see of the actual preparations let them know that the Athenians were going to fight at sea, they had also been informed in advance about the use of grappling irons, and they especially equipped themselves against this in addition to everything else; they put hides over the prow and much of the upper area of each ship, so that if a hook were thrown it would slip off and not catch hold. When everything was ready, the generals and Gylippos exhorted their side, speaking as follows:

[66] "Syracusans and allies, that the deeds already done are noble and those yet to come, the reason for this contest, will be noble is something which we think most of you know, or you would not have undertaken either so enthusiastically, and which we, if anyone falls short of properly understanding it, will make plain. For the Athenians, who came against this country for the enslavement first of Sicily, then, if they succeeded, the Peloponnesos and the rest of Hellas, after they had already acquired a greater empire than any Hellenes of past or present, you, the first to withstand that same navy with which they made all their conquests, have already defeated in sea battles and now, from all indications, will defeat them in this one. For whenever men are brought up short where they claim preeminence, what is left of their diminished self-esteem is weaker than if they had had no such belief in the first place, and when their vaunting is toppled by what goes contrary to expectations, their strength also gives way regardless of resources. And this is what the Athenians are likely to have experienced now.

[67] "But for our part, what already existed and was indeed the basis for our daring ventures even when we were still unskilled is now firmer, and since added to that is the judgment that we are the strongest, if we have defeated the strongest, hope is redoubled in each man. In most cases, the fullest hopes for an undertaking supply it also with the fullest zeal. And the particulars of their imitation of our preparations are normal usage for us, and we are not the ones to be inept in dealing with each; as for them, once large numbers of hoplites are on deck, contrary to their established practice, and many javelin-throwers—terrestrial beings, one might say—from Akarnania and elsewhere also aboard, who will not even be able to find a way to discharge a missile while seated, how can they help fouling their ships and spreading confusion among themselves, all moving in what is not their own style? Since they will not even benefit from their superior number of ships, in case any of you has become alarmed by this, that he will not be fighting against a fleet the same size as his; numerous ships in a limited

space will be unprepared for implementation of any of their intentions but in full readiness for the reception of damage devised by us. And be aware of the main truth emerging from what we believe is reliable intelligence: overwhelming as their troubles are, and because they are under pressure from their present difficulty, they have reached the desperate state of trusting less in their preparations than in fortune as they risk everything in the only way they can, either to break through and sail out or withdraw by land afterward, since they could hardly fare worse than at present.

[68] "Against such disarray, then and the self-betraying fortune of our worst enemies, let us engage with a passion, and let us recognize what is recognized by all in dealing with enemies, the claim of any man to satisfy his soul's rage through punishment of the aggressor, and at the same time that to take vengeance on enemies, which will be within our means, is called sweetest of all. And that these are enemies, the most hateful, you all know, the very men who came against our land to enslave it, whereby, if they had succeeded, they would have conferred on the men the worst pain, on the children and women the greatest disgrace, and on the whole city the most shameful title. In response to that, it becomes no man to show softness or consider it a gain for them to free us from danger by departing. This they will do regardless, even if they win; but if by the fulfillment of our intentions, the likely fulfillment, they are chastised and we bequeath to Sicily in firmer measure that same freedom she enjoyed before, this is a glorious feat. And these are the rarest of risks, which cause least damage from reverses yet the most benefit by ending well."

[69] After the Syracusan generals and Gylippos had in this way exhorted their own men in turn, they too began to man their ships, reacting as soon as they were aware that the Athenians were doing this. Nikias, however, appalled by the situation and seeing what the danger was and how near it had drawn, since they would set sail at any minute, and supposing, as leaders usually feel about great battles, that everything enacted on their side was still inadequate and everything expressed in words was not yet sufficient, called forward each one of the trierarchs once more, addressing him by his father's name, his own name, and his tribe, urging, whenever anyone had some degree of distinction that he not betray that part of himself, and, whenever anyone had famous ancestors, that he not tarnish the excellence of his family, reminding them of their country, which was so free, and the possibilities for all of an untrammeled daily life within it, saying other things as well which men in so great a time of crisis would not mention if they were guarding against appearing to speak in platitudes, especially references to women and children and ancestral

gods, which are brought forward in much the same form for every occasion, but they cry them aloud when they think they might help in a general state of consternation. Then, stepping down after giving not what he thought was sufficient exhortation but barely adequate, he led the troops to the shore and drew them up over the largest expanse possible, so that they might be of the greatest possible use to those on the ships by way of encouragement; Demosthenes, Menandros, and Euthydemos (it was they who went on board as the Athenian generals) setting sail from their camp, sailed right to the barrier and the passageway left in it, intending to force their way to the outside.

[70] The Syracusans and their allies, who had already put out with very nearly the same number of ships as before, were on guard with part of these around the exit, and also completely around the rest of the harbor, so that they could fall on the Athenians from all directions at once, and at the same time their land forces stood ready to help wherever the ships came to the shore. For the Syracusan ships, Sikanos and Agatharchos were in command, each holding one wing of the entire fleet, and Pythen and the Corinthians held the center. When the Athenians drew close to the barrier, they sailed against it and in their first charge overpowered the ships stationed next to it, and they started trying to break the chains; but after this, when the Syracusans and their allies bore down on them from all directions, the sea battle was no longer fought only by the barrier but throughout the harbor, and it was fierce as none had been before. For on both sides there was great enthusiasm among the sailors for charging whenever ordered and much matching of skills and competition among the pilots; and the marines were intent that, whenever a ship struck a ship, what was done on deck should not fall short of skills elsewhere. Everyone was striving to show himself foremost in the position to which he had been assigned.

With many ships meeting in scant space (and these were certainly the most ships to fight a sea battle in the smallest space; for both sides combined came to slightly under two hundred), ramming seldom occurred because there was no backing water or sailing round, but collisions were more frequent, any time one ship ran into another, either because it was in flight or because it was charging another ship. And the whole time a ship was bearing down, men fired countless javelins, arrows, and stones at it from the deck; when the ships met, the marines fought hand to hand trying to board each others' ship. It so happened that, because of the restricted space, in many places ships had rammed others but were rammed themselves, so, around one ship, two, in some places even more, were fused together, and it fell to the helmsmen to ward off some while aiming at others, not one at

a time but many and from all over, and the great din from many ships colliding caused consternation and at the same time inability to hear the voices
of the coxswains. For on both sides there was more than ample exhortation
and shouting on the part of the coxswains, both as part of their work and in
the rivalry of the moment, as they shouted at Athenians, to force their way
out and make the effort now, one more time if they ever had before, for safe
return to their homeland, and at Syracusans, that it was glorious to prevent
their escape and enhance each one's own homeland by winning. And in
addition, the generals on both sides would call out the name of the trierarch
if they saw anyone turning back unnecessarily and ask, if Athenian, whether
it was because they considered the most hostile of shores now more their
element than the sea, which they had made their own with no little toil, that
they were retreating; if Syracusans, whether men whom they knew beyond
all doubt were eager to escape any way they could were putting them to
flight even as they were fleeing themselves.

[71] And on the shore, as long as the sea battle stayed evenly balanced,
the land forces on both sides experienced intense struggles and conflict in
their minds, the local army passionately wanting still more glory, the
invaders fearing that they would be even worse off than they were now.
And for the very reason that the fate of the Athenians depended entirely
on their ships, their fear of the outcome was beyond anything, and because
there was no consistency in their alignment, they were also compelled to
view the sea battle without consistency. For since the spectacle was a short
distance away, and all were not observing the same thing at the same time,
any who saw their own men prevailing would take heart and turn to
appeals to the gods that they not be deprived of their salvation; but those
witnessing defeat would let out cries of lamentation, and by observing the
action they were actually more cowed in spirit than those involved in it.
Still others, looking off at some evenly fought sector of the sea battle, were
kept in the most painful state of all on account of the continued uncertainty
of the conflict, the intensity of their fear making their very bodies sway
back and forth to match their perceptions; for all the while they were either
just on the point of getting away or just on the point of being lost. And all
within the Athenian army, as long as the battle on the sea was about even,
you could hear everything at the same time, lamentation, shouting, "we're
winning," "we're losing," every other possible outcry that would be wrung
from a great army in great danger. The men on the ships were reacting in
much the same way but only up until the Syracusans and their allies, after
prolonged fighting, routed the Athenians and in a decisive offensive, with
much shouting and cheering, drove them to the land.

At that point, the naval forces, driven ashore at one point or another if they had not been captured in the water, emptied into the camp; the land forces, no longer divided in their reactions, with universal wailing and groaning in a single impulse over the unbearable turn of events went in some cases to rescue the ships or to guard the remnant of their walls, but most now thought only of themselves and the means of survival. The shock of this moment went beyond anything. What they had suffered was almost exactly what they had dealt out at Pylos; for when the ships of the Lacedaemonians were destroyed, their men who had crossed over to the island were also as good as lost, and this time there was no hope for the Athenians to reach safety by land unless something unaccountable happened.

[72] After this savage sea battle and the loss of many ships and men on both sides, the victorious Syracusans and their allies collected the wrecks and their dead and then sailed back to the city and set up a trophy, but the Athenians, in reaction to the enormity of their terrible situation, did not even think to ask permission to take up their dead and wrecks but wanted to depart immediately during the night. Demosthenes went to Nikias and made the proposal to man their remaining ship once again and force their way out at daybreak if they could, saying that they still had more remaining ships that were usable than the enemy had; while the Athenians had about sixty left, their opponents had fewer than fifty. And with Nikias in agreement and the generals wishing to man the ships, the sailors were unwilling to go on board, since they were stunned by the defeat and no longer believed they could win.

They were all now of the opinion that they should retreat by land, [73] but Hermokrates the Syracusan, suspecting their intentions and considering it dangerous if such a large army, after retreating by land and settling somewhere in Sicily, were to wish once again to make war on them, went to those in authority and advised them, giving his reasons, that they could not allow the Athenians to retreat during the night but every one of the Syracusans and their allies must go out right now to build barriers across the roads and guard the defiles in the area ahead of time. The authorities themselves were fully as convinced of this as he was, and they thought it had to be done but the men, since they had just gotten a welcome rest after a great sea battle, and besides there was a festival (for this day happened to be their sacrifice to Herakles), would not be willing to obey with equanimity; most, as a consequence of their extreme joy over the victory, had turned to drinking at the festival, and they expected that they would listen to any orders from them sooner than arming and going out at this time. Since it was clear to the officials from their own assessment that the whole business was impracticable, and Hermokrates made no further impression on them, he responded by devising the following scheme on his own, fearing that during the night the Athenians might already get past the most difficult areas undisturbed. He sent some of his own associates to the camp with horsemen when it was growing dark; they rode up just close enough to be heard and called some individual names as though they were friends of the Athenians (for there were certain people who reported to Nikias on matters inside the city), telling them to advise Nikias not to lead the army off during the night, since the Syracusans were guarding the roads, but to withdraw during the day after leisurely preparation.

After saying this they left, and those who had heard them notified the Athenian generals; [74] they stayed on for the night in accordance with the message, not supposing that there was trickery. And since after all they were not setting out right away, it seemed best to them that they wait until the following day for the soldiers to pack what was the most useful, as well as they could, and that they leave everything else behind and start out taking just the supplies that sufficed for bodily sustenance. But the Syracusans and Gylippos, going out ahead with the infantry, blocked the roads in the area where the Athenians were likely to pass, put guards at the fords across the streams and rivers, and, to give the army a reception, stationed themselves at what seemed the best places for obstructing it. Sailing up with their ships, they towed those of the Athenians off the beach; the Athenians themselves had carried out their intentions by burning quite a few, but the Syracusans, at their leisure and without opposition, tied on the others wherever each one had run ashore and conveyed them to the city.

[75] After this, when it seemed to Nikias and Demosthenes that there had been adequate preparation, the departure of the army did now finally take place, on the second day after the sea battle. And what was terrible was not only one aspect of their situation, that they were leaving after they had lost all their ships, and amid danger for both themselves and their city after their great hopes, but for each man abandoning the camp also involved awareness of things that were painful to see and to think about. For since the dead were unburied, whenever anyone saw one of his close friends

7.73. "The authorities . . . going out at this time": an extraordinarily irregular sentence, perhaps intended to convey embarrassment or ambivalence on the part of these authorities. "When it was growing dark," etc.: the "friends" take so many obvious imposters' precautions (see Russell 1994, pp. 194–95) and their message is so implausible (why should the Syracusans only guard the roads this night?) that it seems possible that the Athenians were not wholly unwilling to be tricked, cf. *HCT* IV *ad* 7.74.1 and Kagan 1981, p. 336.

lying there he was stricken with grief along with fear, and those who were being left behind while alive, the wounded and the sick, made the living feel far more grief than they felt for the dead and far more pity than they felt for the departed. In turning to entreaties and lamentations, they drove the men to distraction, begging them to take them along, crying out to each of them whenever anyone saw a friend or kinsman, hanging on to tent-mates who were now departing, following along as far as they could, and, whenever spirit or flesh failed any of them, never dropping behind without many wails and appeals to the gods, so that the whole army, filled with tears and in this distracted mood, found it not easy to set out, even from a hostile land and after they had already experienced suffering too great for tears, while fearing what unknown suffering might lie ahead. There was also a certain mortification and strong self-condemnation. For they resembled nothing other than a city stealing away after capitulation to a siege, and no small city. In the overall crowd, there were no fewer than forty thousand on their way at the same time. The rest of them all carried anything they could that was useful, and the hoplites and cavalry, in contrast to their usual practice, actually carried their own food themselves under their weapons, some lacking servants and some distrusting them; they had long since started to desert, and most did so right now. What they carried was not even enough; for there was no longer food in the camp. Moreover, the general degradation and equal apportionment of misery, although this lightened the load somewhat (in that many were sharing), were not on that account regarded at the time as easy to bear, above all because from such splendor and vaunting at first they had reached such an end in humiliation. For this was certainly the greatest reversal for any Hellenic army, since what resulted for these men was that, in comparison with their arriving to enslave others, they were going away fearing that instead they themselves would suffer this, in comparison with the prayers and paians they sailed off with, they were setting out for home again with contrasting words of ill omen, and they were proceeding as infantry instead of sailors, committed to hoplite rather than nautical arms. Even so, all this seemed endurable in their awareness of the immensity of the danger still hanging over them.

[76] Nikias, seeing the army disheartened and greatly altered, went along the ranks and tried to encourage and cheer them as circumstances permitted, shouting more and more in his urgency as he came to each group and wishing to do some good by projecting his voice as far as possible: [77] "Even in the present circumstances, Athenians and allies, you must still have hope (there are men who have been saved before now from

even more terrible situations than this) and not blame yourself too much for either your disasters or your undeserved wretchedness now. I myself, surpassing not a single one of you in vigor (alas, you see the state I am reduced to by my illness) and giving the impression, I am sure, of being second to no one in good fortune, yes, even I am now caught up in the same danger as the lowliest. And yet I have spent my life in many devout actions toward the gods and many just and irreproachable ones toward men. In consequence, my hopes for the future are confident ones, despite all, and our disasters certainly do not alarm me as to our worth. Perhaps these will even abate; enough has gone well for the enemy, and if we were resented by any of the gods for our expedition we have already been chastised sufficiently. For already, it would seem, other men have attacked their fellows, and what they suffered after behaving in human fashion was endurable. So it is reasonable now for us to expect milder treatment from god (for by now we are more deserving of the gods' pity than their resentment), and as you see at the same time what sort of hoplites you are and how many march in your ranks do not be too demoralized, but bear in mind that you are instantly a city wherever you settle, and no other in Sicily could easily stand up to you if you attacked or drive you out after you were established. See to your own progress so that it is safe and orderly, each of you believing only this, that wherever he is forced to fight he will have that spot as homeland and fortress if he wins. Our journey will be a hurried one, by night and day alike; we are short on provisions, and if we reach some friendly place among the Sikels (for they can still be trusted because of their fear of the Syracusans), you can then consider yourselves in safety. Word has been sent ahead to them, and they were told to meet us and bring food with them. Understand me fully, soldiers, your only choice is to be brave men, since there is no place nearby where you will be safe if you turn coward, and if you escape the enemy now, the rest of you will gain those things I am sure you all long to see again, and you who are Athenians will raise up again, fallen as it is, the great power of the city; men are the city, not walls and ships without men."

[78] As he gave these exhortations, Nikias also passed through the army and wherever he saw it scattered or out of order he brought it together and

---

7.77. This is the culmination of the *leitmotif* of the expedition as a city, yet Nikias stops short of identifying the city as Athens, see Luschnat 1942, pp. 104–5. Assessments of this speech have differed radically; especially interesting are the comparisons Rawlings (1981, pp. 135–66) makes between this and Nikias' other speeches and those of Perikles.

organized it, and Demosthenes did all this with the men near him, saying very much the same things. The army moved in a squared formation, first Nikias' portion in the lead, and that of Demosthenes following. The hoplites kept the baggage handlers and most of the general crowd inside the square. And when they came to the Anapos river, they found some of the Syracusans and their allies drawn up there to oppose them, and after routing these and controlling the crossing they moved on ahead; the Syracusans kept attacking them, both by riding alongside and with javelins thrown by the light-armed. On this day the Athenians advanced about forty stades and bivouacked by a hill; on the next day they got under way early and advanced about twenty stades, then came down to a flat area and made camp there, since they wanted to get something to eat from the houses (this was an inhabited area) and also take their own water along with them from there; for where they were going it was not plentiful for many stades ahead. Meanwhile, the Syracusans had gone forward and were building a wall across the pass up ahead; this consisted of a steep hill and a precipitous ravine on each side, called the Akraian Rock.

The next day, the Athenians went forward, and the cavalry and javelin throwers of the Syracusans and their allies in large numbers kept hindering them from both sides, hurling javelins and riding alongside. The Athenians fought them for a long time, and then fell back on the same camp. And they no longer had provisions as formerly; for because of the cavalry it was no longer possible to leave camp. [79] Starting early in the morning, they set out again and forced their way to the hill with the wall across it and they found waiting in front of them an infantry force drawn up behind the wall, not a few shields deep; for the site was narrow. When the Athenians attacked, trying to take the wall, and were struck by many missiles thrown from the hillside, which was steep (the men up above could reach them more easily), they fell back again, unable to force their way through, and rested. It happened that at the same time there was also thunder and rain, as is apt to occur by the time it is late autumn; as a result, the Athenians became even more disheartened and thought that all this as well was leading up to their destruction. While they were resting, Gylippos and the Syracusans sent one part of the army to build a wall cutting them off from the rear where they had marched previously; but they countered by sending some of their own men and prevented it. After this, the Athenians withdrew with the whole army to more level ground and bivouacked. The next day, they advanced, and the Syracusans surrounded them and attacked on all sides and wounded many, and they would give ground if the Athenians attacked but charge if they withdrew, falling on the hindmost in particular in case by routing them little by little they could panic the entire army. The Athenians held out in this fashion for a long time and then, after advancing five or six stades, rested in the plain; the Syracusans moved away from them and back to their own camp.

[80] During the night, Nikias and Demosthenes, since their army was in a bad state both because of a lack of all supplies by this time and because many had been wounded in many assaults made by the enemy, decided to light as many fires as possible and withdraw the army, no longer by the route they had intended but in the opposite direction from the one the Syracusans were watching, toward the sea; the army's overall route was not toward Katana but over the other part of Sicily toward Kamarina and Gela and the Hellenic and barbarian cities in that area. So after lighting many fires they went forth during the night. And in the way that fears and terrors are likely to descend on armies, and the largest ones most of all, especially when moving at night in enemy country with the enemy not far away, disorder was rampant among them; the army of Nikias, in taking the lead throughout, kept together and got far ahead, but that of Demosthenes, which was about half the total or more, became separated and moved with less order. Nevertheless, they reached the sea at dawn, and they took the road called the Helorine and proceeded, so that when they came to the Kakyparis river they could go up the river through the interior; for they also hoped that the Sikels whom they had sent for would meet them there. When they came to the river, there too they found some Syracusan guards building a wall and palisade across their path. After forcing their way past them, they crossed the river and advanced again to another river, the Erineos; for this was the way the guides advised.

[81] Meanwhile, when day came, and the Syracusans and their allies realized that the Athenians had departed, many held Gylippos responsible for deliberately letting the Athenians go away, and by rapid pursuit along the route recognized with little difficulty as the one taken, they caught up with them around the time of the midday meal. And when they made contact with the men under Demosthenes, who were at the rear and moving in a more dilatory and disorderly way because of being thrown into confusion during the night, they fell on them and began a battle, and the Syracusan cavalry was able to encircle them and drive them together into one spot because of their complete isolation. The army of Nikias was a full fifty stades ahead; for Nikias led his army faster, thinking that safety in such a situation was a matter of not staying to fight if they could help it but retreating as quickly as possible, doing only the amount of fighting that was forced on them. But what happened to Demosthenes was that he was

generally in more continual distress because the enemy closed in on him first as the last component in the retreat, and also that at this point, aware of the Syracusans in pursuit, he did less advancing than forming ranks for battle, until he was surrounded by the Syracusans after taking too much time, and he and his men were in complete turmoil; after they had been jammed together into some spot which a wall encircled, a road on either side and there were a number of olive trees, missiles came from all around them. It was understandable that the Syracusans employed this method of attack and not a battle at close quarters; taking extreme risks against desperate men now favored them less than it did the Athenians, and at the same time a certain chariness developed about throwing one's life away just before a success already apparent, and they thought that in this style they would subdue and capture them anyway.

[82] Accordingly, after they struck the Athenians and their allies with missiles from all sides throughout the day and saw that they were worn out by now from both their wounds and their general misery, Gylippos and the Syracusans made a proclamation, first that any of the islanders who wished were to come over to them on terms of freedom; and some cities defected, not many. Then a later agreement was made with all the rest with Demosthenes, that they were to surrender their arms and that no one was to die by violence, imprisonment, or lack of the most necessary sustenance. So they all surrendered, six thousand of them, and laid down all the money they had, putting it into upturned shields, and they filled four shields. They immediately took these men to the city; on the same day, Nikias and his men arrived at the Erineos river, and after crossing it he made camp on high ground.

[83] The next day, the Syracusans caught up with Nikias and told him that the men with Demosthenes had surrendered, directing him to do the same; incredulous, he arranged a truce to send a horseman to verify this. The horseman went off, and since he brought back word that they had surrendered, he sent a herald to Gylippos and the Syracusans with the message that he was ready, on behalf of the Athenians, to repay all the money that the Syracusans had spent on the war, on condition that they let his army go; until the money was repaid, he would give Athenians as hostages, one for each talent. Rejecting the proposal, the Syracusans and Gylippos attacked and surrounded them and struck these men too with missiles from all sides until evening. And they too were in a miserable condition because of their lack of both food and supplies. Nevertheless, they decided to set out. Watching for the quiet part of the night, they picked up their weapons, and the Syracusans noticed and sang the paian.

And the Athenians, realizing that they were not going undetected, put down their arms again, except for about three hundred men; these forced their way through the guards and went wherever they could in the night.

[84] When day came, Nikias led the army on. The Syracusans and their allies pursued closely in the same way, hurling missiles and shooting down javelins from all sides. And the Athenians pressed on toward the Assinaros river, partly because, pressured on all sides by the assaults of both numerous cavalry and the ordinary soldiers, they thought that it would be somewhat easier for them if they crossed the river, partly out of fatigue and in their craving to drink. When they came to it, they plunged in, no longer in any order but each of them wanting to be the first across, and the enemy closing in now made the crossing difficult; because they were forced to move packed together, they fell and trampled one another, and from contact with both spears and equipment some were killed instantly while others got entangled and pulled under. Standing along the other bank of the river, which was steep, the Syracusans hurled missiles down at the Athenians as they were drinking thirstily in most cases and jostling each other in the shallow part of the river. And the Peloponnesians descended and did the most butchery when they were in the river. The water immediately turned foul but was not only drunk just as much when full of blood along with the mud but fought over by most of them.

[85] Finally, by the time many corpses were lying on one another in the river, and the army had been slaughtered, part of it by the river and part of it, if there were any escapes, by the cavalry as well, Nikias surrendered to Gylippos, since he trusted him more than the Syracusans; he told him to do as he pleased with him but stop the massacre of the rest of the soldiers. After this, Gylippos finally gave the order to take prisoners. They brought back alive in one group all the survivors who had not been smuggled away (there were many of these) and also sent men to pursue the three hundred who had gotten past the guards in the night, and they caught them. Now the portion of the army rounded up as communal property was not large, but the portion stolen away was, and all Sicily was full of them, since they had not been covered by negotiations like the men captured with Demosthenes. Also no small number were killed; for this was certainly the worst massacre and second to none during this war. Not a few also died in the attacks which came frequently during their march. Nevertheless, many escaped, some even at the time, others after they became slaves and ran away later; these had Katana as a refuge.

[86] When the Syracusans and their allies had gathered their forces, they collected all the prisoners they possibly could along with the spoils

and went back to the city. They put the other Athenians and the allies down in the quarries, thinking that this was the safest way to watch them, but murdered Nikias and Demosthenes, against the wishes of Gylippos. For Gylippos considered it a glorious feat for himself, on top of everything else, to bring the opposing generals back to the Lacedaemonians. It happened that the one, Demosthenes, was their worst enemy, on account of the events on the island and at Pylos, and the other the most accommodating because of these very events; for when Nikias was persuading the Athenians to make peace, he was eager for the Lacedaemonians from the island to be released. The Lacedaemonians were well disposed toward him in return, and he put his main trust in this when he surrendered to Gylippos. But since some of the Syracusans had been in communication with him, they were afraid, it is said, that if questioned under torture on such grounds he would confound them in the midst of their success, while others, especially the Corinthians, were afraid that by bribing people, since he was indeed wealthy, he would escape, and there would be trouble from him once again, and they persuaded their allies and put him to death. So for such reasons or very similar ones he died, although of all the Hellenes, at least in my time, certainly the least deserving to reach this level of misfortune because of a way of life directed entirely toward virtue.

[87] The Syracusans treated the men in the quarries harshly during the first stage. For since there were many in a deep and narrow space, the sun and the suffocating heat were still distressing them at first, and the con-

7.86. Translation along the lines of "directed entirely toward virtue" is disputed, cf. *HCT* IV *ad* 7.86.5, Adkins 1975, and Connor 1984, p. 205; "least deserving" remains Thucydides' most puzzling superlative, cf. also Green 1970, pp. 345–47, Pouncey 1980, pp. 129–30, Kagan 1981, pp. 369–72, Connor 1984, pp. 205–6, and Lateiner 1985. That Nikias opposed, often with prescience, the expedition that destroyed him was very much to his credit for Thucydides (although his ruinous faith in his agents inside Syracuse detracts from his sagacity), but his language suggests more. There is something approaching consensus that he viewed Nikias as a decent anachronism, but I doubt this, at least as his main emphasis. Thucydides clearly wanted to show exactly to what extent the expedition's failure was due to Nikias' mistakes in the field, and his portrayal of a reactive commander whose concern for thoroughness drove him to second efforts but tended to result in indecision is consistent and convincing (and reflected in the speaking style displayed at such length). "Least deserving," arguably an overstatement, may have been motivated by certain similarities in the backgrounds of the two men (7.48n and Adkins pp. 390–92), by Nikias' entrapment in the expedition he opposed, and in reaction to Athenian condemnation of his surrender (his name was omitted from the memorial to the casualties in Sicily, see Pausanias, *Description of Greece* 1.29.12).

trasting cold autumnal nights that ensued weakened their condition by the change, and since they had to do everything in the same space because of close confines, and furthermore the corpses were piled together on one another, dead from wounds and because of the change and so forth, there were unbearable smells, and at the same time they were afflicted with hunger and thirst (for eight months they gave each a cup of water and two cups of food a day), and of all the other miseries men thrust into such a place were likely to suffer there was not one that they did not encounter. For up to seventy days, the whole group lived like this; then, except for the Athenians and whatever Sikeliots or Italiots had joined them, they sold them all. The total number captured, while difficult to give out accurately, was nevertheless not fewer than seven thousand. And this Hellenic event turned out to be the greatest connected with this war and, at least in my opinion, of Hellenic events we have heard of, the most splendid for those who won and the most wretched for those who were ruined. For after having been completely defeated in every respect and suffering no little misery at any point in what can truly be called total destruction, army, navy, and everything else was lost, and few out of many returned home. This was what happened concerning Sicily.

7.87. "Total destruction": I agree with Marinatos Kopff and Rawlings 1978 (see also Marinatos 1981, pp. 60–61), against *HCT* IV *ad* 7.87.6, that this is an intentional reference to Herodotos 2.120—but not that Thucydides is reflecting a "Herodotean" theodicy. Such an interpretation would involve Thucydides in offering Nikias a lesson in matters theological, undermine the elaborate comparisons with the Pylos campaign (were the Spartans "punished" then?), and cloud the (admittedly puzzling) authorial statement that the Athenians did not support the expedition adequately (2.65). Rather, Thucydides' choice of words proclaims the parity of his subject, and his treatment of it, with both Herodotos and "Homeric" epic.

BOOK EIGHT

INTRODUCTION

While stunned by the news from Sicily, the Athenians resolve on and quickly implement measures for a last-ditch defense. The Spartans and their allies, old and new, plan a new offensive expecting to finish off Athens quickly. Revolts break out in many areas of the empire, and in large part because of the very multiplicity of opportunities the campaign against Athens lacks cohesiveness from the start, allowing the Athenians to regain the initiative. At the same time, however, the Spartan alliance embarks on a policy that will decisively affect the outcome of the war: collaboration with Persia, sacrificing the interests of some Greeks in the Persian sphere of influence in order to get financial support.

The war is now primarily a naval one fought in Ionian waters, and the Athenians soon display a measure of their old superiority; their main base becomes Samos, which develops a close relationship with Athens after a violent revolt of the common people against the upper classes. Also on Samos, however, occurs the first stage of a revolt by the Athenians against their own democratic government. The catalyst is the machinations of Alcibiades, estranged from the Spartans, who sees his ultimate security first in cultivating the Persian satrap Tissaphernes, then in intriguing for his return from exile. His argument that Persia can be won over to the Athenian side through his influence and if the Athenians form a more conservative government is accepted with some reluctance by the forces on Samos, but when the revolution spreads to Athens, it is soon uncoupled from Alcibiades and spearheaded by ideologues; the oligarchy of the Four Hundred assumes absolute power over the intimidated city.

Meanwhile, however, once again on Samos, an overwhelming democratic counterrevolution occurs, and Athens is for a short time divided between a democratic army and navy and an oligarchic city on the brink of internecine war. This is averted partly by Alcibiades, who has joined the forces on Samos, partly by the spread of counterrevolution to the city; while the most determined oligarchs attempt to come to terms with Sparta, others are disaffected and combine with the rank and file of the hoplites. Faced with mutiny on two fronts and internal dissent, the cowed Four Hundred attempt appeasement, but now the ac-

tual war intervenes. A Peloponnesian fleet deals the Athenians a shattering defeat off Euboia, and the whole island, which has become Athens' most valuable resource, revolts. The Peloponnesians, however, do not exploit their victory by sailing against the Peiraeus, for which Thucydides uncategorically blames Spartan lethargy. Given a reprieve, the Athenians depose the oligarchs and restore the democratic constitution or something very similar to it. Under the leadership of the two men who started the counterrevolution, the Athenian fleet encounters the Peloponnesians in the Hellespont and turns a near-disaster into an encouraging victory at sea. The Peloponnesians had been in that region to find more satisfactory Persian assistance than Tissaphernes had been furnishing; book 8 ends with Tissaphernes about to attempt a rapprochement.

The discursiveness, even fragmentation of book 8 forms the sharpest possible contrast with the intense focus of books 6 and 7, a contrast that has contributed heavily to a perception (going back to antiquity) that this final book is inferior in quality to the rest of our text. And an explanation for inferiority has always seemed ready at hand: book 8 is a rough draft; Thucydides left his account of the events of 413–411 in its present state (or a more inchoate one to which a posthumous editor brought a degree of organization) and turned to revision of the preceding books. While it might be debated where "book 8" actually begins (the opening sentence is intimately connected with the concluding one of book 7, a striking reminder that Thucydides did not make the book divisions), its overall idiosyncrasy is generally and rightly acknowledged. The main arguments for unfinished work are the following: the narrative ends abruptly rather than at a meaningful stopping point (and at a date six years earlier than the end of the war, which Thucydides announced would be his conclusion); rather than speeches in direct discourse, we find short summaries in indirect discourse; several documents are quoted verbatim; there are two extensive flashbacks (one dealing with Alcibiades' intrigues, the other with the oligarchic coup in Athens); inconsistencies and loose ends are more numerous than in other portions of the work.

To a certain extent, these arguments will be addressed in my footnotes (see especially the first). Briefly stated, my opinion is that Thucydides' intellectual vigor and originality is nowhere more apparent than in book 8, whose idiosyncrasy is only marginally due to lack of final revision. In particular, the two flashbacks are an innovation caused by his understanding that the complexity of events occurring in different theaters at the same time could not be adequately dealt with by a continuous linear narrative. This device, moreover, enabled him to emphasize this complexity by taking the reader behind the scenes and by showing how men frequently acted without knowing how they had been overtaken by events; this last aspect is reminiscent of 5.27–84, which has some other affinities with book 8. As for the passages in indirect discourse, I consider them carefully finished work rather than sketches for speeches that would have eventually been inserted.

BOOK EIGHT

[1] And in Athens, when the news arrived, for a long time they would not believe, even from those who were very much soldiers surviving the action itself and reporting it plainly, that everything in its entirety could have been so entirely destroyed; and when they realized, they were angry at the orators who had shared their zeal for the expedition, just as though they had not voted for it themselves, and furious at the oracle-mongers, seers, and anyone whose divinations had made them hope that they would capture Sicily. Everything grieved them on every side, and after what had occurred, terror and the most extreme consternation came over them. For bereft, both as individuals and as a city, of many hoplites and cavalry and of a flowering whose like they could see nowhere, they were oppressed at heart; since they also saw neither enough ships in the shipyards nor money in the treasury nor staffing for the ships, they were without hope of survival in the present situation and thought that their enemies from Sicily would immediately sail against the Peiraeus with their fleet, especially after winning so decisively, and at that point their enemies at home, with all their forces now redoubled, would fall on them in full strength on both

---

8.1–109. The case for book 8 as a rough draft is exhaustively presented in *HCT* V, pp. 369–75 and frequently invoked in Andrewes's commentary. Although it is certain that the book was not intended to end at 8.109 and undeniable that there are a relatively large number of omissions and inconsistencies (e.g., inadequate cross-referencing), I am fundamentally in agreement with Connor 1984, pp. 213–30, and Erbse 1989, *passim*, that book 8 was shaped by Thucydides' continuing development as a writer and as an analyst combined with his response to the new trends in the war (Konishi 1987 certainly goes too far in arguing that 8.109 is the intended conclusion not only of book 8 but of the entire work). The intriguing suggestion by Flory 1988b (I am grateful to Professor Flory for sending me a copy of his paper) that Thucydides' increasing pessimism about the possibility of explaining the course of the war causes him to abandon his enterprise at 8.109 in "something like despair," could be modified; he might rather have felt that revision of earlier portions had become the most urgent priority. He shows a new inclination to share speculations with the reader, see Connor 1984, pp. 215–17.

land and sea, and their own allies in revolt along with them. But they nevertheless resolved that as far as circumstances permitted they should not give in but prepare a fleet, getting together timber and money from wherever they could, make sure of their allies, Euboia in particular, and as for the city, moderate its functions in the direction of economy and select a board of elders who could propose initiatives about the current situation as needed. And they were prepared to be orderly in every respect in accordance with their immediate alarm, just as a democracy is apt to behave. After making these resolutions, they then acted on them, and the summer ended.

[2] In the following winter, in reaction to the great Athenian catastrophe in Sicily, all the Hellenes immediately had exhilarated ideas, those who were allies of neither side that even if no one was calling them in they could no longer stand aside but had to go against the Athenians of their own accord, thinking in each case that the Athenians would have gone against them if they had succeeded in Sicily, and at the same time that the rest of the war, glorious to take part in, would be short, and the allies of the Lacedaemonians for their part sharing a greater zeal than before to find a quick release from severe hardships. And most of all, the subjects of the Athenians were ready, even beyond their strength, to revolt from them because of judging matters in a passion and not even conceding them the argument that they would be able to survive at least over the following summer.

8.1–2. "And they were prepared . . . apt to behave": it can hardly be maintained that this explicitly ideological comment is "scornful" (McGregor 1956, p. 99—but see also pp. 96–97; cf. *HCT* V *ad* 8.1.4, Connor 1984, p. 227, Kagan 1987, p. 7); in indicating that the resilience and flexibility essential to the Athenian recovery was derived from democratic institutions, Thucydides is consistent with his statement that the Syracusans were the Athenians' most formidable opponent (see 7.55n). Several features emphasize the depth of his conviction about this ideological factor. He mentions it at a point when Athenian hopes were certainly less realistic than those of their enemies; moreover, he has made 8.2 an analogue to the description of Athenian emotions in 415 ("And a passion for the expedition . . . ," 6.24), thus foreshadowing that the Spartan-led offensive will implode (conversely, the new Athenian measures are the antithesis of their giddy extravagance and individualistic rivalry in 415 B.C.E.). The Spartan allies feel "shared zeal"—as the Athenians had "shared zeal" for the Sicilian expedition (8.1). Finally, on Thucydides' own later showing, 8.2 is full of exaggeration (especially about the neutrals now wishing to participate, see *HCT* V *ad* 8.2.1), which enables him to make two rhetorical points: it is now the enemies of Athens who are deluded; zeal on the part of all the other Greeks is a precondition for Spartan activism.

The Lacedaemonian state was encouraged by all these things, and especially because their allies from Sicily, now out of necessity strengthened by a fleet, in all probability were going to be with them as soon as it was spring. Feeling hopeful on all counts, they intended to take up the war without reservation, calculating that after its satisfactory conclusion they would in the future be rid of such dangers as would have descended on them from the Athenians if they had added Sicilian resources to their own, and also that after overthrowing them they would then be secure as leaders of all Hellas. [3] Accordingly, Agis their king, setting out immediately from Dekeleia during this winter with some of his forces, levied money from the allies for the fleet, turning toward the Gulf of Malis he exacted money from the Oitaians by taking away most of their livestock, in accordance with their old enmity, and he forced the Achaians of Phthiotis and the other subjects of the Thessalians in the area to give him money and hostages, although the Thessalians were opposed and made objections, and deposited the hostages at Corinth and tried to bring these people into the alliance. The Lacedaemonians fixed the assessment for the cities as the construction of a hundred ships, and they assessed themselves and the Boiotians at twenty-five apiece, the Phokians and Lokrians at fifteen, the Corinthians at fifteen, the Arkadians, Pellenians, and Sikyonians combined at ten, and the Megarians, Troizenians, Epidaurians, and Hermionians at ten. And they made the rest of their preparations, with the idea of pursuing the war as soon as it was spring.

[4] During this same winter, the Athenians, as they had intended, were also preparing, by the construction of ships after getting timber together, by fortifying Sounion so that there would be security for their grain transports as they sailed around it, abandoning the fortress in Lakonian territory which they had built when sailing past to Sicily, cutting back in the interest of economy if there seemed to be any useless spending anywhere, and above all by watching over the allies to keep them from revolting.

[5] While both sides were carrying out these activities and equipping themselves for war just as though they were at the beginning of it, the Euboians were the first to send envoys to Agis during this winter about revolting from Athens. He accepted their proposal and summoned Alkamenes son of Sthenelaidas and Melanthos to take command in Euboia; they arrived with about three hundred neodamodeis, and he made preparations for their crossing. In the meantime, the Lesbians also came, also

---

8.4. For possible book-division here (to account for repetition of 8.1), see *HCT* V *ad loc.*

wishing to revolt; with the Boiotians helping them negotiate, Agis, persuaded to hold off regarding Euboia, prepared for their revolt, giving them Alkamenes, who was supposed to have sailed to Euboia, as harmost, and the Boiotians promised them ten ships, as did Agis.

These negotiations took place independently of the Lacedaemonian state; for as long as he was at Dekeleia with his own forces, Agis had full authority to send an army wherever he wished, to assemble one, and to collect money, and during this time the allies, one could say, were much more influenced by him than by the Lacedaemonians in the city. Since he had his own forces, he was immediately formidable wherever he arrived. So he was acting in the interests of the Lesbians, while the Chians and Erythraians, also ready to revolt, turned not to Agis but to Lacedaemon, and arriving along with them was an envoy from Tissaphernes, who was the general in the coastal area for King Dareios son of Artaxerxes. For Tissaphernes was calling in the Peloponnesians and promising to furnish subsistence. As it happened, he had recently been called to account by the king for the tribute from his province, which he had fallen behind on through being unable to collect the tribute from the Hellenic cities because of the Athenians. He accordingly thought that he would be more likely to collect the tribute if he weakened the Athenians and at the same time would make the Lacedaemonians the king's allies and, just as the king had commanded him, either capture alive or kill Amorges the bastard son of Pissouthnes, who had revolted in Karia. [6] So Tissaphernes and the Chians were negotiating in common for the same end, and Kalligeitos son of Laophon, a Megarian, and Timagoras son of Athenagoras, a Kyzikene, who were both exiles from their countries living at the court of Pharnabazos son of Pharnakes, arrived at Lacedaemon around the same time, sent by Pharnabazos with the idea that they would bring ships to the Hellespont and, if possible, he himself, just as Tissaphernes was anxious to do, would cause the cities in his own

8.5. Since Thucydides comments that the war seemed to be beginning all over again, it may not be chance that he mentions the father of Alkamenes (and not that of Melanthos). Archidamos had predicted that the Spartans would pass on the war to their children (1.81); his son Agis was now the leading Spartan general, while the father of Alkamenes may well have been the Sthenelaidas whose speech (1.86–87) directly and successfully countered that of Archidamos. A complex chain of events will lead to the death of Alkamenes (8.10): the major casualty in the first action of the renewed war. On the other hand, Thucydides' only use of the Spartan term harmost, like the new Spartan war-aim of hegemony (see *HCT* V *ad* 8.2.4) and the autocratic behavior of Agis, looks ahead to the final years of the war and beyond.

province to revolt from the Athenians, in order to get the tribute and make the Lacedaemonian alliance with the king through his own agency.

Since each group was negotiating these things separately, the one from Pharnabazos and the one from Tissaphernes, there was considerable competition among the envoys at Lacedaemon for one group to persuade them to send ships and an army to Ionia and Chios and the other to the Hellespont first. The Lacedaemonians, however, were much more receptive to the arguments of the Chians and Tissaphernes. Alcibiades was helping them with their negotiations, and he was extremely close to the ephor Endios as an ancestral xenos, which was also where his family got the Lakonian name; Endios was named son of Alcibiades. Nevertheless, the Lacedaemonians first sent Phrynis, a perioikos, to Chios as an observer to see whether they had as many ships as they claimed, and in general whether the city matched the reputation given out, and when he reported that all they had heard was true, they immediately made both the Chians and the Erythraians their allies and voted to send them forty ships, since according to what the Chians had said sixty ships were already in the area. At first they were going to send ten of these on their own with Melanchridas, who was their admiral; then, after there was an earthquake, instead of Melanchridas they sent Chalkideus and instead of ten ships they prepared five in Lakonia. And the winter ended, as did the nineteenth year of this war, which Thucydides recorded.

[7] As soon as the following summer began, since the Chians were pressing them to send the ships and afraid that the Athenians would become aware of the negotiations (for all these embassies were kept secret from them), the Lacedaemonians dispatched three Spartiates to Corinth to transport the ships across the isthmus from the sea on the other side to the one toward Athens as quickly as possible and order all ships to sail to Chios, those which Agis was preparing for Lesbos as well as the rest. In all, the number of allied ships there was thirty-nine.

[8] Now in the interests of Pharnabazos, Kalligeitos and Timagoras neither joined the expedition to Chios nor gave out the money, twenty-five talents which they had brought with them for sending ships, but intended to sail later on a different expedition of their own. As for Agis, when he saw the Lacedaemonians pushing for Chios first, he had no different view of his own, but the allies came together at Corinth, deliberated, and decided that first they would sail to Chios with Chalkideus in command, the one who was preparing the five ships in Lakonia, and then to Lesbos with Alkamenes in command, the same one Agis had intended, and come to the Hellespont last (Klearchos son of Rhamphias had already been appointed

as commander there), and that they would bring half the ships across the isthmus first, and these would sail off immediately, so that the Athenians might not give any more attention to those setting out than to those brought across later. For they were making the voyage in this open way out of contempt for the weakness of the Athenians, because an important naval presence of theirs was yet to be seen.

Since they had decided on this, they immediately transported twenty-one ships. [9] But although they were in a hurry to sail, the Corinthians were concerned not to join the voyage until they had celebrated the Isthmian festival, which was at this time. On their behalf, Agis was quite amenable that they should not violate the Isthmian truce in the slightest, but that he should make the expedition his own private one. Since the Corinthians did not concur, and instead there was a delay, the Athenians began to be more aware of the Chians' plan and sent Aristokrates, one of their generals, charging them with it, and when the Chians denied it they ordered them to send ships along with them as a pledge to the alliance; they sent seven. The reasons for sending the ships were that the majority of the Chians did not know about the negotiations, while the oligarchs who were in complicity were not yet willing to have the people hostile to them before they had at least gathered some strength, and they no longer expected the Peloponnesians to come because of their delays.

[10] Meanwhile, the Isthmian festival took place, and the Athenians sent a delegation to it (for there had been a proclamation), and the plans of the Chians became increasingly transparent to them. When they returned, they immediately made arrangements to keep the ships from putting out from Kenchreai without their knowledge. But after the festival these set sail for Chios with twenty-one ships under the command of Alkamenes. And at first the Athenians sailed up to them with an equal number of ships and tried to draw them away into the open sea, but since the Peloponnesians did not follow them very far but turned back, the Athenians also went back; they had the seven Chian ships in their total and did not consider them reliable but later, after manning additional ships to total thirty-seven, they chased the Peloponnesians sailing along the coast into Peiraion in Corinthian territory; this is a deserted harbor and the farthest in the direction of the border with Epidauros. The Peloponnesians lost one ship

8.8. "So that the Athenians might not give any more attention": on the bizarre combination of caution and confidence, cf. *HCT* V *ad* 8.8.3 and Kagan 1987, p. 37.

8.10. "Peiraion" is commonly emended to "Speiraion." See *HCT* V *ad* 8.10.3.

out at sea, but they gathered the rest together and anchored. When the Athenians assaulted them both on the water with their ships and on the ground after making a landing, there was a great disorderly melée, and the Athenians disabled most of the Peloponnesian ships on the shore and killed Alkamenes the commander; some of their men were also killed. [11] After drawing away, the Athenians stationed against the enemy ships a sufficient number to blockade them and anchored with the rest at the small island on which they made their camp a short distance away, and they sent to Athens for help. For on the following day the Corinthians had arrived, bringing reinforcements for the Peloponnesian fleet, and others from the area not much later.

The Peloponnesians, seeing that keeping a guard in a deserted place was troublesome, were at a loss; while it even occurred to them to burn their ships, they then decided to beach them and maintain a guard, settling down with their land forces, until some convenient means of escape should turn up. And Agis, after he learned of this, sent them Thermon, a Spartiate. It had first been reported to the Lacedaemonians that the ships had set sail from the isthmus (for there had been orders from the ephors to Alkamenes to send a horseman whenever this happened), and they immediately wanted to send the five ships of their own with Chalkideus in command and Alcibiades with them; then, in their state of eagerness, they received the news about the ships taking refuge in Peiraion and, in their despondency that just when they had first taken up the Ionian war they had stumbled, had no further inclination to send the ships but even wanted to recall some that had previously set out.

[12] When Alcibiades realized this, he prevailed once again on Endios and the other ephors not to shrink from the voyage, saying that they would complete it before the Chians heard about the disaster for their ships, also that he himself, as soon as he set foot in Ionia, would easily persuade the cities to revolt, telling of the weakness of the Athenians and the zeal of the Lacedaemonians; for he would be more credible than anyone else. And he said privately to Endios that it would be glorious if he caused Ionia to revolt and the king to become an ally of the Lacedaemonians through his agency rather than this being the accomplishment of Agis; he himself happened to be at odds with Agis. After persuading the other ephors and Endios, he set

---

8.12. "If he caused" (probably Endios); "through his agency" (probably Alcibiades'); "he himself" (probably Alcibiades): for the confusion over this passage as well as for later sources about the enmity between Agis and Alcibiades, cf. Tucker 1908, Classen/Steup VIII, and *HCT* V *ad* 8.12.2.

sail with the five ships along with Chalkideus the Lacedaemonian, and they made the voyage in a hurry. [13] And around this same time the nineteen Peloponnesian ships that had been with Gylippos throughout the war were on the way back from Sicily. After they were intercepted off Leukas and battered by the twenty-seven Athenians ships, whose commander, Hippokles son of Menippos, was on the watch for the ships from Sicily, all but one got away from the Athenians and sailed into Corinth.

[14] Alcibiades and Chalkideus arrested all they met as they sailed to keep from being reported and, after landing on the mainland first at Korykos and releasing them there, had a preliminary meeting with some of the Chians working with them, and since these urged them to sail into the city without advance notice, they suddenly appeared before the Chians. The majority were in a state of astonishment and consternation; but among the oligarchs it had been arranged that the council happen to be in session, and when there were statements by Chalkideus and Alcibiades that many more ships were sailing over, while they did not disclose that the ships were blockaded in Peiraion, the Chians and then the Erythraians revolted from Athens. After this, they sailed with three ships and caused the revolt of Klazomenai as well. Immediately crossing over to the mainland, the Klazomenians fortified Polichna, in case there might be need for a withdrawal from the island where they lived.

So those who had revolted were all in the process of building fortifications and preparing for war; [15] the news about Chios quickly reached Athens, and since they thought the danger surrounding them was now clear and great, and that the remaining allies would not be willing to stay quiet after the largest city had defected, in their present fear, having throughout the entire war refrained from touching the thousand talents, they immediately lifted the penalties imposed on anyone who proposed this or put it to a vote, and they voted to use it and man no small number of ships, and to send right now those eight that had returned after leaving the blockade to pursue the ships with Chalkideus and failing to catch them (their commander was Strombichides son of Diotimos), and that twelve more reinforce them not much later with Thrasykles, these also leaving the blockade. Withdrawing the seven Chian ships that were taking part in their campaign against the ships in Peiraion, they freed the slaves on them and imprisoned the free men. They quickly manned ten more ships for the blockade in place of all the ones that had left and dispatched them, and they intended to man thirty more. Their zeal was great, and they took no half measures in sending reinforcements against Chios.

8.15. "The thousand talents": see 2.24.

[16] Meanwhile Strombichides arrived at Samos with his eight ships, and after adding one Samian ship he sailed to Teos and directed it to stay inactive. But Chalkideus also was sailing against Teos from Chios with twenty-three ships, and at the same time the land forces of the Klazomenians and the Erythraians were following along the shore. Strombichides learned this in advance and sailed out, and when he had reached the open sea and saw from there how many ships there were from Chios, he took flight to Samos; and they pursued. At first the Teians would not admit the land forces, but when the Athenians fled, they brought them in. The land forces stayed and waited for Chalkideus to join them from the pursuit, but since he took a long time, of their own accord they tore down the fortification the Athenians had built on the mainland side of the city of the Teians, and a few of the barbarians, whose commander was Stages, a lieutenant of Tissaphernes, came up and helped them.

[17] After Chalkideus and Alcibiades chased Strombichides to Samos, they armed the sailors from the Peloponnesian ships and left these in Chios, and after giving the ships replacement crews from Chios and manning twenty more they sailed to Miletos to cause it to revolt. For Alcibiades, who was on close terms with the leading men among the Milesians, wanted to preempt the Peloponnesian ships in winning them over and, just as he had promised, give credit for the accomplishment to the Chians, himself, Chalkideus, and the one who had sent them out, Endios, through his having joined the Chian forces and Chalkideus in causing the greatest possible number of cities to revolt. Accordingly, after escaping detection during most of the voyage and arriving slightly ahead of Strombichides as well as Thrasykles, who happened to have come just now from Athens with twelve ships and joined in the pursuit, he brought about the revolt of Miletos. The Athenians sailed after them close behind, and since the Milesians did not admit them, they anchored at Lade, the island that lies offshore.

And this first alliance of the Lacedaemonians with the king, right after the Milesians revolted, was concluded by Tissaphernes and Chalkideus: [18] "The Lacedaemonians and their allies made an alliance with the King and Tissaphernes on the following terms. Whatsoever territory and cities the King holds and his ancestors held, this is to belong to the King, and whatsoever money or anything else came in to the Athenians from these cities, the King and the Lacedaemonians and their allies in common are to put a stop to it, so that the Athenians receive neither money nor anything else. The King and the Lacedaemonians and their allies are to conduct the war against the Athenians in common, and it is to be disallowed to make an end to the war unless it is resolved on by both parties, the King and the

Lacedaemonians and their allies. If any revolt from the King, they are to be enemies of the Lacedaemonians and their allies, and if any revolt from the Lacedaemonians and their allies, they are to be enemies of the King in the same way." [19] This was the alliance that was concluded.

After this the Chians immediately manned ten ships and sailed to Anaia, wanting to learn about conditions in Miletos and at the same time to cause the cities to revolt. But when a message came to them from Chalkideus to sail back again, and that Amorges was arriving on land with an army, they sailed to the sanctuary of Zeus; and they observed sixteen ships, with which Diomedon had sailed in from Athens even after Thrasykles. When they saw them, they fled to Ephesos with one ship; the others, to Teos. The Athenians captured four empty ships whose crews had gotten ashore first; the rest took refuge in the city of Teos. The Athenians sailed off to Samos, while the Chians set sail with the rest of their ships and, along with the land forces, caused Lebedos and then Erai to revolt. After this, each made their way home, land forces and ships.

[20] Around this same time, the twenty Peloponnesian ships in Peiraion, which had previously been chased and blockaded by an equal number of Athenian ships, sailed out suddenly and won a sea battle, capturing four Athenian ships, and after sailing off to Kenchreai they prepared once again for the voyage to Chios and Ionia. And from Lacedaemon Astyochos came to them as admiral, the man to whom the entire naval command now passed. After the land forces withdrew from Teos, Tissaphernes, after coming in person with an army and finishing the demolition of the fortifications at Teos, whatever was left, also withdrew. And after he left, Diomedon, arriving not much later with ten Athenian ships, formally arranged with the Teians that they be admitted as well. He sailed along the coast to Erai and assaulted it, and since he was unable to capture the city, he sailed away.

[21] At this same time, an uprising on Samos by the common people against the upper classes also took place in conjunction with the Athenians, who happened to be present aboard three ships. The Samian common people killed about two hundred of the upper classes in all, and after punishing four hundred with exile and distributing their land and houses among themselves, they administered the city from now on, since the Athenians voted on autonomy for them after this in the belief that they

8.19. "Amorges was arriving": see 8.5. It is unclear when he became an Athenian ally (see 8.28); for the problem, cf. *HCT* V *ad* 8.5.5, Kagan 1987, p. 29–32, and Erbse 1989, pp. 95–96.

were now reliable, and they extended no rights to the land-owning classes nor was it allowed any longer for anyone from the common people to give a daughter to them in marriage or take one from them.

[22] After this, in the same summer, the Chians, just as they had been at the start, with no lessening of their zeal to present themselves in force and, even without the Peloponnesians, cause the cities to revolt, and at the same time wanting as many as possible to share their risks, made their own expedition to Lesbos with thirteen ships, in full accordance with the instructions from the Lacedaemonians to go to Lesbos second and from there to the Hellespont, and the land forces of both the Peloponnesians who were present and the local allies followed along the shore to Klazomenai and Kyme; Eualas, a Spartiate, was their commander and Deiniadas, a perioikos, commander of the fleet. The ships put in at Methymna and caused its revolt first, and four ships were left there; the rest then caused Mytilene to revolt.

[23] As for Astyochos the Lacedaemonian admiral, he sailed from Kenchreai with four ships, as he had intended, and arrived at Chios. And on the third day after his arrival, the twenty-five Attic ships sailed to Lesbos, under the command of Leon and Diomedon; Leon had come later with ten ships from Athens as reinforcements. Astyochos, also setting sail late on the same day and adding one Chian ship, sailed to Lesbos in case there was anything he could do to help. He reached Pyrrha and from there, on the next day, Eresos; there he learned that Mytilene had been taken by the Athenians in their first assault; for the Athenians, putting into the harbor unexpectedly in their sailing formation, overcame the Chian ships, and after landing and defeating in battle those who offered resistance they took over the city. Learning this from the Eresians and the Chian ships from Methymna with Euboulos, which had been left there earlier, fled when Mytilene was captured, and (now three, since one was captured by the Athenians) fell in with him, Astyochos stopped heading for Mytilene, but after causing Eresos to revolt and arming the men from his ships he sent them along the coast on foot to Antissa and Methymna, assigning Eteonikos as their commander. He himself sailed along the coast with his ships and the three Chian ships, hoping that the Methymnaians would take courage when they saw him and continue in the revolt. But since everything at Lesbos went adversely for him, he took his men on board and sailed off to Chios. The allied land forces, which had intended to go to the Hellespont, were also brought back to their various cities. And after this

8.23. On the several problems of the text, I have followed *HCT* V *ad* 8.23.4, 5.

six of the allied Peloponnesian ships at Kenchreai joined them at Chios. The Athenians restored the situation on Lesbos, and after sailing from there and capturing the Klazomenian fortifications, which were under construction at Polichna on the mainland, they brought the people back to their city on the island, except for the ones responsible for the revolt; they went off to Daphnous. So Klazomenai passed back over to the Athenians.

[24] In the same summer, the Athenians, using their twenty ships that lay moored against Miletos at Lade, made a landing at Panormos in Milesian territory and killed Chalkideus, the Lacedaemonian commander, who had come to help with a few men, and the third day after that they set up a trophy, which the Milesians took down, as a dedication made without control of the territory. And Leon and Diomedon, using the Athenian ships from Lesbos, carried on the war against the Chians from their ships, setting out from the Oinoussai Islands off Chios, from Sidoussa and Pteleon, which were forts they held in Erythraian territory, and from Lesbos; as marines, they had some hoplites from the register pressed into this service. After they also landed at Kardamyle and Boliskos, defeated in battle the Chian defenders who came up, and killed many of them, they left the countryside desolate in this area, and they won again in another battle at Phanai and in a third at Leukonion.

And after this, the Chians now no longer came out against them, and the Athenians plundered their country, which was well stocked and unharmed from the Persian wars up to this time. For the Chians alone, of all the people I have known of next to the Lacedaemonians, have been prosperous and at the same time prudent, and the more their city increased in stature the more securely they ordered themselves. And even this very revolt, if this seems an action of theirs away from the safer course, was not something they ventured to carry out before they were going to share the danger with many excellent allies and were aware that after the Sicilian disaster not even the Athenians themselves denied any longer that their situation was quite terrible; if they went astray somewhere among the unaccountable aspects of human existence, they committed their mistake along with many who held the same opinion, that Athens would quickly be destroyed altogether. So then, as they were being shut off from the sea and plundered on land, some undertook to bring the city over to the Athenians; the rulers, who knew about them, took no action themselves, but bringing Astyochos the admiral from Erythrai with the four ships accompanying

8.24. "Which the Milesians took down": an unusual and interesting incident, see *HCT* V *ad* 8.24.1.

him, they considered how they could put an end to the plot in the most temperate possible way, whether by taking hostages or by some other means. This was how they were occupied.

[25] And from Athens, at the end of this same summer, a thousand Athenian and fifteen hundred Argive hoplites (of which five hundred Argives were light-armed whom the Athenians had rearmed) and a thousand from the allies, on forty-eight ships, some of which were also troop transports, with Phrynichos, Onomakles, and Skironides as generals, sailed into Samos, and after crossing to Miletos they set up camp. The Milesians came out, eight hundred of their own hoplites, the Peloponnesians who had come with Chalkideus, some auxiliaries of Tissaphernes, and Tissaphernes, present himself with his cavalry, and they engaged the Athenians and their allies. And the Argives, dashing forward out of the formation with their wing in a contemptuous disorderly advance against Ionians who would not stand up to them, were defeated by the Milesians and just under three hundred were killed; but the Athenians, after defeating the Peloponnesians first and driving back the barbarians and the miscellaneous masses but not encountering the Milesians, since after their rout of the Argives they fell back on the city when they saw the rest of their side beaten, came to a halt right by the city knowing themselves now victorious. And in this battle it turned out that the Ionians on both sides conquered the Dorians; for the Athenians defeated the Peloponnesians facing them, and the Milesians, the Argives. After setting up a trophy, the Athenians began preparing to wall off the site, which was shaped like an isthmus, thinking that if they brought Miletos over, the other places would readily come over to them as well.

[26] At this point, when it was already late in the day, the news reached them that the fifty-five ships from the Peloponnesos and Sicily were practically there. For from the Sikeliots, with Hermokrates the Syracusan especially urging them on to contribute now to the final stage of the destruction of the Athenians, twenty Syracusan and two Selinountine ships came, and from the Peloponnesos the ones they had been preparing, now finally ready; and the two combined fleets, assigned to Therimenes the Lacedaemonian to take to Astyochos the admiral, sailed first into Leros, the island lying in front of Miletos. Then, sailing from there into the Iasic gulf when they learned that the Athenians were at Miletos, they wanted to know first what the situation was at Miletos. They learned the facts about the battle when Alcibiades came on horseback to Teichioussa in Milesian territory, right where they had bivouacked on their voyage in the gulf, since Alcibiades had been there fighting alongside the Milesians

and Tissaphernes, and he warned them, unless they wanted to ruin once and for all not only the situation in Ionia but the whole campaign, to come to the aid of Miletos immediately and not allow it to be walled off.

[27] They were going to come to its aid at daybreak; but since Phrynichos the Athenian general had received from Leros a reliable account about the enemy ships, he refused when his colleagues wanted to stay where they were and fight it out at sea; he would not do this himself, would not let them do this, and would not, as far as it was in his power, let anyone else do this. Whereas it was possible to fight at a later time knowing clearly against how many of the enemy ships they would be fighting and with how many of their own, with full and unhurried preparation, he would never, in giving in to the reproach of disgrace, run risks without reason. For it was not disgraceful for the Athenians to withdraw from an enemy fleet if the situation called for it; in any situation, it would be a more disgraceful result if they were defeated, and the city would not only fall into disgrace but into extreme danger as well; it was barely possible for this city, after the disasters it had experienced, to take the initiative somewhere with sound preparation voluntarily, or even in extreme emergency—but to go into danger when there was no compulsion, by free choice? He told them to take up the wounded as quickly as possible, also their land forces and the equipment they had brought with them, and, leaving what they had taken from enemy territory in order to lighten their ships, to sail off to Samos and from there, with all their ships now united, attack if there were opportunities. Phrynichos prevailed and carried out what he had advised; and he seemed, no more at this moment than afterward, not only in this matter but wherever he was involved, a man not without intelligence. So in this way, with their victory incomplete, the Athenians left Miletos as soon as evening came, and the Argives sailed off for home in a hurry and angry over their disaster.

8.27. "Phrynichos prevailed": scholars have tended to approve of his policy, following Thucydides' lead while often noting that his praise of Phrynichos seems not only emphatic but defiant. Kagan (1987, pp. 65–68), in particular, has persuasively argued that Phrynichos exaggerated the risks and ignored the magnitude of the Athenian opportunity (Kagan doubts treasonous intent), and that accepting his advice proved very costly; cf. also Schindel 1970, pp. 294–97, *HCT* V *ad* 8.27.5, and Grossi 1984, p. 24. In any case, Thucydides endows him with formidable speaking abilities; it is unlikely that the powerful effects of repetition ("He would not . . ." and "disgrace—not disgraceful—more disgraceful"; the former instance is strikingly marked by hiatus) were lavished on a rough draft which Thucydides would have eventually replaced with direct discourse, see Hammond 1977, pp. 148, 154.

[28] Getting under way at daybreak from Teichioussa, the Peloponnesians put in there subsequently, waited one day, and on the next, after they had added the Chian ships, which had initially been pursued along with Chalkideus, they wanted to sail back to Teichioussa for the equipment they had unloaded. When they arrived, Tissaphernes came up with his land forces and persuaded them to sail to Iasos, where Amorges, an enemy, was in control. And making a sudden attack on Iasos, without anyone expecting their ships to be other than Attic, they captured it; the Syracusans were especially commended in this action. After taking Amorges alive, the bastard son of Pissouthnes who was in revolt from the king, the Peloponnesians handed him over to Tissaphernes to bring back to the king if he liked, which was the king's command to him, and sacked Iasos, and the army took a very large amount of property; for the place had wealth of long standing. They brought in the mercenaries from Amorges and, rather than harming them, enrolled them in their own ranks, since most were from the Peloponnesos. And after handing over to Tissaphernes the town and all the captives, slaves and free men, for whom they agreed to receive one daric apiece from him, they then withdrew to Miletos. Pedaritos son of Leon, whom the Lacedaemonians had sent out to Chios as a commander, they sent off by land as far as Erythrai with the mercenary force taken from Amorges and also appointed Philippos to Miletos on the spot. And the summer ended.

[29] In the following winter Tissaphernes, after making defensive arrangements at Iasos, came to Miletos, and he distributed a month's pay to all the ships, just as he had promised in Lacedaemon, at one Attic drachma a day for each man, but in the future he wanted to pay three obols until he had asked the king; if the king told him to, he said he would pay the full drachma. While Hermokrates the Syracusan general refused this (for Therimenes, who was not admiral but sailing along with them to deliver the fleet to Astyochos, was lax about the pay), there was agreement nevertheless on a larger amount than three obols for each man for every five ships. For to five ships he paid three talents a month; and this was paid to the rest, in proportion to the number of ships exceeding that figure, at the same rate.

8.29. Tissaphernes originally wanted to cut the pay from a drachma to three obols (which would be two and a half talents for five ships). Interpretation of the compromise agreement is a notorious crux; I have inclined toward an explanation involving limited and plausible emendation, see Boeckh 1857, p. 377, n. 2. On later and more complicated solutions, cf. Tucker 1908 and *HCT* V *ad* 8.29.2; Pearson 1985 suggests that Thucydides is suppressing a rake-off for the officers (then why would he tell us as much as he does?).

[30] In the same winter, when thirty-five more ships and the generals Charminos, Strombichides, and Euktemon had come from home to join the Athenians, after assembling the ships from Chios and all the others the Athenians wanted to draw lots to blockade Miletos with the fleet while sending naval and land forces against Chios. They acted accordingly; Strombichides, Onomakles, and Euktemon, using thirty ships and taking on troop transports part of the thousand hoplites who had come to Miletos, sailed against Chios as their lot, while the others who stayed at Samos controlled the sea with seventy-four ships and made descents on Miletos. [31] Astyochos, who happened to be on Chios at this time collecting hostages because of the treachery there, ceased this activity when he was aware that the ships with Therimenes had come and the situation of the alliance was stronger, and taking the ten Peloponnesian ships and ten Chian ships he set sail and, after attacking Pteleon without capturing it, sailed along the coast to Klazomenai and ordered the Athenian sympathizers there to move inland to Daphnous and come over to his side; Tamos as well, the lieutenant for Ionia, joined in giving the order. Since they did not obey it, he made an assault on the city, which was unwalled, could not capture it, and sailed away on a strong wind, in his own case to Phokaia and Kyme, the rest of the ships to harbors in the islands Marathoussa, Pele, and Drymoussa lying off Klazomenai. All that had been stored there for safe keeping by the Klazomenians they either plundered and consumed while waiting eight days on account of the winds or put on board when they sailed off to Phokaia and Kyme to join Astyochos.

[32] While he was there, envoys from the Lesbians arrived, once again wishing to revolt. They persuaded him, but since the Corinthians and the other allies were unenthusiastic because of the earlier failure, he set sail and went to Chios. After this, Pedaritos, who had previously been coming along the shore with a land force and was at Erythrai, crossed over to Chios with his army; also available to Astyochos were soldiers from the ships, numbering five hundred, who had been left behind by Chalkideus along with their arms. Since some of the Lesbians were proposing to revolt, Astyochos made the argument to Pedaritos and the Chians that they ought to bring up their ships and effect the revolt of Lesbos; for either they would have more allies or, if they failed, they would damage the Athenians. But they would not comply, and Pedaritos refused to turn the Chian ships over to him. [33] He then, taking the five Corinthian ships and a sixth from Megara, one from Hermione, and the Lakonian ships he had brought with him, sailed for Miletos to assume the position of admiral, uttering many threats against the Chians to the effect that he would most

assuredly not come to their aid if they were in any need. And stopping at Korykos in Erythraian territory he spent the night there.

The Athenians from Samos, who were sailing to Chios with their army, were separated from them by the intervening ridge when they anchored there as well, and they failed to notice one another. When a letter came from Pedaritos during the night saying that Erythraian prisoners from Samos, released for the purpose of betraying Erythrai, had arrived there, Astyochos immediately set sail for Erythrai again, after coming this close to encountering the Athenians. Pedaritos also sailed across to meet him, and since on investigating the story about the apparent traitors they discovered that it had all been alleged as a pretext for escaping from Samos, they exonerated them and sailed off, the one voyaging to Chios and the other to Miletos as he had planned.

[34] Meanwhile the Athenian forces on the ships, also sailing from Korykos and rounding Arginon, happened on three Chian warships and pursued as soon as they saw them. A great storm came up, and the Chian ships barely escaped into the harbor, but the three most impetuous of the Athenian ships were wrecked and cast ashore at the city of the Chians and some of the men captured, the others killed, while the rest of the ships escaped into the harbor called Phoinikous at the base of Mimas. From that point, they subsequently anchored at Lesbos and began preparing their fortifications.

[35] In this same winter, Hippokrates the Lacedaemonian, sailing from the Peloponnesos with ten Thourian ships under the command of Dorieus son of Diagoras and two others, one Lakonian ship, and one Syracusan, put in at Knidos; its revolt had by now been brought about by Tissaphernes. When their people at Miletos heard about them, they ordered them to guard Knidos with half their ships and to stay around Triopion with the rest and apprehend the merchant ships stopping there from Egypt; Triopion, a sanctuary of Apollo, is a headland projecting from Knidian territory. The Athenians found out about this, and sailing from Samos they seized the six ships on guard at Triopion; the men from them got away. After this, sailing into Knidos, they attacked the city, which was unwalled, and nearly took it. The next day they attacked again, and, since after the people had built better defenses during the night, and the men

8.32–33. It is not surprising that Pedaritos and the Chians spurned Astyochos' proposal; why would their *failure* damage the Athenians? It is possible that Thucydides deliberately gave Astyochos a clumsy argument, in keeping with a frequent undertone of mockery toward the "admiral"; cf. Erbse 1989, p. 9.

who escaped from the ships at Triopion had come in to join them, they could now do them less harm than previously, they left and sailed off to Samos after plundering the territory of the Knidians.

[36] When Astyochos arrived at Miletos around the same time to take command of the fleet, the Peloponnesians were still well provided with everything for their camp, for adequate pay was being given and the large amount of property plundered from Iasos was at the disposal of the soldiers, and also the Milesians were zealously carrying on the war. All the same, the first treaty with Tissaphernes, the one made by Chalkideus, seemed deficient to the Peloponnesians and not in their favor, and they made another while Therimenes was still there. It is as follows: [37] "The treaty of the Lacedaemonians and their allies with King Dareios and the King's sons and Tissaphernes. Let there be a peace and friendship on the following terms. Whatsoever territory and cities belong to King Dareios or belonged to his father or ancestors, let neither the Lacedaemonians nor their allies go against these either in war or to do any harm, nor let either the Lacedaemonians or their allies exact tribute from these cities; nor let either King Dareios or those whom the King rules go against the Lacedaemonians or their allies in war or to do any harm. If the Lacedaemonians or their allies need anything from the King, or the King from the Lacedaemonians or their allies, whatever they persuade one another, let this be right for them to do. Let both parties conduct the war against the Athenians and their allies in common. If they terminate it, let them do so in common. Whatsoever forces are in the territory of the King, the King having sent for them, let the King pay their expenses. If any of whatsoever cities are party to the treaty go against the territory of the King, let the others prevent this and aid the King to the limits of their power; and if any of those in the territory of the King or in any territory which the King rules go against the territory of the Lacedaemonians or their allies, let the King prevent this and aid them to the limits of his power. [38] Therimenes, turning over the ships to Astyochos after this treaty was made, sailed away in a small boat and disappeared from sight.

The Athenians from Lesbos, who had already crossed over to Chios with their army and were in control of land and sea, fortified Delphinion, a place that was in any case strong on the landward side and also possessed harbors and was not far from the city of the Chians. And the Chians, who had already been drubbed in a number of battles and besides were very far from enjoying good relations among themselves but, since by now the faction of Tydeus son of Ion had been put to death by Pedaritos for atticizing, and the rest of the city was forcibly held down by oligarchs, were suspicious of one another instead, stayed inactive and did not in their own eyes appear a match for the enemy, nor did the mercenaries with Pedaritos. They sent to Miletos, however, and urged Astyochos to help them; when he paid no heed, Pedaritos sent a letter about him to Lacedaemon alleging misconduct. So in Chios the Athenians had a situation that had reached this state; from Samos, their ships made descents against the ones at Miletos, but when these would not put out against them, they withdrew to Samos again and stayed inactive.

[39] In the same winter, the twenty-seven ships prepared by the Lacedaemonians for Pharnabazos through the agency of Kalligeitos the Megarian and Timagoras the Kyzikene put out from the Peloponnesos and sailed for Ionia around the solstice, and Antisthenes, a Spartiate, sailed with them as commander. The Lacedaemonians also sent eleven Spartiates along as advisers to Astyochos, one of whom was Lichas son of Arkesilas. And their instructions were, when they arrived at Miletos, to join Astyochos in attending to matters in general in the way that would be best, to send out either these same ships or a greater or a smaller number to Pharnabazos in the Hellespont, if that seemed best, assigning as commander Klearchos son of Rhamphias, who was sailing with them, and to dismiss Astyochos from his position of admiral, if that seemed best, and appoint Antisthenes; for in view of the letter from Pedaritos they were suspicious of him. They sailed accordingly from Malea across the open sea and stopped at Melos, and on encountering ten Athenian ships they captured three without their crews and burned them. After this, afraid that the Athenian ships that escaped from Melos might inform the Athenians at Samos of their approach, which was just what happened, they sailed toward Crete, making it a longer voyage and staying on guard, and then put in at Kaunos in Asia. From there, considering themselves now at a safe location, they sent a message to the ships at Miletos about being convoyed along the coast.

[40] During this time, the Chians and Pedaritos did not cease to send messages to Astyochos despite his refusal to act, urging him to help them against the blockade with all his ships and not look on while the largest of the allied cities in Ionia was being both shut off from the sea and despoiled by brigandage on land. For the slaves of the Chians, who were numerous and in fact the most numerous for any single city except that of the Lacedaemonians, and on account of their numbers at the same time punished for misconduct with relative severity, immediately, once the Athenian army appeared solidly based behind fortifications, deserted to them in large numbers, and because they knew the country, it was these who did

it the greatest damage. Accordingly, the Chians claimed that he should help them, while there was still a hope and possibility of stopping the Athenians, since Delphinion was being fortified but not yet completely, and a larger rampart was being added around their camp and ships. And Astyochos, even though this had not been his intention in view of his earlier threats, was motivated to send them the help when he saw that the allies were enthusiastic as well.

[41] But meanwhile news arrived from Kaunos that the twenty-seven ships and the advisers from the Lacedaemonians were there, and considering all other matters secondary to convoying this many ships along the coast so as to increase their control of the sea, and getting the Lacedaemonians who had come to observe him across safely, he immediately sailed for Kaunos, giving up the voyage to Chios. Landing at Kos in Meropis during his voyage along the coast, he sacked the town, which was not only unwalled but reduced to ruins, as it happened, by the occurrence of an earthquake, definitely the most severe we can recall, sending the people to the mountains in flight, and through his raids he treated the area as booty, except for the free inhabitants; these he let go. Arriving at Knidos from Kos during the night, he was pressured by the appeals of the Knidians into not sending his sailors ashore but sailing directly, just as he was, against the twenty-seven Athenian ships, which Charminos, one of the generals from Samos, was using to keep a watch against the arrival of the same ships from the Peloponnesos that Astyochos was sailing to join.

The Athenians at Samos had been informed from Melos about their approach, and Charminos had guards watching off Syme, Chalke, Rhodes, and Lycia; for he already knew about their being at Kaunos. [42] So Astyochos, just as he was, sailed on to Syme before there might be time to report him, in case he could overmaster the ships somewhere on the high seas. And rain along with foggy climate caused his ships to wander and fall into confusion. At daybreak, when his fleet was scattered, and one part of it, the left wing, was now visible to the Athenians, with the rest still wandering around the island, Charminos and the Athenians hastily set sail against them with fewer than their twenty ships, on the assumption that these were the ships from Kaunos they had been watching for. Falling on them immediately, they sank three and damaged others, and they had the upper hand in the action until, unexpectedly, the majority of the ships came into view, and they were cut off on all sides. Taking flight at this point, they lost six ships and fled for refuge with the rest to the island of Teutloussa, and from there to Halikarnassos. After this, the Peloponnesians put in at Knidos and were joined by the twenty-seven ships from

Kaunos, sailed with the combined fleet to Syme and set up a trophy, and anchored again at Knidos.

[43] The Athenians, sailing to Syme with all their ships from Samos when they heard about the sea battle, did not rush to attack the fleet at Knidos, nor did it attack them, but sailed back to Samos after getting the naval equipment on Syme and stopping at Lorymoi on the mainland. All the Peloponnesian ships were now at Knidos and making whatever repairs were needed, and the eleven Lacedaemonians held discussions with Tissaphernes when he arrived concerning both what had already been negotiated, in case any of it dissatisfied them, and what way of fighting the war in the future would be the best and the most advantageous for both sides. Lichas in particular looked into the way things were being handled, and he said that neither treaty was a good agreement, not that of Chalkideus and not that of Therimenes, but indeed it was a terrible thing if all land the King and his ancestors once ruled he claimed to be master of now as well (for that made it possible for all the islands to go back to slavery, and Thessaly and Lokroi and places all the way to Boiotia), and instead of freedom the Lacedaemonians would be conferring the rule of the Mede on the Hellenes. He accordingly told them to make other treaties that were better, saying that at any rate the Lacedaemonians would not observe these, nor did they need any of the sustenance on these terms. Offended, Tissaphernes went away in a rage without accomplishing anything.

[44] The Lacedaemonians, on the other hand, had intentions of sailing to Rhodes, since proposals from its most important men had reached them, hoping that they could bring over an island with no lack of strength in its numbers of sailors and land forces, and believing at the same time that they themselves, on the basis of their existing alliance, would be able to maintain their fleet without asking Tissaphernes for money. Accordingly, sailing immediately from Knidos in the same winter and at Rhodes putting in first at Kameiros with ninety-four ships, they terrified most of the population, who did not know about the negotiations and, especially since their city was unwalled, took flight. The Lacedaemonians then called them together, also the people of the two cities, Lindos and Ialysos, and

8.43. The clause in parentheses has a finite verb and so would normally be an authorial observation—yet the tone is unmistakably that of Lichas (despite Classen/Steup VIII *ad* 8.43.3). The construction might be claimed as analogous to 7.42 (see note there), but such a device does not seem motivated in this passage; emendation to the infinitive is almost universal and perhaps warranted (I am grateful to A.R. Dyck for pointing out to me that this would correct a very natural corruption). On Lichas, see Pouilloux and Salviat 1983, also 5.50 and 8.84n.

persuaded the Rhodians to revolt from Athens. And at this juncture the Athenians, who were aware of the situation, sailed from Samos with their fleet hoping to get there in time, but since they arrived slightly too late, they sailed back to Chalke for the moment, and from there to Samos, and subsequently made war against Rhodes by raiding from Chalke and Kos. As for the Peloponnesians, they levied the sum of thirty-two talents from the Rhodians, while otherwise remaining inactive for eighty days with their ships drawn up on shore.

[45] But at this time and even earlier, before they moved to Rhodes, the following negotiations were going on. After the death of Chalkideus and the battle at Miletos, since Alcibiades was under suspicion among the Peloponnesians, and a letter of theirs had arrived from Lacedaemon telling Astyochos to put him to death (for he was a personal enemy of Agis and appeared generally untrustworthy), he first withdrew in alarm to Tissaphernes and then, where Tissaphernes was involved, did as much damage as he could to the Peloponnesian cause, and by getting to be his instructor in every aspect he reduced the payments, so that instead of an Attic drachma, three obols were paid and this with no regularity, telling Tissaphernes to say to the Peloponnesians that the Athenians, out of their longer years of naval experience, paid their own men three obols, not because of poverty so much as to keep the sailors from behaving arrogantly in their prosperity, some getting their bodies in worse condition by spending on the sort of things that would lead to their weakness, others deserting ship because they would not be abandoning pay held back to commit them.

And he instructed him in the way to bribe the trierarchs and generals into agreeing with him in these matters, all but the Syracusans; their Hermokrates alone, on behalf of the whole alliance, opposed him. And when cities asked for money he sent them off with a retort of his own on Tissaphernes' behalf, that the Chians were shameless when, as the richest of the Hellenes, they were being saved by outside assistance and still demanded that others risk their lives and their money on behalf of their

---

8.45–56. "Even earlier": how far back does the flashback take us? The time involved is shorter if 8.29 and 8.45 report separate though similar pay-reduction incidents. While *HCT* V *ad* 8.45.2 inclines toward this view, I believe that in 8.45 Thucydides has retold the incident of 8.29, this time taking us behind the scenes and leaving (insufficient) clues (i.e., the reduction from a whole drachma, the protests of Hermokrates, the prospect of greater bounty from the king) to show that this is the same event; see especially Erbse 1989, pp. 32–36, also (with more emphasis on the unrevised condition of book 8) Brunt 1952, p. 83, Lewis 1977, p. 92, and Kagan 1987, p. 73, n. 16.

freedom. As for the other cities, he said that, since before they revolted they kept paying up to the Athenians, they were in the wrong if they did not consent to contribute as much and still more on their own behalf now. He also pointed out that Tissaphernes, since he was fighting the war with his own funds, was naturally being frugal now, but if support ever came down from the king he would give them their pay in full and offer reasonable assistance to the cities.

[46] Alcibiades also recommended to Tissaphernes that he be neither overly eager to terminate the war nor willing, whether by bringing over the Phoenician ships he was preparing or by providing pay for more Hellenes, to give the same people control on both the land and sea, but that he let the two sides each have one part of the command, and that it be left possible for the king to bring in the other side against the one making trouble for him at any time. If command of both land and sea were unified, he himself would have no one to join with in getting rid of the side in control if he were unwilling at some point to stand up himself and fight the contest through to the end at great expense and risk. The cheaper way was this: at a small fraction of the expense and at the same time with security for himself, to wear the Hellenes out against one another. And he said that the more suitable partners in rule were the Athenians; they had fewer ambitions on land and were fighting with both the rationale and the practice that were most in his interests. For they would be in league with him in making the coastal district subject to themselves and all those living in the king's land subject to him; the others, on the contrary, had come to liberate them. And it was not likely that the Lacedaemonians would now be liberating the Hellenes from the Hellenes themselves but would not liberate them from them as barbarians unless they eventually drove them out.

He accordingly urged him first to wear down both sides and then, after trimming the Athenians down as much as possible, finally get the Peloponnesians out of the country. And Tissaphernes on the whole had these inclinations, at least as far as it was possible to infer from what he was doing. As a consequence, he gave Alcibiades his trust as though he was advising him well on these matters, and he furnished the Peloponnesians with inferior subsistence and would not allow them to fight at sea but instead, by claiming that the Phoenician fleet would be coming and the issue contested from a position of superiority, devastated their cause and brought their fleet down from its top condition, which had become very strong, and in general, that he was not taking part in the war enthusiastically was too obvious to miss.

[47] During his stay with them, Alcibiades gave Tissaphernes and the king this advice partly because he believed it to be the best and partly because he was making the fundamental provisions for his own restoration to his country, since he knew that there was the possibility, if he did not destroy it, that some day he could persuade his way back, and he believed that he would be at his most persuasive if he were seen to be in favor with Tissaphernes. That was what actually happened. The Athenian soldiers at Samos became aware that he had great influence with him, and then, partly because Alcibiades sent word to the most influential men there to get himself mentioned among the best people as willing to return home provided there was an oligarchy rather than the iniquity that had cast him out, to make Tissaphernes their friend, and live with them as a fellow-citizen, but even more on their own initiative, the Athenian trierarchs and the most influential men on Samos were eager to overthrow the democracy.

[48] And this movement first occurred in the camp and subsequently went from there to the city. Certain men crossed over from Samos and had a conference with Alcibiades, and since he held out the possibility that he would first make Tissaphernes their friend and then the king as well, if they were not governed by democracy (for that way the king would have more trust in them), the most influential men had great hopes both for themselves, as the ones enduring the greatest hardships, that they would also get the government into their hands, and that they would prevail over the enemy as well.

When they went to Samos, they organized those who were favorably disposed into a conspiracy and also told the people openly that the king would be their friend and supply money if Alcibiades were restored and they were not governed by democracy. The mob, whatever anger it felt for the moment over these arrangements, kept quiet because of its expectations that the pay from the king would be easy to get; the organizers of the oligarchy, after they had communicated with the masses, once again studied Alcibiades' proposition among themselves and with the majority of their association.

While it appeared feasible and trustworthy to the others, Phrynichos, who was still general, found nothing satisfactory in it but held the opinion that, just as Alcibiades (as was indeed the case) had no more wish for oligarchy than for democracy nor any consideration other than a way of being recalled by his associates through changing the city's existing order, whereas guarding against faction was their own greatest necessity, it was also not rewarding for the king, now that the Peloponnesians were equally a presence on the sea and were in possession of cities within his realm, not the smallest, to take on trouble by aligning himself with the Athenians, whom he did not trust, when it was possible for him to make friends of the Peloponnesians, from whom he had suffered no harm. As for the allied cities, to whom they would of course be promising oligarchy, since they themselves, of course, would not be under democracy, he said that he knew very well that those who had revolted would not be any the likelier to come back to them, just as those who stood by them would not be any the more likely to be loyal; for they would not want to be subjects in either an oligarchy or a democracy in preference to being independent in whichever of these two they ended up. And as for the so-called gallant gentlemen, they believed that these would present them with no less trouble than the common people would, since these were the purveyors and the instigators to the common people of evils, from which they themselves benefited the most. And as far as it was up to them, the allies would be put to death without trial and more violently, whereas the common people were their refuge and a restraint on the gallant gentlemen.

Since this was what the cities had learned from actual events, he was absolutely certain that this was how they thought. Accordingly, he for one was not satisfied with anything about the proposition from Alcibiades or the reaction to it. [49] But the conspirators who were at the meeting accepted the proposition in front of them, which had been their original decision, and they prepared to send Peisandros and other envoys to Athens

8.48. The speech is much too carefully written (Phrynichos again makes effective use of hiatus) for a rough draft; see 8.27n. "They would . . . be promising": emendation to the future tense seems essential; it is not implausible (*pace HCT* V *ad* 8.48.5) that Phrynichos, once he has dealt with Alcibiades' proposals, should devote most of his speech to a new but relevant topic on which he claims to be an expert (on the relationship to 4.85–87, see Plant 1992, and on the popularity of the empire and the factor of class, 1.96.n). Interpretation of that portion is highly controversial, and I briefly state my opinions (where I have not effectively done so through translation) on several points: the faction to be avoided is among the Athenians overall, not among the conspirators; the conspirators were nevertheless a politically heterogeneous group; the group included democrats, Phrynichos among them (his later turn to oligarchy was a matter of survival); not significantly represented in the group were the "gallant gentlemen" (see 4.40n and Bourriot 1995, especially vol. 1, pp. 178–88), ambitious aristocrats presumed to be Alcibiades' strongest supporters; the claim that the democrats protected the allies against abuses by the "gallant gentlemen" is very problematic, especially since Thucydides appears to endorse the speech overall. Cf. Grayson 1972, Hammond 1977, *HCT* V *ad* 48.6, and Grossi 1984, pp. 27–35.

to negotiate for both the return of Alcibiades and the dissolution of the democracy and make Tissaphernes a friend of the Athenians.

[50] Since he realized that there was going to be a proposal for the recall of Alcibiades, and that the Athenians would consent to that, Phrynichos, fearing in view of the opposition expressed in his speech that if Alcibiades returned he would do him harm, resorted to the following. He sent to Astyochos the admiral of the Lacedaemonians, who was then still at Miletos, telling him in a secret letter that Alcibiades was ruining their cause by making Tissaphernes a friend of the Athenians, giving a clear written account of the rest of the situation as well; he said that where an enemy was involved, it was pardonable in himself to do him harm even at cost to the city. Astyochos had no intentions of punishing Alcibiades, especially since he was no longer coming within reach as he once did, but went inland to the residence of Alcibiades and Tissaphernes at Magnesia and told them what was in the letter from Samos, becoming an informer in turn, and then, so it was said, for personal profit proceeded to attach himself to Tissaphernes as a partner in both this matter and the rest; this was the reason he offered weak resistance over the pay when it was not full.

Alcibiades immediately sent a letter against Phrynichos to those in authority at Samos telling them what he had done, also demanding that he be put to death. Alarmed and in the most extreme danger because of the information against him, Phrynichos again wrote to Astyochos, reproaching him because what he had told him earlier had not been kept secret, as was honorable, and also telling him that now he was ready to enable them to destroy the entire Athenian army at Samos, with written details of how (since Samos was unfortified) he could arrange this, and that since his life was now in danger from them he could not be faulted for taking this or any other action before being destroyed by his worst enemies. This information Astyochos also gave to Alcibiades.

[51] And when Phrynichos learned in advance that he was playing him false, and that a letter from Alcibiades about these proposals had just about arrived, he preempted it by being the one to bring the message to the army

---

8.50–51. Scholars have variously interpreted this famous intrigue, with a marked tendency to doubt that Thucydides has told (or understood) the entire story (or even that it ever took place). I find it possible to believe that the "not unintelligent" Phrynichos expected his second letter to be divulged—and that this is consistent with Thucydides' language (especially since there is now no reference to Phrynichos' fear or alarm). Cf. Westlake 1956, Schindel 1970, *HCT* V *ad* 8.50, 8.51, Kagan 1987, pp. 124–30, and Bloedow 1991b. "Weak resistance over the pay": apparently a forward reference to 8.83.

that the enemy intended to attack the camp, since Samos was unfortified, and not all the ships were in the harbor, that he had gotten accurate information about this, and that it was necessary to fortify Samos as quickly as possible and otherwise stay on guard. And as general he himself had the authority to carry this out. They began preparing the fortifications, and as a result of this Samos, while it would have been fortified anyway, was fortified more quickly. Not much later, the letter came from Alcibiades, saying that the army was betrayed by Phrynichos and the enemy about to attack. But since it did not appear that Alcibiades was credible but instead attributing to Phrynichos, out of hatred, a share of his own foreknowledge of the enemy plans, he did Phrynichos no harm but even tended to bear him out by giving the same message.

[52] After this, Alcibiades kept attempting to win over Tissaphernes and persuade him to be a friend of the Athenians, while Tissaphernes, who was afraid of the Peloponnesians because they were on hand with more ships than the Athenians yet was willing to comply if he possibly could, especially since he knew about the disagreement among the Peloponnesians at Knidos over the treaty of Therimenes (at this time they were already at Rhodes, so the disagreement had already taken place), during which Lichas, in claiming that it was intolerable to agree that the king was to be master over any cities either he or his father had ever ruled earlier, had substantiated the argument previously advanced by Alcibiades about the Lacedaemonians liberating all the cities. Alcibiades, like a contender for some great prize, devoted himself zealously indeed to cultivating Tissaphernes.

[53] Meanwhile, the Athenian envoys sent from Samos with Peisandros on their arrival in Athens made a speech before the people, condensing many arguments into their main ones, above all that it was possible for them, if they recalled Alcibiades and were not governed by the same form of democracy, to have the king as an ally and prevail over the Peloponnesians. When, in addition to the large number who spoke in opposition regarding the democracy, the enemies of Alcibiades raised the cry that it was terrible if he returned home after breaking the laws, and the Eumolpidai and the Kerykes testified against him regarding the Mysteries, which had been the cause of his exile, and invoked the gods against restoring him, Peisandros, coming forward in the face of much protest and outrage, called forth each one of the protesters and asked him if he had any hope for the

---

8.52. The problems of this passage are exaggerated in *HCT* V *ad loc.*, see Erbse 1989, pp. 57–59.

salvation of the city, when the Peloponnesians had no fewer ships than they had confronting them on the sea and a larger number of cities in their alliance, and when the king and Tissaphernes were providing them with money, while they no longer had any themselves, unless someone were to persuade the king to switch over to their side.

When they answered "no," that was when he would tell them plainly, "Well then, we will never see that unless we are governed more moderately, give office to fewer persons, so that the king trusts us, and do not deliberate more about government than about salvation at this time (for we will also have the possibility to make changes later, if anything is unsatisfactory), and unless we recall Alcibiades, who is the only man alive able to accomplish this." [54] The people were angry at first when they heard the proposal regarding the oligarchy, but after the clear lesson from Peisandros that there was no other salvation, in their fear and at the same time hoping that it could be changed, they conceded. They voted for Peisandros to sail with ten men and negotiate matters with Tissaphernes and Alcibiades in whatever way seemed best to them.

At the same time, when Peisandros slandered Phrynichos, they removed him and his colleague Skironides from their commands and sent Diomedon and Leon to the fleet as replacements. Peisandros, since he did not consider him useful for the negotiations with Alcibiades, slandered him by claiming that he had betrayed Iasos and Amorges. And Peisandros also went to all the political clubs that happened to exist in the city already to deal with legal cases and public office and exhorted them to band together, make their plans in common, and overthrow the democracy, and after he had made other preparations in keeping with the situation, so that there would no longer be any delays, he himself and the ten men made the voyage to Tissaphernes.

[55] In the same winter Leon and Diomedon, who had now reached the fleet, made a descent on Rhodes. Finding the Peloponnesian ships drawn up on the shore, they made a landing and defeated in battle the Rhodians who put up a defense and then withdrew to Chalke and carried on the war from there rather than Kos; for it was easier for them to keep watch in case the Peloponnesian ships set out in any direction. And at Rhodes Xenophantidas, a Lakonian, came from Pedaritos at Chios and said that the Athenian fortifications were completed by now, and that unless they

---

8.53–54. The Eumolpidai and Kerykes were the clans controlling the priesthoods of the Mysteries. "Slandered" and "betrayed" probably reflect Thucydides' views; cf. *HCT* V *ad* 8.54.3 and Kagan 1987, p. 134.

came to the rescue with all their ships, their cause at Chios would be lost. And they intended to come to the rescue. But meanwhile Pedaritos himself, with both the mercenaries at his disposal and the Chians in full force, assaulted the portion of the Athenian defenses protecting the ships and took control of part of it as well as some ships drawn up on the shore. When the Athenians came out to the rescue and routed the Chians first, the forces under Pedaritos were also defeated, and he himself and many of the Chians were killed and a large amount of weapons captured.

[56] After this, the Chians were even more under siege by land and sea, and there was a great famine locally. And the Athenian envoys under Peisandros reached Tissaphernes and held a conference about their agreement. But Alcibiades (for he had no assurance at all from Tissaphernes, who was more afraid of the Peloponnesians and still, just as he was being trained by him, wanted to wear out both sides), resorted to the following plan, that Tissaphernes fail to conclude an agreement because of making the greatest possible demands on the Athenians. It seems to me that Tissaphernes also wanted the same result, in his case because of fear, while Alcibiades, once he saw that he did not wish to conclude an agreement anyway, wanted it to seem to the Athenians that it was not that he was unable to persuade Tissaphernes, but that the Athenians, after he had been persuaded and was willing to take their side, were not making sufficient concessions. For Alcibiades, speaking himself on behalf of Tissaphernes in his presence, made such excessive demands that, even though for a long time they acquiesced in whatever he demanded, the attitude of the Athenians still bore the blame. He required the concession of all Ionia, then the outlying islands and other items. When the Athenians did not oppose these demands, he finally, now in their third meeting, fearing full detection of his incapability, required that they allow the king to build ships and sail his own coast wherever and with as many ships as he wished. At that point, the Athenians, no longer doubting that there was an impasse and that they had been tricked by Alcibiades, left in a rage and went back to Samos.

[57] Immediately after this, and during the same winter, Tissaphernes came to Kaunos with the intention of bringing the Peloponnesians back to Miletos and, after making still another agreement, any way he could, furnishing subsistence rather than being in a state of complete hostility, since

8.56. "Sail his own coast" is a disputed reading, cf. *HCT* V *ad* 8.56.4 and Kagan 1987, pp. 137–38. "No longer doubting" is a paraphrase where the text appears corrupt, see *HCT* V *ad* 8.56.5.

he was afraid that, in their difficulties over subsistence for a large number of ships, either they would be forced to fight the Athenians on the sea and would be defeated or, with their ships left without crews, what the Athenians were after would come to them without his assistance; and he feared, additionally and above all, that in their search for subsistence the Peloponnesians would ravage the mainland.

Therefore, calculating and taking precautions against all these factors, in full accordance with his wish to balance the Hellenes against each other, he sent for the Peloponnesians, and he gave them maintenance and also concluded this third treaty. [58] "In the thirteenth year of the reign of King Dareios, when Alexippidas was ephor in Lacedaemon, an agreement was made in the Plain of the Maiandros by the Lacedaemonians and their allies with Tissaphernes and Hieramenes and the sons of Pharnakes concerning the affairs of the King and of the Lacedaemonians and their allies. The territory of the King, as much as is in Asia, is to belong to the King; and concerning the territory of the King, he shall plan as he wishes. The Lacedaemonians and their allies are not to go against the territory of the King to do any harm, nor the King against that of the Lacedaemonians or their allies to do any harm. If any of the Lacedaemonians or their allies go against the territory of the King to do harm, the Lacedaemonians and their allies are to prevent them; and if any from the territory of the King go against the Lacedaemonians or their allies, the King shall prevent them. Tissaphernes is to provide maintenance for the ships now present according to the terms agreed on until the ships of the King come; the Lacedaemonians and their allies, after the ships of the King arrive, are to sustain their own ships if they wish, this to be their responsibility; but if they wish to receive the subsistence from Tissaphernes, Tissaphernes is to provide it, but the Lacedaemonians and their allies, when the war has ended, are to repay to Tissaphernes whatsoever money they receive. When the ships of the King arrive, the ships of the Lacedaemonians and those of their allies and those of the King are to fight the war in common in whatever way seems best to Tissaphernes and the Lacedaemonians and their allies. If they wish to end the war against the Athenians, it is to be ended likewise in common." [59] This was the treaty they made. And after this Tissaphernes began preparing to bring the Phoenician ships, just as had been stated, and to do everything else he had promised, and he wanted it apparent that he was at least in the act of preparing.

[60] When the winter was already ending, the Boiotians used treachery to capture Oropos, where the Athenians had a garrison. Their accomplices were men from Eretria and Oropos itself who were plotting the revolt of

Euboia; for since the place is opposite Eretria, it could not fail to cause serious trouble for Eretria and Euboia in general while the Athenians were holding it. Accordingly, now that they held Oropos, the Eretrians went to Rhodes, calling the Peloponnesians into Euboia. But they were more intent on coming to the aid of Chios, since it was in difficulty, and they put out from Rhodes and sailed with all their ships. When they were around Triopion, they observed the Athenian fleet sailing from Chalke on the high seas; since neither sailed against the other, the Athenians ended up at Samos and the Peloponnesians at Miletos, seeing that it was no longer possible for them to come to the rescue at Chios without a sea battle. And this winter ended, as did the twentieth year of this war which Thucydides recorded.

[61] In the following summer, as soon as spring began, Derkylidas, a Spartiate, was sent by land with no small army along the coast to the Hellespont to cause the revolt of Abydos (the people are colonists of Miletos), and the Chians, during the time Astyochos was at a loss for a way to help them, were forced by the afflictions of the siege to fight a sea battle. As it happened, while Astyochos was still at Rhodes, they had received from Miletos, as commander after the death of Pedaritos, Leon, a Spartiate, who had accompanied Antisthenes as a marine, as well as twelve ships which happened to be guarding Miletos, of which five were Thourian, four Syracusan, one was Anaian, one Milesian, and one Leon's. When the Chians marched out in full force and occupied a strong position, and their ships set sail at the same time, thirty-six against thirty-two Athenian, they fought the sea battle. After it had been fiercely contested, the Chians and their allies withdrew to the city (for it was now late in the day), although they were not getting the worst of it.

[62] Immediately after this, when Derkylidas had completed his march from Miletos, Abydos on the Hellespont revolted and went over to Derkylidas and Pharnabazos, as did Lampsakos two days later. When Strombichides found out, he hurried to the rescue from Chios with twenty-four Athenian ships, some of which were transports carrying hoplites, and after defeating in battle the Lampsakenes who came out against him and taking Lampsakos, which was unfortified, at the first assault, treating goods and slaves as plunder while sending the free men back to their homes, he went against Abydos. And since it did not surrender and he was unable to capture it by assault, he sailed off to the coast opposite Abydos and established Sestos, a city on the Chersonesos which the Medes once held, as a fortress and a position for keeping watch over the whole Hellespont.

[63] Meanwhile, the Chians were in greater control of the sea, and Astyochos and the others at Miletos, after hearing about the sea battle, and

that Strombichides and his ships had departed, were emboldened as well. Sailing along the coast with two ships, Astyochos picked up the ships from there and with the whole fleet now united made a descent on Samos; since, on account of harboring suspicions against each other, they did not put out to sea against him, he sailed off back to Miletos.

For around this time and even before, the democracy at Athens had been overthrown. When the envoys led by Peisandros left Tissaphernes and came to Samos, they not only established their control even more firmly over the situation in the army itself but also prompted the influential men among the Samians to persuade them to accept oligarchic government following their own example, even though the Samians had had an internal uprising to avoid being under oligarchy. And at the same time the Athenians at Samos conferred among themselves and reached the conclusion to leave Alcibiades out, inasmuch as he was unwilling (since he was also not well suited to joining an oligarchy anyway), and all on their own, since they were indeed already taking their chances, find a way to keep the enterprise from being called off, and at the same time to hold out concerning the war and contribute money and anything else necessary themselves out of their personal resources with zeal, as men no longer laboring for anyone except themselves.

[64] So after these exhortations to one another, they now immediately sent Peisandros and half the envoys home to manage matters there and with instructions to set up oligarchies wherever they stopped among the subject cities; the other half were sent off in various directions to the rest of the subject lands, and Dieitrephes, who was in the area around Chios but had been elected commander for the area toward Thrace, was sent off to take up his command. When he arrived at Thasos, he overthrew the democracy. And less than two months after his departure the Thasians proceeded to fortify their city, thinking that they were in no further need of aristocracy under the Athenians but in daily expectation of liberation by the Lacedaemonians. For there were even exiles of theirs among the Peloponnesians, driven out by the Athenians, and these, along with sympathizers inside the city, were working hard to bring ships and carry out the revolt of Thasos. So it turned out as they wanted most, that their city was being restored without risk, and the democracy that would have pre-

---

8.63. "Inasmuch as he was unwilling": i.e., the conspirators considered his behavior as Tissaphernes' negotiator both uncooperative in itself and indicative of the further problems they would have with him.

8.64. Dieitrephes: probably the same man as in 7.29, see *HCT* V *ad* 8.64.1.

vented this had been overthrown. For the Athenian establishers of oligarchy, then, what happened was the opposite of what they wanted regarding
Thasos and, I suppose, among many of their other subjects as well. For
after the cities had been given "moderate government" and freedom of
action, they went on to outright independence, attaching no value to the
sham of "law and order" under the Athenians.

[65] Peisandros and his group sailed along the coast overthrowing the
democracies in the cities according to plan, and bringing hoplites from
certain places along with them as supporters they arrived at Athens. And
they found that most of the work had already been accomplished by their
associates. For some of the younger ones had banded together and secretly
put to death a certain Androkles, a preeminent leader of the common people who was also especially responsible for banishing Alcibiades, and they
killed him for both reasons, on account of his demagoguery and because
they believed that they would gratify Alcibiades, since he was being
recalled and was going to make Tissaphernes a friend; and they secretly
did away with some other unsuitable persons in the same way.

Openly, a proposal of theirs had already been circulated, that no one
should receive public pay except for those on military campaigns and no
more than five thousand men should participate in the government, those
who were also especially qualified to serve by virtue of both their property
and their persons. [66] But this was a specious gesture toward the masses,
since those who reshaped the state were also meant to be the ones controlling it.

Despite all, the assembly and the Council of the Bean still continued to
meet; but they discussed nothing except what suited the conspirators, who
moreover furnished the speakers and who reviewed beforehand what was
going to be said. And none of the others spoke in opposition any longer,
since they were afraid and saw the extent of the conspiracy; if anyone did
speak out, suddenly and in some convenient way he was dead, and there
was neither a search for the perpetrators nor legal sanctions if any were
suspected, but the people instead remained immobilized by such terror
that anyone who suffered no violence, even if he had kept silent, considered it a gain. Since they believed the conspiracy to be much more extensive than it was, they were intimidated, and there was nothing they could
find out, reduced to helplessness by the magnitude of the city and and by
their ignorance about one another. For these same reasons, it was impossible for anyone who was aggrieved to voice his sorrows to another, in

8.66. "Council of the Bean": i.e., chosen by lot.

order to plot his revenge; for he would find himself speaking either to a stranger or to an acquaintance who could not be trusted. It was a case of every member of the common people suspecting every other member he approached of being involved in what was going on. For those involved included men no one would ever have thought would turn to oligarchy, and they were the ones who created the greatest distrust for the majority and helped most to provide safety for the minority, confirming the populace in its distrust of itself.

[67] It was during this crisis that Peisandros and his group arrived and immediately dedicated themselves to what remained to be done. They first convened the assembly and proposed a resolution that ten commissioners be chosen with absolute powers to draw up legal measures, and that on a designated day the commissioners introduce their measures for the best way of governing the state. Next, when the day arrived, they confined the assembly within the Kolonos (which is a sanctuary of Poseidon about ten stades outside the city), and the commissioners introduced no measures apart from this, that it was permitted for any Athenian to make any proposal he wished with impunity; in case anyone should indict the speaker for illegal procedure or in any other way hinder him, they imposed severe penalties. At that point, with no further concealment now, it was proposed that no one any longer hold any office belonging to the present system or receive pay, and that they choose five men as presidents, that these choose a hundred men, and each of the hundred choose three men in addition to himself; and that they, the Four Hundred, enter the council house and rule with absolute powers in whatever way they judged best, and that they convene the five thousand whenever they saw fit.

[68] Peisandros was the one who proposed this resolution and generally played the most active visible role in overthrowing the democracy; on the other hand, the one who devised the way in which the entire enterprise reached this point, after devoting his attention to it the longest, was Antiphon, a man second to no Athenian of his time in ability and a master both at developing plans and at stating his conclusions, and while he was not

---

8.68. On Antiphon, see *HCT* V *ad* 8.68.1, also Heitsch 1984. There is a long-standing controversy over whether the speech-writer and member of the Four Hundred was also the sophist Antiphon (some of whose preserved fragments are more consistent with oligarchy than others), see recently Gagarin 1990 (unitarian) and Pendrick 1993 (separatist). Thucydides' high praise is probably the starting point of the ancient tradition that Antiphon was Thucydides' teacher, but the relationship is credible and accepted by a number of scholars (e.g. McGregor 1956, p. 95); fragments of the sophist suggest that he was a formative influence on

one to come forward in the assembly or go willingly into any other scene of contention but was regarded with suspicion by the people because of a reputation for cleverness, he was nevertheless the one man most able to help those contending in law courts or in the assembly whenever anyone consulted him. And in addition, after the democracy had been changed back, and Antiphon was brought to trial at a later time when the actions of the Four Hundred had been reversed and were being dealt with harshly by the assembly, it is clear that he in person, on trial for these very actions, as a collaborator, made the best defense on a capital charge of all men up to my time. Phrynichos as well devoted himself to the oligarchy with a zeal setting him apart from everyone else, since he was afraid of Alcibiades and knew that he was aware of all his dealings with Astyochos at Samos, thinking that in all probability he would never be recalled by an oligarchy; once he was committed, he showed himself by far the most dependable in facing the dangers. And Theramenes son of Hagnon was prominent among those who took part in overthrowing the democracy, a man not lacking ability in either speech or judgment. And so, as the work of numerous intelligent men, the undertaking not unnaturally went forward, although it was a major one; for it was difficult, in close to the hundredth year after the tyrants were overthrown, to end the freedom of the Athenian people, who were not only not subjects but over more than half of that time had themselves been accustomed to rule over others.

[69] When the assembly, as soon as it had ratified the proposals with no voices in opposition, had been disbanded, immediately afterward they brought the Four Hundred into the council house, in the following manner. The Athenians were all at their stations at all times, some on the walls and some in the ranks, on account of the enemy at Dekeleia. Now on that day they let those who were not aware of their plans go off according to their routine, but those who were part of the conspiracy had instructions to remain quietly, not right beside the arms but at a distance, and, if anyone opposed what was being done, to seize their weapons and make that

---

Thucydides stylistically (Finley 1967, pp. 88–117). For the theory that Thucydides heard Antiphon's speech, and therefore that he was recalled from his exile by 411, see recently Piccirilli 1986 (I follow *HCT* V *ad* 8.68.2 in doubting this). "After the democracy had been changed back": on the formidable problems of the text, see *HCT* V *ad* 8.68.2; I have mainly and tentatively followed Tucker 1908 *ad* 8.68.2 in my translation (supposing that Thucydides meant to clarify by overall context a phrase that would more normally mean "when the democracy was taken away"). See also 8.97.

impossible. There were also Andrians, Teneans, three hundred Karystians, and some Aiginetan epoikoi whom the Athenians had sent out as settlers, and they had come with their own arms for just this purpose and had been given the same instructions. When they had all been positioned accordingly, the Four Hundred, each with a concealed dagger, and one hundred twenty youths whom they made use of wherever it might be necessary to use force, came and accosted the Councilors of the Bean who were in the council house, telling them to take their pay and get out; they themselves brought them their pay for the entire period remaining for them and gave it to them on their way out.

[70] When the council had withdrawn in this manner, without a word of opposition, and the rest of the citizens offered no challenge but remained quiet, the Four Hundred entered the council house and at this time chose their own chairmen by lot and also, as for everything pertaining to the gods, carried out prayers and sacrifices as they took office, but later, departing considerably from the democratic administration, except for not recalling the exiles because of Alcibiades, they otherwise governed the city with arbitrary power. They put to death certain men, a rather small number, whom they found it convenient to have out of the way, imprisoned others, and also banished some; and in addition they sent ambassadors to Agis the king of the Lacedaemonians, who was at Dekeleia, telling him that they were willing to make peace, and that it was reasonable for him to be readier to make terms with them than formerly with the untrustworthy democracy.

[71] Agis, thinking that the city was not in a stable condition, and that the people would not so quickly surrender their long-standing freedom, also that if they saw a sizable army of Lacedaemonians they would not stay inactive, made no response to accommodate the heralds from the Four Hundred, since at the time he did not believe that the Athenians were no longer in disarray, and not much later, after sending for a large additional force from the Peloponnesos, on his own initiative he brought the garrison from Dekeleia along with the newcomers right down to the walls of the Athenians, hoping that either the Athenians, in their disarray, would be more likely to yield on his terms, or that on account of the confusion likely to prevail inside and outside the city he could not fail to capture at least the Long Walls on his first assault because of their deserted state. But when he drew close up, and the Athenians, with no element of disturbance inside the city, sent out the cavalry and part of their hoplites, light-armed, and archers, shot down some of his men because of their coming too close, and took possession of some of the weapons and bodies, he now understood the

situation and led his army back. And while he himself and his men remained in their position at Dekeleia, he sent the reinforcements home after they had stayed in the area for a few days. After this, the Four Hundred continued to send envoys to Agis as before and, since he was now more receptive and gave them this advice, to Lacedaemon as well proposing an agreement, since they wanted to make peace.

[72] They also sent ten men to Samos to reassure the army and explain that the oligarchy had not been established to harm the city and its citizens but to save their entire cause, and that five thousand, not merely four hundred, were actually involved—even though the Athenians, what with their campaigns and their business abroad, had never yet come to deliberate any matter so important as to involve a meeting of five thousand. After giving them further instructions in the appropriate things to say, they sent them off immediately after taking power, fearing just what happened, that a mob of sailors would in itself be unwilling to stay under an oligarchic system, and that once the trouble had started there the sailors would go on to overthrow them.

[73] On Samos, there had in fact been revolutionary activity against the oligarchy, and the following events took place around the same time the Four Hundred were banding together. For the Samians who had formerly risen as democrats against the upper classes changed again under the influence of Peisandros, after he arrived, and his Athenian accomplices at Samos, and up to three hundred became conspirators and intended to attack the others for being democrats. They killed Hyperbolos, one of the Athenians, a despicable person who had been ostracized not on account of fear of his power and importance but on account of his evil ways and the shame he brought to the city, and they acted in collusion with Charinos, one of their generals, and some of the Athenians in their midst, demonstrating their good faith, and cooperated with them in other actions of the sort and were also eager to attack the majority. Since the latter were aware of what was in store, they disclosed it to the generals Leon and Diomedon (who submitted to the oligarchy unwillingly because of their high standing with the people), to Thrasyboulos and Thrasylos, one a trierarch and the other a hoplite, and to others thought to be at all times especially opposed to the conspirators and urged them not to look on while they themselves were destroyed and Samos estranged from the Athenians after being their only resource for holding the empire together this far.

8.72. *Pace* Kagan 1987, p. 181, n. 87, the oligarchs cannot merely have been explaining that they had not yet found occasion to convene the Five Thousand.

After listening to them, these men spread the word to each one of the soldiers not to permit this, and above all to the Paralians, all free Athenians who sailed in the Paralos and were forever assailants of oligarchy even when it was not at hand; and whenever Leon and Diomedon sailed somewhere, they left the Samian some ships for their defense. And so, with the help of all these and especially the Paralians, when the three hundred attacked them the Samian populace prevailed. They put to death about thirty of the three hundred who were the most guilty and punished three with exile; taking no reprisals against the rest, they lived with them from now on as citizens of a democratic government.

[74] The Samians and soldiers sent the Paralos off to Athens at full speed to report what had happened, with Chaireas son of Archestratos, an Athenian who had shown zeal for the new developments, on board; for they did not know yet that the Four Hundred were in power. When they reached port, the Four Hundred immediately imprisoned two or three of the Paralians, stripped the others of their ship, put them on board another, a troop-ship, and assigned them to guard duty around Euboia. Chaireas, however, slipping away somehow when he saw the current situation, came back to Samos and gave the soldiers an exaggerated report of all the horrors at Athens, that they were punishing everyone with floggings, and it was not possible for anyone to say a word against those running the government; that the soldiers' wives and children were being abused; and that they intended to seize and lock up the relatives of every member of the forces at Samos who was not of their persuasion, so that if they did not submit these would die; and he told them many other lies in addition. [75] When they heard this, at first they rushed at those who had done the most to bring about the oligarchy and others who had participated, intending to stone them; at this point, however, after being restrained by the moderates with the admonishment that they must not destroy their cause when enemy ships were lined up against them nearby, they stopped.

After this, Thrasyboulos son of Lykos and Thrasylos (these had been especially prominent in the revolution), no longer concealing their desire to change the state of affairs at Samos to democracy, swore all the soldiers, and above all the ones connected with the oligarchy, to the most solemn oaths that they would in truth uphold democracy and concord, carry on the war against the Peloponnesians with zeal, and be enemies of the Four Hundred and make no overtures to them. All the Samians of military age swore the same oath along with them, and the soldiers made common cause with the Samians in all their undertakings and in whatever ensued from the risks they were taking, believing that there was no safe haven for either the Samians or themselves, but if either were to prevail, the Four Hundred or the enemy at Miletos, they would be destroyed.

[76] So they were now locked in a duel, one side attempting to force the city to accept democracy, the other to force the army to accept oligarchy. The soldiers immediately held an assembly, in which they deposed their former generals and any of the trierarchs they regarded with suspicion and chose new trierarchs and generals, including Thrasyboulos and Thrasyllos, to replace them. They stood up and exchanged a variety of exhortations, especially that there was no need to lose heart because the city had revolted from them; it was the smaller number that had broken away from them, the more numerous and in all respects the better providers. For since they had possession of the entire fleet, they would force the other cities ruled by Athens to make their payments, just as though they were operating out of Athens (and Samos, the city that belonged to them, was not weak but had come very close to taking the control of the sea away from the Athenians when it was at war with them and would give them the same base as before for holding off the enemy), and as the ones with the ships they were better able than the people in the city to provide themselves with supplies. Furthermore, that Athens had controlled the approach to the Peiraeus as long as it had was due to the advanced post on Samos held by themselves, who now, if the others refused to give back their constitution, were in a better position to deny the others the sea than to be denied by them. And any service the city could render toward prevailing over the enemy was scant or worthless, and they had lost nothing in men who no longer had either money to send, something the soldiers themselves were providing, or sound guidance, which was the justification for a city to have control over camps. Instead, even in this function, they had gone wrong by abolishing the traditional laws, while they themselves were preserving them and would attempt to force the others to do the same. So not even for men who could guide them soundly were they worse off among themselves. And Alcibiades, if they provided him with immunity and recall, would be glad to bring them the alliance with the king. And most impor-

---

8.76. McGregor 1965, pp. 41–43 offers the attractive suggestion that Alcibiades had been farsighted enough to instigate an oligarchic coup purely so that he could be recalled as the restorer of democracy (his behavior in 8.56 could support this); Ellis 1989, p. 73, and Forde 1989, p. 192, n. 17 are both favorable but consider the theory incapable of proof. And did Thucydides understand that this was Alcibiades' strategy? I think that both questions are moot without Thucydides' account of Alcibiades' actual return to Athens in 407 B.C.E.

tant of all, if they failed totally, their possession of such a large fleet gave them many places of refuge where they would find both cities and land. [77] After holding this meeting among themselves and encouraging one another, they also continued unabated military preparations. The men sent to Samos by the Four Hundred, who had learned about this whole situation by the time they were at Delos, stayed there and took no action.

[78] Around this time, the Peloponnesian soldiers in the fleet at Miletos were spreading word among themselves that their cause was being ruined by Astyochos and Tissaphernes, the former because he was not willing to fight a sea battle either earlier, when they themselves still had their vigor unimpaired and the fleet of the Athenians was small, or now, when they were said to be divided into factions and their fleet was not yet united; instead, by waiting for the Phoenician ships from Tissaphernes, a matter of mere talk rather than action, they were risking attrition; now as for Tissaphernes, he was not bringing these ships, and the talk was that he was damaging the fleet by not giving it regular or full subsistence. Therefore, they said, they must no longer delay but fight it out at sea. The Syracusans were especially insistent. [79] Since Astyochos and the allies were aware of the murmuring, and after a council meeting their decision had been to fight a decisive sea battle, when they were informed as well about the turmoil at Samos, they put out to sea with their entire fleet of one hundred twelve ships and sailed toward Mykale, directing the Milesians to proceed there by land.

When the Athenians from Samos, whose eighty-two ships were just then moored at Glauke in Mykale (here Samos is a short distance from the mainland looking toward Mykale), saw the Peloponnesian fleet sailing against them, they retreated to Samos, thinking that they were numerically insufficient to stake everything on a battle. At the same time (since they had learned in advance from Miletos that the enemy wanted to fight a sea battle), they were also expecting Strombichides to come from the Hellespont and reinforce them with the ships from Chios, which had ended up at Abydos; a messenger had already been sent to him. They accordingly withdrew to Samos, while the Peloponnesians sailed to Mykale and set up camp with the land forces of both the Milesians and the neighboring people.

On the following day, when they were about to sail against Samos, the news came that Strombichides had arrived with the ships from the Hellespont, and they immediately sailed back to Miletos. After they were joined by these ships, the Athenians themselves made a descent on Miletos, wanting to fight a decisive sea battle; and since no one put out to sea against them, they sailed back to Samos. [80] Immediately after this during the same summer, after the Peloponnesians refused to come out against the Athenians even with their own fleet united, thinking they were overmatched, they were at a loss for a source of money for so many ships, especially since Tissaphernes was a poor supplier, and dispatched Klearchos son of Rhamphias to Pharnabazos, in accordance with his original orders on leaving the Peloponnesos, with forty ships. Pharnabazos was inviting them, and he was ready to provide subsistence; and at the same time Byzantion was sending them offers to revolt.

So these forty Peloponnesian ships set out on the open sea to keep the Athenians from knowing about their voyage, and after they were caught in a storm most, with Klearchos, found shelter at Delos and subsequently returned to Miletos (but Klearchos then traveled by land to the Hellespont and took command), while ten with the general Helixos of Megara got through to the Hellespont and brought about the revolt of Byzantion. After this, when the Athenians learned about it, they sent ships as reinforcements and guards for the Hellespont, and a minor sea battle occurred off Byzantion, eight ships against eight.

[81] The leaders at Samos, and particularly Thrasyboulos, who after accomplishing the revolution was always very firm in his conviction that they should recall Alcibiades, at last also persuaded the majority of the soldiers after an assembly, and when they voted to give Alcibiades recall and immunity he sailed across to Tissaphernes and brought Alcibiades to Samos, thinking that their sole salvation was the possibility of his converting Tissaphernes from the Peloponnesian side to theirs. When an assembly was held, Alcibiades complained about the personal misfortune of his exile and lamented loudly, and when he also spoke at length about matters of state he instilled in them no small hopes for the future, and he went to extremes in exaggerating his influence over Tissaphernes, so that the oligarchs at home would be afraid of him and the political clubs be more readily disbanded, the men at Samos would hold him in higher esteem and feel bolder themselves, and the enemy would have their relations with Tissaphernes strained to the breaking point and their existing hopes completely dashed.

He accordingly made these extravagantly boastful promises, that Tissaphernes had made him the solemn pledge that as long as any possessions remained to him, the Athenians, provided he could trust them, would not want for subsistence, even if he ended up having to coin the silver from his own bed, and he would deliver the Phoenician ships, now at Aspendos, to the Athenians instead of the Peloponnesians; but he would trust the Athenians on one condition, that Alcibiades be recalled in safety to be his guarantee. [82] When they heard this and a good deal more, they immediately elected him general along with the ones they already had and entrusted all their affairs to him, and not a man would have traded his immediate hopes of safety and vengeance on the Four Hundred for anything else, and they were now ready, on the basis of what they had been told, to despise the enemies at hand in the immediate future and sail against the Peiraeus. He, however, despite the number who insisted, completely prevented their sailing against the Peiraeus leaving behind the enemies closer at hand, and he said that he would first, as their elected general, sail to Tissaphernes and make arrangements for conducting the war. And he left straight from the assembly, in order to make it seem that he was a close partner of Tissaphernes in all matters, wanting at the same time to increase his standing with him and demonstrate that he had now been elected general and was in a position to do him both good and harm. And the consequence for Alcibiades was that he could use Tissaphernes to impress the Athenians and use them to impress him.

[83] When the Peloponnesians at Miletos found out about the recall of Alcibiades, since they already distrusted Tissaphernes, they were now still more suspicious of him. For what had happened in their own case was that at the time when the Athenians sailed against Miletos, since they were unwilling to go out against them, Tissaphernes by becoming much more remiss in his payments intensified the hatred they had for him even before this because of Alcibiades. And the soldiers, gathering in groups, also some other personnel of importance, took stock just as on the prior occasion, that they had never received full pay, they got short pay and not even that with regularity, and, unless they either fought a decisive sea battle or moved to a location where they could get subsistence, the crews would desert the ships; and Astyochos was to blame for all of this, since he was indulging Tissaphernes' inclinations for his own private gain.

[84] While they were taking stock in this way, a disturbance of the following sort also occurred in connection with Astyochos. In the same degree that the sailors of the Syracusans and Thourians were free men for the most part, they were also the boldest in confronting Astyochos and demanding their pay. He responded somewhat arrogantly and made threats, actually raising his baton against Dorieus when he was speaking up on behalf of his own sailors. When the crowd of soldiers saw this, in true sailor fashion they rushed at Astyochos with shouts, intending to stone him; he saw them in time to take refuge at an altar. He was not actually stoned, however, and they were separated. In addition, the Milesians

in a surprise attack seized the fort built by Tissaphernes at Miletos and expelled the garrison he had installed. Their actions met with the approval of both the allies in general and the Syracusans in particular. Lichas, however, was displeased with them and said that the Milesians and the others living in the king's territory must both slave for Tissaphernes within reasonable limits and curry favor with him in addition until they successfully resolved the war. But the Milesians were furious at him for both this and other things of the same sort, and when he subsequently died of illness they did not allow him to be buried where the Lacedaemonians who were present wanted.

[85] While their relations with Astyochos and Tissaphernes were in this marked state of dissension, Mindaros came from Lacedaemon to succeed Astyochos as admiral and took over the command; Astyochos sailed home. But Tissaphernes sent with him one of his followers and an envoy, a bilingual Karian named Gaulites, to accuse the Milesians over the fort and at the same time offer his own defense, since he knew that the Milesians were on their way to Sparta especially to denounce him, and Hermokrates along with them, who intended to expose Tissaphernes for ruining the Peloponnesian cause and playing a double game. He had always been an enemy of Hermokrates over the payment of the wages; and finally, when Hermokrates was in exile from Syracuse, and other generals for the Syracusan fleet had arrived at Miletos (Potamis, Myskon, and Demarchos), Tissaphernes went after Hermokrates much more than before now that he was an exile and made the accusation, among others, that it was after once asking him for money and not getting it that he displayed hostility toward him. So Astyochos, the Milesians, and Hermokrates sailed off to Lacedaemon; Alcibiades had already crossed from Tissaphernes back to Samos.

[86] The envoys from the Four Hundred, whom at an earlier point they had sent to reassure and instruct the now-alienated men at Samos, arrived from Delos when Alcibiades was already there, and when an assembly was held, they attempted to speak. The soldiers at first were unwilling to listen, clamoring instead for killing those who were overthrowing the democracy; then they managed to quiet down and listen to them. They announced that the revolution was not being brought about for the destruction of the state but rather for its preservation, nor so that it could be betrayed to the enemy (which could have been done when the enemy invaded while they

8.84. Lichas may not have died until shortly after 397, see Pouilloux and Salviat 1983 and 1985 but also strong counterarguments in Cartledge 1984.

were already in power); moreover, all of the Five Thousand would participate in the government in turn, and their relatives were not being abused, as Chaireas had slanderously reported, nor had they suffered any harm but were in every case still just where they had been, in possession of their own property. Although they said a great deal more, the soldiers were not any more inclined to listen but continued to be angry and express many opinions, in particular that they should sail against the Peiraeus.

And it seems that then, for the first time, Alcibiades did the state a service, one that was unsurpassed, in that when the Athenians at Samos were passionately determined to sail against their own people, in which case it is absolutely clear that the enemy would immediately have seized Ionia and the Hellespont, he prevented it. And at that moment not one other man would have had the power to hold back the crowd, but he stilled it and with a scolding dissuaded those who were personally enraged against the envoys. He sent them back with an answer in his own right, that he had nothing against the rule of the Five Thousand, but they were to put an end to the Four Hundred and establish the council just as it was before, that of the Five Hundred; and if there had been any limitations in the direction of economy, if that meant that the soldiers would receive more subsistence, he was all in favor. Otherwise, he told them to hold out and make no concession to the enemy; for as long as the city was kept safe, there was great hope of their also coming to terms among themselves, whereas if either of the parties, the one at Samos or the one back there, took one false step, there would be no one left to be reconciled with.

Envoys from Argos also arrived, promising to help the Athenian democracy at Samos, but after commending them and asking them to be on hand if they were called on, he then sent them away. The Argives had come

8.86. "All of the Five Thousand" (here for the first time designated as an institution, 8.72n): while this translation strains the Greek (cf. *HCT* V *ad* 8.86.3 and Kagan 1987, p. 181, n. 87), the alternate possibility, that all citizens should in turn be members of the Five Thousand, seems impossible in this context, *pace* Gallucci 1986, p. 168, n. 14 (his theories, on which see 8.97n, do not necessitate this translation here). "For the first time, Alcibiades": against the manuscript tradition that would give the sense "Alcibiades first and foremost" (recently accepted by Forde 1989, p. 165, n. 47), see *HCT* V *ad* 8.86.4, Kagan 1987, p. 182, and Erbse 1989, p. 90, and cf. Ramón Pherm 1991; scholars have expressed some surprise that Thucydides should express so negative a view of Alcibiades' prior career (the variant manuscripts probably originated because of such surprise). This incident is not a doublet of 8.82, see especially Erbse, pp. 19–20; for the possibility that, despite Thucydides, Alcibiades' course of action here was actually not the wisest, see especially Bloedow 1973, pp. 39–40, also Kagan, pp. 183–84.

with the Paralos, whose men had previously been assigned to sail around Euboia in the troop-ship and also to bring Athenian envoys from the Four Hundred to Lacedaemon, Laisopodias, Aristophon, and Melesias; when their voyage had taken them to Argos, they arrested the envoys and handed them over to the Argives as in large part responsible for overthrowing the democracy, and they themselves did not go back again to Athens but arrived with the envoys from Argos to Samos on their trireme.

[87] During the same summer, just at the point when the Peloponnesians, on account of both the other factors and the recall of Alcibiades, were particularly resentful against Tissaphernes as now openly pro-Athenian, Tissaphernes, certainly giving every indication of wanting to clear himself of these charges, made preparations to travel to Aspendos to get the Phoenician ships and asked Lichas to accompany him; concerning the army, he said that he would appoint Tamos, his subordinate, to provide subsistence during his absence. Accounts are inconsistent, and it is not easy to know what intentions he had when he went all the way to Aspendos and then did not bring back the ships. For this much is clear, that the Phoenician ships, one hundred forty-seven of them, got as far as Aspendos; the reason for their not coming farther is conjectured in many different ways. For some, he went away in order to exhaust the resources of the Peloponnesians, just as he had planned (at any rate, Tamos, his appointee, provided not better but even worse subsistence); for some, he brought the Phoenicians as far as Aspendos in order to exhort money from them for their release (for in any case he was not going to use them); for others, it was because of the outcry at Lacedaemon, so that it could be said that he was not acting wrongly, he was quite clearly leaving to get the ships, which were genuinely being manned. To me, however, it seems very clear that it was for the purpose of wearing out and immobilizing Hellenic enterprises that he failed to bring the ships, by a process of attrition while he was mak-

8.87. While citing alternate theories, Thucydides carefully makes his own the most authoritative. Some additional modern explanations would undermine this authority: the Phoenician ships were needed to deal with an Egyptian revolt (e.g., Lewis 1977, p. 133); Tissaphernes was aware of the fleet's inferior quality (Lateiner 1976). Scholars have tended to be programmatic in addressing this chapter: Andrewes (*HCT* V *ad* 8.87) suspects that this is an early draft based on incomplete information, Erbse (1989, pp. 20–22) is generally satisfied with Thucydides' account, and Connor (1984, p. 215–17) argues that the more open methodology is one of the innovations of book 8 (which experiment, however, he does not repeat; for citation of two conflicting accounts—rather than explanations—of an event, see 2.5).

ing his way to Aspendos and wasting time, and of equalization, so that he did not strengthen either side by reinforcing it, since if he had actually wanted to he could, of course, have brought the war to an end by putting in an appearance in no uncertain manner; for by bringing in the fleet, he would in every probability have given the victory to the Lacedaemonians, who in fact, even as it was, were closer to an even match than to inferiority in the fleet that confronted their enemies. But what most of all convicts him is the excuse he gave for not bringing the ships. He said that they were fewer than the king had commanded to be collected; but in that case he would certainly have found even greater favor by not spending a large amount of the king's money yet accomplishing the same thing with smaller resources. Whatever his intentions, then, Tissaphernes arrived at Aspendos and met with the Phoenicians; and at his urging the Peloponnesians sent Philippos, a Lacedaemonian, with two triremes to get the ships.

[88] When Alcibiades learned that Tissaphernes was on his way to Aspendos, he took thirteen ships and sailed there himself, promising the men at Samos a secure and major reward (that is, he would either bring the Phoenician ships for the Athenians himself or at least stop them from going to the Peloponnesians), while probably long since aware that it was not Tissaphernes' intention to bring the ships and wanting to discredit him among the Peloponnesians as much as possible for being a friend to himself and the Athenians, so that he would accordingly be under greater pressure to come over to the Athenian side. So he put out to sea and sailed straight in the direction of Phaselis and Kaunos.

[89] Meanwhile, when the envoys sent by the Four Hundred arrived at Athens from Samos and reported the message from Alcibiades, that he told them to hold out and make no concession to the enemy and also said that he had great hopes of both reconciling them with the army and prevailing over the Peloponnesians, they gave a great deal of fresh courage to the majority of participants in the oligarchy, who were already unhappy and would gladly have taken any safe way out of the business. And now they began to gather in groups and criticize the government, headed by men who were very much part of the oligarchy and in office, such as Theramenes son of Hagnon and Aristokrates son of Skelias and others, who were among the foremost of those involved in the government but—afraid of the army at Samos, so they said, of Alcibiades in real earnest, and also

---

8.88. A very revealing episode. While Alcibiades is apparently offering the forces on Samos a reward for supporting him (so Classen/Steup VIII *ad loc.*), the boon he promises and the one he expects to bestow are totally different.

of the envoys who were being sent to Lacedaemon, in case of their failing to consult the majority and doing something harmful to the state—said that they wanted to be rid of so excessively narrow an oligarchy, and that it was necessary instead to designate the Five Thousand in reality not in name and put the government on a fairer basis.

This was the constitutional guise of their arguments, but in their personal ambition most of them were caught up in just the sort of situation in which an oligarchy emerging out of a democracy is surest to be destroyed; for everyone instantly expects not to be equal but far ahead in every single case; but under a democracy, when an election is held, each man can tolerate the outcome more easily in the belief that it was not through his peers that he was denied. But what most obviously spurred them on was the strength of Alcibiades' position at Samos and their impression that the oligarchy did not have long to run; each man accordingly competed to be the foremost champion of the people himself.

[90] Those among the Four Hundred who were particularly opposed to such ideas and were in the forefront, Phrynichos, the one who had been a general at Samos and had come over during that time, Aristarchos, a man of the most extreme and prolonged hostility to democracy, Peisandros, Antiphon, and others of particular influence, who previously, right after coming to power and when the army at Samos revolted from them and turned to democracy, had been sending envoys from their group to Lacedaemon and striving for the accord and also constructing the fort at the place called Eetioneia, did so all the more when their envoys returned from Samos, since they saw that not only the people but men of their own faction who had seemed trustworthy until now were changing sides. So they hurriedly dispatched Antiphon and Phrynichos and ten others, fearful about conditions both at home and at Samos, and directed them to reach an agreement with the Lacedaemonians in any way that was at all bearable.

And with more zeal than ever, they continued constructing the fort at Eetioneia. The fort had this purpose, Theramenes and his group said, not to keep out the men from Samos if they tried to force a passage into the Peiraeus, but rather to let in the enemy at will with both sea and land forces. For Eetioneia is a mole of the Peiraeus, and the entrance runs right along side it. It was accordingly fortified in conjunction with an existing wall facing inland, in a way that enabled the fort, when a few men occupied it, to control the entrance; the old wall on the land side and the new inner wall being built facing the sea ended at the same tower, one of two, right at the mouth of the harbor, which is narrow. They also walled off a very large stoa right next to the inner wall and very closely connected with it inside the harbor and took charge of it themselves, forcing everyone to bring in grain on hand and unload imported grain and sell it by taking it from there.

[91] Theramenes, then, had been calling attention to this activity for some time, and after the envoys came back from Lacedaemon without any results for the people as a whole, he added the statement that this fort threatened to destroy the city. For it happened that just at this time, in response to calls from the Euboians, forty-two ships from the Peloponnesos, including some Italian ships from Taras and Lokroi and some from Sicily, were already anchored off Las in Lakonian territory and preparing for the voyage to Euboia under the command of Agesandridas son of Agesandros, a Spartiate; these ships, Theramenes said, were sailing to help the men fortifying Eetioneia, not Euboia, and unless there were immediate precautions, the Athenians would be ruined before they realized it. And something of the sort was actually under consideration by the men who were accused, and this was not entirely a slanderous account. For they wanted above all to rule the allies as well under the oligarchy, and short of that, at least to keep the ships and fortifications and have autonomy, and if denied this as well, at any rate, rather than letting themselves face more certain destruction than all the others by the return of the democracy, to bring in the enemy and make terms that abandoned the fortifications and ships and allowed any treatment of the city whatsoever, as long as there would be immunity for their own persons. [92] This was their specific purpose as they zealously built this fort, with its entrances and passageways for the enemy, and they wanted it completed in time.

Now up to this point there was talking within small groups, more or less in secret, but when Phrynichos, back from the embassy to Lacedaemon, was stabbed during the busiest time of the marketplace by a member of the militia before he had gone any distance from the council house and died on the spot, the victim of a plot, and after the killer's escape his Argive accomplice was captured and under torture by the Four Hundred told them neither the name of anyone who gave the orders nor anything else except that he knew that there were many men who gathered together both at the

---

8.89–92. Thucydides' hesitation to credit Theramenes with either honesty (note especially the gratuitous "not entirely a slanderous account") or daring is very striking; see *HCT* V *ad* 8.89.3. Antique and modern opinions divide sharply over Theramenes, see Buck 1995 (himself strongly negative). "The slogan" must have been "called out to the crowd" by members of the crowd itself; cf. Kagan 1987, pp. 195–96.

house of the commander of the militia and houses elsewhere, this was the time, since nothing decisive followed the event, when Theramenes, Aristokrates, and all the rest of the Four Hundred and outsiders who shared their views finally moved into action more boldly themselves.

For at this same time, the Peloponnesian ships had already sailed around from Las and, with Epidauros as their anchorage, overrun Aigina; and Theramenes said that it was unlikely that, on a voyage to Euboia, they would have gone into the gulf to Aigina and back to Epidauros to anchor, if they had not come on a summons for that very same purpose he was always denouncing; it was therefore no longer possible to stay inactive. Finally, after many rebellious speeches and expressions of suspicion ensued, they now dealt with the situation through actions as well. The hoplites in the Peiraeus who were building the fort at Eetioneia, and who included Aristokrates, an officer in charge of men from his own tribe, arrested Alexikles, a general who belonged to the oligarchy and was especially partial to the political clubs, led him off to a house, and confined him. There were others who joined in making the arrest, among them Hermon, a member of the militia and commander of those assigned to Mounichia; but what mattered most was that this was the will of the hoplite rank and file.

When this was reported to the Four Hundred, who happened to be in session in the council house, all those opposed to it were immediately ready to get weapons, and they threatened Theramenes and his supporters. He defended himself, saying that he was ready to go right now to help release Alexikles. And taking along one of the generals, a man who shared his views, he proceeded to the Peiraeus; Aristarchos and some youths from the cavalry also went to the rescue. There was great confusion and consternation; in the city they thought that the Peiraeus had now been seized and that the man under arrest had been killed, while in the Peiraeus they thought that the men from the city were just about to fall on them. But since the older men restrained those who were running in every direction and making for their weapons, and Thucydides the Pharsalian proxenos in the city was on hand and assiduously blocked everyone's path shouting at them not to ruin their country while their enemy was in wait nearby, they managed to quiet down and kept from attacking each other. When Theramenes, who was a general himself, came to the Peiraeus, he raged at the hoplites as far as shouting was concerned; on the other hand, Aristarchos and those hostile to them were genuinely angry. But most of the hoplites took a fighting stance, showing no repentance, and they asked Theramenes whether he thought the fort was being built for a good purpose or that it was better for it to be torn down. If they thought it right to tear it down, he said, then that was what he thought too. After that, the hoplites and many of the people of the Peiraeus climbed on top of the fortification and began demolishing it. And the slogan called out to the crowd was that whoever wanted the Five Thousand to rule instead of the Four Hundred should get to work. For they were concealing themselves nonetheless by using the words "the Five Thousand," to avoid directly using the words "whoever wants the people to rule," since they were afraid that the Five Thousand existed in reality, and that anyone speaking to anyone else might make a slip through ignorance. This was the reason the Four Hundred did not want the Five Thousand either to exist or to be exposed as nonexistent, thinking that so many participants would mean outright democracy, but then again the uncertainty would cause men to fear one another.

[93] The next day, the Four Hundred, while badly shaken, met in the council house nonetheless; the hoplites in the Peiraeus, after releasing Alexikles, the man they had arrested, and tearing down the fort, went to the Dionysiac theater in Mounichia, grounded their arms, and held an assembly, and after taking a vote they proceeded directly to the city and grounded their arms, this time in the Anakion. And certain men chosen from the Four Hundred came to them, spoke with them man to man, and began persuading those they saw were reasonable to keep quiet themselves and cooperate in restraining the rest—saying that they would disclose the Five Thousand, and the Four Hundred would come out of these by rotation in whatever way seemed best to the Five Thousand—and in the meantime not to do anything to ruin the city nor force it into the enemy camp. After many of them had heard speeches by many, the entire group was more even-tempered than before, and their fears were mainly for all citizens alike. And so they agreed to hold an assembly in the sanctuary of Dionsysos on a given day to discuss working together.

[94] When the time came for the assembly in the sanctuary of Dionysos, and they had just about convened, it was reported that the forty-two ships with Agesandridas had left Megara and were sailing along the coast of Salamis; and every man thought that this was exactly what had long since been declared by Theramenes and his supporters, that the fleet was sailing to the fort, and it seemed that it had been opportunely destroyed. Although it may well have been through some arrangement that Agesandridas stayed at Epidauros and that area, it is also likely that he waited there with a view to the dissension prevailing among the Athenians, in hopes of arriving at the right time.

When the Athenians received the report, they accordingly proceeded at a run to the Peiraeus in full force, since a war launched by the enemy, greater than their private one, was not far away but approaching their harbor. Some of them manned the ships on hand, some launched additional ones, while others went to defend the walls and the mouth of the harbor. [95] After sailing along the coast and around Sounion, the Peloponnesian ships anchored between Thorikos and Prasiai and later arrived at Oropos. The Athenians, in great haste and forced to use crews that had not trained together, since the city was divided by faction, and they wanted to hurry to the defense of what mattered most (for with Attica closed to them, Euboia meant everything), sent ships to Eretria with Thymochares, a general. When they arrived, combined with those already at Euboia, they numbered thirty-six. And they were forced to fight at sea immediately; Hegesandridas brought his ships forth from Oropos after breakfast, and by sea Oropos is about sixty stades from the city of Eretria.

Now the Athenians, since he was sailing against them, tried to man their ships immediately in the belief that the crews were by their ships; but, as it turned out, they were getting food for breakfast, not from the marketplace (for the Eretrians had seen to it that nothing was on sale there) but from houses at the farthest end of the city, so that while their ships were gradually being manned the enemy could get a head start in attacking and give the Athenians no choice but to set sail whether they were ready or not. And they had a signal for the right time to attack raised from Eretria. This was the state of Athenian preparedness when they put out to sea and fought in front of the harbor of Eretria, yet for a short time they actually held their own; then they turned to flight and were pursued to the shore. And all those who took refuge in the city of Eretria in the belief that it was friendly met the harshest fate, since they were murdered by the people; but all who took refuge in the fort they occupied in Eretrian territory survived, as did all the ships that reached Kalchis. After capturing twenty-two Athenian ships and killing some of the men and taking others prisoner, the Peloponnesians set up a trophy. And not long afterwards, they brought about the revolt of all of Euboia except for Oreos (which the Athenians occupied themselves) and organized its affairs in general.

8.95–96. "Except for Oreos": formerly Hestiaia, see 1.114 and *HCT* V *ad* 8.95.7. The projected disasters are an uncanny forecast of the final Athenian defeat in 405 B.C.E. (especially since at Aigospotamoi the Athenian fleet was again unready for battle partly because the crews were going long distances for provisions, see Xenophon, *Hellenika* 2.1.27–28, Strauss 1983). "Not on this occasion alone": cf. 1.70,

[96] When word of Euboia reached the Athenians, they felt such shock as never before. For neither the disaster in Sicily, great as it seemed at the time, nor anything else had ever frightened them in this way. Since a period when the army at Samos was in revolt, when there were no more ships nor men to embark on them, when they themselves were divided by faction and it was not clear when they might be in conflict with one another, had culminated in so great a disaster as this, resulting in the loss of their ships and above all Euboia, which had been of more value to them than Attica, how could they reasonably be other than disheartened? But what especially and most directly alarmed them was that the enemy might be bold enough after their victory to sail straight at them in the Peiraeus when it was bereft of ships; indeed, they thought the enemy were as good as there already. This is just what the enemy, with more boldness, could easily have done and either divided the city still more seriously by a block-ade or, if they had settled down to a siege, forced the fleet, hostile to the oligarchy though it was, to come from Ionia to the rescue of their own rel-atives and the city as a whole; and in the process the enemy would have had the Hellespont, Ionia, the islands, everything as far as Euboia—practically speaking, the whole Athenian empire. But not on this occasion alone, but on many others as well, the Lacedaemonians proved the most convenient of all people for the Athenians to be at war with. For as the farthest from them in character—the one people being quick, the other slow; the one enterprising, the other timid—they were obliging in general and particu-larly in the case of a naval power. The Syracusans demonstrated this; for because they were the most similar to the Athenians in character, they also fought the best against them.

[97] So the Athenians, in reaction to the news, manned twenty ships and also held assemblies, one of them immediately and now for the first time in the place called the Pnyx, which had also been the customary meet-

---

7.55. Some simplistic elements, especially in the comparison with Syracuse (rightly criticized by *HCT* V *ad* 8.96.5 and Kagan 1987, pp. 201–2) are all the more striking as an indication of Thucydides' convictions.

8.97. For exhaustive analysis of this chapter and its political implications, see espe-cially Donini 1969, *HCT* V, pp. 323–40 and Gallucci 1986. Andrewes upholds the long-standing view that the new government was a moderate oligarchy until late in 411/10, when the franchise was restored to the thetes after the battle of Cyzicus. Building on the revisionist theories of Ste. Croix 1956, Gallucci argues very per-suasively that the thetes were enfranchised from the start but barred from office until the first prytany of 410/9 (pp. 45, 105–6). It is credible that Thucydides

ing place at other times, and in this assembly they voted to depose the Four Hundred and entrust their affairs to the Five Thousand, who were to consist of all who could also afford a suit of hoplite's armor; and no one was to receive pay for any office, and they put a curse on any violation. There were also other frequent meetings later on, at which they voted for legislators and various measures regarding the constitution. And during the first phase, the Athenians clearly had their best government, at least in my lifetime; for a moderate blending between the few and the many came about, and it was this which first lifted the city out of the terrible current condition of its affairs. They also voted to recall Alcibiades and others along with them and sent word to both him and and the forces at Samos urging them to devote themselves to the cause.

[98] During this revolution, Peisandros, Alexikles, and all who had been the most active in the oligarchy immediately made off to Dekeleia; Aristarchos alone, who also happened to be a general, quickly took some archers who were preeminently foreigners and proceeded to Oinoe. This was an Athenian fort on the Boiotian border, and the Corinthians, after calling in the Boiotians for assistance, were besieging it on their own initiative because of a disaster inflicted by Oinoe involving the loss of their men returning from Dekeleia. Now Aristarchos, after contacting the Corinthians, tricked the men in Oinoe, telling them that those in the city had come to a general agreement with the Lacedaemonians, and that it was necessary for them to hand over the place to the Boiotians; the agreement had been made on these terms. Believing him as a general and because they were uninformed on account of the siege, they departed under a truce. The Boiotians took possession of Oinoe after it was captured in this fashion, and in Athens the oligarchy and strife ended.

[99] As for the Peloponnesians at Miletos, around the same time during this summer, since no one among those assigned by Tissaphernes at the time he went to Aspendos had furnished any subsistence, nor had either the Phoenicians' ships or Tissaphernes arrived after all this time, and Phil-

---

would have approved of the earlier restriction, yet he could write that "oligarchy ended" with the downfall of the Four Hundred. Hence, "during the first phase . . . best government"; rather than ". . . not least—for the first time in my experience—do the Athenians appear to have governed themselves well" (Connor 1984, p. 228).

8.98. "Archers . . . preeminently foreigners": the reference is to Athens' police force; Aristarchos wanted those least attached to Athens, or even Greece.

ippos, the man sent with him, and another named Hippokrates, a Spartiate who was at Phaselis, sent a dispatch to Mindaros saying that the ships were not coming at all, and they were being wronged by Tissaphernes, and Pharnabazos kept calling on them to come, eager in his own right to bring in their fleet and, just like Tissaphernes, cause the cities in his domain still under the Athenians to revolt, expecting that he would gain considerably as a result, after all this Mindaros left Miletos, combining good organization with the suddenness of his instructions, an attempt to avoid detection by the forces at Samos, and sailed for the Hellespont with seventy-three ships (sixteen had sailed there earlier in the same summer, and these also overran part of the Chersonesos), but he put in at Ikaros when he was caught by a storm and had no choice, and after being held in the harbor by five or six days of bad sailing weather, he reached Chios.

[100] Thrasylos on Samos, when he learned that he had set sail from Miletos, immediately sailed with fifty-five ships himself, pushing on to keep the other from entering the Hellespont first. Since he found out that he was at Chios and thought he could pin him down there, he stationed lookouts both on Lesbos and on the mainland opposite, so that if the ships did make a move in any direction this would not go unnoticed, and he himself sailed along the coast to Methymna and gave orders to prepare barley and the other provisions with the intention that if this became a longer period he would make raids on Chios out of Lesbos. At the same time, since Eresos on Lesbos had revolted, he wanted to sail against it and if possible seize it. Methymnian exiles, who were among the most influential men, had brought over from Kyme about fifty hoplites associated with them and hired some from the mainland, about three hundred in all, with Anaxarchos, a Theban, in charge because of kinship, and made an assault on Methymna first; when their attempt was beaten back because of the prior arrival of the Athenian garrison from Mytilene, after they were once more driven off in a battle outside the city they got across the mountains and caused the revolt of Eresos.

So Thrasylos sailed there and intended to assault it. Thrasyboulos was there as well, since he had arrived previously from Samos with five ships after the news reached them that the exiles had crossed over; since he was too late, he anchored there on arrival. They were also reinforced by five ships on their way home from the Hellespont and five Methymnian ships. In all, there were sixty-seven ships on hand, and with the forces taken from these they were preparing to use their full strength to capture Eresos by siege engines or any other means if it was at all possible.

[101] Meanwhile, after Mindaros and the Peloponnesian ships spent two days taking on provisions, and each man received three Chian fortieths from the Chians, they hurriedly set out from Chios on the third day, not sailing on the open sea, to avoid encountering the fleet at Eresos, but to the mainland, keeping Lesbos on their left. After putting in at the harbor of Kartereia in Phokaian territory and eating breakfast, they sailed along the coast of Kyme and ate supper at Arginoussai on the mainland opposite Mytilene. From there, with most of the night still ahead, they sailed along the coast and reached Harmatos on the mainland just across from Methymna, hurriedly ate breakfast, sailed past Lekton, Larisa, Hamaxitos, and the places in that area, and before midnight arrived at Rhoiteion, already in the Hellespont, and there were some ships that put in at Sigeion and places elsewhere in the area.

[102] When the Athenians at Sestos with eighteen ships got the signal from their beacons and noticed many fires suddenly blazing on the enemy shore, they realized that the Peloponnesians were sailing in. And on the same night, stealing along the shore of the Chersonesos, they sailed toward Elaious as fast as they could, hoping to sail past the enemy ships into open water. They eluded the eighteen ships at Abydos, although word had already come from their fleet to keep a close watch for the Athenians if they sailed out; but not all of them outran the ships with Mindaros, who gave chase immediately when he spotted them at dawn, and while most of them escaped to Imbros and Lemnos, the four hindmost were overtaken near Elaious. They captured one, stranded near the shrine of Protesilaos, and even its crew, and two others without their crews; and they burned one, which was deserted, near Imbros.

[103] After this, with the ships from Abydos added to the rest, eighty-six in all, he spent that day besieging Elaious, and since it did not give in to him, he sailed back to Abydos. The Athenians, deceived by their lookouts, did not believe that any passage of enemy ships could escape their notice and were taking their time as they assaulted the walls, but when they found out they immediately abandoned Eresos and went in a hurry to defend the Hellespont; they captured two Peloponnesian ships, which encountered them now after sailing recklessly into the open sea in their earlier pursuit, and when they reached Elaious a day later, they anchored,

8.101. "Chian fortieths": Hardwick 1992 explains these as silver coins worth one-fortieth of a Persian gold daric (see 8.28).

8.102. On the problems of the text, see *HCT* V *ad* 8.102.2.

brought in all the ships that had gone there for refuge, and spent five days getting ready for a battle. [104] Then, in the following manner, they went into this engagement.

They were sailing very close to shore toward Sestos in a single line, and the Peloponnesians, who perceived this from Abydos, sailed out against them in turn. Realizing that they were about to fight, the Athenians with their seventy-six ships extended their column along the Chersonesos, from Idakos as far as Arrhiana, while the Peloponnesians, with eighty-six ships, extended theirs from Abydos to Dardanos. On the Peloponnesian side, the Syracusans held the right wing, while Mindaros himself held the left with the best-sailing ships, and on the Athenian side Thrasylos held the left and Thrasyboulos the right; the other generals were distributed in between. With the Peloponnesians eager to initiate the conflict and if possible, by outflanking the Athenian right wing with their own left, cut them off from exit while in the center, they thrust them back to the shore a short distance; the Athenians, who realized this, outsailed the enemy and went beyond the point where they wanted to cut them off; their own left wing was already extended past the promontory called Kynossema. But while this was going on, in the center they ended up with their ships inadequate and scattered, especially since the number they had was smaller, and the area of Kynossema had a sharp, angular outline, so that what was happening on the far side of it was not in sight. [105] Accordingly, falling on their center, the Peloponnesians drove the ships onto dry land and disembarked, since they had an enormous advantage in the fighting. Assisting their center was possible neither for Thrasyboulos and his men from the right wing, under attack by a multitude of ships, nor for those with Thrasylos from the left (there was no visibility because of the Kynossema promontory, and at the same time the Syracusans and their other opponents matched them in numbers and were shutting them in), until the Peloponnesians, fearlessly pursuing ships here and there because they were winning, began growing less organized in part of their formation. When Thrasyboulos and his men realized this, making no further effort now at extending their wing and suddenly turning, they met the ships bearing down on them and routed them, and they took on the errant Peloponnesian ships in the victorious sector, pounded them, and threw most into a panic that permitted no resistance. The Syracusans as well, who as it happened were now giving way before Thrasylos and his men, were more inclined toward outright flight when they saw the others.

[106] After the rout was complete and the Peloponnesians fled, most of them at first to the Meidios river and then to Abydos, the Athenians cap-

tured few ships (for the Hellespont, because it was narrow, provided their opponents with close places for refuge), and yet this sea battle gave them a victory at the best possible time. Afraid all the while of the Peloponnesian fleet, both because of a series of lesser failures and because of the disaster in Sicily, they were done with reproaching themselves or conceding their enemies any further merit in naval matters. Still, of the enemies' number they captured eight Chian ships, five Corinthian, two Ambraciot, and two Boiotian, and one apiece from the Leukadians, Lacedaemonians, Syracusans, and Pellenians; and they lost fifteen themselves. After they set up a trophy on the promontory, where the Kynossema is, bringing in the wrecks, and giving the enemy back their dead under truce, they sent a trireme to Athens to report the victory. When the ship arrived, and the Athenians heard about the good fortune unexpectedly following the recent disasters around Euboia and during the factional strife, they regained their courage and thought that their cause was still capable of prevailing if they embraced it zealously. [107] On the fourth day after the battle, when they had hurriedly repaired their ships, the Athenians sailed from Sestos to Kyzikos, which had revolted; spotting the eight ships from Byzantion anchored off Harpagion and Priapos, they sailed against them, defeated the land forces in battle, and seized the ships. On arriving at Kyzikos, which was unwalled, they brought it back into the alliance and exacted money from it. Meanwhile, the Peloponnesians sailed from Abydos to Elaious and recovered those of their ships that were in good condition (the Elaiousians had burned the others), and they dispatched Hippokrates and Epikles to Euboia to get the ships from there. [108] And around this same time Alcibiades with his thirteen ships sailed to Samos from Kaunos and Phaselis, announcing that he had diverted the Phoenician fleet from coming to the Peloponnesians and that he had made Tissaphernes friendlier to the Athenians than before. After manning nine ships in addition to the ones he had, he exacted a large sum from the Halikarnassians and fortified Kos. After he had done these things and appointed a governor for Kos, since it was now close to autumn, he sailed back to Samos.

And at Aspendos, Tissaphernes, since he had found out that the Peloponnesian fleet had sailed from Miletos to the Hellespont, broke his camp and moved on to Ionia. While the Peloponnesians were in the Hellespont, the Antandrians (who are Aiolians) brought hoplites of theirs overland from Abydos across Mt. Ida and led them into the city, since they

8.106. "The Kynossema": "Tomb of the Bitch," i.e., Hecuba (see Euripides, *Hecuba* 1270–73); apparently the trophy was set up near the tomb.

were being injured by Arsakes the Persian, Tissaphernes' subordinate, also the man who, after the Delians settled Atramyttion when ousted from Delos by the Athenians for the purification of Delos, offered the excuse of a quarrel, which was left vague, invited their most important men to campaign with him, led them out on terms of supposed friendship and alliance, and waited until they were eating breakfast, surrounded them with his own men, and shot them down. Accordingly, since on account of this act they were afraid that he might treat them lawlessly as well, and since he was inflicting other measures impossible for them to bear, they expelled his garrison from their acropolis.

[109] Tissaphernes, when he knew about this action by the Peloponnesians as well, besides their actions at Knidos and Miletos (for there also his garrisons had been driven out), considering his relations with them severely strained and afraid of their doing him still more harm, at the same time chagrined that Pharnabazos, by accepting them as allies, was in some respects going to fare better against the Athenians in less time and at less cost, made up his mind to proceed to the Hellespont in order to complain to them about what had happened at Antandros and defend himself against the slanderous accusations over the Phoenician ships and the other matters as plausibly as possible. Arriving at Ephesos first, he offered sacrifice to Artemis . . .

8.109. Thucydides' concluding sentence is incomplete. Most manuscripts include a following sentence, "When the winter after this summer ends, the twenty-first year will be completed": an (early?) editorial addition, cf. Classen/Steup VIII and Tucker 1908 *ad* 8.109.2.

ABBREVIATIONS

AHB: *Ancient History Bulletin*

AJP: *American Journal of Philology*

BICS: *Bulletin of the Institute of Classical Studies, University of London*

CA: *Classical Antiquity*

CJ: *Classical Journal*

CP: *Classical Philology*

CQ: *Classical Quarterly*

GRBS: *Greek, Roman and Byzantine Studies*

HCT: *Historical Commentary on Thucydides*

JHS: *Journal of Hellenic Studies*

LCM: *Liverpool Classical Monthly*

PP: *La Parola del Passato*

TAPA: *Transactions of the American Philological Association*

GLOSSARY

Archon: "ruler," title given to nine high officials of the Athenian state chosen annually (by lot at the time of the Peloponnesian War); the most important, the *Archon Eponymous*, gave his name to the year in Athenian records.

Atticize: to side with Athens; implying disloyalty to Greek interests, on analogy with *medize* (3.64n).

Boiotarch: official of the Boiotian League; each member state was represented by at least one.

Cleruch: "lot-holder," Athenian citizen sent as settler to another state under Athenian control and allocated land there but (unlike a colonist) retaining Athenian citzenship (3.50n).

Deme: the smallest and most basic unit in the political organization of the Athenian state; every Athenian citizen belonged to one of these villages or parishes (of which there were well over a hundred).

Drachma: monetary unit and coin used by most Greek states, worth six *obols* and approximately a day's pay; one-hundredth of a *mina*.

Ephor: title of five officials chosen annually by the citizens of Sparta and possessing the greatest political and legislative power in the Spartan state; one gave his name to the year in Spartan records.

Epoikoi: "secondary colonists" usually sent out after earlier settlers, and usually in part as military reinforcements (2.27n).

Harmost: originally, a *Spartiate* charged with supervising a community of *perioikoi*; starting late in the Peloponnesian War, also the leader of a garrison installed in other states to enforce subservience to Sparta (8.5n).

Helot: agricultural slave and property of the Spartan state; each *helot* was assigned to a plot of land and responsible for farming it and giving a substantial portion of the produce annually to its *Spartiate* owner.

Hoplite: heavily armored infantryman who fought in close formation, primarily by thrusting with his spear; the most important component of Classical Greek armies, *hoplites* furnished their own arms and armor (and often a slave to carry it on marches) and represented the middle class of the Greek state (4.96n).

Medize: to collaborate with the "Medes," i.e., Persians, implying treason to Greece (1.128–35n, 3.64n)

Metic: long-term resident of Athens, either a freed Athenian slave or citizen of another state, Greek or non-Greek; *metics* were taxed, subject to Athenian military service, and given some of the less important privileges of Athenian citizenship.

Mina: Greek monetary unit, equivalent to a hundred *drachmas*; one-sixtieth of a *talent*.

Neodamodeis: *helots* awarded personal freedom, although probably few if any rights of citizenship (4.80n).

Obol: smallest regular Greek monetary unit, one-sixth of a *drachma*.

Paian: hymn in honor of Apollo, widely used by Greeks on various occasions, including military campaigns; sometimes used as a battle song, but not among the Athenians and Ionians.

Paralos: one of two Athenian state *triremes* (with the *Salaminia*) used for important missions as well as combat.

Peltast: the most highly skilled of Greek light infantry, armed with a javelin and small wicker shield; usually from Thrace, where they originated, or the more backward areas of Greece, *peltasts* were used as mercenaries by many Greek states.

Pentekonter: "fifty-oared" warship, predecessor of *trireme*; obsolete but still in use at the time of the Peloponnesian War.

Perioikoi: "dwellers around," inhabitants of Spartan territory enjoying at least limited autonomy but without Spartan citizenship.

Proxenos: citizen of a Greek state chosen by another state to represent its interests among his fellow–citizens.

Prytany: Athenian committee that presided over the council; one *prytany* from each tribe presided for a tenth of the year.

Salaminia: see *Paralos*.

Satrap: Persian provincial governor; effectively, a vassal-king.

Skytale: Spartan device for sending messages (1.131n).

Spartiate: full citizen of the Spartan state; as such, member of a small elite.

Stade: the length of an athletic stadium and standard Greek unit of distance; six hundred feet (with considerable regional variability).

Stater: coin of variable worth in relation to other monetary units (3.70.n).

Talent: Greek monetary measure (and unit of weight); an Attic *talent* was worth sixty *minas*.

Taxiarch: Athenian commander of *hoplites*, subordinate to the generals; ten (one from each tribe) were chosen annually by the assembly.

Thetes: "laborers," in Athens, members of the poorest of four economic classes of citizens, contributing military service as marines and especially rowers.

Trierarch: commander of a *trireme*; in Athens, also a person required to equip and maintain a *trireme* for one year (a heavy expense).

Trireme: standard Greek warship of the Classical period, named for its arrangement of oars in three superimposed rows and carrying a crew of about two hundred.

Xenelasia: "driving out foreigners," institutionalized Spartan practice of periodically expelling all non-Spartans (2.39n).

Xenos: most literally, "stranger," but with many secondary meanings, including the participant in formal "guest-friendship," often hereditary, between individuals in different Greek states (2.13n).

WORKS CITED

Adkins, A.W.H. 1975. "The *Arete* of Nicias: Thucydides 7.86," *GRBS* 16: 379–92

Allison, J.W. 1984. "Sthenelaidas' Speech: Thucydides 1.86," *Hermes* 112: 9–15

————. 1989. *Power and Preparedness in Thucydides*

Amit, M. 1968. "The Melian dialogue and history," *Athenaeum* 56: 216–35

Arnush, M. 1992. "Ten-Day Armistices in Thucydides," *GRBS* 33: 329–54

————. 1995. "The Career of Peisistratos Son of Hippias," *Hesperia* 64: 135–62

Austin, N. 1966. "The Function of Digressions in the *Iliad*," *GRBS* 7: 295–312

Avery, H. C. 1973. "Themes in Thucydides' Account of the Sicilian Expedition," *Hermes* 101: 1–13

Babut, D. 1986. "L'Épisode de Pylos-Sphactérie chez Thucydide: L'agencement du récit et les intentions de l'historien," *Revue de Philologie, de Littérature et d'Histoire Anciennes* 60: 59–79

Badian, E. 1992. "Thucydides on rendering speeches," *Athenaeum* 80: 187–90

————. 1993. *From Plataea to Potidaea. Studies in the History and Historiography of the Pentekontaetia*

Bauslaugh, R.A. 1979. "The text of Thucydides IV 8.6 and the south channel at Pylos," *JHS* 99: 1–6

Berger, S. 1992. "Seven cities in Sicily: Thuc. 6.20.2–3," *Hermes* 120: 421–24

Bloedow, E.F. 1973. *Alcibiades Reexamined*

————. 1987. "Sthenelaidas the Persuasive Spartan," *Hermes* 115: 60–65

————. 1990. "'Not the Son of Achilles, but Achilles himself:' Alcibiades' Entry on the Political Stage at Athens II," *Historia* 39: 1–19

————. 1991a. "Alcibiades: A Review Article," *AHB* 5: 17–29

————. 1991b. "Phrynichos the 'Intelligent' Athenian," *AHB* 5: 89–100

————. 1992. "Alcibiades 'brilliant' or 'intelligent'?" *Historia* 41: 139–57

————. 1996. "The Speeches of Hermocrates and Athenagoras at Syracuse in 415 BC: Difficulties in Syracuse and in Thucydides," *Historia* 45: 141–58

Boeckh, A. 1857. *The Public Economy of Athens*

Boegehold, A.L. 1979. "Thucydides' Representation of Brasidas before Amphipolis," *CP* 74: 148–51

Bonfante, L. 1989. "Nudity as a Costume in Classical Art," *American Journal of Archaeology* 93: 543–70

Borza, E.N. 1990. *In the Shadow of Olympus. The Emergence of Macedon*

Bourriot, F. 1995. *Kalos Kagathos—Kalokagathia*

Bradeen, D.W. 1960. "The Popularity of the Athenian Empire," *Historia* 9: 257–69

Bradford, A.S. 1994. "The duplicitous Spartan," Powell, A., and S. Hodkinson, eds., *The Shadow of Sparta*: 59–86

Brock, R. 1996. "Thucydides and the Athenian Purification of Delos," *Mnemosyne* 49: 321–27

Brunt, P.A. 1952. "Thucydides and Alcibiades," *Revue des études grecques* 65: 59–96

Buck, R.J. 1995. "The Character of Theramenes," *AHB* 9: 14–24

Canfora, L. 1980. "L'historien Thucydide n'a jamais été éxilé," *Dialogues d'Histoire Anciennes* 6: 287–89

Cartledge, P. 1984. "A new lease of life for Lichas son of Arkesilas?" *LCM* 9: 98–102

————. 1993. *The Greeks: A Portrait of Self and Others*

Christ, M. 1989. "The Authenticity of Thucydides 3.84," *TAPA* 119: 137–48

Classen/Steup = Classen, J., *Thukydides*, revised by J. Steup, 1900–1922, reprinted 1963, 8 vols.

Cogan, M. 1981. *The Human Thing. The Speeches and Principles of Thucydides' History*

Cole, T. 1991. *The Origins of Rhetoric in Ancient Greece*

Connor, W.R. 1977. "A Post-Modernist Thucydides?" *CJ* 72: 289–98

———. 1984. *Thucydides*

Crane, G. 1996. *The Blinded Eye. Thucydides and the New Written Word*

Daverio Rocchi, G. 1985. "Brasida nella tradizione storiografico. Aspetti del rapporto tra ritratto letterario e figura storico," *Acme* 38: 63–81

Debnar, P.A. 1996. "The Unpersuasive Thebans (Thucydides 3.61–67)" *Phoenix* 50: 95–110

Donini, G. 1964. "Thucydides 7.42.3: Does Thucydides agree with Demosthenes' view?" *Hermes* 92: 116–19

———. 1969. *La Posizione di Tucidide verso il governo dei Cinquemila*

Dover, K.J. 1965. *Thucydides Book VII*

———. 1973. *Thucydides*

———. 1974. *Greek Popular Morality in the Time of Plato and Aristotle*

———. 1978. *Greek Homosexuality*

———. 1988. *Collected Papers* II

Edmunds, L. 1993. "Thucydides in the Act of Writing," Pregostini, R., ed.,*Tradizione e Innovazione nella Cultura Greca da Omero all'Età Ellenistica* II: 831–52

Ellis, J.R. 1978. "Thucydides at Amphipolis," *Antichthon* 12: 28–35

———. 1991. "The Structure and Argument of Thucydides' Archaeology," *CA* 10: 344–75

Ellis, W.M. 1989. *Alcibiades*

Erbse, H. 1989. *Thukydides-Interpretationen*

Evans, D. 1974. "Dodona, Dodola, and Daedala," Larson, J.G., ed. *Myth in Indo-European Antiquity*: 99–130

Falkner, C.L. 1992. "Thucydides and the Peloponnesian Raid on Piraeus in 429 B.C.," *AHB* 6: 147–55.

Farrar, C. 1988. *The Origins of Democratic Thinking*

Figueira, T.J. 1991. *Athens and Aigina in the Age of Imperial Colonization*

Finley, J.H. 1942. *Thucydides*

———. 1967. *Three Essays on Thucydides*

Flory, S. 1988a. "Πᾶσα ἰδέα" in Thucydides," *AJP* 109: 12–20

————. 1988b. "Why Did Thucydides Leave His History Unfinished?" *American Philogical Association. Abstracts of the One Hundred Twentieth Annual Meeting*: 23

————. 1990. "The meaning of τὸ μὴ μυθῶδης (1.22.4) and the usefulness of Thucydides' History," *CJ* 85: 193–208

————. 1995. "*Scriptio Continua*, Ancient Literacy, and the Composition of Thucydides' *History*," *American Philological Association. Abstracts of the One Hundred Twenty-Seventh Annual Meeting:* 116

Flower, H. 1992. "Thucydides and the Pylos Debate," *Historia* 14: 40–57

Forde, S. 1989. *The Ambition to Rule. Alcibiades and the Politics of Imperialism in Thucydides*

Gagarin, M. 1990. "The Ancient Tradition on the Identity of Antiphon," *GRBS* 31: 27–44

Gallucci, R. 1986. *Myth of the Hoplite Oligarchy: Athens, 411/10 B.C.*, diss. UCLA

Gantz, T. 1993. *Early Greek Myth*

Garner, R. 1987. *Law and Society in Classical Athens*

Georges, P. 1994. *Barbarian Asia and the Greek Experience*

Graf, D. 1984. "Medism: the origin and significance of the term," *JHS* 104: 15–30

Graham, A.J. 1992. "Thucydides 7.13.2 and the Crews of Athenian Triremes," *TAPA* 122: 257–69

Grant, J.R. 1974. "Towards Knowing Thucydides," *Phoenix* 28: 81–94

Graves, C.E. 1888. *Thucydides. Book IV*, reprinted 1982

Grayson, C.H. 1972. "Two Passages in Thucydides," *CQ* 22: 62–73

Green, P. 1970. *Armada from Athens*

Grene, D. 1965. *Greek Historical Thought*

Grossi, G. 1984. *Frinico tra propaganda democratica e giudizio tucidideo*

Halperin, D.M. 1990. *One Hundred Years of Homosexuality and Other Essays on Greek Love*

Hammond, N.G.L. 1977. "The meaning and significance of the reported speech of Phrynichus in Thucydides 8, 48," Kinzl, K.H., ed., *Greece and the Eastern Mediterranean in Ancient History and Prehistory:* 147–57

Hanson, M.H. 1993. "The Battle Exhortation in Ancient Historiography. Fact or Fiction?" *Historia* 42: 161–80

Hardwick, N. 1992. "The Solution to Thucydides viii.101.1: the 'Chian Fortieths," *American Philological Association. Abstracts of the One Hundred and Twenty-fourth Annual Meeting*: 41

Haslam, M. 1990. "Pericles poeta," *CP* 85: 33

Heath, M. 1990. "Justice in Thucydides' Athenian Speeches," *Historia* 39: 385–400

Heitsch, E. 1984. *Antiphon aus Rhamnus*

HCT = Gomme, A.W., A. Andrewes, and K.J. Dover, *A Historical Commentary on Thucydides*, 1945–1981, 5 vols. (I 1945, II 1956, III 1956, IV 1970, V 1981)

Hogan, J. 1980. "The ἀξίωσις of Words at Thucydides 3.82.4," *GRBS* 21: 139–49

Hornblower, S. 1987. *Thucydides*

———. 1991. *Commentary on Thucydides* I

Hunter, V. J. 1973. *Thucydides, the Artful Reporter*

———. 1977. "The Composition of Thucydides' *History*: A New Answer to the Problem," *Historia* 26: 269–94

Johnson, L.M. 1990–1991. "Rethinking the Diodotean Argument," *Interpretation* 18: 53–62

Jones, N. 1978. "The Topography and Strategy of the Battle of Amphipolis," *California Studies in Classical Antiquity* 10: 71–104

Jordan, B. 1986. "Religion in Thucydides," *TAPA* 116: 119–47

———. 1990. "The Ceremony of the Helots in Thucydides IV, 80," *Antiquité Classique* 59: 37–69

Jung, V. 1991. *Thukydides und die Dichtung*

Kagan, D. 1969. *The Outbreak of the Peloponnesian War*

———. 1981. *The Peace of Nicias and the Sicilian Expedition*

———. 1987. *The Fall of the Athenian Empire*

Kallet-Marx, L. 1993. *Money, Expense, and Naval Power in Thucydides' History 1–5.24*

Katicic, R. 1957. "Die Ringkomposition im ersten Buche des Thukydideischen Geschichtswerkes," *Wiener Studien* 70: 179–96

Kebric, R.B. 1976. "Implications of Alcibiades' Relationship with Endius," *Mnemosyne* 29: 72–78

Kelly, T. 1985. "The Spartan σκυταλε," Eadie, J. W., and J. Ober, eds., *The Craft of the Ancient Historian: Essays in Honor of C. G. Starr:* 141–69

Keuls, E.C. 1985. *The Reign of the Phallus. Sexual Politics in Ancient Athens*

Kirby, J.T. 1983. "Narrative Structure and Technique in Thucydides VI–VII," *CA* 2: 183–211

Konishi, H. 1983. "Ten years and a few more days, Thucydides 5.20.1," *LCM* 8: 69–70

———. 1987 "Thucydides' *History* as a finished piece," *LCM* 12: 5–7

La Rocca, E. 1986. "Prokne ed Itys sull'acropoli: una motivazione per la dedica," *Athenische Mitteilungen* 101: 153–66

Lang, M. 1972. "Cleon as the Anti-Pericles," *CP* 67: 159–69

Lapini, W. 1991. "Tucicide tragico: noterella su 3.113.1–6," *Sileno* 17: 121–38

Lateiner, D. 1976. "Tissaphernes and the Phoenician Fleet (Thucydides 8.87)," *TAPA* 106: 281–88

———. 1985. "Nicias' Inadequate Encouragement (Thucydides 7.69.2)," *CP* 80: 201–13

Lewis, D.M. 1977. *Sparta and Persia*

Liebeschuetz, W. 1968. "Thucydides and the Sicilian Expedition," *Historia* 17: 289–94

Loraux, N. 1986a. "Thucydide a écrit la guerre du Péloponnèse," *Métis* 1: 139–61

———. 1986b. "Thucydide et la sédition dans les mots," *Quaderni di Storia* 12: 95–134

Luginbill, R.D. 1994. "*Othismos*: The Importance of the Mass-shove in Hoplite Warfare," *Phoenix* 48: 51–61

Luschnat, O. 1942. *Die Feldherrnreden im Geschichtswerk des Thukydides*

McDonnell, M. 1991. "The introduction of nudity: Thucydides, Plato, and the vases," *JHS* 111: 182–93

MacDowell, D. 1962. *Andocides. On the Mysteries*

McGregor, M.F. 1956. "The Politics of the Historian Thucydides," *Phoenix* 10: 93–102

———. 1965. "The Genius of Alcibiades," *Phoenix* 19: 27–46

Mackay, L.A. 1953. "Latent Irony in the Melian Dialogue," G.M. Mylonas, ed., *D.M. Robinson Studies* II: 570–72

Mackie, C.J. 1996. "Homer and Thucydides," *CQ* 46: 103–13

Macleod, C. 1977. "Thucydides' Plataean Debate," *GRBS* 18: 227–46 (= Macleod 1983, 103–22)

———. 1978. "Reason and necessity: Thucydides iii 9–14, 37–48," *JHS* 98: 64–78 (= Macleod 1983, 88–102)

———. 1979. "Thucydides on Faction (3.82–3)," *Proceedings of the Cambridge Philological Society* 205: 52–68 (= Macleod 1983, 123–39)

———. 1983. *Collected Essays*

Mader, G. 1993a. "Rogues' Comedy at Segesta (Thucydides 6.46): Alcibiades Exposed?" *Hermes* 121: 181–95

———. 1993b. "Strong Points, Weak Arguments: Athenagoras on the Sicilian Expedition," *Hermes* 121: 433–40

Magnelli, A. 1991. "Naxos, Apollo archegetes e la composizione delle *Storie* di Tucidide," *Sileno* 17: 281–86

Marchant, E.C. 1918. *Thucydides Book 3*

———. 1919. *Thucydides Book VII*

Marinatos, N. 1981. *Thucydides and Religion*

Marinatos Kopff, N., and Rawlings, H.R. III 1978. "Panolethria and divine punishment. Thuc. 7.87.6 and Hdt. 2.120.5," *PP* 33: 331–37

Marr, J.L. 1971. "Andocides' part in the mysteries and hermae affairs," *CQ* 21: 326–38

Maurer, K. 1995. *Interpolations in Thucydides*

Mitchell, B. 1991. "Kleon's Amphipolitan Campaign," *Historia* 40: 170–92

Moles, J.L. 1993. "Truth and Untruth in Herodotus and Thucydides," Gill, C., and T.P. Wiseman, eds., *Lies and Fiction in the Ancient World*: 88–121

Morens, D.M., and Littman, R. J. 1992. "Epidemiology of the Plague of Athens," *TAPA* 122: 271–304

Morgan, T.E. 1994, "Plague or Poetry? Thucydides on the Epidemic at Athens," *TAPA* 124: 197–208

Nikolaidis, A.G. 1990. "Thucydides 4.28.5 (or Kleon at Sphakteria and Amphipolis)," *BICS* 37: 89–94

Orwin, C. 1994. *The Humanity of Thucydides*

Ostwald, M. 1969. *Nomos and the Beginnings of the Athenian Democracy*

————. 1979. "Diodotus, Son of Eucrates," *GRBS* 20: 5–13

————. 1988. *ANAΓKH in Thucydides*

Parry, A. 1957. *Logos and Ergon in Thucydides*, diss. Harvard, published 1981

————. 1969. "The Language of Thucydides' Description of the Plague," *BICS* 16: 106–18

Pearson, L. 1985. "Tissaphernes' Extra Money," *Bulletin of the American Society of Papyrologists* 22: 261–63

Pendrick, G.J. 1993. "The Ancient Tradition on Antiphon Reconsidered," *GRBS* 34: 215–29

Percy, W.A. 1996. *Pederasty and Pedagogy in Ancient Greece*

Piccirilli, L. 1986. "Questioni tucididee," *Studi Italiani di Filologia Classica* 79: 19–27

Plant, I. 1992. "Thuc. VIII.48.5: Phrynichus on the Wishes of Athens' Allies," *Historia* 41: 249–50

————. 1994. "The Battle of Tanagra: A Spartan Initiative?" *Historia* 43: 259–74

Pope, M. 1988. "Thucydides and Democracy," *Historia* 37: 276–96

Pouilloux, J., and Salviat, F. 1983. "Lichas, Lacédemonien, archonte à Thasos, et le livre VIII de Thucydide," *Académie des Inscriptions et Belles-Lettres. Comptes Rendus*: 376–404

————. 1985. "Thucydide après l'exil et la composition de son Histoire," *Revue de Philologie, de Littérature et d'Histoire Anciennes* 59: 13–20

Pouncey, P.R. 1980. *The Necessities of War: A Study of Thucydides' Pessimism*

Powell, A. 1979. "Thucydides and Divination," *BICS* 26: 45–50

Powell, J.E. 1937. "Puns in Herodotus," *Classical Review* 51: 103–5

Pritchett, W.K. 1995. *Thucydides' Pentekontaetia and Other Essays*

Radt, S.L. 1976. "Philologische Kleinigkeiten zum Melierdialog," *Mnemosyne* 29: 33–41

Ramón Pherm, V. 1991. "Notas a Tucídides VIII 86, 4," *Cuadernos de investigación filolólogica* 17: 193–98

Rawlings, H.R. 1977. "Thucydides on the Purpose of the Delian League," *Phoenix* 31: 1–8

————. 1981 *The Structure of Thucydides' History*

Reichenauer, G. 1991. *Thukydides und die hippokratische Medezin*

Rengakos, A. 1996. "Fernbeziehungen zwischen den thukydideischen Reden," *Hermes* 124: 396–417

Rhodes, P.J. 1987. "Thucydides on the Causes of the Peloponnesian War," *Hermes* 115: 154–65

———. 1988. *Thucydides: History II*

———. 1994. *Thucydides: History III*

Richardson, J. 1990. "Thucydides 1.23.6 and the debate about the Peloponnesian War," Craik, E.M., ed., *"Owls to Athens." Essays on Classical Subjects Presented to Sir Kenneth Dover:* 155–61

Rigsby, K. 1987. "Phocians in Sicily: Thucydides 6.2," *CQ* 37: 332–35

Robertson, N. 1980. "The True Nature of the 'Delian League,'" *American Journal of Ancient History* 5: 64–96, 110–33

Roisman, J. 1987. "Alcidas in Thucydides," *Historia* 36: 385–421

Romilly, J. de. 1956. *Histoire et raison chez Thucydide*

Russell, F.S. 1994. *Information Gathering and Intelligence in the Greek World, ca. 800–323 B.C.*, diss. UCLA

Rusten, J.S. 1985. "Two lives or three? Pericles on the Athenian character (Thuc. 2.40.1–2)," *CQ* 35: 14–19

———. 1986. "Structure, Style, and Sense in Interpreting Thucydides: The Soldier's Choice (Thuc. 2.42.4)," *Harvard Studies in Classical Philology* 90: 49–77

———. 1989. *Thucydides, the Peloponnesian War, Book II*

Schindel, U. 1970. "Phrynichus und die Rückberufung des Alkibiades," *Rheinisches Museum* 13: 281–97

Schneider, C. 1974. *Information und Absicht bei Thukydides. Untersuchung zur Motivation des Handelns*

Schreiner, J.H. 1976. "Anti-Thukydidean Studies in the Pentakontaetia," *Symbolae Osloenses* 51: 19–64

Sealey, R. 1984. "The Tetralogies ascribed to Antiphon," *TAPA* 114: 71–86

Seaman, M.G. 1995. "The Athenian Expedition to Melos and the Melian Contribution to the 'Spartan War Fund,'" *American Philological Association. Abstracts of the One Hundred Twenty-Seventh Annual Meeting:* 145

Small, J.P. 1995. "Artificial Memory and the Writing Habits of the Literate," *Helios* 22: 159–66

Smart, J.D. 1972. "Athens and Egesta," *JHS* 92: 128–46

———. 1986. "Thucydides and Hellanicus," Moxon, I.S., J.D. Smart, and A.J. Woodman, eds., *Past Perspectives. Studies in Greek and Roman Historical Writing*: 19–35

Snodgrass, A. 1980. *Archaic Greece*

Spence, I.G. 1990. "Perikles and the defense of Attika during the Peloponnesian War," *JHS* 110: 91–109

Spratt, A.W. 1905a. *Thucydides. Book III*

———. 1905b. *Thucydides. Book VI*

Stadter, P.A. 1993. "The Form and Content of Thucydides' Pentakontaetia (1.89–117)," *GRBS* 34: 35–72

Stahl, H.-P. 1966. *Thukydides. Die Stellung des Menschen im geschichtlichen Prozess*

Ste. Croix, G.E.M. de. 1954. "The Character of the Athenian Empire," *Historia* 3: 1–41

———. 1956. "The Constitution of the Five Thousand," *Historia* 5: 1–23

———. 1972. *The Origins of the Peloponnesian War*

Strasburger, H. 1958. "Thukydides und die politische Selbstdarstellung der Athener," *Hermes* 86: 17–40

Strassler, R.B. 1988. "The harbor at Pylos, 425 B.C.," *JHS* 108: 198–203

———. 1990. "The opening of the Pylos campaign," *JHS* 110: 110–25

Strauss, B.R. 1983. "Aegospotami Reexamined," *AJP* 104: 24–35

Stroud, R.S. 1994. "Thucydides and Corinth," *Chiron* 24: 267–304

Swain, S. 1993. "Thucydides 1.22.1 and 3.82.4," *Mnemosyne* 46: 33–45

Tompkins, D.P. 1972. "Stylistic Characterization in Thucydides. Nicias and Alcibiades," *Yale Classical Studies* 22: 181–214

———. 1983. Review of Rawlings 1981 in *AJP* 104: 93–96

Tucker, T.G. 1908. *The Eighth Book of Thucydides*

Tzifopoulos, Y.Z. 1995. "Thucydidean Rhetoric and the Propaganda of the Persian War Topos," *PP* 281: 91–115

Westlake, H.D. 1956. "Phrynichus and Astyochus," *JHS* 76: 99–104

————. 1960. "Athenian Aims in Sicily, 427–424. A Study in Thucydidean Motivation," *Historia* 9: 385–402

————. 1968. *Individuals in Thucydides*

————. 1971. "Thucydides and the uneasy peace—a study in political incompetence," *CQ* 21: 315–25

————. 1972. "The Two Second Prefaces of Thucydides," *Phoenix* 26: 12–17

————. 1980. "Thucydides, Brasidas, and Clearidas," GRBS 21:333–339

Whitby, M. 1994. "Two shadows: images of Spartans and helots," Powell, A., and S. Hodkinson, eds., *The Shadow of Sparta*: 87–126

Wilson, J.B. 1979. *Pylos 425 B.C. A historical and topographical study of Thucydides' account of the campaign*

————. 1982a. "The Customary Meanings of Words Were Changed—Or Were They? A Note on Thucydides 3.82.4," *CQ* 32: 18–20

————. 1982b. "What Does Thucydides Claim for his Speeches?" *Phoenix* 36: 95–103

————. 1987. *Athens and Corcyra. Strategy and Tactics in the Peloponnesian War*

Winnington-Ingram, R.P. 1965. "τὰ δέοντα εἰπεῖν. Cleon and Diodotus," *BICS* 12: 70–82

Woodman, A.J. 1988. *Rhetoric in Classical Historiography*

Wylie, G. 1992. "Brasidas—Great Commander or Whiz-Kid?" *Quaderni Urbinati di Cultura Classica* 70: 75–95

ADDENDA

The following are relevant works that I did not have adequate opportunity to use:

Cartwright, D. 1997. *A Historical Commentary on Thucydides. A Companion to Rex Warner's Penguin Translation*

Hornblower, S. 1996. *A Commentary on Thucydides*, vol. 2, *Books IV–V*

INDEX OF SPEECHES

INDEX

The references are to book and chapter numbers.

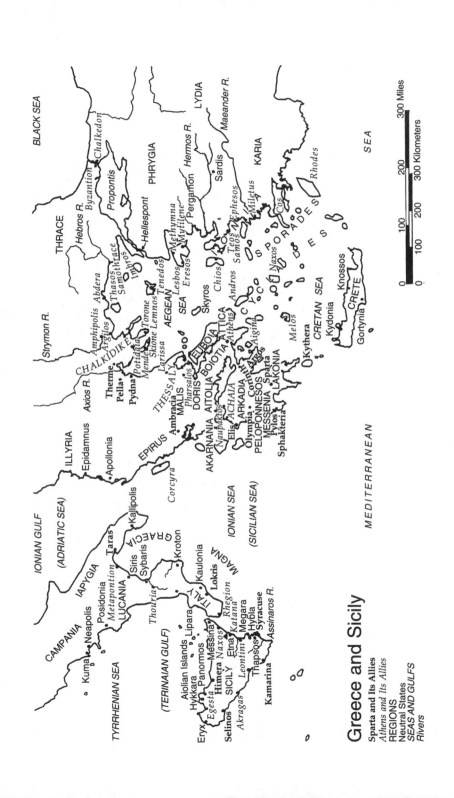

Greece and Sicily

Sparta and Its Allies
Athens and Its Allies
REGIONS
Neutral States
SEAS AND GULFS
Rivers

IONIAN GULF

(ADRIATIC SEA)

ILLYRIA

Epidamnus

Apollonia

KRESTONIA

Amphipolis

Argilos

Eion

LOWER
MACEDONIA

Therme

Pella

Pydna

MYGDONIA

CHALKIDIKE

Olynthos

Akanthos

Torone

Mende

Skione

Potidaia

EPIRUS

Corcyra

Larissa

THESSALY

Pharsalos

Ambracia

MALIS

Idomene

Olpai

Herakleia

DORIS

Delphi

EUBOIA

Chalcis

IONIAN SEA

(SICILIAN SEA)

AITOLIA

Anaktorion

Leucas

AKARNANIA

Naupaktos

Chaironeia

BOIOTIA

Thespiai

Thebes

Plataia

Eretr

Dekeleia

Athens

Mar

Kephallenia

KRISAIAN

ACHAIA

GULF

Sikyon

Megara

ATTICA

Peiraeus

Zakynthos

ARKADIA

Corinth

Mycenae

Salamis

Aigina

Elis

Olympia

Mantinea

Tegea

Argos

Epidauros

Troizen

PELOPONNESOS

Thyrea

Hermione

Pylos

MESSENIA

Sparta
(Lacedaemon)

LAKONIA

Sphakteria

Kythera

Greece

Sparta and Its Allies
Athens and Its Allies
REGIONS
Neutral States
SEAS AND GULFS

MEDITERRANEAN   SEA

Kydoni

0	100	200	300 Miles
0	100	200	300 Kilometers

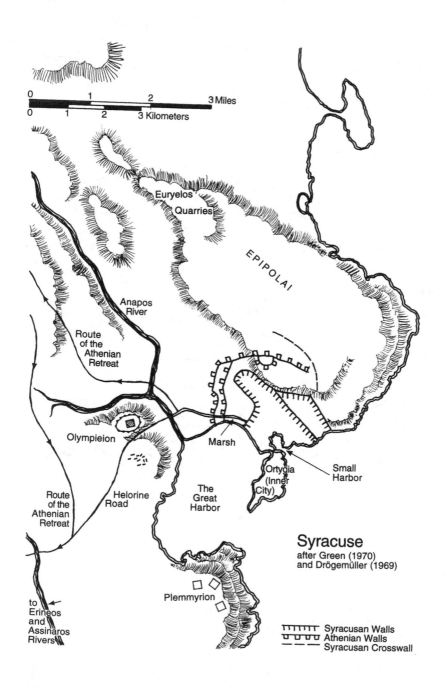

0   1   2   3 Miles
0   1   2   3 Kilometers

Euryelos
Quarries

EPIPOLAI

Anapos
River

Route
of the
Athenian
Retreat

Olympieion

Marsh

Ortygia
(Inner
City)

Small
Harbor

Route
of the
Athenian
Retreat

Helorine
Road

The
Great
Harbor

Syracuse
after Green (1970)
and Drögemüller (1969)

to
Erineos
and
Assinaros
Rivers

Plemmyrion

Syracusan Walls
Athenian Walls
Syracusan Crosswall

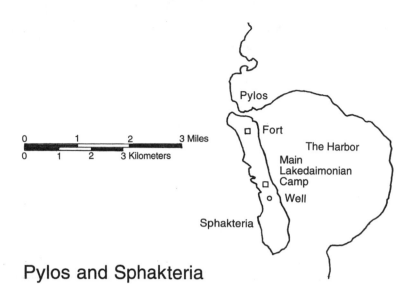

Pylos and Sphakteria

Athens and Its Neighbors